Steffen Fleßa

International Healthcare Management

Steffen Fleßa

International Healthcare Management

—

Towards Efficiency, Effectiveness and Equity of
Healthcare Systems in Low- and Middle-Income Countries

DE GRUYTER

ISBN 978-3-11-914476-6
e-ISBN (PDF) 978-3-11-221729-0
e-ISBN (EPUB) 978-3-11-221737-5

Library of Congress Control Number: 2026930133

Bibliographic information published by the Deutsche Nationalbibliothek
The Deutsche Nationalbibliothek lists this publication in the Deutsche Nationalbibliografie;
detailed bibliographic data are available on the Internet at http://dnb.dnb.de.

© 2026 Walter de Gruyter GmbH, Berlin/Boston, Genthiner Straße 13, 10785 Berlin
Cover image: bamlou/DigitalVision Vectors/Getty Images
Typesetting: Integra Software Services Pvt. Ltd.

www.degruyterbrill.com
Questions about General Product Safety Regulation:
productsafety@degruyterbrill.com

Preface

More than 35 years ago, I was permitted to choose a completely exotic topic for my master thesis. Under the supervision of K. Heidenberger and M. Meyer, I analysed the health economic impacts of HIV/AIDS on the faith-based healthcare services in Tanzania. For a German Diploma in Business Administration, this topic was indeed curious, but since then, international healthcare management has never let me go. It is the most exciting field of research I can imagine.

During my 5 years of service in Tanzania and numerous studies in Africa, Asia, and South America, as well as in my dissertation and habilitation, I focused on international healthcare management. However, I am always aware that the primary goal of this field should not be the academic allure of exploring the new, but rather my research and teaching should serve the people. International healthcare management must put its knowledge at the service of life to remain true to itself. Therefore, this book is more than just an attempt to transfer knowledge. It aims to contribute to improving healthcare in all countries of the world. And it should encourage the reader to consciously decide to use their expertise for the benefit of other people.

This book would not have been possible without the support of numerous friends and colleagues. This includes all who have accompanied me on my journey into international healthcare management. I thank W. Ritter, T. Reichart, H. Becker, H. Waltz, M. Blöcher, K. Hornetz, C. Becker, and many others for their support. My greatest appreciation goes to my African and Asian colleagues who inspired me and opened my mind towards realities beyond European thinking, in particular S. Mmbaga, E. Kweka, B. Kouyaté, T. Su, S. Raj Pandey, K. Hui, Z. Ermatov, and many others. My research was funded by the Evangelical Mission Society, German Research Foundation, European Union, KfW Development Bank, and German Society for International Cooperation (GIZ). Without them, I would not have been able to conduct my studies. I also owe thanks to my colleagues Katharina Schaufler, Johanna Eberhard, Elias Eger, Bishwas Chamling, and my co-workers who have read various versions of the manuscript. Finally, I thank my family, who let me go time and again to truly experience international healthcare management – the suffering of people, the smell of an African hospital, endless meetings in Ministries of Health, but also the laughter of healthy children, the joy of a young mother, and the dignity of an old man who just received his new glasses after cataract surgery.

I hope all readers will be thrilled by the fascination of international healthcare management. This 'virus' infected me in 1988 – and there is no cure. Because there is certainly nothing more fascinating than international healthcare management.

Greifswald, July 2025 — Steffen Fleßa

https://doi.org/10.1515/9783112217290-202

Contents

Preface —— V

1 Introduction —— 1

2 Fundamentals —— 5
2.1 Scientific Classification —— 5
2.1.1 Health —— 5
2.1.2 Health Science —— 9
2.1.3 Health Economics and Healthcare Management —— 16
2.1.4 Health Policy and Ethics —— 22
2.2 Health and Development —— 45
2.2.1 Fundamental Concept —— 45
2.2.2 Development and Developing Countries —— 53
2.2.3 Health and Healthcare in Resource-Poor Countries —— 69
2.3 Conceptions —— 73
2.3.1 Prevention —— 73
2.3.2 Primary Healthcare —— 75
2.3.3 Health Promotion —— 78
2.3.4 Regional Health Planning —— 81
2.3.5 Universal Health Coverage —— 84
2.4 Health Policy —— 88
2.4.1 Historical Pathways —— 88
2.4.2 Developments of the New Millennium —— 95

3 Demand —— 115
3.1 Fundamentals —— 115
3.1.1 Economic Framework Model —— 115
3.1.2 Demographic and Epidemiological Transition —— 120
3.2 Modelling Epidemiological Processes —— 133
3.3 Epidemiology of Infectious Diseases —— 143
3.3.1 Fundamentals —— 143
3.3.2 Case Study: AIDS —— 157
3.3.3 Case Study: Malaria —— 170
3.3.4 Case Study: COVID-19 —— 182
3.4 Epidemiology of Non-infectious Diseases —— 207
3.4.1 Fundamentals —— 207
3.4.2 Case Study: Diabetes Mellitus Type II —— 217
3.4.3 Case Study: Cataract —— 222
3.4.4 Case Study: Cervix Uteri Carcinoma —— 228

3.5   Health Risks —— **236**
3.5.1   Overview —— **236**
3.5.2   Nutrition —— **239**
3.5.3   Water and Hygiene —— **243**
3.5.4   Pregnancy and Birth —— **246**
3.5.5   Substance Abuse —— **249**
3.5.6   Environmental Influences —— **255**
3.5.7   Urbanization and Megacities —— **259**
3.5.8   Unstable Population —— **263**
3.6   Filters Between Need and Demand —— **266**
3.6.1   Distance Filter —— **266**
3.6.2   Price Filter and Health Insurance —— **269**

4   Supply —— 279
4.1   Business Administration of Healthcare —— **279**
4.1.1   Agents of Production —— **279**
4.1.2   Transformation Process —— **292**
4.1.3   Leadership Process —— **293**
4.2   Supply Structure —— **296**
4.2.1   Catchment Areas —— **296**
4.2.2   Levels of Care —— **299**
4.2.3   Provider Portfolio —— **302**

5   Healthcare Systems and Reforms —— 307
5.1   Costs —— **307**
5.2   Healthcare Reform Alternatives —— **309**
5.2.1   Overview —— **309**
5.2.2   Healthcare Financing —— **313**
5.2.3   Healthcare Structure —— **327**
5.3   Health Policy Process —— **332**

6   Outlook —— 339

References —— 341

Index —— 365

1 Introduction

The healthcare sector is an exceptionally complex and dynamic system consisting of numerous actors, sectors, and regulations. Patients and service providers meet in health markets and expect financing through health insurance. Services are provided on an outpatient, inpatient, and various intermediate bases and are regulated by numerous laws, with the speed of various healthcare reforms being enormous and increasing. Those who deal with the management of the healthcare sector today choose a research and working area that could not be more demanding – and this statement applies to all countries.

The development of the healthcare sector and the associated demands on the management of this industry are described in numerous publications, and our knowledge of healthcare management is growing.[1] However, although knowledge and resources of the healthcare sector (e.g. the number of doctors, health budget, buildings, and equipment) have steadily increased over the past decades, the gap between what is technically possible and what can be financed is growing wider. We can create significantly better and more health services today than in the past, but we could do so much more based on our technical knowledge if only we could afford it. At the same time, it is expected that this gap between affordability and potential services will widen further as the aging population will lead to increased demand for health services and strain the financial potential of social systems.[2] There are numerous reasons to engage with the healthcare system and its management.

Why should a student or scholar from one country deal with international healthcare management at all? Is it not more sensible to first solve the problems of his own country before dealing with bottlenecks in other countries? Or should the 'international' aspect not at least be limited to neighbouring countries facing very similar problems? This monograph aims to show that there are good reasons to study international healthcare management and to familiarize oneself with problems and solutions, especially in resource-poor countries. This is justified, among other things, because the 'view over the fence' puts our own problems into perspective. Given the existential dimension of resource scarcity in the healthcare sector of most countries around the world, our own problems appear in a different light, teaching us a bit more modesty and serenity – perhaps even gratitude for our situation. These virtues are a good mindset for fundamentally solving our own problems.

Moreover, there are many concrete experiences in other countries from which we can directly learn. In a globalized world, the healthcare sector is not a closed system but is in constant exchange, ranging from mutual promotion to direct competition for international customers. For instance, before the German healthcare reform

---

1 Compare Zweifel, Breyer, and Kifmann (2014) and Sloan and Hsieh (2017).
2 Compare Howdon and Rice (2018).

https://doi.org/10.1515/9783112217290-001

of 2003, no one would have expected that the German hospital payment system would be developed based on a diagnosis-related group system from the other end of the world. Knowledge of international healthcare management alone opens access to such seeds of innovation.

But healthcare managers[3] can also learn a lot from resource-poor countries. The healthcare systems of many high-income countries are extremely complex and overlaid by an almost incomprehensible number of regulations. Simple relationships, such as the price elasticity of demand for health services, the significance of distance for demand, or the availability of doctors, are distorted by a multitude of institutions and regulations, making it very difficult to study the fundamental relationships. The view of the 'simplicity behind complexity', i.e. the basic systemic interrelationships, is becoming increasingly difficult in these countries. In comparison, the healthcare systems in resource-poor countries can be studied in their pure form. We need to understand how supply, demand, and regulation of health markets function. Resource-poor countries provide a very good learning platform for this purpose.

In addition, other countries can learn from experiences (and failures) of countries such as Germany. For example, there is great interest in Asian and African countries in the Bismarckian health insurance system, although a simple transfer to a different social, economic, and historical situation is not possible. Instead, our concepts must be reflected upon and transformed against the backdrop of these countries to represent a promising ideological export. However, this requires a fundamental knowledge of healthcare management in Africa and Asia. Germany can contribute to improving the health situation of the majority of the world's population. The partner countries would like to learn from us but expect at least a basic sensitivity to their specific situation. Not least, development aid in the healthcare sector is a relevant job market for healthcare managers.

Finally, the necessity of international healthcare management arises from the fact that the classic separation between health problems in higher- and lower-income countries is obsolete. Up to two decades ago, industrialized countries and developing countries were neither structurally nor dimensionally comparable in terms of their problems. The classic platitudes ("In Africa, everyone is poor – in Germany, everyone is rich!"; "In Asia, everyone dies from infections, in Germany from cancer"; "In Central America, nobody has access to modern healthcare, in Germany it doesn't matter where someone lives!") no longer hold true (if they ever did). This monograph emphasizes that the real division in healthcare provision is no longer between industrialized and developing countries, but between urban and rural areas or between poverty groups and wealthier sections of the population. A peripheral, poorer region in Ger-

---

3 For reasons of better readability and easier comprehension, this textbook uses the generic masculine in this text. We hereby explicitly address all gender identities without any judgemental distinction.

many (such as East Pomerania) suffers from structurally comparable problems to the Nouna District in the west of Burkina Faso, while a wealthy Indian from the upper class has access to the same health services nationally and internationally as a well-situated resident of Frankfurt am Main. Therefore, it may be useful for a peripheral region in Europe or Northern America to learn from concepts originally developed for rural care in resource-poor countries, while the upper class in the cities of developing and emerging countries should choose the care in Western metropolises as a benchmark. In both cases, dealing with international healthcare management is a prerequisite for efficient further development and adaptation of one's own system.

From the above explanations, a certain focus on resource-poor countries emerges because they are home to the majority of the world's population, from them, we can learn humility and serenity in the face of our own situation, there is a great demand for well-reflected system solutions, and the structures can be studied in their pure form. Consequently, the term 'international' in this monograph is not – as unfortunately often the case – narrowed down to few neighbouring countries of the same economic level (e.g. the USA, Canada, and German-speaking countries) but is truly defined in a global sense. In contrast to countries that otherwise completely fall out of the focus of textbooks on healthcare management, essential insights into healthcare management are to be worked out.

In this book, we will use the term 'healthcare management' instead of 'health management' because, strictly speaking, health cannot be managed, but only the systems that are supposed to contribute to strengthening the health of the population can be. We understand it to mean the systematic planning, implementation, and control of measures to protect, promote, expand, and restore the health of a population. Healthcare management is clearly prescriptive in orientation, i.e. it should provide concrete instructions on how healthcare systems, interventions, and institutions can be planned, organized, led, monitored, and continuously improved to achieve predefined goals.

International healthcare management can draw on the findings of numerous sciences and put them to use for its own questions. These include demography, epidemiology, public health, health economics, and health policy, which are used for the control of healthcare systems, programmes, and institutions. Chapter 2 thus discusses the interfaces with these neighbouring sciences. Since a focus of this work is on resource-poor countries, the relationship between health and development is also highlighted. Finally, historical and current concepts of international healthcare management are discussed.

Based on these definitions, delimitations, and classifications, the fundamental elements of healthcare management can be discussed. These include, in particular, the demand for and supply of health services. Chapter 3 discusses the determinants of demand based on a framework model. Focuses include the demand for maternity care as well as some exemplary infectious and chronic degenerative diseases. The chapter also presents the most important filters between need and demand (especially distance and purchasing power).

In Chapter 4, the factors of production are first presented, with particular attention to differences compared to Germany. This is followed by discussions on spatial supply structure, levels of care, and the provider portfolio. The book concludes with an analysis of healthcare systems and reforms. A focus is on financing options and healthcare systems in an international comparison. Finally, the values and goals discussed in Chapter 2 are recalled and applied to reform alternatives.

2 Fundamentals

In the following section, the foundations of international healthcare management are laid. It becomes clear that the content of this chapter can only be understood from a multidisciplinary perspective, i.e. healthcare management encompasses aspects of public health, demography, and epidemiology as well as health economics and health policy. Transferring this general concept to the international sphere, it becomes necessary to analyse the relationship between health and development and, in particular, the healthcare systems in resource-poor countries. Finally, international healthcare management is presented in its historical context. Fundamentals here are the concepts of primary healthcare (PHC) and health promotion, and also newer approaches such as the Commission on Macroeconomics and Health, the Paris Declaration, and the sustainable development goals (SDGs). The scientific classification, the international perspective, and the conceptual view form the basis for further analyses of supply and demand for health services as well as for healthcare systems and reforms.

2.1 Scientific Classification

Healthcare management is a relatively new field that can build on the findings of other disciplines. Therefore, it is necessary to briefly describe these neighbouring sciences and, as far as possible, to distinguish them from healthcare management. In addition to health economics, with which there is naturally a close relationship, the (further) disciplines of health sciences are of great importance for understanding healthcare management. Other sciences that are occasionally relevant (e.g. civil engineering and agriculture) will not be considered here.

2.1.1 Health

The starting point of healthcare management is the health of the population. However, it proves difficult to define what health exactly is, and how it can be measured and pursued. Without an approach to this concept, healthcare management must remain vague and arbitrary.

A simple definition of the term is found in the constitution of the World Health Organization (WHO), which defines health as a "state of complete physical, mental, and social well-being and not merely the absence of disease or infirmity".[4] The 'complete' well-being declares health as a maximal value, which is aimed for, but cannot

---

[4] The Constitution of the World Health Organization was adopted by the International Health Conference in New York on 22 July 1946. It entered into force on 7 April 1948 (WHO 1948).

https://doi.org/10.1515/9783112217290-002

be achieved. The WHO term is thus hardly operationalizable and usable for concrete decisions of healthcare management. However, the multidimensionality is helpful, i.e. recognizing the human being as an entity with physical, psychological, and social existence. These dimensions span a space whose volume represents health. Only when the maximal value of 'well-being' is achieved in all three dimensions can a person – according to the relatively simple definition by the WHO – be considered healthy. Diseases indeed threaten human health (and here in particular, but not only, the physical dimension), but curing all diseases does not imply well-being. Rather, health includes the ability to fulfil functions, satisfaction in social structures, self-actualization, etc., i.e. aspects that go far beyond the absence of disease.[5]

Table 2.1 provides an overview of possible dimensions of human health as a translation of the WHO definition and further developments.

Table 2.1: Dimensions of health (with examples).[6]

Physical dimension	Psychological dimension	Social dimension	Spiritual dimension
Genes, nutrition, environment (e.g. water and air), habitat (e.g. living space), and sleep	Emotional balance, relaxation, recreation, affection, contact ability, self-esteem and confidence, security, and freedom	Equality, social network, circle of friends, family, connectedness, conflict, and reconciliation ability	Wholeness, meaning, dedication, shalom, purpose, faith, integration, and harmony

Without doubt, the WHO constitution was highly influenced by the experiences of World War II and its disastrous consequences for mankind. However, the concept was developed on to include other aspects, such as spiritual health. Spirituality has a broad meaning spanning from "meaning, value, transcendence, connecting [. . .], and becoming [. . .]".[7] Today, it is widely accepted that spirituality is a human need and a prerequisite of well-being for many[8] and that the 'spirit' (Latin: *spiritus* meaning breath, courage, and soul) longs for meaning, value, transcendence, connecting, and growth that might not be sufficiently reflected in the psychological dimension.[9] Spiritual health is closely connected to religious perspectives, but it is not identical with it.[10] In particular, patients with chronic degenerative diseases and lifelong suffering might depend on 'spiritual resources' affecting their subjective health that go far beyond the other dimensions of health.

---

5 Consequently, the opposite of health is not simply disease. Although it is not common, it might be helpful to use the term 'unhealth' to express the contrary.
6 Source: Own.
7 Ghaderi, Tabatabaei, Nedjat, et al. (2018).
8 Compare Pesut, Fowler, Taylor, et al. (2008).
9 Compare Jaberi, Momennasab, Yektatalab, et al. (2019).
10 Compare VanderWeele (2024).

The WHO definition with its demand for "complete . . . well-being" is based on a static conception of health. You either have health – or you (mostly) do not. For the practice of healthcare management, it is more useful to understand health as a dynamic process in which health is acquired and lost. Thus, Audy[11] describes health as a "continuing property", which can be measured as the "individual's ability to rally from a wide range and considerable amplitude of insults, the insults being chemical, physical, infectious, psychological, and social", and Huber et al. define health as the "ability to adapt and self-manage".[12] This dynamic concept of health is closely related to the concept of resilience, i.e. "the process and outcome of successfully adapting to difficult or challenging life experiences, especially through mental, emotional, and behavioural flexibility and adjustment to external and internal demands".[13] However, health is not only dynamic in the sense that we can come back to the status quo after an insult, but that our health can improve and grow so that a lifelong change in health becomes possible.

Figure 2.1 demonstrates the dynamics of health before and after an infection with chickenpox. A child has a certain health condition: (a) After the infection, it contracts chickenpox, i.e. its health decreases. However, the child recovers and additionally builds up immunity. By the end of the considered period, a child's health is higher than before (b) because it has acquired an additional capability to respond to viral stimuli. Therefore, the goal of healthcare management must be to enhance the individual's ability to respond to various assaults on human health, not limited to stimuli from bacteria and viruses. Psychological and even spiritual stresses (e.g. loss of meaning) also require an appropriate response, for example, by the individual developing a 'hick skin'.

Viewing health in this dynamic manner over time, a characteristic image emerges. Children initially have low resistance but quickly acquire an immune response, leading to rapid health improvement. In adulthood, their capability to respond to viral and bacterial attacks is relatively high, and their psychological (and spiritual) resilience often increases, all other things being equal. However, susceptibility to chronic degenerative diseases rises in middle age. In old age, protection against infectious diseases declines, leading to a general decrease in health. Figure 2.2 displays the typical progression.

Public health thus sensibly presupposes a dynamic and multidimensional concept of health, thereby implying the possibility and the mandate to improve the population's health through a multifactorial approach. Fighting pathogens is only one of many approaches. Strengthening individual response capabilities to life's stresses, integrating into functional social networks, supporting spiritual life, creating stable political systems,

---

11 Audy (1971).
12 Huber, Knottnerus, Green, et al. (2011).
13 American Psychological Association (2024).

health

b ···

a

Infection   Immunity
                                          time

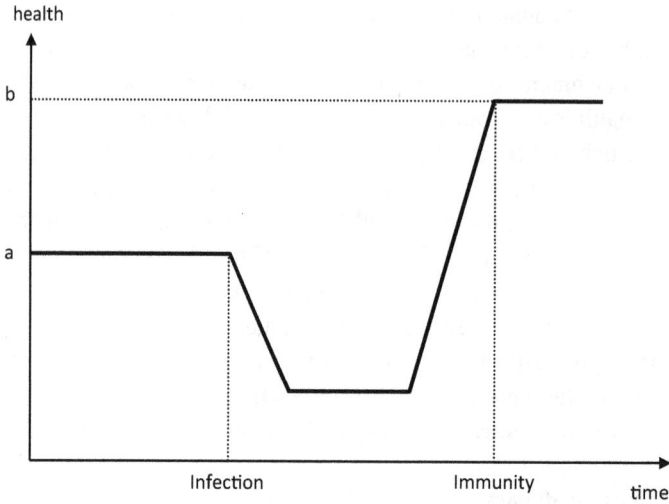

Figure 2.1: Dynamic concept of health.[14]

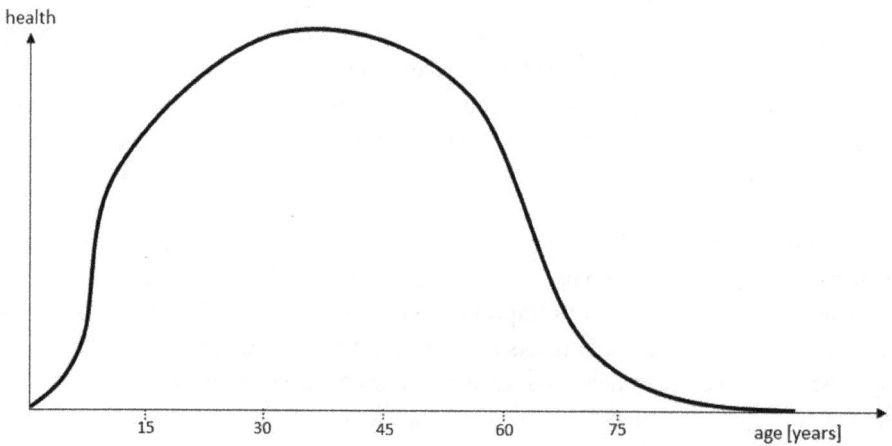

health

15   30   45   60   75   age [years]

Figure 2.2: Health as a function of age.[15]

and enhancing the economic independence of individuals and societies are equally important. International healthcare management specifically addresses health problems that cannot be reduced to the biological-medical dimension, such as access, opportunity costs, or the quality dimensions of healthcare.

---

14 Source: Own, based on Meade and Emch (2010).
15 Source: Own, based on Meade and Emch (2010).

The traditional understanding of health is utterly shaken by the discoveries in genetics and personalized medicine.[16] The immense knowledge about predisposition to diseases renders a person in an asymptomatic health state merely as a 'not-yet-sick' individual. Health becomes a utopia and is replaced by the absence of symptoms. Whether this concept of health can be goal-oriented for operational healthcare management is still undetermined. However, there is an inherent need to extend healthcare management even more towards the phase of prevention, i.e. it also includes the identification of risk factors and the corresponding health-promoting responses to them.

In summary, we can state that the term 'health' is difficult to define and operationalize. A management science, whose goal is the maintenance and improvement of the health of individuals and society, requires specific, measurable, realistic, and time-bound objectives. Diseases, on the other hand, are much simpler to define as deviations from a medically defined normal state and therefore inherently meet the management requirements for a target variable. Consequently, healthcare management in practice is often disease management, i.e. a set of measures for the prevention and cure of diseases. This chapter will also focus primarily on diseases while grossly neglecting social, psychological, and spiritual dimensions of human existence. However, readers should be aware that health is always more than just the absence of disease and that neither disease nor health can be limited to the physical dimension.

2.1.2 Health Science

Due to the high importance of health for every person, the science of human health holds a significant status and is pursued with great differentiation.[17] If one defines humans as a system, then the exploration of their health can start with this system, its subsystems, and supra systems. The science of the system itself is often conducted as clinical research with a strong focus on preventing and curing diseases of and in one person. Subsystems, for example, are the immune system, metabolism, genetics, or the proliferation of bacteria in the human body. The scientist completely abstracts from the individual and researches, especially within the scope of biomedical research, subindividual regularities. Finally, the research subject may not be the health of an individual but that of entire populations, where the supra system population is indeed more than the sum of its individuals, since the material, informational, and organizational relations between people constitute health-relevant facts that cannot be captured solely by the separate analysis of individuals (see Figure 2.3).

---

16 Compare Schleidgen, Klingler, Bertram, et al. (2013) and Jain (2015).
17 For an overview, compare Hurrelmann and Razum (2012).

Health science, in a broader sense, is understood to encompass subindividual, individual, and supra-individual health research. Often, the term 'public health' and 'health sciences' are used interchangeable, but public health has a much stronger focus on the supra-individual dimension of health. The term public health was first mentioned in 1848 in Great Britain in the so-called 'Public Health Act'. The goal of this population-based act (and of public health) was disease prevention and the care of subpopulations at high risk, such as urban workers at the dawn of the industrial revolution. In Great Britain and the USA, degree programmes in public health were established more than a century ago to research how to achieve these goals. The School of Public Health at Johns Hopkins University was the very first independent faculty in this field established by funds of the Rockefeller Foundation in 1916.

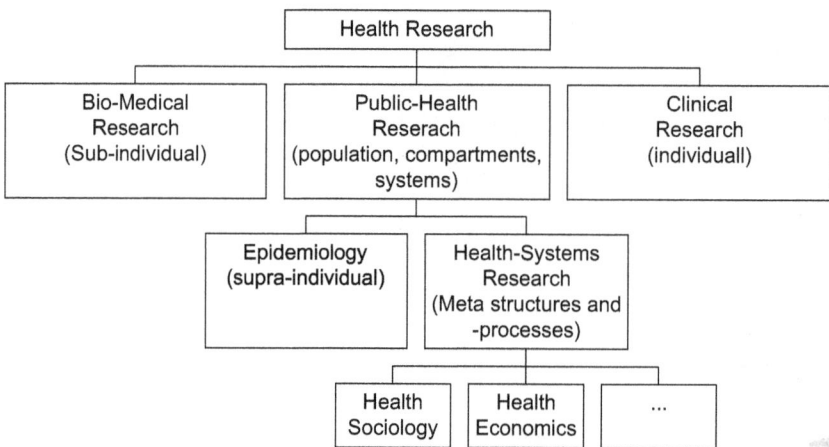

Figure 2.3: Health science.[18]

In Western Germany, it wasn't until the 1980s that public health was established as an academic discipline. This was partly due to the so-called racial hygiene of national socialism, which misused the ways of thinking and arguments of public health research in Germany for its reprehensible goals, resulting in little scientific interest in the questions of supra-individual health research after the end of World War II. In Eastern Germany, public health played a stronger role, but it was less academic but abused as an instrument to build-up a 'socialistic healthcare system'. After reunification, most achievements of public health in Eastern Germany got lost (e.g. higher vaccination rates, lower obesity, and better dental health). Thus, there is a significant need to catch up, less in the methods of public health than in the penetration of the population-based approach to health research in Germany.

---

18 Source: Based on Egger, Razum, and Rieder (2017) and Schwarz (2022).

The fundamental criterion of public health is its focus on the population. One of the oldest definitions comes from C. Winslow in 1920. He defined public health as:

> . . . the science and art of preventing disease, prolonging life, and promoting health and effi-ciency through organized community effort for the sanitation of the environment, the control of communicable infections, the education of the individual in personal hygiene, the organization of medical and nursing services for the early diagnosis and preventive treatment of disease, and for the development of the social machinery to ensure everyone a standard of living adequate for the maintenance of health, so organizing these benefits as to enable every citizen to realize his birth right of health and longevity.

More recent definitions also emphasize this focus, for example, Schaeffer, Moers, and Rosenbrock note that: "Public Health is the theory and practice of measures and strat-egies related to groups or populations for reducing the likelihood of illness and death by lowering risks and strengthening resources. Public Health analyses and influences epidemiologically identifiable risk structures, causal relationships, and coping possi-bilities behind individual cases of disease."[19]

The individual definitions largely agree in their focus on the population, but they differ significantly in their openness to questions that lie outside the immediate influ-ence zone of the medical areas of hygiene and infection protection. Thus, the so-called 'old public health' was still relatively close to the classical understanding of medicine and expanded it to include prevention and the community. On the other hand, 'new public health' adds to 'old public health' through the health policy dimension, which is particularly evident in the more structural view of healthcare system research and values sciences unrelated to medicine (such as political science, economics, and man-agement) for their objectives, thereby creating a fundamentally new conception of public health. For example, Schwarz defines: "Public Health encompasses all analyses and management approaches that are primarily related to entire populations or larger sub-populations, namely organisable approaches or systems of health promo-tion, disease prevention, and combat, using culturally and medically appropriate, ef-fective, ethical, and economically justifiable means."[20]

For the healthcare manager, the definition by Schwarz might be helpful, as it essen-tially defines public health as management focussed on healthcare systems and their populations, raising the criterion of efficiency as a proprium of economics to a condi-tion for public health measures. However, one should not go so far as to equate health-care management with public health, since management, as a prescriptive science, is always decision-oriented and thus may not cover the more analytical approaches of epi-demiology, health sociology, or medical geography. For a practice-oriented public health, on the other hand, healthcare management is needed to translate the findings of these other sciences into decisions and monitor their implementation.

---

19 Schaeffer, Moers, and Rosenbrock (1994).
20 Schwarz (2022).

As important disciplines within public health, whose concepts we will repeatedly refer to in this chapter, medical sociology, hygiene, medical geography, demography, and epidemiology will be briefly presented.

Sociology is the science of human coexistence, with particular emphasis on the formation, action, and accountability within social groups. Medical sociology[21] as a specialty of general sociology, accordingly analyses the complex interdependencies of health, disease, institutions, rules, and human behaviour within the social system. In principle, all aspects of public health are considered, but from the specific perspective of human coexistence. This approach is very helpful for healthcare managers, as diseases always spread within human groups, who work in healthcare institutions or make regulations for dealing with diseases.

Hygiene is the "science of preventing diseases and maintaining and strengthening health".[22] Traditionally, the focus was on infection prevention, with the major successes of microbiology in the second half of the nineteenth century (e.g. the discovery of the cholera pathogen) shaping the reputation of this field and implying a close connection between hygiene and microbiology. From today's perspective, the contribution of curative medicine to the improvements in life expectancy and quality of life appears rather marginal, while improved cleanliness and nutrition were of paramount importance.[23] The importance of hygiene in the era of chronic degenerative diseases is often underestimated, although new infectious diseases (e.g. AIDS and COVID-19) and the increasing resistance of known pathogens are likely to give hygiene new significance. On the one hand, the healthcare manager provides tools for implementing hygiene findings (e.g. management of vaccination programmes), and on the other hand, gains important knowledge about infection systems from this science to test their own theories and concepts against reality.

Medical geography[24] describes and explains the spatial distribution of diseases or of the institutions of the healthcare system. Its specificity, therefore, lies in the interpretation of the phenomena of the healthcare system in space, where the map (e.g. cancer atlas) remains one of its most important tools. Since economics traditionally neglects the spatial dimension and focusses all actors at a single location through aggregation, economists or healthcare managers can learn from medical geography the importance of the spatial dimension for their models and action recommendations.

Demography[25] is the study of populations, particularly analysing their size and structure in terms of temporal and spatial development. A well-known model is the

---

21 Compare Borgetto and Kälble (2007) and Siegrist (2005).
22 Deutsche Gesellschaft für Hygiene und Mikrobiologie (2010).
23 Compare McKeown (1979a) and McKeown (1979b).
24 Compare Meade and Emch (2010).
25 Compare Delvos (2008) and Weinstein and Pillai (2015).

population pyramid, which illustrates the strength of individual cohorts. Modern demography relies on extensive statistical models to explore the rules of population development. Basic knowledge of demography is of great importance for healthcare management, as the structure and growth of the population are crucial for the spread of diseases, for the organization of health services, and for the enforceability of intervention measures.

Epidemiology[26] has traditionally been understood as the study of the spread of diseases in space and time. Today, it increasingly broadens its scope to the systematic identification of population-related risk factors and causations. It is not limited to the spread of diseases but includes the diffusion of health states. For example, analysing vaccination coverage in a population is a task of epidemiology. Fundamental epidemiological concepts (e.g. prevalence, incidence, and study design) are part of the basic knowledge for the healthcare manager, and also advanced models of biometry[27] are helpful for their studies, especially since they are methodologically identical to econometric models, with few exceptions.

It is interesting that at the beginning of epidemiological research, the interdependence of disease, economy, and spatial occurrence was already central. In 1854, cholera raged in London, claiming numerous lives. The English physician John Snow (1813–1858) observed that cholera cases were clustering around a specific water pump and concluded that this must be the source of the infection. The mapping of cholera cases based on Snow's observations (see Figure 2.4) is considered one of the first epidemiological works. The geographical dimension of epidemiology was long neglected, with the focus on analysing temporal patterns. However, Figure 2.5 shows that both aspects are combinable and of great significance.

When examining the contents of degree programmes in public health and healthcare management or health economics, a broad overlap is noticeable. For example, at the Harvard School of Public Health, subjects such as environmental hygiene, epidemiology, statistics and biometry, economics, health policy, decision theory, healthcare management, and healthcare in low-income countries are part of the curriculum, meaning that only environmental hygiene distinguishes the degree programmes in public health and healthcare management or health economics. It is noteworthy that many international schools of public health offer lectures on healthcare in low-income countries, while this is rather an exception in Germany. International healthcare management or international public health in Germany is in dire need of development.[28]

---

26 Compare Gordis and Rau (2001), Bonita, Beaglehole, and Kjellström (2008), and Gordis (2008).
27 Compare Lorenz (1996) and Dümbgen (2009).
28 Compare Razum, Zeeb, and Laaser (2006).

Figure 2.4: Map based on John Snow (1854).[29]

In recent years, the term 'community medicine' has also become established, although the distinction from public health is not sharply defined (compare Table 2.2). In principle, community medicine leans more towards individual-based medicine and analyses the interdependence of health and disease within a clearly defined community. Aspects outside the medical system, such as water management or agriculture, are therefore less likely to be the subject of research in community medicine, even if they are relevant from a health policy perspective. However, making a precise distinction is challenging.

29 Image in public domain. Source: Snow (1854).

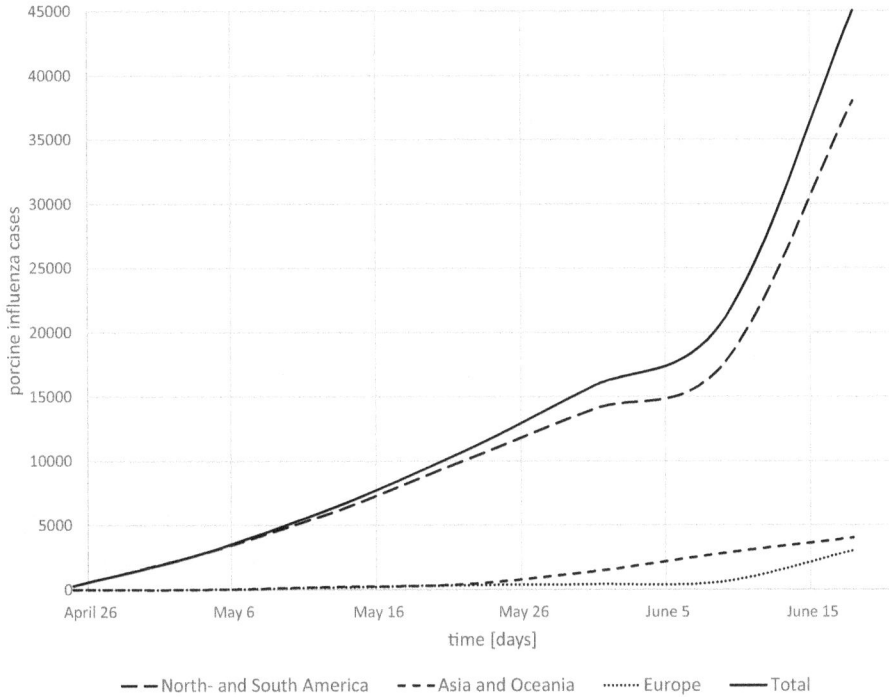

Figure 2.5: Development of the porcine influenza, 2009.[30]

Table 2.2: Public health, community medicine, and curative medicine.[31]

Criteria	Public health	Community medicine	Curative medicine
Target population	Population	Population of the region and individual	Individual patients
Orientation	Prevention	Prevention	Cure of disease on demand
Work characteristics	Key messages	Screening, proactive approach, motivation, and personal interaction	Personal interaction on demand
Cooperation	Social network	Social network, facilities of the region, and medical care of the region	Medical care of the region

30 Source: FluTracker (2012).
31 Source: John (2003).

In summary, we can understand healthcare management both as an independent discipline and as a sub-discipline of public health. Healthcare management is methodologically and fundamentally part of the economic sciences, while its research content is clearly attributable to public health. It shares this dual subordination with other disciplines, such as biostatistics, medical sociology, and medical geography. However, this is not a disadvantage but rather opens up the complete knowledge world of the economic sciences for the health sciences, making it an indispensable element of the same – both in an individual country and internationally.

2.1.3 Health Economics and Healthcare Management

So far, we have defined healthcare management as the systematic planning, implementation, and control of measures to protect, promote, expand, and restore the health of a population, where healthcare management shares the research object of health with many disciplines and utilizes important findings of these sciences. The proprium of healthcare management, like health economics as sub-disciplines of economic science, is efficiency. In contrast to health economics, however, healthcare management is primarily prescriptive in orientation, i.e. it concerns the very concrete design of institutions and processes that positively impact the health of populations. The distinction from health economics is, however, just as fuzzy as the differentiation between modern business administration and economics.

To illustrate this point, we will develop a health economic framework model.[32] In this context, it is important first to distinguish between the object of research and the science itself. Generally, the term 'economy' refers to all households, companies, and institutions collectively striving to overcome scarcity. Economics, on the other hand, is the scientific study of the economy. Consequently, health economics is the application of economics to the problems of the healthcare system.[33]

Figure 2.7 presents the basic, greatly simplified model.[34] The basic assumption here is that demand exceeds supply, meaning the goods to satisfy human needs are insufficient. This assumption can be accepted as given in the healthcare sector, not only but especially in an international context, where a fundamental scarcity of personnel, medications, functional facilities, standardized processes, time, logistics, etc., leads to a general undersupply of healthcare services of acceptable quality. Scarcity, as a real-world phenomenon, underlies all healthcare management actions and is often expressed by the inequality:

---

32 Compare for this purpose Fleßa and Greiner (2020).

33 According to this definition, the term 'health economy' should encompass all entities overcoming scarcity in the healthcare sector. In reality, the health economy often refers only to the commercially active providers in this sector.

34 Compare Fleßa and Greiner (2020) and Zweifel, Breyer, and Kifmann (2014).

$$D > S$$

where D represents the demand variable and S is the supply variable.

The supply side can be analysed on two levels. The micro level is the domain of business administration, where distinguishing between the microeconomics of a company and the theory of business administration is hardly possible. Fundamentally, it examines the transformation of production factors (operating resources, materials, labour, managerial labour, information, and customers) into goods for the customers. The latter are tangible goods or services and have the characteristics of solving a specific scarcity problem or of satisfying the needs of a customer. Business administration typically considers a single productive unit (operation).

Health services administration is an essential element of healthcare management and applies the knowledge of general business administration to healthcare providers such as hospitals, dispensaries, medical practices, and practice networks. For example, in a hospital, the production factors of buildings, beds, laboratory equipment, doctors, nursing staff, and administration are recombined to create hospital services (bed days, discharges, surgical procedures, etc.) that represent the sole reason for the company's existence. Procurement, production, marketing, financing, investment, logistics, and management are the basic functions of these enterprises and are analysed abstractly, but the primary task of healthcare management is the systematic support of concrete management in a real healthcare facility.[35]

Health economics, on the other hand, abstracts more strongly from the specific decision-making processes of individual companies and analyses the supply on a macro level as an aggregate of several providers. For example, supply structures must be defined, which consist of providers of varying scope and depth of service. The traditional supply pyramid (compare Figure 2.6) consisting of village health workers, dispensaries, health centres, primary, secondary, and tertiary hospitals, as advocated by the WHO in many low-income countries, is an example of this aggregated view. Furthermore, health economics considers the distribution of these facilities in space, i.e. in districts and regions of a country. This results in the central and decentralized problem of allocating health resources (e.g. personnel and budget of the Ministry of Health (MoH)) to the individual levels and spatial units of the healthcare system.

The demand for health services is the final link in a process chain that consists of the elements objective lack of health, need, and demand, as well as a series of filters. The starting point of the demand analysis according to Figure 2.7 is, therefore, an objectively detectable physical or psychological illness or a regular, natural process that requires medical assistance (e.g. birth). This objective lack of health can be measured by doctors, but the affected person may not be aware of this condition. For example, conjunctivitis in children of nomadic tribes in Africa is so common that parents only consider it an illness in extreme cases. The objective lack is 'normal' and is not subjec-

---

35 Compare Fleßa (2022).

tively felt as a deficiency. Health economics, therefore, deals with the analysis of diseases and fertility as the basis for the demand for health services. A particular focus of research is on measuring the efficiency of prevention and intervention, i.e. most cost-benefit analyses, cost-effectiveness analyses, and cost-utility analyses measure the ratio of resource consumption of an intervention to the objective lack of health, but rarely the impact of this intervention on the demand for health services.

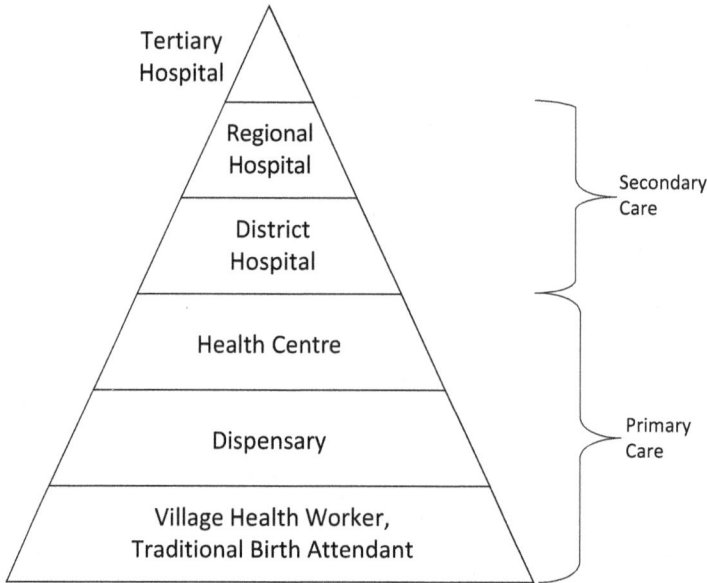

Tertiary Hospital

Regional Hospital

District Hospital

Health Centre

Dispensary

Village Health Worker, Traditional Birth Attendant

Secondary Care

Primary Care

Figure 2.6: Pyramid of healthcare services.[36]

A scientifically detectable lack of health does not automatically create a need for health services. The deficiency must be perceived by the sick individual for a motivation to satisfy the need to arise. The decisive factor in whether an objective deficiency, i.e. the deviation from objectifiable norms of physiological regulation or organic functions, is subjectively perceived, lies in health education. On the other hand, needs that are not based on a scientifically detectable lack of health can also exist. In both cases, healthcare institutions play an important role, as they can ensure that an objective deficiency is also subjectively felt, or conversely, a subjective need not based on objective deficiency is addressed.

Needs become a want when the need is confronted with concrete goods that can serve to eliminate the deficiency. This means that needs are fundamentally similar across all times and cultures, but they can lead to very different wants. For example,

---

36 Source: Phillips (1990).

first-time mothers in rural Africa in the nineteenth century and in Germany at the beginning of the twenty-first century have the same need for maternity care. However, the specific good on which the hope of satisfying this need is placed differs significantly. The African woman would express the want for a traditional midwife, while the German would automatically associate childbirth with a delivery room in a modern clinic. It is again the task of health education to inform patients about the health services available for satisfying their needs, i.e. to create a want.

The want for health services only becomes a demand in the health market if sufficient purchasing power exists, if the urgency of the need is high compared to other needs, if the quality of the offer is adequate, and if the need can be met within a reasonable distance. It is widely centre that the benefit, especially of treating life-threatening diseases, is very high and, therefore, the want for health services has high priority. In acute life-threatening situations, only treatment counts, i.e. alternative uses of the budget are irrelevant. However, this presupposes that a sufficient budget for health services exists within the private household or is supported by (social) insurance payments. Therefore, the financing of health services, especially with the help of health insurance, is a focus of health economics.

Numerous recent health economic research studies focus on the determinants of the quality of health services and the ways to improve it. However, the relationship between perceived outcome quality and demand is less frequently discussed. Likewise, the importance of distance has not been addressed in health economic discussions, even though geographers have often highlighted the paramount importance of this factor. Especially for services requiring customer presence, the distance between the consumer and provider is highly relevant. It is particularly noteworthy that the friction of distance is especially significant in prevention programmes. This means, for example, that a mother might be willing to drive 15 km to her general practitioner for treatment of her child with measles, but she might not undertake the same distance just to have her healthy child vaccinated against measles preventively.

The health market coordinates supply and demand, with numerous submarkets existing according to the hierarchical and regional structure of the supply of health services. The analysis of market processes in healthcare occupies a wide space in health economic discussions. Here, two questions dominate: First, it is debated whether an efficient supply situation (a so-called Pareto optimum) can occur on health markets or whether government interventions are necessary due to market failure. A further discussion analyses whether an efficient situation is even socially desirable or if government interventions are needed to enable access to the market for poverty groups. The question arises whether the government should only guarantee the framework conditions for market activities or whether it should directly intervene in the market activities, for example, by setting prices for health services so that even poor population segments can afford them.

Figure 2.7 summarizes the health economic framework model once again. An objective lack of health may become a subjective experience of deficiency (=need), which turns into want when confronted with concrete goods for satisfying the need. The want becomes a demand on the market when the purchasing power is sufficient, the quality of the offer is right, the offer is accessible, and the benefit for the individual is high enough. Supply and demand meet on the markets.

This – undoubtedly simplified – health economic framework model also encompasses the research objects of healthcare management, meaning health economics and healthcare management research the same subject, but with different objectives and levels of abstraction. To this end, the model of human activity can be referred to.[37]

On the everyday level, one deals with daily problems and their practical solutions without claiming universality, temporal constancy, or reflection. For example, filling out forms at the MoH is an important task that, however, does not pose a scientific challenge.

On the applied practical level, there are concrete problems with a complex structure that often require structured and systematic approaches, where academic training is helpful. For instance, developing an information system for a health insurance company requires scientific structuring methods, without yet achieving the level of universality typical for a science.

The applied scientific level, on the other hand, deals with concrete problem solutions that can claim a certain level of generalizability. They do not encompass all institutions or processes and are not fundamental models or ground-breaking theories of a sector. However, their level of abstraction allows for the transfer of specific questions and solution approaches to other, similar processes and institutions or to sub-problems. An example would be assessing the pros and cons of outsourcing in hospitals. It would be presumptuous to speak of a fundamental theory here – yet, this level is of great importance for practice.

The general level of science develops binding terminology from the findings of the applied scientific level and generalizes experiences into regularities. The scientific process at this level is cyclical, i.e. hypotheses are derived from empirical findings, which in turn are to be empirically or analytically verified. From the system of definitions and regularities proven through hypothesis testing, models and, finally – with a higher degree of complexity and reliability – theories that encompass the entire subject are derived. Examples include the service production model, the principal agent theory, or the Grossman model.

The meta-level of science transcends the individual discipline and provides a framework for addressing general phenomena. Systems theory is such a foundational approach that has found widespread application in almost all empirical sciences.

---

37 Compare Ritter (2001).

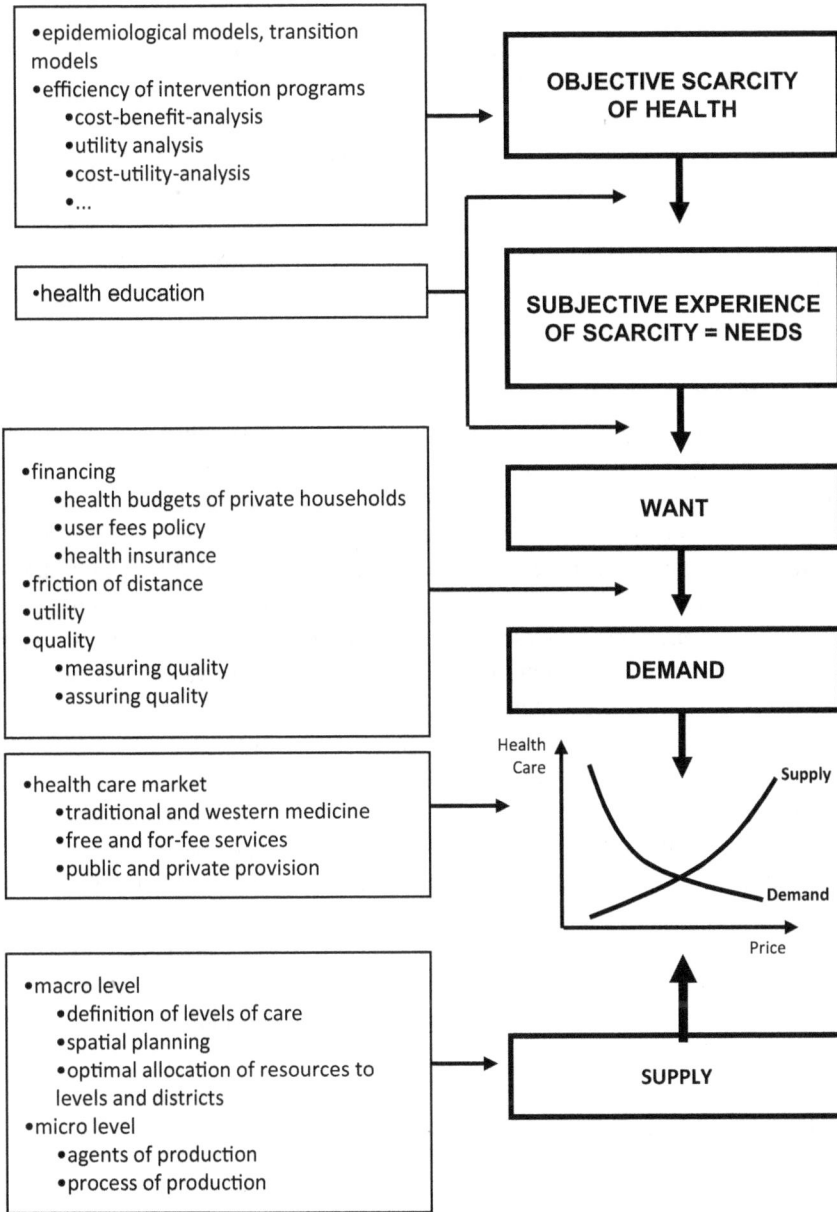

Figure 2.7: Health economic framework model.[38]

---

38 Compare Fleßa and Greiner (2020).

Healthcare management is a relatively young prescriptive science with the goal to produce reliable knowledge for specific decision-making situations. From this perspective, healthcare management predominantly operates at the applied scientific level, making its findings available to the applied practical level. General models and theories of healthcare management are currently scarce, meaning this young science is still in the process of distilling terminology and testing regularities from the applied scientific level before it can be referred to as a theory. Health economics, on the other hand, primarily operates within the realm of general science. Its terminologies, models, and theories are precisely defined and tested – sometimes at the cost of high abstraction, which may imply a certain distance from practice.

The different objectives and classifications also lead to different toolsets. Practice-oriented healthcare management predominantly utilizes business management methods of system control. Healthcare management can thus also be understood as the cybernetics of healthcare systems, incorporating both the control of individual actors (e.g. health service providers and health insurance companies) and the processes of demand, supply, and market. For each actor in the healthcare system and for regulating the overall system, cybernetics implies comprehensive control that includes both classic management (planning, organization, staffing, leading, and controlling) and the analysis of the environment (resources, competition, cooperation partners, value systems, demographic, epidemiological, economic, and social processes). Figure 2.8 illustrates the complexity of controlling healthcare systems.

At this point, a deeper analysis of management or system control will be omitted. In summary, healthcare management can be defined as the science of controlling healthcare systems. This includes all institutions (e.g. service providers, financing organizations, logisticians, information systems, regulators, the population, and civil society) and all processes (e.g. service production, transport, and demand behaviour) that serve to improve, maintain, or restore the health of a population. Healthcare management always intends not just to understand or assess the system but to shape it in accordance with the goal system. Therefore, discussing the value and goal system is directly within the scope of healthcare management's responsibilities.

2.1.4 Health Policy and Ethics

2.1.4.1 Introduction

Healthcare management, on the one hand, encompasses all levels of the healthcare system, i.e. from the micro level (e.g. traditional midwives, pharmacies, general practitioners, dispensaries, health centres, hospitals, and patients) through the meso level (association of statutory health insurance physicians, professional associations, hospital networks, and practice networks) to the macro level (civil society, MoH, legislation, and regulation), covering all actors and processes of planning, implementation, and control of health-relevant measures. Health policy, on the other hand, encompasses

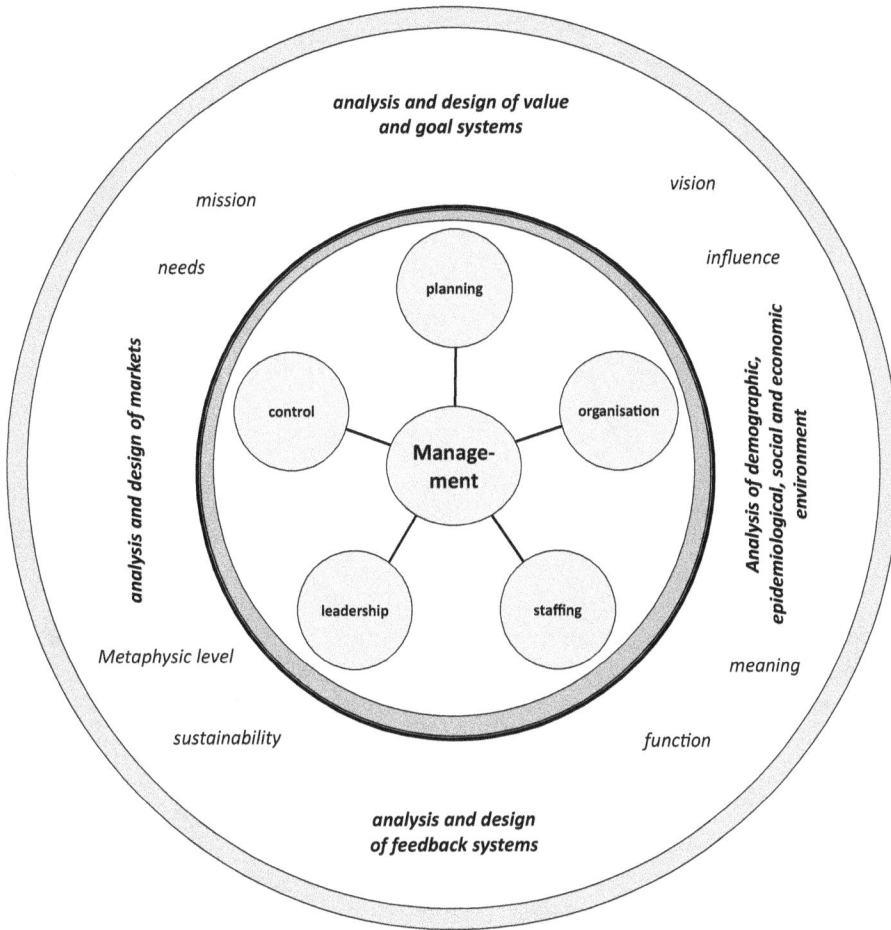

Figure 2.8: Governance of healthcare system.[39]

the macro level and analyses the activities of politics to control the healthcare system. From this perspective, health policy is a subsystem of healthcare management. At the same time, however, health policy as an essential part of social policy extends beyond healthcare management and includes all political influences on areas of life that are relevant to health, such as housing policy, consumer protection, environmental policy, family policy, traffic, and road construction policy. Thus, healthcare management is also an instrument of health policy. Figure 2.9 schematically shows that health policy, health economics, and healthcare management have significant overlaps but are not identical in content and methodology.

---

39 Source: Fleßa (2010a).

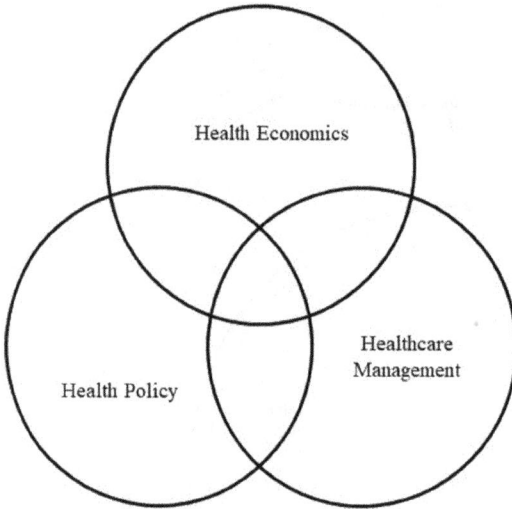

Figure 2.9: Health policy, health economics, and healthcare management.

Health policy is always strategically oriented and thus, like strategic management, involves the analysis and design of the goal system, the environment, resources, and cooperations. The goal system of health policy arises from the fundamental value system of a society, applied to the healthcare system. The discourse on values and goals is the task of ethics and will be delved into further. Environmental analysis encompasses the demographic, epidemiological, social, and economic development of the population. Health policymakers must know, anticipate, and evaluate structures and changes to identify opportunities and risks early on and to be able to respond based on their goal system. When deviations from the goals occur, there is a need for intervention, where, at the strategic level, the focus is particularly on the generation of resources. Health policy does not necessarily have the task of acting directly as a provider of health services but creates a regulatory framework for the activities and elements of the healthcare system by creating leeway for problem-solving and resource generation through laws and regulations. Health insurance companies, hospital operators, doctors, pharmacists, the pharmaceutical industry, etc., use the freedoms created by health policy and, skilfully guided by politics, overcome the deviation of the current state from the health policy goal.

2.1.4.2 Values

The values and goals of health policies in different countries vary in their formulation and prioritization but largely agree in substance. They express for each country's historical path and culture what the Universal Declaration of Human Rights (UN Resolution 217 A (III), 10 December 1948) refers to as 'human dignity' and attributes to every member of the human community. However, the principle of human dignity is difficult to operationalize and demands an articulation of the measures by which it can be achieved. Here, both the Universal Declaration of Human Rights and most constitutions embody the values of the French Revolution – liberty, equality, and fraternity, or liberty, justice, and solidarity. Figure 2.10 shows this derivation.

Freedom, justice, and solidarity are challenging to define but are of central importance to the formulation of health policy. Here, freedom is defined as the ability to choose between different alternatives as an autonomously acting subject, thereby being able to make decisions. For health policy, it is relatively irrelevant to what extent individual decision-making freedom is neurobiologically determined or limited.[40] More importantly, there must be a choice, meaning the individual can select from a bundle of at least two alternatives. Monopolies, therefore, infringe on the individual's right to freedom as much as licensing and establishment regulations. The freedom of the individual must always be limited where the rights of others are endangered by the exercise of freedom (e.g. medical activities by insufficiently trained personnel) or where creating choices is not feasible or only possible with unreasonable effort (e.g. natural monopolies).

In many healthcare systems, creating alternative offerings is a significant problem. For example, hospitals in sparsely populated areas have a natural monopoly, as the fixed-cost-intensive hospital operation makes opening another hospital within a reasonable distance appear economically unfeasible. For potential patient, the choice is merely treatment or no-treatment, but not between different providers. In other areas, choices might be viable, but government regulations or traditions prohibit the establishment of competing providers. Here, the question must be answered regarding the importance of competition, freedom of choice, and pluralism of offerings for a society.

Justice is also a challenging value because different models of justice compete and are ultimately irreconcilable: egalitarian distribution, needs-based justice, and merit-based justice.[41]

Egalitarianism means that everyone receives the same, regardless of their performance or needs. In principle, the bundle of goods is divided by the number of individuals – a procedure as simple as it is dangerous. First, it implies that someone who, due to certain circumstances (e.g. disability), needs particularly many goods to satisfy their needs, receives as much as someone who does not need these goods at all. Second, this approach assumes that the bundle of goods available for distribution is a given. In reality, however, the amount to be distributed is highly variable and depends mainly on the diligence, creativity, and willingness to perform of the economic subjects. The bundle of goods tends to be higher the more these virtues are distrib-

---

40 Compare Roth (2005).
41 Compare Midgley (2020).

uted and the more intensively they are exhibited. Egalitarianism means that someone who is particularly diligent, frugal, creative, and willing to take risks gains nothing from it. Thus, the willingness to perform is at least potentially restricted. In a society where resources are allocated egalitarian, diligence, thrift, creativity, and willingness to take risks, i.e. the sources of progress, are penalized.

The first problem of egalitarian distribution is sought to be overcome by orienting towards needs-based justice, which can generally be described as: "To each, what they need!". It first analyses people's needs. Then, it allocates to each as much as they need to cover their needs. However, this approach proves to be extremely problematic for the practice of health policy. First, there would need to be an all-knowing entity that knows and evaluates the needs and requirements of people. Which needs or demands are legitimate, and which should not be fulfilled? For instance, should the need of an alcoholic for his drug be considered in the needs-based distribution of the gross national product (GNP), or should a higher authority decide that this important need for him should not be satisfied?

Second, "in a world characterized by scarcities, a complete satisfaction of all needs in the sense of the formula 'To each his own' is unattainable"[42]. As long as the limitation of goods meets the boundlessness of needs and demands, a higher authority must weigh the claims and separate those that can be fulfilled from those that cannot. It cannot be ruled out that precisely those needs or demands that an individual considers particularly important will not be satisfied. Alternatively, individuals could rank their needs by importance, which, on the one hand, would be too demanding for many people and, on the other hand, might cater to the selfish needs of some individuals. Subsequently, mechanisms would be needed to reconcile the ranked claims of people.

Third, needs-based justice is contrary to economic development because it hinders diligence, thrift, creativity, and willingness to take risks. The third rule of justice, merit-based justice, on the other hand, encourages these virtues by fundamentally allowing everyone to receive as much as their performance warrants, a principle that is widespread in economics, for example, in the demand that real wages should correspond to the marginal productivity of labour.

The third value is solidarity. It implies the support of the stronger for the weaker, i.e. the young for the old, the healthy for the sick, the rich for the poor, etc. However, solidarity is not identical to altruism or selflessness. Solidarity rather implies a rational weighing of the advantages and disadvantages of providing support to those in need. For example, the young take care of the old (e.g. in the solidarity-based pension insurance) because they know that they will be old one day too. Then, they hope, a younger generation will take care of them. Likewise, the healthy pay into solidarity-based health insurance for the sick because they hope to receive enough support

---

42 Bremer (1996).

themselves if they fall ill. Even the charity of the rich towards the poor has rational reasons, for even the wealthy must fear (albeit with low probability) being poor themselves one day. Then, they hope, others will take care of them. Thus, solidarity within a state is often not an expression of a good heart but a very rational calculus. Solidarity reduces uncertainty in situations of very low probability but which are associated with catastrophic scenarios and high anxiety. At least emotionally, the fears of future uncertainty can be overcome by solidarity today.

Altruism – at least in the tradition of love in the Christian West – differs from this pure utility calculation. The loving individual is willing to forego their own benefit, both short and long terms, to increase the benefit of another. Since this trait is relatively rare, our economic system and our healthcare system cannot be based solely on love. Even if it were possible to build a society of the loving, where almost all people were motivated solely by love, it would be very dangerous. As long as even one individual behaves selfishly, love would lead to the exploitation of the loving. This exploitation would occur in a lawless, helpless space because no one in the 'society of the loving' would expect this behaviour. Therefore, it is better for a society not to assume altruism but to create rules that promote solidarity among social groups. This is undoubtedly an important task of health policy.

2.1.4.3 Goals

Freedom, justice, and solidarity are values that express the fundamental principle of human dignity. However, for the practice of health policy, they are still too abstract and require exemplification. Health policy goals must be specific, measurable, achievable, realistic, and time-bound (SMART goals). The goals of accessibility, effectiveness, sustainability, and participation already meet these requirements much more clearly and are often cited as fundamental goals of health policy.

Effectiveness

Health services should make a positive contribution to people's health, i.e. they should be effective. This implies that these services are offered in the right quantity, at appropriate quality, at the right time, in the suitable place, and in combination with other services. The quality of health services is particularly important here. Cheap but qualitatively insufficient and thus ineffective medicine and care cannot be a health policy goal.

The concept of quality is complex and difficult to specify,[43] making the measurement of its effects challenging. According to Donabedian, quality can be divided into structure, process, and outcome quality.[44] For public health, this concept must be enhanced with the distinction between output, outcome and impact.

---

43 Compare Fleßa (2010a).
44 Compare Donabedian and Bashshur (2002).

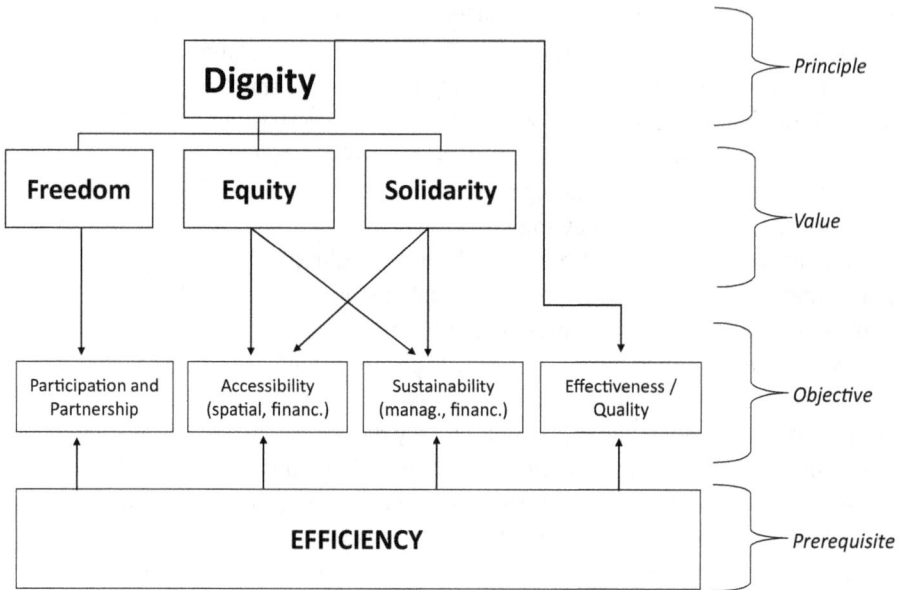

Figure 2.10: Value and goal system of the healthcare sector.

The quantity and quality of resource consumption determine the structure quality. The task of a health institution or programme is the production of health services. For this purpose, production factors are recombined in such a way that the best possible service is produced. The recombination process (=production) determines the process quality. The less resources are wasted in the interaction of the production factors, the better the process quality. It can be determined using flow charts, error rates, service times, etc. The service production process is complicated by the physical presence of the customer (e.g. patient), on whom the service is provided. Unlike the production of commodities, the customer as an external factor is an essential component of the production process. He not only collects his service at the end but is part of the service creation process (Figure 2.11).

The result of the production process is not health but merely a health service, i.e. an output (compare Figure 2.12). It can be measured quantitatively, e.g. by the number of contacts (e.g. consultations), by the number of bed days, and by the number of patients. More challenging is measuring outcome quality and, above all, tracing outcome quality back to the production process, as the customer as an external factor significantly influences the outcome quality. While in the production of goods, a customer has no influence on the product's quality, the success of healing or consultation of a health service cannot be separated from the person and personality of the customer.

Therefore, the outputs of the health service providers' production process are only one determinant of the patients' health (outcome). His genetic disposition, living

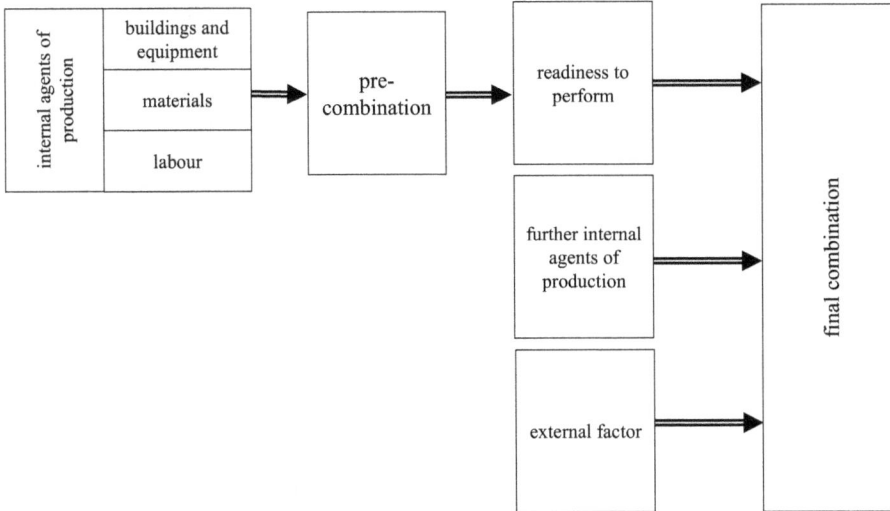

Figure 2.11: Service process.[45]

space, occupation, role, etc., influence the outcome at least as much as the output of the healthcare system.

Finally, the health of an individual serves as an input factor for a societal production function, the result of which is prosperity and growth for the entire society, and also (social) security and reliability. For example, curing a patient with tuberculosis (TB) enables them to be economically active again, relieves their family members from caregiving duties, and prevents the patient from infecting others. The final result will be economic productivity, and also reduction of risks for his family and the entire society. Thus, the impact can be significantly higher than the outcome.

In summary, health policy measures need to be effective in the sense that they produce an outcome that has an impact on society. At the same time, these statistics are relatively difficult to measure, so in practice, focus is often placed on outcomes (e.g. bed days) – a narrow approach that tempts one to confuse performance figures of health service providers with the health of the population.[46]

Accessibility
Health services should be accessible to the population, meaning there should be no barriers preventing a want from becoming a demand. As shown in Figure 2.7, poor quality, lack of purchasing power, and spatial distance are the main barriers.

---

45 Source: Corsten (1998).
46 Compare Murray et al. (2002) and Shengelia, Murray, Adams, et al. (2003).

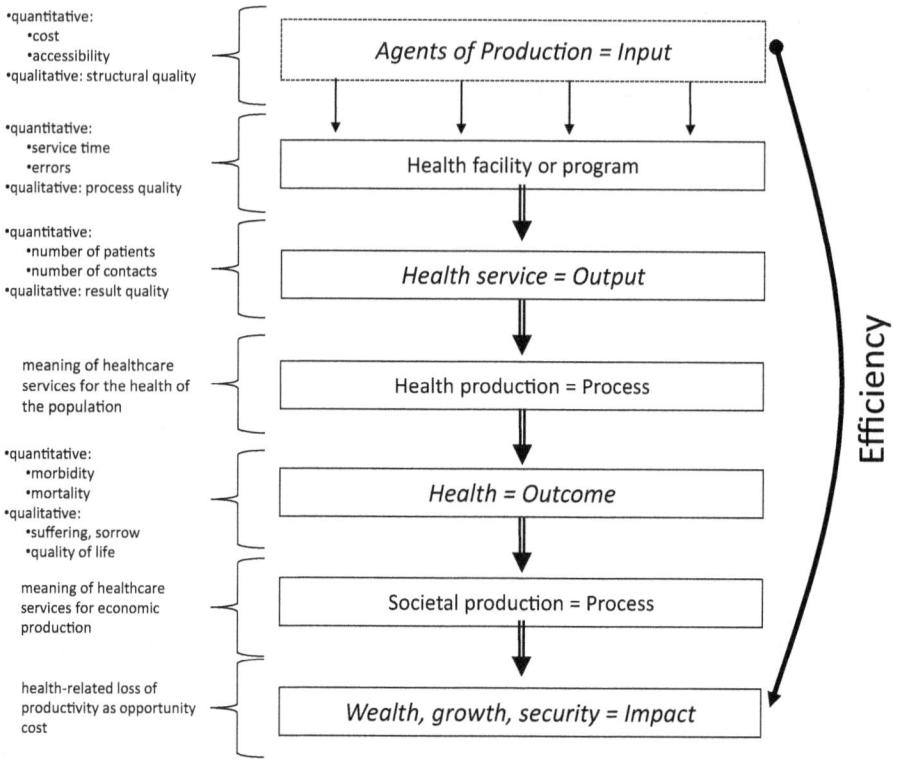

Figure 2.12: Output-outcome-impact model.[47]

Spatial accessibility is a significant issue in peripheral areas of low-income countries. In general, the number of interactions between two elements decreases with increasing distance (distance decay effect) because the costs of interaction increase with distance, where not only monetary costs are considered, but especially the loss of time in overcoming spatial distance. As shown in Figure 2.13, there is a critical distance beyond which no (significant) interactions occur. For instance, a travel distance of 1 day to visit a hospital might be such a limit, as experience shows that no one is willing to spend the night on the way to the hospital. Thus, the maximum catchment area of a hospital, for a population primarily traveling on foot, is about 50 km. This implies that people living more than this distance from a hospital are systematically excluded from receiving hospital services. For dispensaries, even a 10-km walk represents a limit many are unwilling to cross.

This example also shows that overcoming distance depends not only on the spatial distance in kilometres but also on the infrastructure, the gravity of the health ser-

---

47 Source: Own, based on Claeson, Griffin, Johnston, et al. (2002).

number of
transactions

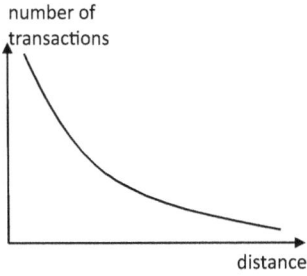

distance **Figure 2.13:** Distance decay model.[48]

vice provider, and the perception of distance, i.e. the friction of distance is just a special case of a gravity model, as expressed in the following formula:

$$G = C \cdot \frac{M_1 \cdot M_2}{d^a}$$

where G is the gravity between two centres, C is the constant, M_i is the mass of centre i, $i = 1, 2$, D is the distance between two centres, and a is the friction constant

The attraction between two centres thus generally depends on the mass of the centres, the spatial distance, and the friction constant. A hospital has a higher significance as a healthcare provider than a dispensary, meaning that, all else being equal, people are more willing to overcome a certain distance to go to a hospital than to visit a dispensary. Tertiary hospitals have a higher mass than secondary hospitals, which in turn are more attractive than primary hospitals. The number of beds in a hospital is only an indicator of the mass of the institution. More significant is the role in a healthcare system, which is expressed, for example, in staffing, facilities, and specialized departments.

The significance of distance depends on infrastructural and cultural mobility. The life radius of many people in resource-poor countries is less than 50 km, meaning that even a trip to the nearest district capital can be a challenge. At the same time, mobility is increasing in rural areas, particularly with the improved availability of public transport, making healthcare providers significantly easier to access. However, a problem remains that spatial accessibility requires adequate financial resources, as public transportation typically incurs costs. Spatial accessibility is further explored in Section 4.1.2.

Therefore, the second component of accessibility is affordability (financial accessibility). In many developing countries, poverty groups lack access to modern health services, resulting in above-average morbidity and mortality rates in these subpopulations. The inadequate medical care of the poor population can have two causes: a lack of willingness to pay (WTP) and a lack of ability to pay (ATP).

---

48 Source: Fleßa (2007).

Many diseases in developing countries are life-threatening, so there is generally a high WTP. Sick people are willing to pay for health services if the service provided promises healing success. Thus, WTP can be increased through quality improvement measures (e.g. staff training and sufficient availability of medicines).

However, the income of the vulnerable in resource-poor countries is low, so they often cannot afford effective healthcare, even though they would like to. The above-average morbidity and mortality rates are thus mostly not due to a lack of WTP but to a lack of ATP. People die from curable diseases because they cannot afford a hospital stay. Sometimes, the ATP can be temporarily increased by selling livestock or farmland. In the long term, however, the loss of agricultural means of production leads to complete impoverishment, i.e. further decrease in the ATP. Financial accessibility is further explored in Section 5.2.

Sustainability

Effectiveness and affordability are crucial goals of health policy. However, they should not only address the needs of today's patients but also take future generations into account. Adequate health services must be provided for them as well, necessitating the inclusion of sustainability as a goal.

Sustainability is a key development policy paradigm. Most development aid agencies require evidence of sustainability for all grants, and there is a vast number of publications on this concept. Despite this, there is no uniform definition, and measuring sustainability is exceptionally challenging.

Originally, the concept of sustainability comes from forestry.[49] To protect forests from overuse, a resource management focussing on maintaining stock levels was legally mandated in the Middle Ages, meaning annual logging could not exceed annual growth. This was termed 'sustainable forestry', ensuring subsequent generations would find at least the same quantity and quality of forests as the present generation.

Sustainability became a buzzword in development economics in 1972. The 'UN Conference on Environment and Development' led to an open conflict between developing countries and the Western world: Developing countries insisted on their right to economic development, while the Western world demanded a higher level of environmental protection in these countries. The conflict was resolved with the concept of 'sustainable development'. Further international conferences and reports, such as the Brundtland Report (1987) and the UN Conference on Environment and Development in Rio de Janeiro (1992), as well as regional consultations and declarations, such as the Khartoum (1988) and the Lusaka Declaration (1999), expanded and specified the concept to include economic, social, and ecological dimensions:
- Development versus growth: A country exploiting its resources beyond their natural regeneration capability can achieve relatively high economic growth in the

---

49 Compare Caradonna (2022).

short term. However, this does not constitute development in the long term, as future generations will not be able to rely on these resources. The concept of sustainability calls for development rather than purely quantitative growth.

- Intergenerational justice: Future generations should have the same access to resources as the current generation. This aligns with the traditional understanding of forestry sustainability.
- Intragenerational justice: In political discussions, the demand for sustainability is often linked with the obligation of wealthy countries to poorer states, i.e. a more egalitarian distribution of resources between the Global North and South. At the same time, intragenerational justice implies reducing regional disparities within a country, such as differences in services between urban and rural areas.
- Environmental protection: Intergenerational justice is only achievable if natural resources are used sparingly. Thus, environmental protection is a crucial goal of sustainable development.

Accordingly, the Brundtland Report defined sustainable development as "development that meets the needs of the present without compromising the ability of future generations to meet their own needs. The demand for this development to be 'sustainable' applies to all countries and people. The ability of future generations to meet their needs is endangered both by environmental destruction and by underdevelopment in the Third World".[50]

While initially focussed on environmental protection in developing countries, the demand for sustainability quickly extended to other areas of development economics. Today, development practitioners speak of 'ecological sustainability', 'sustainable programmes', or 'sustainable institutions', and most development aid organizations require evidence of sustainability for programmes or institutions they aim to support. Sustainability has also become an important term in healthcare, with numerous authors calling for the sustainability of health institutions, technical facilities, projects, or social development. However, the broad application of the term 'sustainability' in practice to anything related to the future necessitates a precise definition and operationalization to be useful for healthcare management.[51]

The expansion of the sustainability concept beyond environmental protection issues to encompass many aspects of development necessitates a redefinition of sustainability as the capacity of an open system to generate services at the current time without compromising the ability of future periods to do the same. The structure of this system must be designed in such a way that the transformation of input into output, i.e. the system's function in its environment, is conducted so that the system's energy level after the transformation is not diminished, ensuring that a transformation pro-

---

50 Compare Hauff (1987).
51 Compare Asante (1998).

cess can also occur in the future. Accordingly, various aspects of economic and social sustainability can be distinguished:

- Sustainability from static and dynamic perspectives: From a static perspective, a system is sustainable if it can survive indefinitely in a constant environment ('viability'). The dynamic view expands this concept, demanding that a system responds to changes in its environment in such a way that it can survive under new conditions. It is entirely possible for a system to have unlimited viability in an unchanged environment (sustainability in a static view) but to be immediately destroyed once those conditions change (sustainability in a dynamic view).
- Sustainability from structural and functional perspectives: A system capable of maintaining its structure (e.g. buildings, machinery, and staff qualifications) over the long term is sustainable from a structural perspective. This is a long-term, but not short-term, prerequisite for the system to fulfil its function in its environment (sustainable from a functional perspective). It is possible for a system to maintain its function in the short term while consuming its structure.
- Sustainability from the perspective of development aid donors and recipients: From the perspective of development aid donors, an institution or programme is sustainable if it is viable after financial contributions from outside have ceased. From the recipients' perspective, an institution or programme is often considered sustainable if it can survive long term with a constant volume of donations.
- Sustainability of disease control programmes: Diesfeld et al. take it even further, defining a health programme as sustainable if the "positive changes achieved continue to exist after its completion".[52] The eradication of smallpox was such a project. After the last patient was discharged cured in October 1977, the vaccination project could be abandoned shortly thereafter. The eradication of the disease was permanent. Most health institutions and programmes cannot meet this high standard.

Sustainability is thus a highly complex goal of health policy. It is absolutely necessary to consider sustainability, but it must be precisely defined and operationalized; otherwise, it is of no use to healthcare management.

More recently, the term 'resilience' became more popular in development economics although it is rather difficult to define. The allegory of health can support the reflection on the term: The traditional understanding of health assumes that threats (e.g. viruses, bacteria, parasites, psychological stress, and air pollution) put a short-term strain on health, but the body has the ability to return to its original state. This return to the original level could be called 'static resilience'. However, as mentioned in Section 2.1.1, health is dynamic, meaning that the body does not return to its original state, but rather to a higher level of health than before the stress. The body has improved its ability to

---

52 Compare Diesfeld, Falkenhorst, Razum, et al. (2001).

react appropriately to the same or similar attacks (dynamic resilience). In some cases of severe illness, the body cannot be resorted on the same level, but still comes back to an equilibrium on a lower level. This could be called 'deformative resilience'.

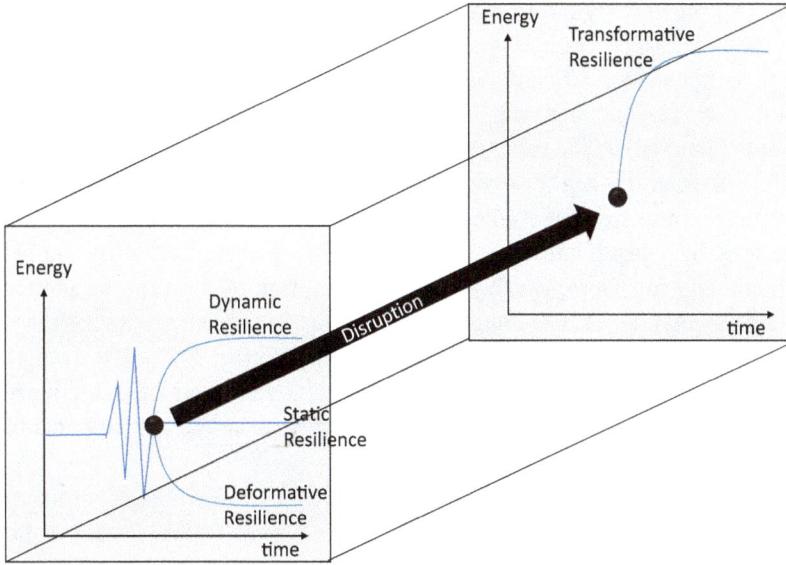

Figure 2.14: Resilience.[53]

Figure 2.14 indicates a dynamic system model facing a diachronic regime up to a bifurcation or tipping point. If the system is sufficiently energetic, it can come back to an equilibrium on the same (static resilience), on a higher (dynamic resilience) or a lower (deformative resilience) level. It could, however, also develop at a much higher level with completely different structures, i.e. the system might be completely transformed (transformative resilience). The healthcare system itself can be viewed from the perspective of how it responds to disruptions. The question is whether it has the power to return to the old balance after a disruption (reconstructive resilience), or whether even after overcoming the disruption it rises to a higher level. This higher level will enable the healthcare system in the future, to the same or similar levels to be able to respond to challenges more appropriately so that they no longer trigger a crisis.

Participation
Participation is a dual process, involving both "allowing others to share in what one is, has, and does" and "enabling all participants or those affected to have a share in

---

53 Source: Own.

the powers, rights, privileges, and possessions established by these structures".[54] Therefore, those affected should have decision-making powers and the freedom to make decisions about their lives, health, care, and future. It is important to distinguish between active and passive participation. The former describes the independent contribution to processes, while the latter refers to participation when decision-makers are legitimized. For example, exercising the right to vote is a form of passive participation, as the elected officials are legitimized to perform their duties for the benefit of the electorate. Both active and passive participation, along with the right to choose between them, reflect the value of freedom as described above.

All stakeholders in the healthcare system, including patients, workers, service providers, public administration employees, civil society groups, and development aid organizations, have legitimate interests that must be considered. A focus is on patients and their right to choose, which is both a human right and a prerequisite for successful implementation. Only healthcare reforms that are socially compatible, i.e. accepted by the majority of the population, can be implemented. The more strongly individual stakeholders are integrated into the decision-making process, the more likely they are to accept new changes. Thus, participation is both a primary goal of health policy and a tool to ensure implementation.

Another expression of participation is the partnership between the government and other service providers. Commercial health service providers, non-profit organizations, and their associations are directly affected by governmental health policy decisions and must therefore be involved in the decision-making process. This goal has been increasingly emphasized in recent years.

Effectiveness, accessibility, sustainability, and participation are health policy goals of great importance for international healthcare management. Healthcare management serves to implement these goals by providing tools that can help achieve them. However, these four goals compete with each other, leading to potential conflicts.

2.1.4.4 Goal Conflicts

Figure 2.15 illustrates the conflict between these goals using the example of communicating tubes. Effectiveness, accessibility, sustainability, and participation are connected to a gas-filled cylinder. Applying pressure to one of these parameters immediately affects the others. For example, attempting to increase effectiveness, all else being equal, will likely worsen accessibility, participation, and sustainability.

Financial accessibility (affordability) and effectiveness or quality are good examples of conflicts in health policy goals. Given state or development aid subsidies, services can either be affordable but of poor quality, or of high quality but unaffordable for the majority of the population. Health policy will try to define a basic package of affordable health services accessible to everyone, regardless of income and location.

---

54 Rich (1991).

However, the conflict remains that a compromise must be made with the given resources regarding which diseases to treat and the quality of care.

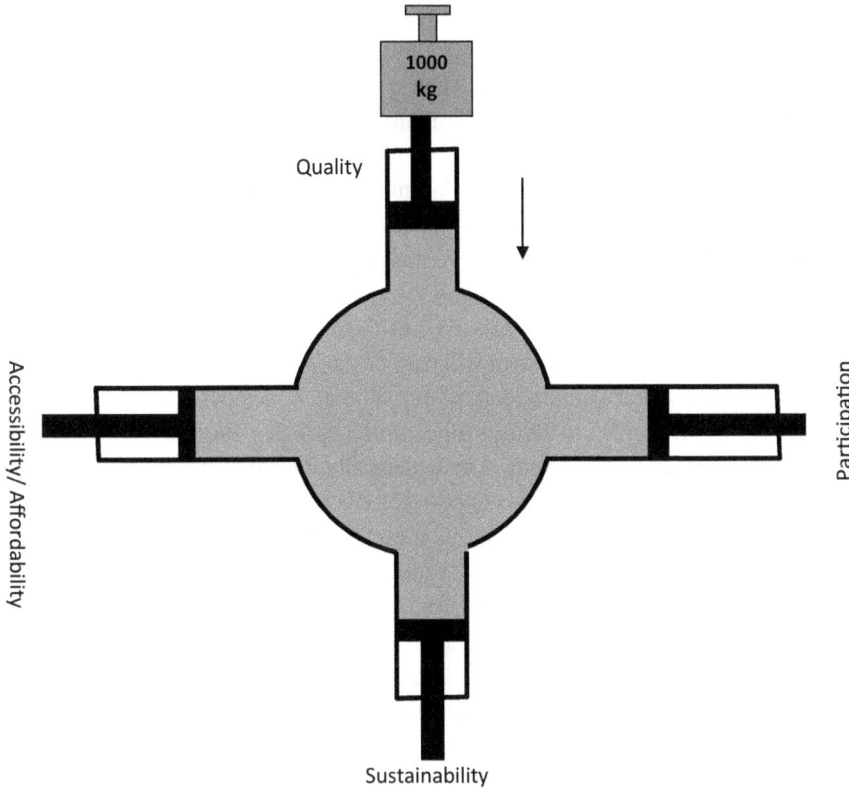

Figure 2.15: Goal conflicts.[55]

The limitation of the scope of services and the adaptation of standards to national
conditions result in many people in resource-poor countries suffering from or dying
of diseases that would be curable in Western countries. Given the existing scarcity of
resources, the 'basic package' in the poorest countries must be so narrowly defined
and the standards so low that this neither corresponds to the guiding principle of
human dignity nor seems politically feasible. Health policymakers, therefore, risk alle-
viating the suffering of the current generation at the expense of future generations,
as there is also competition between the goals of affordability and sustainability.

Affordability implies that a healthcare institution charges low fees or provides
fee waivers to poverty groups. Consequently, revenues will generally not suffice to
fund maintenance, depreciation, and training. The facility cannot be maintained at its

---

55 Source: Own.

original standard, meaning patients will not receive the same quantity and quality of services in the future as they do now. The facility is not sustainable. Therefore, afford-ability and sustainability are competing goals.

Health policy must, therefore, balance the needs of people today against the interests of future generations. Future benefits must be compared with current ones. There is a risk of elevating the suffering of those currently alive as the sole measure of action, thus largely neglecting the goal of sustainability through exclusively short-term-oriented humanitarian aid.

Considering those affected in the decision-making process (participation) does not clearly compete with the other goals. On the one hand, only those alive today can participate in current decisions, potentially emphasizing affordability and quality at the expense of sustainability. On the other hand, participation is an essential prerequisite for the population's identification with the healthcare system. Only if they take responsibility for their healthcare system will they sustainably commit to its existence.

Figure 2.15 shows that simultaneous improvement in achieving all goals is only possible if pressure is applied to all four tubes simultaneously, increasing the gas density. This is a metaphor for efficiency, which generally describes the ratio of outcome to resource input. A system or process is efficient if a given outcome is achieved with minimal resource input or a maximum outcome is achieved with a given resource input. Figure 2.16 illustrates this using a production possibilities curve, which is the geometric locus of all combinations of health for individuals A and B possible with a given production technology. Points on the curve (e.g. 1–5) are efficient (Pareto-optimal) since improving A's health can only come at the cost of worsening B's health. Points above the curve are technically impossible, while points below are technically possible but inefficient. For example, at point (6), the situation of A or B can be improved without detracting from the other, representing a waste of resources.

Achieving the health policy goals of effectiveness, accessibility, sustainability, and participation can, therefore, be improved through two measures simultaneously. Firstly, by reducing the waste of resources, for example, through the application of healthcare management planning methods. The use of modern materials management systems in hospitals means fewer medications need to be discarded, freeing up resources for improving patient treatment (effectiveness), reducing fees (accessibility), maintaining facilities (sustainability), or establishing a public-private partnership (participation). Efficiency thus enables the achievement of health policy goals (compare Figure 2.10).

Alternatively, efforts can be made to shift the production possibilities curve, for example, by employing more efficient technology. The transition to minimally invasive surgery, for instance, results in higher-quality medical services, lower costs, fewer subsequent health issues, and potentially even greater patient participation, as full anaesthesia may not be required. This too is a measure to increase the overall system's efficiency, confirming the fundamental assertion that efficiency creates the room for achieving health policy goals.

H_a

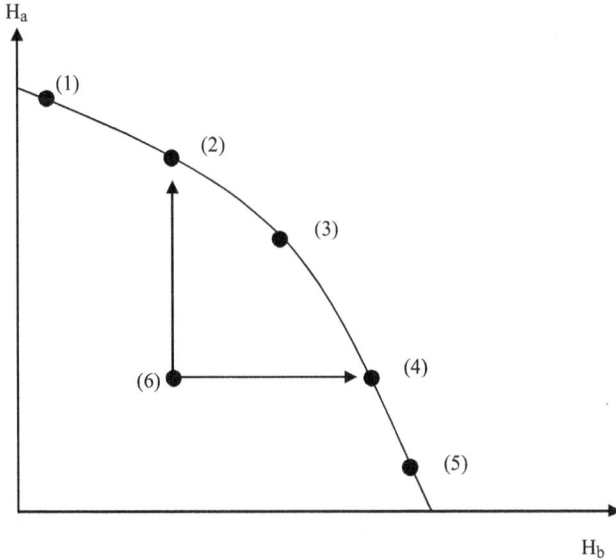

Figure 2.16: Production possibilities curve.[56]

Efficiency is, therefore, a prerequisite for achieving the goals of effectiveness, accessibility, sustainability, and participation. These goals, in turn, can be understood as measures to strive for societal values such as freedom, justice, and solidarity. Consequently, efficiency is also a condition for these fundamental values. Every resource that is wasted is no longer available to defend freedom, justice, and solidarity. However, it is often stated that justice and efficiency are opposites and that politics must settle for a compromise. Therefore, it becomes necessary to analyse the relationship between efficiency and justice more thoroughly.

Justice and Efficiency
Traditional economics maximizes the sum of a variable across all individuals, using variables such as gross domestic product (GDP), consumption, utility, health status, or similar, depending on the application. As shown by target function (1), maximizing the sum equates to maximizing the average if the number of individuals is constant:

$$z = \sum_{i=1}^{n} x_i \rightarrow \text{Max!} \Leftrightarrow Z' = \sum_{i=1}^{n} 1/n \cdot x_i \rightarrow \text{Max!} \tag{1}$$

This target function Z' (1), on the one hand, therefore corresponds to a distribution in which the average is optimized. However, it does not guarantee that a distribution

---

56 Source: Sickles and Zelenyuk (2019).

considered just will be achieved. Target function Z" (2), on the other hand, focusses on the welfare of the weakest member of society and attempts to maximize it. Target function Z"' (3) also concentrates on justice by striving for the smallest possible deviation from the average:

$$Z'' = \underset{i=1..n}{\text{Min}}(x_i) \rightarrow \text{Max!} \tag{2}$$

$$Z''' = \sum_{i=1}^{n} |x_i - \bar{x}| \rightarrow \text{Min!} \tag{3}$$

Only in the case of equal income distribution do the target functions (1), (2), and (3) lead to the same generation of resources. Typically, a situation perceived as just is likely to have lower productivity than a situation resulting from a pure efficiency consideration. Thus, from a pure efficiency perspective, the average population is better off than from a primary justice perspective.

Target function (2) does not automatically lead to equality. Instead, it allows for variance in the variable x, if this leads to an improvement for the weakest in society. This corresponds to Rawls' principle, which accepts inequality as long as it benefits the least advantaged. This complex statement will be illustrated with an example (Table 2.3).

Table 2.3: Principle of Rawls: example of income of persons A, B, and C.[57]

Person	Year 1990	Year 1995	Year 2000	Year 2005
A	300	330	100	300
B	300	600	800	300
C	300	900	1,200	1,200

In 1990, all three individuals had the same income (€300), meaning the average income was also €300. By 1995, the average income had risen to €610, with each person benefiting to varying degrees. Person C tripled their income, person B doubled theirs, and person A saw only a 10% increase. The distribution became more unequal, but everyone was better off.

By the year 2000, income had risen again. On average, it now stood at €700, but the income of the poorest had dropped to a third of its original value. Not only did their situation worsen relative to the other two individuals, but it also worsened absolutely compared to the starting point in 1990. According to Rawls, an increasing average does not justify the absolute worsening of the poorest person's situation.

---

57 Source: Own.

The year 2005 represents a borderline case. The income of persons A and B remained unchanged from 1990, but person C's income increased. The average income also rose from €300 to 600. However, the increasing inequality is perceived as unjust. According to Rawls, the transition from 1990 to 1995 leads to an acceptable level of inequality because even the poorest benefits. All further developments are to be rejected as unjust, even if the increasing income of person C does not result from exploitation or oppression but from their performance.

Rawls, in a way, reconciles justice and efficiency by suggesting that performance should be rewarding and, at the same time, benefit the weakest in society. This idea laid the foundation for modern economics, widely regarded as initiated by the English moral philosopher Adam Smith. In his seminal work, *The Theory of Moral Sentiments* (1759), he emphasized the importance of compassion, sympathy, and dedication in human interactions. Throughout his career, Smith sought practical ways to implement these principles, primarily aiming to combat poverty in England. His research culminated in *The Wealth of Nations* (1776), where he presented a surprising conclusion that still baffles some today: the goals of ethics are best realized through the economy, and a free market economy will eventually lead to everyone being better off.[58] Smith resolved this conflict by advocating for economic growth through free-market economics and suggesting 'sympathy' as a complement to the market order, leaving it to the "humanitarian sentiment of the individual".[59]

We thus face the issue of different distributions competing over which is just. Figure 2.17 exemplifies the relationship between justice and efficiency, similar to Figure 2.16 plotting the respective health benefits of individuals A and B (H_a and H_b). Unlike Figure 2.16, it assumes that individual A naturally has better health and therefore, ceteris paribus, a higher state of health than B.

Point (1) represents the unrealistic scenario where all health resources are allocated to A, leaving B without access to healthcare services, resulting in significantly lower health benefits. Realistically, this situation would make B a source of infection, endangering A as well. Therefore, it is more efficient for B to also have access to healthcare resources, reducing A's risk of infection, as indicated by the shift from point (1) to point (2). Both benefit from redistribution: B gains access to healthcare services, and A becomes healthier than before, despite sharing resources. Beyond point (2), any increase in B's benefit would come at the expense of A, meaning all points between (2) and (4) are Pareto-optimal.

The target function (1) for this example would read:

$$Z^* = H_a + H_b \rightarrow \text{Max!}$$

---

58 Compare Homann and Blome-Drees (1992) and Aßländer (2018).
59 Schöpf (1984).

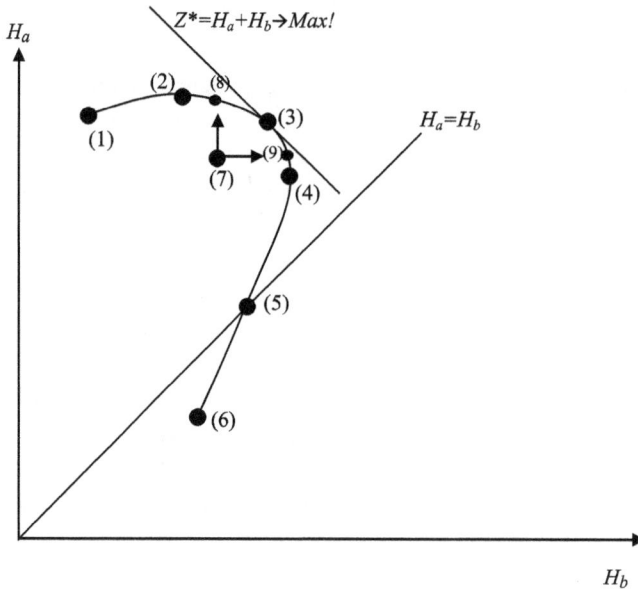

Figure 2.17: Justice and efficiency.[60]

Point (3) symbolizes the maximum health benefit for both individuals. Since the sum of benefits is maximal, the average benefit is also maximal, but maximizing the average benefit does not imply an equal distribution.

From point (4) onwards, further redistribution of health resources from person A to person B results in both being worse off. Due to his weaker natural constitution, B is less able to convert the additional health resources into health, while A, without sufficient health protection, is often sick, thereby increasing the risk of infection for B. If this negative effect of a higher risk of infection outweighs the positive effect of additional health resources, both individuals' benefits may decrease. Figure 2.16 shows this for the extreme, but not unrealistic scenario, where at point (6), all health resources are invested in B, resulting in person A constantly infecting person B, and they both have low benefits together.

Point (4) symbolizes the best possible care for person B, while point (5) represents equal distribution. In the not unrealistic case that A has a better natural constitution than B, the point of equal utility is located to the lower left of the Pareto-optimal points, meaning both individuals are worse off than in the case of inequality. Therefore, according to Rawls , point (4) is preferable to (5), as both persons A and B benefit more from it, i.e. the unequal distribution at point (4) benefits the weaker of the two (B).

---

60 Source: Fleßa (2003a).

The figure shows that the point of maximum sum of benefits (3) and the point of best care for the weaker (4) can be relatively close to each other. Indeed, in this situation, one would likely aim for maximizing the average rather than equal distribution, because it definitely grants both A and B better health.

These explanations show that justice and efficiency are not fundamentally in competition. It is important to acknowledge the limitations of one's own science and define both terms precisely. The limitation of economics is evident at point (7), which lies below the production possibilities curve, thus being Pareto-inefficient. Economists can undoubtedly recommend moving from point (7) to point (8) or (9), or to any point on the curve between (8) and (9). This statement can be made at any time, as moving from point (7) to any point between (8) and (9) does not make any individual worse off. The statement that point (7) is worse than point (2) or point (4) is, however, a value judgment, as a change from (7) to (2) or (4) would imply improvement for one at the expense of another. Economists making such redistribution proposals are leaving the solid ground of their discipline.

Precise definitions of the terms efficiency and justice are important to avoid unnecessary disputes over terminology. Here, the health economic framework model (compare Figure 2.7), proves useful, which for easier illustration is slightly modified and repeated here as Figure 2.18.

Efficiency compares outcomes with resource consumption. Depending on whether one defines disease, need, demand, or supply as the outcome, different concepts of efficiency emerge as follows:
- Disease: The efficiency analysis determines the health status that can be produced with given resources.
- Need or wants: It is examined which needs or wants can be satisfied with given resources.
- Demand: The analysis determines what demand can be met with given resources.
- Supply: It is analysed which services can be produced with given resources.

Clearly, these concepts of efficiency vary greatly. For example, technically optimal surgical procedures (supply efficiency) say little about whether the health of the population in the catchment area is optimally promoted. A hospital may be very efficient from a business perspective but only serves the upper class. The large number of sick people would never dare to visit this expensive hospital, i.e. the resources are relatively inefficiently used to serve the population.

Justice can also be tied to the individual elements of the framework model:
- Disease: The justice analysis identifies health inequalities, i.e. the goal would be equally good health for all.
- Needs: It is examined whether every individual can satisfy their health needs equally well.
- Wants: The analysis describes whether everyone can meet their need for health services, i.e. whether everyone gets the services they wish for.

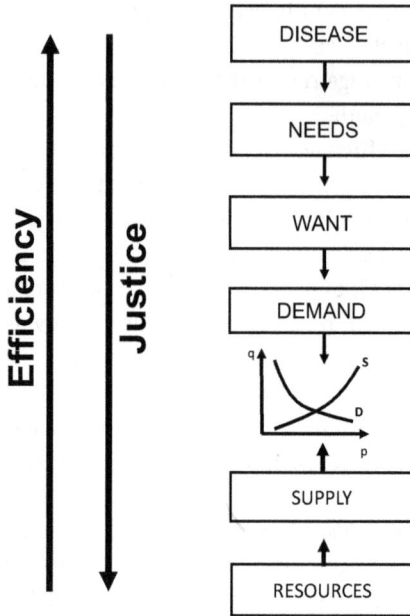

Figure 2.18: Health economic framework model (based on Figure 2.7).[61]

- Demand: The analysis determines whether everyone gets what they can afford and reach.
- Supply: It is analysed whether everyone receives the same health services.

Again, it is evident that the various conceptions of justice are partly contradictory and cannot be fully reconciled. For health policy, it is crucial to precisely define its terms and goals. Ethics is therefore a prerequisite for health policy.

In conclusion, healthcare management is an action-oriented science that supports decision-makers in the healthcare sector in planning, implementing, and controlling health-relevant measures. This leads to a high level of interdisciplinarity, as healthcare management draws from sciences such as public health, epidemiology, demography, sociology, geography, ecology, agriculture, hydraulic engineering, settlement development, and applies their findings for a practice-oriented control of health-relevant processes. The starting point is always the value and goal system of a population, so the discussion of health policy goals forms the basis of all further explanations.

Values and goals differ between societies. Hofstede,[62] for example, distinguishes the criteria of 'power distance', 'individualism', 'masculinity', 'uncertainty avoidance',

---

61 Source: Own.
62 Compare Hofstede (1983), Hofstede, Hofstede, and Minkov (2005), and Hofstede Insights (2024).

'long-term orientation', and 'indulgence' as dimensions of national culture and shows that these values significantly differ among the countries and world regions he studied. From these values arises the historical path that, in turn, shapes the values, so it is expected that the health policy goals of different countries will differ significantly. Considering the path dependency of healthcare systems, different resource allocations, and the diverse epidemiological, ecological, and demographic conditions, it becomes clear that for a practice-oriented science like healthcare management, there cannot be a uniform, culture-independent doctrine. Instead, healthcare management is regionally differentiated, meaning that insights gained in one region can be enlightening for others but cannot be directly and uncritically transferred. Therefore, it is necessary to establish international healthcare management as a science. This chapter aims to serve this purpose.

2.2 Health and Development

International healthcare management analyses and compares the management of health-relevant processes in different regions to derive practical recommendations for efficient healthcare. The varying resource endowments in different world regions are of great importance for this analysis. Therefore, it is essential for further discussions to analyse the relationship between health and development or between disease and healthcare resources.

2.2.1 Fundamental Concept

Health and development[63] are elements of an autocatalytic process, meaning investments in health lead to developmental effects, which in turn induce a health improvement. To investigate this relationship, the terms economic growth and economic development are initially considered equivalent. This assumption will be questioned subsequently.

The second causality (economic growth creates health) is relatively straightforward, as the health of the population is partly the result of health services produced using national economic resources. Therefore, a wealthy nation has more resources available to produce health services, generally improving the health of the population along the development path. This perspective has led to the stance in development policy that the best health policy is economic policy since a growing economy will ultimately provide the resources for improved health.

---

63 Compare also Johnson (2011).

The first causality (health creates economic growth) was long contested. The starting point is the national economic production function, where the factor of human labour plays an important role, for example, in the form of a Cobb-Douglas production function:[64]

$$Y = a \cdot C^\alpha \cdot L^\beta$$

where Y is the GDP, a is the productivity parameter, C is the capital stock, α and β are the partial production elasticities, and L is the labour force.

Key determinants of economic growth include the quantitative increase in the production factors labour and capital. The production function can be easily expanded to include the factors land or natural resources and human capital. Moreover, technological progress plays a crucial role as it can increase the productivity of the production factors. For example, the use of modern machinery means that more can be produced with the same amount of labour.

Health is a factor that influences the quantity and quality of the labour force. For example, combating diseases leads to fewer lost work hours, making the labour factor more available. This relationship can be simplified in the production function as

$$Y = a \cdot C^\alpha \cdot (h \cdot L)^\beta$$

where h is the health status.

Economic growth, therefore, can be expressed as[65]

$$\frac{\dot{Y}}{Y} = \frac{\dot{a}}{a} + \alpha \cdot \frac{\dot{C}}{C} + \beta \cdot \frac{\dot{h}}{h} + \beta \cdot \frac{\dot{L}}{l}$$

or, holding everything else constant, as

$$\frac{\dot{Y}}{Y} = \beta \cdot \frac{\dot{h}}{h}$$

where $\frac{\dot{h}}{h}$ can be interpreted as the rate of health-improving technological progress.

This fundamental connection was placed at the centre of international health policy by the WHO in 2000. Based on the final report of the 'Commission on Macroeconomics and Health', the WHO postulated that health expenditures are not merely humanitarian aid but profitable investments into the health of a population. After extensive debate, this statement is generally accepted,[66] with the basic relationship also considered valid for developed countries. For example, the European Union concluded in its 2005 report, 'The Contribution of Health to the Economy in the European Union':

---

64 Compare Cobb and Douglas (1928).
65 $\dot{Y}$ denotes the difference in time, i.e. $\dot{Y} = Y_{t+1} - Y_t$.
66 Compare Möller, Schmidt, Laaser, et al. (2004), Morrow (2002), and Ivinson (2002).

. . . good health promotes earnings and labour supply. Particularly relevant to Europe, with its aging population, they show how poor health increases the likelihood of early retirement. Together, this evidence offers a powerful argument for European governments to invest in the health of their populations, not only because better health is a desirable goal in itself but also because it is an important determinant of economic growth and competitiveness.

Even for countries with very high incomes, such as Germany, it is proclaimed that health is a prerequisite for economic development and that investments in health pay off.[67]

Especially for developing countries, investments in health could be particularly profitable as they enable overcoming the classic development traps described by Nelson in 1956.[68] Starting with a capital investment (compare Figure 2.19), for example, through development aid, this investment leads to economic growth according to the growth formula, which in many developing countries resulted in a significant increase in population growth. This, in turn, had two consequences. On the one hand, the high birth rate means a long-term overload of public services, notably the healthcare system. An increasingly larger population must be provided with health services, often not feasible, leading to a deterioration of the population's health status.

At this point, it becomes clear that an autocatalytic process can take two directions. Improved health leads to rising economic growth, which in turn leads to improved health, thereby, once initiated, a self-reinforcing process leads to a significant improvement in economic conditions. On the other hand, a reduction in health also leads to a vicious circle, as poor health leads to decreased labour performance and, consequently, a reduction in economic performance, which in turn has adverse effects on healthcare provision. This initiates a downward spiral.

The second effect was often referred to as the 'Malthusian trap'. The English cleric and social philosopher Robert Malthus (1766–1834) predicted that the food supply would grow linearly, but the population would grow exponentially, leading to famine. Indeed, capital investments in some developing countries in the 1950s and 1960s led to a disproportionate increase in population, such that agricultural production could no longer keep up, and the capital investment ultimately fizzled out.

It has been demonstrated in many developing countries that original capital investments remained relatively ineffective in the long term, as they only led to a disproportionate population growth. Investments in health, however, do not have these negative effects. As shown in Figure 2.20, health investments have three effects. First, they directly lead to an improvement in the population's health. Second, they lead to economic growth, as, for example, the renovation of healthcare facilities represents demand for the local economy. Most importantly, however, health investments lead to a perceived security of existential provision. Citizens perceive that the state cares for them, that they are better off, and their quality of life increases. This is partly due

---

67 Compare Siadat and Stolpe (2005).
68 Compare Nelson (1956).

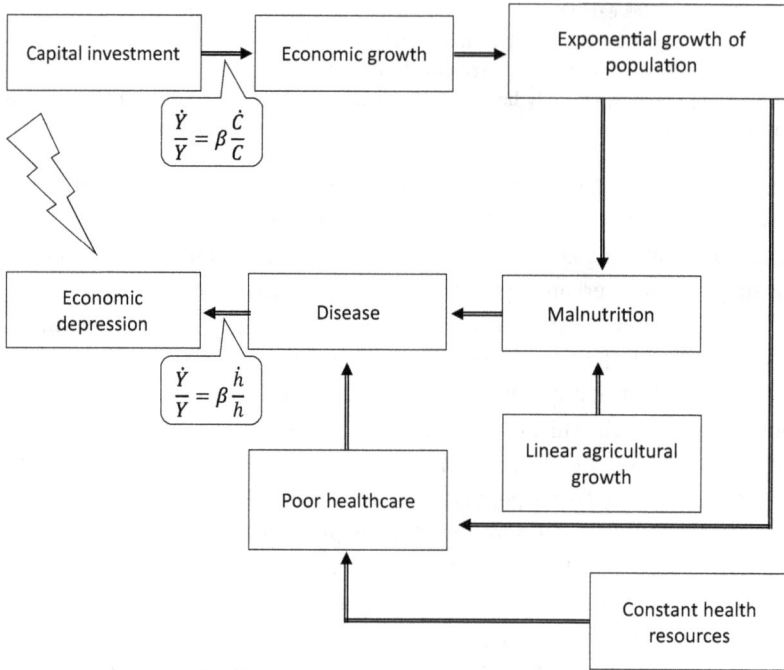

Figure 2.19: Development trap.[69]

to the health status itself, but to a greater extent, health investments imply a transformation process in the population's perception. For example, parents experience that it is no longer necessary to have ten children so that at least two survive to later support the parents. Instead, a sense of life security, quality of life, and improved need satisfaction develops, reducing the birth rate.

Economic growth therefore still tends to lead to an increase in the birth rate, but perceived security reduces it, so that, ceteris paribus, there may even be a reduction in population growth. This results in a positive development spiral of health and development that can overcome development traps.

Figure 2.21 shows that there is a positive correlation between GNP per capita and life expectancy (0.65 for all data), but the correlation is not the same for all income groups (compare Table 2.4). It seems that lower-middle-income countries and high-income countries benefit most from higher incomes. The relationship between the national product and child mortality (Figure 2.22) is similar. The correlation coefficient is −0.142 for all countries, but again, it is the strongest for the lower-middle-income and the higher-income countries.

---

69 Source: Own.

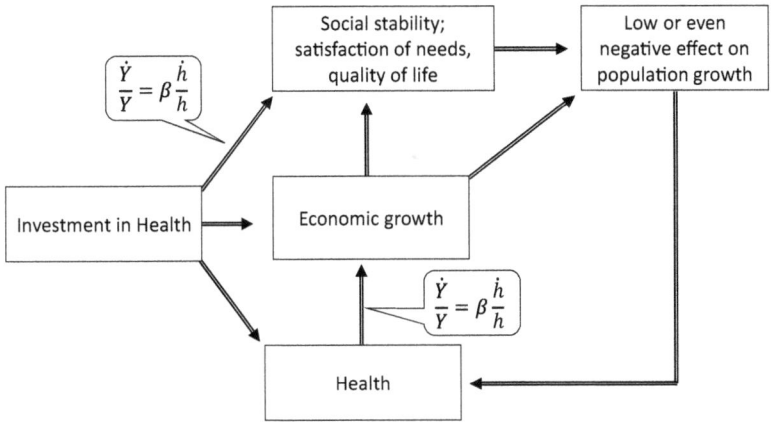

Figure 2.20: Health and development.[70]

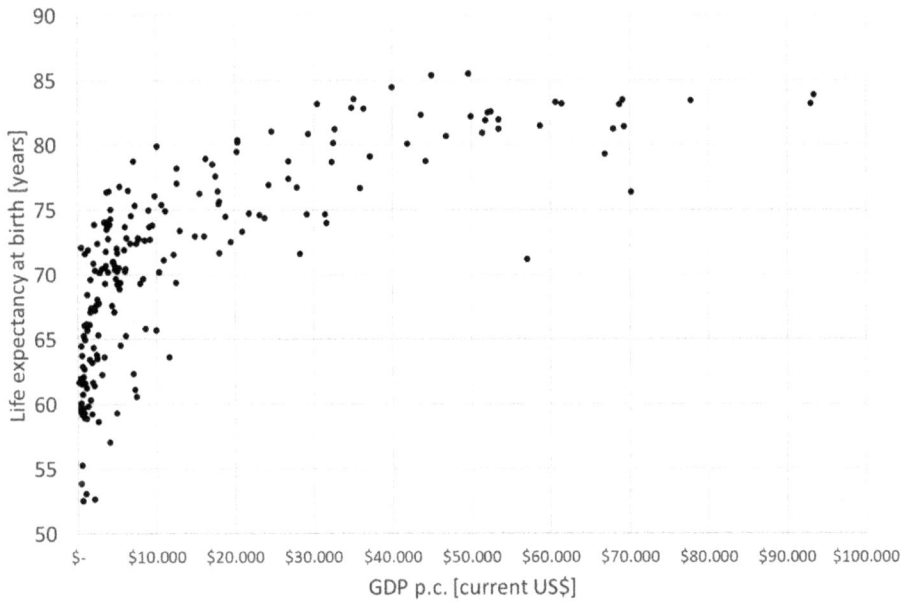

Figure 2.21: Gross national product and life expectancy at birth globally (2008).[71]

70 Source: Own.
71 Source: Own, based on World Bank (2024b). Most statistics used in this chapter are retrieved from the World Development Indicators and can be updated by the readers: https://databank.worldbank. org/source/world-development-indicators.

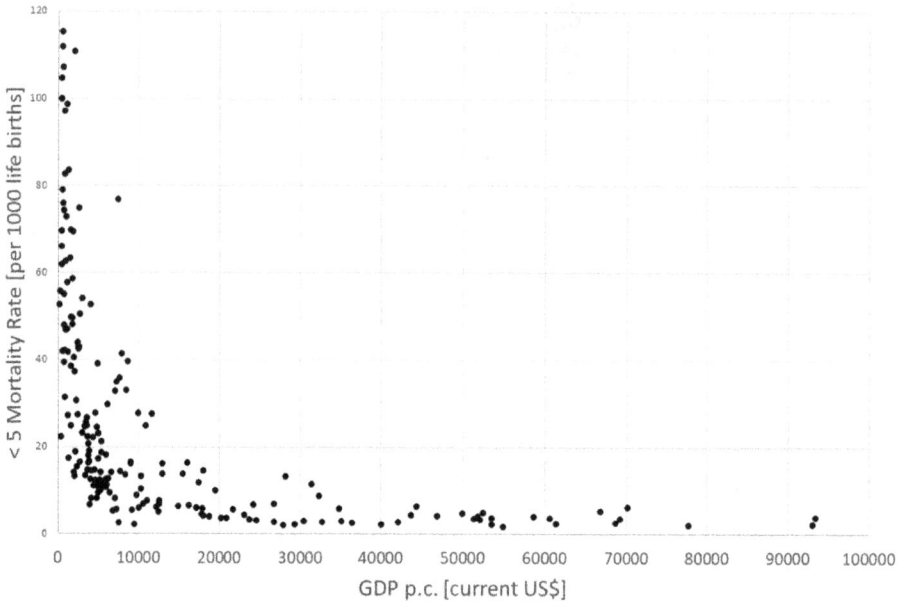

Figure 2.22: Gross national product and child mortality globally (2008).[72]

Table 2.4: Correlation between income per annum per capita (p.a. p.c.) health outcomes.[73]

	Income (US$ p.a. p.c.)	Correlation with	
		Life expectancy	Child mortality
Low-income countries	<1,045	−0.02	−0.01
Lower-middle-income countries	1,045–4,125	0.53	−0.54
Higher-middle-income countries	4,126–12,745	0.21	−0.12
High-income countries	>12,735	0.52	−0.39
All		0.65	−0.42

The general relationship between health and development also applies to the social groups within these countries. Figure 2.23 illustrates the vicious cycle of poverty and disease, which is particularly relevant for poverty groups within a society.[74] Poverty leads to low schooling or training. Therefore, the poor or children from poor families are predominantly open to low-paid jobs with high health risks. The living conditions also pose a health risk. At the same time, the poor have fewer coping resources, as

---

72 Source: Own, based on World Bank (2024b).
73 Source: World Bank (2024b).
74 Compare Mielck (2000) and Hoebel, Michalski, Baumert, et al. (2025).

many health-promoting leisure activities (e.g. vacations) are unaffordable for them. Due to their material poverty, they receive poorer medical care. Even services that would be entitled to them for free cannot be claimed due to their low education. Since the poor are generally not social pressure groups, they cannot enforce their claims. These factors lead to poor health behaviour, i.e. the poor smoke relatively more, drink more alcohol, and are more often overweight than the average. Most importantly, however, they seek medical help only when symptoms become severe (symptom tolerance). All these factors result in a significantly increased risk of illness and mortality.

The higher morbidity and mortality, in turn, lead to growing poverty. Those who are often sick have a higher risk of unemployment. They have no energy to participate in further training and qualifications. In some cases, a portion of the household's labour is absorbed by caring for the sick. Material poverty has increased. Thus, a vicious cycle develops: poverty leads to illness, and illness to increasing poverty. Once this process is set in motion, it catalyses itself over and over again.

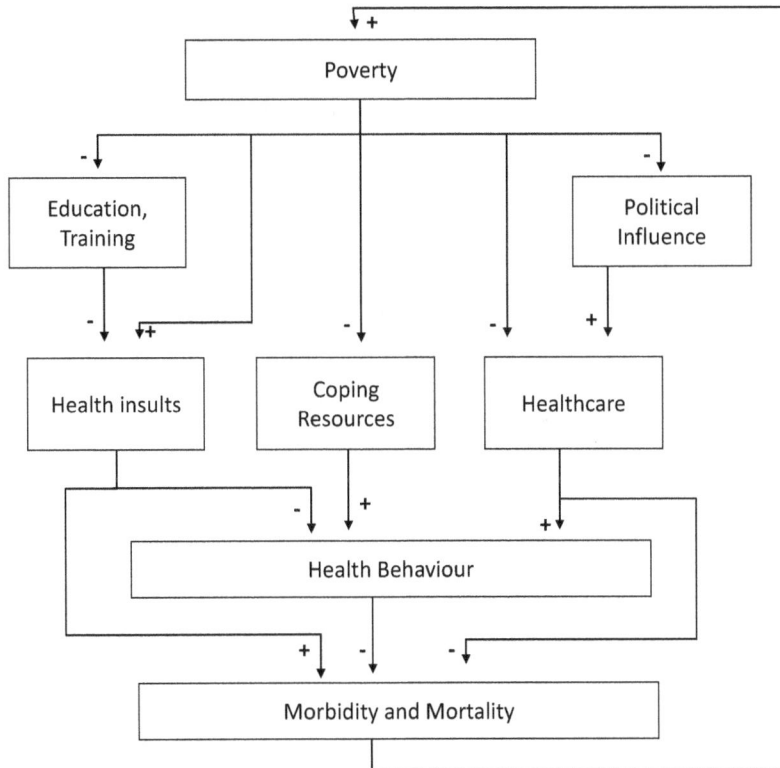

Figure 2.23: Health and poverty as a closed loop.[75]

---

75 Source: modelled after Elkeles and Mielck (1997).

The social gradient, i.e. the fact that a lower socioeconomic position has a negative impact on the health of an individual,[76] is documented: the risk of unhealthy depends on social class. For example, the risk of heart attack is 150% higher in the first income quintile than the fifth, the diabetes risk is increased by 85%, and the cancer risk by 126%. Poor men have an average risk of being overweight, which is 126% higher, while for women, this statistic is even 318%. As a result, the life expectancy is 82 years for the wealthiest quintile and 72 years for the poorest quintile, meaning poverty costs 10 years of life in Germany.[77] The social gradient is dominant: childhood mortality,[78] diabetes,[79] and even cancer incidence and mortality are negatively correlated with the social status[80] resulting in a different life expectancy of years or even decades between the poor and the rich.[81]

The traditional assumption that heart attack is a 'manager's disease', i.e. a problem of the upper class, is therefore false. To a large extent, heart attack is a poverty problem. The lower classes consume more fatty foods and exercise less than the upper classes, as healthy eating is expensive and physical fitness in cheaper residential areas is difficult or costly. Interestingly, the mortality risk in the upper class decreased by 54% from 1970 to 1991, while it increased by 10% in the lower class.

In summary, we can state that health and development or economic growth are the poles of an autocatalytic process. Investments in the health of a population lead to economic growth, which in turn can promote health. Once this process is initiated, it continuously strengthens itself, so that the health and prosperity of a population continuously increase. The classic development traps, primarily based on the effect of economic growth on the population, can be overcome by the stabilizing consequences of health-promoting investments. On the other hand, declining investments in health or external shocks (such as new diseases) can lead to a self-reinforcing vicious cycle of poverty and disease. This fact has been underlined again and again by economists and international organizations. For instance, the European Commission declares that:

> [. . .] good health promotes earnings and labor supply. Of particular relevance to Europe, with its ageing population, they show how poor health increases the likelihood of early retirement. Taken together, this evidence provides a powerful argument for European governments to invest in the health of their populations, not only because better health is a desirable objective in its own right, but also because it is an important determinant of economic growth and competitiveness.[82]

---

76 Compare WHO (2024m).
77 Compare Geyer (2001) and Helmert and Voges (2001).
78 Compare WHO (2024m).
79 Compare Lampert, Kroll, Kuntz, et al. (2018).
80 Compare Berger, Engelhardt, Möller, et al. (2022).
81 Compare Iacobucci (2019).
82 Suhrcke, McKee, Stuckler, et al. (2006).

And the Lancet Commission (2035) notes that:

> [. . .] there is an enormous payoff from investing in health. The returns on investing in health are impressive. Reductions in mortality account for about 11% of recent economic growth in low-income and middle-income countries as measured in their national income accounts. [. . .] Between 2000 and 2011, about 24% of the growth in full income in low-income and middle-income countries resulted from VLYs [value of additional life-years] gained. This more comprehensive understanding of the economic value of health improvements provides a strong rationale for improved resource allocation across sectors.[83]

2.2.2 Development and Developing Countries

So far, we have equated the terms 'development' and 'economic growth', and intuitively used the terms 'developing country' and 'developed countries'. Therefore, before fundamentally examining the structure of the healthcare sector in developing countries, it is necessary to define these terms as precisely as possible.

2.2.2.1 Static Concept of Development

To date, there is no clear definition of 'development' or 'developing country'. "Exaggeratingly, it could be said that there are as many definitions of development as there are institutions dealing with this topic."[84] The development economics literature is also exceptionally extensive, and an exhaustive overview will not be attempted here.[85] Instead, the concept of developing countries will only be clarified as far as necessary for understanding the relationship between health and development and for delineating the affected areas.

Fundamentally, a distinction can be made between a static and a dynamic concept of developing countries. The static concept analyses criteria indicating a certain level of development, while the dynamic concept of developing countries focusses on the development process of certain countries. Thus, countries whose social and economic indicators suggest that a low level of development is referred to as developing countries in the sense of the static concept. Typical indicators include per capita income (compare Figure 2.24), the Gini coefficient of income distribution, literacy rate, and child mortality rate. Based on these indicators, 'developed countries' and 'underdeveloped countries' were distinguished, although the term 'underdeveloped countries', formerly common, is no longer officially used today as it tends to sound pejorative. Since the early 1970s, UN organizations have referred to countries with low per capita incomes as 'less developed countries' to avoid the term 'developing countries'.

---

83 Jamison, Summers, Alleyne, et al. (2013).
84 Lachmann (2003).
85 See here, for example, Lerner (2018).

Within this group, the poorest countries were called 'least developed countries' (LDCs compare Figure 2.25).[86]

The UN General Assembly established criteria for LDC membership in 1971, which were valid until 1990. A country was classified as LDC if it met at least two of the following criteria:

– an annual per capita income of less than $355,
– the share of industrial production in the GNP of less than 10%, and
– an adult literacy rate of less than 20%.

Following the second UN Conference of LDCs (1990), new criteria were developed that, with slight adjustments, are valid today and allow for a more precise classification of poverty. The current criteria that must be met are:[87]

– Income: The annual per capita income must not exceed $1,018 on average over 3 years.
– Economic vulnerability index: This index describes the 'vulnerability of societies', primarily arising from dependence on a single source of income, e.g. export revenues, the share of agricultural production, and the share of manufacturing and services in the GDP.
– Human assets index (HAI): This index provides information about human capital, e.g. food security, malnutrition, child mortality, enrolment rates, and adult literacy.

In the year 2024, 45 countries were classified as LDCs, with 33 countries in Africa. Eight Asian countries and one American country (Haiti) are considered LDC. Three of the countries are in the Pacific region (Kiribati, Solomon Islands, and Tuvalu).[88]

There are several other categorizations of countries by their level of development. Until 1990, countries were often divided by their economic system. The First World referred to countries whose economies were predominantly market-oriented, while the Second World consisted mainly of socialist countries with centrally planned economies. The Third World included economies characterized primarily by barter transactions. This designation is considered outdated since there are hardly any countries primarily based on barter, but the term has persisted to this day.

Another way to categorize countries is the human development index (HDI). It is published annually by the United Nations Development Programme and combines health and education as social components with income as the economic component of development in a single figure. Less developed countries typically have an HDI of under 0.4, and LDCs under 0.25, although a complete assignment is not possible.

---

86 Originally, the abbreviation LDC was used for less developed countries, while LLDC stood for least developed countries. Today, LDC indicates least developed countries while LLDC means land-locked developing countries.
87 Compare UN (2024a).
88 Compare UNCTAD (2024).

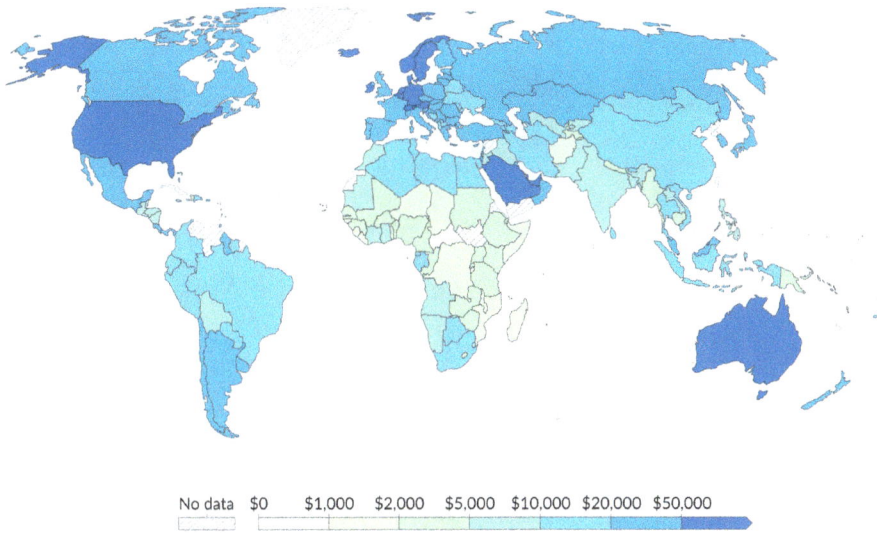

Figure 2.24: GDP per capita (2022).[89]

Another categorization is made by the World Bank, which differentiates (based on the gross national income per capita, calculated using the World Bank Atlas method) low-income economies (≤$1,145) lower-middle-income economies ($1,146–$4,515), upper-middle-income economies ($4,516–$14,005), and high-income economies ≥$14,005 (categories of 2025).[90] This grouping is particularly relevant for the credit terms offered to the respective countries, e.g. low-income countries usually receive grants that have not to be paid back, while lower-income countries are offered long-term loans at very low interest, but the respective amounts have to be paid back.[91]

Finally, the UN also distinguishes 'small island developing states' as well as the landlocked developing countries, with the latter group including European countries for the first time (Armenia, Azerbaijan, Moldova, and Macedonia). These countries share common development challenges due to their island location or lack of access to ports and thus international trade.

As complex as the static categorization of developing countries may seem, the situation regarding sub-Saharan Africa is clear. In a static definition, this continent has

---

89 Source: OurWorldinData – CC-BY@: https://ourworldindata.org/grapher/gdp-per-capita-worldbank (18 February 2025).
90 Source: World Bank (2024a).
91 It is questionable whether investments in healthcare should be financed by loans, i.e. future generations have to pay back better healthcare for the current generation.

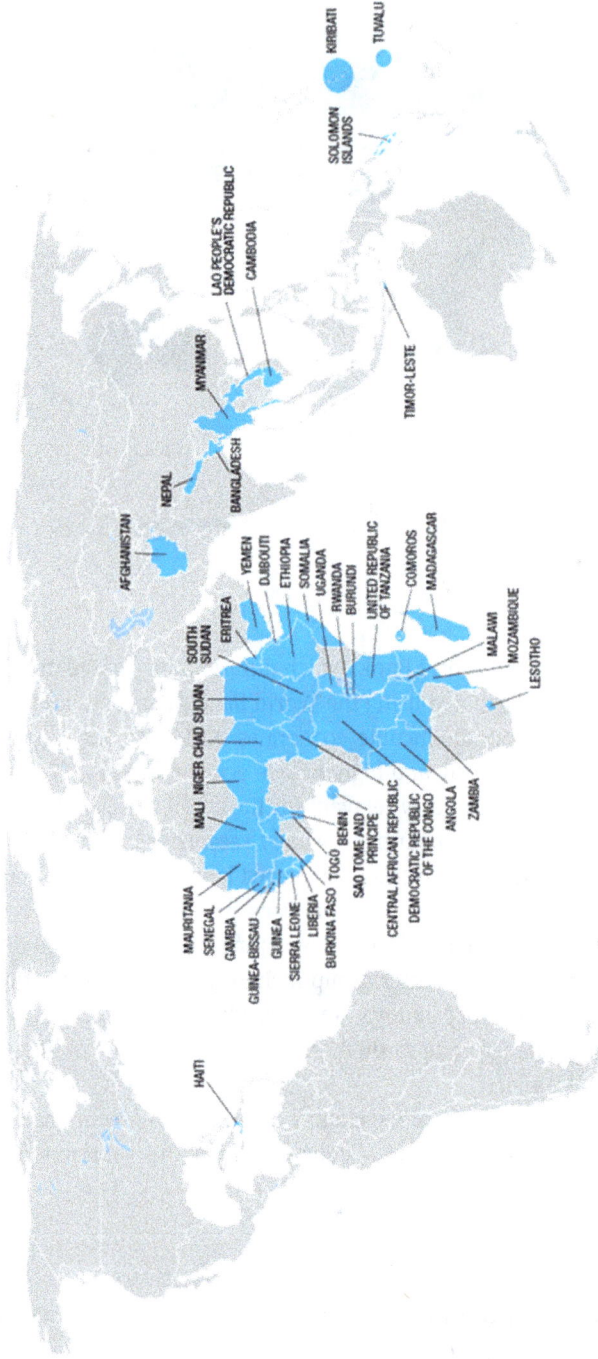

Figure 2.25: Least developed countries.[92]

92 Source: UNCTAD (2024). ©(copyright 2024) United Nations. Reprinted with the permission of the United Nations.

the lowest level of development – and accordingly the most severe development and health problems. This is particularly evident in the high loss of health-related quality of life, which the World Bank first comparatively determined in 1993. In no other major region do people die as young and suffer as dramatically from diseases and disabilities as in Africa (compare Figure 2.26).

In summary, we can conclude that the static concept of developing countries is useful for categorizing countries and identifying certain regularities. The health problems of developing countries or the specific difficulties of their healthcare systems are indeed largely dependent on the available national income. Except a few countries that have higher incomes but are structurally considered developing countries (e.g. Maldives), developing countries are primarily characterized by low overall economic production, resulting in limited health resources (compare Figure 2.27). From this perspective, it is therefore justifiable to equate economic power and level of development. However, the static concept of development is solely prescriptive, i.e. it is insufficient to explain the development process and to derive action guidelines for healthcare management. For this purpose, it is necessary to consider the development process, i.e. to introduce a dynamic concept of development.

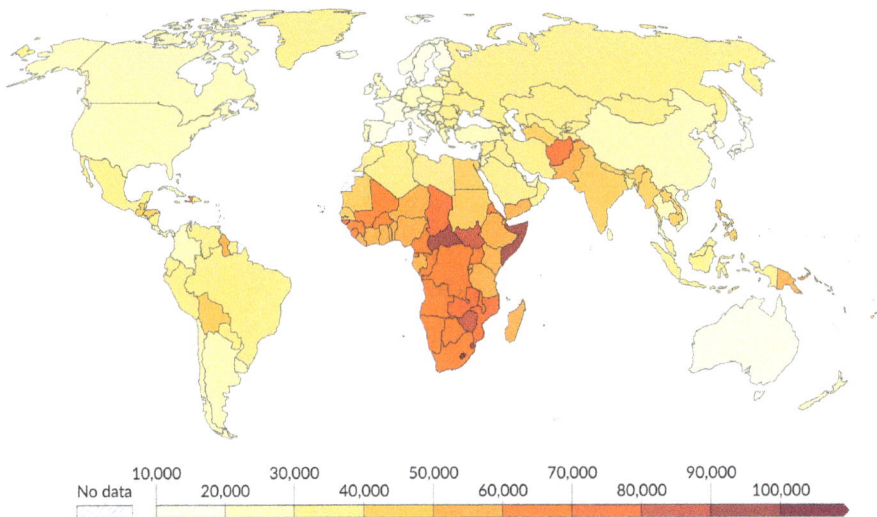

Figure 2.26: Global disease burden (yearly loss of disability-adjusted life years per 1,000 inhabitants).[93]

---

[93] Source: OurWorldinData – CC-BY@: https://ourworldindata.org/grapher/dalys-rate-from-all-causes (18 February 2025).

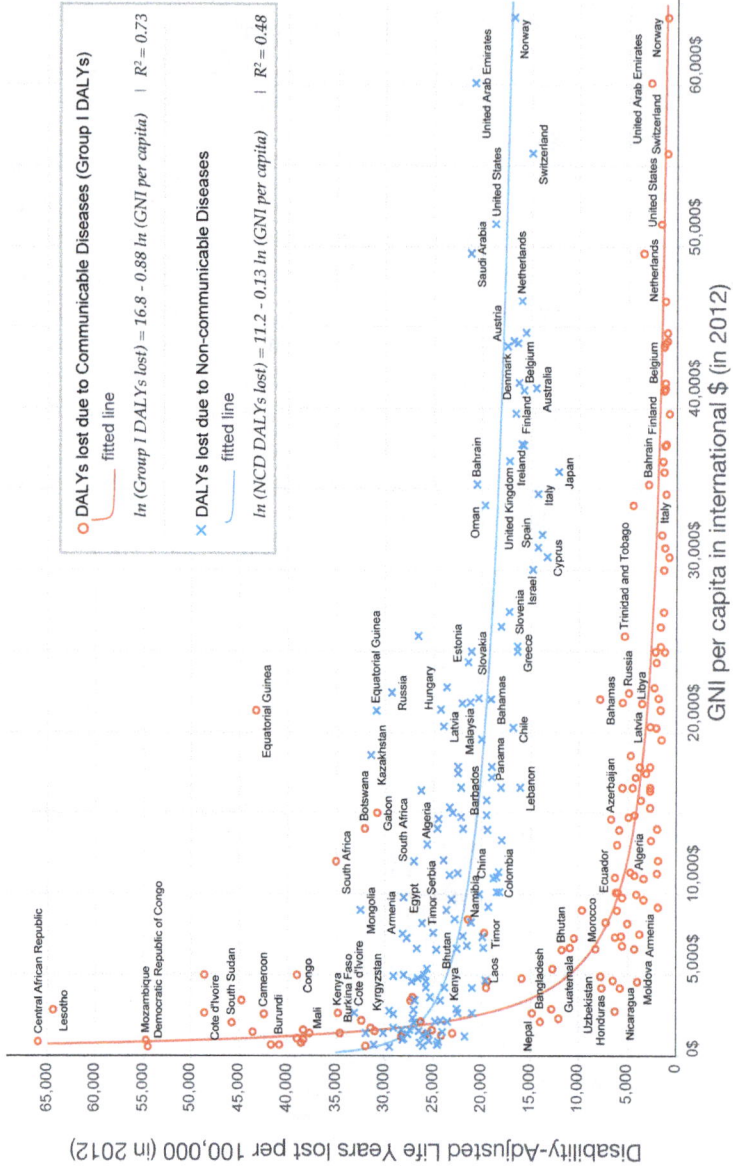

Figure 2.27: DALYs' lost and GNI per capita. [94]

94 Source: OurWorldinData – CC-BY@: GNI per capita versus DALYs' lost due to communicable and non-communicable diseases (18 February 2025).

2.2.2.2 Dynamic Development Concept

In contrast to the static concept of a developing country, for which the level of development of a country is decisive, a dynamic understanding of the concept sees development as a process. Developing countries would thus be those states that are evolving. Here, development is defined as an increase in system complexity,[95] which is fundamentally different from the mere expansion of the existing system structure (growth). Growth increases the number of elements in a system, while development describes an increased specialization of elements, a higher degree of division of labour, and an expansion or intensification of the relations between these elements (communication and transportation relationships). Thus, development in biology never means the mere growth of an individual, but an evolutionary act can be seen in the metamorphosis of a caterpillar into a butterfly. The butterfly is not larger or heavier than the caterpillar, but biologically more complex because it is capable of reproduction.

Similarly, economic development is not solely described by a higher gross social product, but also by specialization and division of labour, which necessitates more intensive exchange relationships. For example, Bobek[96] as a representative of a stage theory[97] describes human development in six stages: hunters and gatherers, specialized fishermen and hunters, peasantry clan-based farming, feudal agricultural society, unproductive capitalism (older urban society), and productive capitalism (new urban society). Each stage differs from the previous one by a higher degree of division of labour and specialization, resulting in exponentially increasing efficiency.

In this context, the question of what comes after the cultural stage of 'productive capitalism' is interesting. Assuming that the development to a higher stage was triggered by overcoming the limiting factor of production, it could be postulated that many countries today are on their way into an information society, whose primary resource is information. However, it might be more accurate to speak of a knowledge age, as information per se is irrelevant to the productivity of a social system. Efficiency advantages are provided only by knowledge tied to the person, which forms the basis for decision-making ability. In this sense, one could also speak of an age of wisdom, where the managerial factor, especially its ability to discern and differentiate, represents the scarce factors of production, while pure information can be assumed as given.

Ritter describes the transition from one stage to another as development[98] while the (sometimes millennia-long) perseverance in a stable phase is referred to as persistence. A purely quantitative increase in output, based solely on an increase in the number of identical system elements, does not constitute development; it can even lead to involution. However, the increase in system complexity will, in turn, generally

---

95 Compare Ritter (2001).
96 Compare Bobek (1959).
97 Compare Corsten and Gössinger (2007) and Stavenhagen (1969).
98 Compare Ritter (2001).

be accompanied by an increase in output (e.g. gross social product) and the carrying capacity of the system (e.g. population number).[99]

Looking at the development of national economies since the Industrial Revolution, the long-term waves that show 50- to 70-year cycles are striking. Kondratieff (1892–1938) attributed the long waves of economic activity to basic innovations that would initiate a decades-long upswing phase. Such basic innovations have so far been the steam engine and cotton (K1), steel and railways (K2), electrical engineering and chemistry (K3), petrochemicals and automobiles (K4), and information technology or computers (K5). The basic innovation leads to the valorization of a resource that was previously hardly used. In the first to fourth cycles, these resources were material, in K5, they are informational (compare Figure 2.28).

Currently, there is speculation about what dominant force could initiate the next long-term upswing. Nefiodow[100] postulates that the "psychosocial health and competence of people" could become the dominant basic resource in the future, on which everything else will be built. Health services would thus become key technology.

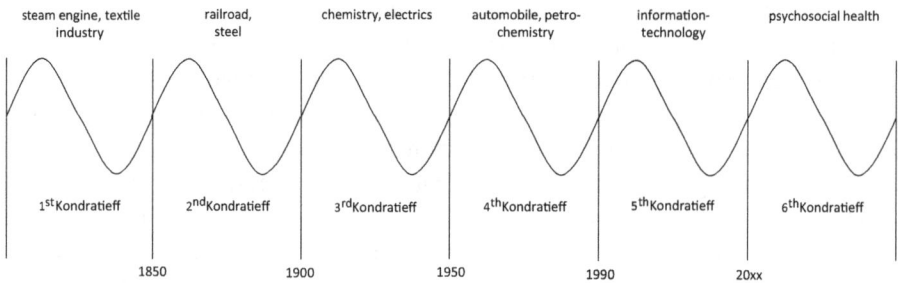

Figure 2.28: Basic innovations.[101]

Other authors take a somewhat broader approach and declare human technology as the basic innovation of the sixth Kondratieff.[102] Unlike the industrial and information age, where technical and methodological competencies were the key factors for successful economies, social and self-competencies now appear as the limiting factor of economic development. The well-educated, mobile, and self-confident workers require leaders who derive their authority not from threat, reward, legitimacy, or expertise, but primarily from their personality. Self-management, self-assessment, time management, proactivity, integrity, and trust competence (in oneself, in employees, in

---

99 Compare Affemann, Pelz, and Radermacher (1998).
100 Compare Nefiodow (2001).
101 Source: Fleßa (2007).
102 Compare Baaseke (2002).

life) are at the stage of the sixth Kondratieff the decisive factors of production, whose strengthening will decide the efficiency of economic systems. This also includes questions of spirituality and the major philosophical themes that have come back into the focus of management in recent years.[103]

Neumann[104] questions the thesis of spontaneously arising basic innovations and attributes the Kondratieff waves to the long-term change in the time preference rate. He defines time preference as the systematic underestimation of future benefits and empirically demonstrates that a high orientation towards the present leads to low (to negative) growth rates of national income, while a high orientation towards the future leads to strong investments and thus to the basic innovations. Here, the time preference must change cyclically, as the propensity to consume is shaped in childhood and youth. Poor parents raise their children, who carry a deep desire to improve their living situation but at the same time have not developed excessive consumer expectations. They invest, i.e. they have a low time preference. Richer parents, however, spoil their children, who consequently have a high level of consumption and expect this for a lifetime. The propensity to invest will be low. Neumann calls the phenomenon of changing time preference rates across generations the Buddenbrook syndrome, as this merchant family experienced this cycle in three generations: The founding generation built a fortune through a combination of luck, frugality (low time preference!), and diligence. The maintaining generation already had a higher propensity to consume (medium time preference) and a somewhat lower inclination to work. The squandering generation, on the other hand, was characterized by a high time preference rate, primarily interested in consumption and leisure. Thus, the 50- to 70-year Kondratieff cycles emerge in generational succession.

Neumann thus culturally justifies an economic phenomenon (business cycle) and connects the meta-level of sciences (here: time preference as a cultural value) with the real level of economics.

Stage and wave theories share the idea of progressive development, from which increasingly efficient economic systems evolve, each overcoming the limiting factor through product and process innovations. A developing country is thus a regional entity that is making its way to a higher level of development, regardless of its current level. A consistent application of the dynamic definition of development would therefore lead to some LDCs not being classified as developing countries because they are hardly evolving qualitatively. Many Western industrial countries, on the other hand, would be classified as developing countries because they are in a transition from an industrial to a service society or an information society.

The following will present the healthcare system in resource-poor countries. In terms of the static concept, these are developing countries. In a dynamic sense, some

---

103 Compare Rieckmann (2005) and Ladkin (2020).
104 Compare Neumann (1990).

of them (e.g. Myanmar, Sudan, and Haiti) are more characterized by persistence than by genuine development.

2.2.2.3 Causes of Poverty

Since healthcare and health status are primarily a function of the available resources, a brief discussion of the causes of poverty is necessary at this point. It should be noted that poverty and wealth are, to a certain extent, the result of the same factors, so understanding the causes of poverty also provides insights into the sources of wealth and vice versa. The analysis here cannot be all-encompassing but aims to provide a basic understanding of the factors that explain the global distribution of poverty and wealth and thus health.

Figure 2.29 provides an overview of possible causes of poverty, although not all factors apply equally to the individual, a social class, and a larger population. For example, factors such as ethnicity, habitat, and culture are, by definition, only relevant for larger groups. Similarly, the reverse conclusion (that populations or individuals who can be described as poor fulfil the causes of poverty mentioned here) is not entirely correct, as chance also plays a certain role. Under no circumstances should an accusation (e.g. 'the poor lack diligence') be derived.

The causes of poverty can be categorized into physical disposition, living environment, and behaviour. The physical dimension had a very dominant influence in human history but should not be neglected even today. For example, a disability (especially in resource-poor countries) represents a significant risk of poverty because economic performance is usually reduced or can only be valorized with higher effort. Thus, regions where disabilities occur particularly frequently tend to be poor. This can be demonstrated, for example, in areas where onchocerciasis still implies a higher risk of blindness (e.g. Burkina Faso), so that a high percentage of adults go blind and have to leave the fertile river valleys.[105]

Another disposition is cognitive intelligence,[106] the importance of which is significantly debated. In the industrial age, mathematical-scientific thinking ability plays a major role, so a child born with below-average cognitive intelligence will also, ceteris paribus, have a higher likelihood of having a below-average lifetime income. Below-average mathematical-scientific intelligence thus appears as a risk of poverty in the industrial age. However, this does not mean that the influence of innate cognitive intelligence is dominant. It is somewhat changeable through education. Even if one makes the bold assumption that mathematical-scientific thinking ability is 60% genetically determined, the remaining 40% still decide whether someone develops an IQ of 80 or 120, thus whether they tend to be poor or wealthy. The significance of genetic disposition for cognitive performance and thus the risk of poverty should not be overemphasized.

---

105 Compare Hoerauf, Büttner, Adjei, et al. (2003).
106 Compare Murray (1998).

Moreover, purely mathematical-scientific thinking ability is by no means a guarantee that someone will be successful in life. For one, the measurement of intelligence is very problematic, as it only allows a limited statement about coping with life and life success.[107] The intelligence tests are tailored for a very specific thinking ability for certain cultural groups and are not easily transferable to other thinking traditions (e.g. the personal logic of Africa vs. the factual logic of Europe). On a supra-individual level, mathematical intelligence is thus hardly definable as a cause of poverty. On the other hand, emotional and social intelligence[108] play a much larger role in the service society than the often overestimated cognitive intelligence. If global economic development tends more and more from industry to relationship economics, the wealth of nations could be completely redistributed.

Disability and intelligence are partly genetically determined, though the extent of disposition is disputed. Other characteristics, such as skin colour and certain intolerances, are practically fully genetically determined and can thus be differentiated. For example, the strong pigmentation of populations adapted to strong sunlight in the tropics is an effective protection against some forms of skin cancer. The indigenous people of Australia are therefore less affected by malignant melanoma than the predominantly fair-skinned population that settled the land after 1770. Fair skin thus represents a certain risk of poverty – although one that is greatly reduced by cultural systems (welfare state) and overlaid by numerous other factors (e.g. social disadvantage of indigenous people). Another example of a predominantly genetic disposition is food intolerance. For instance, dairy farming could not develop among the Bantu tribes in Southern Africa because the vast majority of adults are lactose intolerant.[109] Dairy farming could, therefore, not achieve the high importance for nutrition and economic development in wide parts of Africa which it had in parts of Europe.

The living environment can also represent a comparative disadvantage, especially for entire populations. Habitat was highly influential in economic development before modern times, while cultural factors have become significantly more important since then. However, factors such as natural resources, animals and plants, climate, relief, axes, maritime aspects, and diseases remain crucial for poverty and wealth to this day.

Natural resources are an essential factor of production and, thus, a basis for the wealth of individuals, groups, and nations. The upswing of mining areas and the 'bonanza' of oil-producing countries are attributable to the presence of natural resources. However, the conclusion that 'the more natural resources, the richer' is not correct in every case. For example, Spain's decline as a superpower was at least partly due to the enormous resources of gold and silver in the South American colonies, which allowed Spain to buy virtually anything it wanted in terms of consumer goods without produc-

---

107 Compare Goleman (2008).
108 Compare Goleman (2008) and Goleman (2006).
109 Compare Meade and Emch (2010).

```
                              ┌─────────────────────┐
                              │  Causes of Poverty  │
                              └─────────────────────┘
        ┌───────────────────────┬──────────────────────────┐
┌────────────────────┐  ┌──────────────────┐       ┌──────────────────┐
│ Physical Disposition│  │    Environment   │       │     Behavior     │
└────────────────────┘  └──────────────────┘       └──────────────────┘
   ── Genetic Disposition  ── Mineral Resources   ┌──────────────────┐  ┌──────────────┐
   ── Disability           ── Flora and Fauna     │Individual Behavior│ │   Culture    │
   ── Intelligence         ── Climate, Relief, Axes └──────────────────┘  └──────────────┘
   ── ...                  ── Access to sea           ── Diligence          ── Religion
                           ── Diseases                ── Frugality          ── Political System
                           ── ...                     ── Risk-Taking        ── Economic System
                                                      ── Aggressiveness     ── Social System
                                                      ── ...                ── ...
```

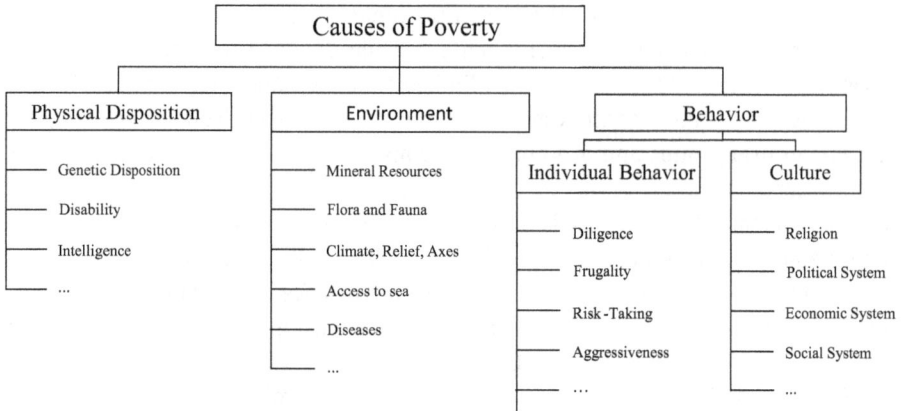

Figure 2.29: Causes of poverty.[110]

ing itself or developing technologically.[111] With the depletion of natural resources, Spain's power faded, unable to keep up with the technological development of the seemingly poorer European countries. Thus, the Netherlands became a superpower, while Spain became impoverished – a fate that could threaten some oil-producing countries if they failed to transfer their resource revenues into capital and labour.[112]

Even in a globalized world, natural resources do not always imply wealth. The Commission on Macroeconomics and Health[113] shows that especially developing countries with lucrative natural resources are affected by poverty, as the supposed wealth can induce civil war, international interventions, and corruption. For example, countries with diamond deposits in West Africa or the eastern regions of the Congo are significantly more often affected by unrest and poverty than resource-poor neighbouring countries.

Climate and relief are also significant for the development of a region. Steep slopes, drought, flooding, cold, heat, and especially high variability of these parameters pose significant challenges to agriculture, giving 'temperate latitudes' a natural economic advantage over extreme regions. Climates, in particular, shape culture. For example, the harsh winters in Central Europe require intensive storage and preventive maintenance to survive the cold season, while year-round vegetation periods and high temperatures tend to make storage and maintenance unnecessary and pointless.

In addition to natural resources, climate, and relief, the prevailing animals and plants are of great importance for the economic development of a region. For instance, Jared Diamond[114] explains that the conditions for the domestication of plants

---

110 Source: Fleßa (2003a).
111 Compare Landes, Enderwitz, Noll, et al. (1999).
112 Compare Landes, Enderwitz, Noll, et al. (1999).
113 Compare Sachs (2001).
114 Compare Diamond (1999).

and animals, and thus for the Neolithic Revolution, were extremely unevenly distributed among the major regions. For example, plants, to serve quickly and easily as the basis for new agricultural products, must meet the following conditions: They must be annual plants since a multi-year investment period is inhibitive for beginning agriculture. The plants must be relevant to nutrition, i.e. have a high protein content. They should be plants with large seeds that already have a high yield by nature. For instance, the original forms of wheat are already very starchy, while the natural variants of maize are very far from today's cobs. Well-suited are climates with a definite, time-limited fruit phase, so a reliable planting and vegetation period exists. Additionally, these plants should exhibit uncomplicated fertility, i.e. hermaphroditic self-pollinators are preferred. As shown in Table 2.5, for example, the occurrence of large-seeded grasses as the basis for the breeding of cereals is very unevenly distributed on Earth. Just on this basis, it is not surprising that the Neolithic Revolution took place in various locations in Asia, Europe, and America, yet the effectiveness of agriculture and its diffusion potential varied considerably. The so-called 'Fertile Crescent' was predestined from the start to become the centre of the agrarian economy and has fed large populations since antiquity.

Table 2.5: Distribution of large-seeded grasses across the world.[115]

Region	Number of species
Mediterranean region (Western Asia, Europe, and Northern Africa)	32
England	1
Eastern Asia	6
Sub-Saharan Africa	4
Northern America	4
Central America	5
Southern America	2
Northern Australia	2

Table 2.6: Emergence of agricultural centres.[116]

Region	Plants	Animals	Time
Fertile Crescent	Wheat, peas, and olives	Sheep and goat	8500 BC
China	Rice and millet	Pigs and silk worm	7500 BC
Central America	Corn, beans, and pumpkin	Turkey	3500 BC
Andes/Amazon	Potato and manioc	Llama and Guinea pig	3500 BC
Eastern USA	Sunflower	–	2500 BC
Western Africa	Yam and oil palm	–	3000 BC
New Guinea	Banana and sugarcane	–	7000 BC

---

115 Source: Diamond (1999).
116 Source: Diamond (1999).

The natural occurrence of animals also met the requirements for domestication very differently. Successful candidates for livestock farming had to be efficiently and relatively easily fed in captivity, exhibit a high growth rate, and have few reproduction problems in captivity. Also important is a certain docility – why, for example, the aurochs were easier to domesticate than the rhinoceros. For herd animals, it is also important that they do not have a tendency for panic-stricken flight and exhibit a high social hierarchy so that humans can take on the role of the leader (e.g. dogs). Again, it becomes apparent that the natural stock of domesticable animals was particularly high in Europe and Asia (and especially in the Fertile Crescent), while, for example, in America, only the llama and alpaca and, to a lesser extent, the guinea pig were available as domestication candidates.

According to Diamond, the natural existence of animals and plants at least explains the unequal global distribution of poverty and wealth since secured nutrition through effective agriculture was the basis for the emergence of the first stable communities, cities, states, and empires. The argument is mainly historical, but even today, the availability of plants and animals, and thus effective agriculture, is a foundation of food security. Thus, we can explain – at least partly – malnutrition and nutrient deficiencies in parts of contemporary Africa by the sparse availability of effective food plants on this continent. Global food crops, such as potatoes, do not come from Africa and have not fully adapted to the African tropical conditions.

However, the question arises as to why domesticated plants did not quickly spread from the centres of the Neolithic Revolution and adapt, for example, in Africa. It is important to note that plants are generally adapted to specific climates (temperatures, amounts of rainfall, and rainy seasons) and to a terrain or altitude. Naturally, spreading a plant along a latitude (i.e. from east to west or west to east) is easier than along a longitude (i.e. from north to south or south to north) because no fundamentally different climate regions have to be overcome. The spread of agricultural plants from the Mediterranean region to Africa largely failed because these crops, accustomed to the Mediterranean climate, perished on their way to the inner tropics. The climate in Southern Africa would indeed have been suitable for these plants. Still, they could not survive the journey through Africa's deserts and rainforests, nor could they adapt over longer periods to first become suitable for the tropics and then transform back into their Mediterranean predecessors. Only when Europeans brought their seeds from Europe to Southern Africa could effective agriculture be practiced there. As shown in Figure 2.30, the spread of agricultural innovations is therefore particularly effective in Eurasia, while it is extremely difficult, for example, in America.

Maritimity refers to the proximity to the sea. Landlocked countries have no access to the resources or the trade routes of the seas, especially if they are not connected by navigable rivers. Therefore, it is logical that landlocked countries, all else being equal, have a higher risk of poverty. The United Nations (UN) addresses this fact with their category of landlocked developing countries because, even in the age of global transport means, this location poses a significant competitive disadvantage for a nation.

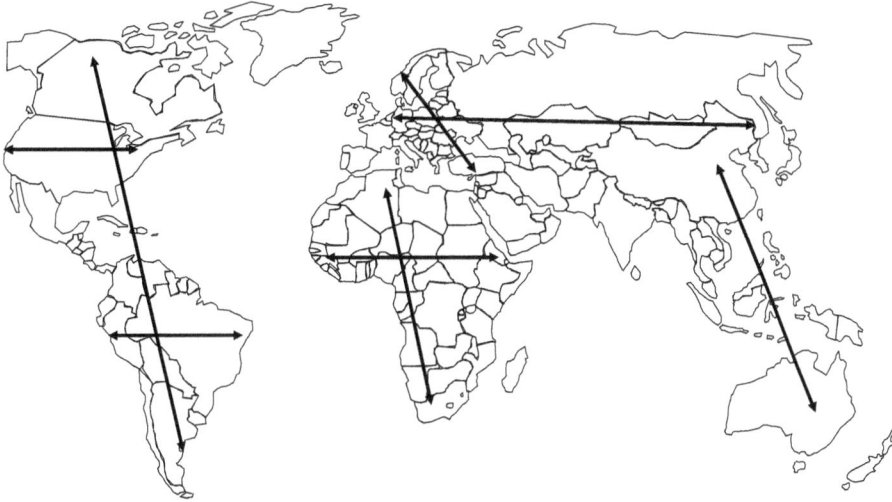

Figure 2.30: Continental axes.[117]

These countries cannot produce goods cheaply enough to offset their higher transportation costs to ports, and there are only a few products light enough for transportation costs to be irrelevant.

Finally, diseases (especially infectious diseases) play a significant role in economic development. The Black Death in the Middle Ages, measles and smallpox in America, and cholera in the early Industrial Revolution had a significant impact on the impoverishment of entire regions. For example, the Spanish under Cortés could only gain a foothold in South America because, after a devastating defeat, they inadvertently infected enemy groups with measles and smallpox, against which there was no immunity in South America.[118] The majority of the Aztec population and many other peoples of Central and South America were not killed by Spanish weapons but by European pathogens such as smallpox, measles, influenza, typhus, diphtheria, malaria, mumps, whooping cough, plague, TB, and yellow fever, all of which were unknown in America before the Europeans' arrival. In return, Spanish sailors and soldiers likely brought syphilis back to Europe, though this is contested. Naturally, the question arises as to why the exchange of pathogens was so one-sided.

It is important to note that many human infectious diseases have an animal origin. The close coexistence of humans and domestic animals in rural societies provides the opportunity for pathogens to effectively transfer from animals to humans, in numbers likely to adapt to the pathogen to the new host probable. Table 2.7 shows that the dreaded pathogens, which were particularly responsible for the political, mil-

---

117 Source: Diamond (1999).
118 Compare Landes, Enderwitz, Noll, et al. (1999).

itary, and economic decline of North, Central, and South America, as well as 350 years later of countries in sub-Saharan Africa, predominantly came from animals that had been domesticated in Europe or had existed there in close community with humans for millennia. In America, on the other hand, only the llama could have had a similar potential, but to this day, the closeness of llama farming cannot compare with the almost domestic coexistence between humans and cattle in Europe or Asia. Diseases thus played a central role in the emergence of poorer and wealthier regions.

Table 2.7: Animal origin of infectious diseases.[119]

Disease in humans	Animal origin
Measles	Cattle (bovine pox)
Tuberculosis	Cattle (bovine tuberculosis)
Smallpox	Cattle (cowpox) and other species with related pox viruses
Influenza	Pig and ducks
Whooping cough	Pig and dogs
Malaria	Chickens and ducks

As outlined in Section 2.2.1, diseases are a significant factor hindering development and thus a cause of poverty. The emergence of diseases, their spread, and their mortality rate depend heavily on the climate, natural barriers (rivers, mountains, etc.), and maritimity. To some extent, therefore, poverty and wealth are also conditioned by geofactors, i.e. the striking differences in the history of people of different continents over broad periods are not due to innate differences among the people themselves but to differences in their environments.

In addition to physical disposition and habitat, human behaviour determines poverty or wealth. This applies both to the individual and to the culture of population groups. Diligence, thrift, risk-taking, and assertiveness are important prerequisites for individual economic success. Hofstede[120] uses these characteristics as dimensions of national culture, meaning individual values shape primary culture, but religion, political, economic, and social systems are manifestations of secondary culture that can promote or reduce poverty beyond individual behaviour.

The relationship between the economic system and economic growth has been frequently discussed. Jay[121] shows, for example, that the Industrial Revolution in England was only possible in a relatively free economic system, and Sen[122] demonstrates

---

119 Source: Diamond (1999).
120 Compare Hofstede (1983).
121 Compare Jay (2000).
122 Compare Sen (1983).

the importance of democracy for economic progress. Religion also plays an important role, with recent research[123] confirming Weber's classic thesis[124] that religion or denomination has a significant impact on savings rates, innovation, and economic growth. For instance, religious taboos on animal use could limit agricultural development, the traditional role of women in certain world regions is likely to reduce the pool of ideas in a population, and fatalism and cyclical thinking of some beliefs might lead to low initiative.

In summary, the poverty of individuals, social groups, and populations has numerous causes, which themselves form an interdependent system with strong mutual dependencies and autocatalytic processes. A simple, linear linkage of one cause to one effect is not possible. Today, and for entire populations, cultural factors are of higher importance than other influences, meaning the political system, economic order, and social system play a defining role. However, focussing solely on economic circumstances (such as the propensity to save) cannot explain poverty and wealth in the world – and thus falls short of justifying the inequality in the distribution of health and disease. When an overview of the basic structure of the healthcare system in resource-poor countries is given next, the reader should be aware that there are many reasons for being categorized into this group of countries. Accordingly, healthcare systems and health problems will vary across different resource-poor countries.

2.2.3 Health and Healthcare in Resource-Poor Countries

All statistics indicate that we live in many worlds of health. There is no 'global health' in the sense that all human beings have equal chances to a healthy life of high quality. Instead, the place of birth and living determines our healthcare, health, quality of life, and life expectancy. Looking at childhood mortality, we cannot even state that the start chances are equally distributed.

Morbidity and mortality in resource-poor countries differ significantly from those in richer world regions. The life expectancy at birth in low-income countries was 63.0 years in the year 2022, in lower-middle-income countries 67.2, in upper-middle-income countries 75.7, and high-income countries 79.5. In sub-Saharan Africa, it was 60.8 and 53.0 in Chad and Lesotho.[125] The difference between the highest (Macao) and the lowest (Chad) life expectancy per country is 32.38 years. Worldwide, the life expectancy of women is 74.5 years and of men 69.6, i.e. a difference of 4.9 years. A span of more than 10 years can be seen in Armenia and Belarus.

---

123 Compare Berger (1994) and Iannaccone (1998).
124 Compare Weber (1958).
125 Source: World Bank (2024b).

At the same time, the life expectancy at birth and at any other year of life has been constantly growing all over the world. With the exemption of the COVID-19 crisis of 2020–2022, worldwide life expectancy has grown by 4.2 months per year since 1950 (compare Figure 2.31). However, the difference between high- and low-income countries is still tremendously high, i.e. much remains to be done to reduce the mortality in poorer regions of the world, in particular of children.

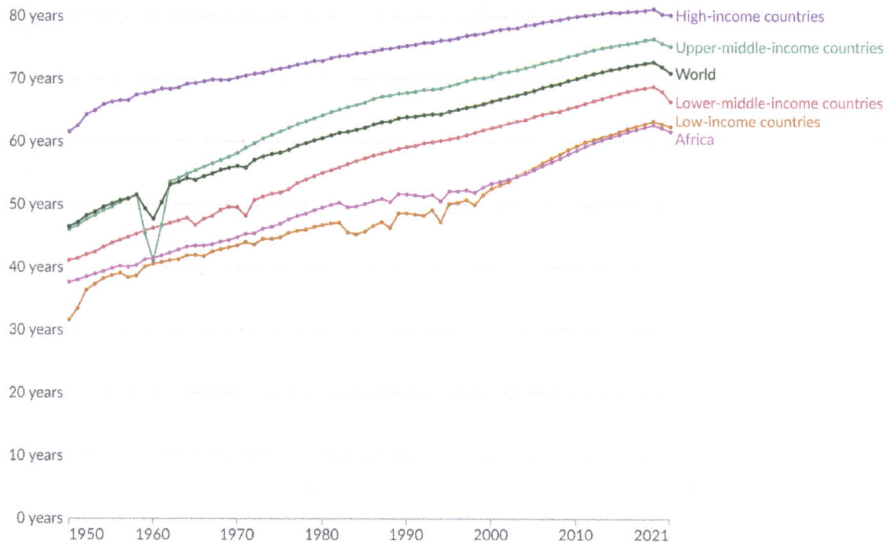

Figure 2.31: Life expectancy globally.[126]

As outlined in Section 3.1.2, not only the rates but also the causes of mortality differ. In developing countries, more than half of disease cases and slightly less than half of deaths are attributable to infectious diseases, while inhabitants of developed countries predominantly suffer and die from chronic degenerative diseases. The AIDS epidemic significantly reduced life expectancy in developing countries in the 1990s and has amplified the significance of infectious diseases, although – as we will show later – chronic degenerative diseases were indeed present and on the rise in these countries. Currently, many low-income countries suffer from a "double burden of disease",[127] i.e. chronic degenerative and infectious diseases at the same time and with high incidence and prevalence rates.

---

126 Source: OurWorldinData – CC-BY@: https://ourworldindata.org/grapher/life-expectancy (18 February 2025).
127 Marshall (2004).

Healthcare resources also vary considerably and are correlated with the economic power of a nation. For this analysis, we use the GDP converted to international dollars using purchasing power parity rates (PPPs). Data are in constant 2021 international dollars (World Bank 2024). High-income countries have a GDP (PPP) of $56,396 per capita, while it was $2,300 in low-income countries. Burundi had a GDP (PPP) per capita of $857, Luxembourg of $137,059 (compare Table 2.8). In the first group of countries, an average of $6.498 (PPP) or 13.1% of the GDP was invested in healthcare, while in the low-income countries, it was only $112 or 5.3% of the GNP. The country with the highest healthcare expenditure per capita is the USA with more than $12,014, while South Sudan was the country with the lowest healthcare expenditure ($33.77). Papua New Guinea had the lowest current health expenditure as a rate of GDP with 2.3%. Generally, it can be stated that health expenditures in developing countries are very low, both in absolute terms and relative to their GDP, and that absolute and relative spending on healthcare increases with rising economic strength.

Table 2.8: Basic healthcare statistics (2021 and 2022).[128]

Income category	Life expectancy at birth, total (years)	GDP per capita, PPP (constant 2021 int. $)	Current health expenditure per capita, PPP (current int. $)	Current health expenditure (% of GDP)	Physicians (per 1,000 people)	Nurses and midwives (per 1,000 people)	Hospital beds (per 1,000 people)
High	79.5	56,396.17	6,497.98	13.1	3.62	10.07	6.07
Lower middle	67.2	8,049.42	273.17	3.9	0.69	1.60	0.63
Upper middle	75.7	19,874.74	1,071.99	5.8	2.11	3.55	3.25
Low	63.0	2,299.52	111.80	5.3	0.35	0.97	–
SSH Africa	60.8	4,350.22	203.57	5.1	0.24	1.28	–
World	72.0	20,214.79	1,638.78	10.4	1.70	3.75	2.88

The availability of material and human resources also varies significantly between countries. In high-income countries, there were on average 3.62 physicians per 1,000 inhabitants (2022), while in low-income countries, there were only 0.35.[129] Cuba had the highest number of doctors per inhabitant (9.54), Niger the lowest (0.038), Germany

128 Compare World Bank (2025).
129 Compare WHO (2025a).

is placed 179 of 197 countries with 4.53 doctors per 1,000 inhabitants, i.e. one doctor had to serve more than 26,000 inhabitants in Niger, 221 in Germany, and 105 in Cuba.

The number of nurses and midwives per 1,000 people also varies widely. In 2022, there were 0.97 per 1,000 inhabitants in low-income countries, but 10.07 in high-income countries. Finland topped the list with 22.32 nurses per 1,000 inhabitants, more than twice as many as Germany (12.35). Even within low-income countries, the ratio of nurses to population varies greatly. While countries like Tanzania seem to meet their nursing needs, others (e.g. Niger) have only one nurse per 4,500 inhabitants.

The bed density varies strongly as well. A standard value that has been aired long ago by the WHO and the World Bank assumes that one hospital bed per 1,000 inhabitants should suffice under the conditions of a developing country in the tropics to ensure adequate care.[130] This value never had an empirical basis and might be obsolete, but it is still used. Unfortunately, the data on hospital beds is very incomplete and/or old. In high-income countries, the average is 6.07 beds per inhabitant, and in lower-middle-income countries, it is 0.63. Both values are the latest from 2017. For low-income countries and sub-Saharan Africa, no values are provided by the World Bank. However, it is obvious that the range is wide: one hospital bed for 5,000 inhabitants of Madagascar, and one bed for 60.8 inhabitants of Monaco. In Germany, the respective statistic is 119.3. Certainly, it is very difficult to compare the epidemiological and care situation between these countries, but it is obvious that poor nations have extremely limited financial and personnel resources to take care of the sick and needy.

At this point, the reader must proceed with great caution, as the reliability of data is low. Often, economic, demographic, and epidemiological values are based on estimates, since statistics are either not collected, incomplete, or incorrectly collected. Conflicting or deviating values in official statistics (e.g. World Bank and WHO) are common. What Lane wrote about the data situation in Tanzania in the early 1980s probably still applies to many developing countries today: "Perhaps the major problem of any researcher in Tanzania is the lack of data, the almost complete unreliability of what data is available and the absence of any recent data", so that "scarcity of information inhibits governments from making informed choices about the allocation of public resources for better health, as well as improvements in the management of publicly provided and/or financed services".[131] However, even with great caution, we can state that the healthcare situation is disastrous for the majority of people living in low- and lower-middle-income countries. The averages might be even misleading as the rich minority might consume the lion's share of healthcare resources leaving even less for the vast majority of the poor. Inequity in healthcare is not only an international challenge – it is sometimes even worse within one country. We live in many worlds of health.

---

130 Compare World Bank (1993).
131 Compare Ferranti, Lovelace, and Pannenborg (1999).

2.3 Conceptions

2.3.1 Prevention

The healthcare system has traditionally been focussed on curing diseases, meaning that the emphasis of all healthcare systems lies in treating existing illnesses. The field of curative medicine has advanced technologically and has produced impressive institutions. To this day, the guiding thought process of doctors, nursing staff, and health policy makers is primarily healing-oriented, even though Hippocrates already placed the importance of preventing diseases at the centre of his activities. Many still view medicine as synonymous with cure, and the recurring waves of appeals for prevention have done little to change this.[132] In the global, national, and professional policy arenas, prevention is, despite contrary proclamations, at best a budding innovation, still waiting for its systemic breakthrough.

However, this state of affairs is not a reason for the foundation of healthcare management to neglect prevention. On the contrary, numerous studies show that prevention is often efficient and, in some cases, even the only way to combat diseases sustainably. Despite the marginal existence of prevention in international healthcare management, we will now focus on concepts of healthcare that are not seen as alternatives to, but rather as equally important partners of cure. We proceed historically, evolving from prevention to PHC and health promotion initiatives. The section concludes with brief remarks on the more recent developments in international healthcare management.

Prevention simply means the avoidance or preclusion of a negative event or process (Latin: *praevenire* meaning to prevent and to forestall), i.e. in healthcare, it refers to the avoidance of a disease, the deterioration of a health condition, or new illnesses.[133] The term 'health prevention' used lately is nonsensical because it is not health that should be avoided but rather the disease. Health should be fostered and promoted, not prevented.

As Figure 2.32 illustrates, prevention is categorized into primary, secondary, and tertiary levels. Primary prevention aims to prevent diseases from occurring in the first place. It can be differentiated into behavioural and environmental prevention. Reducing emissions is an example of environmental prevention, benefiting individuals from the general improvement of living conditions. Conversely, abstaining from smoking is a behavioural change for an individual.

Once an infection has occurred or a chronic degenerative disease has developed, it must be identified as soon as possible to address it before its clinical manifestation. Most screening examinations fall into this category. For example, regular dental

---

132 Compare Werner, Sanders, Weston, et al. (1997).
133 Compare Walter and Schwartz (2003).

check-ups do not prevent caries but aim to detect carious teeth early on, so they can be treated at the earliest stage, thereby stopping the progression of caries. Fluoride prophylaxis, on the other hand, aims to prevent caries and thus represents primary prevention.

Tertiary prevention follows successful treatment. It aims to prevent the cured (or treated) individual from falling ill again or their condition from deteriorating further. For example, individuals who have suffered a heart attack then undergo rehabilitation to learn healthy eating and physical exercise.

Prevention, therefore, is a very comprehensive concept that encompasses extensive elements such as vaccination programmes, screening (e.g. breast cancer screening), mother-child programmes (e.g. prenatal care and screenings for children and adolescents), nutrition and dietary supplements, drinking water control, hygiene monitoring, meat inspections, building standards, product safety, healthy workplace conditions, and traffic safety, with the latter aspects of health protection predominantly situated outside the core healthcare sector and largely being sovereign tasks. This corresponds to the classic understanding of hygiene as developed in the nineteenth century and manifested in public health policies.

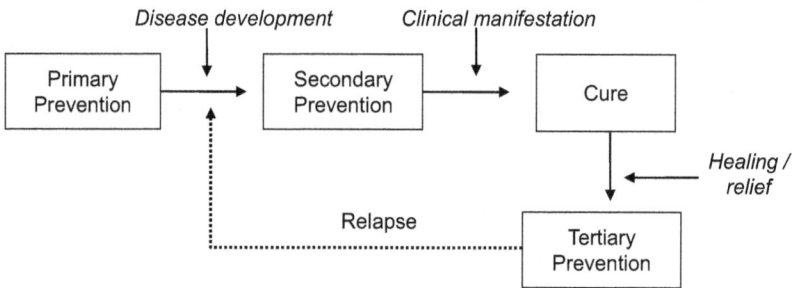

Figure 2.32: Phases of prevention.[134]

Numerous prevention programmes focus on combating communicable diseases since they usually have a clear cause and are therefore easily preventable (single-cause models, compare Section 3.1.1). For instance, dengue fever is caused by the dengue virus, transmitted by clearly identifiable mosquitos (particularly *Aedes aegypti* and the Asian tiger mosquito), so combating the carrier mosquitos leads to a reduction in dengue. Accordingly, mosquito control programmes formed an early focus of prevention measures, e.g. by the Rockefeller Foundation or the WHO (compare Section 3.3.2). Dengue threatens an estimated 2.5 billion people worldwide and can occur in the dan-

---

134 Source: Fleßa (2007).

gerous form of haemorrhagic fever.[135] Disease control programmes for dengue can reduce the number of adult mosquitos by insecticide spraying indoor and outdoor, traps, toxic sugar baits, and spatial repellents. The number of larvae or pupae can be reduced by water disinfection with insecticides or chlorination as well as by *Wolbachia*-based biocontrol and the breeding sites by drainage of swamps, insecticide-treated materials such as water bucket covers and by the reduction of water containers in settlements. More recently, the reproductive capacity of mosquitos is targeted, for instance, by the release of transgenic or sterilized insects (e.g. sterilized by irradiation).

It turns out that the prevention of dengue – as with many diseases – is primarily not a medical issue.[136] Instead, the disease arises as a consequence of an unstable (drinking) water supply, forcing people to maintain larger water reserves at home to have enough water during periods of scarcity. These water reserves are often stored in barrels, providing ideal breeding conditions for *Aedes* mosquitos. This example is typical of the interdisciplinarity field of prevention, which goes far beyond medicine – a fact that was heavily emphasized in the PHC declaration.

2.3.2 Primary Healthcare

PHC was proclaimed as the principal concept of healthcare in all member countries of the WHO at the World Health Conference in 1978. It is based on considerations and concepts that had already been expressed and tried out 10–20 years earlier in various countries.[137] Among others, Protestant churches and missions were significant because they increasingly viewed their role, their successes, and their future opportunities as essential service providers of healthcare in the 'mission fields' during the 1950s and 1960s with increasing criticism and sought alternative concepts of healthcare. First, it was centre that the vast majority of the population in the colonies at the time were not reached by the existing services. Looking back on this period, McGilvray, the long-time director of the Christian Medical Commission (CMC), writes, ". . . these church-related institutions, together with all the other available facilities of Western medicine, were reaching only 20% of the population in these countries and were thus sustaining a grave injustice to the 80% who remained deprived of any services at all".[138] The churches and missionary societies realized that focussing on hospital services was contrary to their mission of comprehensive evangelization. The second point of criticism concerned the financial side: the case costs of medical treatment in existing institutions were getting higher and higher. McGilvray notes that "in the early 50s,

---

135 Compare Nimmannitya (2004) and WHO (2011a).
136 Baly, Flessa, Cote, et al. (2011).
137 Compare Flessa (2016a) and Flessa (2016b).
138 McGilvray (1979).

there was a drastic increase in the cost of medical care".[139] Missionary societies that wanted to participate in medical-technical progress and equipped their mission hospitals with laboratories, x-ray machines, and modern medications increasingly came under cost pressure. Eventually, they could no longer cover the costs.

Third, the practice of purely curative and institution-based medicine in mission hospitals was increasingly questioned for its compatibility with the Christian understanding of healing. The main focus was that medical mission must always include preventive medicine[140] and cannot be fully delegated to doctors or nurses but must be perceived by the church as a whole.[141]

These issues were discussed at two international conferences in Tübingen, known far beyond ecclesiastical circles as Tübingen I (May 19–24, 1964) and Tübingen II (September 1–8, 1967). The delegates of these conferences designed a new conception of church health services:[142]

- Christian health work is always holistic. Therefore, purely physical healing contradicts the biblical image of man.
- It should involve as many community members as possible, not just doctors and nurses.
- It should be oriented towards prevention.
- It cannot be seen detached from other development planning; it is always interdisciplinary.

The resolutions of Tübingen I and II had a profound impact on further developments in healthcare system research. Immediately following the conferences, numerous regional conferences were held to disseminate the findings and resolutions, particularly in developing countries (e.g. Makumira Consultation 1967) and to allow reflection on the specific cultural background. This work was coordinated and supported by the CMC, especially since 1973, in close contact with the WHO, facilitated by their shared location in Geneva.[143]

Thus, the WHO had to recognize that 25 years after its founding (April 7, 1948), the most significant health problems had not decreased. Instead, financing the already existing health services became increasingly difficult. In search of solution strategies, the then Director of WHO, Halfdan Mahler, centre that the resolutions of Tübingen I and II were indeed relevant for all health services in developing countries. As a result, regular conferences were agreed upon. The CMC magazine *CONTACT* became mandatory reading at the WHO for some years. The concept of PHC, presented

---

139 McGilvray (1982).
140 Compare Ewert (1990).
141 Compare Scheel (1987).
142 Compare McGilvray (1982).
143 Compare Diesfeld, Falkenhorst, Razum, et al. (2001).

in the Alma-Ata in 1978 (September 6–12),[144] can be interpreted as a secular development of the Tübingen declarations.

'PHC' is "an updated term for hygiene, [. . .] expanded to include Health Policy demands in the broadest sense of the word and a strong participatory element".[145] Thus, PHC[146] is a concept of health policy. It is not a tier in the pyramid of health services but a comprehensive philosophy that should underlie all health policy decisions at all levels. The primary goal is to improve the population's health status, so that "Health for all by the year 2000" (Alma-Ata Declaration, §V) can be achieved. PHC includes elements of prevention and curative medicine, following these principles:[147]

- PHC is oriented towards the specific needs of the target group; PHC pursues the alignment of health opportunities among different population groups, i.e. the target group is not a social or economic elite but the majority of the population.
- PHC fundamentally involves the community in determining relevant goals and measures. The participants thus take responsibility for their health (community-based healthcare, CBHC).
- PHC or CBHC primarily relies on the available resources and considers the financial limitations of the community. In LDCs, this implies a partial redistribution of health resources to primary health services and prevention programmes.
- PHC demands that curative and preventive measures be carried out as close to the base as possible. This implies a central role for health education in CBHC/PHC. The upper levels of the health pyramid are not excluded; however, they are reserved for cases that cannot be treated at lower levels.
- PHC is an integral part of the national healthcare system.
- PHC is fundamentally multisectoral, meaning the activities of PHC are fully integrated into other sectors of human development (e.g. agriculture, education, and water management).

The Alma-Ata Declaration was partly rejected as politically biased because § III directly refers to a 'New International Economic Order'. Section X attributes poor healthcare in developing countries to high military expenditures. Werner and Sanders write:

> Many of the principles of Primary Health Care were garnered from China and from the diverse experiences of small, struggling non-governmental Community-Based Health Programs (CBHP) in the Philippines, Latin America, and elsewhere. The intimate connection of many of these initia-

---

144 Compare WHO (1978).
145 Diesfeld and Bichmann (1989).
146 'Healthcare' means the provision of health-related services, while 'healthcare' describes the system required to offer healthcare. Thus, it is correct to talk about 'primary healthcare', but several authors talk about 'healthcare' referring to both aspects.
147 WHO (1978).

tives to political reform movements explains to some extent why the concepts underlying PHC have received both criticism and praise for being revolutionary.[148]

Nonetheless, the declaration was signed by all WHO member countries.

However, health policy makers quickly expressed their concerns, considering the goals as utopian. They demanded strict prioritization, i.e. focussing on a few goals and measures that were particularly efficient. The WHO still pursues a comprehensive concept today, called 'comprehensive primary healthcare' . Other institutions, such as UNICEF, advocate focussing on a few easily combatable diseases, known as 'selective primary healthcare' . The mother-and-child programmes ('maternal and child healthcare') have proven to be particularly efficient. However, the implementation of WHO's comprehensive PHC concept at the country level has been largely unsuccessful. Although there were promising initial successes, it is evident today that the expectations were not met. Nevertheless, WHO titled its World Health Report (2008), i.e. 30 years after Alma-Ata, "Primary Health Care – now more than ever!" and still sees this concept as fundamental for fair and efficient healthcare, not only in resource-poor countries.[149]

2.3.3 Health Promotion

The direction of thought from Alma-Ata was revisited in 1,986 at the first International Conference on Health Promotion in Ottawa and condensed into the concept of health promotion. The starting point was a paradigm shift in public health research. While until the 1980s, the focus was primarily on why people become ill and what can be done against it (pathogenesis) , questions increasingly revolved around why people stay healthy and what can be done to improve health (salutogenesis) . The Ottawa Charter[150] was adopted by the World Health Assembly and is thus a binding document for (almost) all countries of the world, demanding the inclusion of health promotion in all areas of life and policy.

As the term implies, health promotion aims to strengthen all structures, institutions, and processes that positively affect the health of individuals and populations. It therefore starts from a dynamic understanding of health (compare Section 2.1.1) and the possibility of salutogenesis. It "encompasses all measures that aim at changing and promoting both individual and collective health behaviours as well as the living conditions, i.e., the framework conditions that influence the health and health behaviour of each individual and entire populations".[151] Here, one can distinguish between the political and practical approach. The Ottawa Charter is primarily a political docu-

---

148 Werner, Sanders, Weston, et al. (1997).
149 Compare WHO (2008b).
150 Compare WHO (1986).
151 Brößkamp-Stone (2003).

ment that places health promotion in the service of combating the "inequalities in the health and life expectancy of different social groups" and demands "social justice and equality of opportunity, [. . .] peace, adequate living conditions, education, nutrition, a stable ecosystem, and careful use of existing natural resources".[152] Subsequent conferences (e.g. Adelaide 1988, Sundsvall 1991, Jakarta 1997, Mexico City 2000, Bangkok 2005, and Nairobi 2009) further specified individual areas of action.

Practically relevant are the action strategies of the Ottawa Charter:[153]

- Advocacy for health: All decision-makers are called upon to include the health dimension in all political decisions, i.e. always to ask how a decision affects people's health. They should thus shape the political, economic, social, cultural, and biological environment in a way that it has a positive effect on the population's health. Reducing health promotion to the healthcare sector or even medicine is thereby excluded. Rather, systems should act health-promotionally, which found little consideration in the PHC concept, e.g. financial policy and companies.
- Enabling and empowering: The goal of reducing existing differences in health status can only be achieved by strengthening individuals and groups in their own health potential. However, this requires strengthening their competencies, their level of information, and their willingness and ability to take responsibility for their own health and to advocate for it. Empowerment, competence promotion, and access to relevant information are thus core elements of health promotion.
- Mediating and networking: Since health is a complex process influenced by numerous actors, a health-promoting overall conception requires active and continuous cooperation of all stakeholders regardless of whether they are attributed to the healthcare sector.

These action strategies should be implemented in various fields of action (compare Figure 2.33), especially in the development of a health-promoting overall policy, the creation of health-promoting living environments, the support of health-related community actions, the reorientation of health services and other health-relevant services, and the promotion of personal skills development. Crucial here is the so-called settings approach, which – simply put – states that health promotion primarily does not occur in special places (e.g. doctor's office) or in particular programmes but where people live. Thus, health-promoting living conditions, means of transport, roads, workplaces, recreational opportunities, friendships, clubs, etc., must be strengthened. This requires not only structural conditions but also the support of health-promoting behaviour within the framework conditions. WHO programmes of healthy cities, health-promoting regions, health-promoting schools, health-promoting hospitals, and workplace health promotion are programmes that follow this model.

---

152 WHO (1986).
153 Compare Kickbusch (2003).

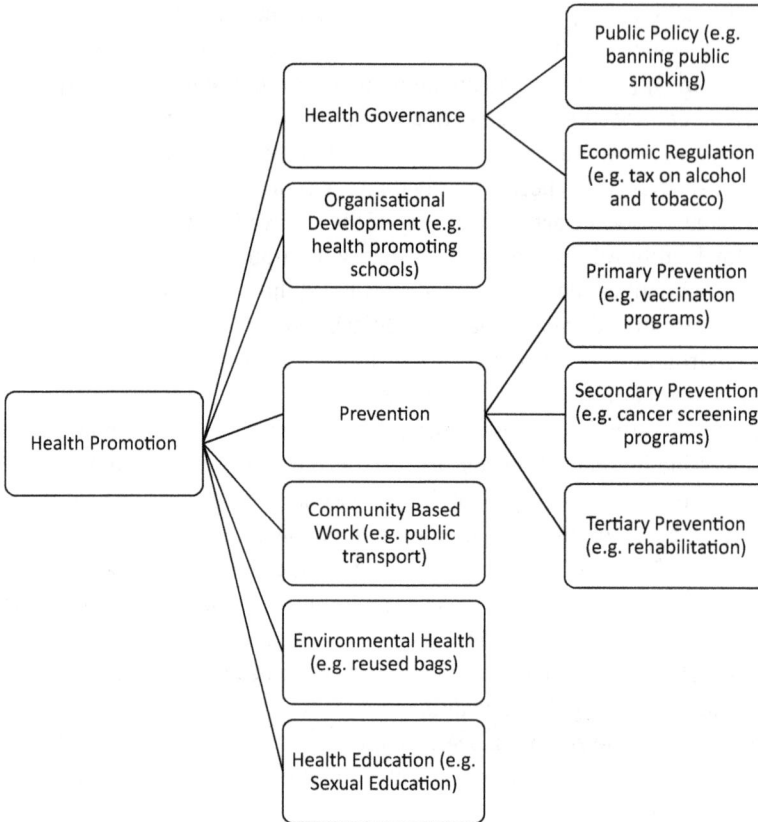

Figure 2.33: Health promotion.[154]

The adoption of these programmes in resource-poor countries was minimal until a few years ago. Since a large part of the population were independent subsistence farmers or seemed replaceable as day labourers of low qualification, health promotion was essentially limited to classic forms of prevention, such as vaccination programmes and hygiene. In addition, the pressing burden of acute diseases in healthcare facilities made health promotion appear as a secondary issue.

However, this has changed in recent years. For example, the health aspect of urban planning is becoming increasingly important as, for instance, air pollution poses a significant threat. Also, companies are beginning to think about health promotion since the growing middle and upper classes in low-income countries and, in particular, the 'young professionals' in cities are valuable resources that need to be nur-

154 Source: Own.

tured and preserved. Alcohol and tobacco abuse, obesity, and AIDS pose existential threats to companies if their workforce is affected. Increasingly, these companies take responsibility and support their employees in a health-conscious lifestyle.

One would expect that companies, cities, hospitals, etc., would promote the health of their stakeholders out of ethical conviction. However, this often happens only due to economic pressure. On the one hand, this is regrettable, but on the other hand, it opens up room for action. If it can be demonstrated that health promotion has significant advantages for all parties involved, the concept can be adopted and implemented. As sobering as this is – often, it is not the quality of life of people that decides health policy but the economic benefits. Here, it is the task of international healthcare management to demonstrate these benefits.

2.3.4 Regional Health Planning

Central planning of healthcare is essential to safeguard equitable and efficient services. This does not mean that the government has to provide healthcare services on its own, but it must take the responsibility that services of all levels are available in all locations for all subsets of the population. The levels of care indicate a hierarchical referral system, frequently depicted as a healthcare pyramid (compare Figure 2.34).[155]

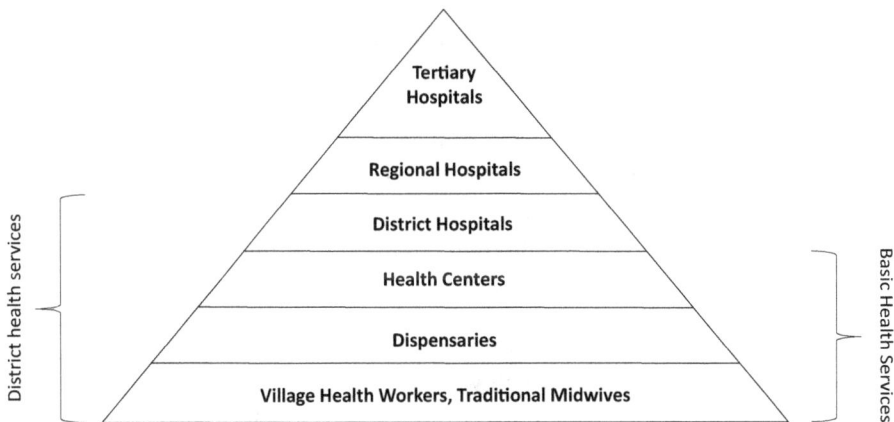

Figure 2.34: Healthcare pyramid.[156]

The WHO advocates for a healthcare system centred around a largely independently planning health district, integrating prevention programmes (e.g. vaccination pro-

---

155 Compare Phillips (1990).
156 Source: Fleßa (2006). Compare also Figure 2.6.

grammes and education), curative facilities, traditional medicine, and intersectoral measures (e.g. water construction and agriculture). All actors who can directly or indirectly impact the population's health should be involved in the health district.[157] As a geographical unit, the health district should be small enough to ensure the population's participation (§ 4) but large enough to guarantee efficient planning and management of all health-promoting and improving activities (Recommendation 15). The WHO Global Programme Committee defined:

> A district healthcare system based on primary healthcare is a more or less self-contained segment of the national healthcare system. It comprises, first and foremost, a well-defined population, living within a clearly delineated administrative and geographic area, whether urban or rural. It includes all institutions and individuals providing healthcare in the district, whether governmental, private, or traditional. A district healthcare system, therefore, consists of a large variety of interrelated elements that contribute to health in homes, schools, workplaces, and communities, through the health and other sectors. It includes self-care and all health workers and facilities, up to and including the hospital at the first referral level and appropriate laboratory, other diagnostic, and logistic support services. Its component elements need to be well-coordinated by an officer assigned to this function in order to draw together all these elements and institutions into a fully comprehensive range of promotive, preventive, curative, and rehabilitative health activities.[158]

The district healthcare system thus encompasses village health workers, traditional midwives, dispensaries, health centres, and district hospitals. The bottom three levels (compare Figure 2.34) make up the basic healthcare services. There is some dispute whether the term 'primary care' is identical with basic or with district healthcare, i.e. whether first-line hospitals belong to primary care. We take the position that smaller hospitals with beds, laboratory, and surgical facilities indeed belong to primary care, but the term 'district healthcare' is more an administrative category, i.e. it describes the way of organizing healthcare in a geographical unit. More important is the distinction between primary care and primary healthcare (see Section 2.3.2). The latter will be described as a philosophy of providing healthcare at the lowest possible level, while the former addresses a level of care.

The WHO has long advocated for comprehensive coverage with village health workers and traditional midwives to ensure non-institutional primary care. The village health worker (community health workers) manages the village health post, offering curative medicine at the most basic level, with a clear focus on prevention and health promotion.[159] Their area of responsibility should cover a maximum radius of 1-h walk, maintaining the orientation towards primary care. The traditional midwife (traditional birth attendant) is usually a mother of multiple children who supports

---

157 Compare WHO (1978).
158 Compare WHO (1996).
159 Compare Adegoroye (1989) and Shaffer (1987).

other mothers during childbirth and has no formal training. In many resource-poor countries, they assist with the majority of births to this day.

The second level of the health pyramid consists of dispensaries, distinguished from health centres by their lesser functionality and lack of beds. Both institutions have only paramedical staff, with no doctors present. In the district hospital, more severe cases can be treated, as physicians, as well as operating rooms and a laboratory are available. The district hospital and the primary care services together form the fundamental components of the health district.

The district hospital, as an integral part of the health district, can coordinate and administer the health services in the district.[160] This includes training and continuing education for village health workers and traditional midwives, as well as the staff of dispensaries, health centres, and prevention programmes. Additionally, all actors in the health district (employees, institutions, and programmes) are administratively and logistically supported here. Furthermore, the district hospital serves as a referral hospital, with severe cases being referred from health centres to the district hospital. Offering basic surgical services (e.g. Caesarean section, hernia surgery, and appendectomies) and better diagnostic capabilities in hospitals strengthens the district population's trust in the healthcare system and promotes the acceptance of prevention programmes.[161] For example, it is difficult to convey to expecting mothers why they should participate in prenatal care if no hospital can perform a Caesarean section.

Traditionally, most patients in low-income countries used to walk to the dispensary and health centre. It was often assumed that they will travel a maximum of 2 h to the dispensary and 4 h to the health centre. For district hospitals, it was often assumed that the maximum travel distance is a day's journey. For rural areas, this implied a maximum distance of 50 km, as the majority of the population arrives on foot or with simple vehicles (e.g. donkey carts) at the hospital. For areas with functioning public transportation, the catchment area can be larger. However, these figures were merely estimates, and modern mobility has changed the friction of distance. The actual distances depend on infrastructure, terrain, urgency of illness, etc. For instance, Africa and Asia have experienced a tremendous increase of public and private transport within the last 30 years with tremendous results on the mobility of patients. Mothers who used to walk for 2 h to a dispensary for a delivery, take a TukTuk today, bypass the dispensary, and go directly to the next district town to the district hospital in order to deliver. Thus, smaller facilities are getting less relevant, at least for some interventions. They receive, however, an increasing role in offering services for chronic degenerative diseases (e.g. hypertension and diabetes).

According to the WHO, the district healthcare system is the foundation of healthcare. The district management team sets priorities for curative and preventive medi-

---

160 Compare Tarimo (1991) and WHO (1992).
161 Compare Metelmann, Flessa, and Busemann (2020).

cine, creates plans, and independently implements measures to achieve these goals. Moreover, there are rarer and more severe diseases that cannot be treated at the district hospital. These patients are referred to a regional hospital, which offers specialized departments (internal medicine, general surgery, gynaecology and obstetrics, and psychiatry). Most resource-poor countries also have one or more tertiary hospitals offering further specializations (e.g. orthopaedics, ophthalmology, and ear-nose-throat) and are typically teaching hospitals. The coordination of health districts, regional, and tertiary hospitals is the responsibility of the MoH, which also allocates the health budget across the different levels of the healthcare system.

Regional health planning is crucial to provide services on all levels to all compartments of the society living in all locations. The market alone will safeguard an efficient allocation of resources and efficient production of services in the long run. However, this will not guarantee a fair distribution of services and it might induce side effects such as radicalism in remote and 'forgotten' locations. However, planning might also be too strict and lead to inefficiency. For instance, the Russian Federation and some former republics of the Soviet Union still have very strict and centrally administered healthcare systems. A major difference is the separation of functions in different hospitals. In Uzbekistan, for instance, national hospitals are separated according to medical specialities (e.g. emergencies, obstetrics, and paediatrics) and hospitals are in different sectors of the capital city Tashkent. Cooperation between these separate hospitals is poor, and accessibility is difficult as well. Attempts to change the system and have one comprehensive hospitals in each sector of the city face strong resistance. Consequently, regional healthcare planning is required to provide the best possible services to the population.

2.3.5 Universal Health Coverage

PHC, health promotion, and regional health planning were incorporated into a comprehensive concept called universal health coverage (UHC), calling for universal access to healthcare services for everybody in this world.[162] "Universal coverage (UC), or universal health coverage (UHC), is defined as ensuring that all people can use the promotive, preventive, curative, rehabilitative and palliative health services they need, of sufficient quality to be effective, while also ensuring that the use of these services does not expose the user to financial hardship."[163] In comparison to PHC, the focus is on "obtainment of good health services de facto without fear of financial hardship"[164] and "universal financial protection",[165] i.e. the focus is on economics!

---

162 Compare Evans, Hsu, and Boerma (2013a) and Reich, Harris, Ikegami, et al. (2016).
163 WHO (2024l).
164 Evans, Hsu, and Boerma (2013b).
165 Kutzin (2013).

UHC is a very comprehensive concept with the dimensions of health, coverage and universality:

- Health: The Alma-Ata Declaration had the vision of a 'Health For All by the Year 2000' where "health is to be brought within reach of everyone in a given country. And by 'health' is meant a personal state of well-being, not just the availability of health services".[166] UHC is no reprint of 'Health for All', but it puts strong emphasis on healthcare delivery and social security. While 'Health for All' might be idealistic, 'Coverage of All' might be realistic.

- Coverage: A population is covered by healthcare services if they are spatially, financially and culturally accessible and healthcare services are provided in sufficient quantity and quality. Spatial accessibility means that patients and their relatives can reach the point of care, while financial accessibility implies that the patients can afford to reach the service provider and afford the fees as well as other costs. A service provider is culturally accessible if the population accepts the provider and no social or cultural barriers prevent them from seeking help. The quantity of services depends on the capacity of the provider (e.g. beds, staff, and drugs), while the quality refers in particular to the result quality visible to the patient and his relatives.

- Universality: This criterion has the dimensions population, services, and cost recovery. Firstly, it asks who is covered in case of illness and analyses the coverage rate of different social groups (extremely poor, near-poor, formal and informal sectors, employed and unemployed, middle class, etc.), of population in different locations (e.g. urban and rural, and central and peripheral regions) as well as of family members (spouse and children).[167] Secondly, universality ask what services are covered, i.e. what phase of the service process (health promotion, prevention, out-patient, in-patient, rehabilitation, and palliative care), which conditions and diseases (e.g. reproductive health, nutritional conditions, communicable diseases, chronic degenerative diseases, and lifestyle medicine) and which price level of interventions (e.g. highly active antiretroviral therapy, dialysis, or cancer treatment) are covered. Thirdly, the dimension of universality analyses which proportion of costs is covered by public health expenditures, health insurance ,or out-of-pocket payments. Figure 2.35 shows the dimensions of universality as a cube with these three dimensions. In high-income countries, the UHC cube might fill the entire feasibility space of maximum health, access, and universality. The main problem of these countries is the fact that the cube constantly grows due to demographic and technological changes. In resource-poor countries, the UHC cube covers only a small share of the feasibility space, and a lot has to be done to improve the situation in all dimensions.

---

166 Mahler (2016).
167 Compare Kaiser, Rotigliano, Flessa, et al. (2023).

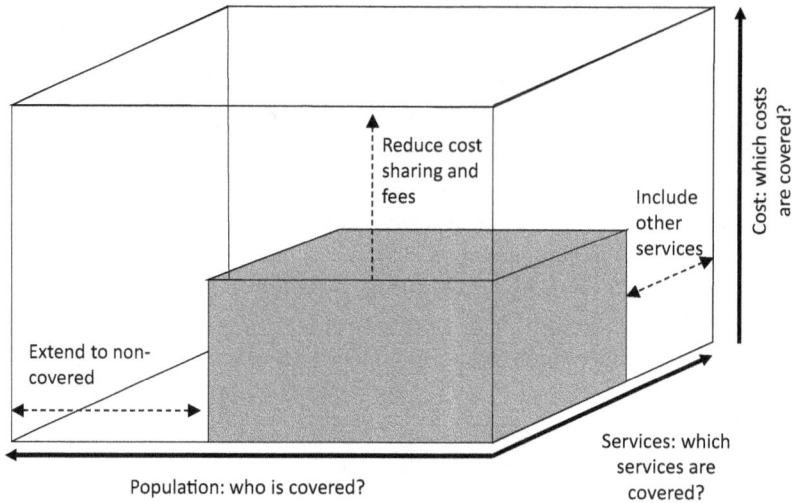

Figure 2.35: Universal health coverage.[168]

UHC is a central objective of international politics and the SDG (see Section 2.4.2) target 3.8: "Achieve universal health coverage, including financial risk protection, access to quality essential health-care services and access to safe, effective, quality and affordable essential medicines and vaccines for all".[169] It is generally accepted that UHC requires that national governments take responsibility for the social protection of their population. Thus, social health protection and subsidies for the poor are the two most important instruments of UHC.[170]

The World Bank calculates a UHC coverage index[171] (compare Figure 2.36) incorporating all three dimensions (World Bank 2019). The world index of the year 2021 (latest data) was 42 in low-, 58 in lower middle-, 79 in upper middle-, and 85 in high-income countries. Somalia had the lowest UHC coverage index (27), Canada the highest (91). Fourteen of 15 countries with an index below 40 are in sub-Saharan Africa, merely Papua New Guinea with an index of 30 is in this group. The index shows that, in particular, Asian countries have strongly improved the social protection for their citizens. More and more countries offer social insurance coverage at least for parts of the population.[172]

---

168 Source: Own, based on Cattaneo, Tamburlini, Stefanini, et al. (2015).
169 Compare WHO (2019b).
170 Compare Cattaneo, Tamburlini, Stefanini, et al. (2015). See also Section 5.2.2.
171 The UHC coverage index for essential health services is "based on tracer interventions that include reproductive, maternal, newborn and child health, infectious diseases, noncommunicable diseases and service capacity and access). It is presented on a scale of 0 to 100" (World Bank 2024b).
172 Compare Adhikari (2018). See also Section 5.2.2.

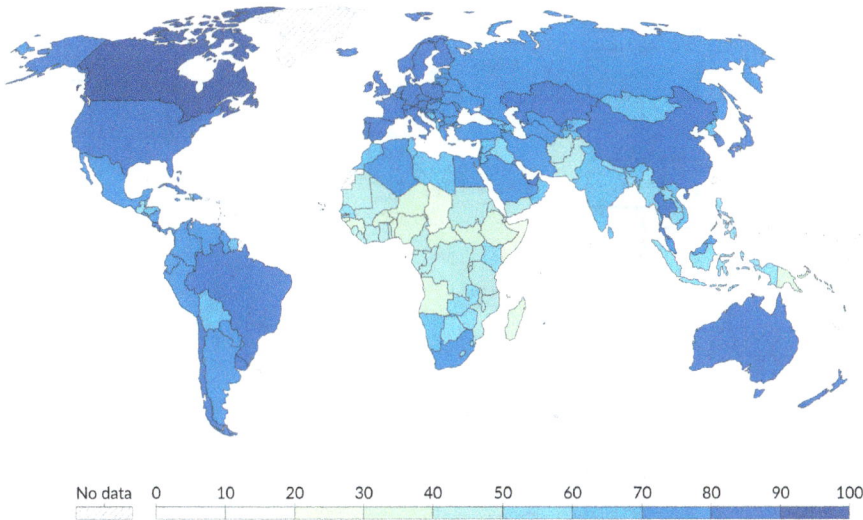

No data 0 10 20 30 40 50 60 70 80 90 100

Figure 2.36: Universal health coverage index (2021).[173]

The year 2012 was the 'big year' of UHC with a number of resolutions calling for UHC, such as the Mexico City Political Declaration on Universal Health Coverage (2012), the Bangkok Statement on Universal Health Coverage (2012), the Tunis Declaration on Value for Money, Sustainability, and Accountability in the Health Sector (2012), and the UN-resolution Transition of National Health Care Systems towards Universal Coverage (2012). Since then, UHC is a standard concept of international health policy and development cooperation. The charm for the healthcare manager is that this concept can easily be combined with the health economic framework model described in Section 2.1.3 and the production model of Section 4.1.2. As shown in Figure 2.37, the demand and supply side meet on the market. The result of the market processes is the coverage of the population. Thus, UHC is an essential component of the health economic model – even if it is usually not called that.

173 Source: OurWorldinData – CC-BY@: https://ourworldindata.org/grapher/universal-health-coverage-index (18 February 2025).

| DEMAND-SIDE | SUPPLY-SIDE |

•Demography
•Epidemiology
•Transition

SCARCITY

Disease Pattern

•Contacts
•Risk of admission
•Length of stay

AGENTS

Staffing
Equipment
Buildings
Location

Prevention

•Emergencies, accidents
•Seasonality

Health Education

NEEDS

Population density

Excess Capacity

PRODUCTION

Time per
Service Unit

Management

Distance Barriers
•Transport time/distance
•Infrastructure
•Mental mobility
•Attraction
•Cultural / natural barriers
•Type of medicine

WANT

•Input-Based
•Output-Based

•Daily Rate
•Flat Rate
•Fee-for-Service

Financial System

PRODUCT

Quantity
Quality

Perceived Quality
•Opening times, presence
of staff, waiting times
•Attitude of staff
•Drugs, grounds,
buildings, equipment,
cleanliness
•Adequate medical
examination
•Results

Elasti-cities
Excess
demand

Priority
•Utility of health care
•Utility of alternative goods
•Costs of alternative goods

Price Barriers
•Costs
•Indirect costs
•Direct costs
•Fees
•Transport
•Food
•Income/wealth
•Subsidy
•Insurance

DEMAND
•Disease Panorama
•Levels of Health
Care
•Service units p.c.
•Regions

MARKET
•Competition
•Functionality
•Regulation

SUPPLY
•Levels of Health
Care
•Service Profiles
•Regions

•Existence
•Quality/Functionality
•Referral

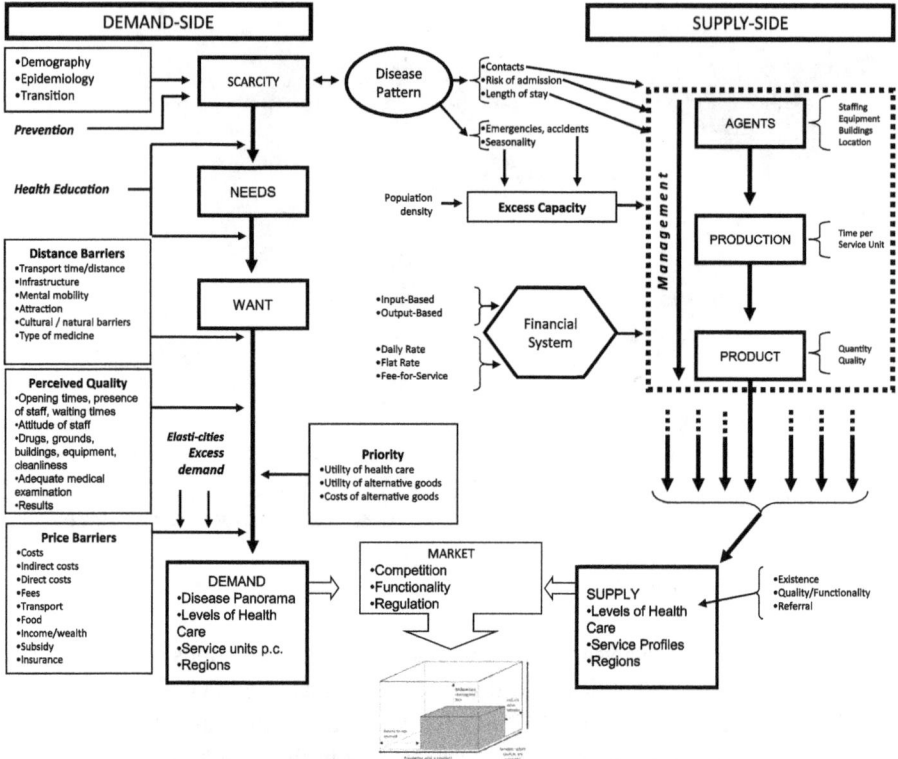

Figure 2.37: Universal health coverage and healthcare management.[174]

2.4 Health Policy

2.4.1 Historical Pathways

Healthcare systems and health policies can only be interpreted within their historical context. Thus, the following will describe the historical paths on which healthcare systems have evolved.

It is fundamentally assumed that all cultures and cultural groups generate healthcare systems based on the resources of their habitat and the demands of their developmental stage.[175] Although Western, scientific medicine has found worldwide distribution, it has not been able to completely displace the traditional systems of many

---

174 Source: Own.
175 Compare Leiniger (1970) and Leiniger (2005).

regions. For instance, Chinese medicine, developed during the Chou (1121–225 BC) and Han Dynasty (206 BC to AD 225),[176] continues to exist alongside Western medicine and has spread almost globally. Indian traditional medicine (Ayurveda) and Arab medicine (Unani) are widely practiced to this day. These systems were developed by high cultures that, according to Bobek[177] belong to the era of older urban societies. They have diffused across entire cultural spheres, and official training programmes for the healing professions exist.

Cultures at the stage of nomadism and clan-based farming, as well as feudal agriculture societies develop healthcare systems with their own profession of the healer. However, the respective system or understanding of healing and disease is usually tied to the individual tribe and thus narrowly distributed. These are societies with particular (as opposed to universal) religions. Characteristic of them is that an individual is born into the tribe and ancestral beliefs, thereby automatically adopting the religious views. A subsequent change of religion is thus not possible: "Membership is inherited. Belonging to the religion coincides with belonging [. . .] to tribe or people as well as to shared culture. Conversion to the religion seems as impossible as it is unthinkable."[178] Therefore, the understanding of healing is always limited to tribal boundaries.

In societies with particular religions, there were also no institutionalized schools where one could learn the profession of being a healer. Moreover, the connection between healing and religion was much closer than with Chinese, Indian, or Arab traditional medicine. In traditional religions, health and disease are seen as expressions of an individual's harmony with their social and spiritual environment.[179] The cause of a disease is often seen in a violation of a taboo or the disrespect of an ancestor or spirit, so only an act of reconciliation (e.g. an animal sacrifice) can eliminate the cause of the disease.[180] In most LDCs before the arrival of Europeans (particularly in Africa) or Chinese (especially in Southeast Asia), there were hardly any herbalists or traditional surgeons who did not use magical elements in their healing rituals.[181]

Before World War I, the influence of Western medicine on the lives of people in developing countries was very minimal.[182] The few colonial officers and missionaries were convinced of the superiority of their civilization and thus their medicine. However, their resources were too limited to reach larger portions of the indigenous population. While the colonial health service primarily followed the central place structures and hospitals were mainly built in larger cities, missionaries went to remote

---

176 Compare Meade and Emch (2005).
177 Compare Bobek (1959).
178 Drehsen and Baumotte (1995).
179 Compare Feierman and Janzen (1992a), Mbiti (1992), and Mbiti (1994).
180 Compare Mbiti (1994).
181 Compare Kasiloo (2000).
182 Compare Schott (2000) and Schweikart (1992).

rural areas. The original goal of mission medicine was "to unlock the soul of Africans",[183] which, of course, applies to the population of all missionary areas outside Africa as well. However, it was already lamented in 1873 that "the medical missionaries won confidence was not necessarily a blessing, since blind and ignorant confidence in the omnipotent doctor was more harmful than beneficent [. . .]. As a converting agency, [. . .] the hospital had been a failure".[184]

There are numerous reports of the selfless service of the first mission sisters and doctors.[185] As impressive as the results of these early institutions may have been in their immediate catchment area, they were of no significance to the majority of the indigenous population, who lived too far away from these facilities to be able to avail of their services. The early colonial period is marked by a strict dichotomy between Western medicine in the cities or mission stations and the traditional medicine of the rural majority.

The period after World War I meant an intensification of Western medicine for many colonies (or protectorates). On the one hand, existing institutions were expanded, and on the other hand, efforts were made to reach remote areas with so-called 'outreach programmes'. A team of doctors and nurses would regularly visit distant villages from a hospital to conduct outpatient consultations. Initially, only curative individual medicine was offered, which was later expanded to include elements of prevention to avoid epidemics of communicable diseases. These prevention programmes were mostly directed at combating specific diseases in certain regions, e.g. sleeping sickness.[186] This leads some authors to doubt they were carried out for humanitarian reasons. It is suspected that these measures primarily served to secure the labour force potential of colonial farms or administration, i.e. public health activities were implemented to fight diseases that could affect the European populations (e.g. malaria and sleeping sickness) or to maintain a healthier labour force resulting in higher profits for the colonials.[187] Therefore, by the end of the colonial era, the majority of the population in today's LDCs still relied exclusively on traditional healers as providers of health services.

In 1949, Mao proclaimed the People's Republic of China, and thousands of missionaries had to leave China. They looked for new fields of activity, especially the doctors among them were welcomed in the poor countries of Africa and Asia. There, they continued the tradition of the China Mission, which had begun in the mid-nineteenth century. When the first missionary doctors came to China at that time,[188] they found a functioning indigenous medicine that was more advanced in many areas of internal

183 Anderson (1988).
184 Scarborough (1873). Compare also Young (1973).
185 Compare, e.g. Weishaupt (1936) and Gilmurray, Riddell, and Sanders (1979).
186 Compare Calwell (1993).
187 Compare Bruchhausen (2020).
188 An introduction into the history of medical missions is given by Grundmann (1992). Here, we refer in particular to pages 130–168.

medicine than European conventional medicine at the time. However, there was no surgery in China, as the opening of a dead body – a basic prerequisite for training surgeons – was a traditional taboo. Consequently, China missionaries specialized in surgery, i.e. medical mission and surgery became almost synonymous.[189]

When the medical missionaries had to leave China 100 years later and came to Southeast Asia and Africa, it was mainly surgeons who began working in these new 'mission fields'. Since a surgeon needs a large, functional hospital with a modern operating room, wherever former China missionaries worked, hospitals were expanded and large operating rooms were built. Grundmann describes this development since 1949: "Subsequently, mission doctors continued to focus mainly on surgery, which required a stability of location for observation and aftercare [. . .], which is why medical mission and hospital became virtually identical."[190]

The new mission areas differed from China in that there was no efficient, indigenous internal medicine. However, this fact was overlooked under the pressure of surgeons seeking new fields of activity, and the 'disease palaces' were created:[191] large, modern hospitals with high costs that, however, benefit only a comparatively few people. For example, own surveys in Central Tanzania (Dodoma Rural health district) showed that only 0.368% of all disease cases implied the need for surgical intervention. However, the costs for surgery accounted for about 20% of the total costs of the health district.

The end of the colonial era and the first decades of the independent states focussed on rural areas, where the majority of the population lived, in the centre of health policy. New, modern hospitals were built in rural areas, so the number of hospitals increased significantly while the distance to travel decreased. For instance, in Tanzania, the average travel distance decreased from 36.57 km (1963) to 25.39 km (1996). This period also saw the establishment of most tertiary hospitals in major cities. Initially celebrated as a great achievement, they consumed the majority of the national health budgets,[192] which is why they are sometimes called 'white elephants'.

In some countries, this era of large hospital constructions coincided with the nationalization of private and faith-based[193] health institutions. The young states were financially able to maintain these new, large operations because, on the one hand, they received extensive foreign aid, and on the other hand, the 1960s were a period of high economic growth in many LDCs. Thus, a hospital infrastructure was created in the

---

189 For instance, Skinsnes (1952) phrased his experiences in the medical mission field of China with the book title *Scalpel and Cross in Honan*.

190 Grundmann (1992).

191 Morley and Lovel (1986).

192 Compare Barnum, Kutzin, and Roemer (1993).

193 The majority of these institutions belonged to Christian churches. However, the older term 'church-based' is frequently replaced by the term 'faith-based' because some other religious groups do also provide healthcare services, e.g. the Agha Khan Foundation or Buddhist for Health.

1960s and 1970s, which still forms the backbone of scientific medicine in low-income countries, especially in Africa. However, Western medicine was only able to partially displace traditional healers. In some countries, they were officially integrated (e.g. in Vietnam and China), elsewhere they were tolerated or fought against. Nonetheless, it is estimated that to this day, 50–80% of the population in Africa and Asia seek the services of traditional healers. In other countries (e.g. Cambodia), traditional knowledge is lost to a high extent, but non-professional healers have found their market as quacks with abilities far below the traditional healer. In locations where traditional healers with a long-term (formal or informal) training still exist, they have comparative advantages such as their spatial proximity to patients, the acceptance of non-monetary compensation (e.g. food and labour), cultural proximity (e.g. same tribal language), and especially the integration of the spiritual dimension into the healing process.

In the mid-1970s, a global crisis of healthcare in developing countries became apparent, requiring a rethinking. However, the Declaration of Alma-Ata and the PHC concept (compare Section 2.3.2) have only been implemented very hesitantly to this day, leading to a dramatic escalation in the healthcare situation in low-income countries during the 1980s and 1990s. The following elements of a global health crisis are only outlined here and will be discussed in more detail later:

– Technical efficiency: The ratio of services provided to resource consumption in healthcare facilities in developing countries indicates low technical efficiency and significant potential for rationalization. Although personnel costs in Africa were relatively low in the mid-1990s, the cost per unit of service at African dispensaries was 200% of comparable Asian institutions. For hospitals, it was even 500%.[194] Studies indicate that the productivity of facilities at the same level of care within a country varies significantly.[195] Aspects of technical efficiency will be delved into in Section 4.1.

– Allocative efficiency: Despite the self-commitment of all countries and the numerous appeals by the WHO to promote primary healthcare services, little changed in the priorities of government health budgets after the Alma-Ata conference. The World Bank found for sub-Saharan Africa that:

> – major urban hospitals (so-called tertiary facilities) often receive half or more of the public funds spent on health and commonly account for 50 to 80% of recurrent healthcare sector expenditures by the government. In the mid-1980s, for example, the major hospitals' share of public recurrent health expenditures was 74% in Lesotho, 70% in Somalia, 66% in Burundi, 54% in Zimbabwe, and 49% in Botswana.[196]

---

194 Compare Tarimo and Webster (1996).
195 For example, patients per doctor, patients per healthcare worker, infusions per operation, and units of malaria medicine per case of malaria. Compare Beiter, Koy, and Flessa (2023).
196 Weltbank (1994).

- We will revisit the allocation to the levels of care in Section 4.2.1.
- Reduction of government health budgets: In the 1980s and 1990s, most governments in developing countries were no longer financially able to maintain or increase health budgets.[197] Low government revenues, a large number of government employees, and economic mismanagement (e.g. overvalued currencies) led to numerous developing countries only being able to
- Low government revenues, a large number of civil servants, and economic mismanagement (e.g. overvalued currencies) led to many developing countries remaining solvent only with the help of loans and grants from international organizations, such as the World Bank and the International Monetary Fund. However, these financial organizations could only offer their support if it was guaranteed that these resources were effective, necessitating the implementation of so-called structural adjustment programmes. These regularly included a reduction in health and social budgets, although the impact on social indicators is disputed.[198]
- Reduction of private purchasing power: In the twentieth century, a significant portion of the population in developing countries primarily lived from subsistence farming. Cash income, which is needed, for example, to pay for health services, is usually generated by cash crops (e.g. coffee, tea, sisal, cotton, and cocoa) that are traded on the world market. Dependence on climate variations, harvests, and world market prices leads to high inter- and intra-annual fluctuation in private purchasing power. Especially in the 1990s, the payment ability of the rural population in many developing countries declined, leading the World Bank, for example, to note for Tanzania: "The really poor – the bottom 10% or so of the income distribution – appear to have fallen behind. They need special attention. Income inequality between cities and the countryside, and even within the countryside, has increased."[199] The reduction in private purchasing power also led to a decrease in the ATP for health services, thereby worsening the average health condition.
- Population growth: The existing infrastructure or a constant health budget was not sufficient to provide the constantly growing population with health services of the same quantity and quality. The average population growth rate of the LDCs between 1978 (Declaration of Alma-Ata) and the year 2000 (target of 'Health for All by the Year 2000', compare Section 2.3.2) was about 2.5% per annum. This means that in 2000, almost twice as many people lived in the LDCs as in the year of the Alma-Ata Declaration, and about three times as many as at the independence of most developing countries (approximately 1960–1965). High investments

---

197 Compare Creese and Kutzin (1997).
198 Compare Gaag and Barham (1998).
199 Weltbank (1999). Compare also Ferreira (1994) and Rösch (1995).

would have been necessary to equip them all with an equivalent range of health institutions and programmes.

– Deterioration of infrastructure: Many healthcare facilities in the LDCs were built towards the end of the colonial period or in the first decade after independence. Consequently, the infrastructure is 35–45 years old. Replacement investments were not made for a long time, jeopardizing the sustainable provision of medical services.[200]

– Epidemics: The emergence of new diseases (e.g. AIDS), the worsening situation of known infectious diseases (e.g. malaria), and the aging of the population lead to an increased demand for health services. There was also an increase in so-called lifestyle diseases (e.g. obesity and tobacco abuse).[201] Therefore, the WHO has determined these negative side effects of economic development as the focus of its actions for a 'Health for All' in the twenty-first century.[202]

The threats to health and human development in resource-poor countries were recognized by national and international politics. Since the end of the 1990s, the healthcare sector has gradually moved from a shy niche of humanitarian aid organizations to the centre of development policy. The Millennium Summit was particularly important in this regard. It is important to note that parallel to the demographic and epidemiological transition, there has also been a mobility transition, significantly influencing the disease panorama as well as the possibilities and limits of health policy. In 1970, only about 750 million people in the then developing countries lived in cities, but by 1990 this number had already risen to about 1.3 billion. In 2023, 4.6 of the 8 billion inhabitants of this planet lived in towns, the majority of them in countries which are still or were developing countries in the 1970s.[203] The particular importance of megacities for the healthcare system in developing countries is discussed in Section 3.5.7.

The World Development Report 1993 was such an innovative leap. In 1987, the World Bank published the report "Financing Health Services in Developing Countries – An Agenda for Reform"[204] which received little attention. However, the subsequent document, "Investing in Health" from 1993, sparked extensive political debate.[205] It called for an orientation towards efficient intervention measures with clarity previously unknown, where efficiency measurement was conducted using disability-adjusted life years (DALYs) (see Section 3.1.1).[206] DALYs were developed by

---

200 Compare Yudkin (1999).

201 Compare Seidell (1999), Okosun, Forrester, Rotimi, et al. (1999), and Jones and Kirigia (1999).

202 Compare WHO (1998).

203 Compare Heineberg (2000) and Destatis (2024).

204 Compare Akin, Birdsall, and De Ferranti (1987).

205 Compare World Bank (1993).

206 From the mathematical formulation (see Section 3.1.1), a DALY is defined as a 'disability-adjusted life year lost', so the term 'loss of DALYs' is technically incorrect. Often, the characterization 'lost' is omitted, which makes the term commonly used.

World Bank economist Murray[207] and represent a measure of disease-related loss of life years and quality of life. The logic of the World Development Report is straightforward: it calculates how many DALYs can be gained by investing US$1 in health and demands financing only for interventions with the highest returns. Therefore, the report represents both a methodological and political advance, making health economics increasingly significant in international health. Even the WHO, which had long fought against the application of DALYs and efficiency measures, eventually had to adopt this concept, evidenced by Murray's move to the WHO.

The World Development Report 1993 demanded a health budget of US$12 per capita per year for the LDCs, with 33% allocated for prevention and 67% for curative measures – targets that have been reached neither then nor now. The follow-up document "Better Health for Africa" (1994)[208] added another US$2 per capita per year for organizing health services but confirmed the figures from the World Development Report.

2.4.2 Developments of the New Millennium

Since Alma-Ata and Ottawa, numerous other international declarations and documents significant for international healthcare management have been created. In the following, we will describe the most important ones since the year 2000. Often, these strategies and policies bring nuances of novelty and sell 'old wine in new bottles', but sometimes they represent quantum leaps in public perception.

Millennium Development Goals
In 1978, the WHO defined (minimum) goals for international health policy (compare Section 2.3.2) to achieve 'Health for All by the Year 2000':[209]
– Life expectancy at birth >60 years
– Infant mortality <50/1,000 live births
– Child mortality <70/1,000 live births

By the end of the planning period up to the year 2000, it became clear that these goals were largely missed in most resource-poor countries. In 2000, the 55th General Assembly of the United Nations agreed at the so-called Millennium Summit on the goals of development policy to combat extreme poverty by 2015. The respective result and instrument of the summit were the millennium development goals (MDGs). The importance of these goals lies in the fact that for the first time, politicians from the major

---

207 Compare Murray (1994b) and Murray (1994c).
208 Compare The World Bank (1994).
209 Compare WHO (1998.)

economic nations took responsibility for the living conditions of people in developing countries. Additionally, the goals were quantified and given a deadline, making their achievement measurable and assessable, unlike many other targets of international politics. As shown in Table 2.9, goals 4–6 are primary health goals, while goals 7 and 8 contain health-relevant aspects in their specifications.

Table 2.9: Millennium development goals.[210]

No.	Goal	Health specification
1	Combat extreme poverty and hunger	
2	Universal primary education	
3	Gender equality/ empowerment of women	
4	Reduce child mortality	For details, see Table 2.10
5	Improve maternal health	For details, see Table 2.10
6	Combat HIV/AIDS, malaria, and other diseases	For details, see Table 2.10
7	Ensure environmental sustainability	Halve, by 2015, the proportion of people without sustainable access to safe drinking water (from 65% to 32%) Achieve significant improvement in lives of at least 100 million slum dwellers, by 2020
8	Develop a global partnership for development	In cooperation with pharmaceutical companies, provide access to affordable essential drugs in developing countries

The MDGs were defined in detail, and respective indicators were attached (compare Table 2.10). For instance, goal 4 (reduce child mortality) had two targets and two indicators. For each indicator, a baseline value of the year 1990 and target values of the year 2015 were to be given. For instance, the under-five mortality rate in the LDCs was 175 per 1,000 live births in 1990 and it was the objective to reduce it by 2/3 to 58 until 2015. The infant mortality rate was 109 per 1,000 live births in 1990 and it was the objective to cut it down by 2/3 to 36 in 2015. Figure 2.38 shows the child mortality for selected regions from 1990 to 2022. It is obvious that the situation strongly improved in all regions. However, the majority of low- and middle-income countries has not reached the MDG 4.A. At the same time, the differences between regions and in particular between high-, middle- and low-income economies are still significant.

---

210 Compare United Nations (2010).

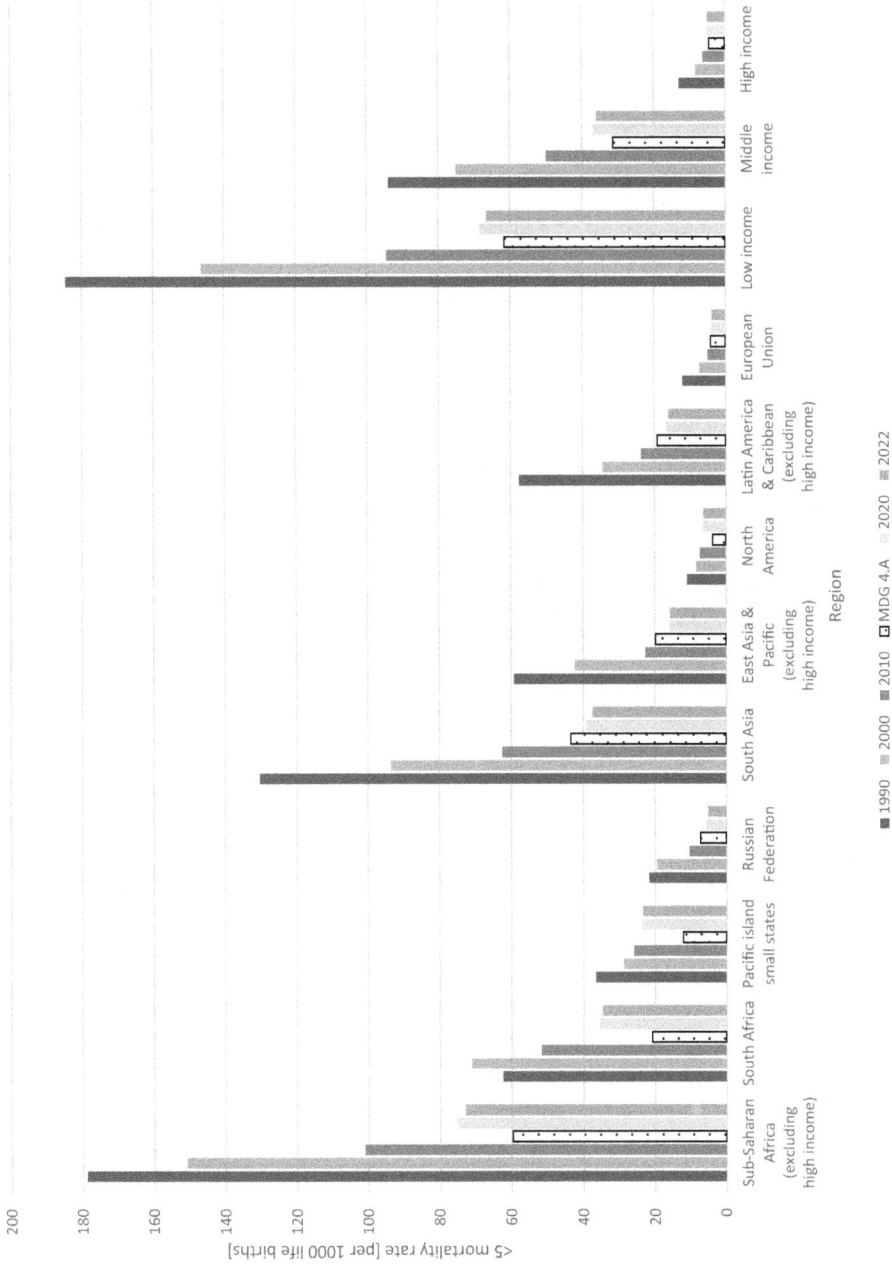

Figure 2.38: Millennium development goal 4.[211]

211 Source: United Nations (2010).

Table 2.10: Health-related millennium development goals in LDC.[212]

MDG	Target	Indicator	Baseline 1990	Target level	Level 2015
Goal 4: Reduce child mortality	Target 4.A: Reduce by two-thirds, between 1990 and 2015, the under-five mortality rate	4.1 Under-five mortality rate (per 1,000 live births)	175	58	71
		4.2 Infant mortality rate (per 1,000 live births)	109	36	50
		4.3 Children immunized against measles (%)[213]	55	100	75
Goal 5: Improve maternal health	>Target 5.A: Reduce by three-quarters, between 1990 and 2015, the maternal mortality ratio	5.1 Maternal mortality (per 100,000 live births)	903	95	436
		5.2 Births attended by skilled personnel (%)	59	100	64 (2019)
	Target 5.B: Achieve, by 2015, universal access to reproductive health	5.3 Contraceptive prevalence rate (%)	19	100	40 (2019)
		5.4 Adolescent fertility rate (births per 1,000 women aged 15–19)	136		101
		5.5 Antenatal care coverage (%)	–	100	?
		5.6 Unmet need for family planning	–	0	?
Goal 6: Combat HIV/AIDS, malaria, and other diseases	Target 6.A: Have halted by 2015 and begun to reverse the spread of HIV/AIDS	6.1 HIV prevalence among population aged 15–24 years (%)	1.52	0	1.98
		6.2 Condom use at last high-risk sex	–		54.9
		6.3 Proportion of population aged 15–24 years with comprehensive correct knowledge of HIV/AIDS			
		6.4 Ratio of school attendance of orphans to school attendance of non-orphans aged 10–14 years			

---

212 Source: World Bank (2024b), UN (2003), and UN (2015). Some data is not available for LDCs, in some cases not for all respective countries.
213 The original MDGs focus on children <1 year, while the statistics are available for children aged 12–23 months.

Table 2.10 (continued)

MDG	Target	Indicator	Baseline 1990	Target level	Level 2015
	Target 6.B: Achieve, by 2010, universal access to treatment for HIV/AIDS for all those who need it	6.5 Proportion of population with advanced HIV infection with access to antiretroviral drugs (%)	0	100	49
	Target 6.C: Have halted by 2015 and begun to reverse the incidence of malaria and other major diseases[20]	6.6 Incidence and death rates associated with malaria (new cases per 1,000 at risk)	158 per 1,000 12.5 per 10,000	<158 per 1,000 ?	94 per 1,000 10.2 12.5 per 100,00
		6.7 Proportion of children under 5 years sleeping under insecticide-treated bed nets			
		6.8 Proportion of children under 5 years with fever who are treated with appropriate anti-malarial drugs			
		6.9 Incidence, prevalence, and death rates associated with tuberculosis (new cases per 100,000 people)	172	<172	143
		6.10 Proportion of tuberculosis cases detected and cured under directly observed treatment short course			

Table 2.10 shows the health-related MDGs with their targets and indicators. For the researcher, it is a disaster that many MDG indicators have no proper baseline value, and even statistics from WHO and World Bank focussing on MDGs do not provide all indicators.[214] For the entire world, most indicators are available, but for LDCs, quite a number of baseline values and final values for 2015 do not exist. Sometimes, values are only available for 2019, but not for the end of the MDG era in 2015. In total, the health-related MDGs were not achieved in LDCs. Merely the fight against malaria and TB appears to be progressing more successfully. The availability of impregnated bed nets has strongly increased, and the case detection and treatment of TB is much better than before. However, the focus on malaria, TB and HIV/AIDS has caused the emergence of 'neglected diseases'.[215]

214 For example, https://databank.worldbank.org/source/millennium-development-goals-.
215 Compare Moran, Guzman, Ropars, et al. (2009).

Sustainable Development Goals

Some years before the deadline of the MDGs (Millennium Development Goals Summit 2010), disappointment with the MDGs was universal. Firstly, it became obvious that most MDGs would not be achieved. Secondly, it was strongly discussed that the MDGs were too narrow to address the complex and interdependent system of development. Thirdly, the MDGs were still strongly driven by the 'rich' North while participation of the South was limited. Consequently, it was decided to develop a new target and indicator system (post-MDGs) called SDGs. The vision was 'transforming our world: the 2030 Agenda for Sustainable Development' with 17 global goals and 169 targets (compare Table 2.11).

Table 2.11: Sustainable development goals.[216]

No.	Goal
1	End poverty in all its forms everywhere
2	End hunger, achieve food security and improved nutrition, and promote sustainable agriculture
3	Ensure healthy lives and promote well-being for all at all ages
4	Ensure inclusive and equitable quality education, and promote lifelong learning opportunities for all
5	Achieve gender equality and empower all women and girls
6	Ensure availability and sustainable management of water and sanitation for all
7	Ensure access to affordable, reliable, sustainable, and modern energy for all
8	Promote sustained, inclusive and sustainable economic growth, full and productive employment, and decent work for all
9	Build resilient infrastructure, promote inclusive and sustainable industrialization, and foster innovation
10	Reduce inequality within and among countries
11	Make cities and human settlements inclusive, safe, resilient, and sustainable
12	Ensure sustainable consumption and production patterns
13	Take urgent action to combat climate change and its impacts[3]
14	Conserve and sustainably use the oceans, seas, and marine resources for sustainable development
15	Protect, restore, and promote sustainable use of terrestrial ecosystems, sustainably manage forests, combat desertification, and halt and reverse land degradation and halt biodiversity loss
16	Promote peaceful and inclusive societies for sustainable development, provide access to justice for all and build effective, accountable, and inclusive institutions at all levels
17	Strengthen the means of implementation and revitalize the global partnership for sustainable development

---

216 Source: UN (2024b).

Table 2.12 indicates that a major number of SDGs relate directly (SDG 3) or indirectly to health. The UN has defined 13 targets and 28 indicators for SDG 3, i.e. health is still a crucial component of SDGs. In comparison to the MDGs, the SDGs are much broader and cover many more dimensions of health and well-being. Non-communicable diseases (NCDs), mental health, health workforce, suicide, environmental pollution, etc., are determinants of health, which shift to the focus of the SDGs.

Table 2.12: Health-related sustainable development targets and indicators.[217]

MDGs/targets	Indicators
1.a Ensure significant mobilization of resources from a variety of sources [. . .]in order to provide adequate and predictable means [. . .] to implement programmes and policies to end poverty in all its dimensions	1.a.2 Proportion of total government spending on essential services (education, health, and social protection
2.1 By 2030, end hunger and ensure access by all people, in particular the poor and people in vulnerable situations, including infants, to safe, nutritious, and sufficient food all year round	2.1.1 Prevalence of undernourishment
	2.1.2 Prevalence of moderate or severe food insecurity in the population, based on the Food Insecurity Experience Scale (FIES)
2.2 By 2030, end all forms of malnutrition, including achieving, by 2025, the internationally agreed targets on stunting and wasting in children under 5 years of age, and address the nutritional needs of adolescent girls, pregnant and lactating women, and older persons	2.2.1 Prevalence of stunting [. . .] among children under 5 years of age
	2.2.2 Prevalence of malnutrition [. . .] among children under 5 years of age, by type (wasting and overweight)
	2.2.3 Prevalence of anaemia in women aged 15 to 49 years, by pregnancy status (percentage)
3.1 By 2030, reduce the global maternal mortality ratio to less than 70 per 100,000 live births	3.1.1 Maternal mortality ratio
	3.1.2 Proportion of births attended by skilled health personnel
3.2 By 2030, end preventable deaths of newborns and children under 5 years of age [. . .]	3.2.1 Under-5 mortality rate
	3.2.2 Neonatal mortality rate
3.3 By 2030, end the epidemics of AIDS, tuberculosis, malaria and neglected tropical diseases and combat hepatitis, water-borne diseases and other communicable diseases	3.3.1 Number of new HIV infections per 1,000 uninfected population, by sex, age, and key populations
	3.3.2 Tuberculosis incidence per 100,000 population
	3.3.3 Malaria incidence per 1,000 population

217 Source: UN (2024b) and UN (2020).

Table 2.12 (continued)

MDGs/targets	Indicators
	3.3.4 Hepatitis B incidence per 100,000 population
	3.3.5 Number of people requiring interventions against neglected tropical diseases
3.4 By 2030, reduce by one third premature mortality from non-communicable diseases through prevention and treatment [. . .]	3.4.1 Mortality rate attributed to cardiovascular disease, cancer, diabetes, or chronic respiratory disease
	3.4.2 Suicide mortality rate
3.5 Strengthen the prevention and treatment of substance abuse, including narcotic drug abuse and harmful use of alcohol	3.5.1 Coverage of treatment interventions (pharmacological, psychosocial and rehabilitation, and aftercare services) for substance use disorders
	3.5.2 Alcohol per capita consumption (aged 15 years and older) within a calendar year in litres of pure alcohol
3.6 By 2020, halve the number of global deaths and injuries from road traffic accidents	3.6.1 Death rate due to road traffic injuries
3.7 By 2030, ensure universal access to sexual and reproductive healthcare services, including for family planning, information and education, and the integration of reproductive health into national strategies and programmes	3.7.1 Proportion of women of reproductive age (aged 15–49 years) who have their need for family planning satisfied with modern methods
	3.7.2 Adolescent birth rate (aged 10–14 years; aged 15–19 years) per 1,000 women in that age group
3.8 Achieve universal health coverage [. . .] for all	3.8.1 Coverage of essential health services
	3.8.2 Proportion of population with large household expenditures on health as a share of total household expenditure or income
3.9 By 2030, substantially reduce the number of deaths and illnesses from hazardous chemicals and air, water and soil pollution and contamination	3.9.1 Mortality rate attributed to household and ambient air pollution
	3.9.2 Mortality rate attributed to unsafe water, unsafe sanitation, and lack of hygiene [. . .]
	3.9.3 Mortality rate attributed to unintentional poisoning
3.a Strengthen the implementation of the World Health Organization Framework Convention on Tobacco Control in all countries, as appropriate	3.a.1 Age-standardized prevalence of current tobacco use among persons aged 15 years and older
3.b Support the research and development of vaccines and medicines [. . .]	3.b.1 Proportion of the target population covered by all vaccines included in their national programme

Table 2.12 (continued)

MDGs/targets	Indicators
	3.b.2 Total net official development assistance to medical research and basic health sectors
	3.b.3 Proportion of healthcare facilities that have a core set of relevant essential medicines available and affordable on a sustainable basis
3.c Substantially increase health financing and the recruitment, development, training, and retention of the health workforce [. . .]	3.c.1 Health worker density and distribution
3.d Strengthen the capacity [. . .] for early warning, risk reduction, and management of national and global health risks	3.d.1 International Health Regulations (IHR) capacity and health emergency preparedness
	3.d.2 Percentage of bloodstream infections due to selected antimicrobial-resistant organisms
4.2 By 2030, ensure that all girls and boys have access to quality early childhood development, care, and pre-primary education so that they are ready for primary education	4.2.1 Proportion of children aged 24–59 months who are developmentally on track in health, learning, and psychosocial well-being, by sex
	5.6.1 Proportion of women aged 15–49 years who make their own informed decisions regarding sexual relations, contraceptive use and reproductive healthcare
5.6 Ensure universal access to sexual and reproductive health and reproductive rights [. . .]	5.6.2 Number of countries with laws and regulations that guarantee full and equal access to women and men aged 15 years and older to sexual and reproductive healthcare, information and education
12.4 By 2020, achieve the environmentally sound management of chemicals and all wastes throughout their life cycle [. . .] in order to minimize their adverse impacts on human health and the environment	12.4.2 (*a*) Hazardous waste generated per capita; and (*b*) proportion of hazardous waste treated, by type of treatment

The UN publishes annually a "Sustainable Development Goals Report" showing developments and achievements. For the year 2024, it indicates that merely target 3.9 (health impact of population) was on track, while targets 3.2 (child mortality), 3.5 (substance abuse), 3.a (tobacco control), and 3.b (immunization coverage) were assessed as 'moderate progress, but acceleration needed'. Targets 3.3 (communicable diseases), 3.4 (NCD and mental health), 3.6 (road traffic accidents), 3.7 (sexual and reproductive health), as well as 3.c (health workforce) showed only marginal progress and required significant acceleration. Stagnation was indicated for maternal mortality (3.1) and UHC (3.8). The data for assessing the management of health risks was insufficient.[218] In other words, the achievement of the health-related SDGs is at stake, and the situation is even worse in low-income countries.[219] There is much to be done if the goals are to be achieved by the year 2030 – but the system of goals forms a vision that goes far beyond indicators. It is the vision of a healthy planet with well-being for every human being with a clear dedication of the UN and (almost) all nations.

Health-Related Data

The most updated and reliable comprehensive database are the World Development Indicators (WDIs) provided by the World Bank. They cover time series of a wide variety of data for all nations and groups of nations, including health-related statistics.[220] However, some statistics or data of relevance do not exist in the WDI.

As stated before, Murray developed the concept of DALYs for the World Development Report 1993,[221] which became the foundation of the Global Burden of Disease (GBD) study. It is implemented by the Institute of Health Metrics and Evaluation (IHME) at the University of Washington and funded by the Gates Foundation. Based on the updated data on mortality and disability (morbidity) of all major diseases and health conditions in different regions of the world, this database is the most important source of epidemiological data for many countries and health-related decisions. The most recent study was published in *The Lancet*,[222] and fact sheets are available for all health-related topics.

Based on the GBD, WHO developed the Global Health Estimates (GHEs) coving not only the loss of quality of life (DALYs) but also a wide variety of indicators, such as life expectancy, healthy life expectancy, mortality, and morbidity.[223] Thus, the availability of global data is much better than it was. The main problem frequently is the inconsistency between databases (e.g. data from GHE and WDI) and between data from national and international statistics. It is preferable (but not always possible) to use statistics from one source and as original as possible (e.g. country statistics instead of global statistics).

Health and Development

Towards the new millennium, the WHO, barely visible on the political stage since the early 1990s, reassumed leadership under Gro Harlem Brundtland (Director General, 1998–2003) who established the 'Commission on Macroeconomics and Health'[224] to inves-

---

218 Source: UN (2024c).
219 A detailed tracking of SDGs is available at https://ourworldindata.org/sdgs/good-health-wellbeing.
220 Compare World Bank (2024b).
221 Compare Murray (1994b), Murray (1994c), and World Bank (1993).
222 Compare Murray (2024) and IHME (2024).
223 Compare WHO (2024d).
224 Compare Feachem (2002), Ivinson (2002), and Sachs (2002).

tigate under what conditions the MDGs could be achieved. The commission was high profile, led by economist Jeffrey Sachs and health scientist Robert Feachem, among others.

The researchers concluded that health is a crucial production factor and that investments in population health are rational, as better health does not lead to an increase in birth rates like many other measures. An investment in health, therefore, has a higher return than many other investments, meaning investments in health can help overcome the development trap! This insight was not exactly innovative (compare Section 2.2.1), but for the first time, it was empirically proven as they employed extensive econometric models.

However, the positive effects of health investments require a certain minimum amount. Sachs and Feachem calculated that expenditures for health in developing countries needed to be raised to US$30–40 per capita per year to achieve these successes. They called for donor organizations to cover a difference of up to US$30 per capita per year or US$27 billion per year compared to the expenditures at that time. Since an estimated US$5 billion per year was flowing into supporting health services in developing countries in 2000, this would have meant an additional US$22 billion was needed.

Sachs is quoted as saying: "For a macro-economist 22 billion are just peanuts." However, in reality, it proved impossible to raise these funds. Although significant additional sums were promised for combating diseases in developing countries in recent years, only a portion has been delivered. This attitude was sometimes met with great anger in developing countries.

One outcome of the Commission on Macroeconomics and Health was the UN's willingness to engage more intensively with healthcare in developing countries. Hence, under the leadership of Kofi Annan (UN Secretary-General, 1997–2006), the 'Global Fund to Fight AIDS, Tuberculosis and Malaria' was founded in 2001. The Global Fund, as it is commonly called, is a financing instrument that doesn't implement projects itself but raises funds (e.g. from governments and foundations) to finance projects combating these three diseases. Initially, a financial volume of US$10 billion per year was targeted, which was never reached.

The Global Fund focusses directly on goal 6 of the MDGs but has had significant side effects. First, the focus on these three diseases led to the neglect of other conditions, giving rise to the so-called "neglected diseases"[225] or exacerbating their problems. Second, projects supported by the Global Fund are frequently so extensive that they often exceed local capacity. If a country's absorption capacity is smaller than the financial influx, this typically leads to corruption. Third, developing countries quickly learned the criteria for grant allocation. Many consultants make a living by drafting appropriate applications, and the formal correctness of an application can take precedence over its content. Fourth, the projects lead to an unequal distribution of resources. For example, HIV patients are relatively well-treated, while others suffer from

---

225 Compare Hotez (2021).

miserable health services. Fifth, projects funded by the Global Fund draw staff from other facilities because GF-supported projects can pay better.

The Global Fund often responds to this criticism by pointing out that it was given this mandate by the UN General Assembly. In reality, this argument is not convincing because organizations and mandates can evolve, and the health of the global population urgently needs a 'Global Fund of Health Promotion' that finances projects based on clear efficiency criteria, which have the most significant impact on population health. Global Fund projects have a tendency to be vertical, i.e. focussing only on one or a small set of conditions or diseases instead of covering the entire healthcare sector (horizontal). Originally, Alma-Ata was to replace vertical programmes, but it took quite some years until the Global Fund became less focussed on the three diseases. The grant budget of GF for 2023–2025 is roughly 49% on HIV/AIDS, 27% on malaria, 14% on TB, and 10% on other diseases or programmes.

Some years later, the Lancet Commission 'Global Health 2035: a world converging within a generation' broadened the scope again beyond these three diseases and took up the vision of the Commission of Macroeconomics and Health.[226] In principle, they repeat the findings of the Commission of Macroeconomics and Health that investments in healthcare are profitable by calculating the so-called 'full income' as the total of GN and the value of an additional life year (expressed in WTP for an additional year of life). They state that the reduction in mortality is the reason for 11% of expected increase in 'full income' and forecast a 'grand convergence', i.e. low- and lower-middle-income countries would reach the 2013 level of upper-middle-income countries by the year 2035. They put more focus on fighting NCDs by national policies, in particular fiscal instruments such as taxation of risk factors (e.g. tobacco).

The relation between development and health has been proven several times, and has become standard knowledge. However, as the health panorama and the healthcare landscape changes, we can expect that the instruments of achieving economic development by better health and healthcare will have to be reassessed time by time.

Paris Declaration

A major problem, not limited to the healthcare sector, is the lack of coordination among donors, preventing the optimal overall interests of donors and recipients of development aid. This issue was addressed at the Paris Conference in 2005 (28.2.2005–2.3.2005).[227] The goal of the 'Paris Declaration' was to increase the effectiveness of development cooperation, among other things by strengthening the partner countries' ownership, aligning development cooperation with national development strategies, institutions, and procedures (alignment), harmonizing donor activities (harmonization), introducing results-oriented management (managing for results), and mutual accountability.

---

226 Compare Jamison, Summers, Alleyne, et al. (2013).
227 Compare OECD (2005).

Table 2.13 exhibits different concepts of global development assistance for health (DAH).[228] Traditionally, most external development partners (EDPs) initiated projects of limited scope and time, e.g. establishing a hospital. Most of these projects were hardly coordinated with other projects and with healthcare activities of the respective government. It was soon realized that many healthcare problems cannot be addressed by stand-alone projects or a discontinuous series of projects. Instead, development programmes are required which run until a problem is solved or until the effort is taken over by the country's healthcare services. Prevention (e.g. an AIDS control programme), training or running certain curative facilities can still be initiated and operated by EDPs, but they require more long-term coordination, in particular with the government of the respective country.

The sector-wide approach (SWAp) coordinates all healthcare activities of the government and EDPs as:

> . . . an approach to a locally-owned program for a coherent sector in a comprehensive and coordinated manner, moving towards the use of country systems. SWAps represent a [. . .] shift in the focus, relationship and behaviour of donors and Governments. They involve high levels of donor and country coordination for the achievement of program goals, and can be financed through parallel financing, pooled financing, general budget support, or a combination.[229]

Ideally, all partners (i.e. government and all EDPs) pay into one basket out of which all healthcare activities are paid for without earmarking certain donations for certain activities. Sometimes, this is not possible, so the basket fund is supplemented by a single-donor trust fund, still contributing to the sector budget but with a limitation on the application of his funds.

While the SWAp is limited to a certain sector (usually health or education), the general budget support provides funds for a government without limitation to a certain sector. The control by the EDP is very low, i.e. funds might be used in a manner which does not reflect the value system of the EDP.

Following the Declaration of Paris, many bi- and multilateral healthcare programmes changed towards SWAps. All stakeholders of the (health) sector jointly decide on their priorities and allocate their resources accordingly. Particular interests are overcome in favour of the overall optimum of a sector. In some countries, a basket fund was developed for this purpose, which does not only include the pooling of resources but collective decision-making on healthcare resources as well. For example, this could mean that funds from the Global Fund flow into this basket but are partially used for infrastructure measures because the healthcare stakeholders of a country currently consider this to be a priority. The Global Fund and some other major foundations (e.g. Clinton Foundation and Gates Foundation) have so far rejected this.

---

228 Compare Flessa (2024).
229 Vaillancourt (2009).

Table 2.13: Conceptions of development assistance for health.[230]

Method	Horizon	Content	Ownership	Target	Coordination	Financing	Risk
Project	Fixed	Tailor-made intervention with limited scope	Can be external development partner	Specific challenge	Limited	One source or consortium	Poor coordination and alignment, poor sustainability, and poor ownership
Programme	Until problem is solved or taken over	Tailor-made intervention with broader scope	Can be external development partner	Specific challenge	Limited	One source or consortium	Poor coordination and alignment, medium sustainability, and poor ownership
Sector-wide programme	Phases of a continuous sector programme	Entire sector	Government	Entire health sector	Completely within health sector	Basket financing or single-donor trust fund	Limited control by external development partners
General budget support	Annual support	Entire government	Government	All sectors	Completely with all sectors	Non-earmarked budget	Very limited control by external development partners

230 Source: Own, based on UNFPA (2005).

Output-based aid (OBA) is another measure derived from the Paris Declaration. Developed by the Reconstruction Loan Corporation and used in numerous countries, OBA does not simply channel funds into the basic funding of health services but only for certain services. Unlike 'pay for performance', not all services are rewarded, but only selected services for particularly needy population groups. For example, pregnant women from poverty groups are entitled to purchase heavily subsidized vouchers for childbirth. The healthcare provider submits this voucher to an agency after the service and receives the corresponding payment. OBA is thus a concept for 'management by results'.

Finally, the Paris Declaration brings a development aid concept back into focus that was deliberately abandoned in the 1970s: the promotion of elites, e.g. through special training programmes in donor countries. Elite promotion is double-edged. On the one hand, elites are crucial for economic development; on the other hand, elites also need legitimacy from civil society, which can be challenging in some partner countries. Therefore, elite promotion must be linked with democratization and good governance measures.[231]

The implementation of 'Paris' was discussed in a number of conferences and programmes. For instance, "Providing for Health" (P4H, 2007) with a focus on social security, "International Health Partnership" (IHP, 2012) with a focus on harmonization, "Accra Agenda for Action" (AAA, 2008) with the aim to strengthen the implementation of the Paris Declaration and the "Helsinki Statement" (The Eighth Global Conference on Health Promotion, 2013) to mainstream health in all political dimensions can be seen as outcomes of the Declaration of Paris.

Finally, the international partners agreed on criteria to assess development cooperation. Figure 2.39 shows that the so-called Development Assistance Committee (DAC) criteria[232] are based on the five dimensions of the Declaration of Paris of effective aid, namely (1) ownership of partner countries, (2) alignment of EDPs, (3) harmonization among EDPs, (4) managing for results, and (5) mutual accountability. These universal principles are influenced by a frame of parameters for successful implementation for the case of a health SWAp, i.e. (a) government commitment, (b) legitimacy, (c) accountability, (d) leadership of the government, (e) focus on systems strengthening, (f) institutional development, and (g) EDP commitment. The evaluation of these parameters is based on the DAC criteria of development cooperation, i.e. relevance, cohesion, effectiveness, efficiency, impact, and sustainability (Chianca 2008).

The DAC criteria build on each other. The interventions with a certain input (e.g. budget) are supposed to produce certain outputs that will generate outcomes. It is assumed that these outcomes will have an impact on the general objectives of the society or the healthcare system. For instance, procurement of contraceptives (input)

---

231 Compare http://www.betteraid.org.
232 OECD Development Assistance Committee (DAC).

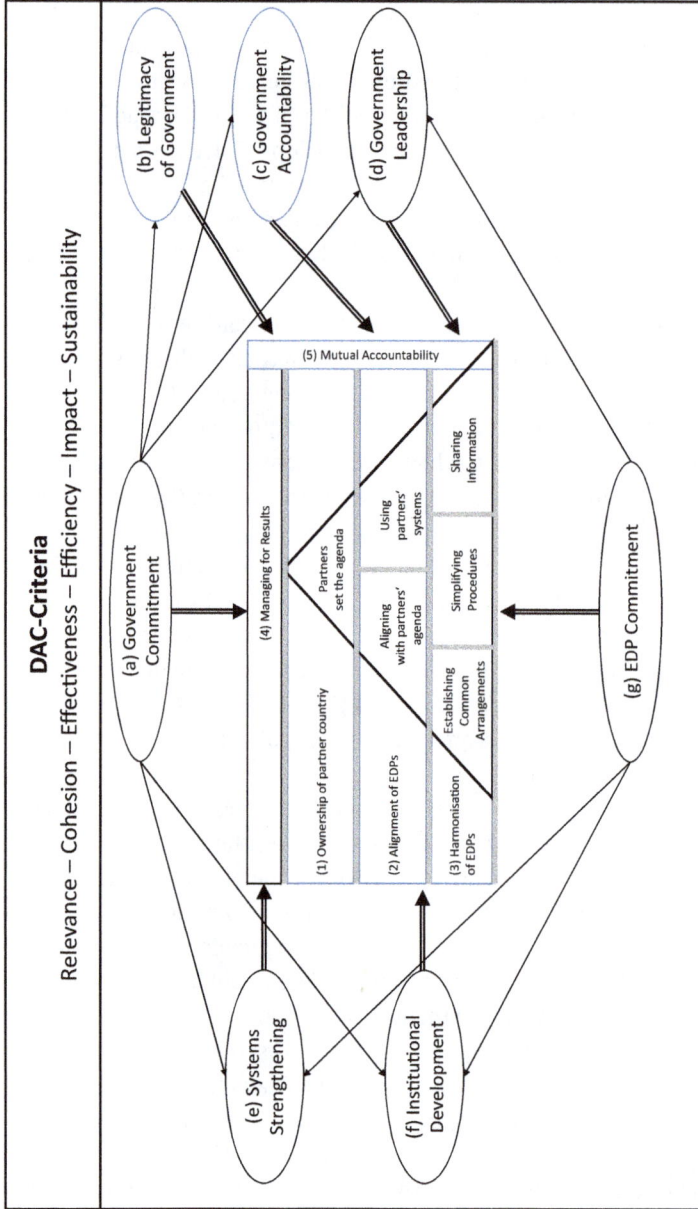

Figure 2.39: Effective aid and DAC criteria.[233]

233 Source: Own, based on D'Aquino, Pyone, Nigussie, et al. (2019).

will increase the availability of contraceptives in health centres (output) which is the prerequisite that contraceptives are used (outcome). This might reduce the total fertility rate of the population (impact). The input is a necessary but insufficient condition of the output, which is a necessary but insufficient condition of the outcome, which is a necessary but insufficient condition for the impact. The criteria of efficiency compare the input with the output, outcome and impact, while the criteria of relevance ask whether all of these achievements were not only done right but were the right things to do. Finally, sustainability analyses the long-term viability of efforts.

The DAC criteria are used by many national and international partners (e.g. governments, development agencies, and UN organizations) to assess the quality of their work. They have become a standard.

Private Sector

The new millennium has also experienced an intensive discussion on the role of the private sector in healthcare in low-income countries. Traditionally, the division was simple for most resource-poor countries: Government and faith-based health service providers care for the poor, while the few wealthy individuals visit private service providers. However, this has changed. Firstly, state and church institutions are increasingly unable to care for the poor. For example, subsidies from European and North American churches for partners in developing countries have significantly decreased. Secondly, there is a growing middle class preferring fast, local, and higher-quality services, even if they have to pay for them. Thirdly, in developing countries, the boundaries between private, government, and non-profit are increasingly blurred, as there are numerous forms of cooperation, public-private partnerships, and mergers.

The consequence is that in some developing countries, the private sector provides a large portion of the population's healthcare. The World Bank report "The Business of Health in Africa"[234] attests to this and attributes growing importance to the private sector. However, it should be noted that this report was prepared by the International Finance Corporation (IFC), a subsidiary of the World Bank, whose primary goal is the promotion of private enterprise. Therefore, the empirical findings are mixed with normative statements, i.e. the belief in the superiority of the market and private economy. In reality, the 'Business for Health' is likely to be limited to cities in poor countries, while the majority of the population will probably still rely on government and charitable institutions in the coming years. A major exemption are the private pharmacies that are available in almost all villages. However, most of them are simple retail shops and the shopkeepers have no training at all in pharmacology. Thus, the quality of drugs and consultation services is at stake, and there is a need for improved licensing of these 'wild' pharmacies in almost all low-income countries. It is the state's task to regulate these emerging markets and particularly to ensure quality standards.

---

234 IFC (2008).

Revisiting Health

Section 2.1.1 defined health under the assumption that this chapter is about the health of and healthcare for human beings. The starting point was the health of the individual, but public health as the health of a population became more and more relevant. Furthermore, it was realized that these populations are connected, and the interdependencies become more and more intense and global. Due to intensified global networking and the insight that health extends far beyond national borders, Global Health developed to a powerful concept during the last quarter of the twentieth century, which includes global public health as well as global clinical care. However, in this context, health still means the global health of human beings, although it is obvious that environmental and animal health have always been connected to human health.

By the end of the twentieth century, the relation between human health, animal health, and the environment shifted even more to the focus of researchers. This concept of interdependency of these three dimensions is called One Health as an approach of "the collaborative efforts of multiple disciplines working locally, nationally, and globally, to attain optimal health for people, animals and our environment",[235] as the One Health Initiative Task Force phrased it. It has to be stressed that One Health is by far more than zoonosis research. Instead, the interdependencies of human, animal, and environmental health are the object of research, including a wide range of interdependencies, such as healing forests or soil microbiomes for healthy human and animal food. One Health as a policy goes far beyond research and attempts to change the political and regional system in the One Health Region. The latter is a spatial unit (e.g. district, region, and state) in which the health of people, animals, and the environment in their interdependence is taken into account in all economic, political, social, and legal decisions. The aim of a One Health Region is to regionally promote the health of people, animals, and the environment.

If we combine One Health and Global Health, we receive Planetary Health as "the health of human civilization and the state of the natural systems on which it depends".[236] The depletion of natural resources, the environmental pollution, and climate change have a major impact on the health of humans, animals, and the environment of the entire planet. Thus, the different concepts are not contradicting put pointing at different facets or dimensions of health in a broader sense.

Until today, it is not clear whether these 'new' concepts will actually have a major impact on international healthcare management which has and most likely always will have a focus on human health. Animals and the environment are seen by healthcare managers as important components of the health ecosystem in which human health is promoted or harmed. They are seen as instruments in the fight for human

---

235 Adisasmito, Almuhairi, Behravesh, et al. (2022). See also the WHO 'One Health High-Level Expert Panel' (OHHLEP), WHO (2025b).
236 Horton and Lo (2015).

health. However, this approach is termed 'anthropocentrism' by some philosophers proposing that the environment and animal health would have the same right as human health.[237] For the practical healthcare manager, however, there is enough to be worked on to defend and strengthen human health. For him, animals and the environment are important factors determining human health and the interdependencies between these systems call deeper insights into the environmental and animal dimension, but the priority of this chapter will be granted to humans.

Undoubtedly, there are a number of other declarations and programmes that have influenced healthcare in low-income countries (e.g. the Bamako Initiative, 1987; International Health Regulations, 2005; Muskoka Summit, 2010; Cairo Workshop on Capacity Development, 2011; and Global Health Commitments, 2021). However, the examples presented should suffice to demonstrate that healthcare and health policy are dynamic processes. Ultimately, all initiatives are based on the attempt to shape the framework of the health economics model (compare Figure 2.37). This model also determines the further structure of this discussion. In the next section, we will address the left-hand side of the model (demand), followed by the right-hand side (supply). An analysis of the interface, i.e. the markets and the corresponding reforms seeking to influence this market relationship, will follow.

In summary, the task of international healthcare management can be seen in describing and analysing health-relevant institutions, frameworks, and processes in various world regions to derive recommendations for an efficient structure of healthcare provision and to factually improve the practical control of processes in the healthcare system and all its service providers. Often, these processes in resource-poor countries are still in pure form and thus more clearly analysable than in the complex industrial countries, which is why this monograph will often focus on healthcare management in resource-poor countries. However, this should not lead to the erroneous conclusion that the phenomena, regulatory systems, structures, and processes presented here are only relevant for low-income countries. Instead, the control mechanisms can be well researched in these countries and then transferred to the economically developed world. This is particularly evident in some healthcare concepts discussed in Section 2.3.2. For example, important components of PHC were developed in and for resource-poor countries but are now an innovative seedling for area-wide provision, particularly in structurally weak regions of higher-income countries, demonstrating significant importance.[238]

---

237 Compare Lederman, Magalhães-Sant'Ana, and Voo (2021).
238 Compare Flessa (2023b).

3 Demand

The demand for health services is generally based on an objective lack of health. Although it is not common in literature, it is appropriate to call this opposite of health 'unhealth'. It is a condition that can be diagnosed by a physician, but it does not mean that the respective person feels sick (compare Figure 2.7). Hypochondria has so far played a minor role in low-income countries, although the demand for health services without a physiological cause is certainly based on a deficiency, which is more likely to be psychological than physical. More importantly, as discussed in Section 2.1.3, not every objective deficiency results in a demand for health services.

The following will discuss the determinants of demand for health services. We proceed from the health economic framework model mentioned above and specify the parameters that determine demand. Subsequently, selected demand determinants will be discussed. These include demographic and epidemiological transitions, as well as infectious and chronic degenerative diseases. This is followed by a discussion of risk factors and the main filters between need and demand. The goal of this extensive section is to understand the demand for health services as a complex process of different factors, which are starting points for healthcare management.

3.1 Fundamentals

3.1.1 Economic Framework Model

The starting point of the following considerations is the health economic framework model, which was discussed in detail in Section 2.1.3, so only the key points will be specified here. The fundamental observation is that the objective lack of health is the starting point for demand, but not every deficiency results in demand. Therefore, it is not correct to measure the disease burden using service statistics. Instead, epidemiological data are needed, such as those collected in 'Demographic Surveillance Systems' that determine the disease burden through regular surveys in selected districts of many countries.[239] This often includes a so-called 'verbal autopsy', i.e. determining the cause of death by interviewing the relatives of the deceased.[240]

The causes of the objective lack of health, and thus the demand, are multifaceted. A common distinction is made between non-communicable and infectious diseases. Furthermore, a disease is considered chronic if it lasts for an extended period, meaning that acquired immune deficiency syndrome (AIDS) and tuberculosis (TB) are chronic (without treatment) just like rheumatism or arteriosclerosis. However,

---

239 Compare also http://www.indepth-network.org/.
240 Compare Zahr (2007).

https://doi.org/10.1515/9783112217290-003

chronic degenerative refers to non-communicable diseases that arise from age-related wear and tear. Separate from this is the demand for health services due to pregnancy and childbirth, as well as disabilities and accidents. International statistics often use terms inconsistently, leading to some confusion.

From the objective deficiency, a subjective experience of deficiency emerges and eventually becomes a need when there is sufficient information about the problem and the possibilities for healing or alleviation. Therefore, health education plays a significant role in the transition from deficiency to demand.[241]

Ultimately, filters must be overcome that prevent a need from becoming a demand. The most significant filter is likely the financial filter (compare Section 3.5.8), meaning that if financial resources are insufficient, a demand cannot arise, even if there is an urgent need. Distance and quality filters also play a certain role.

Therefore, the demand in healthcare facilities only partially reflects the actual disease burden. It is also important to note that it only allows for statements about case numbers (morbidity and mortality) but not about the actual burden that a disease represents in society. Particularly for economic evaluation, the quality of life plays a significant role. Therefore, the concept of disability-adjusted life years (DALYs), which is of great importance in international healthcare management, will be briefly discussed below. As outlined in Section 2.4.1, DALYs were first defined in 1993 as the measure of the global disease burden (GBD) of a population[242] and have since become a kind of standard in health economics, in particular in low- and middle-income countries. For each death, the number of lost life years is calculated, with life expectancy estimated at 82.5 years for women and 80.0 years for men.[243] Each lost life year corresponds to one lost DALY. Future years are discounted at a rate of 3%. In addition, there is an age-specific weighting of lost life years, i.e. 'life years lost at different ages are assigned different relative values'. The weighting of a life year (x) follows the function $x \cdot 0.16243 \cdot e^{-0.04 \cdot x}$, so that the value of a life year is highest in adulthood, while it is lower for children and the elderly. Figure 3.1 shows the weighting.

The combination of age weighting and discounting emphasizes adult health, while the neonatal mortality (and morbidity) becomes less significant. Figure 3.2 shows two curves: the first curve results if the loss of life years is valued equally at all ages and no discounting occurs. The second curve represents the loss in DALYs. It is evident that the gap between the two curves is maximum for newborns. Therefore, the use of DALYs as a measure for evaluating health economic interventions tends to reduce the focus on child mortality, while increasing the focus on adult health.

The global burden of disease includes not only the loss of DALYs due to premature death, but also a component that captures the loss of quality of life due to disabil-

---

241 Compare Fleßa (2007).
242 Compare World Bank (1993), Murray (1994a), Murray (1994b).
243 We present the original version of the DALYs of the year 1990. Further adjustments and regionalizations were made in the past years (WHO 2017).

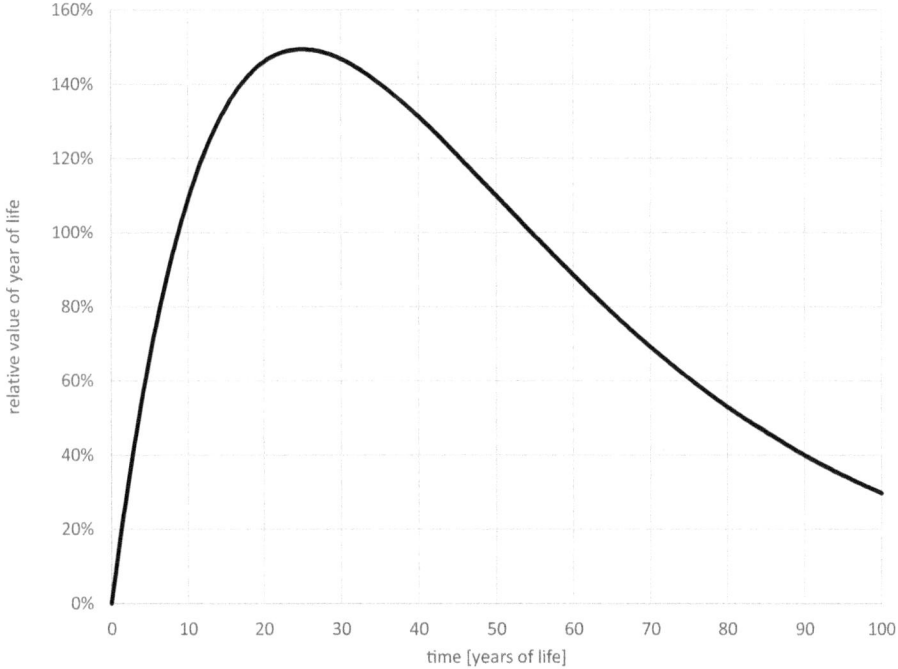

Figure 3.1: Value of a life year for the calculation of DALYs.[244]

ity. Depending on the severity of the disability, a utility value between 0 and 1 is assigned to the health state (constant D), as is customary in the calculation of 'quality-adjusted life years' (QALYs). Table 3.1 shows the categories.

With a discounting of 3% and the age adjustment described above, the loss of DALYs due to a disease or disability is calculated as follows:

$$\int_{a}^{a+L} D \cdot x \cdot 0.16243 \cdot e^{-0.04 \cdot x} \cdot e^{-0.03 \cdot (x-a)} dx =$$

$$- \frac{D \cdot x \cdot 0.16243 \cdot e^{-0.04 \cdot x} \cdot}{0.07^2} \cdot \left\{ e^{-0.07 \cdot L} \cdot [1 + 0.07 \cdot (L+a)] - (1 + 0.07 \cdot a) \right\}$$

where D-is the disability weight, L-is the duration of disability or loss of life years due to premature death, a-is the age at which the disability begins or year of death, and x-is the age.

Thus, it is possible to combine the loss of quality of life due to disability and premature death into a single figure and, with the help of mortality statistics and expert

---

244 Source: Murray (1994b).

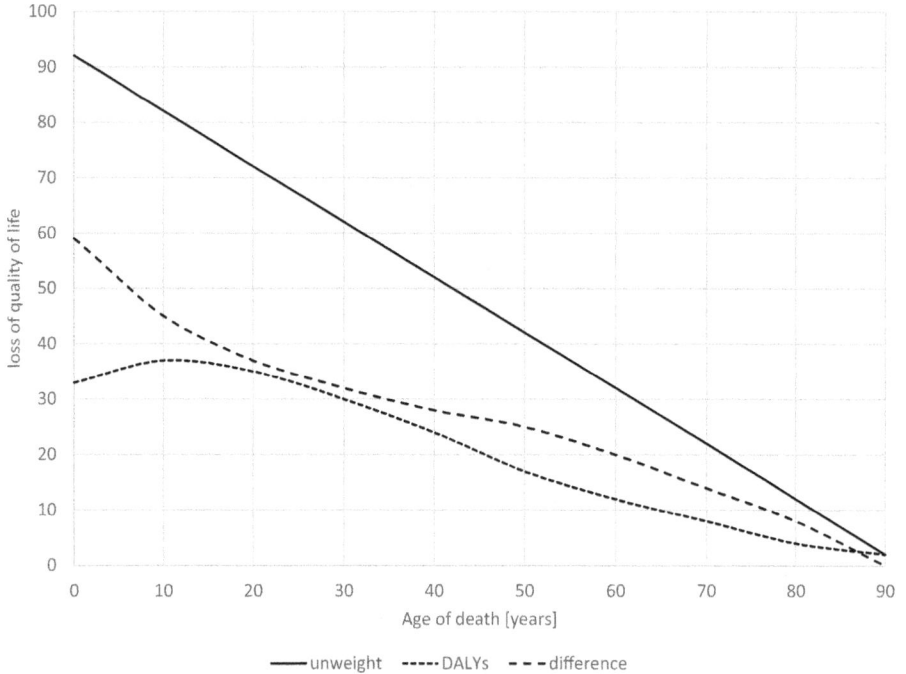

Figure 3.2: Loss of quality of life for the calculation of DALYs.[245]

estimates, to make statements about the global burden of disease. In 1990, the BGD was 50,766 DALYs per 100,000 people, and by 2019, the respective figure had fallen to 33,760. In 2021, it was 36,203 due to COVID-19. The worst situation existed in sub-Saharan Africa with a loss of DALYs of 85,342 in 1990, but this sub-continent also strongly improved to 60,445 in 2021 (compare Figure 3.3), i.e. the decline in sub-Saharan Africa was almost identical to the rest of the world (−29%). In 1990, about 44% of DALYs were lost due to non-communicable diseases, some 45% due to communicable, maternal, and nutritional diseases, and about 11% due to injuries. The respective figures for 2021 were 62%, 30%, and 9% (rounding errors). In 2019 (before COVID-19), the respective figures were 65%, 26%, and 10%.[246]

The introduction of DALYs as an efficiency criterion for health economic measures was undoubtedly an important step, as it guarantees an international standard and thus the comparability of intervention studies. However, the calculation of DALYs

---

245 Source: Author's own figure, based on World Bank 1993. The figure shows the cumulative loss of quality of life when a person dies at a certain point in time. Since women and men have different life expectancies, the loss of DALYs must be different for men and women depending on the age at death. The figure above represents the course for women.
246 IHME (2025).

Table 3.1: Definition of disability levels for DALYs.[247]

Health condition	Disability weight (D)
Limited ability to perform at least one activity in one of the following groups: leisure, education, reproduction, and occupation	0.096
Limited ability to perform most activities in one of the following groups: leisure, education, reproduction, and occupation	0.220
Limited ability to perform activities in two or three of the following groups: leisure, education, reproduction, and occupation	0.400
Limited ability to perform most activities in all four groups	0.600
Need for assistance in instrumental activities of daily living, such as preparing meals, shopping, and housework	0.810
Need for assistance in activities of daily living, such as eating, personal hygiene, and toilet use	0.920
Death	1.000

contains assumptions[248] that make their transferability to other problems doubtful. First, the discounting with 3% lacks an objective basis. It would be quite possible to calculate scenarios with different interest rates. In reality, epidemiological studies almost always use a discount rate of 3%, because they simply determine the age at death or the point of disability and then read off the loss of DALYs from the World Bank's tables. While this improves the international comparability of studies, it does not solve the problem of the lack of a scientific foundation.

Second, the different weighting of various ages is not always justifiable. It is certainly sensible if the goal of health policy is to promote productive years and thus contribute to an increase in gross domestic product (GDP). For all other health policy goals, however, this weighting represents an overemphasis on this age stage. It is ethically questionable why a lost year of life for a newborn should be worth less than that of a 35-year-old. Third, linking certain health states with quality of life values is problematic when they are assumed to be inter-culturally constant. The calculation of DALYs assumes that a disease means the same loss of quality of life everywhere in the world. This is doubtful, as the subjective suffering from a disease is always influenced by the culture of a people.

Nevertheless, DALYs are a standard in international healthcare management. The World Health Organization's (WHO) 'Global Burden of Disease Database'[249] regularly

---

247 Source: Murray (1994a).
248 Compare Anand and Hanson (1997).
249 http://www.who.int/healthinfo/global_burden_disease.

provides calculations for regions and diseases based on the DALY concept. This is undoubtedly an important aid, but the discounting leads to systematic undervaluation of preventive measures. Diseases that primarily affect the productive age groups, such as TB and AIDS, are rated higher due to the emphasis on adult years.

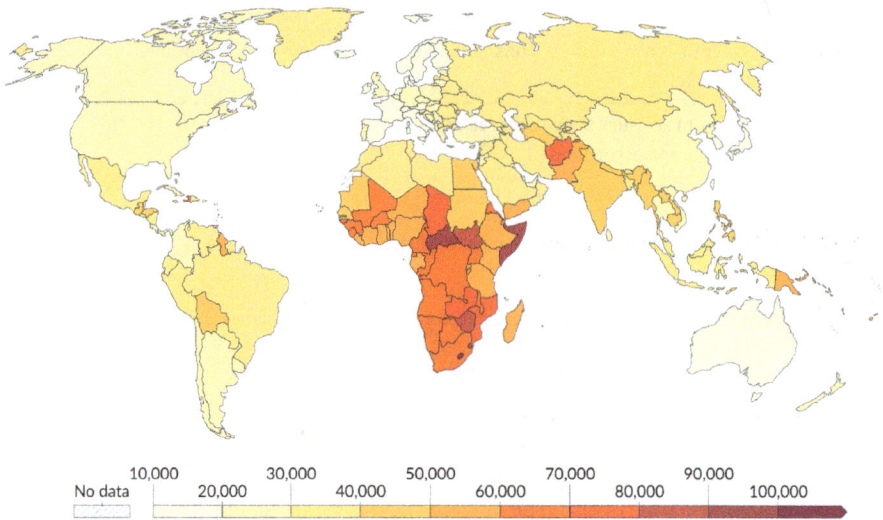

Figure 3.3: Global burden of disease 2021.[250]

In summary, we can state that there are no incontrovertible standards for the burden of disease in a population. It is important to note that the level and composition of the disease burden depend on the age structure of the population, so an analysis of the demographic and epidemiological transition is necessary.

3.1.2 Demographic and Epidemiological Transition

3.1.2.1 Basic Parameters
As defined in Section 2.1.2, demography is the study of the structure and development of a population, i.e. demography is always the foundation for a discussion of the demand for health services. The primary influences on demographic development are the number of births and deaths. The crude birth rate is the rate of live births in a year to the mid-year population of the same year.[251] The mid-year population is con-

---

250 Source: OurWorldinData – CC-BY@: https://ourworldindata.org/grapher/dalys-rate-from-all-causes (18.02.2025).
251 Compare Esenwein-Rothe (1982) and Dinkel (2002).

sidered the population number on 30 June. It approximates the average population number for the year. In the case of a growing population, the mid-year population underestimates the average population; in the case of a declining population, it overestimates it. The crude birth rate is currently under 1% in Germany, while in some developing countries, it is more than 5% (compare Table 3.2).[252]

Table 3.2: Crude birth and death rate.[253]

	Crude birth rate		Crude death rate	
	1990	**2022**	**1990**	**2022**
High income	14.1	9.4	9.1	10.3
Middle income	28.3	16.3	8.8	8.0
Low income	45.5	34.3	16.8	7.8
Sub-Saharan Africa	44.4	34.2	16.2	8.2
World	26.1	16.6	9.3	8.4
Highest	55.5(Niger)[254]	45.3 (Niger)	25.5 (Liberia)	18.4 (Bulgaria)
Lowest	10.0 (Greece, Italy, and Japan)	4.4 (Hong Kong)	2.2 (Qatar)	1.1 (Qatar)

The crude birth rate applies to the entire population, i.e. not only to women of child-bearing age, but also to men, children, and older people. If the number of live births is related to the number of women of childbearing age, one obtains the fertility rate. Again, the mid-year population of women is taken, where it is normally assumed that women are of childbearing age between 15 and 45 years. Age-specific fertility rates (e.g. for women in their twenties) can thus be determined. Another fertility parameter is the net reproduction rate. It indicates the number of girls that a newly born girl will give birth to during her lifetime if she behaves according to the statistical average.

Fertility is countered by mortality. The crude death rate is the number of deaths in a year relative to the mid-year population. It has strongly gone down in the last decades, but it is still much higher in low-income countries than in high-income countries. The current rate for Germany (2021) is 12.8%.[255] Mortality is often related to a specific population group. Thus, under-five mortality (sometimes also called child mortality) represents the probability of not surviving the first 5 years of life, i.e. the number of children who die before their fifth birthday is set in relation to the number of live births. Accordingly, infant mortality is the probability of not surviving the

---

252 For present data compare http://data.worldbank.org/indicator/SP.DYN.TFRT.IN.
253 Source: World Bank (2024b).
254 The World Development Indicators indicate that South Sudan had even higher figures in 1990, but South Sudan gained independence only by 2011.
255 Source: World Bank (2024b).

first year of life. Maternal mortality refers to the number of (pregnancy-related) deaths of mothers in relation to the number of live births.

Mortality refers to a mortality rate that applies to a general population (e.g. the total population). When analysing the ratio of deaths to cases, one speaks of fatality. The age-specific mortality of the population can be taken from so-called life tables, which play a role especially in actuarial mathematics.

Life expectancy is the result of mortality. It usually indicates the expected age of death for a newborn. However, it is also possible to define remaining life expectancies for higher age groups. They correspond to the difference between the expected age of death and the current age of a person. The older a person already is, the more likely he or she is to reach a higher age group. Fertility, mortality, and migration (immigration and emigration) determine population development. First, the well-known age structure (population pyramid) emerges. Figure 3.4 exemplarily shows the population pyramids of Tanzania, Thailand, Germany, and Japan. Tanzania is an example of a pre-industrial country, Thailand is in the midst of industrialization, and Germany and Japan have largely completed this process. Tanzania's population pyramid corresponds to the state of Germany in 1880, and Thailand's pyramid represents the demographic structure of Germany in 1950.

Other important statistical sizes are the youth quotient (proportion of the population under 15 years) and the old-age quotient (proportion of the population that has reached the age of 65). Moreover, some basic epidemiological measures are relevant for understanding the demand for health services.[256] Prevalence refers to the number of cases of a disease in a period relative to the mid-year population in a period. Incidence is the number of new cases in a period relative to the mid-year population in the period. Therefore, the disease panorama, i.e. the spectrum and intensity of diseases in a population, is an important determinant of the demand for health services.

3.1.2.2 Model of Demographic Transition

The concept of demographic transition is comparatively old. Based on time series analyses of fertility and mortality in various countries in Europe, North America, and the Pacific, Thompson[257] showed that these countries exhibited a similar pattern of fertility and mortality during their development: starting from high fertility and mortality, both fertility and mortality decreased over the course of their economic development. He called this a 'transition' and posited that the relationship between demographic and economic development is a universally valid rule. Building on this, Notestein[258] and Blacker[259] developed the theory of demographic transition (compare Figure 3.5).

---

256 Compare Gordis (2008).
257 Compare Thompson (1929).
258 Compare Notestein (1945).
259 Compare Blacker (1947).

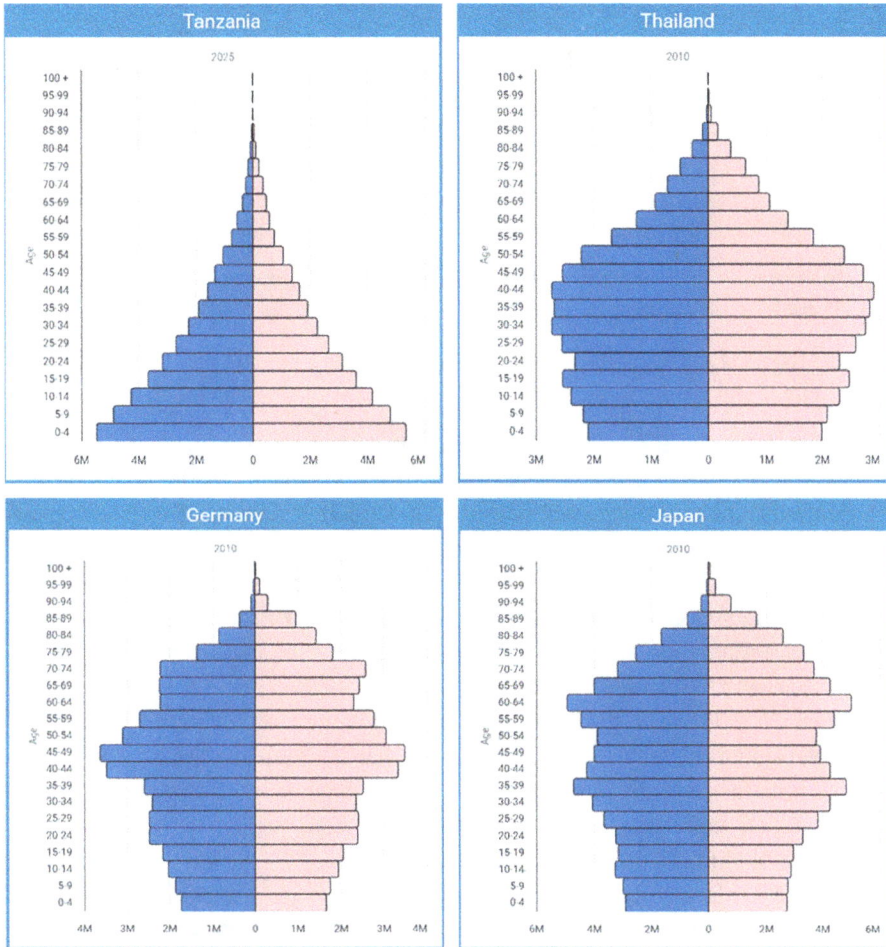

Figure 3.4: Population pyramids of different countries.[260]

- **Phase I**: The crude birth rate and crude death rate are equally high ($\approx$5% p.a. (per annum)), so the population barely grows. Phase I is typical for agrarian societies. Population growth can only be achieved through additional agricultural land or improved soils.
- **Phase II**: Mortality begins to decline, while fertility remains practically constant. In some countries, fertility can even increase above the original value of Phase I. Improved hygiene, medical progress, and increased accessibility to medical services are cited as reasons for the declining mortality. As a consequence, there is strong population growth, which, however, can only continue if additional resources

260 Source: U.S. Census Bureau. (2025).

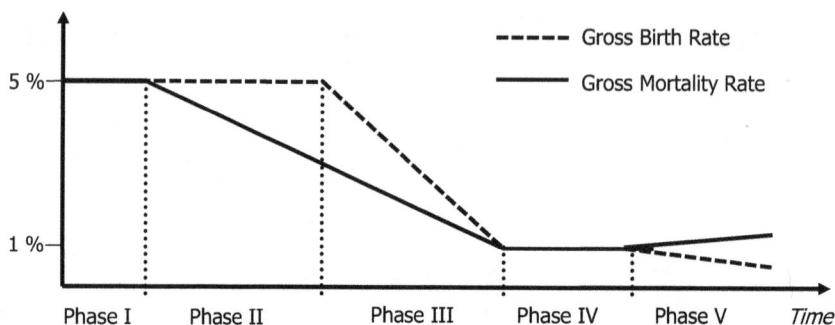

Figure 3.5: Model of demographic transition.[261]

can be provided for the growing population. Most Central European countries reached the second phase of demographic transition during the Industrial Revolution, which not only increased industrial, but also agricultural production, thus creating the basis for the food supply of a constantly increasing population.

- **Phase III**: Mortality continues to decrease, but fertility also begins to decline. The population still grows, but at a decreasing rate. The reasons for the fertility decline are numerous, e.g. increasing urbanization,[262] the introduction of social insurance, and the change in cultural values.
- **Phase IV**: In Phase IV, the crude birth rate and crude death rate are again approximately identical, but at a much lower level than in Phase I (≈1% p.a.). The population remains constant. Most Western countries have reached this phase. According to their experiences, the transition process (from the beginning of Phase II to the end of Phase III) lasts about 80 years.
- **Phase V**: In later years, the originally four-phase model has been extended by a fifth phase[263] in which the birth rate is constant or slightly decreases, while mortality increases due to the age structure. In this phase, the population number decreases – without immigration.

---

261 Source: Fleßa (2003b).
262 The phases II to V of the demographic transition are accompanied by a constant increase in the urban population. Meade & Earickson thus refer to a 'mobility transition', during which the mental and infrastructural ability for relocation constantly increases. Meade and Emch (2005).
263 Compare Minde (2007).

Economists have shown early interest in demographic developments, primarily re-searching the determinants of fertility. Malthus already demonstrated in his famous work *An Essay on the Principle of Population* in 1798 that income and fertility of a population are positively correlated.[264] Since Becker succeeded in tracing fertility back to general utility theory, a series of approaches to determining fertility have emerged.[265] Figure 3.6 shows some important determinants of the birth number.

The starting point is the desire of women and men to have children, which is deter-mined by economic and cultural factors. In a traditional society, children are required as human workforce, in particular to fetch water or firewood and herd the animals. Further-more, children are an instrument of social protection, in particular a 'living pension fund', i.e. a society without a functioning social protection system will ceteris paribus have a stronger reproductive rate. Children have, however, also a value of their own (utility mo-tive), which is determined by cultural, and in particular, religious imprinting.

Frequently, the desire for a certain number of children is not identical between spouses, so the role and power of male and female determines the couple's desire for children. In some cultures, the mother-in-law also does have a major influence on the number of children. The real number also does depend on the availability and price of contraceptives, in particular, modern forms of contraceptives such as the pill, injec-tions, or implants. However, in some cases, the desire might also be higher than the ability, i.e. the ability to conceive and carry to term might also determine the fertility rate. In vitro fertilization (IVF) is an issue, even in countries with a high birth rate, in particular, in urban rich minorities.

It becomes clear that the simple pattern of a linear transition from about 5% at the beginning of the transition to about 1% at the end is not inevitable. The large num-ber of parameters of the interdependent system prevents inevitability. Therefore, in some regions of Africa, people are still waiting for the beginning of the third phase with a strong decline in births, although the beginning of the second phase in some countries dates back 80 years.

3.1.2.3 Model of Epidemiological Transition

The determinants of mortality were analysed significantly later. Omran examined the spectrum of diseases in countries at different phases of the demographic transi-tion.[266] He observed that infectious diseases dominate in countries that are in the first or second phase of the demographic transition. Conversely, chronic degenerative diseases are the main causes of morbidity and mortality in developed countries. Figures 3.7 and 3.8 show how mortality attributable to infectious diseases decreases over the course of a country's economic development, while mortality from chronic degenerative diseases in-

---

264 Compare Malthus (1888).
265 Compare Lee and Mason (2010) and Cervellati and Sunde (2007).
266 Compare Omran (1971) and Omran (1977b).

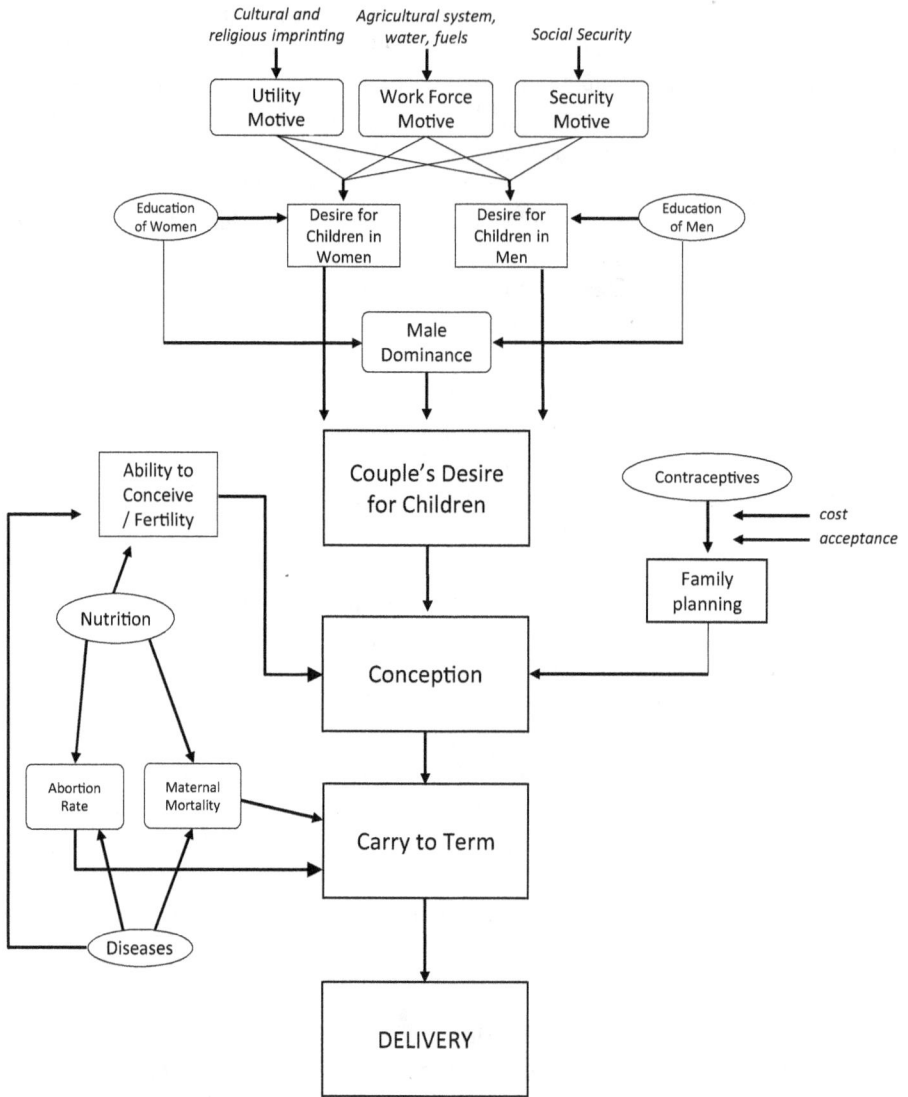

Figure 3.6: Determinants of the crude birth rate.[267]

creases. While chronic degenerative diseases dominant in North Carolina in the 1930s, the shift happened in Vietnam in the 1990s. Worldwide, 45% of the total disease burden (measured in DALYs) were due to communicable, maternal, and nutritional diseases in

---

267 Source: Fleßa (2007).

1990; 45% due to non-communicable diseases; and 11% due to injuries. By the year 2019 (before COVID-19), the respective rates were 26%, 64%, and 9.7%.

Following the demographic transition, Omran termed the shift in morbidity and causes of death from infectious diseases to chronic degenerative diseases as the epidemiological transition.[268] It forms the basis for analysing the demand for health services in countries at different phases of the demographic transition.

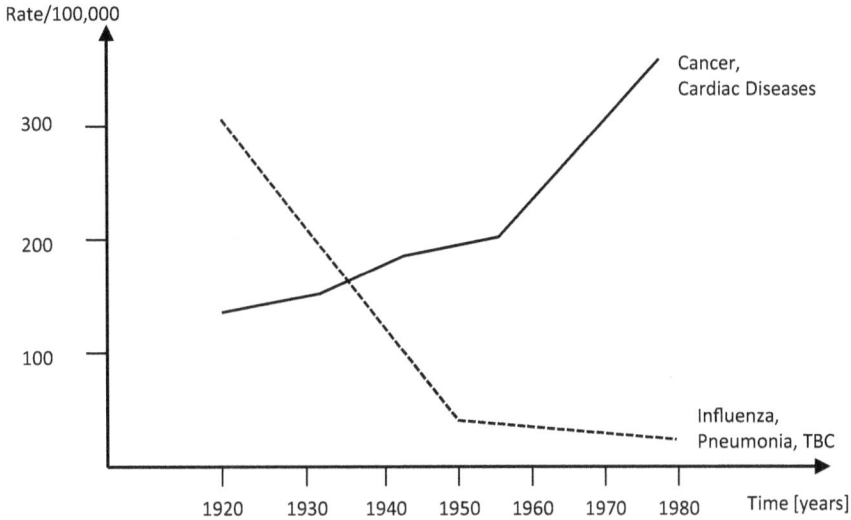

Figure 3.7: Mortality transition in North Carolina.[269]

During the demographic transition, there is a change in the age structure of a society. In the second phase, the population becomes increasingly younger, and the youth ratio rises from about 40% in the first phase to up to 50% at the end of the second phase. It then continuously decreases until it only accounts for 15–20% at the end of the fourth phase. The same development can be seen for the average age and life expectancy. The average age drops from 23 years in the first phase to 21 years at the end of the second phase, then increases to over 40 years. Accordingly, life expectancy is 38 years in the first phase, 40 years at the end of the second phase, and up to 80 years at the end of the transition. The population becomes, therefore, older, and the proportion of the elderly increases.

---

268 Compare Omran (2005).
269 Source: Omran (1977a).

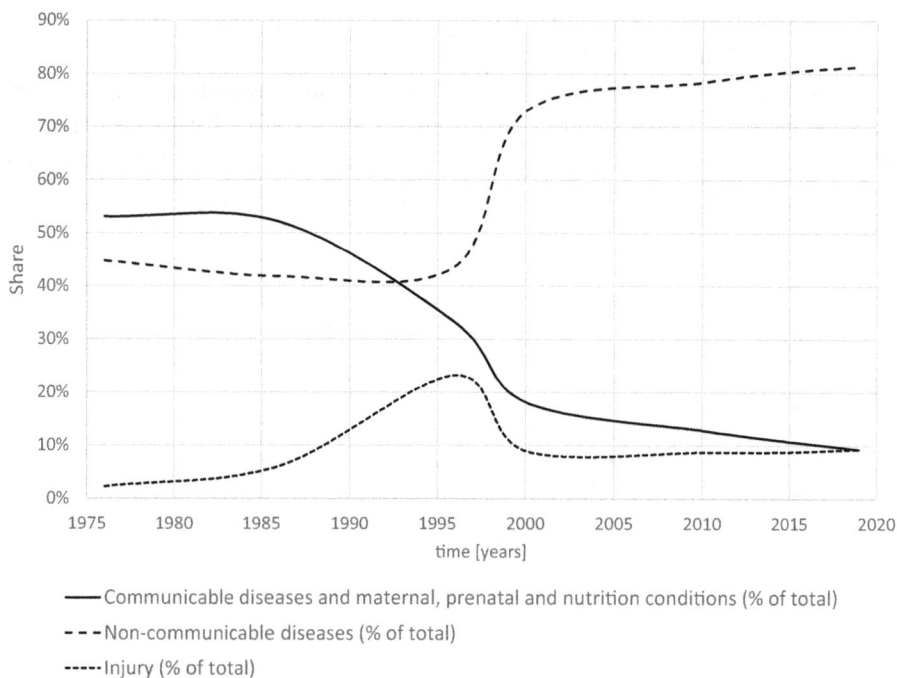

Figure 3.8: Development of mortality in Vietnam (1976–2001).[270]

The changed age structure induces a shifting disease panorama. Each survived infection reduces the future risk of infection. Adults therefore a significantly lower risk of contracting an infection or dying from it than children do. Newborns are weak in terms of immunity. In old age, immunity decreases again, leading to higher susceptibility to infectious diseases. Chronic degenerative diseases, as the name suggests, require a long-term development process. For example, skin cancer may only occur decades after harmful radiation exposure. Therefore, the probability of a chronic degenerative disease increases over the course of life (compare Figure 3.9).

Considering the relationships described, societal morbidity and mortality change during the transition. Child mortality (i.e. the proportion of newborns who do not survive the first five years) drops from almost 30% to 1–2%, and the crude death rate drops from 5% to under 1%. Nevertheless, towards the end of the fourth phase, the mortality of the total population begins to rise again due to changes in the age structure. The demographic transition leads to a transformation of the population pyramid. It resembles an onion with few children, many adults, and an increasingly large

---

270 Source: Socialist Republic of VietNam (2002).

Susceptibility

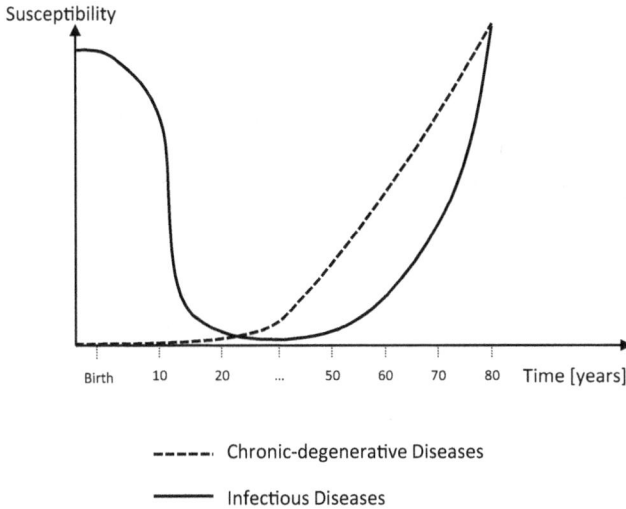

Birth   10   20   ...   50   60   70   80   Time [years]

----- Chronic-degenerative Diseases

——— Infectious Diseases

Figure 3.9: Model of susceptibility.[271]

number of elderly people who are highly susceptible to chronic degenerative diseases. An ageing population will therefore lead to a renewed increase in mortality.

It is evident that the health status of a population is a direct function of the point in time within the demographic transition. Figure 3.10 results from a simulation,[272] showing that in the first phase of the transition, on average, 77% of the population is healthy, 14% suffers from infectious diseases, and 9% has chronic degenerative diseases. The significant impact of infectious diseases is primarily due to the high proportion of children in the total population. They have not yet acquired natural immunity and are therefore particularly vulnerable to infections. The general health status of the population improves during the epidemiological transition, so that in the middle of the third phase, 85% of the population is healthy. However, the increasing average age from the third phase of the transition onwards leads to a steady increase in chronic degenerative diseases, so the average health status of the population deteriorates again. At the end of the fourth phase, in the simulation, on average, only 72% of the population is considered healthy, meaning the ageing of society leads to unprecedented morbidity. It is not surprising that the number of chronic degenerative diseases increases in an ageing society. However, it is also shown that in the fifth phase, the number of infectious diseases increases again, as older people have a lower defence against infections.

---

271 Source: Own.
272 Compare Fleßa (1998).

It is obvious that the epidemiological transition completely reverses the health situation of a country and thus the demand for health services. The changed proportions of infectious and chronic degenerative diseases require differentiated health policy that takes into account the changed morbidity in different phases of the transition (compare Figure 3.11). Additionally, the available health resources during the transition generally increase significantly, which in turn has implications for the optimal resource allocation during the transition.

Countries around the world are at different phases of the demographic and epidemiological transition, and therefore health services must be country-specific. However, there are also sub-populations within a country that are at different phases of the transition. For example, the rural population in Africa suffers primarily from infectious diseases, while the affluent urban upper class seeks medical services mainly for diabetes, stroke, and heart attack. Frenk et al. even speak of "epidemiological polarization".[273]

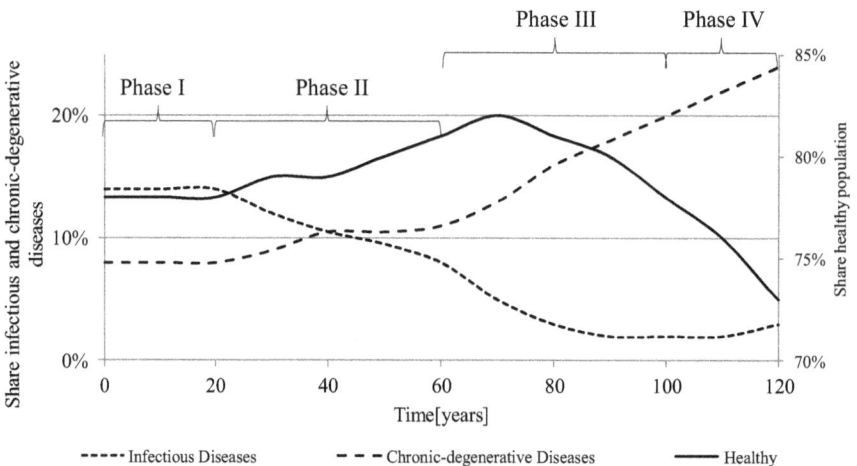

Figure 3.10: Health conditions during the transition.[274]

3.1.2.4 Epidemiological Concepts

The demographic and epidemiological transition also influences the paradigms of the healthcare system. Table 3.3 shows that the age of infectious diseases was managed with comparatively simple epidemiological model concepts, whereas chronic degener-

---

273 Frenk, Bobadilla, Stern, et al. (1991).
274 Source: Own.

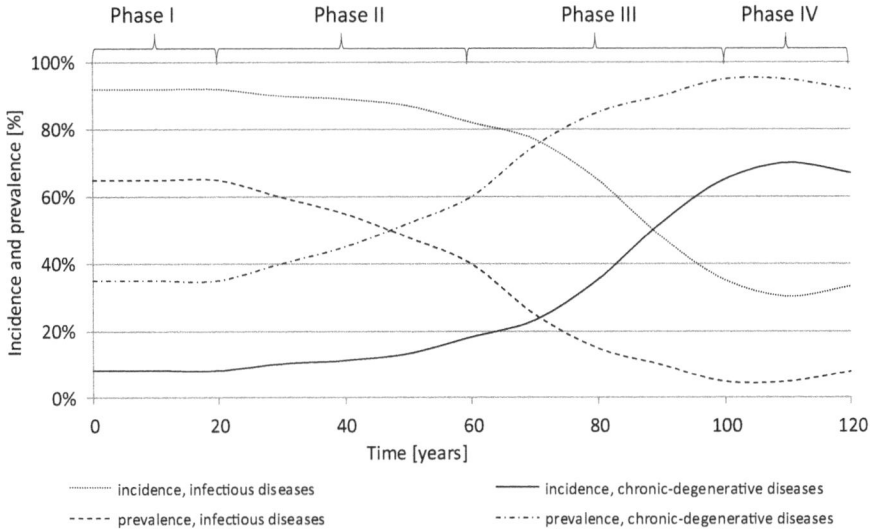

Figure 3.11: Prevalence and incidence of infectious and chronic degenerative diseases.[275]

ative diseases require complex concepts of illness and health. Therefore, societies in the first and second phases of the transition can measure their success with simple indicators (e.g. incidence), while from the third phase onwards, only complex indices can approximately provide insight into the effectiveness of the healthcare system. For example, measles can be combated with vaccination because there is an almost linear, deterministic, and exclusive relationship between the virus and the disease. For most malignant neoplasms, however, individual causes cannot usually be precisely attributed to cancer. Instead, they merely increase the risk of disease, making prevention and combat significantly more difficult. In the case of mental illnesses (e.g. depression, attention-deficit disorder, etc.), the causes are even more complex and require the inclusion of the patient's entire environment.

The need for a paradigm shift and the relevance of the epidemiological transition are underlined by the statistics from the WHO's 'Burden of Disease Database'.[276] Table 3.4 shows the causes of death for income groups and sub-Saharan Africa. It is obvious that low-income countries have a high burden of communicable diseases and maternal, perinatal, and nutrition conditions, while high-income countries have moved towards non-communicable diseases. Injuries are particularly relevant as causes of death for resource-poor countries. The probability of dying within a certain year of life is nowhere higher than in sub-Saharan Africa although missing or

---

275 Source: Own.
276 Source: https://www.who.int/data/gho/data/themes/mortality-and-global-health-estimates.

Table 3.3: Epidemiological concepts.[277]

Time	Causal models	Concept of health	Health indicators
1900	Single-cause model (infectious diseases)	Ecological model (agent-host-environment)	Mortality and morbidity
1920	Multiple-cause model (infectious diseases and transition to chronic diseases)	Social-ecology model (host-environment-behaviour)	Work-related disability measures (occupational health and inability to work)
1940		WHO model: 'complete physical, mental, social well-being'	
1970	Multiple-cause model Multiple-effect model (chronic diseases)	Risk factor model Holistic model (environment, biology, lifestyle, and healthcare system); WHO model: 'Health for all by 2000'	Measures for risk factors (smoking, alcohol, cancer registries, etc.)
1980		Wellness model (increasing conditions of wellness)	Measures for wellness and quality of life
1990	Multiple-cause-multiple-effect model (social transformation disease cycle)	WHO: health promotion; development of healthy policies	Measures for equity; measures for social index

erroneous statistics must also be considered.[278] However, this should not obscure the fact that significant disparities exist within these regions and within individual countries. Furthermore, the corresponding statistics for prevalence, incidence, mortality, and quality of life vary considerably – a discrepancy that is particularly important for optimal resource allocation (compare Section 5.2.3).

If we analyse the disease panorama and the burden-of-disease pattern, the differences between low- and high-income countries are confirmed. Figure 3.12 shows the share of the total burden of disease by cause for the two categories of countries. In low-income countries, only one condition of the top five is from the group of non-communicable diseases (cardiovascular diseases, CVDs), while for high-income countries, only one of the top five diseases is not from this group.

In summary, we can conclude that the impoverished population in developing countries is predominantly in the second phase of the transition, so that infectious diseases are still the primary cause of illness and death. The urban middle and upper classes of these countries, as well as large parts of the emerging economies, are al-

---

277 Schwartz, Siegrist, Troschke, et al. (2003).
278 Compare Jamison (2006).

Table 3.4: Causes of death (% of total).[279]

Category	Communicable diseases and maternal, perinatal, and nutrition conditions	Non-communicable diseases	Injury
Low income	47%	42%	11%
Lower middle income	30%	61%	9%
Upper middle income	8%	84%	8%
High income	6%	88%	6%
Sub-Saharan Africa	54%	36%	10%
World	18%	74%	8%

ready in the third or fourth phase of the transition and are developing a disease panorama similar to that of most European countries, i.e. many countries experience a double burden of disease. Thus, it is necessary for international healthcare management to analyse both communicable and non-communicable diseases.

3.2 Modelling Epidemiological Processes

The international healthcare manager must be able to forecast morbidity, mortality, and cost statistics for years in order to assess the impact and cost-effectiveness of interventions. Thus, modelling epidemiological processes is a crucial instrument for scientists and practitioners of healthcare management.

Mathematical models are used in many sciences because they are faster, cheaper, and less dangerous than reality.[280] Frequently, prognostic models are the only way to forecast the future and make early decisions because waiting for the results would take too long and make decision-making a gamble. However, not every model is appropriate for a specific situation and the selection of the type of model is crucial for the validity of the results.[281]

Many decisions in healthcare require forecasting of epidemiological and economic parameters, such as incidence, prevalence, mortality, intervention cost, treatment cost, and quality of life in future periods. Frequently, it is insufficient to compare the costs and benefits of alternative within 1 year, but the respective costs and utilities might occur in many different years. For instance, a vaccination programme will require an investment in the year of the vaccination, but it will yield results years later when the vaccinated person is immune against a disease. Thus, predicting the epidemiological and economic processes is crucial for the decision whether to

---

279 Source: World Bank (2024b).
280 Compare Meyer (1996).
281 Compare Klein and Scholl (2012).

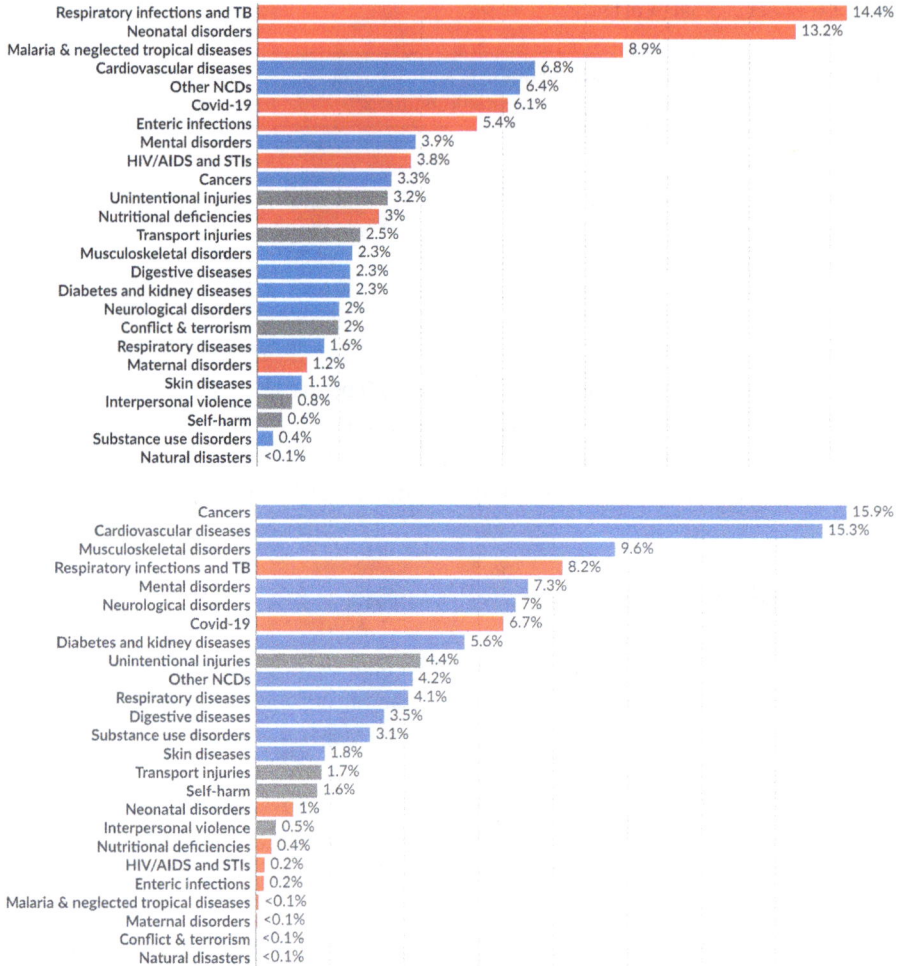

Figure 3.12: Share of burden of disease in low- (upper chart) and high-income (lower chart) countries.[282]

start a vaccination programme. Consequently, decision-making in healthcare requires the selection of the most appropriate mathematical model for the epidemiological and economic process, i.e. the international healthcare manager should know how to predict the consequences of healthcare interventions on the epidemiology, cost, and benefits.

Figure 3.13 shows the typology of models used in health economics to forecast epidemiological and economic processes. To our knowledge, the first mathematical

282 Source: OurWorldinData – CC-BY@: https://ourworldindata.org/grapher/share-of-total-disease-burden-by-cause (18.02.2025).

model of an epidemiological process was developed by En'ko in 1889. He focussed on the spread of measles in a school of St. Petersburg between 1875 and 1888. It took 100 years until it was published in English.[283] Just a few years after this model, Ross published a mathematical model for the prevention of malaria based on data from Mauritius,[284] which became the foundation of biomathematical models.

Many models consist of a set of equations that describe certain properties, such as the basic reproductive rate or the number of infections. The respective equations can be independent of each other (non-simultaneous equations) or form a finite set of equations for which common solutions are sought (simultaneous equations). The simplest form is a simple equation with a set of constants calculating an epidemiological parameter, such as the basic reproductive rate:[285]

$$R_0 = \frac{m \cdot a^2 \cdot b_1 \cdot b_2 \cdot e^{-\mu t}}{r \cdot \mu}$$

where R_0 is the-basic reproductive rate, m is -mosquitoes per human, a is -bites per mosquito per night, b_1 is the-infection risk for humans, b_2 is the-infection risk of mosquitoes, r is the-recovery rate of humans, μ is the-mortality of mosquitoes, and t is the-time.

This first, simple model was followed by several other analytical models,[286] but none of them could be sufficiently realistic to cover the complexity of infectious diseases with one or a set of few equations. In reality, the parameters are not constants but change dynamically. For instance, in the case of malaria and Ross's model, the number of mosquitoes per human (m) depends on the mortality of mosquitoes (μ), and the recovery rate of humans (r) depends (via semi-immunity) on the basic reproduction rate. Thus, in reality, we do not have a simple equation, but have dynamic variables and a system of interdependent equations with time loops.

Econometric models are frequently used to forecast costs and benefits in healthcare. While these models were used in general economics before, the first models predicting epidemiological and health economic parameters were developed in the second half of the twentieth century, initially mainly for healthcare planning,[287] but later also

---

283 Compare En'Ko (1989).

284 Compare Ross (1908).

285 Compare Macdonald (1957).

286 Compare Hudson, Rizzoli, Grenfell, et al. (2002).

287 Compare Feldstein (1967) and Butter (1967).

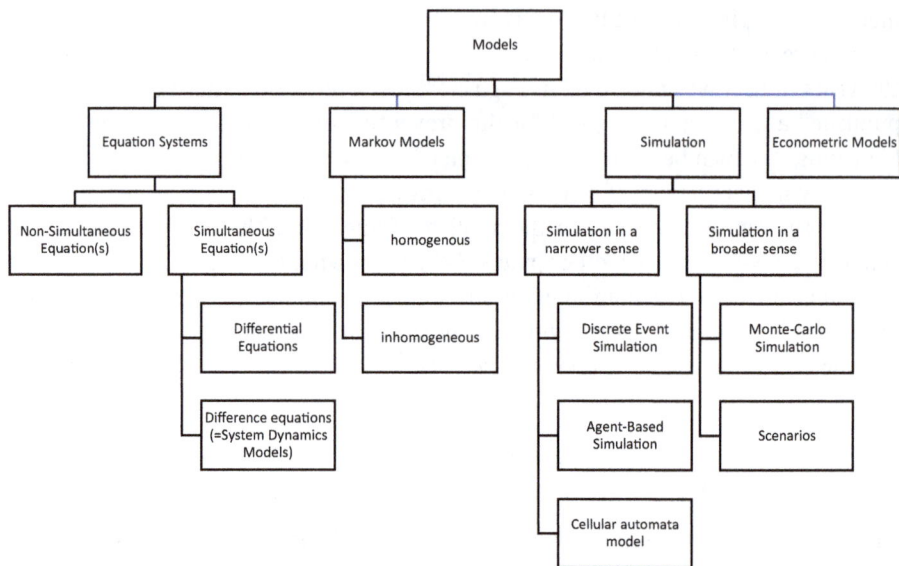

Figure 3.13: Typology of mathematical models in forecasting.[288]

for demand and supply of healthcare services[289] and for specific diseases.[290] However, econometric models are more frequently used to predict the impact of diseases on macro-economic parameters[291] than to forecast the spread of the disease itself. The complex, nonlinear, and sometimes non-monotonic relationship between interdependent parameters of the ecological and epidemiological systems make the application of econometric models rather cumbersome. They are, instead, commonly used to estimate parameters utilized by other models.

The most frequently used model in health economics is the Markov model.[292] The Russian mathematician Andrey Andreyevich Markov (1856–1922) did research on stochastic processes, with the Markov chain being the most relevant model type for healthcare because the states (e.g. healthy, sick, and dead) can be clearly distinguished, and the transition probabilities do not depend on the decisions of policy-makers (e.g. mortality rate). For a Markov chain, it is assumed that the future states depend entirely on the current state, i.e. events that have occurred before have no impact on the transition probability from state i to j (Markov property). The transition probabilities (a_{ij}) form a transition matrix (A), and the vector of states at time t (w_t) is calculated as

---

288 Source: Own.
289 Compare Dars (1971).
290 Compare Egbendewe-Mondzozo, Musumba, McCarl, et al. (2011).
291 Compare Orem, Kirigia, Azairwe, et al. (2012).
292 Compare Siebert, Alagoz, Bayoumi, et al. (2012).

$$w_t' = w_0' \cdot A, \text{ with } A = \begin{pmatrix} a_{11} & a_{12} & \cdots & a_{1n} \\ a_{21} & a_{22} & \cdots & a_{2n} \\ \cdots & \cdots & \cdots & \cdots \\ a_{m1} & a_{m2} & \cdots & a_{mn} \end{pmatrix} \text{ and } w_t = \begin{pmatrix} w_1 \\ w_2 \\ \cdots \\ w_m \end{pmatrix}$$

where a_{ij}-is the probability to change from state i to state j in Δt; $i = 1,\ldots, m$; $j = 1, \ldots,$ n; w_i-is the population in state i; $i = 1, \ldots, m$; t-is time.

The first applications of Markov models in healthcare appeared in the second half of the twentieth century, for instance, for planning clinical trials[293] or allocating healthcare resource.[294] They became very popular for forecasting the development of chronic -degenerative diseases, and the number of publications using Markov models in this field is abundant. In most cases, they start with a cohort which is followed during a number of periods, i.e. no additions to the population of the cohort are made. For instance, such a model can follow a cohort of human immunodeficiency virus (HIV)-infected individuals through various stages of infection (infected but antibody-negative; antibody-positive but asymptomatic; pre-AIDS symptoms, clinical AIDS; and death due to AIDS) for the next 20 years.

Markov chains can be homogeneous or inhomogeneous. The vast majority of these models assume that the transition probabilities remain constant, i.e. they are homogenous. Other models re-calculate the transition probabilities (e.g. after each time interval). The new probabilities can be provided by the modeller (e.g. change of mortality rate assuming that a new medication is available at a certain time) or they are re-calculated based on the results of the last period. In the latter case, the Markov model becomes dynamic, as the probabilities change over time.

System dynamics models are also frequently used in health economics. Forrester developed these models[295] for applications in the industry (e.g. storage and stock control), but the principle was applied to many settings, such as environmental protection, urbanization,[296] and diseases.[297] System dynamic models express the dynamics of a system by a set of difference equations, which are usually solved numerically by calculating in fixed time steps. For instance, the following two equations present a highly simplified population. The population growth in period t (birth) depends not only on the fertility rate, but also on the population in this period t. Consequently, the population in period $t + 1$ is the old population plus the new population depending on the old population. Mortality, migration, etc. are neglected here for simplicity:

---

293 Compare Weiss and Zelen (1965).
294 Compare Davies, Johnson, and Farrow (1975).
295 Compare Forrester (1964).
296 Compare Forrester (1971).
297 Compare Fleßa (2005) and Sterman (2016).

$$\Delta P_t = f \cdot P_t$$

$$P_{t+1} = P_t + \Delta P_t$$

where P_t-is the population in t, ΔP_t-represents births in t, and f-is the fertility rate.

System dynamic models are calculated using modern IT and can become highly complex with thousands of compartments (states), interdependent states, and delay variables (e.g. for ageing). The precision of the computation depends on the time interval (Δt, e.g. years, months, and days). The results of an inhomogeneous Markov model and a system dynamics model with the same time intervals are identical, but Markov models allow a very flexible formulation of the interdependent equations. The model is in particular applied to infectious diseases where the probability of being infected depends on the prevalence rate, i.e. the share of the infected population in the total population. The SIR model (S: susceptible; I: infectious; R: removed) is frequently used[298] and even taught in business schools.[299]

Dynamic models of infectious diseases can usually be represented by one of the types shown in Figure 3.14. The simplest model has three health states, i.e. susceptible (S), infected (I), and recovered (R). In some cases, the agent (e.g. virus, bacteria) is cleared after some time and the patient returns to the status S. SIS and SIR models can be combined, i.e. a part of the infected clears and becomes susceptible again while another part will recover and remain immune. The SIR model can be enhanced towards a SEIR model, in which a special compartment of people exposed to the agent is introduced. The SVIR model, finally, introduces a compartment of vaccinated population which cannot be infected. In some cases, the immunity does not last lifelong so that the recovered person will return to the susceptible compartment (SIRS). Finally, some models combine SIRS with SVIR and allow for two types of immunity. A short-term immunity due to the recovered infection and a long-term immunity due to vaccination.

Markov and system dynamics models allow the prediction of demographic, epidemiological, and economic parameters based on a set of constants. A major challenge is the uncertainty of these constants.[300] Therefore, the modeller has to safeguard that his results are reliable by re-calculating the models with different parameters. Experimenting with an existing analytical model can be called macro-simulation or simulation in a broader sense. The constants can be deterministic (e.g. minimum, maximum, most frequent value) or stochastic. In the latter case, a random number is generated for each stochastic constant following a specified distribution and the simulation is repeated many times in order to receive a reliable distribution of the result (e.g. cost). This form of stochastic simulation is called 'Monte Carlo'.[301]

---

[298] Compare Keeling and Rohani (2011).
[299] Compare Sterman (2016).
[300] Compare Hey, Lotito, and Maffioletti (2010) and Briggs, Weinstein, Fenwick, et al. (2012b).
[301] Compare Rubinstein and Kroese (2011) and Briggs, Weinstein, Fenwick, et al. (2012a).

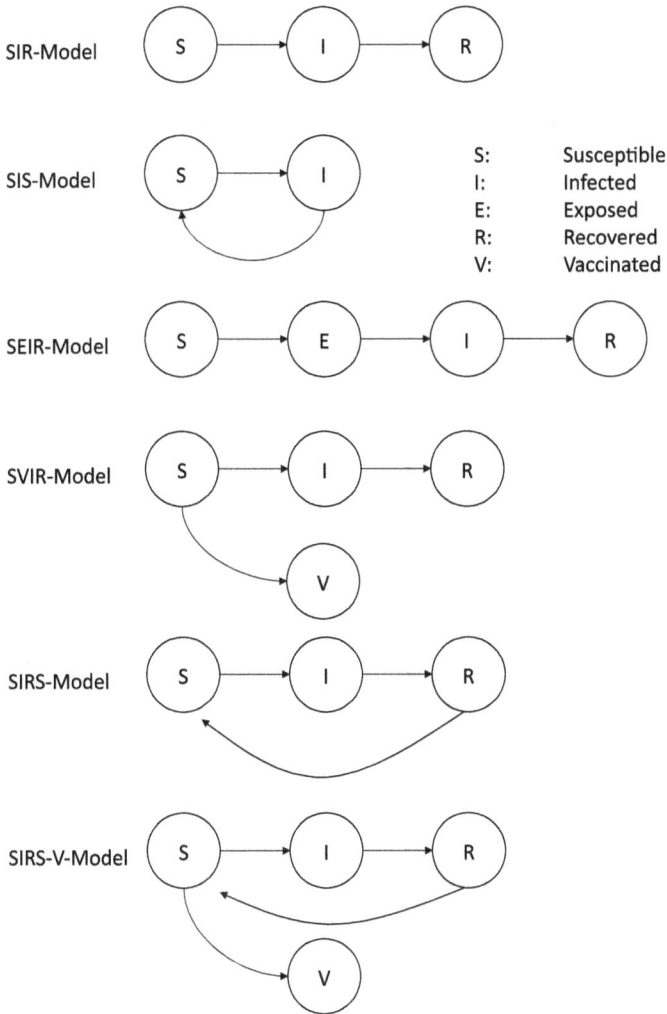

Figure 3.14: Models for infectious diseases.[302]

Micro-simulation, or simulation in the narrower sense, does not rely on other models, but develops the (computer) model specifically for the scientific purpose. For epidemiological and economic problems, it is sufficient if the states change their values only at discrete times (discrete-event simulation, DES), e.g. each event occurs at a particular instant in time, but no change in the system is assumed to occur between consecutive events. The computer develops a list of events, containing all pending events that

302 Source: Sterman (2016), Wang, Sawleshwarkar and Piraveenan (2024), Kermack and McKendrick (1927), and Kermack and McKendrick (1927).

will happen in future (e.g. patient will recover at $t = 120$). For realistic simulations, these events will be stochastic so that micro-simulations only make sense with many runs.[303]

DES has the advantage of generating individuals that can be related to each other. Unlike Markov or system dynamics models, we do not simply generate compartments with homogeneous members (e.g. healthy population), but a set of rather independent entities within a compartment. In this way, we can, for instance, assign an individual newborn to an individual mother, which is relevant to simulate the risk of mother-to-child transmission of HIV before and during birth, as well as during breastfeeding.[304] Traditional DES models assume, however, that all entities of a certain type (e.g. mother, child) have similar characteristics.

DES offers an "intuitive and flexible approach to representing complex systems"[305] and is used frequently in health economics, particularly in health technology assessment (HTA). They can focus on one disease[306] or a bundle of diseases at the same time,[307] but more frequently, it is used to model healthcare service processes.[308]

A specific type of DES is the agent-based simulations (ABSs), where the agents (e.g. persons) interact with other agents and their environment. When an agent is created in a simulation, a set of characteristics is attached to it, which will have an impact on his behaviour. Furthermore, the likelihood of his decisions will depend on former experiences. In this way, it is feasible to distinguish individuals with their typical (e.g. risky sexual) behaviour without assuming that every person of a set is alike. ABS was used for many different diseases and healthcare situations.[309]

Simulations in the narrower sense can also be used to simulate the spatial spread of a disease, in particular by cellular automata models.[310] However, the geographical dimension of disease spread has received less attention from health economists and will be neglected in this paper.

Homogenous Markov models should be applied to chronic degenerative diseases, where a certain cohort is followed for a certain time, and where probabilities (e.g. transition to another health state or mortality) are unchanged throughout the entire process.[311] Contrary, communicable diseases require a model where the "probability

303 Compare Günal and Pidd (2010) and Vázquez-Serrano, Peimbert-García, and Cárdenas-Barrón (2021).
304 Compare Rauner, Brailsford, and Fleßa (2005).
305 Karnon, Stahl, Brennan, et al. (2012).
306 Compare McKenzie, Wong, and Bossert (1998).
307 Compare Young, Taetgmeyer, Zulaika, et al. (2019) and Sterman (2016).
308 Compare Zhang (2018).
309 Compare Smith, Trauer, Gambhir, et al. (2018).
310 Compare Podolski and Nguyen (2021) and Flessa (2023a).
311 Compare Siebert, Alagoz, Bayoumi, et al. (2012).

of a susceptible individual becoming infected at any one point in time (the infectiousness) is related to the number of infectious individuals in the population".[312] The models are nonlinear and "produce transmission dynamics that require specific consideration when modelling an intervention that has an impact on the transmission of a pathogen".[313]

Table 3.5 summarizes the pros and cons of different models and their applicability to different epidemiological situations. Non-simultaneous equation models are the simplest models, which can be computed on a calculator or a spreadsheet. With that structure, models are simple but might be misleading. For instance, an intervention (e.g. vaccination) will not only protect the vaccinated person, but also reduce the likelihood of other people being infected in future. Thus, vaccinating one person today increases herd immunity and consequently reduces the infection risk for all other individuals. The effect of one vaccination goes, thus, far beyond the direct impact on the vaccinated person, but this cannot be reflected in static models.

Markov models require the definition of states and transition probabilities, but the calculation itself is usually based on standard software (e.g. TreeAge). System dynamics models usually require the definition of difference equations, which can be much more demanding. There is standard software (e.g. VenSim), but many researchers prefer to programme the model themselves in a high-level general language, such as C++, Delphi, and Java. All of these models can be combined with a Monte Carlo simulation, but this makes the work even more demanding. The workload of developing DESs is quite high, although standard simulation software for DES is available. The highest workload is required for ABS, even if software exists.

Non-simultaneous equation models and Markov models do not allow a feedback loop, i.e. the results of period t have no impact on transition probabilities in period $t + i$ with $i \geq 1$. Inhomogeneous Markov chains allow re-calculating the transition probabilities every period, but they are very close to system dynamics models. Merely the calculation methodology (matrix multiplication vs. difference equations) differs. The other models permit feedback loops, e.g. the infection probability is a function of former infections. ABS even permit 'learning', i.e. the individual can change their behaviour based on past experiences.

The requirement of empirical data is rather low for non-simultaneous equation models. Markov models need the population in each compartment, as well as the transition probabilities. As most cohort models simply follow the transition of a cohort through the stages (e.g. infected→incubation→sick→death), the data requirements are not very high, e.g. the average duration in a stage is sufficient to calculate the transition process. System dynamics models can be very comprehensive and require a lot of data, for instance, on infection and (sexual) behaviour. However, these models can

---

312 Compare Pitman, Fisman, Zaric, et al. (2012).
313 Compare Pitman, Fisman, Zaric, et al. (2012).

also be rather simple without stronger data requirements. ABS and DES can become quite strong with large data requirements, but smaller models are also feasible. The data availability is particularly challenging in low-income countries with dysfunctional health information systems.

The purpose of the models is also different. Most models allow forecasting of future events, whereas non-simultaneous equation models are static. They permit to calculate cases, costs, or reproduction rates, but the results represent a kind of equilibrium, not a process. All other models are suitable for forecasting. A major difference is the capability of the model to simulate smaller numbers. Non-simultaneous equation, Markov, and system dynamics models analyse cohorts or compartments, but do not distinguish individuality. Consequently, Monte Carlo simulations building on these models do not consider individuality as well. This is appropriate for the 'average person' in a cohort or compartment without considering individual behaviour or probabilities. At the beginning of an epidemic, the spread of the disease is highly stochastic because each infection is a stochastic process. While cohort models use averages, DES and ABS see each infection as an event and the respective variable as binary, i.e. infection or no infection. Even with a base reproduction rate greater than one, an epidemic could end soon after the first case appears simply because the infection is a stochastic process and that patient might not infect another person. Thus, the beginning of an epidemic and small numbers of infected will require stochastic models, i.e. DES or ABS. Monte Carlo simulations based on other models cannot consider individual infection risks and thus are also focussed on larger cohorts of later stages of an epidemic.

In summary, we can state that each type of model has a right of its own. Non-simultaneous equation models are easy to use and rapid instruments that permit a simple epidemiological and/or economic assessment of the spread of a disease. We can, for instance, calculate the basic reproductive rate as an average for a certain population. Markov models can predict the epidemiological and economic processes of a cohort of infected through the stages of the disease and allow analysis, in particular, the impact of screening programmes. For short forecasts, the newly infected have only limited impact on the infection risks of other people, so that the infection risk can be taken as a constant. In this case, Markov models can also be used to forecast the entire process. Over longer periods, the infection risk changes because former infections will increase the risk in later periods. Thus, we would need an inhomogeneous Markov chain where the respective probabilities are re-calculated each period.

Too often, interventions are based on 'guesses' about future epidemiological and economic processes. The international healthcare manager should be familiar with these models in order to base an evaluation on reliable forecasts. With these models, the future still remains uncertain – but we develop an understanding of the impact of uncertainty and the corridors of sound decision-making.

Table 3.5: Applicability of epidemiological models.[314]

	Non-simultaneous equation models	Markov	System dynamics	Monte Carlo	DES	ABS
Workload	Low	Medium	Medium	Medium	High	Very high
Computation	Calculator and spreadsheet	Specific software	Specific software	Partly included in specific software	Simulators	Simulators
Feedback loops	No	No	Yes	Depends on model	Yes	Yes
Data requirement	Low	Some	Some	Some	Some	Comprehensive
Forecasting cohort	No	Yes	Yes	Yes	Yes	Yes
Small numbers	Yes	No	No	No	Yes	Yes
Individuality	No	No	No	No	Partly	Yes
Main use	'Quick and dirty' assessment	Forecasting chronic degenerative diseases and cohorts	Infectious diseases	Sensitivity analysis for Markov and system dynamics models	Smaller numbers, e.g. begin of epidemic	Smaller numbers with individual behaviour

3.3 Epidemiology of Infectious Diseases

The following sections analyse the spread of infectious diseases in time and space. After presenting the state of the art of the epidemiology of these diseases, some examples are discussed to illustrate the role and feature of infections.

3.3.1 Fundamentals

3.3.1.1 Models of Transmission Paths
Modelling transmission paths is of great importance for healthcare management because statements about the efficiency of intervention programmes depend signifi-

---

314 Source: Own.

cantly on the specific transmission route. It is essential to distinguish whether the transmission of the agent occurs from person to person or whether animals (and/or the environment) are involved. The term anthroponosis refers to infectious diseases that are transmissible from humans to humans without involving animals, i.e. human beings are the only host and reservoirs, while animals are neither vectors (transmitters) nor hosts.[315] Many diseases are directly transmissible from person to person, where all body fluids can be the medium. For example, sexually transmitted diseases (STDs, such as AIDS, syphilis)[316] are predominantly transmitted through blood and semen, gastrointestinal diseases (such as cholera, amoebas) through excrement, and respiratory diseases (such as TB, influenza) through secretions. A significant part of the burden of infectious diseases is based on direct transmission from person to person (e.g. plague, measles, smallpox, leprosy, Ebola, hepatitis, whooping cough, diphtheria, typhoid, and COVID-19).[317]

Most of these diseases are likely of animal origin (compare Section 2.2.2.3), but they have adapted to humans so that no animal as a vector, host, or reservoir is needed anymore.[318] Zoonoses, conversely, are infectious diseases that cross the species barrier between humans and animals. Originally, this term only referred to animal diseases (as opposed to human diseases), but during the nineteenth century, the current usage of the term developed, with some authors distinguishing among diseases transmitted from humans to animals (anthropozoonosis), those transmitted from animals to humans (zooanthropozoonosis), and diseases transmissible in both directions (amphixenosis). In some cases, humans may act as incidental hosts,[319] contracting the infection from animals, and becoming ill, but unable to further transmit the disease. These 'one-way street infections' include brucellosis, typically transmitted from animals to humans through unpasteurized milk. Individuals consuming unpasteurized milk or milk products, or those living in close contact with animals, are particularly at risk. Humans develop symptoms such as fever, headaches, and nausea, but transmission from humans to other humans is not possible.[320]

To fully understand the dynamics of zoonotic transmission, it is important to define the different roles within the host-pathogen relationship. Generally, a host is any

---

315 Compare Krauss, Weber, Enders, et al. (1997).

316 Even an anthroponosis might have started as a zoonosis including several several interspecies jumps. However, the anthoroponosis currently has no animal reservoir.

317 Compare Cook and Zumla (2009).

318 Compare Diamond (1999) and Jones, Patel, Levy, et al. (2008). However, a jump from the original animal reservoir to humans is feasible.

319 Compare Hinz (1987).

320 This pathway illustrates the difference between infectious and contagious (or communicable) diseases. The former are caused by germs, i.e., bacteria, viruses, or fungi enter the (human) body, multiply, and can cause an infection. Contagious (or communicable) diseases are capable of spreading from one person to another. Thus, brucellosis is an infectious disease, but it is not communicable from human to human.

organism that provides nutrients to another organism. If this is also beneficial to the host, it is called symbiosis; otherwise, it is called parasitism, where the parasite benefits at the host's expense. An incidental host is an organism that is infected but cannot transmit the pathogen. If the incidental host dies quickly from the disease, it does not interrupt the life cycle of the pathogen. An end host, or definitive host, is an organism where a pathogen reaches its mature stage and reproduces, requiring the host to survive long enough for this process. An intermediate host facilitates a developmental stage of the pathogen, while a transport host, or paratenic host, physically carries the pathogen without developmental changes, and a storage host, or reservoir host, accumulates the pathogen, serving as a source of infection.

The concept of a reservoir is also important for modelling zoonoses. It refers to a population in which the pathogen is 'stored'. Critically, these animal reservoirs often carry pathogens without showing symptoms themselves, and thus pose a persistent threat to human health.

Within the group of zoonoses, various transmission routes can again be modelled. Vector-borne diseases, where an animal takes over the transmission of the disease from human to human, are of great importance. In the case of malaria, a prime example, various *Anopheles* mosquito species act as vectors and transmit the human-pathogenic *Plasmodium* parasites from person to person.[321] Other animals may have their own forms of malaria, but they generally play no role in humans.

The interdependency of human and animal health is much closer for diseases that have an animal reservoir. For example, the rat is the natural end host for the bacterium that causes the plague, which is transmitted by the rat flea as a vector.[322] In exceptional situations (e.g. when too many rats die from the plague), rat fleas also bite humans, causing the plague to spread within the human population. Here, other flea species typically serve as vectors. The control of these diseases is significantly more complex because eradication within the human population is not sufficient. As long as an animal reservoir exists, the disease can always re-occur during an outbreak. Another example is yellow fever, which is feared in the tropics, where monkey populations and *Aedes* mosquitoes serve as reservoirs and vectors.

Finally, there are disease transmissions where animals serve as intermediate hosts but are not simultaneously active as vectors. For example, the *Bulinus* snail is so involved in the reproductive cycle of schistosomiasis (bilharzia) that it picks up pathogens that humans release into the water. There, they mature to another stage and are then released back into the water, where they could infect humans. The *Bulinus* snail also acted as a transport host, as it was unknowingly brought on slave ships from Africa to America in water barrels, thus contributing to the spread of schistosomiasis.[323]

---

321 Flanigan (2007).
322 Compare Meade and Emch (2010).
323 Compare Morgan, Dejong, Adeoye, et al. (2005).

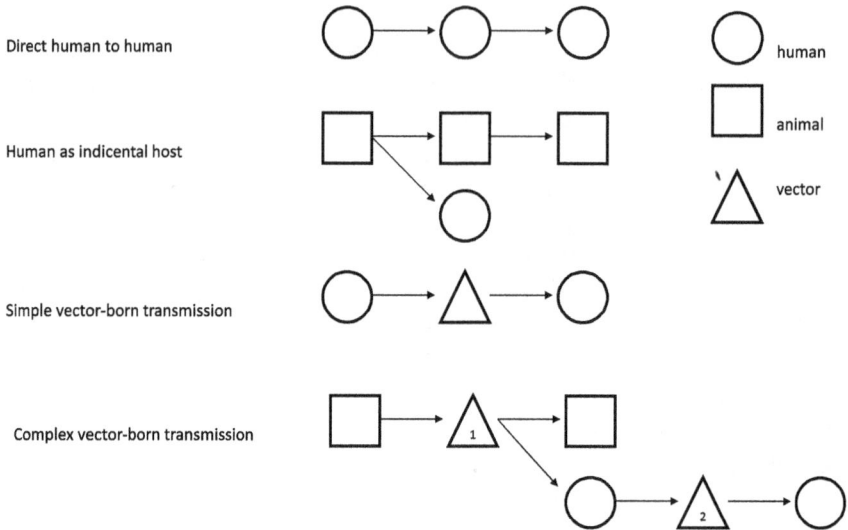

Figure 3.15: Modelling of transmission paths.[324]

Figure 3.15 summarizes the transmission paths. It must be emphasized that the health-care manager can only understand the dynamics of infectious diseases and assess the efficiency of interventions if he comprehends the infection cycles.

3.3.1.2 Diffusion of Infectious Diseases

The speed of the diffusion of an infectious disease in space and time depends on a number of factors. If a disease occurs regularly within an area or community, the disease is endemic. If more people fall sick than what would be expected normally, we talk about an outbreak. An epidemic is defined as a wave of illness where the number of new cases increases significantly in a limited area. If the spread is cross-country and cross-continental, it is referred to as a pandemic.

Diseases diffuse in time and space. Figure 3.16 shows the temporal progression of a simulated measles epidemic on an island with 100,000 non-immune children.[325] It is assumed that five infectious children enter the island on day $t = 1$. The graphs of the number of infections, the exposed children, and the infectious children clearly show exponential growth for about one and a half months. The maximum number of infections per day is 6,485 at $t = 42$, and at $t = 48$, about half of the population is infectious. After about 3 months, the epidemic comes to a standstill because the whole population of formerly susceptible children is immune or has died (1,943 at $t = 100$).

---

324 Source: Meade and Emch (2010).
325 Compare Flessa (2023a).

Figure 3.17 shows the spatial diffusion on the island for six different points of time under the assumption that the five children enter the island on the north-west corner (e.g. through a harbour) and the infection spreads over the island with a homogenous population. It is obvious that the epidemic has already disappeared in its original hotspot while it is still rolling over the rest of the island ($t \geq 51$).

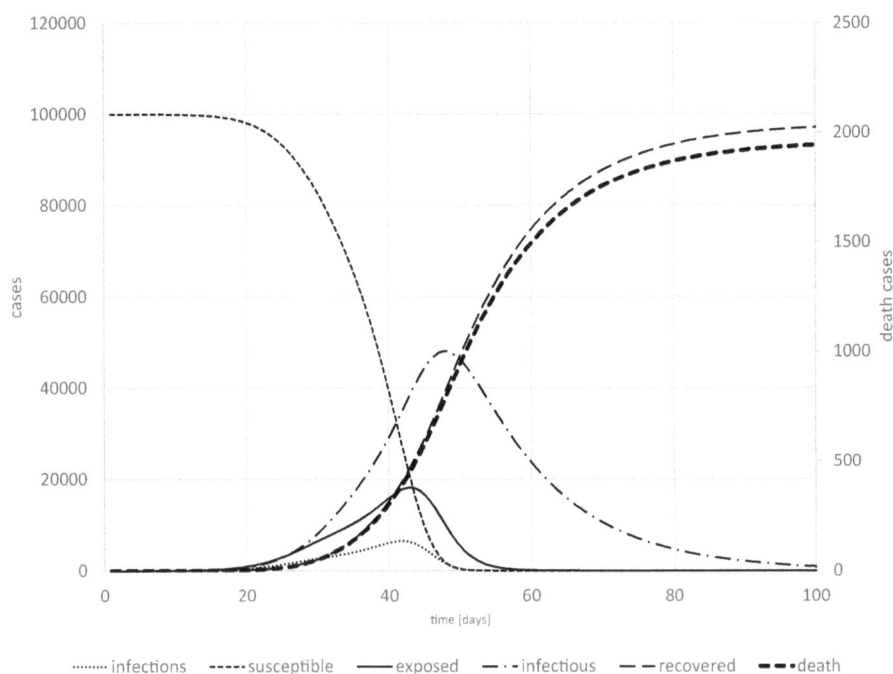

Figure 3.16: Diffusion in time.[326]

The intensity and speed of disease diffusion is expressed and measured by the basic reproductive number (rate), R_0, as the expected number of cases directly generated by one case in a population where all individuals are susceptible to infection. Figure 3.18 shows the principle with the examples of Ebola and SARS-CoV-1. Every person infected with Ebola infects – on average – two other persons, while every person infected with SARS-CoV-1 infects four other people. If $R_0 < 1$, the disease will disappear by itself because each infected person cannot infect at least one more person. If $R_0 > 1$, we will see the exponential growth shown in Figure 3.16.

The basic reproductive numbers of human diseases have a wide range. Influenza, for instance, has a value as low as 1.3, AIDS of 4, smallpox of 5, polio of 6, chickenpox

---

326 Compare Flessa (2023a).

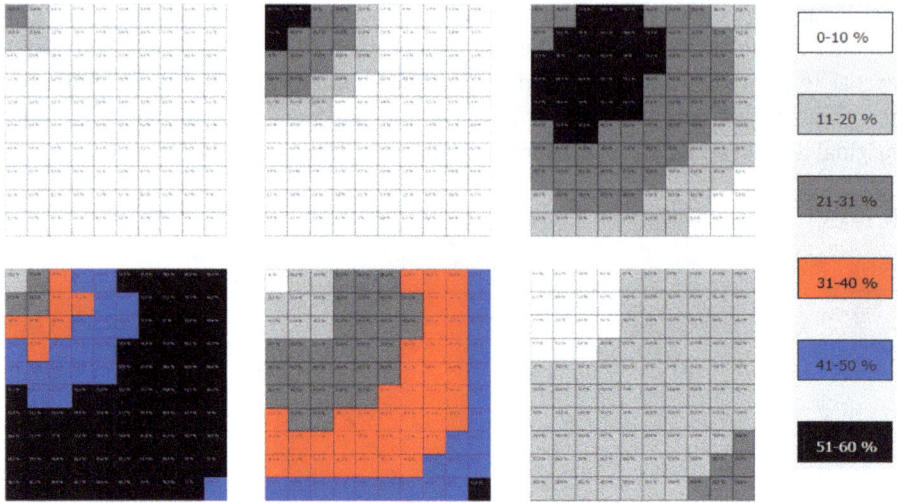

Figure 3.17: Diffusion in space. Simulation for t = 22, 28, 35, 43, 51, and 61.[327]

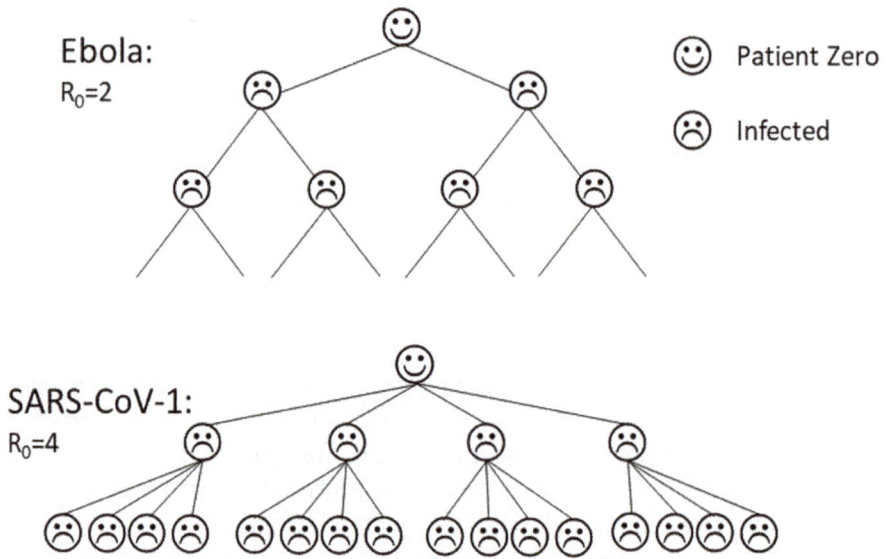

Figure 3.18: Basic reproductive number.[328]

327 Compare Flessa (2023a).
328 Compare KieraCampbell (2024).

of 11, and measles of up to 18,[329] but different stems of one disease might have different basic reproductive numbers. These figures clearly indicate that the diffusion pattern of diseases can be quite different. The higher R_0, the faster a disease spreads, and the more likely we will see an epidemic or pandemic. However, the basic reproductive rate is only relevant as long as no immunity exists or if the infectious person meets only non-immune. The resistance to the spread of an infectious disease within a population is called herd immunity. It is expressed as the percentage of immune (due to previous infections or effective vaccination) in the total population.[330]

The net reproductive number (N_0) expresses the number of people an infectious person will (on average) infect if a part of the population is immune either because it survived the disease or was successfully immunized. If n denotes the share of the immune population (herd immunity) in percent, N_0 can be calculated as

$$N_0 = \frac{R_0(100 - n)}{100}$$

Based on this number, we can calculate the herd immunity required to stop the spread of a disease (herd immunity threshold) as

$$n \geq 100 - \frac{100}{R_0} \ (\%)$$

For instance, if the basic reproductive number is two, one person will – on average – infect two others. If the herd immunity is 50%, every infectious person will only infect one other person because every second person is already immune. Thus, a herd immunity of more than 50% will suffice to end the diffusion of the disease. If R_0 is 3, we will need a herd immunity of 67%, if it is 18 (e.g. measles), we need an immunity of 94.4%.

If an infection leads to permanent immunity, the herd immunity will be eventually achieved. However, this might take long and cause many casualties. An effective vaccination[331] will lead to a sufficient herd immunity, but for some diseases, the immunization coverage must be very high. For instance, influenza with an R_0 of 1.3 will come to a standstill if at least 23.1% of the population is immune, while chickenpox with an R_0 of 11 will require a herd immunity of 90.9%. If the vaccine is not fully effective and/or does not provide long-term protection, the respective rates must be much higher. The eradication of smallpox was possible (herd immunity 80%) because the

---

329 These figures are estimates (CEBM 2024.)
330 Compare John and Samuel (2000).
331 The efficacy of a vaccine is a measure of how much a vaccine lowers the risk of getting sick in a controlled clinical trial. The effectiveness of a vaccine is a measure of how well vaccines work in the real world, i.e. in a communities as a whole. Efficacy and effectiveness usually focus on the protection of the person vaccinated, not necessarily on the transmission risk. Some vaccinations lead to life-long immunity, but many have a limited duration of effective protection.

vaccine was almost 'perfect' and international, as well as national, efforts to immunize the entire population were high.

Generally, vaccinations are the most efficient intervention. For instance, measles was a disastrous disease before vaccinations were introduced worldwide. Before 1963, 90% of children had measles before they reached adulthood, and some two million of them died per year and some 15,000 suffered life-long blindness per year due to this disease. Measles is still a burden, particularly in low-income countries with some 500,000 cases and some 25,000 deaths per year. It is estimated that vaccination programmes are responsible for some 40% of the observed decline in global infant mortality, and 52% in the African region.[332]

In addition to natural or vaccine-based immunity, numerous geographical, biological, and cultural factors determine whether a disease goes extinct, persists, or becomes epidemic.[333] Temperature is an important determinant. For example, the *Plasmodium* requires a minimum temperature of over 20 °C to mature in the *Anopheles* (compare Section 3.3.3). Colder regions are thus hardly affected by malaria, but global warming poses the risk of spreading infectious diseases (e.g. West Nile Virus).[334] Temperature also depends on altitude, as the average temperature typically drops by 0.5 °C for every additional 100 m in elevation.[335] Therefore, the higher an area, the lower the risk of malaria. This is the main reason why traditional settlements in the tropics were often located above 1,500 m, as malaria was virtually not feared there.

Precipitation is also correlated with altitude and determines the spread of disease. Numerous diseases need sufficient rainfall, as, for example, vectors require water to breed. Thus, diseases like dengue, yellow fever, and malaria often occur seasonally. Water bodies (lakes, streams, rivers) also play a significant role. For instance, the blackfly as a vector of onchocerciasis (river blindness) requires oxygen-rich water for its larvae, so it primarily breeds in fast-flowing waters. The *Bulinus* snail, on the other hand, prefers still lakes, so schistosomiasis is predominantly a problem of lake landscapes.

The migrations of animals are a significant problem for the spread of diseases. For example, bird flu (H5N1, avian influenza) is spread by migratory birds across Asia, Europe, Australia, and Africa. Indeed, the introduction of the virus can be quite accurately traced along the main flight routes of these animals (compare Figure 3.19). The spread through animal migration (hoofed animals) also played a crucial role in the major sleeping sickness epidemic at the beginning of the twentieth century in East Africa when the western and eastern forms of sleeping sickness met in Uganda[336] and

---

332 Compare Shattock, Johnson, Sim, et al. (2024) and Berche (2022a).
333 Compare Fricke (1987).
334 Compare Erazo, Grant, Ghisbain, et al. (2024).
335 Compare Meymen (1985).
336 Compare Queen (1911).

made large parts of the fertile land by Lake Victoria uninhabitable to humans to this day.

In addition to geographical and biological factors, culture also plays a significant role in the spread of diseases. For example, the traditional division of labour between men and women, or the understanding of gender roles, leads to a specific pattern of illness. For instance, in some areas of Africa, women are much more frequently affected by bilharzia (compare Section 3.3.1.1) than men are because they traditionally wash clothes and fetch water from the lake, i.e. they have prolonged contact with contaminated water. Men, on the other hand, are more often on the fields or fishing in their boats without standing in the water. The cultural pattern of labour division induces a specific pattern of disease spread – another example of how closely diseases and economic activity are linked.

Figure 3.19: Main migration routes of migratory birds.[337]

The speed of disease diffusion is predominantly influenced by the mobility of the population. Therefore, the increase in long-distance travel, especially air travel, has significantly accelerated the diffusion of diseases. In principle, diseases can spread according to two patterns: spatial and hierarchical diffusion or neighbourhood and hierarchy effects.[338] Spatial diffusion occurs through direct human-to-human contact, without the

---

337 Source: http://www.vogelgrippe.de.ms/.
338 Compare Oswald (2009); Ritter (2001).

need for these individuals to travel to distant centres. Spatial diffusion is often compared to a juice stain on a tablecloth, spreading equally in all directions. Hierarchical diffusion, however, follows the structure of centres, meaning the spread from one centre to another is much faster due to higher traffic density than to the periphery. For example, the spread of the seventh cholera epidemic from 1961 can be seen to have spread almost according to the juice stain pattern. From its origin in Southeast Asia, it developed simultaneously northward (China), eastward (New Guinea), and westward (Pakistan and Iran). About 10 years after its origin, the epidemic reached Africa and Europe almost simultaneously and continued to spread spatially.[339] In contrast, the short but severe SARS epidemic (severe acute respiratory syndrome, SARS) of the winter of 2002/2003 predominantly followed global flight routes after an initial period, meaning all continents and centres were affected relatively quickly, while areas of only short distances from the supposed centre in southern China were affected late or hardly at all. As flight connections have become faster and cheaper, the speed of infectious disease spread has become an increasingly significant problem.[340]

Clothing can also influence the spread of infectious diseases. Most cultures have adjusted their clothing to the dangers of disease over millennia, but modern fashion often runs counter to this. For example, the full-body veiling found in some Islamic countries was less of a medical issue when the clothing was predominantly made of breathable wool. The transition to synthetics, however, significantly increases the risk of fungal infections. At the same time, the light clothing of some tourists in tropical countries provides ideal access for mosquitoes.

The design of residential buildings and settlements also influences infectious diseases. For instance, houses with roofs and walls made of natural materials (e.g. coconut mats and leaves) are ideal breeding grounds for pests that can transmit numerous diseases. As a countermeasure, smoking fires are often stoked in these huts, which can have devastating effects on the respiratory tract and are considered triggers for asthma, and as risk factors for other respiratory diseases. The form of settlement (e.g. street villages, circular villages, and fortified cities) affects ventilation and the accessibility for vectors that breed outside the settlements.

There are also a number of other factors that can influence the spread of diseases. For example, the form of marriage (monogamy vs. polygamy) could determine the spread of STDs just as much as the belief in predestination could influence the readiness for prevention. This means that the international healthcare manager must carefully study the geographical, biological, and especially cultural conditions of the respective country, and sometimes even the sub-region, before making statements about an efficient containment strategy. As always in healthcare management, the principle holds: diagnosis first, then therapy. And this means above all studying the complex interdependent system of agent, vector, and host with all its demographic, ecological, and cultural determinants in detail.

3.3.1.3 Epidemics and Pandemics

Most infectious diseases have spread across the world over centuries without necessarily being referred to as pandemics. Besides the cross-country and cross-continental phenomenon, a pandemic must also demonstrate a certain speed of spread and relevance in terms of larger case numbers. A 'perfect storm' condition for this occurs when a previously unknown pathogen encounters a population that has not yet built up immunity against this pathogen. For example, the great plague epidemic in Europe (starting in 1347) encountered a population that had no immunity and thus reduced the population by an estimated one-third or 25 million people within a few years.[341] Even more devastating were the effects of diseases (measles and smallpox) that Europeans introduced to South America (compare Section 2.2.2.3).

Another factor in the emergence of a pandemic is the natural speed of spread. Droplet infections (e.g. influenza, SARS) are particularly suited to spreading quickly over long distances, while diseases that depend on intermediate hosts or vectors progress relatively slowly or are confined to an ecologically limited habitat.

Diseases that kill the host very quickly have a lower chance of spreading than infections with low lethality. For example, most Ebola epidemics have essentially died out on their own because the affected individuals died so quickly that they could hardly transmit the infection outside of particular environments (e.g. hospitals with low hygiene standards). Transmission is particularly efficient when the patient appears to have recovered but continues to be a carrier. Figure 3.20 simplifies the infectivity (i.e. the probability of infecting another person) of a patient. After a latency and incubation period, the disease breaks out and the patient is usually highly infectious. However, the symptoms are so visible that the transmission of the disease is less likely, as the patient may withdraw or even be isolated. Many cultures practice the isolation of the sick until the acute signs of suffering are no longer visible. The classic quarantine was first imposed in July 1377 by the city administration of Dubrovnik for 40 days ('quaranta giorni') to protect the city from the plague.[342]

Problematic are diseases where the (former) patient can still contribute to the spread of the agent after they appear to have recovered, i.e. are symptom-free (compare Figure 3.20). Such active and passive carriers lead to an effective chain of infection that can only be broken by testing former patients or larger population groups. Amoebas and numerous worm diseases are often transmitted through carriers.

Controlling diseases that do not occur uniformly but in irregular waves is particularly challenging. The annual flu wave is a good example. The healthcare manager

---

341 Compare Kiple, Graham, Frey, et al. (1993).
342 Compare Tartalja (1981).

must predict it to make financial, personnel, and material preparations (e.g. vaccines). The wave motion is partly based on immunity. After recovering from an infection, many people are immune for life against the same strain. This population group forms a natural barrier to the spread. If a population is small and relatively isolated, the epidemic can completely disappear.

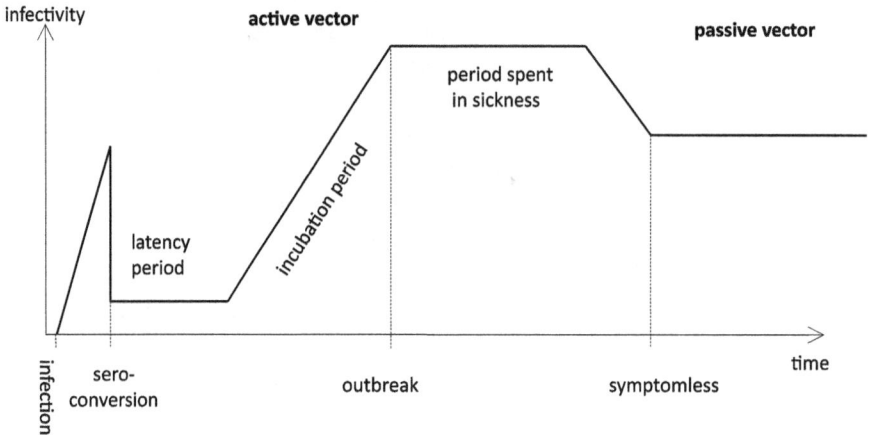

Figure 3.20: Active and passive carriers.[343]

Vaccinations create immunity artificially. In extreme cases, a disease that has no natural reservoir can be completely eradicated, as was declared by the WHO for smallpox in December 1979.[344] The last case occurred on 26 October 1977, in Somalia. The herd immunity of a population must drop below a certain threshold for a disease to break out in the population. The measles on Iceland is a well-documented example of this.[345] Iceland is sparsely populated and remote. The country is so small that measles disappears completely after an epidemic because no small groups of uninfected children can sustain themselves. However, measles is continually reintroduced via the port of Reykjavik. As long as herd immunity is high enough, these cannot lead to an epidemic. Over time, however, more and more children are born who have not yet come into contact with measles. After about 3 years, a sufficient number of children have grown up to let an epidemic to break out. This results in characteristic waves (compare Figure 3.21), similar to predator-prey cycles (compare mouse-fox). In honour of the two mathematicians/biologists who first mathematically modelled this cycle, it is called the 'Lotka-Volterra cycle'.[346] A very similar cycle, albeit with higher ampli-

---

343 Source: Own based on Ignatius (2006).
344 Compare Vutuc and Flamm (2010).
345 Compare Cliff and Haggett (1988).
346 Compare Schuster (2009).

tude, occurs when individual immunity wanes over time, as is the case with cholera. A past cholera infection only protects for a short time against re-infection.

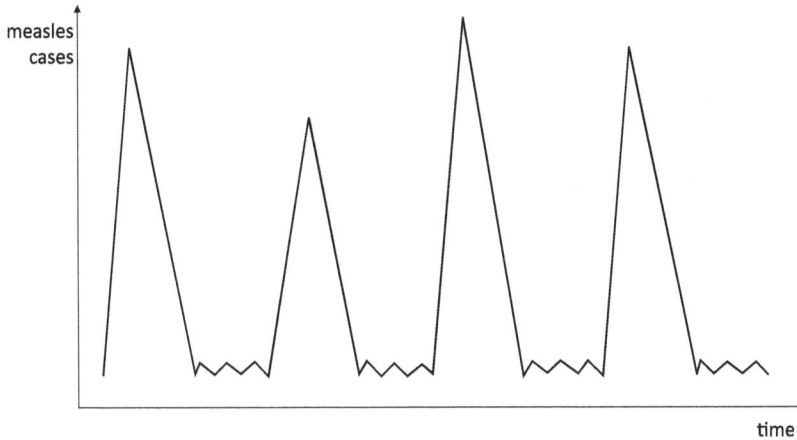

Figure 3.21: Progress of measles in Iceland.[347]

Even when lifelong immunity is established, a typical progression can still occur if the agent, particularly the virus, mutates. These mutations can occur when a subject is simultaneously infected with two related strains of the pathogen, allowing the recombination of genetic material from two viruses to create a new, highly pathogenic virus for which no individual has immunity, even if they have successfully combated the original viruses.

The regular pandemics of influenza are an example of the extensive changes a virus can undergo, making the flu an "unchanging disease due to a changing virus".[348] Major changes are referred to as 'shifts', while minor ones are called 'drifts'. Thus, people who have previously suffered from the flu and its close relatives become susceptible again. These cycles are overlaid by seasonal influences, as influenza occurs primarily in the dry, cold season.

Figure 3.22 shows the progression, which is defined as the Kilbourne model.[349] A mutated virus is introduced into the population, resulting in a very strong epidemic that will break out worldwide, delayed in time, i.e. a pandemic. After the initial subsidence, the virus persists in small population groups. A minor drift occurs, triggering another wave of infection. However, it will be significantly less than the first pandemic, as a large part of the population is already immune or still recognizes the

---

347 Source: Own, based on Cliff and Haggett (1988).
348 Zuckerman, Banatvala and Griffiths (2009).
349 Compare Cliff and Haggett (1988).

virus despite the drift. Thus, the epidemics become progressively weaker until a new shift occurs and a new pandemic begins.

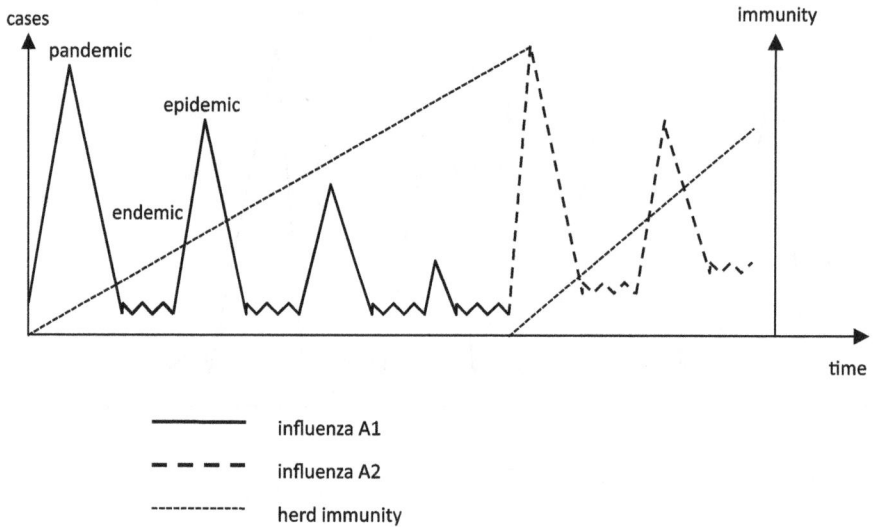

Figure 3.22: Kilbourne model.[350]

Pandemics are regular disasters that have existed for a long time and are likely to threaten mankind also in the future. The 'Black Death' (bubonic plague) killing 1/3 of the European population, the so-called 'Spanish flu' of 1918/19 (H1N1 influenza) with 500 million cases and 50 million deaths, the so-called 'Asian flu' of 1957/57 (H2N2 influenza) with 1.1 million deaths, the HIV/AIDS since the 1980s with estimated 40 million deaths until today, and the COVID-19 pandemic of 2019–2024 with some 800 million cases and more than 7 million reported COVID-19 deaths clearly show the fatal potential and the regularity of zoonotic diseases for global disasters. In all cases, the pandemic started with a new agent (e.g. strain of an existing virus or new virus). With the exemption of AIDS, all of these diseases rolled as a series of waves over the world while the waves got smaller each time.

However, epidemics and pandemics are not primarily a biological or medical issue. The main accelerators are dysfunctional social and health systems, poor nutrition, low education, superstition, and other social and economic conditions and behaviours, which have to be addressed by the international healthcare manager. Infectious diseases are complex systems that can only be understood in their temporal and spatial spread if biological, ecological, and cultural systems are included and understood in their interdependencies. The healthcare manager can only effectively combat

---

350 Source: Cliff and Haggett (1988).

infectious diseases if they recognize these relationships and model them to determine efficient interventions. This will be demonstrated by several examples.

3.3.2 Case Study: AIDS

3.3.2.1 Relevance

AIDS is an example of an infectious disease transmitted directly from person to person. It is classified as a STD since sexual intercourse is the primary mode of transmission. From a modelling perspective, AIDS has a relatively simple transmission mechanism, which has led to the development of numerous models for AIDS transmission that are helpful to healthcare managers.

AIDS is also an example of a disease that quickly became a pandemic, but it is not a "public health emergency of international concern" (PHEIC) . A PHEIC is declared by WHO as "an extraordinary event which is determined to constitute a public health risk to other states through the international spread of disease and to potentially require a coordinated international response".[351] Furthermore, the threat must be "serious, sudden, unusual, or unexpected" and have "implications for public health beyond the affected state's national border" and "may require immediate international action".[352] The International Health Regulations (IHR) were passed as late as 2005, i.e. AIDS would have been such a concern in the 1980s, but the term was not used at that time. Meanwhile, AIDS is global and rather constant.[353]

AIDS has received the greatest attention from the international health community. With the establishment of a dedicated UN agency to combat AIDS globally (UN-AIDS)[354] and the significant financial importance of the 'Global Fund to Fight AIDS, Tuberculosis, and Malaria' (compare Section 2.4.2) there was – at least in the first decade of the new millennium – a risk that AIDS was seen as the only or at least the primary global health problem. As shown in Table 3.6, AIDS is a pandemic with a tremendously high burden of disease. Millions of people have died, millions are living with a fatal disease requiring antiretroviral therapy (ART), and millions are infected every year. There is no doubt that the worldwide effort to fight this disease was necessary. However, there was and is no global 'exceptionality' of AIDS.

---

351 WHO (2019a).

352 WHO (2019a).

353 PHEIC declarations since 2005: wine flu pandemic (2009–2010), polio (2014–today), Ebola in Western Africa (2013–2016), Zika virus epidemic (2015–2016), Kivu Ebola epidemic (2018–2020), COVID-19 pandemic (2020–2023), mpox outbreak 2022–2024. SARS, smallpox, wild type poliomyelitis, and any new subtype of human influenza are automatically declared as PHEICs and without a formal decision of the IHR Emergenccy Committee.

354 http://www.unaids.org/en/.

Globally, HIV/AIDS is 'only' number 16 on the list of major causes of death and number five of the worst infectious disease (2021, compare Figure 3.23). From 1998 to 2008, the disease was number nine on the list and number three of the infectious diseases. Sub-Saharan Africa is the most severely affected (sub-)continent. Here, HIV/AIDS is number seven on the list of major killers, while it was number one from 1997 to 2008 (compare Figure 3.24). Thus, the term 'exceptional' might have been adequate in sub-Saharan Africa for some years, but this time is over and the situation has improved. In 2008, the immune deficiency was responsible for about 3.1% of global deaths, in 2023, it was less than 1%. However, in the African WHO region, about 4.6% are still dying from AIDS.[355] Globally, the figures were not extraordinary[356] and comparing AIDS to the medieval plague, as it was often done, was inappropriate.

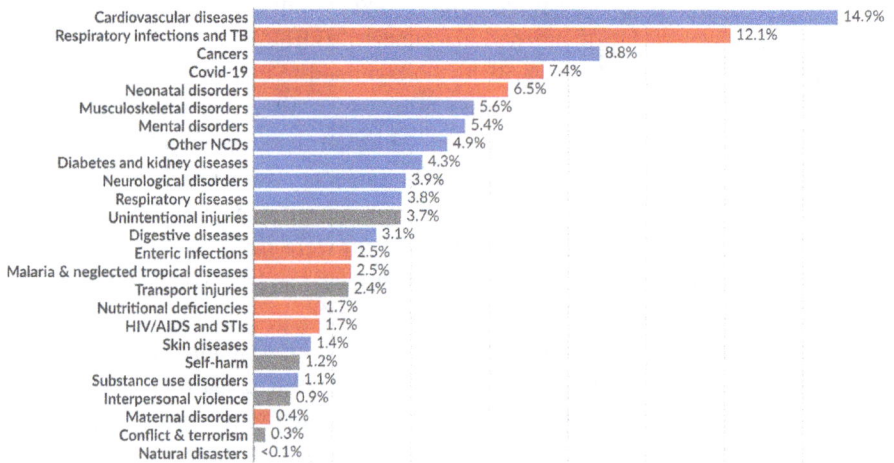

Figure 3.23: Burden of disease by cause, world (2021).[357]

Nevertheless, AIDS is a precarious health problem that the above statistics inadequately capture. Firstly, the situation can be dramatic in some regions, societies, or communities, particularly in sub-Saharan Africa (compare Figure 3.24 and Figure 3.25) where AIDS can still be the top cause of death and the prevalence rates can be very high in certain pockets of the society. Secondly, the death figures say relatively little about the social significance of the disease. Rather, the loss of DALYs is higher, as the middle age groups most affected by HIV infections are weighted more heavily. Thus, HIV/AIDS (and other sexually transmitted infections) accounts for 3.84% of all DALYs

---

355 Source: WHO (2024e).

356 Compare UNAIDS (2010).

357 Source: OurWorldinData – CC-BY@: https://ourworldindata.org/grapher/burden-of-disease-by-cause (18.02.2025).

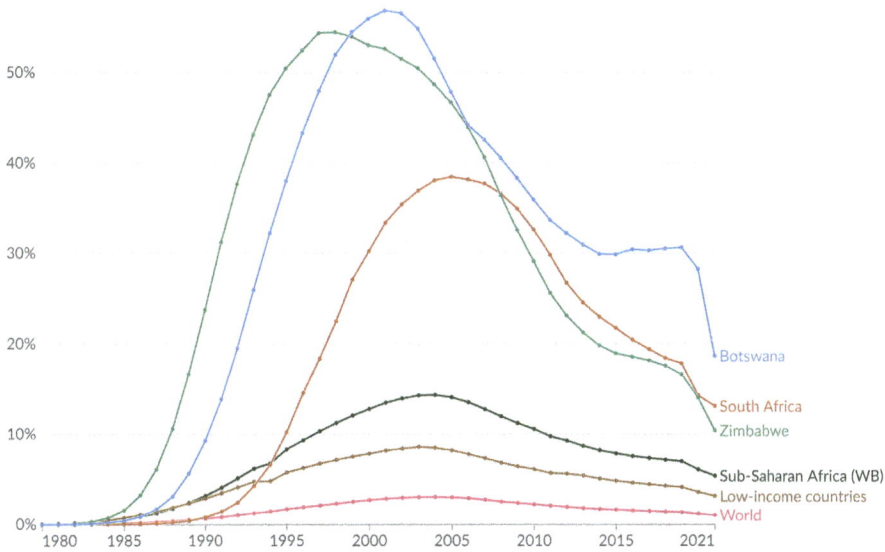

Figure 3.24: Share of all death caused by HIV/AIDS.[358]

Table 3.6: Fact sheet AIDS in 2023.[359]

Statistic	Value
People living with HIV in 2023	39.9 million
Newly infected in 2023	1.3 million
Infected accumulated	88.3 million
Maximum newly infected in 1995	3.3 million
Deaths in 2023	630,000
Deaths accumulated	43.2 million
Maximum deaths in 2004	2.1 million
ART	30.7 million
ART coverage	77%

lost worldwide, and 5.8% in sub-Saharan Africa (2021).[360] In Lesotho, 11,876 DALYs are lost due to HIV/AIDS per 100,000 inhabitants, 8,114 in Zimbabwe, 8,245 in Botswana, and 6,001 in South Africa (2001).[361]

358 Source: OurWorldinData – CC-BY@: https://ourworldindata.org/grapher/share-deaths-aids (18.02.2025).
359 Source: UNAIDS (2024).
360 IHME (2024).
361 WHO (2024f).

Thirdly, the dynamics of HIV spread are extremely high, meaning AIDS has rapidly gone from being a niche phenomenon to a global pandemic and a threat to all development efforts. It is therefore understandable that the global community responded to this infectious disease with measures and intensity that were previously rare. Whether this has always been economically sensible remains to be questioned. However, if all efforts to control the infection were terminated today, we can expect exponential growth again.

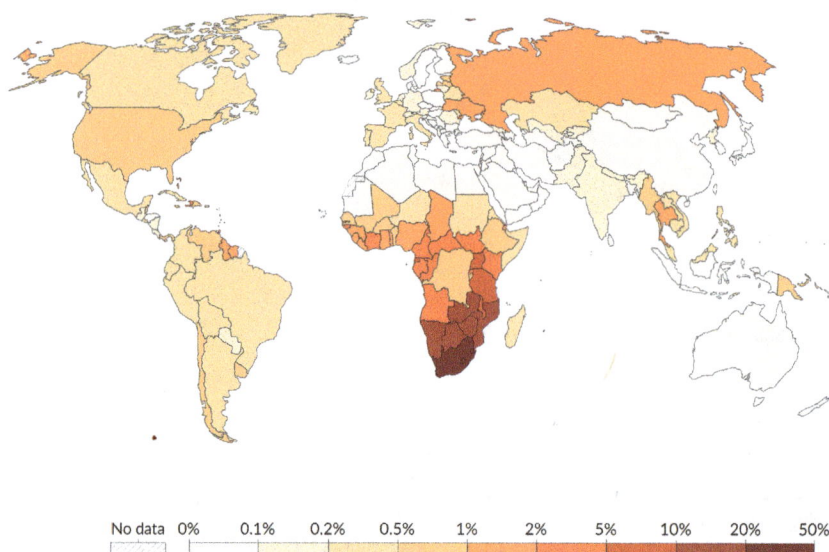

No data 0%   0.1%   0.2%   0.5%   1%   2%   5%   10%   20%   50%

Figure 3.25: Global HIV prevalence (2022).[362]

It is highly likely that the immune deficiency had long persisted in small social groups in Central Africa, but the problem was globally perceived with the appearance of the first cases in the USA in 1981.[363] Just 4 years later, the human pathogenic virus (HIV) was discovered, and since then, no other disease has been researched as extensively as AIDS.

The statistics from UNAIDS show a clear decline in new infections and deaths. The maximum incidence was reached in the year 1997 with 3.02 million new infections. Since then, the statistic almost halved to 1.65 million in the year 2021. In the year 2004, 1.6 million people died from AIDS, while 718,000 people suffered that fate in 2021. With persisting incidence and due to medication, the number of people

---

362 Source: OurWorldinData – CC-BY@: https://ourworldindata.org/grapher/share-of-the-population-infected-with-hiv. (18.02.2025).
363 Ex post some cases could be retroactively tracked back to the year 1959. Compare WHO (1994).

living with AIDS is constantly growing reaching some 40 million in the year 2021. Due to the improved effectiveness of ART, people with HIV can live long and healthy lives if they are diagnosed early and receive effective and sufficient ART. However, in low-income countries, diagnosis and treatment options are not available everywhere.

AIDS is also of great significance because the direct and indirect costs of this disease are comparatively high. If AIDS is not treated with antiretroviral drugs, it leads to death. The loss of human labour during the patient's illness, due to early death, and care by relatives causes significant indirect costs.[364] In the 1990s, many qualified societal leaders fell ill, meaning AIDS had catastrophic effects on the human capital of states, which generally have a very low academic rate. Meanwhile, prevention has significantly improved in the middle and upper classes, so that AIDS is increasingly becoming a problem of the lower class. However, this should not lead to devaluing the deaths of people, even if the monetarily measured indirect costs are lower for them.

In recent years, international aid has also improved access to antiretroviral medications, including highly active antiretroviral therapy (HAART).[365] This was only possible due to international cooperation, including the programmes of the Global Fund. It is estimated that the "scale-up of treatment cost $301billion globally in 1995–2015",[366] and the continued rollout of treatment will require a further $880 billion for drugs and service delivery to achieve the 90-90-90 target of UNAIDS, i.e. that 90% of people living with HIV should have received a diagnosis, and 90% of those should be under ART, and 90% of those should be treated successfully so that no more virus load can be detected. By 2018, the target achievement was 81-82-88. The final objective (or vision) is to end the AIDS pandemic by 2030.

Besides the direct costs of patient treatment, there are also direct costs for prevention. Since the primary mode of transmission of the pathogen is through sexual intercourse, the use of condoms ('safer sex') is considered the most effective prevention. The production cost of a condom is extremely low (estimated at €0.02), but logistics and cultural acceptance pose significant challenges. However, the efficiency evaluation must also consider that condoms prevent the transmission of other STDs.

The second most important route of infection is the transmission from HIV-positive mothers to their children during pregnancy, childbirth, and breastfeeding.[367] It is estimated that without countermeasures, 15–30% of HIV-positive mothers will infect their children during pregnancy and childbirth. An additional 5–20% of infections occur during breastfeeding. The probability of transmission can be significantly reduced through timely administration of antiretroviral drugs, abstaining from breastfeeding, and having a Caesarean section, although the latter two measures are hardly

---

364 Compare Gilliam, Patel, Talwani, et al. (2011) and Forsythe, McGreevey, Whiteside, et al. (2019).

365 Compare Obiako and Muktar (2010) and Ford, Calmy, and Mills (2011).

366 Forsythe, McGreevey, Whiteside, et al. (2019).

367 Prenatal infection: during pregnancy. Perinatal infection: infection post-28th week of pregnancy and up to including the 7th day of life after birth, compare Pschyrembel (1993).

advisable in regions with weak healthcare systems and poor hygiene. These measures (especially antiretroviral medication) are known as 'prevention of mother-to-child transmission' (PMTCT).

Although AIDS is a disease directly transmissible from person to person with low ecological complexity, the possible intervention measures are relatively complex because nonlinear progressions arise in the interdependent system. This will be demonstrated below.

3.3.2.2 Complexity

The following figures are based on a disease dynamic model that simulates HIV spread in a model region.[368] First, the course of HIV infection without intervention will be described. Subsequently, various intervention scenarios will be discussed, focussing on phenomena that typically occur with infectious diseases: nonlinear and time-delayed progressions.

Diffusion Without Intervention

Without AIDS, the population of the region would have raised ceteris paribus to 6,593,482 by 2020 (compare Figure 3.26). Despite the large number of infections and deaths from AIDS, it takes a long time for the demographic effects of this disease to show in the overall population. According to these simulation results, 2,670,096 people lived in the region in 1990, without AIDS, there would have been 2,676,902 (0.25% more). The difference was hardly noticeable; in 1990, AIDS had almost no impact on the overall population. By the year 2000, the population had risen to 3,365,139 inhabitants, without AIDS, it would have been 3,622,042. The difference of 256,904 inhabitants or 7.63% was not considered dramatic by many (health) politicians, and some even regarded the slowed population growth as a success. Only from 2008 did the population begin to decline absolutely. In the first 33 years since the start of the epidemic, AIDS merely reduced population growth, not the population number.

The long incubation and disease duration mean that demographic consequences only become visible with significant time delays after infection. Thus, the number of healthy individuals peaks in 1996 at 2,671,226. Subsequently, this segment of the population declines. The number of HIV-infected individuals peaks in 2011 at 1,083,229, the number of AIDS cases in 2016 (169,294 cases), and the number of AIDS deaths in 2017 (124,921 victims).

The proportions of HIV-infected and AIDS-cases in the total population rise until about 2010, then stabilize at levels of 31% (HIV-infected) and 5% (AIDS cases) of the total population. It is also noted that AIDS played virtually no role until 1990. The case

---

[368] The examplary region had a population of one million inhabitants in the year 1960. For the mathematic model compare Flessa (2002).

numbers were low, and the treatment costs correspondingly insignificant. Even in 2000, AIDS was a disease among many. With 46,336 deaths (in 2000), it was ubiquitous, yet the full dimension of the epidemiological tragedy had not yet become apparent. Since nearly ten times as many HIV-infected individuals live without full-blown AIDS (698,129) as there are AIDS patients (72,537), the burden that AIDS represents for the healthcare system was not fully effective until the year 2000.

The significance of transmission routes (compare Figure 3.27) changes over time. Until 1991, the majority were infected through one-time contacts, with prostitutes as a particularly important high-risk group. Thereafter, the virus had spread so extensively in rural areas that sexual relationships within partnerships became the most important source of infection. About 50–60% of infections are attributable to them.

Remarkably, the increasing number of infections from mother to child is rising. While in 1990 only 2,975 children were infected in this way (4% of the total incidence), the number rises to 24,671 by 2020 (or 19% of all infections). This is primarily due to the increasing prevalence of the virus among women in rural areas leading to constantly rising infection numbers among children. As long as AIDS was confined to prostitutes and men in the city, hardly any perinatal infections were possible. Considering that infected newborns have a very short life expectancy, it becomes clear that AIDS will lead to a significant increase in child mortality. According to the simulation results of this model, the child mortality rate in 2020 without the influence of AIDS would be 109.67 per 1,000 live births, but with AIDS, the figure rises to 181.23. Thus, AIDS completely negates the achievements in combating child and infant mortality of the last decades.

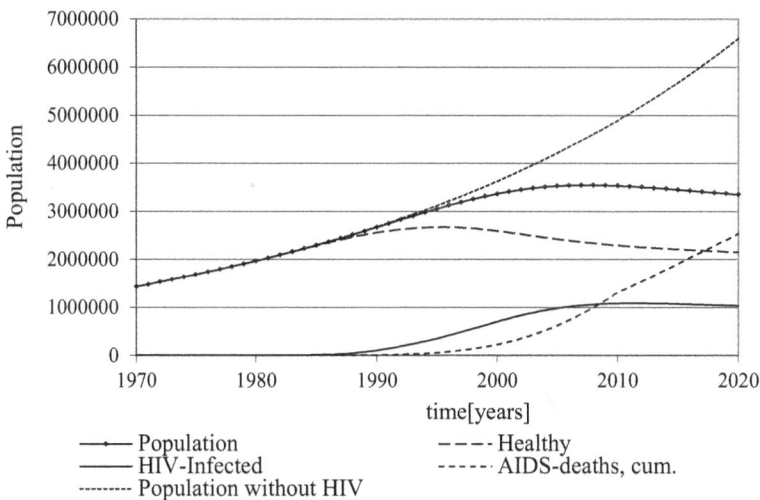

Figure 3.26: Population development and AIDS-related deaths, base simulation.[369]

---

369 Source: Own simulation.

Of a million children whose mothers are HIV-positive, an average of 250,000 is perinatally infected. By the age of 12, the HIV prevalence is nearly 0. At this age, all children who were infected by their mother have already died (compare Figure 3.28).

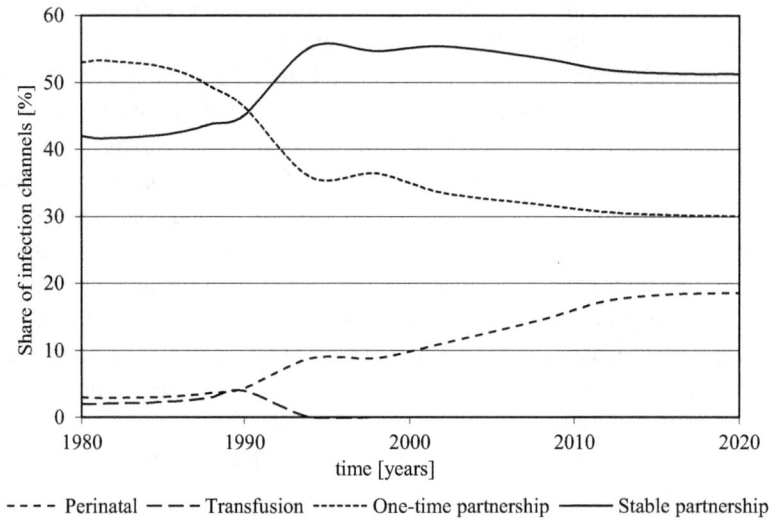

Figure 3.27: Proportions of infection routes, base simulation.[370]

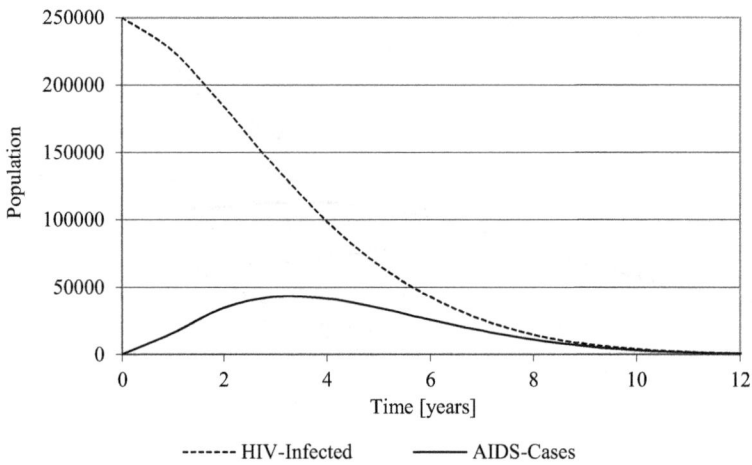

Figure 3.28: Health statuses of 250,000 HIV-positive live births, base simulation.[371]

---

370 Source: Own simulation.
371 Source: Own simulation.

The courses of Figures 3.26–3.28 illustrate the complexity of the epidemiological dynamics of AIDS. The courses are nonlinear and significantly time-delayed, carrying the characteristics of dynamic systems that typically overwhelm human thinking.[372] The healthcare manager must practice this thinking to effectively combat infectious diseases.

Interventions

The consequences of interventions occur with a time delay and are nonlinear. This requires sustainable and consistent implementation planning.

The most effective intervention against AIDS would be an effective vaccine against the HIV virus. Figure 3.29 shows the consequences of vaccination in various scenarios. The standard run represents the case numbers without vaccination. The second curve (Scenario Vaccine) assumes that the vaccination was carried out on 1 January 2001, and protects against AIDS for life. Another simulation (Scenario Half) shows the progression of case numbers when the vaccination is only 50% effective, assuming that this limited effectiveness lasts for life. A scenario (Scenario Short) represents the case where the vaccination is fully effective but loses its protection after 5 years and no booster vaccination occurs. The last curve shows the development of AIDS cases if a lifelong and 100% effective vaccination is only available on 1 January 2006 (Scenario Delayed).[373]

As expected, both a delayed vaccination and a vaccination with limited effectiveness lead to increasing case numbers. Since the prevalence progressively rises, a vaccine that is only available later but is highly effective (delayed) is preferable to a vaccination with low effectiveness (half). Particularly interesting is the trend in case numbers when the vaccination is only effective for 5 years (short). As expected, the curves for vaccine and short are identical until the end of 2005. Subsequently, however, the number of new infections increases so much that by 2020, more people are suffering from AIDS than if no vaccination had been carried out at all. This is due to the fact that people who were protected from HIV infection for five years subsequently have a high risk of infection.

A vaccine that does not provide lifelong protection can thus lead to an acceleration of the demographic and economic consequences if no regular booster vaccinations are carried out. Therefore, vaccination campaigns must be sustainable, otherwise they exacerbate the economic and epidemiological catastrophe that AIDS represents for low-income countries.

---

372 Compare Fleßa (2010b).

373 The purpose of these scenarios is not to forecast the development in a real region and for a certain year, but to point at general rules and processes. Although no vaccine exists against HIV/AIDS, the scenarios can be enlightening about the consequences of vaccination programmes for this disease and many others.

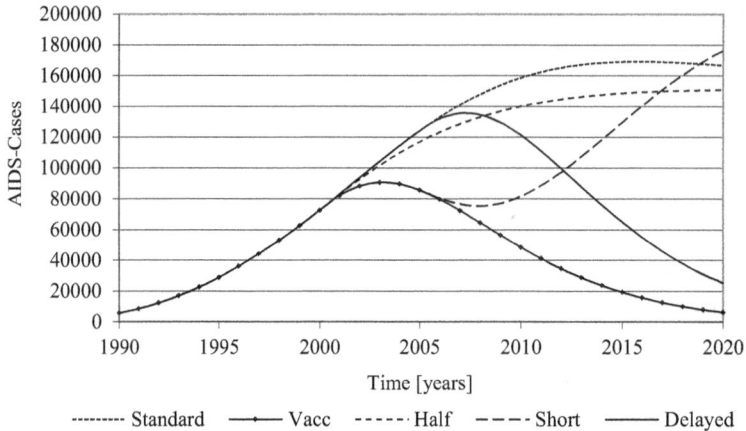

Figure 3.29: Vaccination scenarios.[374]

Since between 92% (in 1990) and 81% (in 2020) of all infections are due to unprotected sexual intercourse, reducing risky sexual relations is the most important means of behavioural prevention. It can be pursued through two strategies: on one hand, education programmes aim to reduce the frequency of intercourse, particularly the number of promiscuous contacts. On the other hand, infections can be reduced by the proper use of condoms, so increasing the acceptance of this contraceptive and knowledge of its use is a focus of many AIDS control projects.

The weighting of both strategies in the optimal portfolio of AIDS control is controversial. Numerous AIDS control programmes distribute condoms free of charge or subsidize the sales price. Many church education programmes, however, advocate sexual abstinence as the most important means of infection prevention. In particular, the Catholic Church rejects the distribution of condoms, as they not only protect against AIDS but are also an effective contraceptive. However, many church leaders of Protestant and Islamic faith communities associate condoms with high promiscuity and a sinful sexual behaviour before or outside of marriage.

Figure 3.30 demonstrates the development of the number of AIDS cases in the model region for different scenarios. The top curve shows the case number without any intervention (Scenario Standard). Another curve depicts the progression if, from the year 2001, a condom is used in all promiscuous relationships that provides 100% protection (Scenario Promis). The frequency of intercourse within the partnership should remain unchanged. Another scenario is the reduction of unprotected sexual intercourse within partnerships by 30% and promiscuous relationships by 50% (Scenario Part). Finally, a scenario should be considered where only professional and occasional prostitutes use condoms (Scenario Prost).

---

374 Source: Own simulation.

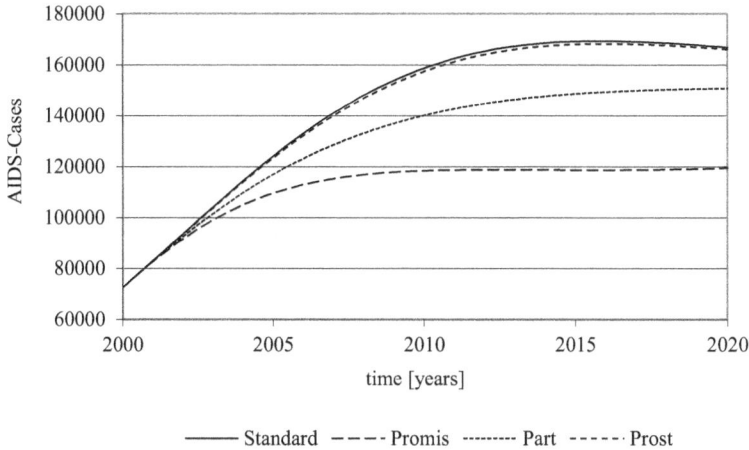

Figure 3.30: Behavioural scenarios.[375]

As expected, the interruption of HIV transmission is most effective when condoms are used in all promiscuous sexual relations (Promis). In this case, the number of AIDS cases in 2020 is only 71.60% of the cases determined in the standard model without any prevention (Standard). A partial reduction of unprotected sexual intercourse, both within the partnership and in one-time relationships (Part), delays the spread of HIV somewhat, but the number of AIDS cases in 2020 will only be 9.60% below the case number without any intervention. Eliminating the route via professional and oc-casional prostitutes (Prost) reduces the number of AIDS cases in 2020 by only 6,861 (0.41%).

The number of condoms required strongly depends on the choice of scenario. If condoms are to be provided for all sexual relations, up to 236 million condoms need to be provided. If only promiscuous contacts are protected, 11.5 million condoms are needed. In the case of a 30% reduction in unprotected relationships within partner-ships and a 50% reduction in promiscuous relationships, 150 million condoms must be used. The number of condoms to protect against infections through contact with pros-titutes is relatively low, totalling only 740,000. The high number of needed condoms points to another complexity factor: logistics. Both the procurement and distribution of condoms in countries with low GDP, large area, and weak infrastructure pose a significant problem. Therefore, social marketing projects often accompany AIDS con-trol measures to ensure widespread availability.[376]

In the literature, the complexity of the epidemiological dynamics of other trans-mission routes (perinatal, transmission in healthcare, and traditional rites) is de-

---

375 Source: Own simulation.
376 Compare Bichmann (2010).

scribed.[377] The few impacts should suffice to demonstrate that the practical healthcare manager must always be an expert on the particular disease they are combating.

3.3.2.3 Antiretroviral Medication

An infection with HIV is still not curable. However, the replication of the virus in the body can be almost completely suppressed by antiretroviral drugs, and in particular by HAART. Various classes of drugs are now available for this purpose, and some are generic and rather cheap. For a long time, HAART was hardly affordable for the majority of low-income countries, but the support of the Global Fund made drugs available for many. By the year 2000, only 2% of the HIV-positive world population (0% of sub-Saharan Africa and 0% of low-income countries) were under ART, in the year 2021, 79% of people with HIV in sub-Saharan Africa, 78% in low-income countries, and 75% in the world were under the appropriate drug regime. The Global Fund alone claims that 24.5 million people were under ART based on its programmes, and 59 million lives would have been saved by their anti-AIDS activities.

Access to ART is viewed by many as a human right, and doubts about this intervention are rarely expressed, as it would be against 'political correctness'.[378] Who would want to deny suffering AIDS patients the lifesaving medications? However, from the perspective of healthcare management, there is at least a need to reflect on the medication policy, as three fundamental problems must be centre and addressed: opportunity costs, sustainability, and absorption capacity.

Opportunity costs are the costs of the lost alternative through a specific use of resources, i.e. resources that flow into ART are not available for alternative use. This affects both the prevention of HIV and the treatment of other diseases. Every euro spent on HIV medications is missing from educational programmes. And every euro that flows into ART can no longer be used to strengthen the overall healthcare system, and thus the treatment of other diseases. The statement by the Global Fund that it has saved x lives through ART is meaningless unless it is also specified how many lives could have been saved if the resources had been invested in education or the treatment of diarrhoea and birth complications.[379]

The opportunity cost argument is meaningless if there is no resource scarcity or if the resources are only available for a specific purpose, i.e. if there is no resource competition. In fact, it is often argued that donors who provide their funds for ART would not finance anything else. However, this shows a lack of strategic perspective,

---

377 Compare Farrar, Hotez, Junghanss, et al. (2023).
378 Compare Marseille, Hofmann, and Kahn (2002), MacKellar (2005), Shiffman (2006), Boerma and Stansfield (2007), and Lyman and Wittels (2010).
379 The dilemma of opportunity costs was first described by Fuchs in his famous book *Who Shall Live?* Fuchs (1974).

as in the long term, it would certainly be possible to redirect funds from ART to prevention and from AIDS to general health promotion, if desired.

Estimates of what ART would cost in developing countries vary widely.[380] However, there is agreement that ART will likely need to be subsidized on a large scale for at least another generation. This raises the issue of sustainability, i.e. it must be clarified which institutions are willing and able to finance ART and all its consequences long-term. Since there are also (fashion) waves in international healthcare, it can be doubted that HIV/AIDS will still have the same priority in 20 years, even if its epidemiological significance remains the same.

For the individual patient, of course, extending their life by a few years is a significant success. Systemically, however, ART only makes sense if financing can be maintained until medications are available that not only prevent the outbreak of AIDS but truly heal the disease. Otherwise, long-term consequences develop that are hardly justifiable.

In the short term, ART significantly reduces AIDS-related mortality. However, the long-term complexity is much higher, as there are feedback effects. On one hand, the use of an antiretroviral drug can contribute to resistance development, especially in areas where regular medication logistics and intake cannot be guaranteed. On the other hand, it is disputed how the availability of a medication affects sexual behaviour. The message that AIDS can be 'cured', which is objectively false but subjectively very tempting, could reduce the fear of unprotected intercourse.

Thirdly, the absorption capacity of a country must also be considered, i.e. "ability of a country or organization to receive aid and use it effectively".[381] From the perspective of healthcare management, it is the recipient's ability to receive financial resources and use them according to the contract, where the unit of measurement is the impact of the received resource on the original goal. Corruption, high overhead costs, and especially inefficiency are the major problem areas here. The higher the amounts to fight AIDS compared to their own health budget, the more likely the funds are to promote corruption, produce a bureaucratic overhead, and ultimately mostly disappear on the way to those actually affected. Given that subsidies from abroad make up a significant portion of the funds for some countries and not a few non-governmental organizations, one should not be surprised that corruption has become one of the main problems in healthcare, and promoting so-called 'good governance' has become a focus of international co-operation.[382]

Figure 3.31 summarizes the first two aspects again. This is not about rejecting ART in developing countries. Rather, the side effects, feedback, and consequences must be centre and considered from the beginning to act responsibly. This requires thinking in terms of interdependencies, nonlinearities, and time delays.

---

380 Compare Editorial (2006).
381 Bhutta (2006).
382 Compare Lewis (2006).

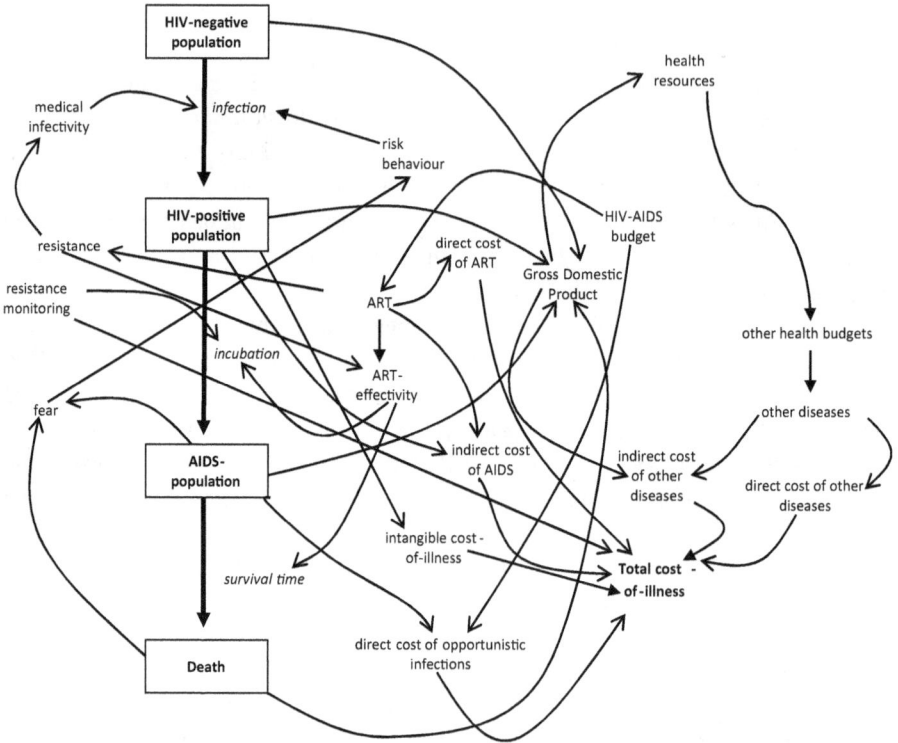

Figure 3.31: Long-term effects of antiretroviral therapy.[383]

In summary, AIDS continues to be an infectious disease of great importance for international healthcare management in the coming years. Monocausal conclusions, short-term interventions, quick actions, and simple thinking will fail due to the complexity of the epidemiological dynamics. International healthcare management is challenged to analyse these interconnections and propose solutions that accommodate this complexity.

3.3.3 Case Study: Malaria

3.3.3.1 Relevance

Malaria is an example of a disease transmitted by a vector, thus having a more complex transmission route than AIDS. It is a parasitic disease caused by protozoa of the genus *Plasmodium* and is by far the most widespread tropical disease. Estimates of the number of cases vary significantly and are strongly dependent on rainfall. Only a

---

383 Source: Own.

few decades ago, a number of up to 500 million cases and up to 4 million deaths were cited annually,[384] but the figures went down. In 2022, some 249 million cases with 608,000 malaria deaths were recorded globally (in 2019 before the COVID-19 pandemic, the numbers were 232 million and 568,000),[385] i.e. the mortality rate was 14.3 deaths per 100,000 population at risk. Currently, 85 countries have endemic malaria, and about 50% of the world population is at risk of contracting malaria. In some countries, malaria was eradicated but they are latently threatened by re-invasion (compare Figure 3.32). However, the vast majority of cases (96%) and deaths (98%) occur in sub-Saharan Africa, and here in particular in a few countries. "More than 50% of all deaths occurred in just four countries – Nigeria (31%), the Democratic Republic of the Congo (12%), Niger (6%), and Tanzania (4%). Around 70% of the global malaria burden is concentrated in 11 countries: Burkina Faso, Cameroon, the Democratic Republic of the Congo, Ghana, India, Mali, Mozambique, Niger, Nigeria, Uganda, and, Tanzania."[386]

As shown in Figure 3.23 in Section 3.3.2.1, malaria (and other neglected diseases) is only number 15 of the top causes of burden of disease worldwide, but it is number three in sub-Saharan Africa, where about 10% of the burden of disease are caused by malaria (and other neglected diseases) in sub-Saharan Africa (2.5% worldwide). However, malaria has still a higher relevance than HIV/AIDS in most countries and regions of the world. Africa is the focus of malaria research, and only 7% of the population in sub-Saharan Africa lives outside malaria areas.[387]

The clinical picture of malaria was described in antiquity. The term derives from the Latin 'mala aria' ('bad air'), as it was suspected that the frequent fevers in the marshes of central Italy were caused by miasmas. In reality, it was malaria that claimed numerous lives even in Roman times.[388] In Europe, malaria was feared until the beginning of this century. However, the disease was of greater significance in the USA. The most dangerous form of malaria (malaria tropica) was likely introduced by African slaves and became the infectious disease with the highest prevalence in the southern states. During the Civil War, 8,000 soldiers died from malaria, and more than 1.2 million cases were counted among the soldiers.[389]

The eradication of malaria in many parts of the world is partly due to the control measures initiated at the beginning of this century by various states and foundations (e.g. Rockefeller Foundation). In 1955, the 14th World Health Assembly resolved to eradicate malaria worldwide, primarily through the control of the carrier (*Anopheles*

---

384 Compare Greenwood, Bojang, Whitty, et al. (2005), Breman, Alilio, and Mills (2004), and WHO (2008c).
385 Source: WHO (2023).
386 Venkatesan (2024).
387 Compare Müller (2011).
388 Compare Oaks (1991).
389 Compare Bruce-Chwatt (1988).

mosquito) using cyclic spraying of house interior walls with DDT. At that time, many shared the euphoric illusion that malaria could be eradicated worldwide by 1970.[390]

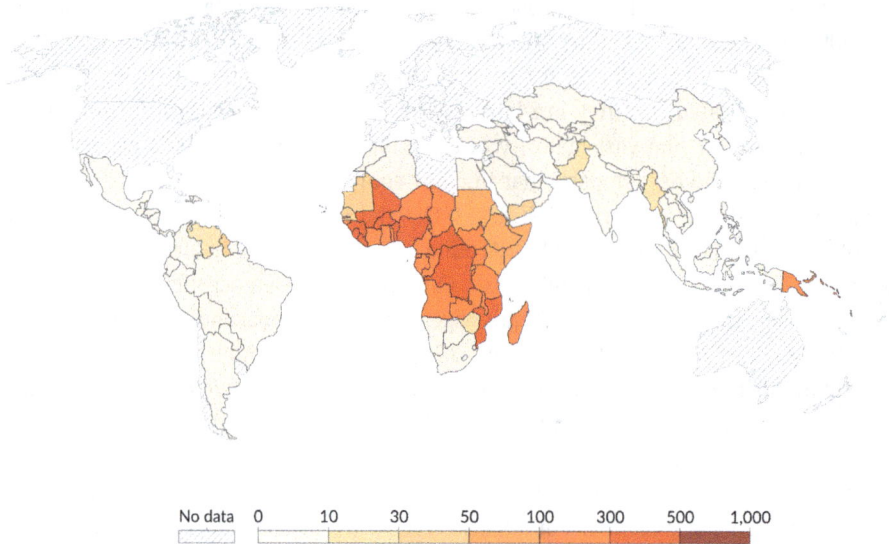

No data   0   10   30   50   100   300   500   1,000

Figure 3.32: Incidence of malaria (2022): new cases per annum per 1,000 population at risk.[391]

While significant successes have been recorded in the subtropics and temperate zones, there is general frustration today regarding the successes of these control measures in the tropics. In the 1970s, the attempt to eradicate malaria was abandoned and later reduced to malaria containment ('Roll Back Malaria') as both *Anopheles* mosquitoes and *Plasmodia* became resistant to cost-effective drugs.[392] Despite considerable investments (e.g. by the Global Fund and the Gates Foundation) in malaria control, the goal of eradicating the disease remains illusory as long as there is no effective vaccine.

Plasmodium is a protozoa (unicellular organism) which is much more complex and difficult to attack than a virus (e.g. smallpox). Consequently, it took long to develop a vaccine that has at least some effectiveness. However, to date, there are two vaccines on the market that promise the prevention of malaria tropica in children living in malaria endemic areas. RTS,S vaccine was prequalified by WHO in 2022, R21

---

390 "This is the DDT era of malariology. For the first time it is economically feasible for nations, however undeveloped and whatever the climate, to banish malaria completely from their borders" (Russell 1955).
391 Source: OurWorldinData – CC-BY@: https://ourworldindata.org/malaria (22.04.2025).
392 Compare Jamison, Creese, and Prentice (1999).

malaria vaccine in 2023, i.e. WHO ensures vaccine safety and quality of the vaccines and (partly) recommends their use. The main problem is the complex logistics: both vaccines must be provided to children in a schedule of four doses from around 5 months of age. A fifth dose is not obligatory and might be given 1 year later in holoendemic areas.[393] However, a vaccine requiring mothers to bring their (healthy) children 4–5 times to a dispensary is a challenge.

The spread of malaria depends on temperature and rainfall. Figure 3.33 shows the dependency. This arises firstly because the carrier mosquito needs water for breeding, and secondly from the dependence of *Anopheles* larvae and *Plasmodium* maturation on temperature. If the temperature falls below 20 °C, the larvae cannot mature into adult insects, and the *Plasmodium* does not develop further within the *Anopheles*. Therefore, dry areas and high altitudes in the tropics are free of malaria. Traditionally, dense rainforests were also malaria-free. However, human interventions (e.g. irrigation, deforestation) are making more and more areas risk-pron.

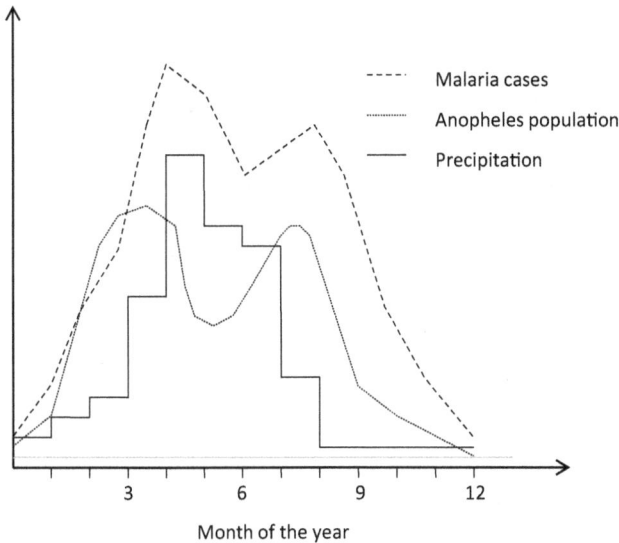

Figure 3.33: Rainfall, Anopheles population, and malaria cases.[394]

The economic significance of malaria as a development barrier for tropical countries cannot be overstated. On one hand, malaria control itself requires significant resour-

393 Compare WHO (2024h).
394 Source: Diesfeld, Falkenhorst, Razum, et al. (2001).

ces, and on the other hand, important labour forces are lost to the economy due to illness and death.[395]

Various authors have estimated the loss of labour due to malaria. They assume that between 5 and 20 (average of 7) man-days per malaria infection are lost to the national economy. A study from India shows that the number of working days lost for an adult case of malaria (11.0) is higher than for the caregiver of a paediatric case (7.1), but this is still a relevant loss of productivity. In addition, children lose on average 9.9 days at school.[396] For Africa, the WHO assumes a loss of 10 man-days per malaria attack, where primarily severe cases of malaria tropica occur. Since up to eight attacks per year can occur in some areas, this corresponds to a malaria-related loss of up to 22% of annual labour. As shown in Table 3.7, the indirect cost (due to loss of labour) is always higher than the treatment cost. Particularly problematic is that malaria occurs especially during the planting season (rainy season), thus endangering the food base of subsistence farmers.[397]

Table 3.7: Cost of malaria (US$).[398]

	Mozambique (2017–2018)		Ethiopia (2018)	India (2005–2014)	
	Uncomplicated malaria	Severe malaria		High transmission	Low transmission
Provider cost	0.35	2.16	1.10	60.90	42.50
Medication and non-medical cost	0.04	0.23	13.50	122.10	99.00
Transport cost	0.34	1.16	12.00	63.30	29.20
Indirect cost	16.67	154.30	12.40	410.00	385.10
Total	17.40	157.85	39.00	656.30	555.80

The treatment of malaria patients absorbs a significant part of the private and public health budget. Table 3.7 shows some examples of treatment costs of malaria patients. However, the burden on the health budget from malaria is greater than these averages suggest, as malaria in most areas exhibits strong seasonal fluctuations.[399] Thus,

---

395 Compare Goodman, Coleman, and Mills (2000), Andrade, Noronha, Diniz, et al. (2022), and Conteh, Shuford, Agboraw, et al. (2021).

396 Compare Singh, Saha, Chand, et al. (2019).

397 Compare Oaks (1991).

398 Source: Alonso, Chaccour, Elobolobo, et al. (2019), Tefera, Sinkie, and Daka (2020), and Singh, Saha, Chand, et al. (2019).

399 Regions that display high levels of malaria transmission throughout the whole year (holoendemic regions) also feature significantly seasonal fluctuations.

relatively large emergency capacities need to be maintained. Accurate planning of workloads is difficult due to the weather dependence of malaria case numbers.

An analysis of the epidemiological processes of malaria requires understanding the complex system of different interdependent regulatory circuits. This includes vector ecology, i.e. the cycle of egg laying, larval stage, and adult insects. Furthermore, the biting behaviour of the mosquitoes must be considered. Ecological parameters (e.g. availability of breeding sites, rainfall, and temperature) thus play a significant role in the spread of malaria. Furthermore, human cultural behaviour must be included. Since *Anopheles* only bite in the evening and at night, the human's location (outside or inside the house, in bed, etc.) is significant. Also, the place of residence (e.g. altitude) and living conditions (e.g. window tightness) must be considered. Finally, population growth and the corresponding pressure to migrate to malaria areas play a role. Accordingly, the model complexity is significantly higher than with AIDS.

3.3.3.2 Complexity

The spread of malaria depends on temperature and precipitation, as demonstrated by the following strategic simulation results, which provide insights into the complexity of epidemiological processes and potential interventions. The model distinguishes two regions (300 and 1,500 m altitude) and maps temperature and precipitation patterns in East Africa. Initially, the dynamics of the *Anopheles* population are examined. Subsequently, the incidence and prevalence of malaria in the human population are considered. Finally, the simulation results of various scenarios are presented.[400]

Figure 3.34 shows the deviations of *Anopheles* populations from their annual average (100%) over time. In both region 1 and region 2, the largest number of *Anopheles* is present in April, at the peak of the major rainy season. At this time, sufficient breeding sites are available, and temperatures are high enough to ensure successful breeding. Decreasing rainfall until July leads to a significant reduction in the number of *Anopheles* in both regions because the breeding sites diminish, and the temperature prolongs the breeding period, thus requiring relatively more breeding sites. In August, it is too cold in both regions to sustain successful breeding. The number of mosquitoes strongly declines, but it is never zero for both regions (although the graph might indicate this with 4.8% of the average in region 1 in September and 0.4% in region 2 in October).

In September, the average temperature rises above 20 °C in region 1, allowing larvae to develop. Increasing rainfall during the minor rainy season then leads to another rise in *Anopheles* populations. Consequently, in October, at the peak of the minor rainy season, a second maximum of the *Anopheles* population occurs in region 1. In region 2, however, the average temperature during this period is not sufficient for the eggs to develop into *Anopheles*. Eggs and larvae die off, and the increase in

---

400 Compare Fleßa (1999) and Flessa (2002).

suitable water bodies for breeding has no impact on the *Anopheles* population. It is not until November that the average temperature rises above 20 °C, allowing eggs to develop into *Anopheles* again. However, the population does not exhibit high dynamics, as rainfall decreases this month.

The number of infectious mosquitoes, however, does not fluctuate as significantly as the total number of mosquitoes or the number of non-infected mosquitoes. The proportion of infectious mosquitoes increases during the major rainy season in region 1, but their rise is much less pronounced than that of the entire population. Accordingly, the risk of transmission per bite decreases. During the colder months, the population decreases, especially since no new mosquitoes are bred. The high proportion of older insects, which have lived long enough to be likely infected, causes the probability of infection per bite to significantly increase during this period. Since *Anopheles* have an average lifespan of only 1 month, the number of older mosquitoes at the onset of the minor rainy season in October is relatively low. The rainy season and warm temperatures lead not only to a rapid increase in the *Anopheles* population but also to a decrease in the proportion of older animals in the population, thus reducing the infection risk per bite. Consequently, the total number of mosquitoes can only provide limited information on the malaria risk at any given time of year.

The average infestation of *Anopheles* in region 1 is 25.64%. This means that, on average, one-quarter of all bites throughout the year are potentially infectious. In region 2, due to climatic conditions, malaria is significantly less prevalent, so, on average, only 4.52% of *Anopheles* is dangerous. Here too, the proportion of infectious mosquitoes in the total population is inversely related, in months with high mosquito activity, relatively few mosquitoes are infectious, while in months with low *Anopheles* density, an individual bite is relatively dangerous. For example, in November, the probability of being bitten by an infectious *Anopheles* is only 4.42% in region 1, while it is 16.05% in region 2.

Morbidity also varies between regions. While region 1 suffers an average of 4.05 infections per year, region 2 only experiences 0.37 infections. Thus, only 0.65% of the population in region 2 suffers from malaria on average, while the morbidity in the valley region is 7.50%. Consequently, malaria prevalence in region 1 is approximately 11.5 times as high as in region 2. This is also reflected in the mortalities: on average, about 2.02% of the population in region 1 dies from malaria each year, compared to only 0.24% in region 2. The percentage risk of death per malaria case in region 2 (0.63%) is higher than in region 1 (0.50%), as 53.14% of the population in region 1 are semi-immune, while only 7.47% of the population in region 2 have this protection.

Figure 3.35 exemplarily presents the incidence and prevalence of malaria in region 1. As expected, the incidence (number of new infections) precedes the prevalence (number of sick individuals) by about 15 days, as there is an incubation period from infection to the outbreak of the disease. According to the occurrence of *Anopheles*, there are two peaks of malaria in region 1 at the beginning of May (global maximum) and the beginning of January (local maximum). In region 2, there is a unimodal

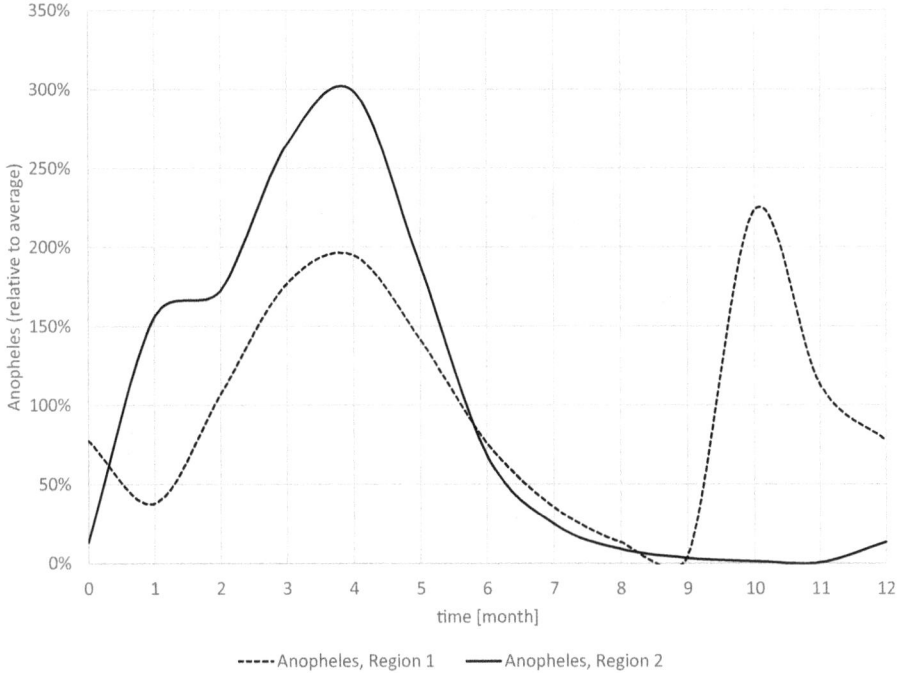

Figure 3.34: Anopheles population.[401]

course with significantly higher variation. The coefficient of variation is 61.33% in region 1, and 135.19% in region 2, indicating that fluctuations are much less in holoendemic regions (region 1) than in other regions (region 2).

The incidence of malaria strongly depends on the mosquito population, which is governed by temperature and precipitation. Since transmission and larval development are subject to minimum temperatures, the daily emergence rate is not a continuous function but can increase suddenly. Consequently, the incidence does not progress smoothly either. Only the prevalence appears as a smoothed curve. Since at time $t = 270$ (September) in region 1, *Anopheles* can successfully breed for the first time after the dry season, fluctuations are particularly strong during this period. Later, they become less pronounced.

In region 1, the number of infections does not fluctuate as much as the number of *Anopheles* (coefficient of variation of *Anopheles*: 69.36%; coefficient of variation of malaria: 60.30%). Especially, the strong growth of the mosquito population during the minor rainy season (October and November) is not reflected in high incidence or prevalence rates. This is primarily because the higher mosquito density is compensated by a lower risk per bite, as many young mosquitoes live and bite, which are not

---

401 Source: Own simulation.

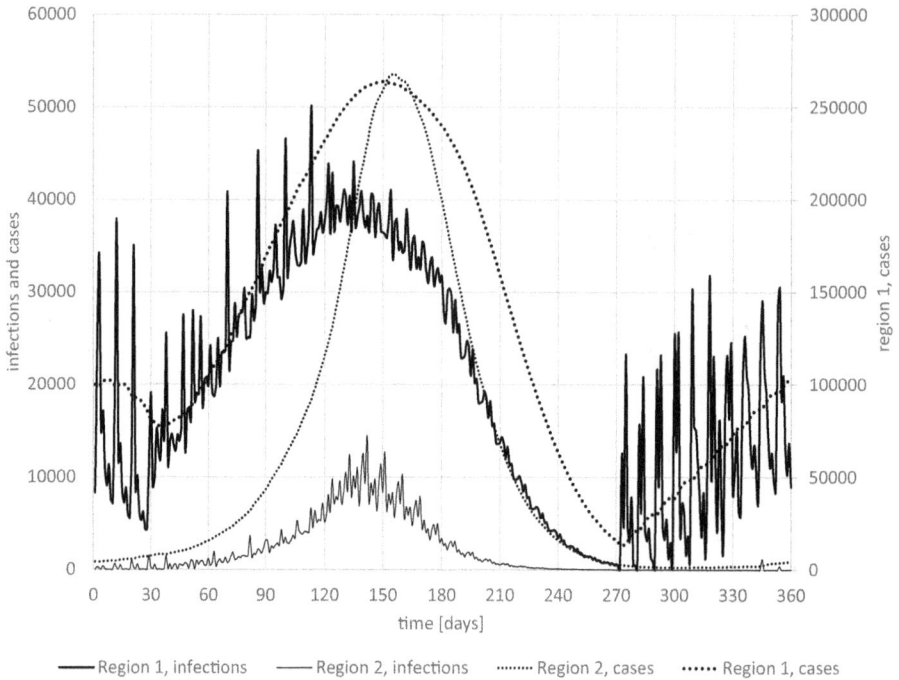

Figure 3.35: Malaria incidence and prevalence in region 1.[402]

yet infectious. In region 2, malaria occurs epidemically in June, with fluctuations in malaria prevalence (coefficient of variation: 131.24%) being higher than the variation in the *Anopheles* population (coefficient of variation: 105.79%). Consequently, region 1 and region 2 behave oppositely.

The complexity of the ecosystem is also reflected in the low predictability of the impact of intervention measures. Simple, linear models must fail. This will be demonstrated using the example of vector control and a bed net programme.

Larvae and adult *Anopheles* are killed using chemical (larvicides, insecticides) or biological (e.g. larva-eating fish, sterile insect technique) measures. The method of choice for a long time was the regular indoor spraying of house walls with DDT ('indoor spraying').[403] This has proven to be an efficient method of vector control, as the relevant *Anopheles* species are endophilic and endophagic, typically seeking their victims inside houses and resting on the inner walls after feeding before they set off to lay eggs. A certain portion of the mosquitoes is thereby killed. Figure 3.36 shows the consequences of indoor spraying. The figure assumes that a constant annual budget is invested.

---

402 Source: Own simulation.
403 Compare Müller (2011).

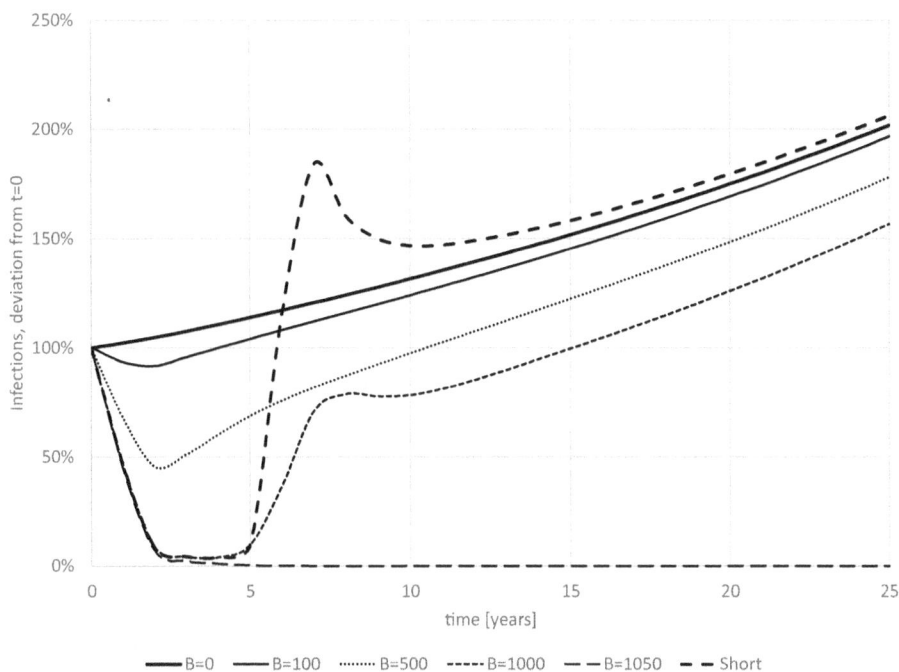

Figure 3.36: Consequences of indoor spraying (region 1).[404]

The solid bold line represents the standard without intervention, where 100% refers to the number of infections before the intervention starts. The incidence increases proportionally to the population number, meaning a growing population also leads to an increasing number of infections. The introduction of indoor spraying with a constant annual budget of US$100,000 ($B = 100$) reduces the number of infections in both regions compared to the initial situation. In region 1, 12.62 million fewer infections are counted over 25 years, while in region 2, 4.43 million infections are prevented. The same applies to a fivefold annual budget ($B = 500$).

With high annual budgets ($B = 1{,}000$), an interesting pattern emerges, the number of infections initially decreases significantly. However, the intensity of indoor spraying is not sufficient to completely eradicate malaria in the holoendemic region. This is only possible with an even higher budget ($B = 1{,}050$), where after about 4 years, malaria is completely eradicated. Now the spraying programmes can be discontinued without leading to a new outbreak of the disease.[405] With lower budgets ($B = 1{,}000$), however, the effectiveness of the spraying diminishes. This is partly due to the declining immunity of the population. As the number of infections decreases, so does the

---

404 Source: Own simulation.
405 The model excludes an external reinvasion.

protection of the population, increasing the risk of infection per bite. Additionally, the population grows, so the annual budget must be spread over an increasing number of houses. There is a critical point beyond which the proportion of sprayed houses is no longer sufficient to contain malaria. This leads to a new wave of infections. Consequently, long-term prevention programmes can only be sustainable if their budget grows in parallel with the population. This has been insufficiently considered in international healthcare management so far.

If we assume that malaria, with its host-vector-breeding ground interaction, is an ecosystem in equilibrium (although a very unhealthy equilibrium for humans), indoor spraying can be seen as a perturbance of this ecosystem. For all budgets <1,050, this ecosystem is resilient, i.e. it has the ability to find back into a new equilibrium of constant growth. Most impressive is the behaviour of the system under the condition that indoor spraying is terminated after 5 years (Short). Such a limited intervention has only a temporary effect while the epidemic beats back after the interventions is terminated. Already in year $t = 6$, the number of infections is as high as it had been without interventions because the huge number of unprotected children without semi-immunity, who grew up in years without major malaria threat, are 'victims' of the plasmodia. In future years, the situation is worse than it would have been without the interventions. Thus, interventions must be highly financed to eradicate the disease ($B = 1,050$) or they must be financed for a very long time and with a growth rate that is at least as high as the population growth rate.

The mosquito net is currently the most important form of primary prevention against malaria. *Anopheles* primarily bites at night while humans are in bed and asleep. During this time, they can be effectively protected by bed nets. Since the early 1990s, there has been intense debate about whether the widespread use of impregnated bed nets has a sustainable effect on the prevalence and incidence of malaria. The impregnation is toxic, causing some of the *Anopheles* that attempt to bite to die. Most importantly, the impregnated nets have a repelling effect, preventing most *Anopheles* from attempting to bite from the outset.

Proponents argue that, especially toddlers, can be relatively easily protected from bites, as they spend the entire night in bed. They have a particularly high malaria-related mortality, so they are especially worth protecting. Older children and adults are active at night, so they will not benefit as much from nets. Some short-term field studies by proponents of impregnated bed nets have shown that mortality among toddlers can be significantly reduced.

However, there were also scientists who warned against a widespread use of bed nets.[406] They argued that immunity, particularly during the first years of life, is built up. Nets prevent toddlers from being bitten and thus becoming immune. Older children and adults will then become sick more frequently and severely. Moreover, the

---

406 An overview is provided by Enayati and Hemingway (2010).

total number of bites will hardly decrease. *Anopheles* will instead focus their activities on older age groups, as they are deterred from biting toddlers. This can lead to a "mortality rebound"[407] significantly reducing the cost-effectiveness of bed nets.

The following will examine the effects of discontinuing the bed net programme after 5 years. Figure 3.37 shows the results for region 1.

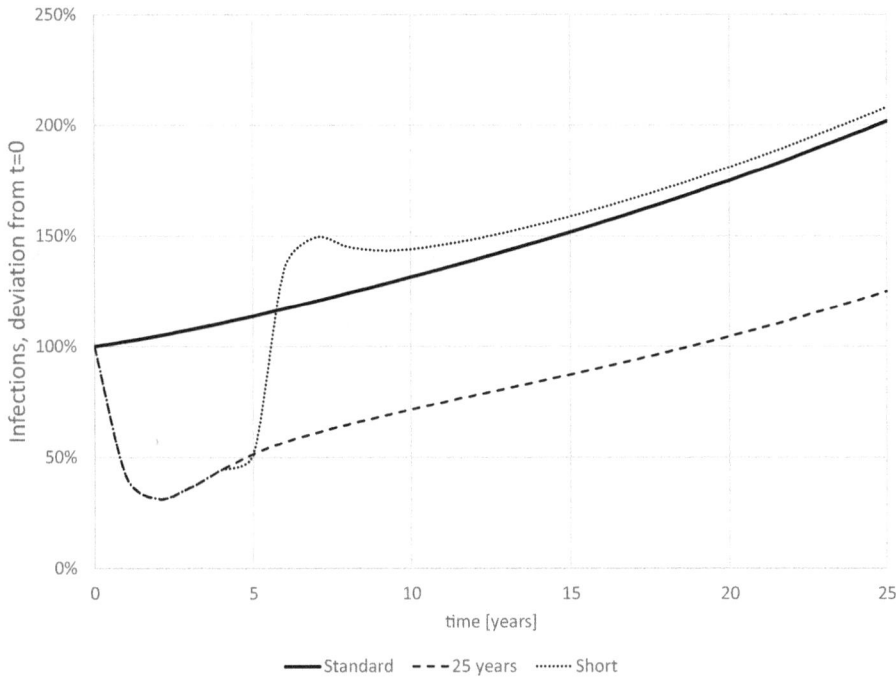

Figure 3.37: Bed net programme, region 1.[408]

The continuous use of bed nets for children under 5 years has a clearly positive effect on malaria incidence and mortality. However, the impact in region 1 is greatest in the first 2 years. Afterwards, the number of infections and deaths begins to rise again. Thus, short-term studies provide a misleading picture of the effectiveness of bed nets.

The analysis also demonstrates that bed net programmes can have catastrophic consequences if they are not long-term. A mosquito net tears easily, and the impregnation (especially in older models) can lose its effectiveness unless it is re-applied several times a year. Then, the number of infections increases significantly. During the 5-year bed net programme, no immunity is built up in toddlers. They are now unprotected, get

---

407 Goodman, Coleman, and Mills (2000).
408 Source: Own simulation.

bitten, and infected. Older children and adults, who were semi-immune before the introduction of bed nets, have lost their resistance and are therefore highly vulnerable. In region 1, the population's immunity rebuilds relatively quickly. In region 2, it takes much longer due to the low frequency of bites. Thus, the number of infections and deaths in region 2 from the sixth year onwards is significantly higher than without a bed net programme. At its peak, there are 62.5% more infections than without the programme. This again shows that health interventions must be long-term, otherwise they can backfire.

3.3.4 Case Study: COVID-19

3.3.4.1 Relevance

Coronavirus disease 2019 (usually referred to as COVID-19) is an infectious disease primarily transmitted by airborne particles and caused by the coronavirus SARS-CoV-2.[409] Like SARS-CoV-1, the virus crossed-over from animals to humans, i.e. COVID-19 is a zoonosis. It is highly likely that it persisted in a bat population for long and took the pathway to humans (with pangolins as intermediate hosts) in Hubei Province, China. After the virus infected first humans, it caused one of the most severe pandemics in recorded history with some 764 million (officially confirmed) cases and more than 7 million deaths during the time of the official pandemic from 11 March 2020 to 5 May 2023.[410]

In comparison to former pandemics, the outbreak is well documented and the diffusion happened in speed of the rocket age. The first cases were reported in December 2019 in Wuhan, Hubei Province, China. The number of cases and deaths in this city rose exponentially with tremendous challenges to the healthcare system and the society.[411] On 7 January 2020, the Chinese Centre for Disease Control and Prevention (CDC) detected the new human coronavirus and sequenced the whole genome of the virus, which was subsequently identified as the pathogen of the disease.[412] Not even a month later (30 January 2020), WHO declared a PHEIC, and only 6 weeks later, WHO had to declare a COVID-19 pandemic (11 March 2020). While the virus is still causing victims, Figure 3.38 shows that the incidence has strongly declined. The figure indicates that the disease did not affect all locations equally and at the same time. The pandemic flowed in waves over the regions, countries, and continents depending on the emergence of new stems, the seasons (with cold seasons causing a new wave), and the respective counter measures.

---

409 Severe acute respiratory syndrome (SARS). SARS-CoV-1 caused the SARS outbreak in 2002–2003.
410 Compare WHO (2024o).
411 Compare Li, Guan, Wu, et al. (2020).
412 Compare Zhu, Zhang, Wang, et al. (2020), Lu, Zhao, Li, et al. (2020), Wu, Zhao, Yu, et al. (2020), and Zhou, Yang, Wang, et al. (2020).

The symptoms are – most likely – well known to all readers by personal experience. The majority of cases are asymptomatic or have mild symptoms such as fever, sore throat, cough, fatigue, loss of taste and smell, etc. The first wave caused a higher mortality, but later waves had a rather low death toll due to the reduced fatality rate and improved medical responses. In total, about 0.92% of all recorded cases died during the pandemic.

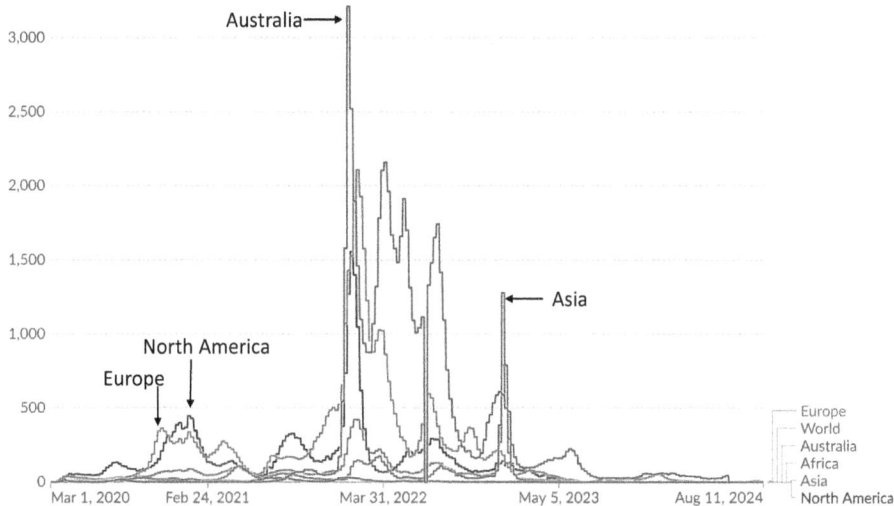

Figure 3.38: Daily new confirmed COVID-19 cases per million people.[413]

Countries reacted differently to the new threat and developed various strategies ranging from laissez-faire to zero COVID.[414] Tanzania, for instance, denied the risk of COVID-19 for quite some time under its late president John Magufuli (1959–2021) so that the country hardly implemented any measures against the disease until his successor, Samia Suluhu Hassan, changed the strategy.[415] Other countries, such as the Great Britain and Sweden, tried to achieve a herd immunity by giving the virus a free rein while protecting specifically vulnerable groups, such as the elderly. Few countries, such as Australia, New Zealand, and Southern Korea,[416] followed the zero-COVID strategy, which could only be achieved by aggressive containment. Once the virus was eradicated in a country, outbreaks could be prevented by strict border control. The majority of countries, however, tried to find the right balance between laissez-faire and aggressive containment.

---

413 Source: OurWorldinData – CC-BY@: https://ourworldindata.org/explorers/covid (18.02.2025).
414 Compare Wu, Neill, De Foo, et al. (2021).
415 Compare Hamisi, Dai, and Ibrahim (2023) and Mtani and Ngohengo (2023).
416 Compare Blakely, Thompson, Carvalho, et al. (2020), Baker, Kvalsvig, Verrall, et al. (2020), and Philippe and Marques (2021).

They accept that the disease cannot be eliminated so that a certain number of infections, cases, and deaths will occur. However, by tailored interventions, the epidemic can be delayed and certain population groups can be protected until a vaccine is available and/ or the herd immunity is sufficiently high without overburdening the healthcare system ('flatten the curve').[417] For this purpose, they have developed a wide set of instruments.

Figure 3.39 gives an overview of mitigation measures applied by individuals and governments to control the pandemic. It is obvious that the dimensions of individual and governmental interventions overlap, e.g. a reduction of mobility can be achieved by law (e.g. temporary border control and border closure) or by individual decisions in self-responsibility. For instance, the Swedish government did not restrict individual liberties as much as the German government, but the Swedish population decided on their own to increase social distancing and limit their mobility.[418] The actual behaviour of the Swedish and German population was quite similar during the first waves.

Most interventions have been well-known for decades. In particular, personal protective equipment (PPE), such as face masks, have been analysed before and after the COVID-19 pandemic.[419] Community masks and surgical masks (white masks) have been in use in the healthcare field for third-party and in particular patient protection for a long time. Masks with a filtering face piece (FFP) have a high capacity to filter aerosols (FFP2 $\geq$ 94%, FFP3 $\geq$ 99%). All of them help to protect other people, but certainly, an FFP has a higher potential of protection than a community mask. Community mask do hardly reduce the risk of getting infected, but if everybody wears a community mask, the individual risk also declines (compare Table 3.8). Whether the filter is sufficient to avoid an infection depends on the viral load, the infectivity of the respective strain, and the immunity of the human. However, the face mask was the most widely used, and likely, also the most important rapid response to COVID-19.

Table 3.8: Effectiveness of face masks.[420]

	Third-party protection	Self-protection
Community mask	X	–
White mask	X	$\approx$
FFP(2,3)	X	X

---

417 Compare Palomo, Pender, Massey, et al. (2023).
418 Compare Hale, Angrist, Kira, et al. (2023).
419 Compare Gurbaxani, Hill, Paul, et al. (2022) and Brienen, Timen, Wallinga, et al. (2010).
420 Source: Own. Based on Brienen, Timen, Wallinga, et al. (2010).

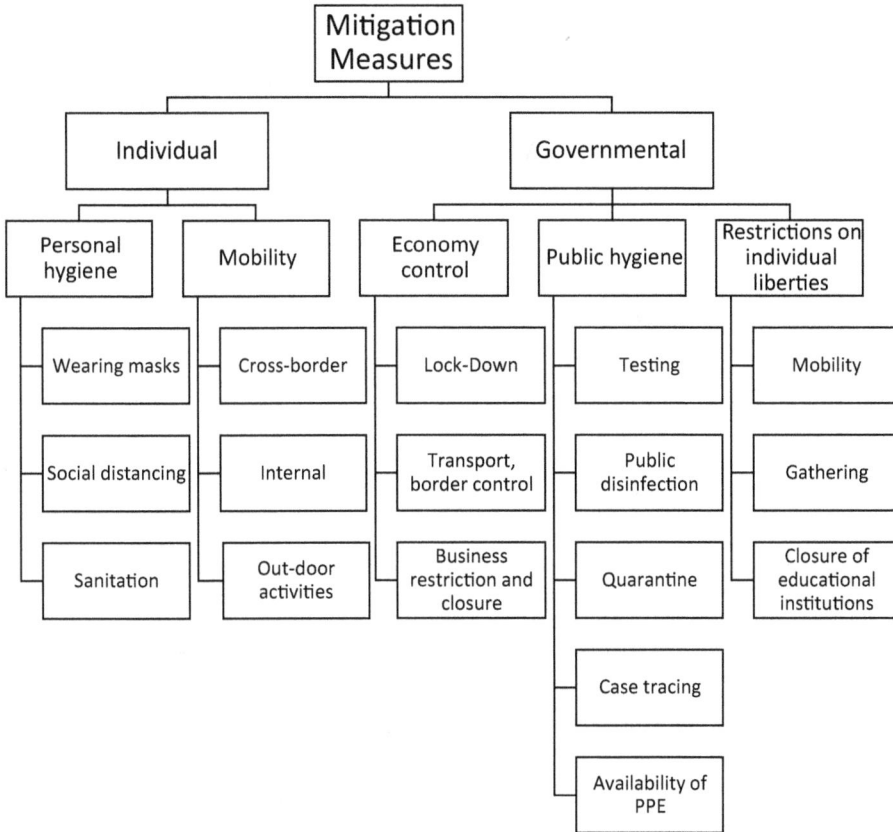

Figure 3.39: Overview of mitigation measures of COVID-19.[421]

The interventions applied by governments can be quite intensive as indicated by the example of China after the first outbreak had ended in 2020.[422] Table 3.9 shows the measures taken by the government of China to safeguard that new cases could not become a new wave. For this purpose, they distinguished different risk areas. Low-risk areas were areas where no new cases were confirmed for 14 consecutive days. Medium-risk areas have newly confirmed cases within 14 days, but the cumulative number of confirmed cases does not exceed 50, or the cumulative number of confirmed cases exceeds 50, and no cluster epidemic occurs within 14 days. High-risk areas refer to more than 50 cumulative cases and a cluster of epidemics occurred within 14 days.

---

421 Source: Own.
422 Compare Wang and Fleßa (2021).

Table 3.9: Prevention and control measures taken by the Chinese government.[423]

Measures	High	Medium	Low
Area traffic control	√		
Close public facilities	√		
Close business	√		
Close primary schools and kindergartens	√		
Close colleges and universities	√		
Delayed start of school	√	√	√
Gathering activities are prohibited	√	√	Reduce
Suspected cases are quarantined	√	√	
Close contacts are subject to isolation medical observation	√	√	√
Use a mobile app	√	√	√
Comprehensive screening of fever patients	√	√	Medical institutions
Door to door testing	√	√	
Wear masks in public places	√	√	√
Measuring body temperature	√	√	√
Keep social distance	√	√	√
Information registration of outsiders	√	√	√
Check health code, itinerary card	√	√	√
Negative nucleic acid test certificate	√	√	√
Disinfect relevant places	√	√	√

With these mitigation measures, China was quite successful for some time. However, with a growing infectiveness and basic reproductive rate of the virus, it became obvious that even very strict measures would not be able to stop the spread of the disease completely. 'Zero COVID' was quite successful in a number of countries, but it worked only in countries with very limited inflow from outside (e.g. New Zealand) and as long as the infectivity was still rather low. The Omicron variant made an end to all attempts of zero COVID.

Figure 3.40 shows the fatality and basic reproductive rate of SARS-CoV-2 in comparison to other diseases. The wild type (i.e. naturally occurring, non-mutated strain) of the virus in Wuhan City had a high fatality rate of 5.25%, and the Alpha variant had a fatality rate of 2.62%.[424] The Beta variant had a higher fatality rate of about 4.19%, but this could also be due to the fact that health systems were even more overwhelmed than in the Alpha wave. Since then, the fatality declined (Gamma: 3.6%, Delta: 2.0%, and Omicron: 0.7%).[425] The basic reproductive numbers also vary signifi-

---

423 Source: State Council (2020); National Health Commission of China (2020a); National Health Commission of China (2020b); National Health Commission of China (2020).
424 There is a very high heterogeneity of the estimated fatality rates and reproductive numbers, i.e. different studies found different rates.
425 Compare Xia, Yang, Wang, et al. (2024) and Yang, Cao, Du, et al. (2020).

cantly between the variants.[426] It was about 2.5 in Wuhan, about 5 for the Delta variant, and has increased to some 9 for Omicron. This development is typically for the adaption process of a new pathogen: the infectivity increases while the fatality declines. The agent has an advantage of leaving the host alive by increasing its reproduction. However, it is much easier to control a disease with a reproductive rate of about 2 than of about 9. Actually, it is almost impossible to avoid infections with a basic reproductive rate of 9.[427]

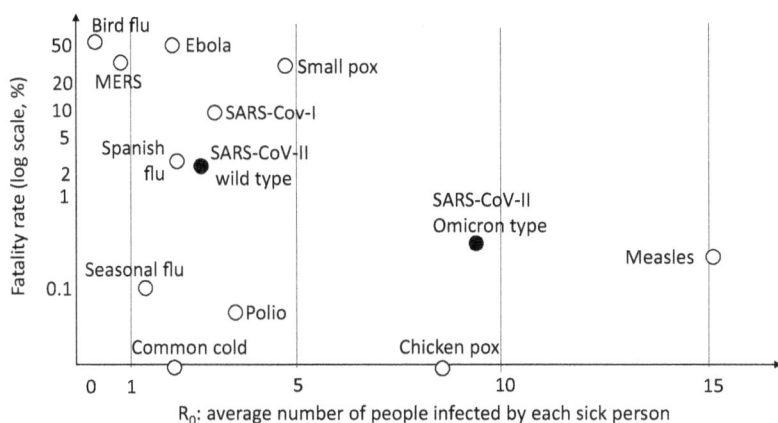

Figure 3.40: Fatality and reproductive rates in comparison.[428]

The pandemic had tremendous economic consequences globally and in almost all countries. Figure 3.41 shows the tree of the cost of the pandemic. The costs of diseases have been systematically recorded for more than 50 years,[429] and the left-hand branch of the tree belongs to the essentials of health economics. There are numerous studies that implement this concept to determine the costs of an illness, but to date, the social follow-up costs have hardly been taken into account. This was hardly necessary, because before the COVID-19 pandemic, the social impact of an illness was limited or resulted directly from the limitations of the sick person and their relatives. A patient who is unable to work during the harvest will of course have major economic disadvantages, but these can always be attributed to the individual illness and are therefore part of the left-hand branch of the costs of a pandemic in Figure 3.41.

---

426 Compare Karimizadeh, Dowran, Mokhtari-Azad, et al. (2023).
427 Compare Wang and Fleßa (2021).
428 Source: Khafaiea and Rahim (2020) and Liu and Rocklöv (2022).
429 Compare Section 5.1 and Rice (1967).

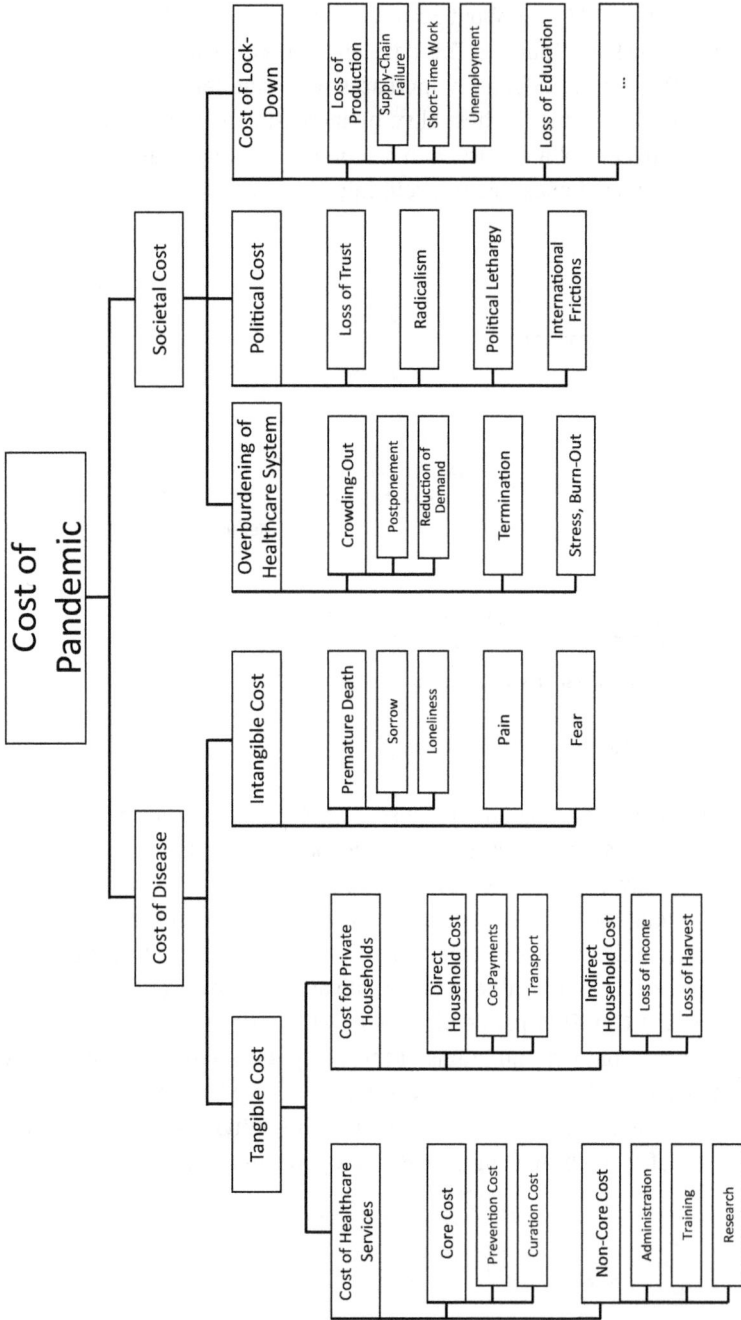

Figure 3.41: Cost of pandemic.[430]

430 Source: Own, based on Fleßa and Greiner (2020).

The COVID-19 pandemic, however, entailed social costs that can no longer be attributed to the individual case of illness. For example, the lockdown, which was intended to prevent the spread of SARS-CoV-2 in many countries, undoubtedly led to production losses and thus to lower national income, even beyond the individual illness. The consequences are short-time working, unemployment, and supply shortfalls that affect society as a whole. As supply chains are highly complex and therefore vulnerable, the consequences can last for years. The consequential costs of a pandemic can therefore also include rising poverty, hunger, and even many more deaths.

In many countries, the lockdown has led to the closure of schools and other educational institutions. This implies a loss of education that may only be compensated for to a limited extent. In poorer countries, however, the closure of schools and kindergartens has also significantly worsened the nutritional situation of children, because the closure has also put an end to free meals for children, which are often the only reliable source of nutrition during the day, especially for poor groups. Figure 3.41 indicates that the costs of the lockdown go far beyond the loss of productivity and education. So far, they have hardly been included in the cost of illness, but are essential for assessing the COVID-19 pandemic.

However, the pandemic also had political follow-up costs. The dynamics of the pandemic and the uncertainty and complexity of the interventions led to a situation in which governments and institutions could be perceived as unreliable and incompetent. This implies a loss of trust of the population towards their leaders, which in turn could promote radicalization and disenchantment with politics in a country. The long-term consequences of the COVID-19 pandemic will be felt for years to come and can only be accurately assessed ex-post. This also includes international tensions resulting from the pandemic and the measures taken (in particular, border closures, export bans, etc.).

Finally, the healthcare system is also affected beyond the treatment of individual patients. Firstly, the overloading of the healthcare system during the pandemic led to the postponement of necessary treatments, which in many cases, has health consequences (e.g. postponement of necessary operations and chemotherapy for carcinomas). In some cases, however, demand also fell because patients no longer dared to visit healthcare services despite clear symptoms for fear of becoming infected or not being treated properly.

However, the heavy overload during the pandemic has also had a knock-on effect on healthcare staff. In several countries, the number of nursing staff fell during the pandemic, with staff resigning or falling ill due to stress, excessive demands, and burnout. It is not yet clear whether the obvious threat to staff will affect the demand for training places in the healthcare sector in the long term.

Figure 3.41 shows that focussing on the treatment costs of COVID-19 patients does not do justice to the situation. However, most of the cost items are difficult to assess. The initial estimates at the beginning of the pandemic assumed a U-shaped course of the pandemic with a sharp slump and a slow but full recovery. In summer 2020, the estimators then tended towards a V-shaped course with a rapid and complete recovery. At the turn of the year 2020/21, a W-shaped course emerged, i.e. the V was followed by another V with a second sharp slump, but also a rapid and full recovery. Finally, a ZZ (zigzag) pattern was assumed, i.e. a series of slumps and recoveries with a decline of amplitudes and a tendency towards a new equilibrium.

The simplest indicator for measuring the economic consequences of a pandemic is the GDP (per capita, p.c.). The first estimates were a decline in GDP of 2.9–3.5% for 2020 with a rapid recovery in 2021. Global GDP amounted to US$87,751,541 million in 2019, and according to the loss of global economic power, for 2020, it would have amounted to between US$2.5 and US$3.1 trillion in a V-shaped curve. Later estimates for the year 2020 for a W-shaped trajectory amounted to up to 6.7% or US$6.9 trillion, with Latin America being the most affected at 8.5% and the low-income countries the least at 4.8%.[431]

Figure 3.42 exhibits the GDP p.c. (PPP, constant 2021 international $) with 2015 as the starting point of 100%. Already before COVID-19, sub-Saharan Africa showed very poor economic progress with annual growth rates of less than 0.5%, while middle-income countries had the highest growth rates. Sub-Saharan Africa was also most severely affected in 2020 with a decline of GDP p.c. of 4.32%, while other low-income countries were in a better situation. Already in 2021, most high- and middle-income countries made good for the loss of 2020, but low-income countries and sub-Saharan Africa were still suffering. In 2023, the poorer nations still had not recovered from the COVID-19 shock, but the world economy, and in particular, high- and middle-income countries, were back to their growth path.

Low-income countries experienced consequences that cannot be expressed in GDP alone. For example, a study by the Congressional Research Service found that "65 million to 75 million people worldwide may have entered into extreme poverty in 2020 with 80 million more undernourished compared to pre-pandemic levels. In addition, some estimates indicate that the decline in global trade in 2020 exacted an especially heavy economic toll on trade-dependent developing and emerging economies".[432] However, many consequences of COVID-19 for the societies and economies will not be recorded in official statistics.

COVID-19 pandemic acts like an exemplification of what was written in Section 3.3.1. The most important learnings are relevant for future pandemics likely to come.

---

431 Compare Szmigiera (2021).
432 Compare Jackson, Weiss, Schwarzenberg, et al. (2021).

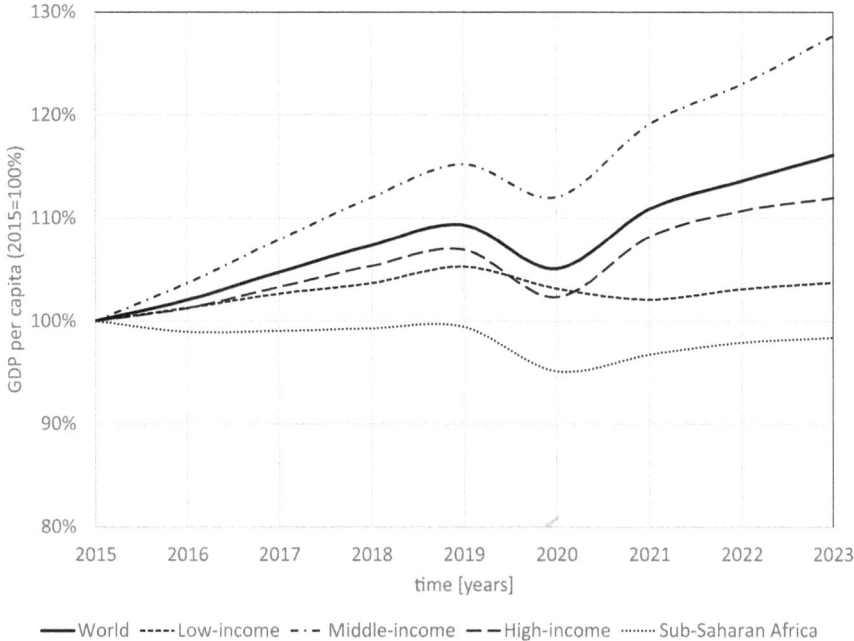

Figure 3.42: GDP per capita, PPP (constant 2021 international $).[433]

3.3.4.2 Epidemiological Processes

A New Virus Can Cause a Pandemic

The COVID-19 pandemic started with a virus crossing-over to humans who had no immunity against this new agent. Most likely, there are thousands of viruses persisting in wild animal populations with the potential of a pandemic. The more humans enter into the realm of wild animals, the more likely a new 'jump' will happen. Consequently, it is obligatory to see the health of animals and of human beings in their habitats and environments as a unity – a fact that is stressed by One Health (see Section 2.4.2).

That a virus infects humans for the first time is not extraordinary. The speed of the diffusion, however, was amazing. From Wuhan in China, it took only weeks until the vast majority of countries were affected. As described in Section 3.3.1, SARS-CoV-2 had several comparative advantages. Firstly, it is a communicable disease without intermediate hosts or vectors. It is transmittable directly by droplets, which is the most common and easiest form of all infection pathways. Secondly, SARS-CoV-2 is infectious before the infected has developed symptoms. For other diseases (e.g. SARS), it was much easier to separate infectious persons because they only became infectious when

---

433 Source: Own, based on Fleßa and Greiner (2020).

they already felt sick. For SARS-Cov-2, this was not possible. Thirdly, the disease has a comparable low fatality and patients will die after several days or weeks, i.e. the infected have sufficient time to infect others. Fourthly, the virus does not depend on special conditions, such as temperature or humidity. It is a matter of fact that the number of infections increases with falling air temperature, but this is mainly a consequence of human behaviour and gathering in small and warm rooms during winter. Finally, modern mobility made it easy for the virus to travel all around the world. Infected but healthy patients could enter an aeroplane in one part of the world and arrive thousands of miles away still without any symptoms. A century ago, it would have taken years to cover the distances that SARS-CoV-2 made good within few weeks.

The disease started to diffuse in time and space. Figure 3.43 shows the simulated diffusion of COVID-19 in Wuhan City under the assumption that no mitigation measures were taken. It is assumed that the first patient was infected on day $t = 1$. Firstly, it is obvious that it takes several months until the new infection becomes visible. Afterwards it starts growing strongly. This is the typical exponential development of an infectious disease: the disease grows 'in silence' without public notice. Once it becomes visible, it can be too late. Secondly, without interventions, the number of cases can become very high. At $t = 200$, about 20% of the population are cases (exposed, infectious without symptoms, infectious with symptoms). After this peak, the number declines exponentially again. Thirdly, the disease disappears rather rapidly after about 60% of the population are immune. This figure responds to the assumption of $R_0 = 2.5$. The model assumes that the immunity is sufficiently strong for at least 1 year. Fourthly, about 1.5% of the population will have died at the end of the wave.

The diffusion of COVID-19 did not only happen in time, but also in space.[434] The wave rolled over continents and countries, and the patterns described in Section 3.3.1.2 could be studied in pure form. Some areas or countries were spared during the first wave because they were sufficiently remote and were not reached before they had implemented mitigation measures.

A Changing Virus Causes Waves
COVID-19 is also an example of a changing virus that caused waves rolling over the globe. A minor reason of waves was the seasonality, i.e. warmer temperature with less crowding in narrow rooms reduced the infection intensity. However, the main reason was the evolutionary adoption process of the virus. It mutated and increased its likelihood of persistence in the human host society by declining fatality and increasing infectiveness (see Figure 3.40). In addition, the mutations safeguarded that the immunity was insufficient to protect the recovered from new infections. Usually, a new strain of SARS-CoV-2 has (at least some) ability to escape the immunity and infect again, i.e. like influenza, COVID-19 is likely to be an "unchanging disease due to a

---

434 Compare Bonnet, Grigoriev, Sauerberg, et al. (2024).

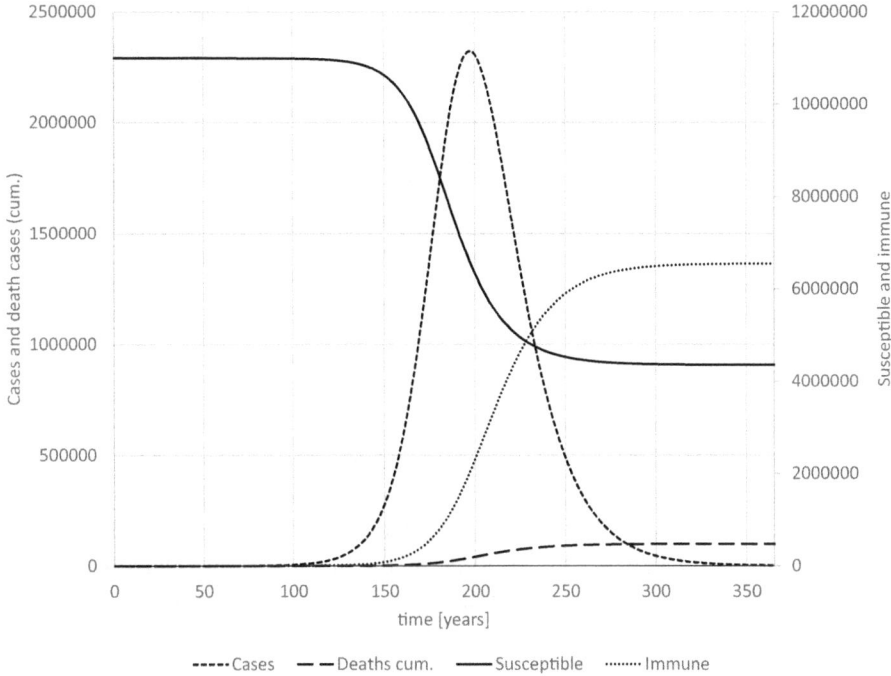

Figure 3.43: Diffusion of COVID-19 in Wuhan.[435]

changing virus"[436] following the Kilbourne model described in Figure 3.22. The idea of reaching a herd immunity by a 'natural' flow of the disease was naive.

The consequences are waves of COVID-19, but also a limited effectiveness and efficiency of the vaccine. With an R_0 of the Omicron variant of about 9, a vaccine of perfect efficacy would require a coverage of about 89% of the population to reach a herd immunity. However, no vaccine could protect perfectly against COVID-19, no country reached 89% coverage, the immunity declined with time, and the virus mutated with new stems capable of escaping immunity. Thus, new waves are also likely within a population covered by vaccines. The vaccination is meaningful nevertheless as it protects against severe forms of the disease and is likely to reduce the infectivity.

Risks Depend on Many Variables
The risk of severe COVID-19 and mortality depends on a number of factors, including viral factors (e.g. strain), environmental factors (e.g. socioeconomic status and air pol-

---

435 Source: Wang and Fleßa (2021).
436 Zuckerman, Banatvala, and Griffiths (2009).

lution), and host factors (e.g. sex, lifestyle, comorbidity, genetic factors, and age).[437] From the beginning, it was obvious that severity of the disease, and in particular, the death rate, depends on age. Ceteris paribus, the death rate grows exponentially with age with the age-set of 80+ having a risk of up to 10% to die from an infection, while fatal outcomes of SARS-CoV-2 among children and young people are rare exemptions. At the same time, the likelihood of dying from COVID-19 increases strongly if a patient has a CVD, diabetes, respiratory disease, hypertension, or obesity. At the same time, comorbidities and age are highly correlated, i.e. older people have chronic degenerative diseases, usually more than one.

The socioeconomic status includes the education, profession, income, wealth, and other variables. As stated before, the richer population usually lives in healthier environments, has more resources to avoid infections, enjoys better healthcare in case of sickness, and has developed more coping strategies to live with impairments (compare Section 2.2.1). Thus, the pandemic was not egalitarian or 'fair', but it hit most the poor in each society and globally, who could not protect themselves. Other factors, such as blood group and ethnic background,[438] might play – if at all – a minor a role in the severity and morbidity of COVID-19. As the factors are correlated with each other, professional statistics must be applied to safeguard proper reasoning.

Interventions Are Complex

As Figure 3.39 indicates, the infection chain can be interrupted in manifold ways. In theory, stopping a viral pandemic is simple because the virus can only replicate if it is absorbed by cells in a (human) body. Outside of the host, the viral capsid will degrade so that the virus will not survive for a longer time. Thus, a viral pandemic can be ended by avoiding new infections for a certain time (e.g. 2 weeks). However, in practice, this is extremely difficult because individual liberties must be strongly restricted to achieve that goal.

It is feasible to eradicate a viral disease if the political will is sufficiently high. For instance, smallpox united the world for the 'Intensified Eradication Programme' (1967).[439] Until the final goal of eradication was achieved, vaccinations, quarantine, and very strict case control were obligatory all over the world.[440]

---

437 Compare Zsichla and Müller (2023).
438 Compare Ijaz, Cheema, Rafiq, et al. (2023).
439 Compare Fenner (1982).
440 Example of case control:"She was isolated at home with house guards posted 24 h a day until she was no longer infectious. A house-to-house vaccination campaign within a 1.5-mile radius of her home began immediately. A member of the Smallpox Eradication Program team visited every house, public meeting area, school, and healer within 5 miles to ensure the illness did not spread. They also offered a reward to anyone who reported a smallpox case". (CDC 2024)

This interference with personal liberty was only accepted because of the tremendous burden of disease. Variola major (Asian smallpox) had a mortality of 20–45% and it is estimated that smallpox caused 300–500 million deaths worldwide in the twentieth century before its elimination was finally declared by WHO in 1980.[441] Five years before, the last case in history had been recorded in Bangladesh. There are several reasons why this eradication became possible. Firstly, high fatality and tremendous burden of disease inspired the world community to invest into the eradication and to accept restrictions, as well as interventions. Secondly, the virus had no animal reservoir. Thirdly, natural immunity after survival of the disease was (almost) perfect and the virus is far less prone to spontaneous mutations than many other viruses. Consequently, the smallpox vaccine had a high efficacy (95%) and guaranteed lifelong protection.

As shown above, the COVID-19 pandemic differs strongly from smallpox. The case fatality is much lower, immunity persists only for a comparably short time, and the mutation rate is much higher.[442] is a DNA-virus, while SARS-CoV-2 is an RNA-virus. DNA is far less prone to spontaneous mutations unlike RNA. An average fatality rate of 1% with a strong focus on the elderly simply did not produce sufficient pressure for even stricter interventions. The impression that COVID-19 was 'just a flu' – as wrong as it is from a medical and epidemiological perspective – still exists and challenges all efforts to implement strict interventions. The wild type of Wuhan with a lower basic reproductive rate could have still been eradicated. Today, COVID-19 is here to stay and has become part of the human living conditions.

A major difference and challenge is the fact that COVID-19 came unexpected and without warning. The selection of the intervention strategy always requires dealing with some degree of uncertainty and assessing risks. However, all decisions during the COVID-19 pandemic were decisions under extreme uncertainty. On the one hand, complex biological events, such as pandemics, are fundamentally dynamic with stochastic influences and the probabilities of occurrence of certain environmental alternatives were unknown or had to be estimated without recourse to experiences. For example, the vaccination behaviour of the population was difficult to predict. Which population groups would be vaccinated, to what extent, and how quickly could not be deduced from other vaccination campaigns. No real experience was available and studies would have taken too long or been too imprecise. Even with the greatest care, 'bold' assumptions had to be made about the probabilities of occurrence.

Secondly, the environmental conditions that might occur were largely unknown. For example, the development of an alpha, delta, or omicron variant could not be predicted at the beginning of the vaccination campaign. Although it was known that there would be mutations, the direction in which they would mutate was not only un-

---

441 Berche (2022b).
442 Smallpow

predictable in terms of probability, but also in terms of their complete content. It can therefore be concluded that important decisions had to be made in the face of complete uncertainty.

It is in the nature of uncertainty that it is possible to say with certainty what the right decision would have been after the random event has occurred, but not before. Often, a decision situation occurs ex ante, which is referred to in science as an 'insurance situation', i.e. decision-makers can distinguish between two alternatives, one of which is more expensive but safer.

Figure 3.44 demonstrates this decision situation for the example of a vaccination or for the establishment of a vaccination programme. The decision-maker must decide whether to carry out a vaccination or to set up the programme. In both cases, a wave of infection can occur or not. If vaccination has been carried out, the vaccination costs will be incurred, but there is a high probability that only minor damage will occur. If there is no wave of infection, the vaccination costs remain constant, but the damage is minor. If, on the other hand, vaccination was not carried out and a wave of infection occurs, this implies high (treatment) costs and a high level of damage. If, on the other hand, there is no wave, there are neither costs nor damage.

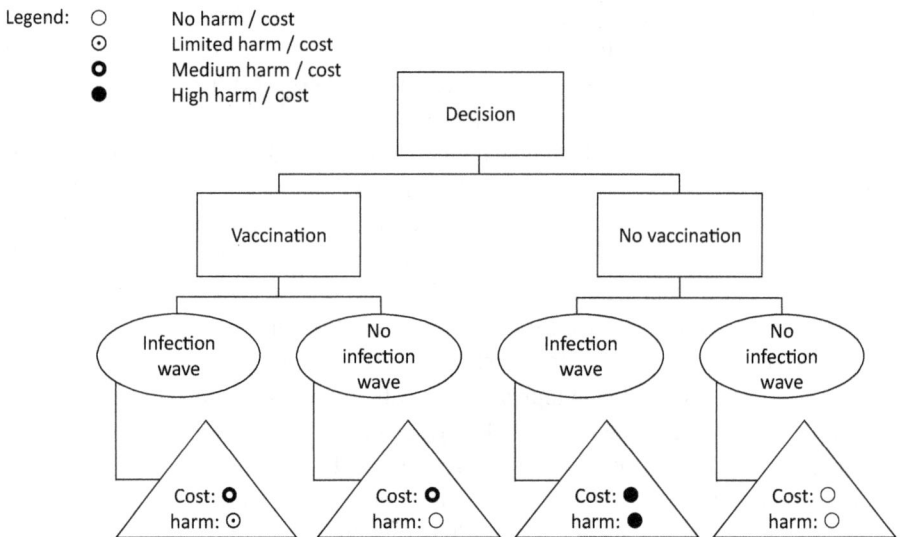

Figure 3.44: Decisions under uncertainty.[443]

This highly simplified example shows some important characteristics of decisions in the face of uncertainty:

---

443 Source: Own, based on Fleßa (2010b).

- If the occurrence of the risk is known in retrospect, the best decision in each case is simple. The problem arises from the uncertainty or the need to make decisions before the loss event occurs.
- If one decides on a safe option (here: vaccination) and then the risk event does not occur, this does not imply that the costs for the safe event were wasted. Rather, this investment was used to acquire a valuable asset: the certainty of not suffering greater damage in any case – regardless of which risk event occurs. The cost of the intervention is therefore not in vain, even if no further wave occurs, but is the price for the certainty that no catastrophic event will occur. Even with insurance, the premium is not in vain if the loss event does not occur. The premium is the price for the certainty that there will be no catastrophic payout.
- It is therefore systematically wrong to dismiss interventions as a waste if there is no further wave. Rather, the (financial and non-financial) costs of the intervention represent a price for the certainty that no more catastrophic damage can occur.
- The question is therefore only whether the price for this value ('safety') is too high. There is no doubt that security is a high social (and political) value with ethical and moral implications, which also justifies a price. Whether the possible protective effect of the mitigation measures justifies the costs must be discussed. But these costs are offset by a value even if there is no further wave, namely safety from catastrophic events.

For a final illustration of the complexity of assessing risks of COVID-19, we would like to refer to the relationship between infectivity and potentially infectious contacts, as shown by Wang et al.[444]

$$R_0 = \sum_{i=1}^{m} \left(1 - (1-p)^{n_i}\right)$$

with the following variables and constants: R_0,-basic reproductive rate; p,-Infectivity; n_i,-number of contacts with person i during infectious period; and m,-number of persons met during infectious period. The uncertainty of the waves of the pandemic and the consequences of interventions is the result of a highly dynamic system with many interrelated elements. Simple answers, strategies, and models are likely to fail. It is the obligation of the international healthcare manager to make decision situations transparent and weigh up risks based on latest evidence.

---

444 Compare Wang and Fleßa (2021).

A Pandemic Causes Tremendous Human Suffering

Human suffering due to COVID-19 has many facets spanning from minor pain to death, from absence from work to poverty, or from delayed funerals to complete breakdown of the healthcare system even for patients with other diseases. However, for many people, death is likely to be the most severe consequence. Here, it is important to note that causality is not always easy. For instance, if an (old) person dies during his infection, it might have also happened that he would have died anyhow, i.e. the person died with COVID-19, but not because of COVID-19. At the same time, a cancer patient might have survived his disease if he had been operated on in time, but due to the COVID-19 pandemic, the healthcare system was so overloaded that his surgery was delayed until it was too late. His death is due to COVID-19, but he died without an infection. Consequently, it is most appropriate to assess the excess mortality instead of the SARS-CoV-2 mortality.[445]

The excess mortality is defined as "the difference in the total number of deaths in a crisis compared to those expected under normal conditions",[446] i.e. the number of deaths from all causes during a period of time beyond what we would have expected under 'normal' conditions. Thus, a person dying with COVID-19 not caused by SARS-CoV-2 will not lead to excess mortality while a person dying from cancer due to delayed surgery during the pandemic will induce excess mortality. From a statistical perspective, however, it is not easy to assess what 'normal' conditions are, i.e. how high the number of deaths would have been without the disease of interest. The international healthcare manager will have to co-operate with professional statisticians in order to get a proper number of projected deaths.

In order to compare the excess between countries with different populations, the *P*-score is introduced as the relative excess mortality:

$$P = \frac{E}{D_p} \cdot 100\% = \frac{D_r - D_p}{D_p} \cdot 100\%$$

where *P* is the-*P*-score, *E* represents-excess deaths, D_r represents-reported deaths, and D_p represents-projected deaths.

Msemburi et al. estimated for the years 2020 and 2021 a loss of 14.83 million excess deaths globally, which is almost three times as much as the official 5.42 million COVID-19 deaths reported.[447] Globally, the *P*-score was 7.97% for 2020 and 18.30% for 2021, i.e. the world experienced an increase of almost 1/5th in 2021 compared to what we would have expected if the pandemic had not occurred. Individual countries were

---

445 Compare Msemburi, Karlinsky, Knutson, et al. (2023).
446 Woodruff (2006).
447 Compare Msemburi, Karlinsky, Knutson, et al. (2023).

affected much more. For instance, the *P*-scores for Peru (97%), Ecuador (51%), and Bolivia (49%) indicate the tremendous human suffering during the pandemic. For many low-income countries (in particular in sub-Saharan Africa), no *P*-values were calculated.

As indicated in Table 3.10, lower- and middle-income countries had the highest *P*-scores while low-income countries were not so severely affected, in particular, sub-Saharan Africa. The special situation of this continent calls for further analysis in the next section.

Table 3.10: P-score of income groups.[448]

Income group	Reported COVID-19 deaths (million)	Excess deaths (million)	P-score (%)
High income	1.93	2.09	9.46
Upper middle income	2.26	4.24	11.53
Lower middle income	1.18	7.86	17.58
Low-income country	0.04	0.64	7.02

Without doubt, mortality is not the only burden caused by the COVID-19 pandemic, and other consequences, such as Long Covid, still have to be analysed in more details in future. Furthermore, the economic consequences for individuals and societies are tremendous. It is obvious that millions of lives could have been saved if the outbreak could have been stopped already in Wuhan. Early detection of potential threats is crucial and requires more funding (and political will).

3.3.4.3 COVID-19 in Africa

COVID-19 was a pandemic affecting all countries, regions, and continents. However, for a long time, it was stated that sub-Saharan Africa was hardly affected.[449] As shown above, the numbers of (official) cases and deaths (including *P*-scores) were comparably low in this region, but this neglects the disastrous economic consequences, as well as some specific features of COVID-19, in Africa that could help to understand this and future pandemics better.

Figure 3.45 shows the four major waves in Africa. In comparison to Figure 3.38 and other continents, the absolute and relative statistics are small, but the waves are clearly visible. As of 2024, the WHO Africa region registered some 9 million cases and 175,000 deaths, or 8,390 cases and 161 deaths per 1 million inhabitants.[450] The prevalence varies greatly. The Republic of South Africa alone reported some 4.2 million cases and about

---

448 Source : Msemburi, Karlinsky, Knutson, et al. (2023).
449 Compare Soy (2020).
450 Compare WHO African Region (2024).

103,000 deaths, which are about 45% of all cases and some 59% of all deaths in the WHO Africa region. Other highly affected countries are Mozambique, Kenya, Namibia, and Ghana.

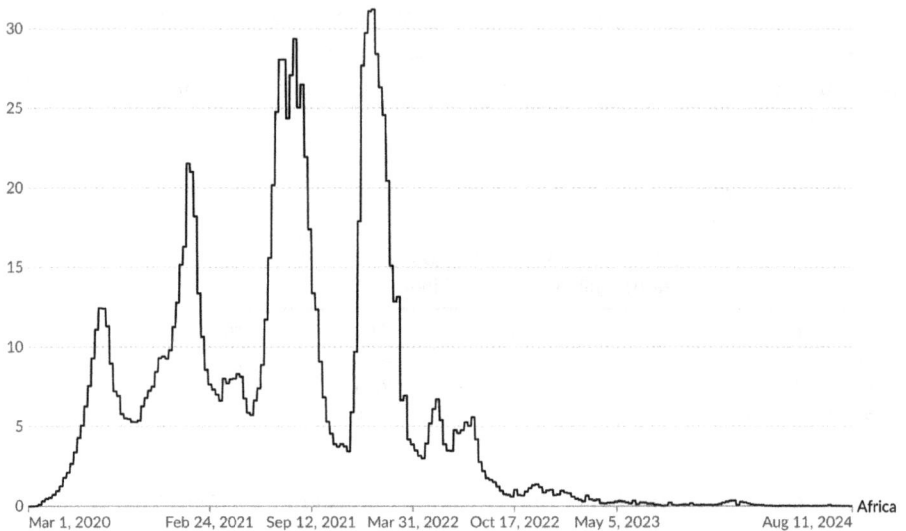

Figure 3.45: COVID-19 cases in Africa.[451]

WHO African Region, Africa CDC, the African Union, and the individual governments quickly took action, but ultimately the world was amazed at the extremely low number of cases. It was quickly assumed that there was a gross underreporting of the COVID pandemic in the region. In fact, there is still insufficient testing capacity today, and at the beginning of the spread, it was practically non-existent outside a few large cities (e.g. Johannesburg, Nairobi).[452] In addition, PCR tests are expensive compared to the health budgets of these countries, and rapid tests have sensitivity and specificity too low to truly reflect the pandemic situation. In rural regions in Africa, they are barely available, so it is reasonable to assume that a large proportion of cases remained undetected. Estimates amount to "six in seven COVID-19 infections go undetected in Africa".[453]

But even if many cases and deaths remain undetected, this does not change the overall picture that COVID-19 in Africa has led to relatively few cases and deaths. The consequences of a dramatic COVID-19 epidemic in a country or region do not have to be detected by laboratory tests: the number of new graves in Brazil or burial fires in

---

451 Source: OurWorldinData – CC-BY@: https://ourworldindata.org/explorers/covid (18.02.2025).
452 Compare Oleribe, Suliman, Taylor-Robinson, et al. (2021).
453 Compare reliefweb (2022).

India could be detected even by satellite. At the same time, reports of completely over-crowded intensive care units and massive shortages of oxygen for ventilation could not be kept secret. Even though there have been local outbreaks in Africa that have reached a threatening intensity (e.g. Nigeria, Uganda), the overall pandemic on this continent was comparatively mild – a fact that needs explanation.

Figure 3.46 depicts a transition model of COVID-19 with factors influencing the flow. There are quite a number of environmental, cultural, and medical factors that might influence the death rate. Here we would just like to focus on the most impor-tant factor: demography. Other factors (e.g. stimulated immunity due to high preva-lence of infectious diseases, climate, and cultural social distancing) are relevant, but the main explanation is most likely the age structure.

The number of infections, severe cases, and, in particular, deaths, depends heavily on the age of those affected. Table 3.11 first looks at the absolute and relative age distri-bution in Tanzania and Germany. About 27% of the German population is in the age group over 60, which is particularly at risk from COVID-19, but only 5% of the Tanzanian population. Table 3.11 also shows the deaths in Germany as of 23 March 2021, i.e. before a nationwide vaccination, from which, an age-specific mortality rate can be determined. The last column shows the number of deaths in Germany that would have occurred ce-teris paribus in the first year of the pandemic if Germany had the age structure of Tan-zania. The age structure alone implies a reduction in the number of deaths from 85,752 to 5,917. About 53.4% of the Tanzania's population is under 20 years of age, and 90.7% under 50. Even under the condition that a young population in Africa is just as likely to be infected as an aged people in Europe, we will expect significantly less severe cases and deaths.[454] The demographic differences are also expressed by Table 3.12 and can also explain the differences between South Africa and other African countries. The Re-public of South Africa has a much older and consequently much more endangered pop-ulation than the other regions of this continent. Other factors, such as obesity and cli-mate, might also play role in the heavy burden of COVID-19 for South Africa, but the main explanation remains demography.

The economic impact of COVID-19 on sub-Saharan Africa exceeds considerably the epidemiological figures. As shown in Figure 3.42, the GDP strongly declined during the pandemic and the countries have severe problems to make good for the loss of these years. However, the picture is quite different for African countries. Figure 3.47 shows the development of the GDP p.c. for selected sub-Saharan African countries. On average, the GDP p.c. fell strongly in 2020, and in 2023, it was only 98% of the level of 2015. Guinea, Benin, and Tanzania did hardly react on the challenge and continued their development path almost untouched. The countries most affected were those in which tourism plays a very dominant role (Seychelles: 14%, Mauritius: 15%, and Cabo Verde: 16%). Other coun-tries were affected in 2020 and could not make good for it afterwards.

---

454 Compare Adams, MacKenzie, Amegah, et al. (2021).

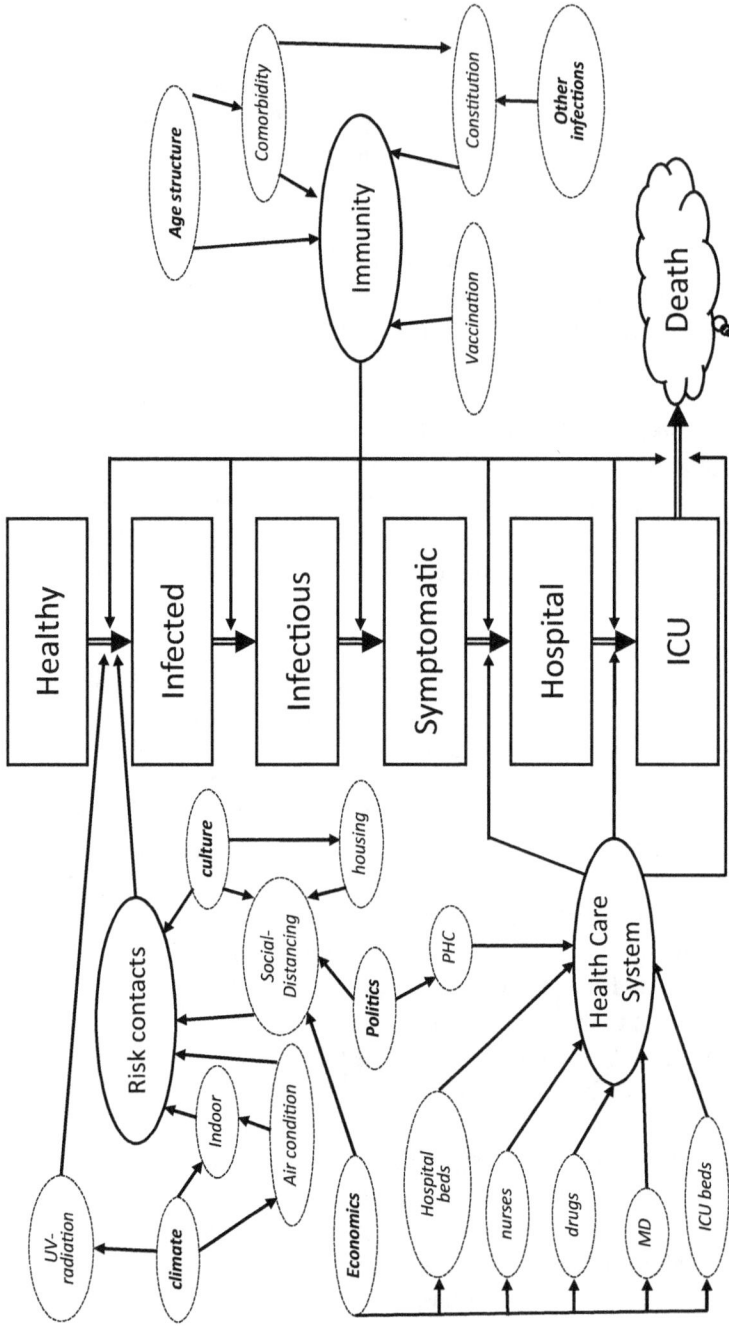

Figure 3.46: COVID-19 transition model.[455]

Table 3.11: Mortality in Tanzania and Germany (data from 2022).[456]

Age	Tanzania Population	Share	Germany Population	Share	COVID-19 deaths (real)	COVID-19 deaths (fictive)
0–9	18,362,316	31.38%	7,752,706	9.61%	8	19
10–19	12,868,924	21.99%	7,581,868	9.40%	3	5
20–29	9,846,249	16.83%	9,483,430	11.76%	52	54
30–39	7,161,928	12.24%	10,871,964	13.48%	137	90
40–49	4,820,727	8.24%	10,070,748	12.49%	413	198
50–59	2,926,635	5.00%	13,304,542	16.50%<	1,975	434
60–69	1,622,800	2.77%	10,717,241	13.29%	5,825	882
70–79	741,236	1.27%	7,436,098	9.22%	14,512	1,447
80–89	157,938	0.27%	2,712,502	3.36%	45,698	2,661
90-	5,342	0.01%	718,000	0.89%	17,129	127
Total	58,514,095	100.00%	80,649,099	100.00%	85,752	5,917

Table 3.12: Demographic statistics of Tanzania, South Africa, and Germany (2022).[457]

Statistics	Tanzania	South Africa	Germany
Growth rate (%)	2.78	1.06	0
Birth rate (‰)	33.3	19.5	9.3
Death rate (‰)	5.09	11.0	11.8
Fertility rate (children per women)	4.39	2.34	1.35
Share 0–14 years (%)	42.7	27.94	12.83
Share 15–24 years (%)	20.39	16.8	0.98
Share ≥65 years (%)	3.08	6.09	22.36

The 'real' cost of COVID-19 in Africa are difficult to assess. The following components must be considered:

– Direct costs: the capacity to treat severe COVID-19 patients was very limited in most African countries. For example, an analysis of the healthcare system in Kenya showed that only 58% of hospitals had a reliable oxygen supply, with significant differences between counties. Only 22 of the 47 counties had at least one intensive care unit in a hospital, with ventilator units mainly in Nairobi and Mombasa. Although capacities have been expanded with international aid, there is a lack of qualified staff for the most part. Laboratory capacities also had to be

456 Source: Own calculations based on Janson (2022); World Population Review (2024).
457 Source: World Population Review (2024).

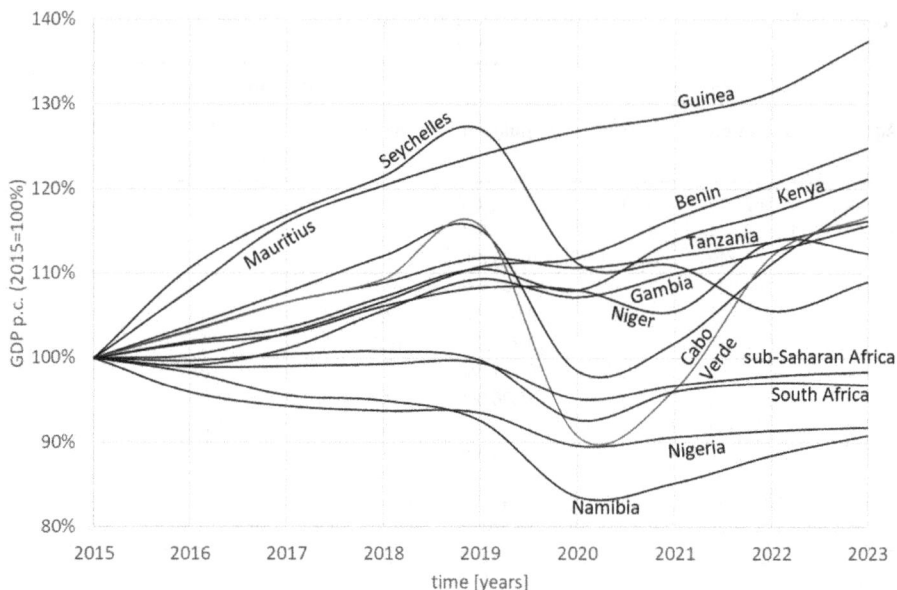

Figure 3.47: Gross domestic product per capita in selected African countries.[458]

built up at great expense.[459] For South Africa, a rough estimate of the treatment costs of COVID-19 patients was given as US$243,161,226 for 2020 and 2021.[460] It is important to bear in mind that only a small proportion of the African population has health insurance. Although the proportion of the population with social security has increased, for the majority of the population in Africa, being admitted to intensive care due to COVID-19 meant a catastrophic health expense for which they may have to sell (productive) property or take on debt. Thus, it can be concluded that the costs per patient were very high for African countries. Even if the number of cases was comparably low, the treatment of COVID-19 patients was a considerable financial burden for the individual, the social systems, and the governments.

- Indirect costs: there are currently no reliable estimates of the indirect costs of COVID-19. For South Africa, the indirect cost due to mortality of the years 2020 and 2021 was calculated as US$1,493,159,262 and due to loss of working time was US$319,388,300.[461] However, it can be assumed that only a fraction of those infected are actually patients, meaning that the actual indirect costs are likely to be lower.

458 Source: World Bank (2024b).
459 Compare Barasa, Ouma, and Okiro (2020) and Oladipo, Ajayi, Odeyemi, et al. (2020).
460 Compare Fleßa (2023).
461 Compare Fleßa (2023).

– Overloading of the healthcare system: the overload of the healthcare system in African countries due to COVID-19 appears to have been rather temporary and localized. Nevertheless, there are indications of negative consequences of COVID-19 on the healthcare system. For example, a survey of slum dwellers in Kenya and Nigeria (as well as Bangladesh and Pakistan) shows that the accessibility of healthcare services deteriorated significantly during the lockdown. In particular, providers were avoided if the service was not urgent. For example, interviewees reported that they had foregone preventive services (e.g. vaccinations, prenatal check-ups). Demand also declined because respondents feared they would be diagnosed with COVID-19, which could lead to exclusion or stigmatization.[462]

Another study conducted in Kenya showed a significant reduction in hospital occupancy. At the same time, however, the demand for outpatient services due to domestic violence increased.[463] It was also reported that international supply chains were disrupted and essential medicines were not available, so that some patients refrained from visiting the healthcare facility.[464] However, compared to the situation in other countries or regions (e.g. Wuhan January 2020, Bergamo March 2020), the situation in healthcare facilities in Africa appears comparatively mild.

– Education: the loss of education is another negative consequence of the COVID-19 pandemic. As a measure against the spread of COVID-19, schools and other educational institutions were closed worldwide from March 2020. Although children very rarely fall seriously ill with COVID-19, they can spread the disease, so school closures were seen as a way of combating the pandemic. In many countries, remote teaching was continued with the help of modern media and in some cases switched to block teaching, alternating teaching, or hybrid forms of learning after a short time so that the proportion of pupils of industrialized countries, who continued their schooling after the lockdown, is relatively high.

In African countries, the situation is different. Firstly, school closures lasted longer in many African countries than in the rest of the world. For example, schools in Uganda did not re-open at all from March 2020 to January 2022 (83 weeks).[465] Although other countries re-opened their schools in the meantime, they reacted to rising COVID-19 case numbers during the second and third waves by closing again. For example, UNICEF found that in July 2021 (at the peak of the third wave in Africa), 40% of school-age children in East and Southern Africa were not attending school. Nearly 32 million children were excluded from school in this region, almost doubling the estimated number of school-age children not

---

462 Compare Ahmed, Ajisola, Azeem, et al. (2020).
463 Compare Kourti, Stavridou, Panagouli, et al. (2021).
464 Compare Barasa, Kazungu et al. (2021).
465 Compare Staude (2022).

attending school. At that time, only 12 of the 21 countries in this region kept their schools open.[466]

Secondly, distance learning opportunities are very limited in most African countries. Books are often not available to all students and access to the internet is mostly limited to the wealthier sections of the population in the larger cities. Closing schools in Africa therefore means something different than in Europe, for example. It implies the complete abandonment of all teaching. Thirdly, in some countries, teachers were not paid during school closures, so they had to look for other jobs. Whether they returned once the schools were re-opened cannot be verified.

The consequences are considerable. UNICEF estimates that pupils in South Africa were between 9 and 12 months behind in July 2021. These statistics do not include the 400,000–500,000 pupils who did not return to school after the lockdown [72].[467] In many cases, the closure of schools had far-reaching social consequences. Many had to work to support families affected by the pandemic (e.g. unemployment of parents). Others married and/or became parents at a very early age, and it was already known before COVID-19 that the number of cases of domestic sexual violence increases during an epidemic without the protection of schools.[468]

As a result, UNICEF estimates that the proportion of illiterate people in Africa will increase significantly in the coming years and it is unclear whether this lack of education and individual and social future opportunities can ever be addressed. At the moment, at least, there are no specific programmes to make up for what has been lost [74].[469] This is particularly dramatic, as a solid school education is often the only way to escape poverty in these countries. Without a good school-leaving certificate and basic reading/writing/math skills, all opportunities for further development remain closed. While in the economically more developed countries of the world, there are usually (sufficiently funded) programmes that make it possible to catch up on schooling later on, dropping out of school in Africa often implies a lifelong stay in the poverty group, even long after the end of the pandemic.

COVID-19 is an example that can elucidate much of the content explained in this book so far. Infectious diseases remain of great importance to international healthcare management. Their absolute and relative decline in Europe, the USA, and other high-income regions is primarily due to the age structure of the population, but also the climate of the temperate latitudes, the availability of water for hygiene, and changed

---

466 Compare UNICEE (2021a).
467 Compare UNICEF (2021b).
468 Compare Bandiera, Buehren, Goldstein, et al. (2019).
469 Compare IFPRI (2021).

working conditions with less exposures are likely to be of great significance. It is therefore questionable whether the ageing of populations in tropical countries will similarly lead to a decline in infectious diseases, or whether they will see the challenge of a double burden of disease. And there is always a threat of new infections coming up – the era of pandemics and infections has not passed and calls for preparedness and wise international healthcare management.

3.4 Epidemiology of Non-infectious Diseases

3.4.1 Fundamentals

3.4.1.1 Relevance

Non-infectious diseases[470] are the most common causes of death and induce the highest burden of disease globally. In the year 2021, non-infectious diseases accounted for about 75% of worldwide deaths and about 62% of DALYs . In comparison to the situation 20 years ago, the relevance of non-infectious disease has strongly increased. The most important 'killers' are CVDs (heart attack, stroke), cancers, and chronic respiratory diseases (such as asthma, chronic obstructive pulmonary disease, occupational lung diseases, and pulmonary hypertension). The highest burden of disease is caused by CVDs, cancers, and musculoskeletal disorders (MSD). The latter demonstrates the difference between burden of disease and deaths: while about 1.7 billion people globally live with MSDs and respective pain and limitations in mobility, the mortality of MSD is low. As the DALY includes disability, as well as premature death, a disease with a high prevalence, pain, and functional limitation can cause a high burden of disease without high mortality.

The share of neonatal, maternal, and nutritional deaths and burden of disease is comparably low, i.e. about 3.3% of global mortality is due to neonatal death, 0.4% due to maternal death, and 0.4% due to nutritional deficiencies. Accidents, suicides, and homicides do play a role globally as well. However, the relevance of the causes of mortality and of burden of disease differs strongly between countries and regions as presented in Table 3.13.

CVDs are globally the leading cause of death (19.4 million) and of DALYs lost (428 million). More than 80% of CVD deaths are caused by heart attacks and strokes with an increasing incidence in particular of younger people. This is – partly – due to changing nutrition and habits of physical activities.

---

470 Many official statistics (e.g. WHO) differentiate three categories: (I) communicable, maternal, neonatal, and nutritional diseases; (II) non-communicable diseases; (III) other diseases (incl. injuries). This categorization makes the distinction difficult because many maternal, neonatal and nutritional diseases are also non-communicable.

Neoplasms are the second most important chronic degenerative diseases in terms of deaths and loss of quality of life. A neoplasm is an abnormal mass of tissue that forms when cells grow and divide more than they should or do not die when they should. Neoplasms may be benign (not cancer) or malignant (cancer). Benign neoplasms may grow large but do not spread into, or invade, nearby tissues or other parts of the body. Malignant neoplasms can spread into, or invade, nearby tissues. They can also spread to other parts of the body through the blood and lymph systems. Also called tumor.[471]

The global burden of disease records neoplasm, including benign neoplasm. However, the vast majority of deaths and DALYs are caused by cancers.

The WHO estimates that in 2022, some 20 million new cancer cases and 9.7 million cancer-related deaths occurred. About 20% of people will develop cancer during their lifetime, and some 10% of the deaths are caused by cancer globally. The absolute and relative numbers are steadily growing.[472]

It is obvious that incidence, prevalence, mortality, and burden of disease (DALY) differ. Some diseases or conditions have very high incidences, for instance, skin diseases.[473] However, the duration of the diseases is rather short, and the mortality is very small. Thus, the incidence of skin diseases is high, while the prevalence is lower, and mortality and burden of disease is almost negligible. When we include other diseases, the difference is even more obvious: in 2021, there were 4.9 billion diarrhoeal disease cases, and 13 billion upper respiratory infections, but 'only' 1.2 million died from diarrhoea and 20,000 from upper respiratory infections worldwide. Nearly 586 million cases of nutritional deficiencies (mainly Vitamin A) were recorded, but 'only' 222,000 deaths.

Simplified, the prevalence is the product of incidence and duration of the disease. Consequently, most chronic degenerative diseases have a much higher prevalence than infectious diseases even if the incidence is identical. Thus, iron-deficiency anaemia, iodine deficiency, and protein deficiency are the most common diseases globally, followed by migraine and visual impairment, i.e. diseases that are usually chronic. If deficiency symptoms are not counted as diseases, asthma, diabetes mellitus, and hearing loss are the next top diseases. As the table shows, the differences between WHO regions are smaller than between the statistical measures (incidence vs. prevalence).

---

471 National Cancer Institute (2024c).
472 Compare WHO (2024).
473 "Skin and subcutaneous diseases", including fungal skin diseases, bacterial skin diseases, scabies, dermatitis, and others.

Table 3.13: Top four non-infectious diseases according to WHO regions in 2021.[474]

WHO region	Incidence (million cases)	Prevalence (million cases)	Deaths (million deaths)	Burden of disease (million DALYs)
Global	Skin diseases (4,693) Neurological disorders (824) Digestive diseases (530) Mental disorders (444)	Neurological disorders (2,870) Digestive diseases (2,381) Skin diseases (2,032) Musculoskeletal disorders (1,687)	Cardiovascular diseases (19.4) Neoplasms (9.9) Chronic respiratory disease (4.4) Diabetes and kidney diseases (3.2)	Cardiovascular diseases (428) Neoplasms (253) Musculoskeletal disorders (162) Mental disorders (155)
African	Skin diseases (910) Neurological disorders (102) Mental disorders (64) Digestive diseases (57)	Skin diseases (335) Neurological disorders (330) Digestive diseases (287) Mental disorders (132)	Cardiovascular diseases (1.2) Neoplasms (0.5) Diabetes and kidney diseases (0.4) Digestive diseases (0.3)	Cardiovascular diseases (33) Mental disorders (20) Neoplasms (18) Diabetes and kidney diseases (14)
Americas	Skin diseases (547) Neurological disorders (123) Digestive diseases (91) Mental disorders (72)	Neurological disorders (428) Digestive diseases (331) Musculoskeletal disorders (291) Skin diseases (277)	Cardiovascular diseases (2.1) Neoplasms (1.6) Diabetes and kidney diseases (0.7) Neurological disorders (0.5)	Cardiovascular diseases (44) Neoplasms (38) Musculoskeletal disorders (29) Mental disorders (26)
Eastern Mediterranean	Skin diseases (341) Neurological disorders (78) Mental disorders (51) Digestive diseases (50)	Neurological disorders (266) Digestive diseases (242) Skin diseases (147) Musculoskeletal disorders (122)	Cardiovascular diseases (1.4) Neoplasms (0.4) Diabetes and kidney diseases (0.3) Digestive disease (0.2)	Cardiovascular diseases (38) Mental disorders (16) Neoplasms (13) Musculoskeletal disorders (13)
European	Skin diseases (543) Neurological disorders (117) Digestive diseases (78) Musculoskeletal disorders (67)	Neurological disorders (416) Digestive diseases (310) Musculoskeletal disorders (267) Skin diseases (258)	Cardiovascular diseases (3.9) Neoplasms (2.2) Neurological disorders (0.7) Digestive disease (0.4)	Cardiovascular diseases (72) Neoplasms (49) Musculoskeletal disorders (26) Mental disorders (21)

---

474 Source: IHME (2025); Ferrari, Santomauro, Aali, et al. (2024).

Table 3.13 (continued)

WHO region	Incidence (million cases)	Prevalence (million cases)	Deaths (million deaths)	Burden of disease (million DALYs)
Southeast Asia	Skin diseases (1,272) Neurological disorders (226) Digestive diseases (136) Mental disorders (489)	Neurological disorders (780) Digestive diseases (580) Skin diseases (489) Musculoskeletal disorders (399)	Cardiovascular diseases (4.5) Chronic respiratory disease (1.7) Neoplasms (1.3) Diabetes and kidney diseases (0.8)	Cardiovascular diseases (116) Neoplasms (43) Chronic respiratory diseases (43) Mental disorders (39)
Western Pacific	Skin diseases (1,058) Neurological disorders (175) Digestive diseases (115) Musculoskeletal disorders (95)	Neurological disorders (639) Digestive diseases (616) Skin diseases (516) Musculoskeletal disorders (469)	Cardiovascular diseases (6.2) Neoplasms (3.7) Substance use disorders (5.7) Chronic respiratory disease (1.5)	Cardiovascular diseases (125) Neoplasms (90) Musculoskeletal disorders (43) Mental disorders (32)

Looking at death, the diseases that become prominent are those described in Table 3.4. Cancer (15%), CVDs (29%), chronic respiratory diseases (7%), and other chronic degenerative diseases account for more than 70% of deaths worldwide annually, depending on the statistics and year. Notably, the significance of accidents is comparatively higher in regions with a lower economic development level than in other WHO regions.

The assessment of DALYs finally combines prevalence weighted by quality of life and mortality into a single measure. It is noticeable that in some regions, mental disorders (e.g. depression) imply a greater loss of quality of life than accidents, CVDs, and cancer. In other regions, visual impairment or hearing loss contributes more to the loss of quality of life than cancer. However, this varies regionally. For instance, in Europe, accidents are of lower importance than CVDs and neuropsychiatric cases, while in Southeast Asia, accidents are a primary reason for the loss of DALYs.

The high number of infections in countries with lower incomes and in the early phases of transition should not obscure the fact that chronic degenerative diseases also play a significant role here. Firstly, many people in these countries are at greater risk of disease. For example, the likelihood of suffering from a chronic respiratory disease is significantly higher in countries where open fires in buildings are the standard method of cooking and heating. Even for diseases traditionally called 'diseases of civilization', there might be a higher incidence in poor than in rich countries if living conditions are similar (e.g. population in urban centres). A study[475] shows that the risk of stroke for the population of Dar-es-Salaam (Tanzania) is higher for all age groups than the corresponding risk for those in North Manhattan.

Secondly, chronic degenerative diseases are less frequently and later diagnosed in poorer countries, since medical staff has only very limited training to detect these diseases. Thirdly, there are fewer treatment options. For example, the age-adjusted cancer risk in sub-Saharan Africa is 120, and the death risk from cancer is 95 per 100,000.[476] The comparable statistics for the European Union are 264 and 115 per 100,000 inhabitants, respectively. This means that the likelihood of getting cancer is 2.2 times higher in Europe than in sub-Saharan Africa, while the death risk is only 1.2 times higher. Late detection and poorer treatment lead to 80% of cancer patients in the African WHO region dying from their cancer, while this figure is only 44% in the European Union.

In Section 3.1.2.4, it was noted that chronic degenerative diseases require a different way of thinking, as simple explanation models (single-cause-single-effect) do not justify the complexity of these diseases. Instead, thinking in complex and stochastic interdependencies that consider numerous causes, potential consequences, and relations is required (multiple-cause-multiple-effect). Indeed, it can be doubted whether the necessary paradigm shift in medicine has already taken place. We do not possess a complete model for understanding chronic degenerative diseases, which is reflected, for example, in the fact that the common pattern for explaining and classifying cancer is primarily oriented towards organ groups (e.g. breast cancer, tongue cancer, and pancreatic cancer), but does not start from the (e.g. genetic) cause.[477] The classification and structuring of chronic degenerative diseases are complex and will still take some time.

This is further complicated by the fact that infectious diseases and chronic degenerative diseases are not absolutely distinct. On one hand, infectious diseases can become chronic and are thus de facto treated like chronic degenerative diseases. For instance, caries behaves like a chronic degenerative disease, yet it is ultimately due to a bacterial infection.

On the other hand, infections play a certain role in the development of some chronic degenerative diseases. For example, the most common tumour worldwide, cervical cancer, is caused by an infection with the human papillomavirus (HPV). An infection with hepatitis can also cause liver cancer.

In summary, we can conclude that chronic degenerative diseases are of great importance in resource-poor countries as well. Their classification is significantly more difficult than for infectious diseases. On the other hand, they are less demanding for

475 Walker, Whiting, Unwin, et al. (2010).
476 Ferlay, Shin, Bray, et al. (2010b).
477 Compare Meade and Emch (2005).

healthcare managers since their spread does not represent a control loop. For infectious diseases, the probability of transmission depends on the prevalence, while for chronic degenerative diseases, it is not determined by the number of affected individuals. Therefore, simpler models (e.g. Markov) are also suitable for forecasting the spread of these diseases.

Only in recent years has international healthcare management become aware that these diseases are of increasing importance worldwide.[478] The following will briefly delve into the two single most important chronic degenerative diseases as far as mortality and burden of disease is concerned in order to provide insights into the international dimension of these diseases.

3.4.1.2 Cardiovascular Diseases

The term 'cardiovascular disease' is not universally defined. It commonly refers to the diseases in Chapter IX of ICD-10[479] or Chapter XI of ICD-11 'Diseases of the circulatory system', i.e. diseases of the heart, blood vessels, and circulation. This includes chronic rheumatic heart diseases, hypertension, ischemic heart diseases, cerebrovascular diseases, diseases of arteries, arterioles, and capillaries, and thrombosis. The primary causes of death are ischemic heart diseases and stroke, accounting for 13.3% and 10.7% of global deaths, respectively.[480]

Ischemia means 'bloodlessness', i.e. very low or absent blood flow to a tissue or organ. If it affects the coronary arteries (coronary vessels), it is referred to as ischemic heart disease. It is usually triggered by arteriosclerosis (arterial calcification), i.e. deposits on the arterial wall preventing adequate oxygen supply to the tissue. The result is coronary insufficiency, a weakness of the heart. If the circulatory disorder is prolonged and severe, parts of the heart muscle can die. This is known as a myocardial infarction. Besides chronic narrowing of an artery, the formation of a blood clot in a coronary artery altered by arteriosclerosis is considered a trigger for such a massive event.

Stroke is the second most common form of CVD. A cerebral infarction has similar causes as a heart attack, i.e. an interrupted or reduced oxygen supply to the brain due to a blood clot in a brain-supplying artery. This is distinct from cerebral haemorrhage, where there is bleeding into the brain (e.g. due to high blood pressure). About 20% of strokes are due to cerebral haemorrhages.

The incidence, and especially, the mortality, of these diseases vary regionally and have changed. It is estimated that in the first phase of transition, stroke and heart attack remain limited to a few privileged population groups. With increasing life expectancy and broader availability of food and luxury goods, the significance of these

---

478 Compare WHO (2008a, 2011c).
479 ICD: International Statistical Classification of Diseases and Related Health Problems. ICD-10 was endorsed by WHO in 1990. In 2022, it was replaced by ICD-11 which had been endorsed in 2019.
480 Compare IHME (2025).

diseases increases strongly during the third and fourth phases of transition. However, most countries in the fourth phase have also learned to prevent CVDs and significantly reduce case fatality. For example, in the USA, the incidence and mortality due to CVDs have steadily declined, although individual population groups have benefited more significantly.[481] For instance, women are significantly less likely to suffer from these diseases before menopause than men are, although this difference levels out later. White Americans die less frequently from these diseases than African Americans, which is likely not due to genetic reasons but primarily due to better healthcare. Especially, the rate of second and third heart attacks depends heavily on the respective milieu.

CVDs are good examples of chronic degenerative diseases having numerous causes, the existence and severity of which vary regionally. The age-standardized death rate from CVDs between both sexes (deaths per 100,000 people) declined from 283.0 (in 2000) to 162.0 (in 2021). This is a great success, but still some 20 million people die from CVDs per year.

Figure 3.48 shows that even within developed countries, the mortality risk due to CVDs varies significantly. The age-standardized rate of death due to CVDs in Germany is twice the respective risk in Japan (120.7 vs. 69.3 per 100,000 inhabitants, year 2021). The respective figures for the year 2000 were 213.8 and 105.5. Africa is the continent with the highest risk of dying from CVDs. In 2021, the age-standardized risk was 287.1 (2000: 312.0): place matters, i.e. there are many worlds of cardiovascular health(care).

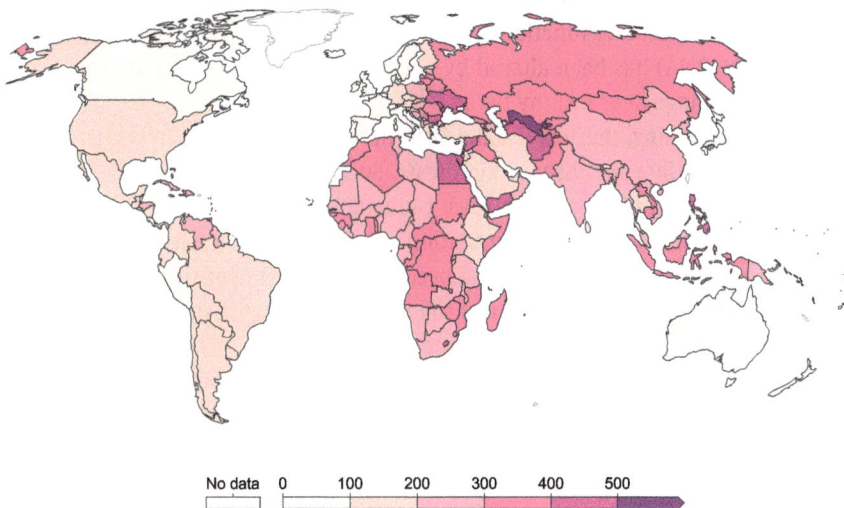

Figure 3.48: Death rate from cardiovascular diseases (2021).[482]

---

481 Compare Meade and Emch (2010).
482 Source: OurWorldinData – CC-BY@: https://ourworldindata.org/grapher/death-rate-from-cardiovascular-disease-age-standardized-ghe (18.02.2025).

The risk factors have been known for decades. Hypertension, nicotine abuse, and elevated blood lipid levels (associated with obesity) are considered primary risk factors, with additional influences including genetic predisposition, age, gender, and physical and psychological stress. They also explain the regionally different distribution of the diseases, although some factors are hardly known. So far, only estimates on the global distribution of hypertension or results from very small samples are available. More precise data is available for obesity, which varies extremely between countries. For example, it is assumed that more than 50% of women aged ≥25 years in South Africa are overweight, while this is only a tiny proportion in Indonesia. Conversely, Indonesia is a country with extremely high tobacco consumption, while comparatively less South African women smoke. Traditionally, East Asians have been considered comparatively less susceptible to CVDs. However, the dietary change of the upper and middle class in this region is likely to have drastic effects on the future prevalence of these ailments.

3.4.1.3 *Cancer*

Cancer is a collective term for more than 100 malignant, i.e. malicious tumours that can affect any part of the body. The 'malignancy' arises because the balance between cell growth and cell death is disturbed, allowing cancer cells to grow almost unhindered and indefinitely. A key role in some of the diseases plays the defect of guardian genes, which leads to cancer arising in the first place or gaining significant aggressiveness in its course. A functional loss of these genes prevents cells, whose genetic information (DNA) has been altered by various causes, from dying, thereby gaining a survival advantage over healthy tissue.[483]

At the beginning, there is usually DNA damage that may have occurred years or even decades before the disease manifests. Such damage can be caused by ionizing radiation (e.g. ultraviolet light, X-rays, radioactivity), chemicals (e.g. benzene, chromium), or viruses (e.g. HPV). A mutation generally also increases the likelihood of further damage, so that the cells may become malignant over time, meaning they exceed their own tissue boundaries, destroy the surrounding tissue, and form secondary tumours (metastases) in more distant parts of the body.[484]

Globocan, the global cancer observatory of the International Agency for Research on Cancer (IARC) as a specialized cancer agency of the WHO,[485] shows that some 20 million new cancer cases occur per year worldwide resulting in about 10 million deaths p.a. This corresponds to an age-standardized incidence rate of 196.9 per

---

483 Compare Bertz (2010).
484 Compare z.B. Meade and Emch (2005).
485 Compare https://gco.iarc.fr/en. (Ferlay, Shin,et al. 2010a). "GLOBOCAN 2008 v1.2, Cancer Incidence and Mortality Worldwide." CancerBase No. 10 Retrieved 1.2.2012, 2012, from http://globocan.iarc.fr.

100,000 inhabitants, with males bearing a higher risk than females (212.6 vs. 186.3). Some 20% of people will develop cancer before the age of 75, and about 10% will die from it, with rates being higher in men than in women (11.4 vs. 8.0%, compare Table 3.14).

The incidence of cancers is higher in countries in the fourth and fifth phase of the epidemiological transition given the strong association of cancer with increasing age due to accumulation of gene mutations with each cell division. Thus, the incidence of many forms of cancer is higher in high-income countries than in low-income countries. However, the instruments of secondary prevention, treatment, and tertiary prevention are much better in high-income countries, so that about 70% of cancer deaths occur in developing countries, with an increasing trend. Even beyond the income classification, there remain significant regional differences that provide insight into the complex inherited and acquired risk factors for developing cancer.[486]

Like most other diseases, cancer develops in the interplay of genetic disposition, exposure in the environment, and culture. The genetic disposition is evident in a disease primarily triggered by mutations. There is a clear familial aggregation of certain cancers. At the same time, certain population groups are protected from some forms of cancer. For example, melanoma is much less common in dark-skinned people than in light-skinned people.

The exposure to DNA-damaging factors depends on the living environment. For example, the fair-skinned Scandinavian or the red-haired Irishman is sufficiently protected against skin cancer in his original habitat, but the same person must be very cautious after migrating to countries with higher UV light exposure, e.g. to Australia. Humans respond to the increased risk with cultural means, such as large hats or UV-absorbing clothing. Generally, however, cultural habits are often responsible for cancer, such as smoking for lung cancer or alcohol abuse for liver cancer.

Table 3.14: Cancer statistics (2022).[487]

Statistics	Men	Women	Total
New cases ('000)	10,311,610	9,664,889	19,976,499
Age-adjusted incidence rate	212.6	186.3	196.9
Risk of illness before age 75 (%)	21.8	18.5	20.0
Deaths ('000)	5,430,284	4,313,548	9,743,832

486 Compare https://gco.iarc.fr/today/en/dataviz/tables?mode=population.
487 Source: Globocan (2024).

Table 3.14 (continued)

Statistics	Men	Women	Total
Age-adjusted mortality rate	109.8	76.9	97.7
Mortality risk before age 75 (%)	11.4	8.0	9.6
Most frequent types of cancer	Lung, prostate, and colorectum	Breast, lung, and colorectum	Lung, breast, and colorectum

From the interaction of genetic disposition, exposure, and cultural behaviour, patterns emerge as shown in Figure 3.49. The extremely different incidences are partially due to different survey standards, but for the most part, they likely reflect human risk behaviour. Alcohol, particularly home distilling common in many developing regions, and mold (*Aspergillus flavus*), as found in peanuts or rice, are among the most significant risk factors with highly variable global distribution.[488]

Modelling cancer for health economic analysis is simple in one sense, as incidence does not depend on prevalence. However, it quickly pushes healthcare managers to their limits since, so far, only correlations of risk factors with diseases are known, while the underlying causality often appears more than questionable. Thus, cancer, like many other chronic degenerative diseases, presents a massive and steadily increasing problem for international healthcare management that an in-depth examination of this demand component is mandatory for anyone who wants to design and manage healthcare systems and facilities.[489]

These few examples of chronic degenerative diseases should suffice to show that they are also of high and especially increasing importance for resource-poor countries. Since they usually do not have a single cause, the analysis of risk factors becomes central. The most important risk factors for chronic degenerative and infectious diseases have already been briefly mentioned and will be presented in more detail below (compare Section 3.5), as they provide access to the complexity and to prevention and intervention options.

---

488 Compare Wu and Khlangwiset (2010) and Liu and Wu (2010).
489 Compare Bosanquet and Sikora (2006).

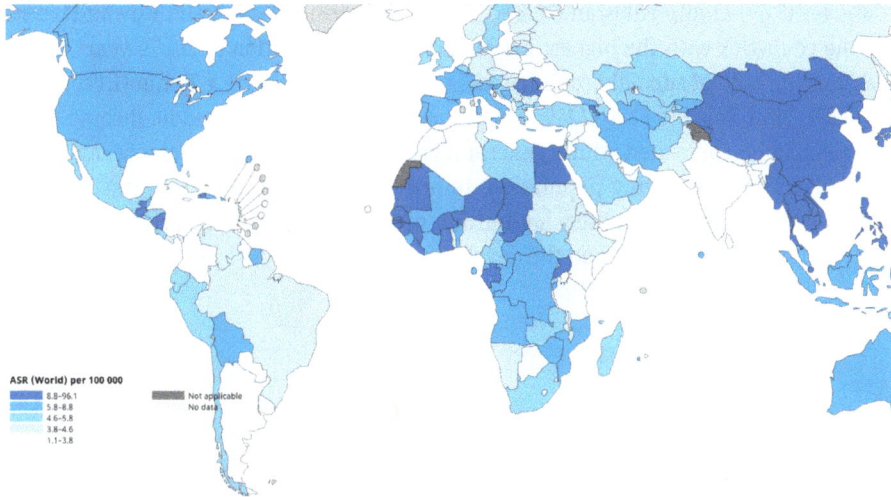

Figure 3.49: Liver and intrahepatic bile duct cancer 2022 (age-adjusted incidence per 100,000, both sexes).[490]

3.4.2 Case Study: Diabetes Mellitus Type II

3.4.2.1 Relevance

Diabetes mellitus type II (T2DM) is a non-communicable disease with a high prevalence and an increasing incidence worldwide. The International Diabetes Federation (IDF) estimates that about 537 million adults (20–79 years) are affected worldwide and more than 75% of diabetes patients live in low- or middle-income countries.[491] The estimated global direct health expenditure on diabetes was estimated as US$760 billion (2019).[492] IDF also expects a strong increase of diabetes cases (2030: 643 million cases, 2045: 783 million cases) resulting in tremendous human suffering, deaths, and costs of treatment.[493] Thus, T2DM is a disease of high public health importance and a good representative to analyse the economic impact of NCDs on the healthcare systems.

In 2021, diabetes was the top nine cause of global loss of DALYs worldwide with 78,938,587 DALYs lost (2.74% of all causes). For causes of death, diabetes held the same position (no. nine globally) with 1.656 million deaths or 2.44% of all global deaths. As shown in Figure 3.50, there is a huge variety between regions and development levels. For instance, diabetes (and kidney diseases) rank on position 16 in low-income countries concerning loss of DALYs (2.3% of all), but on position 7 in upper-middle-income

---

490 Source: Ferlay, Shin, Bray, et al. (2010b).

491 Compare IDF (2021).

492 Compare Williams, Karuranga, Malanda, et al. (2020).

493 Compare Bommer, Sagalova, Heesemann, et al. (2018).

countries (5.6% of all). Pakistan (30.8%), French Polynesia (25.2%), and Kuwait (24.9%) are the countries with the highest prevalence in the population of 20–79 years, while the 'starving belt' of sub-Saharan Africa hardly knows diabetes, e.g. Benin (1.1%), Gambia (1.9%), and Burkina Faso (2.1%). The transition from a low- to middle-income country seems to be correlated with a general increase of incidence, prevalence, and mortality of T2DM. The ageing population, improved supply of food, and less physical activity contribute to an increasing burden of the disease, particularly in countries successfully moving forward on the development pathway.

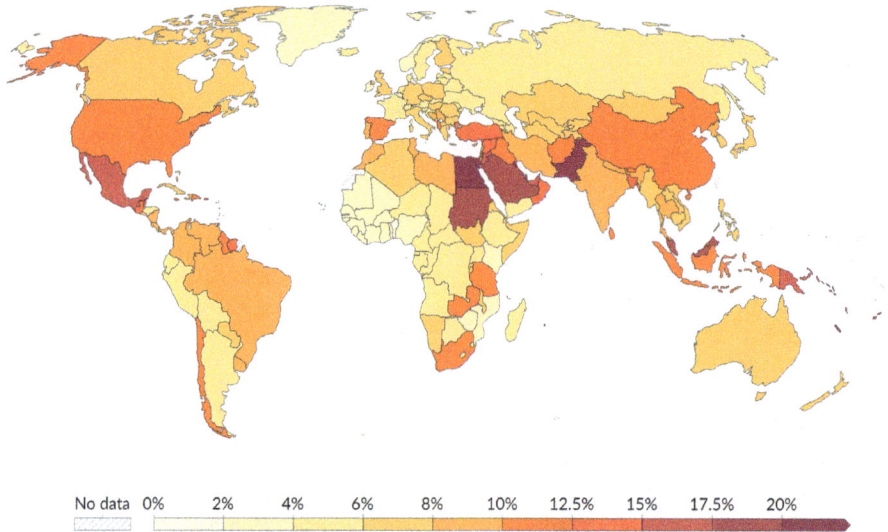

No data 0%   2%   4%   6%   8%   10%   12.5%   15%   17.5%   20%

Figure 3.50: Diabetes prevalence 2021 (share of people aged 20–79 years who have diabetes, both sexes).[494]

Diabetes is a risk factor for chronic complications, such as micro (retinopathy, nephropathy), macro (heart attack, stroke), vascular complications, neuropathy, and circulatory disorders of extremities (diabetic foot ulcers), i.e. theoretically, patients do not die directly from diabetes but from the complications resulting from T2DM. Thus, secondary prevention of complications is crucial for all patients with hyperglycaemia that requires diet, oral antidiabetic drugs (OAD), or insulin.

Prevention and treatment of T2DM in low-income countries is limited. Frequently, the public health services do hardly provide any diabetes care while still concentrating on communicable diseases. T2DM is not included in the basic package of healthcare, and OAD and insulin are not available, particularly in rural places. Where insu-

---

494 Source: OurWorldinData – CC-BY@: https://ourworldindata.org/grapher/diabetes-prevalence (18.02.2025).

lin is available and affordable, logistic challenges constitute another barrier as the material must be kept in a refrigerator and requires sterile syringes and needles.

3.4.2.2 Complexity

In this case study, we will analyse the economics of T2DM in Cambodia. The public health services in health centres and hospitals of this Southeast Asian country provide a basic package of state-guaranteed healthcare services including medication. Most patients have to pay highly subsidized fees, and the poor are exempted. The package is, however, rather limited, and does not include OAD or insulin. Consequently, diabetic patients have to seek services from private providers including a wide set of private pharmacies with very different quality and price level.

Most diabetic patients in Cambodia are undiagnosed until they have severe complications, as blood sugar testing is usually not performed in health centres. As antidiabetic drugs are only available in private pharmacies for comparably high prices, even those who are diagnosed will receive proper treatment only if they can afford it. The same is true for insulin. Consequently, self-help groups and 'peer-educator' groups have been started.[495] MoPoTsyo (Patient Information Centre), for instance, supports diabetes patients with drugs and insulin. At the same time, it teaches them to become peer educators for their villages. This includes the search for potential diabetic cases. Peer educator networks have been accepted by the government as an important contribution to the fight against NCDs,[496] but until now, no funds are allocated by the ministry so that most Cambodians remain without any support if they develop diabetes.

The calculation and prognosis of the costs of different interventions against T2DM is of high importance. In addition, the Ministry of Health is obliged to include new interventions into the basic package of services only if they are cost-effective in comparison to other possible interventions. For that purpose, we developed a Markov model following a cohort of from 2008 to 2028. Figure 3.51 shows the fundamental structure of the Markov model recalling the biological life of a T2DM patient.

The basic simulation projects the epidemiological and economic consequences if the government does not change its current policy, i.e. if the prevention and treatment of T2DM is not included in the basic healthcare package. In this case, only 12.5% of people requiring OAD and insulin can afford them by own funds or have access to them by charitable organizations. The basic simulation assumes that this rate remains stable.

Under this assumption, the number of people with T2DM is steadily increasing from 145,000 in the year 2008 to 264,000 in the year 2028 (+82%). At the same time, the

---

495 Compare van Pelt, Lucas, and Men (2012).
496 Compare Royal Government of Cambodia (2014).

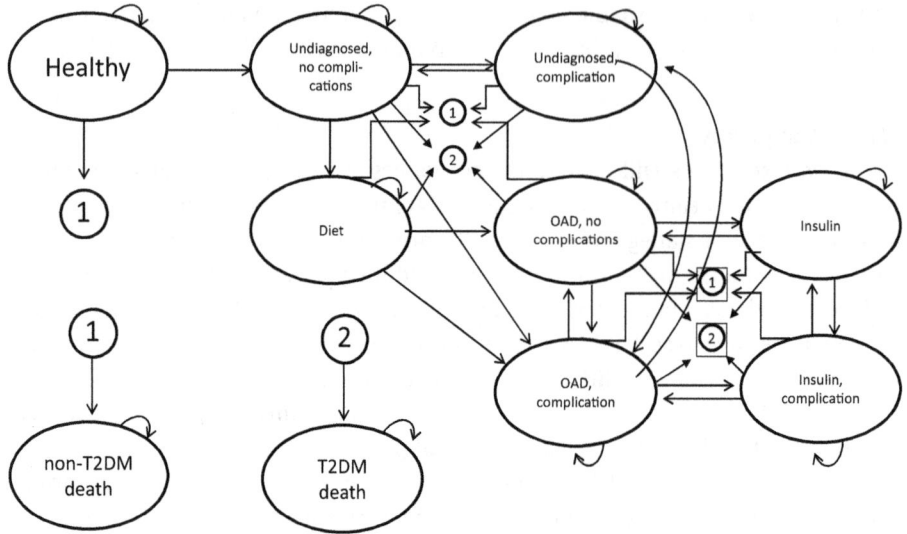

Figure 3.51: Markov graph of T2DM.[497]

population of this age group increases by 67%, i.e. the prevalence rate increases from 4.0% to 4.4% in the age group of ≥35 years.

The majority of T2DM cases remain undiagnosed. The rate is almost stable (63–64%) as the basic simulation assumes that no additional interventions are implemented. The number of diagnosed patients with complication, however, is increasing to a higher extent than the number of diagnosed patients without complications. In 2008, 59% of diagnosed patients had complications, in the year 2028, this rate will have increased to 68%. This is due to the fact that the ageing population and the longer duration of diabetes will result in more cases with complications.

Figure 3.52 shows the number of diagnosed T2DM cases requiring different forms of therapy. 'Diet' means that a diagnosed patient does not receive any medication. Regularly, he is obliged to live a specific diet and modify the lifestyle. OAD are the next stage, followed by injection of insulin. In 2008, 2% would not require any form of medication, 84% would need OAD therapy, and 14% would need insulin. In the year 2028, 8% of diagnosed cases will not require medication, 76% would need OAD therapy, and 17% would need insulin therapy. Thus, a higher share of the population will be in the severe state of requiring insulin. The increase of 114% is much higher than the increase of the total number of diabetic cases in Cambodia. The decision-makers in Cambodia can expect that the worst medical and economic consequences of T2DM are still to come.

---

497 Source: Flessa and Zembok (2014).

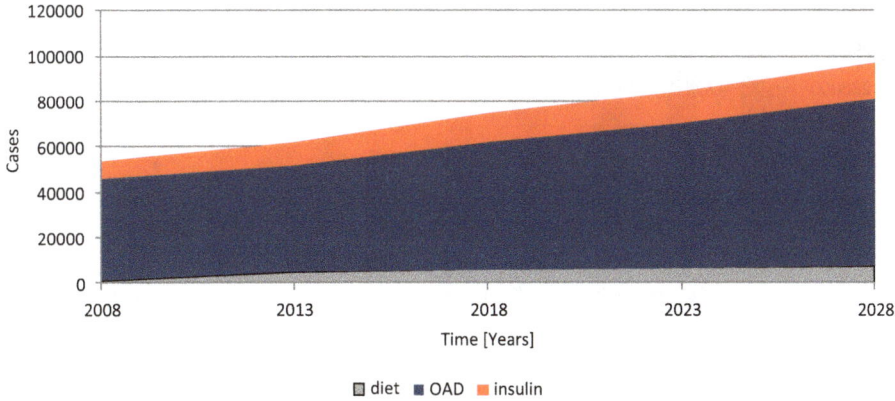

Figure 3.52: Therapy options for T2DM.[498]

This is also reflected by the steadily increasing costs of treatment of patients with T2DM in Cambodia. In the moment, it is estimated that 12.5% of people requiring OAD and insulin therapy do actually receive it (MoPoTsyo 2012; Cambodia 2013). In the year 2008, the 54,000 diagnosed T2DM patients would incur costs of US$2 million to cover all of diabetes treatment. About 57% of this amount would have to be spent for OAD therapy, and the rest for insulin therapy. In the year 2028, this amount will have grown to US$4 million to cover 97,000 patients. If all patients (incl. non-diagnosed) had to be paid-for, the respective figure would be US$5.5 million and US$11 million. These calculations assume stable prices and no discounting. Thus, the costs will double due to a shift of patients towards the expensive patients with complications and requiring insulin. The expected average cost per diagnosed diabetic patient p. a. was US$38 in the year 2008 and will be US$42 in the year 2028.

Early screening and the provision of drugs and insulin are crucial for an improvement of the situation. Here, we would like to concentrate on insulin therapy. Currently, only some 12.5% of those requiring insulin therapy have access to it. In the following, we will analyse the consequences of improved access to insulin therapy.

Figure 3.53 shows the impact of different coverage rates of insulin therapy on the number of deaths. As expected, many deaths will be averted and many years of life saved if more diabetic patients requiring insulin have access to it. If all patients requiring insulin receive it, 43,000 years of life could be saved and 5,800 deaths averted between 2008 and 2028. The number of people living with insulin therapy increases so that the share of diabetic patients with insulin therapy among all diagnosed diabetic patients increases from 17% to 22%. Consequently, the total cost increases from US$42 to US$63 per diagnosed diabetic case.

---

498 Source: Flessa and Zembok (2014).

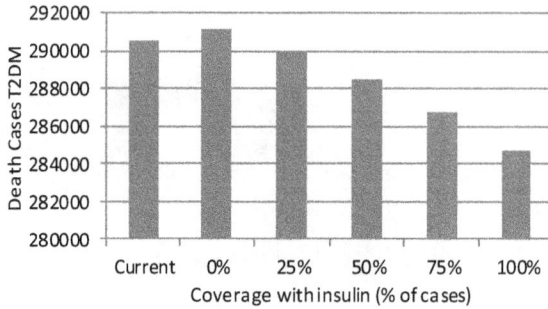

Figure 3.53: Coverage with insulin for T2DM.[499]

If the insulin coverage increases from 12.5% to 25%, the present value of these additional cost will be US$2.3 million, if the entire population is covered, it will be US$20 million. Insulin therapy is quite expensive per person, so that the cost-effectiveness of improved access to insulin is lower than the cost-effectiveness of a higher coverage by OAD therapy. The ICER is US$451 per year of life saved if the access improves from 12.5% to 25%. For an increase from 12.5% to 100%, the respective figure is US$457 ($r = 5\%$).

Consequently, improved access to insulin is cost-effective in Cambodia, but not as effective as improved access to OAD therapy. From a purely economic perspective, improving OAD therapy would have a higher priority than insulin therapy. However, patients requiring insulin are most likely suffering more than patients who can still deal with OAD therapy. Thus, insulin therapy must have a high priority. However, the cost of improved access to insulin is considerable. If all patients requiring insulin are to receive full insulin coverage, the additional cost of the year 2008 will be US$2,473,319, i.e. 6.5 million instead of US$4.1 million. Cambodia will have to seek funds for this additional demand.

The case study demonstrates that T2DM comprises a complex epidemiological and economic process calling for systematic modelling in order to assess the impact of interventions. For a chronic degenerative disease, a Markov model is an appropriate instrument to forecast the budget impact and cost-effectiveness of different interventions.

3.4.3 Case Study: Cataract

3.4.3.1 Relevance

Blindness and vision impairment are major medical and economic problems worldwide. The "Lancet Global Health Commission on Global Eye Health: vision beyond 2020" states that some 1.1 billion people are suffering from some kind of vision im-

---

499 Source: Flessa and Zembok (2014).

pairment,[500] and other organizations estimate even higher numbers.[501] Roughly, half of the people living with vision impairment or blindness have distance vision impairment, and the other half have near-vision impairment[502] with presbyopia, cataract, refractive errors, and glaucoma, as the main causes. The prevalence of vision impairment is much higher in low- and middle-income than in high-income countries, and in particular, prevention and cure of eye diseases is a major issue of concern in many least developed countries.[503]

Cataract is a cloudy area in the lens leading to decreased vision.[504] It is estimated that about 50% of all blindness and 33% of visual impairment are caused by cataracts[505] although a comparably simple lens replacement (cataract surgery) can effectively restore vision in most cases. Consequently, cataract is mainly a medical problem of low- and middle-income countries to be faced by the vulnerable population, in particular, people living in rural areas, older people, women, and illiterate.[506] With the demographic transition of these countries, it is expected that the prevalence of cataracts will increase dramatically unless cataract surgery will be made available even in rural and impoverished settings in Africa and Asia.[507]

The tangible cost of blindness and vision impairment are consequently high and cover cost of treatment (direct provider and household cost), as well as opportunity cost. The latter occurs because a person with reduced vision or blindness will not be as productive as a person without impairment. At the same time, a severely impaired or blind person will frequently need a caregiver to support him who himself will face some opportunity cost of reduced productivity. As mentioned in the "Lancet Global Health Commission on Global Eye Health: vision beyond 2020", the annual productivity loss due to visual impairment or blindness was highest in low- and middle-income countries (e.g. South Asia: 0.6% of GDP) and lowest in high-income countries (e.g. Western Europe: 0.15% of GDP).[508] Marques et al. calculated the global annual productivity loss due to moderate to severe visual impairment (MSVI) or blindness as US$411 billion PPP or 0.3% of global GDP.[509] The WHO estimates the costs of addressing the coverage gap of services to prevent or address MSVI and blindness. As shown in Table 3.15, the required resources to treat or prevent the respective conditions would be quite high calling for a cost-effectiveness analysis in order to allocate scarce healthcare resources to those conditions with the highest efficiency.

---

500 Compare Burton, Ramke, Marques, et al. (2021) and Burton, Ramke, Marques, et al. (2021).
501 Compare WHO (2022).
502 Compare Burton, Ramke, Marques, et al. (2021).
503 Compare IAPD (2022).
504 Compare Psychrembel (2022).
505 Compare Burton, Ramke, Marques, et al. (2021).
506 Compare Rao, Khanna and Payal (2011).
507 Compare Teller and Hailemariam (2011).
508 Compare Burton, Ramke, Marques, et al. (2021).
509 Compare Marques, Ramke, Cairns, et al. (2021).

Table 3.15: Costs of addressing the coverage gap of visual impairment and blindness.[510]

MSVI or blindness causes that are . . .	Disease	US$ (2018)
. . . treatable or addressable	Cataract	8,768,759,000
	Unaddressed refractive error (distance)	6,988,223,000
	Unaddressed refractive error (near)	9,035,476,000
	Total	24,792,458,000
. . . preventable	Diabetic retinopathy	19,858,251,000
	Trachoma	494,077,000
	Glaucoma	11,744,642,000
	Total	32,096,970,000

A number of studies have shown the cost-effectiveness of cataract surgery, particularly in high-income countries.[511] However, our knowledge about the economic dimension of cataract treatment in low-income countries is limited.[512] Lansingh et al. calculated the cost-effectiveness for 'developed countries' as 730 to international $2,400 per DALY averted, the respective figures for 'developing countries' ranged from international $90 to $370 per DALY averted.[513] However, the composition of costs and the relevance of the age of the patient for the cost-effectiveness analysis have not been addressed appropriately.

3.4.3.2 Complexity

In order to assess the cost-effectiveness of a cataract surgery, we calculate the net value of the total direct and indirect lifetime cost of a patient with cataract from the onset of the disease to death for the case with and without a cataract surgery at a certain age (from 40 to 98 years). If the net value of the lifetime cost with surgery is lower than without the surgery, the intervention is called cost-saving. Otherwise, the difference is the net value of the additional cost. The quotient between the net value of this additional cost and the net value of the additional quality of life is the cost-effectiveness, i.e. it shows how much has to be invested to gain one quality of life year. If this cost-effectiveness ration is lower than or equal to the average GDP p.c., we call an intervention highly cost-effective. If it is higher than the average GDP p.c. but lower or equal to twice the GDP p.c., we call it cost-effective.[514] The respective data is given by Flessa.[515]

---

510 Source: World Health Organization (2019).
511 Compare Busbee, Brown, Brown, et al. (2002) and Baltussen, Sylla, and Mariotti (2004).
512 Compare Kuper, Polack, Mathenge, et al. (2010) and Polack, Eusebio, Mathenge, et al. (2010).
513 Compare Lansingh, Carter, and Martens (2007).
514 Compare WHO (2011b).
515 Compare Flessa (2022).

The baseline scenario assumes that the surgery is done at the beginning of the second stage (severe visual impairment) 10 years after the onset of cataract with mild or moderate impairment. Based on the estimates of the experts, it also assumes that the patient is 60 years of age when he is operated on, i.e. all costs and benefits are discounted for a 50-year-old person. The 60-year-old patient has a life expectancy of 77 years. If not operated on, the net value of the total cost is US$2,048.45, and with the surgery, it is US$801.47, i.e. the cataract surgery is cost-saving. In total, 68% of costs are opportunity cost of the caregiver, as the patient will be blind for 12 years, and 22% are productivity loss of the patient, as he will have a reduced productivity until he retires (in the year of the surgery). The remaining 11% are the direct treatment costs. The main difference between the patient with and without the surgery is the productivity loss of the caregiver, which is, in particular, high when the patient is blind which will be avoided completely by the surgery when severe visual impairment starts.

It is relevant to ask how the time of surgery determines the cost-savings. Figure 3.54 shows the result for three scenarios. A later surgery can have two reasons. Firstly, because the onset of the cataract is later in life, and secondly, because the surgery is postponed. The figure shows that the gain in quality of life is lower for both reasons, i.e. an early surgery results in higher increase in quality of life. At the same time, the cost-savings are lower if the patient is operated on early. For instance, if a patient has the onset of cataract with 80 years, the additional lifetime costs are US$225.54 with an increase of quality of life of 0.909. The 80-year-old patient has a rest life expectancy of 5 years, and he will not live long enough to develop severe visual impairment due to cataract. He retired so that no productivity loss is experienced, and with mild/moderate impairment, he will not require a caregiver. Thus, without operation, he will have only low costs. At the same time, the 80-year-old blind person will have high opportunity costs for the caregiver so that the surgery saves US$19.24 and improves the quality of life by 0.19 QALYs. Consequently, there is a good reason to perform the surgery for all blind patients irrespective of their age. For patients with mild/moderate impairment, it is cost-saving to do the surgery before the age of 65, for patients with severe impairment, it is cost-saving to operate on the patient until age of 78.

For the case of surgery in the beginning of the severe impairment, the cost-saving corridor extents to a patient with onset of cataract in the age of 68 and a surgery in the age of 78. For older patients, it is not cost-saving, e.g. the onset with age of 69 leads to a net value of additional lifetime costs of US$21.95 and a gain of 0.69 QALYs. Still, the operation is highly cost-effective with cost of US$32.01 per QALY. If the onset and the surgery are later, the cost-effectiveness will decrease, e.g. the cost per QALY are US$117.21, US$287.81, and US$800.00 for onset age of 75, 80, and 85. For patients older than 95 years, the remaining rest life expectancy is lower than 1 year; thus, it is insufficient to have any gain of quality of life.

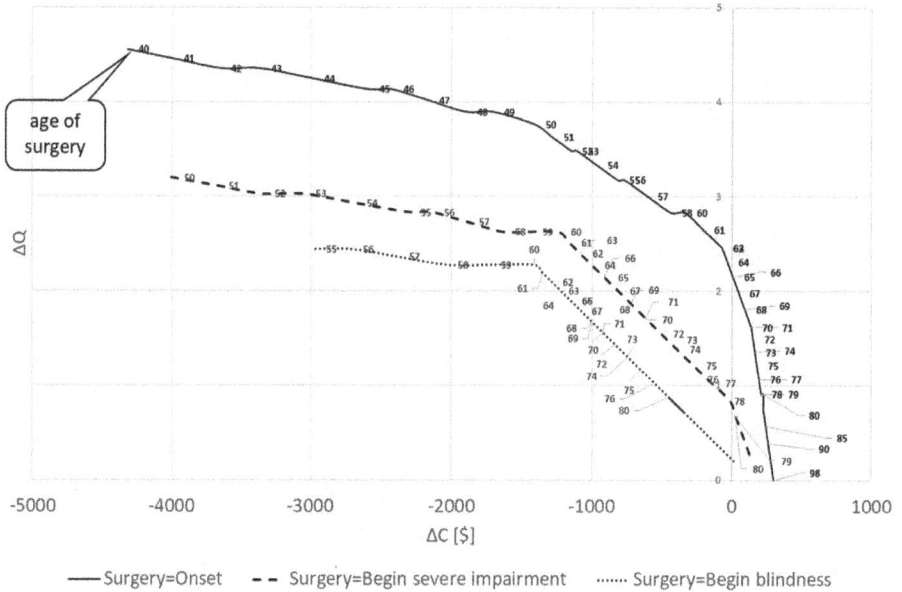

Figure 3.54: Cost-saving and quality of life of cataract surgery.[516]

If the surgery is done in the same year as the onset of cataract, the corridor of cost-saving is smaller. A patient with onset age of 65 years (surgery age of 75) is not cost-saving any more. Thus, the cost per QALY is only US$2.88 in this age. The statistic increases progressively. If the surgery is done in the age of 90, the cost is US$668.29 per QALY, and if it is done in the age of 92, it is US$1,400.00 per QALY. Finally, if the surgery is done when blindness is fully developed, the procedure remains cost-saving until the onset age of 76 (surgery age of 91). At the onset age of 77, the cost per QALY is US$100.00. However, we have to state that the statistics for the three alternatives cannot be compared easily because the life expectancy is different. For instance, a person who is operated on in age 65 (i.e. at the beginning of mild/moderate impairment) has a life expectancy of 78.8 years; a person who is operated on in age 75 (i.e. at the beginning of severe impairment) has a life expectancy of 82.5 years; and a person who receives surgery in the age of 80 (i.e. at the beginning of blindness) has a life expectancy of 85.0 years. Thus, the longer we wait for the surgery, the higher is the likelihood that the patient will get old and thus, the more cost-saving the surgery will be.

Figure 3.55 generalizes these findings. For most ages of onset and surgery, as well as for all relevant parameter variations, cataract surgery is cost-saving in low-income countries. For patients with an onset of the mild/moderate impairment at ages be-

---

516 Source: Flessa (2022).

tween 65 and 70, the intervention is not cost-saving, but still highly cost-effective. Only for very high ages, it is 'only' cost-effective. The only case where cataract surgery in low-income countries is not cost-effective at a threshold of 2·GDP p.c. is if the rest life expectancy is less than 1 year with an age of 93 or higher.[517] However, these cases are so rare in low-income countries that each individual has to be assessed separately. Generally, this analysis confirms that cataract surgery in low-income countries is a good deal.

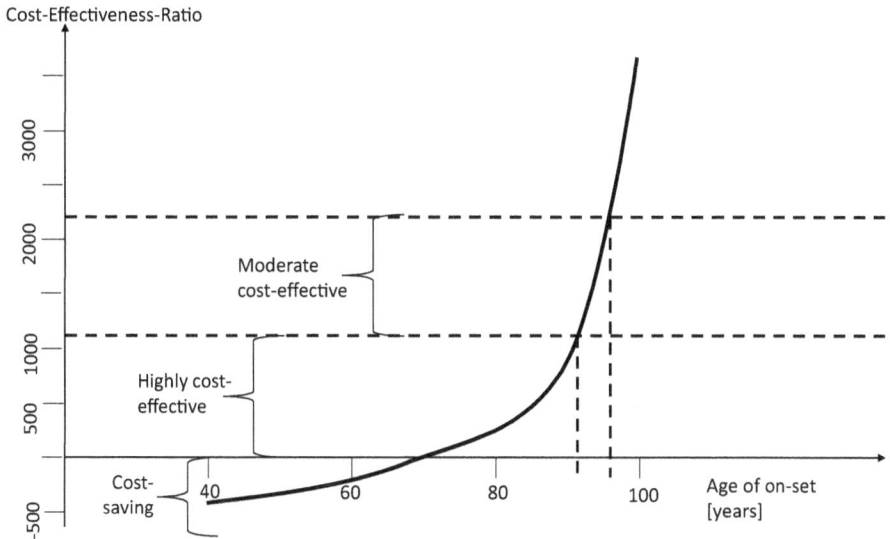

Figure 3.55: Cost-saving and cost-effectiveness corridor.[518]

It is also a matter of fact that financing cataract surgery in low-income countries is only one element of overcoming blindness. Even middle-income countries are still struggling to reach the entire population and overcome barriers, i.e. uptake and coverage of cataract surgery in low- and middle-income countries is a challenge as limited accessibility, poor quality of services, cultural habits, and believes make it difficult to cover the population in need even if financial resources were sufficient.[519] In a systematic review, Mailu et al. identified factors reducing the uptake of cataract surgery.[520] Economic parameters on the side of the demander, as well as the supplier,

---

517 Common cost-effectiveness thresholds: highly cost-effective: cost per year of life ≤1 GDP p.c.; moderate cost-effective: cost per year of life ≤2 GDP p.c. In some studies, an intervention is still called cost-effective if cost per year of life ≤3 GDP p.c. Compare Kazibwe, Gheorghe, Wilson, et al. (2022).
518 Source: Flessa (2022).
519 Compare Lindfield, Vishwanath, Ngounou, et al. (2012) and Grimes, Bowman, Dodgion, et al. (2011).
520 Compare Mailu, Virendrakumar, Bechange, et al. (2020).

play a major role, e.g. socio-economic characteristics, costs of surgery, distance to the healthcare facility, and perceived quality of services.

Economic, social, demographic, and cultural barriers lead to a situation where effective cataract surgical coverage (as the number of people in a population who have been operated on for cataract with a good outcome divided by the number of people operated on or requiring surgery) can be as low as 3.8% (Guinea Bissau) with a median of 14.8% in low-income countries.[521] Consequently, there is general agreement that there is a need to investment more into respective cataract interventions, and costs are not the only prohibiting factor, but an important one.[522] However, the actual cost of the respective programmes and interventions are unknown or obsolete for most low-income countries, and respective estimates of cost-effectiveness based on these older publications are outdated themselves (Horton).[523]

3.4.4 Case Study: Cervix Uteri Carcinoma

3.4.4.1 Relevance
Cervical cancer (cervix uteri carcinoma, CUC) is a malignant neoplasm that is almost exclusively caused by an infection with a specific virus, the HPV. This disease is the second most common cancer in women worldwide with some 667,000 new cases and 297,000 deaths resulting in a loss of almost 10 million DALYs annually (2021).[524] The incidence depends strongly on the region (see Table 3.16). As the infection is sexually transmitted, sexual behaviour determines it to a high extent. At the same time, the CUC can take decades to develop. Consequently, countries with a high life expectancy have a greater risk of a high incidence of cervical cancer. Furthermore, in some areas, this disease might be highly underdiagnosed and underreported.

Table 3.16: Incidence and mortality of cervical cancer.[525]

WHO region	Incidence (new cases p.a. per 100,000)	Mortality (deaths p.a. per 100,000)	Ratio (mortality/ incidence)
Global	16.97	7.55	44.5%
African region	18.2	10.04	55.2%
Region of the Americas	23.79	8.46	35.6%

---

521 Compare McCormick, Butcher, Evans, et al. (2022).
522 Compare Ramke, Evans, Habtamu, et al. (2022).
523 For example Horton, Gelband, Jamison, et al. (2017).
524 Source: IHME (2025).
525 Source: IHME (2025).

Table 3.16 (continued)

WHO region	Incidence (new cases p.a. per 100,000)	Mortality (deaths p.a. per 100,000)	Ratio (mortality/ incidence)
Eastern Mediterranean region	5.23	2.70	51.6%
European region	15.85	6.39	40.3%
Southeast Asia region	16.26	8.44	51.9%
Western Pacific region	18.27	6.98	38.2%

CUC is a complex disease. The modelling of this disease is more complex than for many other diseases. Firstly, caused by HPV, i.e. it is an infectious disease and therefore the likelihood of being infected depends on the number of people who were previously infected and have become infectious, i.e. the infection cycle is dynamic and requires feedback loops between the previously infected and the current infections.

Secondly, the infection can (with a certain probability) lead to cancer, i.e. it is an infectious-disease that 'behaves' like a chronic degenerative disease. The WHO categorizes CUC as a 'malignant neoplasm' in the 'non-communicable diseases' category,[526] although it is clearly a communicable disease. Modelling the processes related to CUC requires characteristics or features of chronic degenerative and communicable diseases in the same model.

Thirdly, CUC is highly complex, as decades can lie between infection and death. On average, lesions will appear about 16 years after the infection, the transition from first lesions to cancer takes another 8 years, and if untreated, the patient can die within 2 years.[527] In reality, these values have a wide deviation. Any intervention will have impacts that will become more pronounced over time.

A realistic model and health economic analysis of CUC (compare Figure 3.56) is more complex and combines the models given in Section 3.2. The healthcare manager has to consider:
– Women or men: the virus is usually transferred from one sexual partner to the other through intercourse, but only women develop CUC.
– Stems: several stems of the papillomavirus exist simultaneously.
– Infection: for some purposes, it is sufficient to start with a cohort of infected and follow them for the rest of their lives (cohort models), while for other purposes, it is crucial to include the infection. The risk of infection depends on the prevalence of HPV in a population, i.e. on the incidence of former periods, i.e. the infection is dynamic. For very short forecasting periods, assuming a constant infection rate is acceptable, for longer periods, it is misleading.

526 Compare WHO (2024b).
527 Compare Seinfeld (2013), Goldie, Kuhn, Denny, et al. (2001), and WHO (2006, 2013).

- Age: CUC is a STD, and sexual activity is found to be dependent on the age of the sexual partners. Thus, the healthcare manager will have to distinguish between age sets.
- Sexual behaviour: as a STD, we have to distinguish between individuals and their sexual behaviour, i.e. long-term partnerships, short-term relations, and coitus frequency that have an impact on the infection probability. Including this distinction is feasible but complex.
- Vaccination: if the economist wants to analyse the impact of a vaccination programme, separate compartments of vaccinated and immune populations are established. The efficacy of the vaccine can be modelled by transferring only a certain percentage of the vaccinated to the compartment of the vaccinated.
- Clearance: the immune system can defeat the virus, i.e. a share of the population of the compartment of the infected and the healthy will be transferred back to the compartment of the non-infected population.
- Screening: different models analyse different screening strategies, such as self-testing (e.g. ELEVATE),[528] point-of-care tests (e.g. VIA),[529] or laboratory tests (e.g. Pap smear).[530] All of these alternatives have advantages and disadvantages and have to be assessed concerning effectiveness, budget-impact, and cost-effectiveness (e.g. compliance, sensitivity, specificity, and cost). Figure 3.56 confronts the visual inspection at a health centre (VIA, left-hand side) with the combination of VIA with a self-testing device. It is obvious that the assessment of the advantages and disadvantages if quite complex.
- Treatment: pre-cancerous lesions can be treated e.g. by cryotherapy, but cancer treatment requires surgery and radiation. After a lesion is removed or a patient is successfully treated, the patient has the same risk as infected women who never had a lesion. The treatment of cancer is very costly and difficult under the conditions of low-income countries. Usually, it is only offered in few tertiary hospitals in the capital city inaccessible for most women.
- Transition: on average, an infected woman will develop a pre-cancerous lesion 16 years after infection, and it takes another 8 years on average for the lesion to develop into cancer.[531] This long-term feature of the disease challenges all economic analyses. Fighting back a disease that kills after 20 or 30 years is not in the focus of policy-makers.

---

528 "EarLy dEtection of cerVical cAncer in hard-to-reach populations of women through portable and point-of-care HPV Testing".
529 "Visual Inspection with Acetic acid".
530 Compare Legood, Gray, Mahé, et al. (2005), Sankaranarayanan, Nene, Shastri, et al. (2009), Huchko, Sneden, Leslie, et al. (2014), and Bedell, Goldstein, Goldstein, et al. (2020).
531 Compare Seinfeld (2013), Goldie, Kuhn, Denny, et al. (2001), and WHO (2006, 2013).

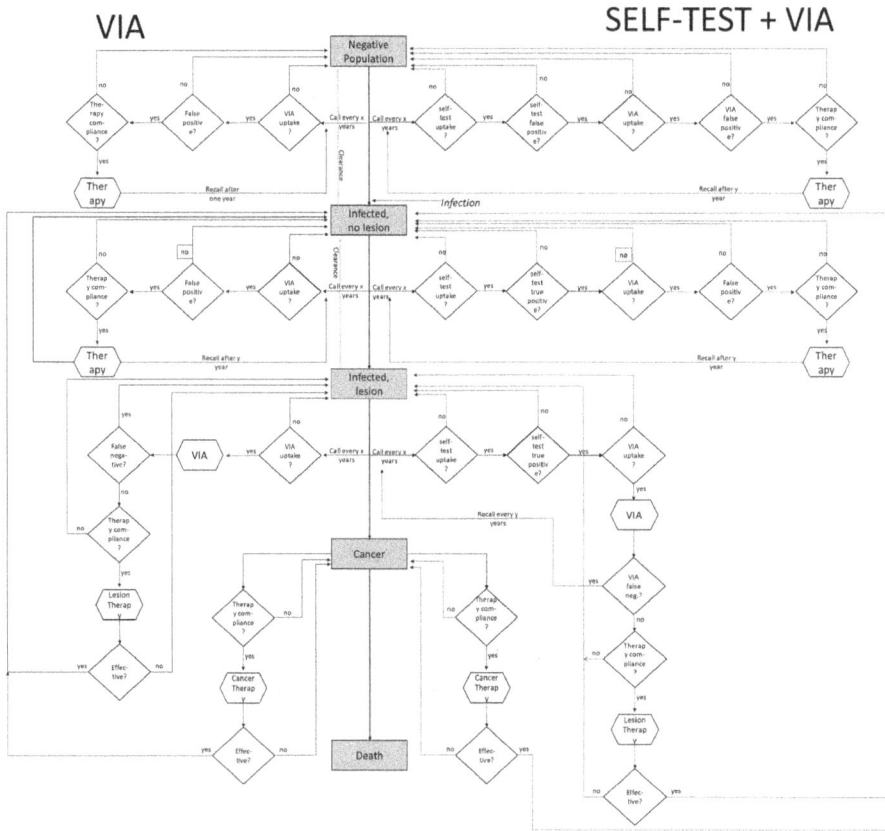

Figure 3.56: Cervical cancer model.[532]

To summarize, CUC is a highly complex disease requiring a complex health economic analysis because of the two aspects of the disease: infection and chronicity. However, cervical cancer is not the only disease with this dual characteristic. A number of viruses are known to cause cancer, such as Epstein-Barr virus (lymphoma), hepatitis B virus (liver cancer), hepatitis C virus (liver cancer), HIV (e.g. Kaposi sarcoma, lymphoma), human herpes virus 8 (Kaposi sarcoma), and human T-lymphotrophic virus (leukaemia/lymphoma).[533] These dual diseases pose a challenge even for the compilation and evaluation of statistics, as the WHO classifies all of them as category II diseases (non-communicable diseases), although their origin is infectious and should be considered category I diseases (communicable, maternal, neonatal, and nutritional diseases). Other examples include the links between pathogenic fungal infections or

532 Source: Own, based on Kim, Brisson, Edmunds, et al. (2008).
533 Compare Schiller and Lowy (2014).

aflatoxins (*Aspergillus flavus* and *Aspergillus parasiticus* causing liver cancer) and cancer development and pathogenesis.[534] In all of these cases, it is difficult to model the pathway from the contact with the agent (virus, fungus, . . .) to cancer, as it is a multiple-cause-multiple-effect model of epidemiology (compare Section 3.1.2.4): contact with the agent can be completely harmless or cause a variety of diseases. At the same time, however, the disease can be triggered by other causes. In comparison to some other forms of cancer (e.g. liver cancer), the complexity of cervical cancer is still manageable. Still, it is a challenge that will be demonstrated by the example of CUC in Cambodia.

3.4.4.2 Complexity

Figure 3.56 exhibits the two alternatives of screening and lesion treatment model applied in Cambodia. The figure shows that there is a need for many variables. In addition to the epidemiological (incidence, prevalence, mortality), demographic (age-sets, fertility, rest mortality), and social (marriage, sexual behaviour) parameters, specific variables for screening technologies are required. Based on a system dynamics model,[535] we collected the respective data from literature and expert interviews. Retrieving this data is frequently very complex for the healthcare manager. However, cervical cancer can also be used as an example that sometimes insufficient data is no challenge as long as we safeguard that the resulting uncertainty is handled professionally.

Firstly, in some cases, uncertain data has no impact on the results. For instance, the risk of being infected during a long-term partnership (if one partner is positive and the other negative) depends on the coitus frequency (f), the length of partnership (l), and the infectivity of the virus (q). While we can estimate the average length of partnerships and the infectivity, the coitus frequency is very difficult to retrieve. However, Figure 3.57 shows that the coitus frequency does not matter as long as the average length of a partnership is more than 100 months. The respective formulae are rather simple. As q denotes the infectivity, $1 - q$ is the likelihood that one sexual intercourse does not lead to an infection. Consequently, $(1 - q_{t,s,a})^{f \cdot l}$ is the likelihood that all sexual intercourse during the partnership will not lead to an infection. $\{1 - (1 - q_{t,s,a})^{f \cdot l}\}$ is the likelihood that at least one sexual intercourse will lead to an infection.[536] Thus, for realistic lengths of partnerships, the coitus frequency can be neglected.

---

534 Compare Garber (2001), Wu and Santella (2012), and Hosseini, Ahangari, Chapeland-Leclerc, et al. (2022).
535 Flessa (2016).
536 Compare Roth and Heidenberger (1998).

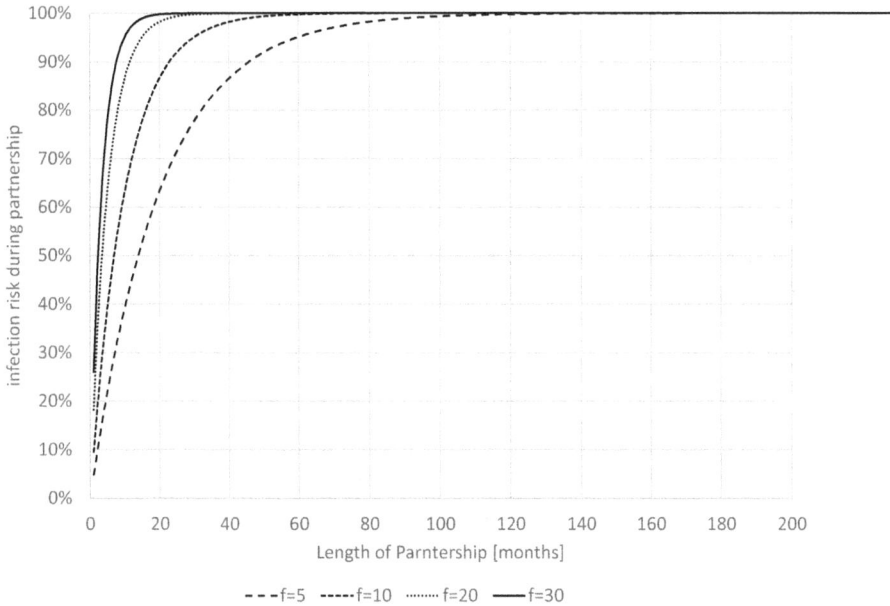

Figure 3.57: Infection risk during partnership.[537]

Secondly, uncertainty can be handled by sensitivity analysis. For this purpose, we change the uncertain parameters and analyse the impact of these changes on the outcomes of the model. Frequently, the change of parameter changes the quantitative (e.g. cost-effectiveness ratio), but not the qualitative results (e.g. an intervention is cost-effective). The sensitivity analysis frequently uses best, likely, and worst values from expert opinion and/or minimum and maximum values from the literature. In addition to this 'What-If?' approach, we can also ask 'How-to-Achieve?' questions, e.g. how much must the cost of an intervention decline so that the intervention becomes cost-effective.

Thirdly, uncertainty must be reflected in the analysis and policy-relevant interpretation of results. All results of a model under extreme uncertainty must be handled with great caution. The figures frequently suggest a degree of precision, which the simulation cannot offer. However, there is still a lot to learn from these models. It is generally accepted that these strategic models are "modelling for insights, not for numbers".[538] The health economic model is designed to understand the system much better, to point at research gaps, and to give some principle answers to pressuring questions of policymakers. These answers will not be precise figures, but still allow policy advice. Even under extreme uncertainty, models can produce robust insight – but the international

---

537 Source: Own, based on Wang and Fleßa (2021).
538 Compare Peace and Weyant (2008).

healthcare manager must have the integrity to caution his audience that there is always a risk of wrong results.

For the case of cervical cancer in Cambodia, Figure 3.58 shows the consequences of different interventions on the years of life lost (YLL). Without intervention, there will be a steady increase in infections, cancer cases, deaths, and YLL. Screening has the potential to rapidly increase detection of lesions or cancer cases and decrease the number of related deaths while the number of infections remains (almost) unchanged. The introduction of a HPV self-test before VIA screening will be even more effective to further reduce the number of cancer cases and deaths and especially YLL. However, only vaccination can (effectively) eradicate cervical cancer in the country, even if it takes decades. If the vaccination campaign starts in 2025 with offering a highly effective vaccine covering all girls of the respective ages, it will take until 2081 for CUC to be eradicated. However, this does not account for re-invasion by, e.g. migration.

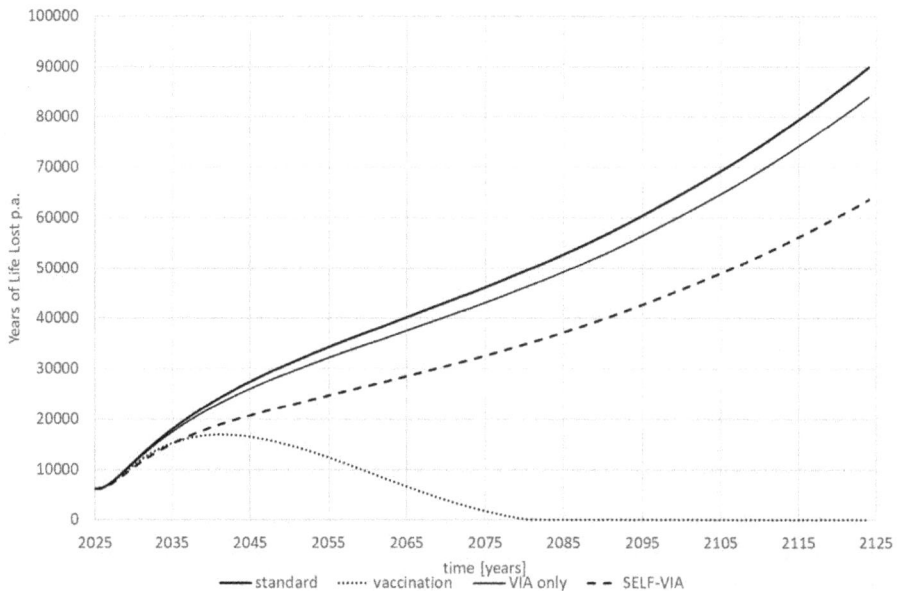

Figure 3.58: Years of life lost due to cervical cancer in Cambodia.[539]

Figure 3.59 depicts the cost per year of life saved for different interventions targeting CUC. It is obvious that the interventions to combat a chronic disease are only cost-effective if the time horizon is sufficiently long. If we assume that the cost per year of life saved must be lower than the gross national income per capita (2023) to be highly

---

539 Source: Own.

cost-effective, VIA screening is highly cost effective from 2031 onward. A combination of HPV self-testing and VIA screening is highly cost-effective from 2033, and a vaccination-only programme from 2035. From 2025 to 2039, the combination of self-testing and VIA screening is more cost-effective than vaccination; until 2066, VIA-only screening is more cost-effective than vaccination. Additionally, a self-test has a major impact on deaths and YLL, but as the tests are quite expensive, the ratio between years of life saved and intervention costs will always be comparably high.

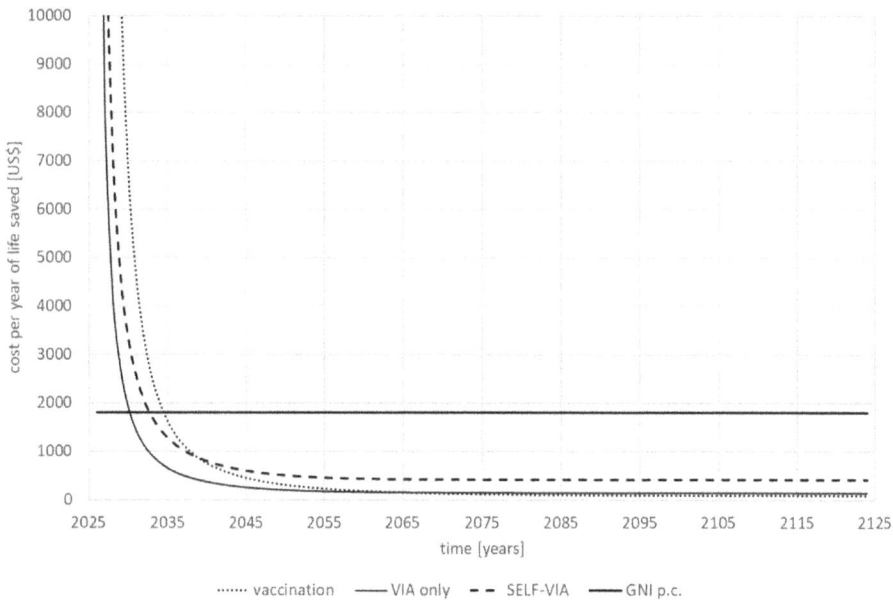

Figure 3.59: Cost per year of life saved by different interventions against cervical cancer in Cambodia.[540]

The results underline that low- and middle-income countries face different economic situations. An intervention can be cost-saving, i.e. the present value of the cost with intervention is lower than the present value of the future cost without intervention. From a business perspective, it might be worthwhile to take a loan and finance the intervention. However, governments or social health insurance are not likely to follow this strategy. Instead, even cost-saving interventions may not be implemented due to budget limits.

Although some measures are not cost-saving, they are nevertheless cost-effective because they 'buy' a comparably large gain in quality of life, life years, or other outcome measures. For this category, it is crucial to compare the cost-effectiveness ratio between this intervention and others in order to allot the scarce resources to the most

---

540 Source: Own.

cost-effective one. Sometimes, we have to consider a bundle of interventions as an alternative (e.g. screening plus vaccination). If the intervention is not cost-effective, it might still be possible and necessary to fund it because of political priorities. However, this will mean that better health could be achieved by another allocation of funds.

With these few scenarios regarding CUC, we close the section on the epidemiology of non-infectious diseases. It was demonstrated that the distinction between infectious and chronic degenerative diseases is blurred, which requires an even more rigorous assessment of the most effective intervention strategies by the international healthcare manager. It has also been shown that a number of factors determine the spread of infections and non-infectious diseases. These risk factors will be analysed in the next section.

3.5 Health Risks

3.5.1 Overview

Health risks are the non-medical determinants of health, i.e. "any attribute, characteristic or exposure of an individual that increases the likelihood of developing a disease or incurring an injury".[541] The main factor determining the incidence, prevalence and diffusion of communicable diseases is the respective agent (virus, bacteria, parasite, and fungus). Here, non-medical factors set the framework for the transmission process. For chronic degenerative diseases, non-medical factors dominate the epidemiological processes.

Table 3.17 shows the most relevant health risks for premature death globally and for income groups. It has to be noted that risks are hardly exclusive, i.e. the sum of death attributed to the factors is usually higher than the total number of deaths. It is obvious that the impact of a particular risk on the number of deaths strongly depends on the income group. Globally, high blood pressure is the worst risk factor, followed by air pollution (indoor and outdoor) and smoking. If we sort for high-income countries, high blood pressure, smoking, high blood sugar, and obesity are the big 'killers'. For low-income countries, air pollution (in particular indoor air pollution), high blood pressure, and low birthweight are of highest importance. Each development status has its own risk factors, and some risk factors are highly relevant for one country and rather unimportant for another.

---

541 Rojas-Rueda, Morales-Zamora, Alsufyani, et al. (2021).

Table 3.17: Health risks (million death) (2021).[542]

Risk factor	Global	Low-income	Lower-middle-income	Upper-middle-income	High-income
High blood pressure	10.850	0.479	3.950	4.630	1.780
Air pollution	8.080	0.567	4.030	2.950	0.429
Smoking	6.180	0.141	1.820	3.040	1.170
High blood sugar	5.290	0.224	1.970	2.950	1.170
Obesity	3.710	0.167	1.130	1.450	0.965
Indoor air pollution	3.110	0.545	0.210	0.466	0.003
High cholesterol	3.110	0.125	1.350	1.520	0.639
Diet high in sodium	1.860	0.054	0.491	1.070	0.243
Alcohol use	1.810	0.089	0.565	0.729	0.424
Diet low in fruits	1.680	0.111	0.859	0.486	0.226
Diet low in grains	1.550	0.069	0.561	0.641	0.301
Low birthweight	1.540	0.380	1.050	0.095	0.018
Secondhand smoke	1.290	0.500	0.486	0.640	0.113
Unsafe sex	0.901	0.190	0.386	0.279	0.440
Unsafe water sources	0.802	0.171	0.601	0.016	0.003
Low physical activity	0.657	0.230	0.229	0.263	0.141
Unsafe sanitation	0.595	0.146	0.595	0.432	0.001
Child wasting	0.493	0.162	0.493	0.240	0.024
Drug use	0.463	0.120	0.147	0.133	0.424

Figure 3.60 illustrates that the risks can be the result of the individual biology (genetics, age, gender, family history) and (almost) unamendable. Other risks are caused by the habitat (e.g. settlement, housing, air pollution) which cannot be changed by the individual easily, but the whole society can mitigate the risk. Most risks, however, are a consequence of individual behaviour and can be addressed by the individual. However, the risk factors are correlated, e.g. obesity is a risk factor which itself is partially caused by genetics, diet, stress, and insufficient exercise (among others). The figure exemplifies the multiple-cause-multiple-effect model: while infectious diseases are primarily caused by the agent (e.g. virus), chronic degenerative diseases usually have more than one risk factor, and the risks are accumulating. At the same time, no risk factor is fully responsible for the development of this disease.

In the following, we will analyse some of these risk factors in more detail in order to determine the portfolio of potential interventions. The multiple-cause-multiple-effect model does also mean that allocating success and cost of an intervention directly is very difficult. At the same time, addressing one disease by reducing one risk factor will have positive impacts on other diseases as well which will improve the cost-effectiveness of the intervention if we comprehend the full picture and not only one disease.

---

542 Source: IHME (2025).

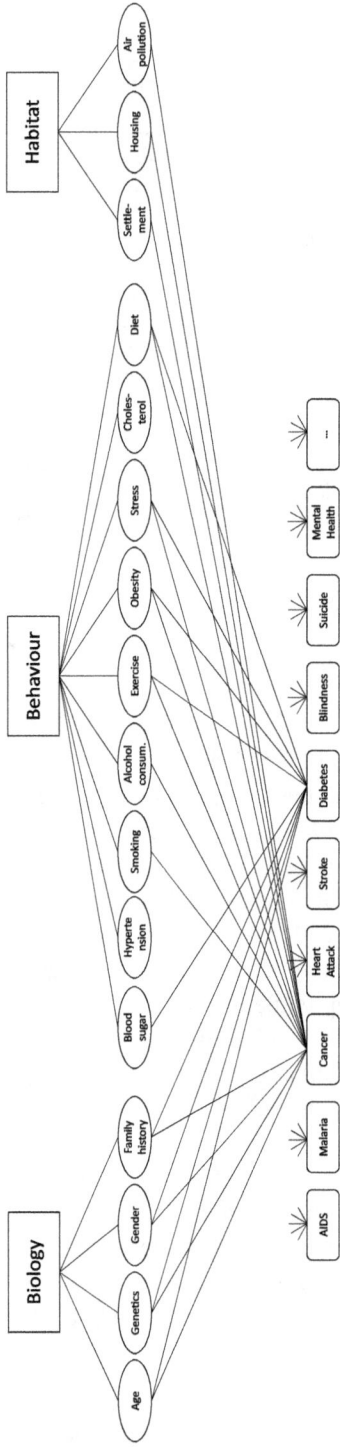

Figure 3.60: Health risks.[543]

543 Source: Own.

3.5.2 Nutrition

Nutrition is fundamental to human health.[544] Malnutrition occurs when certain food components (e.g. protein, iodine, and vitamin A) are lacking. If caloric intake is consistently too low, it is referred to as undernutrition, whereas consistent caloric intake above needs can lead to overnutrition and thus obesity. Nutrition is thus a crucial prerequisite for human development, work capacity, and immunity. Children who are chronically malnourished can hardly compensate for developmental brain damage even in later years, making hunger during child development a human and economic issue. Natural disasters, wars, and civil wars, which often lead to nutritional problems, thus have consequences for people's health even decades later.

The common perception that all people in poorer countries are undernourished is usually incorrect. Rather, it is the poverty groups that suffer from poor nutrition, which includes both partial deficiencies (e.g. vitamins) and unhealthy overnutrition. Except in real hunger regions, poverty groups are often more likely to be obese and suffer more from so-called lifestyle diseases than those who can afford a healthy and balanced diet. This leads to a complex nutritional situation, and there are often several 'nutrition worlds' within a country.

It is important to note that physical access to food is only one component of food security. Cultural and political factors also play an important role, as education (especially of women, who are often responsible for family nutrition) is just as important. Additionally, the health status of the population is a crucial determinant of food security, as sick individuals require more food than healthy ones. Illness and nutrition thus form the poles of a control loop, as poor or deficient nutrition makes one more susceptible to diseases, while diseases in turn lead to poor and deficient nutrition. Diseases of the digestive system (e.g. worm infections),[545] are particularly significant, but the connection can also be seen for many other diseases.

Nevertheless, the availability and affordability of food are central determinants of food security and consequently of health. As shown in Figure 3.61, the demand for food arises from an objective deficiency of food components, which leads to a subjective experience of deficiency and ultimately to a need. However, the need for food competes with other uses of these resources. For example, the production of biofuels has been promoted in recent years, leading to sharp competition between biomass for fuel production and food production in some countries. At the same time, the demand for food is also strongly motivated by speculation, as commodities like wheat, corn, or rice are often bought and sold speculatively long before harvest. A part of the extreme price fluctuations in food in recent years is due to this speculative motive.[546]

---

544 Compare Semba and Bloem (2008).
545 Compare Hunt (2005).
546 Compare Lawson, Alam, and Etienne (2021).

The demand for food is countered by the supply. In principle, food production is a commodity process like any other, although the natural dependence on production factors, which are relatively uncertain, is noticeable. Precipitation and temperature are the dominant factors, but the availability and quality of soils are also crucial. Additionally, hardly any industry is as heterogeneous. Especially in developing countries, the spectrum ranges from simple subsistence farmers with a hoe to industrial agricultural factories, and from latifundia or kolkhozes to large landowners. Food security thus always has a highly political dimension to healthcare.

The link between hunger and the level of development is obvious. Interestingly, countries in the 'hunger belt' of the Sahel zone are less affected than the comparatively richer countries of southern Africa. This is partly due to international programmes, but also partly due to poor statistics. However, these figures say nothing about 'hidden hunger', which does not result from protein-energy malnutrition but from a deficiency of individual nutrients (e.g. vitamin A, iron, and iodine). Iron deficiency anaemia is one of the most common deficiency symptoms worldwide, but women in resource-poor countries are particularly affected. This has various reasons. First, women often receive too little iron through their diet, as, for example, in many cultures, green leaves are rejected and, in some regions, meat is reserved for men. Second, the comparatively frequent pregnancies lead to iron deficiency. Third, frequent worm infections (e.g. hookworms) are associated with iron deficiency.[547]

Furthermore, we have little insight into the distribution of food within a country. Often, hunger, malnutrition, and overnutrition exist concurrently in the same country. Thus, even in countries that traditionally had no issues with obesity, the proportion of obese individuals is rapidly increasing.[548] For instance, the urban elite in China is developing into a population with high potential for diabetes, heart attacks, and strokes, as they have quickly switched their diet to high-fat foods[549] – a fact referred to in analogy to demographic transition as the "Nutrition Transition".[550]

'General hunger' is usually a threat only in agriculturally disadvantaged areas (e.g. Sahel zone) and during crises, such as (civil) wars (e.g. Somalia). Sub-Saharan Africa is still the continent with the most alarming nutritional situation, but also in India and Northern Korea, the situation is serious.

In some low-income countries, the nutritional situation of the average population is acceptable, while children are still suffering from malnutrition. Consequently, development and growth monitoring of children, breastfeeding propagation, and food

---

547 Compare Dossa, Ategbo, De Koning, et al. (2001).
548 Compare James (2008).
549 Compare Fu, Xiang, Zhao, et al. (2011).
550 Compare Caballero and Popkin (2002).

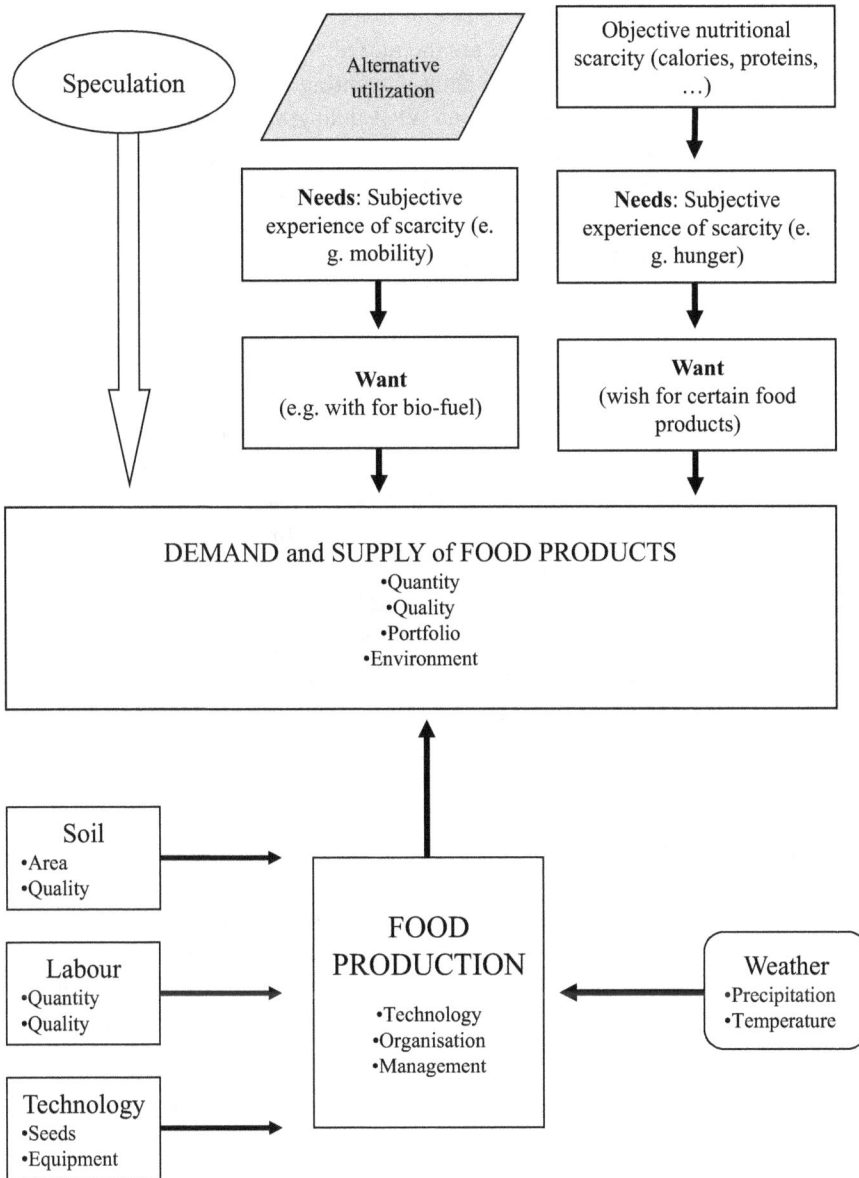

Figure 3.61: Supply and demand for food.[551]

---

551 Source: Own.

supply for malnourished children are essential elements of many primary healthcare programmes. At least three parameters are monitored:[552]

- Stunting (chronic malnutrition): A child is stunting if the height for age is less than twice the standard deviation of the WHO child growth standards median.[553]
- Wasting (acute malnutrition): A child is wasting if the weight-for-height is less than twice the standard deviation of the WHO child growth standards median.
- Underweight: A child is underweight if the weight for age is less than twice the standard deviations of the WHO child growth standards median; contrary, the child is overweight if the weight-for-height is more than twice the standard deviation of the WHO child growth standards median.

The situation is worst during famines and in unstable population, but also structural challenges resulting in global inflation of agricultural products might cause malnutrition of children. For instance, the Russian war against Ukraine increased the world market prices for wheat and other agricultural products leading to starvation in particular in sub-Saharan Africa.[554] While the adults might find solutions, children are usually suffering most with life-long damages.

On the other side, obesity is a worldwide problem, and frequently, it coexists together with malnutrition in the same country or region. This results in increasing incidences and prevalence of chronic degenerative diseases such as heart attack, stroke, and diabetes even in countries where the majority of children are malnourished. It is likely that foetal malnourishment during pregnancy is a cause of a metabolic syndrome in later life.[555] Under this condition, many children and later adults in low-income countries are threatened twice: by poor development during pregnancy and childhood, as well as a higher likelihood of developing chronic degenerative diseases as adults.

In summary, nutrition emerges as a key factor in understanding the demand for health services. Both unbalanced and insufficient, as well as too energy-rich diets, lead to increased demand for health services. Pure nutritional security continues to play an important role in health policy, but the importance of health-promoting nutrition is steadily increasing.

---

552 Compare WHO (2024i).
553 Example: A 5-year-old boy should be 110 cm of height (median). The standard deviation is 5 cm, i.e. the boy is chronically malnourished and consequently too small for its age, if he is shorter than 100 cm (100 cm – 2*5 cm).
554 Compare Yingi (2024).
555 Compare Barker and Osmond (1986).

3.5.3 Water and Hygiene

Water is of central importance for health. Water is, the most important material for hygiene,[556] a carrier of infections, and a basis for nutrition, and it plays such a significant role that the Alma-Ata Declaration defined the provision of water as a core of primary healthcare. From Hippocrates, who in his treatise "Air, Water, and Places"[557] extensively discussed the significance of water for health, through the Alma-Ata Declaration, which demanded an "adequate supply of safe water and basic sanitation" (§7 No. 3), to the Millennium Development Goals (No. 7: "Reduce by half the proportion of people without sustainable access to safe drinking water and basic sanitation") and the Sustainable Development Goals (No. 6: "Ensure availability and sustainable management of water and sanitation for all"), water has always been a focus of public health.

Despite numerous calls to action, "in 2022, 2.2 billion people still lacked safely managed drinking water, including 703 million without a basic water service; 3.5 billion people lacked safely managed sanitation, including 1.5 billion without basic sanitation services; and 2 billion lacked a basic handwashing facility, including 653 million with no handwashing facility at all".[558] The consequences affect particularly children. It is estimated that 10% of the GBD overall, but 30% of child mortality in low-income countries, are caused by unsanitary water and inadequate sanitation.[559]

Diseases can be differentiated into water-borne, water-washed, and water-resident illnesses.[560] In water-borne diseases, the (drinking) water acts as the transmission medium, i.e. the pathogens are ingested with the drinking water. Cholera, hepatitis A, diphtheria, *Salmonella*, polio, and many other diseases are transmitted in this way. Boiling or filtering drinking water is therefore of central importance for prevention but typically requires fuel (e.g. firewood), which especially poorer populations cannot afford and which is becoming increasingly scarce and thus expensive

---

556 Hygiene was defined in Section 2.1.2 as the "science of preventing diseases and maintaining and strengthening health". For this section, hygiene can be defined more practical as the "conditions and practices that help to maintain health and prevent the spread of diseases. Medical hygiene therefore includes a specific set of practices associated with this preservation of health, for example environmental cleaning, sterilization of equipment, hand hygiene, water and sanitation and safe disposal of medical waste" (WHO 2024g).

557 Compare Adams (2022).

558 UN (2024d).

559 OECD (2011). The term 'sanitation' is not identical with water and hygiene, but strongly related as it "generally refers to the provision of facilities and services for the safe disposal of human urine and faeces. Inadequate sanitation is a major cause of disease world-wide and improving sanitation is known to have a significant beneficial impact on health both in households and across communities. The word 'sanitation' also refers to the maintenance of hygienic conditions, through services such as garbage collection and wastewater disposal". (WHO 2024)

560 Compare Diesfeld, Falkenhorst, Razum, et al. (2001).

(deforestation). Technical alternatives include either central water supply or local treatment (e.g. thermal water treatment using solar panels), which, however, require considerable investments and are hardly available especially in slums.

Frequently, there is a cycle in water-borne diseases, as illustrated in Figure 3.62 for diarrhoeal diseases. An infected person excretes the pathogens through stool or urine. Without functioning toilets, it is conceivable that the drinking water becomes contaminated, leading to further infection (either directly by drinking or through food contamination). Other transmission routes include flies, pets, and toddlers, especially if they come into contact with food and do not wash their hands.[561] The most effective prevention is a functioning toilet, although this does not necessarily have to be a water closet. A ventilated dry latrine with a fly trap is also considered hygienic if properly constructed.[562]

Water-washed diseases can be prevented by water, i.e. water acts as a medium of prevention. For example, many colds, worms, and diarrhoeal diseases can be prevented simply by washing hands. Again, this presupposes that water is quantitatively sufficient and not itself contaminated. Those who must carry water over long distances on their heads to their homes will avoid 'wasting' the precious water on personal hygiene.

Finally, there are diseases that either reside in water or can be found in water-rich environments. Often, water is the habitat or breeding ground for these pathogens. For instance, schistosomiasis requires the *Bulinus* snail for development and is thus primarily transmitted in standing waters. The vector mosquitoes of malaria, dengue, and river blindness also need water bodies for their breeding.

Another disease component to consider today is chemical pollution, as, for example, over-fertilization, industrial, and household wastes contaminate the drinking water and pollute the watercourses. Many slums are located near industries so that (especially after rainfall) streams of excrements and chemicals flow through these residential areas, endangering the population. Health problems are caused by water withdrawal (e.g. desertification), flooding, and the opportunity costs (costs of water procurement) that can be significant for international healthcare management in certain regions (e.g. flooding in Bangladesh). The disastrous consequences of the man-made transformation of the Aral Lake to the Aral Desert have been docu-

---

561 WHO addresses the dimension of water, sanitation and hygiene with its WASH-concept (WHO 2025c).
562 This is an example of the great importance of adapted construction in international healthcare management, although we cannot go into detail here. However, it should be emphasized that 'western' concepts of sanitation are not appropriate everywhere, for example, because the water consumption is much too high.

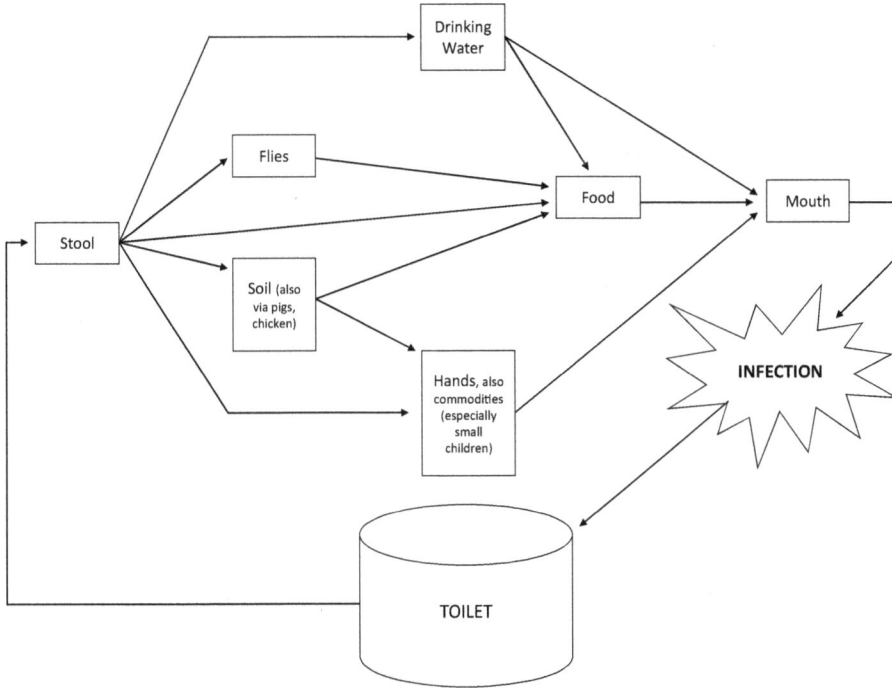

Figure 3.62: Transmission of diarrhoeal diseases.[563]

mented extensively: water means health and life – and desertification means sickness and death.[564]

Water has long been considered ubiquitous, and even today, many people claim the right to have free access to water. In reality, however, water has had to be accessed and managed in many regions for millennia, resulting in regulations and pricing for water access early on. Today, water is almost universally an economic good because it is often scarce and can only be made valuable to humans through labour and investment. Clean drinking water is an exclusive consumer good, meaning the water consumed by one person cannot be consumed by another (without costly processing). Therefore, it is justified that water has a price.

The assertion that water has a price is not the same as claiming that water must be provided by private companies. Traditionally, water supply has always been seen as a public task, i.e. cities and communities usually provided a public water system and sometimes subsidized water. However, attempts were made in the 1990s to pri-

---

563 Source: Own, based on Diesfeld, Falkenhorst, Razum, et al. (2001).
564 Compare Anchita, Zhupankhan, Khaibullina, et al. (2021); Khaibullina, Amantaikyzy, Ariphanova, et al. (2022).

vatize water supply, with examples from South America (e.g. Bolivia) clearly showing that water supply for poor groups deteriorated significantly. Since access to water is considered a human right, the privatizations were partially reversed. A greater problem today is the intense competition for water, as it is an important factor in industrial and agricultural processes.[565]

In summary, the availability of water, the disposal of wastewater, and the control of water accumulations are crucial for the spread of infectious diseases. The increasing chemical contamination of water also means that water is becoming more significant for the prevalence of chronic degenerative diseases such as allergies and cancer (compare Section 3.4.1.3). Beyond that, the example of the Aral Lake teaches that the incidence of stress, heart attacks, and strokes increase with declining or disappearing water. Thus, international healthcare management must also encompass water management.

3.5.4 Pregnancy and Birth

Pregnancy and childbirth still represent a great health risk in many countries.[566] The Alma-Ata Declaration ("maternal and child healthcare, including family planning"),[567] the Millennium Development Goals (Goals 3–5), and the Sustainable Development Goals (particularly goals 3.1 and 3.2) consider the improvement of maternal and child health as central elements of international health policy. The main indicators are the share of pregnancies covered by antenatal care (ANC), proportion of births attended by skilled health personnel, maternal mortality ratio, under-5 mortality rate, infant mortality rate, and neonatal mortality rate. Thus, the "Maternal and Child Healthcare Programmes" (MCH) are always in the focus of international health policy and healthcare management. Examples are the WHO constitution (1948), the Alma-Ata Declaration (1978), the Safe Motherhood Initiative (1987), the Safe Motherhood Actions (1999), the UN Global Strategy for Women's and Children's Health (2010), the Muskoka Initiative (2010), and "The Global Strategy for Women's, Children's and Adolescents' Health (2016–2030)".[568]

Despite of all efforts, maternal mortality (the number of relevant deaths during pregnancy and childbirth per 100,000 live births) remains unacceptable high in many countries. In the year 2021, 191,152 women died due to pregnancy or delivery resulting in a loss of more than 12 million DALYs. About 95% of maternal mortality occurs in low- and lower-middle-income countries (in sub-Saharan Africa alone 111,046 deaths

---

565 Compare Crabtree (2005).
566 Compare WHO (2005).
567 §7 No. 3, Declaration of Alma-Ata.
568 Compare Brizuela and Tunçalp (2017), Moller, Patten, Hanson, et al. (2019), and Kuruvilla, Bustreo, Kuo, et al. (2016).

in 2021) while maternal mortality is close to zero in high-income countries (2003 cases in the year 2021). The respective rates vary even more between countries (compare Figure 3.63). In South Sudan, Chad, and Nigeria, more than 1,000 women die from maternal conditions per 100,000 live births, in countries of the European Union, usually less than 5.[569]

Key elements in combating maternal mortality include ANC, childbirth care by trained midwives, provision of referral capacities for high-risk pregnancies, and family planning, where of course women's health cannot be discussed separately from women's rights. The starting point is family planning, which includes professional counselling and access to contraceptives, as well as the cultural acceptance contraceptive use in order to reduce the total number of children of a women, teenage pregnancies, and pregnancies in older ages. At the same time, contraceptives are a prerequisite for 'optimal child spacing', i.e. increase the time between two pregnancies. A child should be the desire of the women (and husband), not the consequence in poor accessibility of contraceptives.

Oral contraceptives ('the pill') are still the most frequently used contraceptive method in most countries. However, they have the disadvantage that the entire household might be informed about the intervention. Where family pressure to have more children is high, long-term contraceptives (e.g. implants, injections) might be more appropriate. The woman can, for instance, receive the implant while visiting a health centre with a child and be protected for about 2 years without anybody else noticing it. The provision of contraceptives is, however, also a managerial challenge in many countries, including (international) purchasing, logistics, and distribution. Frequently, the provision has been a core element of development cooperation.

ANC is crucial for protecting the health of women and unborn children, but availability and accessibility is poor in particular in sub-Saharan Africa. A fundamental problem with ANC is the accessibility of facilities, as the friction of distance for preventive services is significantly higher than for curative services. Therefore, ANC must be local (max. 10 km) and expertly conducted so that expectant mothers are willing to overcome the distance.

A task of the mother-child care workers in dispensaries is the identification of high-risk pregnancies that must be referred for further clarification and especially for childbirth to higher-level facilities. The definition of what constitutes a high-risk pregnancy must be adapted to the local situation. For instance, the uncritical transfer of criteria from Europe to Africa has led to practically all pregnancies being classified as high risk in some regions because most women of a certain tribe were shorter than 150 cm and had experienced more than three births or were underage at their first delivery. This has rendered the concept of risk selection meaningless.

---

569 Source: WHO (2024j) and IHME (2025).

Another important discussion is the role of traditional midwives. On one hand, they are locally available and still accepted by many women, but on the other hand, they have often proven resistant to any hygiene education. The training of these traditional birth attendants was a focus of the MCH programmes in the 1980s, but it has failed in many regions.[570]

The biggest problem is likely the referral system. Still too few high-risk pregnancies are identified, and very few of risky cases detected actually go to hospitals for delivery. Instead, the hospital delivery beds are occupied by mothers from the upper class, who would not necessarily need a hospital delivery. Distance regularly presents a problem, as pregnant women can hardly cover 50 km on foot. In some cases, hospitals have therefore established so-called 'maternal waiting homes' where mothers can wait for the birth near the hospital.[571]

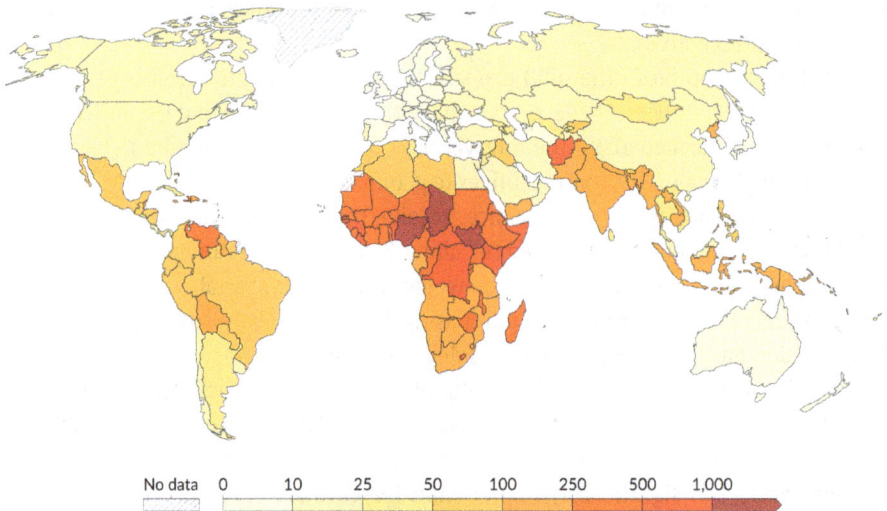

| No data | 0 | 10 | 25 | 50 | 100 | 250 | 500 | 1,000 |

Figure 3.63: Maternal mortality (per 100,000 live births).[572]

A significant portion of maternal mortality is caused by unsafe abortions performed illegally by untrained individuals. It is estimated that about 73 million children are aborted worldwide each year, meaning about 29% of pregnancies end in induced abortion.[573] In many low-income countries, abortions are illegal, so an estimated 33 million abortions are performed clandestinely, without professional personnel and

570 Compare Sibley and Ann Sipe (2004).
571 Compare von Both, Jahn, and Fleßa (2008).
572 Source: OurWorldinData – CC-BY@: https://ourworldindata.org/grapher/maternal-mortality (18.02.2025).
573 Compare Sedgh, Henshaw, Singh, et al. (2007) and WHO (2024a).

under unsterile conditions.[574] The mortality rate of professionally performed abortions is negligible, while up to 200 of 100,000 unsafe abortions end with the deaths of mother and child. Consequently, up to 13% of maternal deaths were found to be linked to abortive pregnancy outcomes.[575]

The debate on abortion is often conducted with great intensity, in particular, in low-income countries. It is discussed whether legalizing abortion would actually increase their number. It cannot be the task of international healthcare management to influence this discussion, which must take place within the civil societies of the countries. However, the healthcare manager can simplify the process by providing targeted facts and thus basing it on evidence.

The high number of 'unwanted' pregnancies is countered by a growing number of childless couples who seek IVF treatments in resource-poor countries, spending significant (private) funds. For example, clinics in India offer artificial insemination to upper-class African couples for cash. Traditionally, it was common in many African societies to give children of close relatives to childless couples. The fact that more and more couples no longer consider this form of family formation sufficient and pursue their own child with much effort shows how strong a cultural change is taking place among the 'young professionals'. The great complexity is exemplified by the fact that sometimes in the same hospital, IVF is performed, an embryo is aborted because it is of an unwanted gender, and the consequences of an unprofessional abortion are treated.

In summary, it can be stated that pregnancy and childbirth pose a significant health risk in developing countries. No other stage of life is as dangerous as pregnancy and delivery/birth, and in no other area can so much be achieved with comparatively little means.

3.5.5 Substance Abuse

Psychoactive drugs constitute significant health risks to the user and to others. Alcohol is most harmful drugs with a very high impact of the social environment (family, work place, . . .), followed by methamphetamine, synthetic cannabinoids, and tobacco products (cigarettes, cigars, pipes, chewing tobacco, snuff, and others).[576] The vast majority of these substances are illegal in almost all countries, but alcohol and tobacco products are readily available in almost all countries for adults and in many countries even for teenagers. The combination of high dependency potential, devastating harm (see Figure 3.64), and free access is the cause why tobacco and alcohol are major risk factors (compare Table 3.17).

---

574 Compare Grimes, Benson, Singh, et al. (2006) and WHO (2024a).
575 Compare Say, Chou, Gemmill, et al. (2014).
576 Compare Crossin, Cleland, Wilkins, et al. (2023).

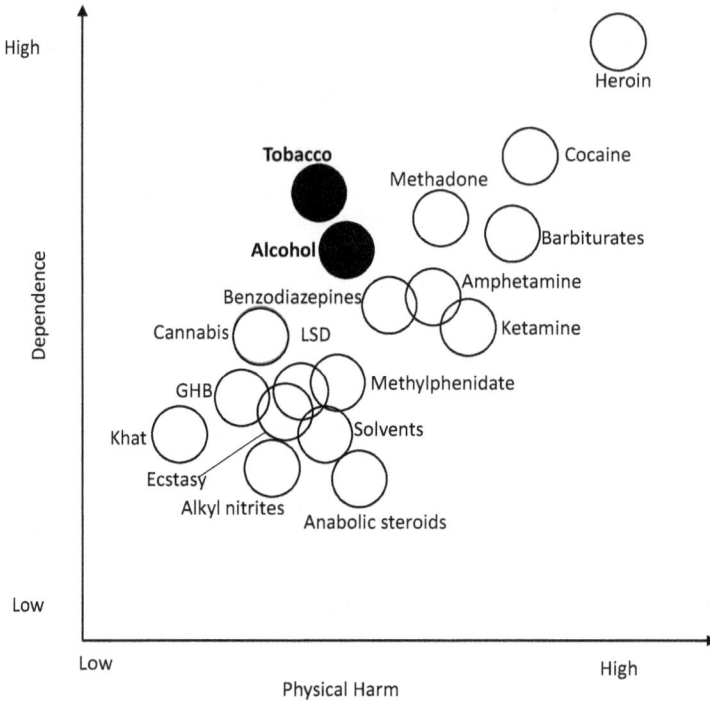

Figure 3.64: Dependence and harm.[577]

Smoking tobacco is considered the most significant cause of preventable deaths worldwide. The WHO estimates that in 2020, 22.3% of the global population (36.7% of men, 7.8% of women) used tobacco more or less intensely, leading to about 8 million deaths and numerous serious illnesses each year.[578] Over 60 carcinogenic substances and toxins in tobacco smoke cause CVDs, respiratory diseases, lung cancer, and many other morbidities. It was estimated that the total economic cost of smoking (direct and indirect cost) was US$1,850 billion in 2015 or 1.8% of the world's annual GDP.[579]

The greatest burden is again borne by resource-poor countries. Firstly, cigarettes smoked there often contain higher levels of harmful substances (e.g. tar) or additives (e.g. cloves in Indonesia). Secondly, unfiltered cigarettes are commonly preferred in these countries. Thirdly, there are fewer antismoking programmes, making tobacco advertising much more prevalent and aggressive. Finally, the healthcare system can only offer limited help in the case of tobacco-related diseases (e.g. lung cancer) be-

---

577 Nutt, King, Saulsbury, et al. (2007) and Crossin, Cleland, Wilkins, et al. (2023).
578 Compare WHO (2024n).
579 Compare Goodchild, Nargis and d'Espaignet (2018) and tabacconomics (2019).

cause the expensive treatments are often unaffordable. Consequently, both the prevalence of smoking and the morbidity and mortality related to tobacco are comparatively high. Alternative tobacco products such as the so-called e-cigarettes are booming, also in low-income countries. They might have a lower risk than traditional
cigarettes, but the risk is still considerable.

There are few studies on the economic significance of smoking in low-income countries. This is partly due to methodological issues (e.g. the limited applicability of methods for calculating indirect costs in subsistence farmers) and partly due to poor data
availability. This is regrettable since smoking not only has economic consequences but
is also determined by economic variables. For instance, poverty groups use tobacco as a
stimulant to suppress hunger. Simultaneously, the quality of the consumed tobacco depends on the economic situation. The lower the educational level and the lower the income of a populations within a country, the higher is the prevalence of tobacco use.[580]
The poor smoke more frequently, and they smoke unhealthier products. The consequence is an over-proportional burden of disease for the poor within a country, as well
as a high burden of disease in particular in Asia (compare Figure 3.65).

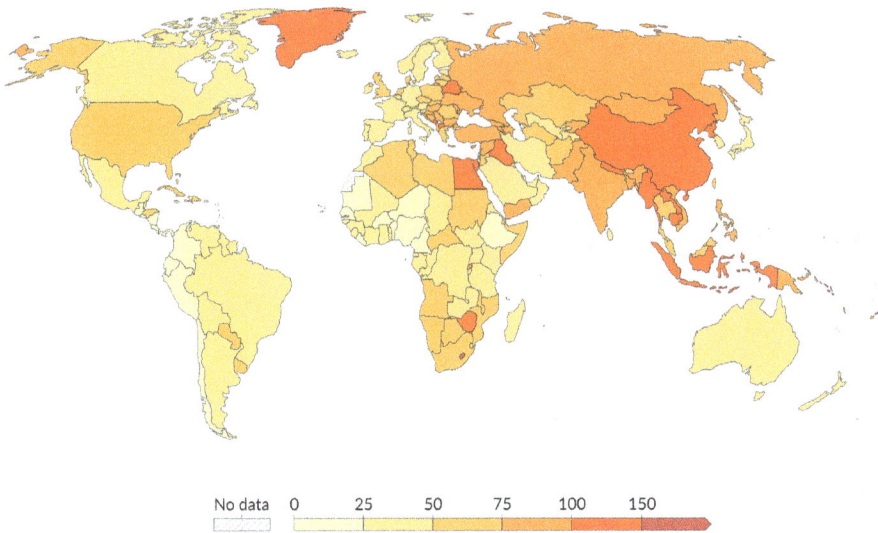

Figure 3.65: Death rate from smoking, 2021.[581]

The prevalence of tobacco consumption is expected to increase in the coming years,
but the consequences of abuse will only fully manifest decades later. As shown in Fig-

---

580 Compare Brady (2020) and Mentis (2019).
581 Source: OurWorldinData – CC-BY@: https://ourworldindata.org/grapher/death-rate-smoking
(18.02.2025).

ure 3.66, the mortality curve of smokers follows the prevalence with a delay of 30–40 years. As men are typically among the first to start smoking, four typical phases occur. In Phase I, only a few men and almost no women smoke. Mortality due to smoking is negligible. Some countries in sub-Saharan Africa still belong to this phase. In Phase II, the proportion of smoking men rapidly increases, while the proportion of smoking women only slowly increases. At its peak, almost 70% of men are smokers. Accordingly, tobacco-associated mortality among men also increases. Many developing and emerging countries are in this stage, e.g. China and Indonesia. In the third phase, the proportion of smoking men decreases, while women significantly 'catch up'. However, the number of male deaths due to smoking now increases significantly, while relatively few women die from tobacco abuse. This phase has been reached by countries in Eastern Europe and some countries in South America. In the fourth phase, women and men are at about the same prevalence level, but women's mortality continues to rise. Most high-income countries are in this stage.

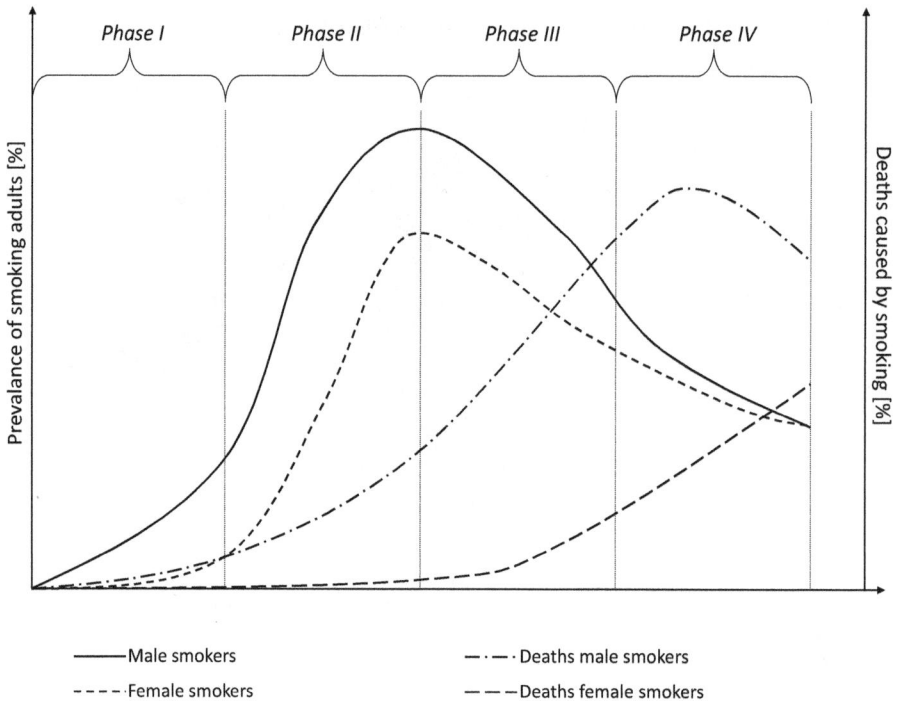

Figure 3.66: Phase model of the tobacco epidemic.[582]

582 Source: Lopez, Collishaw, and Piha (1994).

It is beyond question that combating tobacco abuse must be a high priority in international healthcare. The WHO Framework Convention on Tobacco Control[583] (2003) thus also represents a legally relevant document that obliges individual countries to fight smoking (e.g. through strong restrictions on advertising, reduced accessibility, prohibition of misleading labelling, etc.). Intense discussions revolve around whether the demand for cigarettes is price elastic. Indeed, many states have taxed tobacco, where typically the tax revenues only cover a fraction of the costs of smoking. In the long term, higher prices for tobacco products will likely deter especially young people from starting to smoke.[584] For people who are already addicted, a price increase also implies a search for substitutes, e.g. smuggled cigarettes, self-rolled cigarettes, or lower-quality products, which may in turn have negative health effects.

Alcohol consumption also poses a global risk. In the year 2021, 1,809,438 deaths and a loss of 72,254,239 DALYs were caused by ethanol, a psychoactive and toxic substance contained in alcohol or alcoholic beverages, and the numbers are increasing.[585] Alcohol is the cause of many accidents and non-communicable diseases, such as cancer, but also infectious diseases can be worsened by alcohol consumption. Men are globally more likely to show hazardous drinking habits than women are. For a long time it was discussed whether moderate drinking could be beneficial for the health or at least without harm. It has been accepted by now, that ethanol is a neurotoxin and any quantity of alcohol has negative impacts on the health.[586] However, heavy episodic or heavy continuous alcohol consumption definitely holds a higher risk than moderate drinking does.

The consumption of alcohol and the resulting health impacts strongly depend on regions, countries, and cultural groups. The alcohol consumption per person measured in litres of pure alcohol per person aged 15 or older per year was highest in Romania, Georgia, Czech Republic, Latvia, and Germany, and it was (officially) zero in countries with predominantly Islamic population, such as Kuwait, Saudi Arabia, Sudan, Somalia, and Bangladesh. Table 3.18 shows that the consumption increases with income, but the death toll is also high in some of the poorest countries of the world.

The pattern of different alcoholic beverages is notable. While wine and beer are predominantly consumed in Western Europe and North America, the highest consumption in Eastern Europe falls on spirits. In poorer countries, the homemade production of spirits is also a problem, as these are often significantly more harmful than commercially distilled variants. In sub-Saharan Africa, it is noticeable that intoxication is often the goal of drinking, so that even with relatively low alcohol consumption

---

583 Compare WHO (2003).
584 Compare Lauterbach, Klever-Deichert, Stollenwerk, et al. (2005).
585 Source: IHME (2025).
586 Compare Rheumatology (2023).

Table 3.18: Alcohol consumption, deaths, and DALYs lost due to alcohol (2021).[587]

Region	Consumption pure alcohol (≥15 years, L p.c. p.a.)	Deaths	DALYs
Global	5.43	1,809,439	72,254,239
Sub-Saharan Africa	4.47	194,229	8,339,606
Upper middle income	5.52	729,407	24,332,632
High income	9.22	424,471	28,634,281
Lower middle income	4.04	564,965	3,974,721
Low income	2.88	88,588	15,237,416
Georgia	14.33	1,735	60,068
Czech Republic	13.29	5,106	189,794
Germany	12.22	47,456	510,204
Romania	16.99	16,648	61,730
Lithuania	13.09	1,730	1,455,574
Kuwait	0.00	19	37,194
Saudi Arabia	0.00	445	2,822
Bangladesh	0.01	8,998	468,519
Somalia	0.00	1,023	24,371
Sudan	0.00	315	53,432

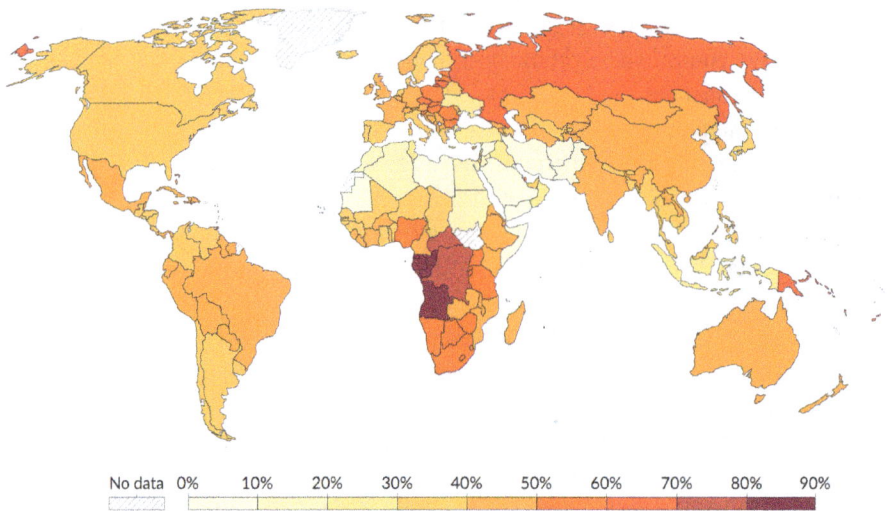

No data 0% 10% 20% 30% 40% 50% 60% 70% 80% 90%

Figure 3.67: Share of heavy drinkers, 2021.[588]

---

587 Source: IHME (2025) and World Bank (2024b).
588 Source: OurWorldinData – CC-BY@: https://ourworldindata.org/grapher/drinkers-had-a-heavy-session-in-past-30-days (18.02.2025).

p.c., the number of severe alcohol-related damages is large.[589] The statistics indicate that the average consumption of pure alcohol (4.47 L p.c. p.a. for population of ≥15 years) is comparable small, but the share of 'heavy episodic drinking' (proportion of adult drinkers who have had at least 60 g or more of pure alcohol on at least one occasion in the past 30 days) is very high on this (sub-)continent.

Figure 3.67 shows the share of adult drinkers who have had a heavy drinking session in the last 30 days (2016). Only Gabon (86.2%), Angola (81.6%), Central African Republic (77.3%), and the Democratic Republic of Congo (77.1%) have rates of more than 70% with comparable little average consumption (Gabon: 7.33 L; Angola: 6.17 L; Central African Republic: 1.99 L; DR Congo: 2.12 L). Alcohol remains a global killer, but drinking habits and health consequences differ significantly.[590]

3.5.6 Environmental Influences

In a multiple-cause-multiple-effect model, environmental influences play an important role in explaining chronic degenerative diseases. Numerous substances are classified as carcinogenic, cause allergies or asthma, and increase the risk of CVDs. Carcinogens are either naturally present in the environment (e.g. mold) or are exploited or produced by humans, such as asbestos, benzene, or arsenic acid. Indoor smoke, which occurs from the burning of excrement, wood, charcoal, coal, or oil, is also considered a cancer risk factor. It also exemplifies the special exposure to environmental hazards that poverty groups face.[591] Furthermore, noise (e.g. traffic noise) plays an important role in the development of diseases, such as psychological and CVDs, as well as hearing loss.

In the last two decades, the relationship between climate change, economy, and health has been intensively studied.[592] The Lancet report "Countdown on health and climate change" expresses deep concern about the "record-breaking human costs of climate change", including heat-related mortality of older people (> 65 years), effects on physical activity, sleep quality and mental health. Extreme weather events are more frequent and severe, including draughts, storms and flooding.[593] The pledges of the Paris Agreement of 2015 were wide ranging, but the political will to reduce, in particular, global warming, seems to be limited.

The primary cause of climate change is economic development. For instance, CO_2, methane, and N_2O have been released into the atmosphere in increasing amounts since the Industrial Revolution, as the vastly increased consumption desires of economically prosperous countries induce a steadily rising demand for goods whose pro-

589 Compare WHO (2012).
590 Source: World Bank (2024b).
591 Compare Desai, Mehta, and Smith (2004).
592 Compare Stern (2007), DeCanio (2003), and Bauer (2011).
593 Compare Romanello, Walawender, Hsu, et al. (2024).

duction releases these gases. Regularly, as a country's economic growth increases, so too does its output of climate-hostile gases.

At the same time, climate change has enormous economic significance, with both negative and positive effects to be distinguished. Figure 3.68 provides an overview of the possible economic consequences of climate change. It is clear that the health effect of climate change is just one of many impacts and that the complex, interdependent system of economic, ecological, and epidemiological parameters requires a differentiated and ideally model-supported analysis.

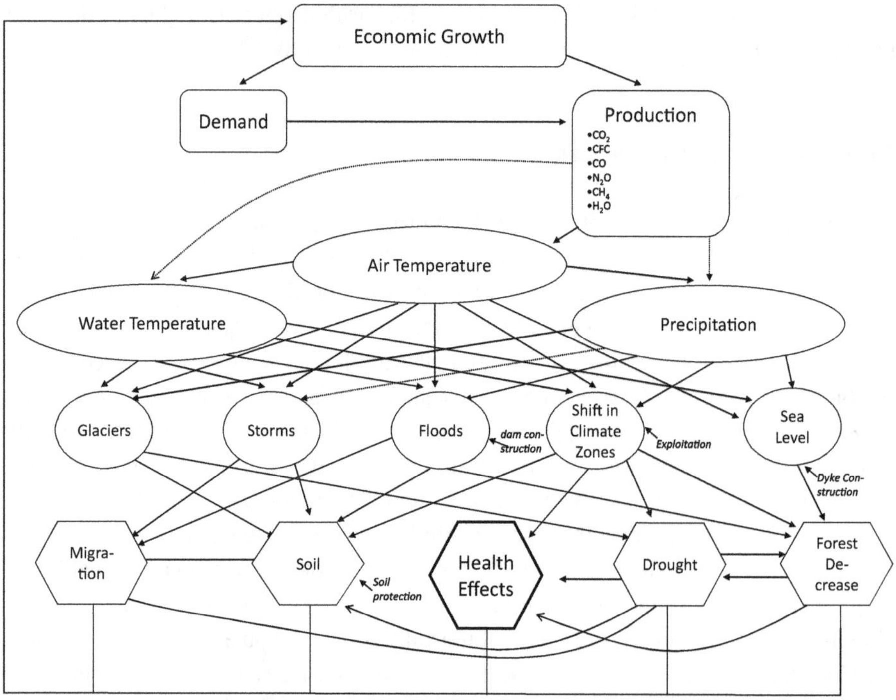

Figure 3.68: Climate change and economy.[594]

Changes in precipitation and air temperature are likely to have a significant impact on the spread of diseases that require a climate-sensitive vector or host. The relationship between global warming and health can be exemplified by using the example of malaria tropica. The model presented in Section 3.3.3 assumes that the maturation of *Anopheles* larvae depends on both the amount of rainfall and the water temperature. At the same time, the maturation of *Plasmodium falciparum* in *Anopheles* depends on the external temperature, so a direct connection between climate changes and the

---

594 Source: Own, based on Weltbank (2010).

spread of malaria is expected. Using a system dynamics model (compare Section 3.2), a cost forecast for malaria treatment in a health district in Africa will be carried out as a function of global warming and the expected reduction in rainfall.

Figure 3.69 shows the development of the costs of malaria treatment in the district with an assumed temperature increase of 0.1 °C per year. Initially, it is noticeable that the treatment costs do not increase linearly with the temperature but take on a wave-like course. Although no random fluctuations are built into the model, local maxima occur. In these years, the *Anopheles* population increases significantly. However, the population then encounters natural limits, as the water surfaces suitable for breeding present a natural restriction. There is a reduction in the *Anopheles* population. Only when the temperature continues to rise, allowing the larvae to develop faster, can the population increase again. Waves are created, as described by predator-prey models.[595]

Furthermore, it should be noted that the costs after 25 years are 51% above the comparative values without temperature increase. In a situation of extreme resource scarcity, such an increase represents a severe developmental obstacle that must be countered with appropriate measures.

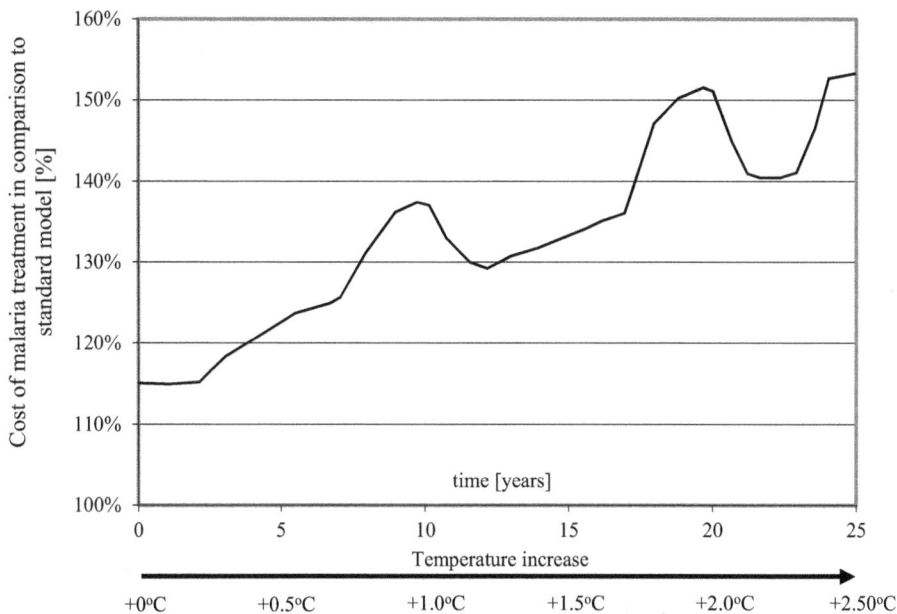

Figure 3.69: Development of malaria treatment costs with an assumed temperature increase of 0.1 °C per year.[596]

---

595 Compare Lotka and James (1956).
596 Source: Own simulation.

The simulation shows that the effects of climate changes on malaria spread are extremely complex. The wave patterns, increases or reductions in infection numbers, are not intuitively understandable. Therefore, healthcare managers should be very cautious in making statements about the relationship between environmental influences and morbidity. An initial analysis suggested that the repeatedly observed increase in malaria morbidity and mortality in the highland regions of East Africa over the last 20 years could be attributed to climate changes.[597] However, a study conducted in the countries of Kenya, Uganda, Rwanda, and Burundi found no evidence of such a phenomenon.[598] The observed increase in malaria in these four countries was mainly attributed to the dramatic rise in chloroquine resistance, failures of the government health services, as well as agro-ecological changes and migration. Newer studies, however, again indicate a closer connection between malaria and global warming, although the significance of reduced rainfall has been overlooked so far.[599]

It is demanding to estimate the economic impact of climate change. Older estimates suggest an economic loss of US\$7.9 trillion by 2005, recent studies estimate the global annual damages to be at 38 trillion dollars (year 2050, PPP US\$2005) with a likely range of US\$19–59 trillion. However, the disastrous impact affects mainly warmer countries, while some countries (e.g. Greenland) might even benefit.[600] It is estimated that the average real GDP loss by 2050 is 'only' 1.7% in Western Europe, but 4.7% in Africa and 3.8% in Latin America.[601]

For some countries, global warming might be absolutely disastrous, in particular, countries where the majority of people live close to the sea level, such as Bangladesh, Cambodia, or the Republic of Maldives. The estimates of mean sea level rise range from 0.4 to 1.2 m until the year 2100 and from 0.8 to 5 m until 2300.[602] This would, for instance, mean that the areas of high population density in Bangladesh, Cambodia, and Southern Vietnam will be permanently under the sea level, a 1 m rise would mean for the Maldives that 80% of the country is permanently under water. However, the mean sea level is insufficient to explain the impact of global warming. As the storm surge will be even higher when the average sea level is higher, an increase of 1 m of average sea level might easily mean an increase of 2.5 m during the monsoon season in Southeast Asia. It is needless to explain that the mangroves of the Ganges in Bangladesh, the river delta of the Mekong in Southern Vietnam, or the Tonle Sap Delta in Cambodia cannot be protected by walls and dams. Global warming will have disastrous consequences with life-threatening health impacts in particular for those nations, which hardly contributed to its underlying cause of CO_2 emission.

---

597 Compare Bouma, Sondorp and Van der Kaay (1994) and Lindsay, Bødker, Malima, et al. (2000).
598 Compare Hay, Cox, Rogers, et al. (2002).
599 Compare Bradfield, Samuel, and Stephen; and Ostfeld (2009).
600 Compare Kotz, Levermann and Wenz (2024).
601 Source: Galey (2019) and Kotz, Levermann, and Wenz (2024).
602 Source: Nazarnia, Nazarnia, Sarmasti, et al. (2020).

The effects of global warming on malaria spread are an example of the numerous interactions between habitat, genetic predisposition, and human behaviour that shape the disease landscape while the example of rising sea levels demonstrates that the environment, as well as economic development, will moderate these health processes. The healthcare manager must be aware of these interdependencies for both infectious and chronic degenerative diseases and incorporate them into their decisions.

3.5.7 Urbanization and Megacities

The location of humans in space represents another significant risk factor for the spread of diseases. In addition to the peculiarities of rural areas (e.g. long distances to the nearest health service provider, frequency of wild animals, influence of agriculture, etc.), the so-called megacities are increasingly coming into focus. They should serve as a paradigmatic example of the health problems in urban zones.

A megacity is generally defined as a city that exceeds a certain, relatively high population threshold.[603] Frequently, cities are considered megacities if they have 10 or more million inhabitants. Since cities often expand beyond their administrative boundaries, the term 'mega-urban area' is more informative. It can also encompass several cities in close spatial proximity and functional integration. Worldwide, more people live in cities than in rural areas, with mega-urban areas growing rapidly.[604] Table 3.19 shows the development of megacities from 1980 to 2020. The number exploded, particularly in China (18) and India (7).

In low-income countries, urbanization began later parallel to the demographic transition, so the proportion of urban population is not as high. However, Figure 3.70 shows that this urban population in least developed countries is steadily increasing and is expected to exceed the rural population by 2035. The strong population pressure during the second and third phases of the demographic transition leads to a continuous influx into cities, with large urban areas growing significantly.[605] For instance, the population of Lagos grew from 1950 to 2023 from 0.29 to 14.23 million (factor 49.1), and the population of Kinshasa in the same period from 0.2 to 14.67 (factor 73.4).[606] The international healthcare manager must consider what it means to provide healthcare services for a population growing by – on average – 6% per year (Kinshasa). It is obvious that the healthcare situation in meta cities is a challenge.

---

603 Compare Bähr (2004).
604 Compare UNFPA (2007).
605 Compare Habitat (2010).
606 Compare UNHABITAT (2010) and Laenderdaten (2024).

Table 3.19: Development of meta-cities (1980–2020).[607]

1980	1990	2000	2015	2020
New York, Mexico City, Sao Paulo, Shanghai, and Tokyo	New York, Mexico City, Sao Paulo, Shanghai, Tokyo, Los Angeles, Buenos Aires, Mumbai, Calcutta, Peking, and Seoul	New York, Mexico City, Sao Paulo, Shanghai, Tokyo, Los Angeles, Buenos Aires, Mumbai, Calcutta, Peking, Seoul, Rio de Janeiro, Lagos, Cairo, Karachi, Delhi, Dhaka, Jakarta, and Manila	Tokyo, Jakarta, Delhi, Karachi, Seoul, Shanghai, Mumbai, New York City, Mexico City, Beijing, Sao Paulo, Lagos, Osaka, Manila, Cairo, Los Angeles, Dhaka, Moscow, Buenos Aires, Lahore, Bangkok, Istanbul, Rio de Janeiro, Tehran, London, Guangzhou, Kinshasa, Paris, Shenzhen, Kolkata, Rhine-Ruhr, Tianjin, Bengaluru, Chennai, Hyderabad, and Chongqing	Shanghai, Chongqing, Peking, Guangzhou, Delhi, Kinshasa, Karachi, Shenzhen, Istanbul, Lagos, Tokyo, Moscow, Mumbai, São Paulo, Chengdu, Lahore, Tianjin, Jakarta, Bangkok, Lima, Seoul, Cairo, Hyderabad, Mexico City, Hangzhou, Ho Chi Minh City, London, Dhaka, Wuhan, Teheran, New York City, Bangalore, Shenyang, Dongguan, Bagdad, Riad, Hong Kong, Bogota, Foshan, Xi'an, Chennai, Rio de Janeiro, Zhengzhou, Nanjing, Dar-es-salaam, Santiago, Surat, Qingdao, Singapore, Ankara, Ahmedabad, Shantou, Sankt Petersburg, Alexandria, Rangoon, Casablanca, and Harbin

Urbanization in least developed countries structurally resembles the development in the nineteenth century in Europe. Industrialization had greatly reduced the proportion of people employed in agriculture, thus exerting pressure on cities, which was significantly enhanced by strong population growth and a beginning decrease in child mortality in rural areas. Cities grew immensely within a few years, with neither hous-

---

607 Source: Laenderdaten (2024).

ing supply nor hygiene able to keep up with this growth. At that time, unlike today, life expectancy in cities was lower than in rural areas. This fact was known as 'urban penalty'.[608] However, growing wealth, hygiene, social insurance, and housing programmes led to a significant decrease in mortality in cities, so that at least equal life expectancies as in rural areas could be achieved in most European cities by the early twentieth century. The existing differences today are primarily due to lifestyle differences. For instance, the rate of fatal traffic accidents is higher in rural areas than in cities.

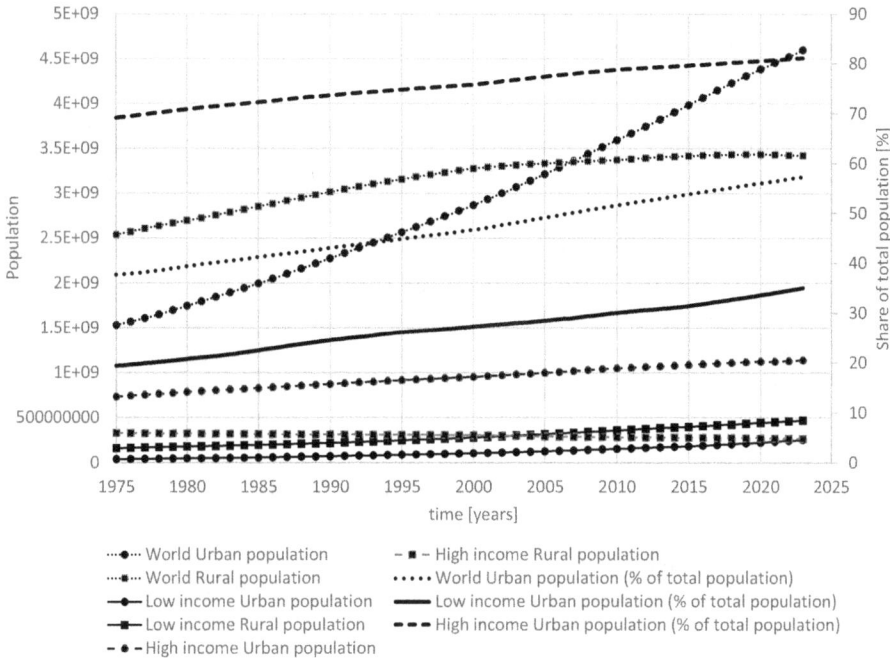

Figure 3.70: Urbanization.[609]

In the slums of developing countries, however, an 'urban penalty' still exists. It is necessary to distinguish between 'slums of hope' and 'slums of despair'.[610] The former arise when cities have sufficient attraction to create a pull on the rural population. The attraction is primarily due to the existence and security of jobs. Slums of hope are way stations for the rural population, who usually leave after some time for better residential areas in the cities. Slums of despair arise from a migration pressure from

---

608 Compare Leon (2008).
609 Source: own, based on World Bank (2024b).
610 Compare Stokes (1962).

the countryside that encounters no corresponding pull factors in the cities. The population of these slums often remains in poverty areas for a long time. They usually do not develop an urban lifestyle, so that slums of despair often resemble giant villages on the outskirts of major cities, without, however, having the social and infrastructure of cities.

Figure 3.71 shows the relationship between living conditions and health status in slums.[611] Low and irregular income of the inhabitants implies poor living conditions. These manifest not only in the poor quality of drinking water or sanitation but also in a building density that almost eliminates the possibility of physical recreation. Slum residents therefore suffer from infectious diseases (such as diarrhoea, worm infections, and malaria), but also from obesity and diabetes. The low income is associated with hazardous workplaces that imply numerous accidents and with social inequality in cities, which fosters crime.

Another problem in megacities, especially in the slums of developing countries, is the severe pollution of air, soil, and water bodies. This leads to respiratory diseases, as well as allergies. For example, ozone levels in Mexico City are above the WHO limit on an average of 6 days per week, particularly affecting the elderly and children. In the megacities of least developed countries, the burden from traffic emissions, power plants, and unregulated industrial emissions is tremendous. Noise is also a significant issue in cities. It leads to premature hearing loss, nervousness, communication, and sleep disorders – diseases commonly associated with industrialized countries. Indeed, urban health problems in developing countries are very similar to those in industrialized nations.

A specific feature of slums in developing countries is the loss of social bonds. In villages, strict moral standards still govern co-existence in almost every respect. Moving to the city often implies leaving the clan structure with its strict norms. Gangs in slums can hardly compensate for this loss of social control. Without social sanctions, crime increases, as does the propensity for changing sexual contacts, so that the spread of HIV in slums is often particularly high.

The risk factors in the slums of megacities in least developed countries induce a high demand for health services, which, however, is hardly met by any supply. The distances to healthcare providers are shorter than in the countryside, but the financial barriers are considerable. Children, women, the elderly, and disabled people in slums often have no or only rudimentary access to healthcare. Healthcare reforms in cities often reach the middle class rather than the poverty groups, so the health situation, especially in the slums of despair, is often even more precarious than in rural areas. It is clear that sustainable improvement of national health indicators can only be achieved if the health problem in cities, especially in mega-urban regions, is addressed politically.

611 Compare Razum and Voigtländer (2010).

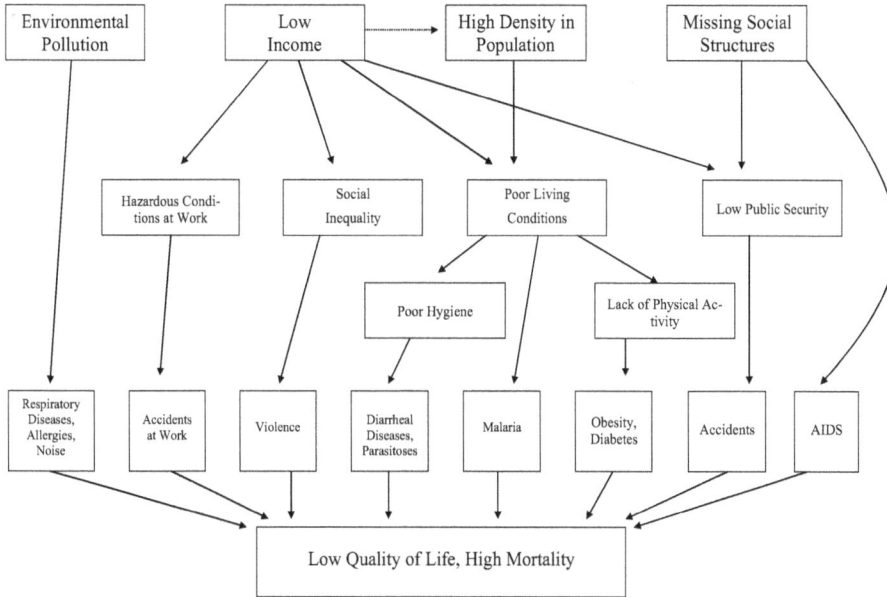

Figure 3.71: Living conditions in slums.[612]

3.5.8 Unstable Population

Healthcare services are usually planned under the assumption that stable organizations and processes can be established for a population that resides at a certain location with social structures, permanent housing, and the possibility to earn one's living and survive at this location. However, this assumption is not correct for millions of people living in unstable situations. The UNHCR (UN High Commissioner for Refugees) estimates that some 123 million people worldwide were forcibly displaced people worldwide by mid-2024. The main reasons are persecution, war and other forms of conflict, violence, human rights violations, or events seriously disturbing public order. About 65% of refugees in 2024 came from only four countries (Syria, Venezuela, Ukraine, and Afghanistan), while five countries hosted 32% of all refugees (Iran, Turkey, Columbia, Germany, and Uganda). Low- and middle-income countries had to shoulder the biggest share, i.e. about 71% of all refugees found their host in these poorer countries. For instance, about one million Rohingya came as refugees from Myanmar to Bangladesh, about 800,000 of them within 1 month of August 2017. The vast majority of them still reside in Kutupalong refugee camp in Cox's Bazar in the east of this lower-middle-income country. This

---

612 Source: Own.

tremendous inflow of vulnerables living under miserable conditions until today has severe consequences for refugees, as well as for the local population.[613]

In order to analyse the health consequences, it is important to distinguish three different groups of unstable populations. Refugees flee their own country and are under the special protection of UNHCR. Frequently, camps are established and new international aid is organized to support refugees. Internally displaced persons also leave their homes and livelihoods behind, but they remain in their own country. They also receive some international attention and support is organized in particular if the respective governments do not support them. The third group are residents affected by complex emergencies but residing in their original location. However, the living conditions in this place of origin are precarious. These people are not displaced, but the population is unstable as well with destroyed or non-existing infrastructure, insufficient shelter, and poor nutrition. UNHCR estimates that by the end of 2023, the number of internally displaced people worldwide (68 million) was much higher than the number of refugees (38 million), asylum-seekers (8 million), or other people in need of international protection (6 million).

The health impact of instability is tremendous:

- Violence: the main reasons for leaving one's location are hunger, political suppression, and violence. The majority of persons in unstable situations have left their home because of wars, including genocides. However, violence is not only a cause of instability, but also an accompanying threat as refugees, internally displaced persons, and residents affected by complex emergencies face multiple threats of violence on their migration, in camps, and even in their original locations without governmental protection. Refugee camps are prone to gang criminality, and many people in unstable populations have to pay 'protection fees' or trafficking charges to criminals. Physical and psychological harm to these vulnerables is common under these conditions.

- Poor public health support: forcibly displaced people cannot easily be covered by public (health) services, such as vaccination programmes, ante-natal care, or food distribution. Children are particularly at risk of illness due to poor public health support. UNHCR estimates that about 40% of displaced persons are below 18 years of age.[614] They require prevention programmes (incl. vaccination and monitoring), and insufficient nutrition will have life-long consequences. It is more likely that official refugee camps under the wings of UNHCR, Red Cross, Red Crescent, or other organization will provide these services, but it is very difficult to cover internally displaced persons and residents affected by complex emergencies. Thus, the two latter groups are more likely to suffer from poor health.

---

613 Compare Joarder, Sutradhar, Hasan, et al. (2020).
614 UNHCR (2024).

- Closely related to the insufficient public health support is the scarcity of drugs and other medical materials. For instance, patients suffering from diabetes will face severe problems to obtain drugs or insulin under the conditions of displacement, nor will they be able to obtain syringes. Even well-financed refugee camps do hardly provide sufficient drugs for chronic degenerative diseases.
- Shelter and sanitation: insufficient housing or shelter to protect against heat, cold, rain, dust, and wind can be a cause or fortifier of many diseases. Poor sanitation is a cause in particular for infectious diseases. The high population density in camps increases the likelihood of being infected. Thus, TB is very common in camps.
- Access to safe food and water: unstable populations have nutritional challenges. Children particularly are at risk of malnourishment. While official refugee camps are frequently supported by international organizations, internally displaced persons and vulnerables under extreme conditions in their original locations will find only insufficient or unhealthy food. Delayed brain development of children and anaemia are common diseases of unstable population. Unsafe drinking water will also lead to infectious diseases, e.g. bacterial and parasitic diseases of the digestive system.
- Stress and mental diseases: the experiences of leaving one's home, violence during the displacement, and in camps, as well as the uncertain future, can induce a post-traumatic stress disorder. Many forcibly displaced people suffer from stress symptoms leading to other diseases. Poor diet and stress can also result in CVDs, e.g. heart attacks.
- Maternal health: ante-natal care and birth-giving are quite difficult for the population without a home. Contraceptives are less likely available under these conditions, so that STDs and pregnancies are frequent. Many women have to rely on untrained birth attendants (frequently other mothers in a similar situation) resulting in suffering and deaths of mother and child.

The majority of unstable populations do not live in official refugee camps. Even refugees who migrate to other countries (illegally) reside in cities, many of them without any social protection.[615] For instance, many Syrian refugees live in Turkey as illegal immigrants without any protection of UNHCR or other institutions. It could be shown that the emergency death rate of residents under severe crisis and of internally displaced persons is much higher than the baseline death rate without crisis. However, the mortality of 'official' refugees is not significantly higher.[616] The health challenges which the healthcare manager might be officially aware of while following the reports of UNHCR might be only the peak of the iceberg.

---

615 Compare König, Sappayabanphot, Liang, et al. (2024).
616 Compare Heudtlass, Speybroeck, and Guha-Sapir (2016).

Thus, we can summarize that the demand for health services primarily derives from the burden of disease. The population structure, the level of economic development, and the presence of risk factors determine the amount and composition of the needs. However, not every need automatically leads to demand. Instead, the purchasing power must be sufficient, the quality of the offered services must be right, and the distance must be surmountable, i.e. the filters between need and demand must be overcome. In the following, the distance and price filters will be discussed in more detail.

3.6 Filters Between Need and Demand

3.6.1 Distance Filter

In Section 2.1.4.3, the importance of distance for the demand for health services was discussed. From the service character, it follows that the bundle of properties includes lack of storage capability, lack of transportability, and the necessity for customer presence, meaning that production and sales coincide in place, time, and action. Health services are often urgent, so timely overcoming of distance is essential.

In principle, distance can be overcome in various ways:

1. The patient visits the service provider independently: normally, the service provider is stationary, i.e. the patient walks or drives to the dispensary, health centre, or hospital. Thus, the transportation costs are borne entirely by the patient and their relatives, meaning both transport and time costs can restrict demand.

2. Patient transport is officially organized: in some countries, regular shuttles pick up patients at home or at collection points and take them to the healthcare provider. Ambulances or emergency services (including helicopter services) is a particularly expensive special form.

3. The service provider visits the patient: in many countries, there are mobile health services where, for example, a team of nurses and a doctor visit remote villages to perform treatments and prevention. The unit costs of this variant are relatively high, as a significant portion of working time is lost to transport and organization.

4. Partial functions of the service provider are outsourced locally or mobile: the distance to the point of service can also be overcome by distributing services, typically centralized, among various local service providers. The satellite-like establishment of dispensaries by hospitals can be interpreted in this way.

5. Telemedicine: the distance between service provider and patient (business-to-customer, B2C) can be overcome through telemedicine (e.g. tele-monitoring). Simultaneously, smaller local units can offer a service range through a central partner (business-to-business, B2B) that they could hardly maintain themselves (e.g. tele-diagnosis in radiology). Telemedicine has become a mainstream of health ser-

vice provision in low-income countries, as well as in development cooperation. Manifold projects focus on tele-monitoring, tele-diagnosis, tele-consultation, etc. within a country and beyond that. In remote areas, data lines are still weak, making more demanding applications (e.g. tele-radiology) difficult, but transmission of data including remote ECG diagnosis are available.[617]

The friction of distance can empirically be determined, and analysing the catchment area is part of a healthcare manager's toolkit. Figure 3.72 shows a scatter diagram of a hospital's catchment area. It is created by randomly selecting a certain number of patient records (here: 200) and plotting the places of origin on a map. From this, the actual catchment areas can be derived. The figure shows the 90% catchment area, meaning 90% of the patients live in this area.

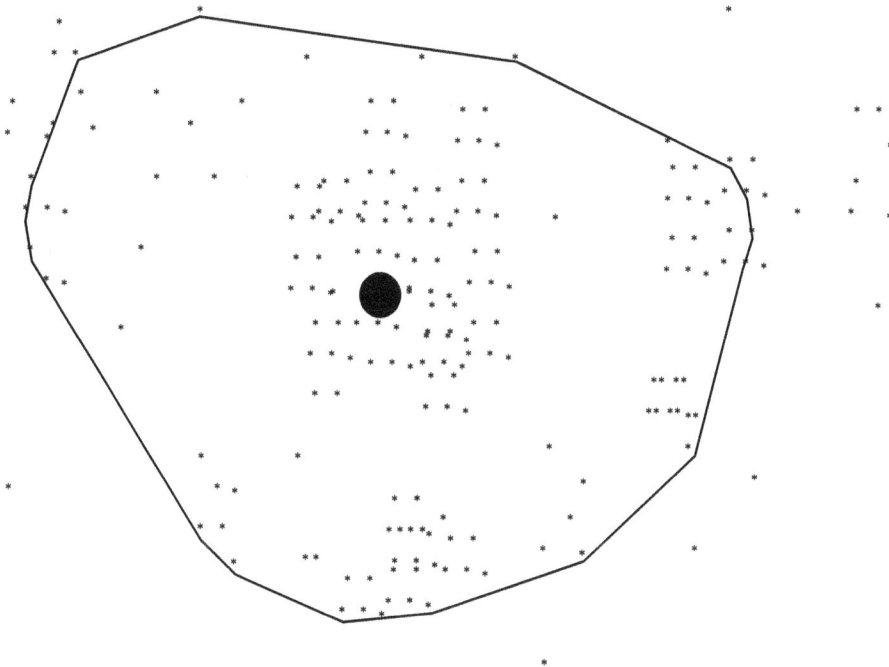

Figure 3.72: Catchment area: scatter diagram.[618]

When plotting the distance against the number of patients, one gets an impression of the friction of distance. Figure 3.73 shows the distances patients travelled to Masasi Hospital (Tanzania). It is noticeable that the number of patients decreases with in-

---

617 Compare Wootton, Patil, and Ho (2009).
618 Source: Own.

creasing distance. From a distance of 50 km, actually no patients come to Masasi Hospital, although there is no other hospital nearby. Comparing the proportion of patients to the population share, it is clear that the hospital disproportionately serves the population within a 5 km radius, i.e. the district hospital is in reality a city hospital for Masasi.

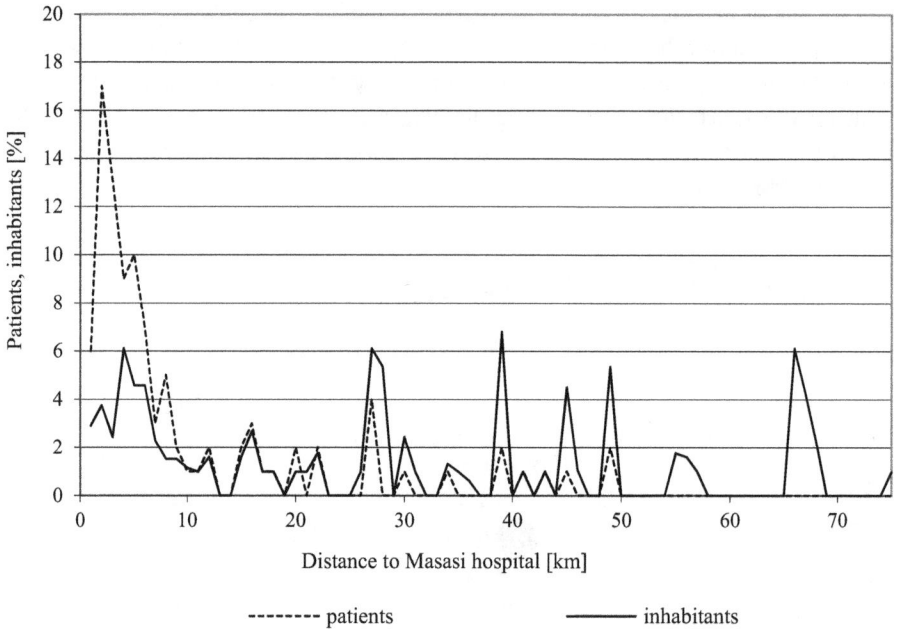

Figure 3.73: Catchment analysis of Masasi Hospital, Tanzania (2003).[619]

The friction of distance depends on the existing infrastructure. Therefore, the pure Euclidean distance, as used in the figures above, may only be an indicator of the actual distance. It would be more sensible to use travel time, i.e. to include roads, public transport, and barriers (e.g. river courses, mountains, national park boundaries, etc.). In this case, however, the survey is more costly and requires in-depth local knowledge.

In rural areas of resource-poor countries, distance is one of the main reasons why people who are ill and urgently needing medical help do not become demanders. This is especially true for preventive services, as their priority is usually low. Therefore, often only mobile provision remains, e.g. in the form of vaccination camps.[620]

---

619 Source: Own.
620 Compare Schweikart (1992).

3.6.2 Price Filter and Health Insurance

The costs of health services are often so high that the income or assets of many people are not sufficient to cover these costs. In particular, severe illnesses requiring hospitalization are a burden for many people. Their ability to pay is less than their willingness to pay, and demand in no way reflects the real need.

The price filter can be overcome in several ways. First, user fees can be subsidized, i.e. the government or donors cover part of the costs. Second, fees can be partially or fully waived if it exceeds the capacity of the patient and their family. In this case, the service provider has to bear the costs. Third, fees can be completely or partially covered by health insurance. The role of the state is discussed in Section 4.2.3, so here, we can focus on the exceptions and the role of health insurance.

3.6.2.1 User Fees and Poverty

The public health services of many developing countries were free of charge until the 1990s. However, this led to massive underfunding and significant quality deficiencies due to concurrently decreasing real government health budgets. As a consequence, most countries introduced user fees (cost-sharing) for patients.[621] The implementation of these programmes has proved to be very difficult. On the one hand, many institutions were organizationally overwhelmed; on the other hand, user fees systematically excluded certain patient groups. Accordingly, they were criticized as unfair.

The primary group disadvantaged by user fees are the poor who cannot afford these fees. Therefore, exemption regulations for poverty groups were developed. The second group consists of people with special needs who, however, do not have decision-making power over the financial resources of the private household, especially children and women. It has been proven that family heads were often unwilling to pay for the health services of these patients. Accordingly, exemption regulations were also developed for these groups.[622] In many cases, chronically ill patients are also poor and/or women/children, i.e. vulnerable groups in many dimensions must be considered for exemptions.

The implementation of the exceptions poses difficulties.[623] First, it must be determined on a case-by-case basis whether a patient is poor. Almost every country has corresponding regulations, but often it is the middle class that benefits from the 'removal of user-fees' rather than the truly poor, who can hardly articulate themselves as, for example, illiterates cannot file a written complaint. Moreover, there are catch-

---

621 Compare z.B. Brandt, Horisberger, and Wartburg (1979), Akin, Birdsall, and De Ferranti (1987), and Abel-Smith and Rawal (1992).
622 Compare Nabyonga, Desmet, Karamagi, et al. (2005).
623 Compare Fernandes Antunes, Jacobs, Jithitikulchai, et al. (2022) and Fernandes Antunes, Jithitikulchai, Hohmann, et al.(2024).

ment areas where the majority of clients are poor and would be eligible for the exception. In this case, health service providers face a significant funding gap, unless the government or a donor re-finances the exemption. This is usually only possible to a limited extent.

Poverty is a difficult term. Firstly, we have to distinguish between income and asset poverty. A person can have hundreds of cows without any cash income. Secondly, absolute and relative poverty have to be discriminated. A person is absolutely poor if he has less than a certain threshold to finance his daily living, e.g. US$1 p.c. per day. The threshold depends on the economic status of a country, and most countries define national poverty levels.

Relative poverty compares the income (or assets) of a person or family with the average. However, it is not so easy to define what the average is (mean, median, and mode) and what threshold should be taken (e.g. 40%, 50%, and 60% of average). It makes a major difference whether somebody is called poor if he earns less than 40% of the median or less than 60% of the mean. Thirdly, the family income must be distributed between family members, but the relationship between the number of family members and poverty is not linear, e.g. a family of mother, father, and five children does not need seven times the income of a single to have the same income level. Fourthly, the assessment of poverty is particularly cumbersome in subsistence farming societies with little or no cash income.

The exemption of fees based on national poverty levels and identification of the poor is a standard in many countries, but it is also a stumbling block. Figure 3.74 exhibits a Lorenz chart of the income distribution of a 'typical' low-income country. The distribution is quite unequal, i.e. the richest 10% of the population have 40% of the total income of this country, while the poorest 10% have only 2.5% of the entire income. The difference between the bold line (line of equal distribution) and the actual income distribution (normal line) expresses the inequality. The Gini coefficient as a well-known statistic for inequality is double the area between the two lines.

The consequences of income inequality are manifold, including health service inequality, health inequality, and wealth inequality. The figure also shows that the first 60% of the population have about 30% of income. The dashed line represents the line of equality for the first 60% of the population. It is obvious that the differences between the actual distribution and the equality of this subset of the population is very small, i.e. the first three quintiles have almost the same income – they are almost equally poor. Thus, it is very difficult to distinguish between the poor and non-poor.

Figure 3.75 shows the density function of income from two different years. At a first glance, the development is very positive, as a big part of the population below the national poverty line has moved beyond this threshold. On the other hand, these very-poor have not become rich – they are just beyond the poverty line (here: 150 currency units). They are always at risk to fall back into poverty. This is in particular problematic as poverty is dynamic and any unforeseen event can set the individual and the family back into poverty. The life of the poor is an up and down between the

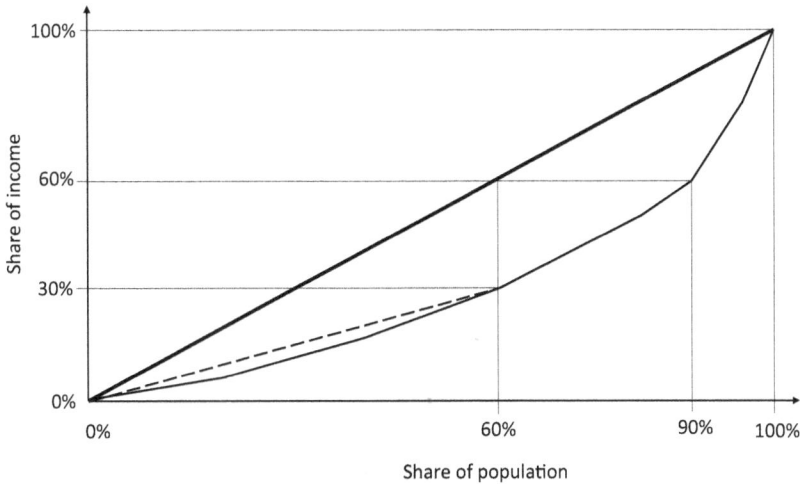

Figure 3.74: Lorenz chart of income distribution.[624]

groups of extreme-poor and near-poor.[625] If a person is near-poor, he will not get exempted to pay user fees. In case of an adverse event, such as a hospitalization, he will become very poor again just because he has to pay the user fees, but he is still officially beyond the threshold and will not get any support. He will be very poor again after the treatment, and when he fights his way back beyond the threshold, it is likely that another event will throw him back. In the absence of social protection, many poor will be under constant risk of impoverishment due to health issues.

The question of how to finance a healthcare system so that those who can contribute to the financing actually do so, while at the same time not excluding the poor, is one of the most pressing problems of international healthcare management. In many countries, pilot projects are being conducted, with international development aid often setting the direction. For example, German development co-operation advocates a social insurance system based on the Bismarck model, while the British promote a government healthcare system without user fees (Beveridge model).[626]

3.6.2.2 Health Insurance
For about 30 years, it has been scientifically investigated whether the introduction of health insurance in resource-poor countries is possible and what effects it has on the healthcare of the population. A treatable disease is, statistically speaking, a rare event

---

624 Source: Own.
625 Compare Vuong, Flessa, Marschall, et al. (2014).
626 Compare GtZ (2007).

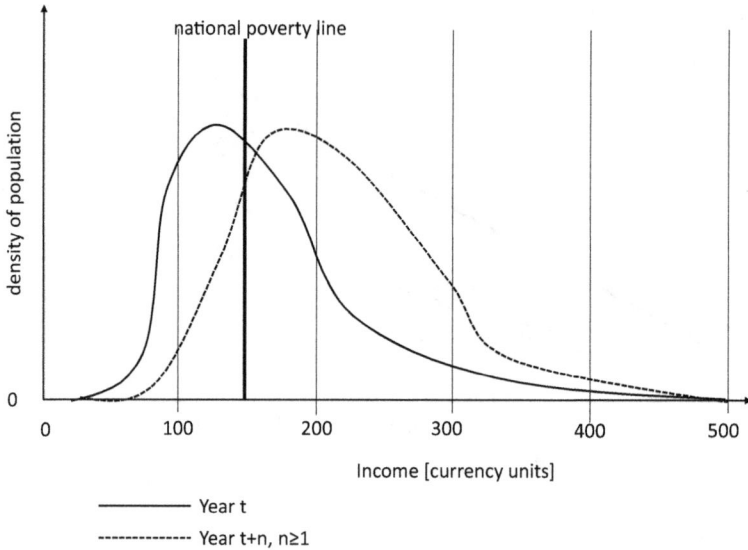

Figure 3.75: Poor and near-poor.[627]

for an individual with a high expenditure. This suggests risk shifting through insurance.

After independence, numerous governments in low- and middle-income countries established health insurances. Pioneers in Africa were Ghana, Kenya, Mali, Zaire, Senegal, and Zimbabwe, while in Asia, especially Thailand, Indonesia, and China were keen to develop a health insurance system. Typically, however, these insurances remained limited to government employees and a few wealthy individuals. Only in China, the majority of the population could benefit from insurance coverage, which, however, quickly declined. Hence, at the beginning of the 1990s, less than 5% of the inhabitants of developing countries were insured. Typically, only the wealthy, urban elite enjoyed this protection.[628]

The minor importance of health insurance in developing countries up to 30 years ago was mainly because the existing health insurances were linked to wage income, yet a large part of the population of these countries lived from subsistence agriculture and thus were not wage earners. This has fundamentally changed. On the one hand, the proportion of people with regular income is also rising in resource-poor countries; on the other hand, health insurance systems have been developed for the rural population without wage income. The majority of these programmes were (co-)financed by major development aid organizations.

---

627 Source: Own.
628 Compare Barnum, Kutzin, and Roemer (1993).

The solidarity system within immediate family ties has a long tradition in most developing countries, meaning the individual's disease risk has always been borne by the family. However, the immediate family is not large enough to absorb the treatment costs of serious diseases without the family facing serious financial difficulties. An institutional health insurance aims to transfer the traditional family solidarity system to a larger group of people, with whom there is no family connection.

The basics of insurance management can certainly be applied to corresponding institutions in developing countries, but often need adjustment in the following areas:

- Trustee: the state, a community, a health institution, or a private enterprise can be the trustee of health insurance. The majority of older health insurances in developing countries are state-run and mainly serve to secure government employees. The wealthy minority of these countries often enjoys private insurance coverage. The trustees of health insurances developed since the early 1990s for people without regular wage income are often the health institutions itself, thus creating health maintenance organizations (HMOs). In many cases, a community also manages insurance. It is usually organized co-operatively and referred to as 'community-based health insurance' (CBHI) or 'community-based health fund' (CBHF).[629] A special form are health insurances tied to other insurances. For example, there are microcredit companies that only grant loans to members who also have health insurance. Often, therefore, microcredit lenders also have health insurance in their portfolio.
- Membership: some health insurances only accept members who meet certain criteria. In developing countries, belonging to a certain community determines who can be included in a CBHI. However, defining the community is extremely difficult, as distant relatives often emotionally belong to the community. HMOs in developing countries typically insure residents of the catchment area, while private health insurances accept anyone who can pay the premium.
- Insurance benefits: the insurance coverage can include outpatient and/or inpatient services. In developing countries, the insurance can therefore cover dispensaries, health centres, and/or hospitals. Including preventive medicine in the portfolio of insurance benefits is also possible. Furthermore, it must be determined to what extent patients are required to make co-payments. In addition, insurances in resource-poor countries often exclude certain services. On the one hand, an annual maximum amount for the treatment of insured individuals can be set; on the other hand, the exclusion of specific diseases is also possible. For example, the treatment costs of AIDS are sometimes not reimbursed.
- Premium payment: health insurances must determine the amount of the premium, as well as the method and timing of payment. The premium can be paid either in cash or in kind. Subsistence farmers will probably prefer payment in

---

629 Compare Rösner, Leppert, Degens, et al. (2011) and Ouedraogo and Flessa (2016).

rice or maize. The annual premium can be paid either in instalments or in one lump sum. In rural areas, it makes sense to demand the complete annual premium after the harvest.

- Service reimbursement: the reimbursement of fees for health services can be retrospective or prospective and can occur as a care rate or as a flat rate per case. In this respect, health insurances in developing countries do not differ from those in Western industrialized countries.

While we will address the financing function of social protection systems again in Section 5.2.2, this section focusses mainly on the filter between want and demand for healthcare services, the insurance being the prime instrument to overcome the price filter. However, implementing health insurances in low-income countries is cumbersome because well-known problems of health insurances from high-income countries are even more pronounced in international healthcare management, while specific challenges arise. The general problems include:[630]

- Demand increase: insurance coverage leads to increased demand for health services. This is partly because price elasticity is relatively high, so with insurance coverage, people who previously avoided the high costs of treatment are now more likely to visit healthcare institutions. It must be emphasised here that this increase in demand is not 'immoral'. Rather, a well-justified need becomes a demand that would otherwise have been unmet or postponed. A different picture arises when, for example, insurance coverage reduces one's own prevention efforts (moral hazard) or when there is an attitude that one should expect adequate service for the premium paid. In these cases, certain filters must be installed, such as a co-payment or a strict review of admission indications.

    Generally, it can be assumed that the demand for health services at least doubles when user fees are removed. This must be considered in the premium calculation when introducing health insurance.

- Adverse selection: generally, a potential policyholder will consider insurance worthwhile when they expect a financial benefit for themselves. This results in those who expect a strong susceptibility to illness being more likely to enter the insurance. The smaller the proportion of insured individuals in the total population, the greater the likelihood that the high-risk cases will apply for insurance. Coverage is only possible for them if the premiums are very high. This prevents people with average risk from joining and can lead to the long-term dissolution of the insurance pool. Family insurance is one way to prevent mostly high-risk groups of the elderly and sick from pushing into the insurance while the healthy do not participate in the pool. However, 'adverse household selection'[631] can also occur here.

---

630 Compare De Allegri, Sauerborn, Kouyaté, et al. (2009).
631 Compare Arhin (1994).

- Overhead costs: the introduction of health insurance means creating a new institution with an appropriate administrative apparatus. Financing these costs through insurance premiums leads to a higher average burden on the insured. This means that the expected value of healthcare costs is always lower than the insurance premium, as the insurance must add a portion of its overhead costs. Therefore, the advantage of health insurance lies not in reducing average costs but in reducing (sometimes completely) the uncertainty. However, the overhead cost shares in some insurances in developing countries are over 50% of the premium income, i.e. the insured 'purchases' the reduction of the risk of catastrophic expenses at significant costs.
- Security surcharge: the frequency of hospital treatments and the severity of cases are uncertain, so hospital costs also fluctuate around an expected value. Therefore, health insurances generally add a security surcharge to compensate for this risk. Especially in developing countries, the variation is relatively large since epidemics are more frequent. If the premium is set exactly at the expected value, the insurance will suffer a loss with a probability of 50%. Consequently, the premium must always be higher, with the surcharge being smaller the larger the insurance pool.

In developed countries, these general problems are solved by having insurances with efficient administration and a large number of insured who have at least a basic understanding of the insurance concept. In low-income countries, this is often not possible since the following specific problems occur:
- Educational level of the insured: the higher the level of education of the potentially insured, the easier it is to communicate the concept of insurance. It is generally difficult to explain to people without formal education why an insured person does not get their premium refunded at the end of a period, even though they were not ill.
- Administrative competence: existing health facility administrations in developing countries often lack the capacity to manage insurance premiums in a fiduciary manner. Accounting is rudimentary, used for recording but not as a management tool.
- Premium payment: For most subsistence farmers, insurance is only attractive if the premium does not have to be paid in regular cash amounts. Most insured individuals only have larger cash inflows once a year (usually after the harvest of global commodities such as coffee), so they prefer to pay the annual premium all at once shortly after the harvest. Many farmers would prefer to pay the premium entirely in kind or as labour. On one hand, this increases acceptance among farmers, but on the other hand, it places the marketing risk entirely on the insurance. A cash premium payment excludes pure subsistence farmers and thus the majority of the poor in developing countries.

- Insured demarcation: most people in developing countries have a very strong community bond. This means that they will reject the insurance of an individual, as the whole family must be insured. In countries where most people do not have a personal ID or a family register, it is difficult to delineate who belongs to the family. Given the inherent administrative problems of health institutions in developing countries, it is hardly possible to ensure that no people are covered for whom payment has not been made. Often, a passport photo is required for each insurance member, which, however, increases administrative costs.
- Identification with institutions: in some developing countries, the population mistrusts large institutions because they were cheated by governmental agricultural cooperatives. Generally, the organizational form of a primary cooperative would be suitable for a CBHI. Currently, however, it is hardly to be expected that the communities themselves will take the initiative. Instead, a 'top-down development' is attempted, in which the state, church leadership, or international development aid organizations build health insurance for the affected people, but without their participation.
- Ethnological problems: in analysing the extent to which insurances are accepted by the population, the culture of a people is the central moment. This particularly affects the traditional handling of the future since some tribes avoid any statement about the future, as fate is considered inevitable. Accordingly, no precautions for future diseases should be taken, otherwise, evil would be invoked. In such a situation, it seems almost impossible to introduce health insurance, as it requires considering future illnesses.
- Independence of the insurance: the sustainable functionality of a health insurance depends on its management and its reserves. There is a risk that higher authorities will exert the same intense influence on the insurances as they currently do on hospitals.

In summary, we can state that health insurance is an effective measure to overcome the price filter between need and demand. However, the willingness to join a health insurance is just as little guaranteed as its long-term existence. Therefore, establishing health insurances requires a national policy that promotes institutional stability, low overhead costs, efficient administration, and structures adapted to local needs, especially for social health insurance.[632]

With these few remarks on the filters between need and demand, the extensive chapter on the demand for health services should be concluded. As shown, demand is not fixed but is influenced by numerous institutions, framework data, and processes.

---

632 Compare Normand and Weber (2009) and Hsiao, Shaw, and Fraker (2007).

The primary goal of international healthcare management is to strengthen health and thus – unlike many consumer goods – to prevent demand in the first place. At the same time, demand based on real needs should be met as comprehensively as possible, as deferred or suppressed health needs usually have significant side, back, and sequelae effects. Therefore, an appropriate offer must be available to meet the demand.

4 Supply

The supply of health services can be analysed on two levels. Primarily, it involves managing the individual economic transformation process of production factors into health services. Figure 2.12 hints at this by showing how production factors in an institution or programme are transformed into output. Figure 4.1 elaborates on this connection, as can be described for a hospital, for example.[633] In principle, the service provision in a healthcare facility or programme only differs in a few points in different countries. The primary differences are likely to be in the availability of production factors, the management process, and quality management.

On the second level, individual healthcare organizations work together to create a supply function. Here, the spatial structure, levels of care, and financing must be considered. The principles of how a supply structure emerges from individual providers are identical for all countries, so the advantages and disadvantages of monopolistic healthcare providers are not fundamentally discussed here. However, we will address the specifics that arise from resource scarcity, low population density, large distances, and low privatization of healthcare in resource-poor countries.

4.1 Business Administration of Healthcare

4.1.1 Agents of Production

The agents of production (i.e. operational labour, managerial labour, capital goods, and materials, possibly supplemented by information and the customer as an external factor) apply to all business units regardless of location. In international healthcare management, however, it must be considered that they are often scarcer, differently defined, and must meet different requirements than in high-income countries. This is particularly true for buildings and facilities as well as for personnel.

4.1.1.1 Buildings and Equipment

In resource-poor countries, in addition to the traditional questions of equipment provisioning, there are problems with appropriate technology, lack of maintenance culture, and the consumption of one's own infrastructure.

Appropriate technology refers to methods and techniques that do not align with what is technically feasible or the technical world standard but consciously ask which technology is appropriate for a particular situation. Typically, appropriate technologies are simpler, cheaper, and smaller than standard technologies and take more account of

---

633 Compare Fleßa (2008) and Fleßa (2010a).

https://doi.org/10.1515/9783112217290-004

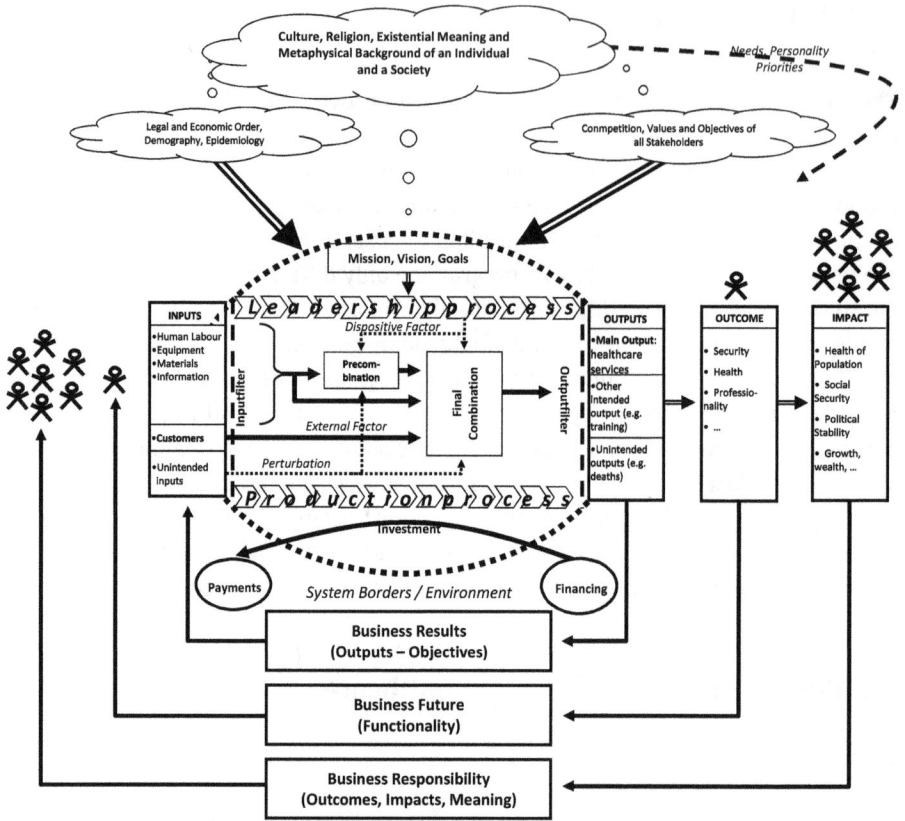

Figure 4.1: Transformation process of a healthcare facility or programme.[634]

the local population. For example, almost all infusions worldwide are industrially produced through distillation. This process is energy-intensive, particularly incurring high transport costs, as industrial production tends to take place in a smaller number of central locations. An appropriate technology is infusion production through osmosis (filter techniques), which can be done locally in a hospital. The units are correspondingly small (e.g. with a capacity of 20,000 L per year), operable by a lab technician independently, and comparatively inexpensive. Further examples are solar sterilizers, ramps as a substitute for elevators, sterilized bicycle spokes as external fixators, a basic radiographic system, and motorized stretchers as a substitute for an ambulance vehicle. Recently, the term frugal innovation is preferred with a focus on technology that is

---

634 Source: Fleßa (2022).

cheaper ('substantial cost reduction'), easier to operate ('concentration on core function-alities') and tailored to wards the needs of the situation ('optimal performance level').[635]

Most Europeans assume the superiority of Western technology and demand it for other countries. However, this leads to two problems: First, it often overburdens local resources, and second, Western technology can be dangerous and inferior if not used within an overall system. The first case occurs, for example, when buildings and equipment cannot be maintained with local funds and local personnel. Often, inappropriate technology leads to high maintenance costs that significantly exceed the original purchase costs or the donation amount. Mastery of the technology by local staff is a fundamental condition for efficient healthcare provision.

The second case occurs, for example, when Western standard solutions remain non-functional under the conditions of other countries, thus endangering staff, patients, and the public. For example, there is a risk that the radiation dose will continuously increase with classic x-ray technology as the developer solution ages. Hospitals often cannot afford regular renewal of chemicals, so this technology leads to significant radiation exposure. Simple devices, like those produced in India for rural hospitals, are superior here to the complex European systems.

A technology can only be considered applied if it is strategically planned. It is important to include the complete life cycle. It begins (1) with a needs assessment, presupposing that there are goals for the equipment provision. Only what can be derived from the goal system of the healthcare facility should be purchased, regardless of whether a donor or another programme is currently available that would like to 'gift' something to this facility. Often, one finds dumps of such 'gifts' from developed countries in hospitals of resource-poor countries that were unusable or unmaintainable under local conditions. When operational failures occur, they cannot be repaired and are stored – with all the risks to the environment.

This also contradicts the effort to standardize (2). Especially in least developed countries, there are numerous partnerships that result in each healthcare facility having different devices that were obtained 'for free' or cheaply from their partners. Standardizing equipment within a facility and region would allow for specific training of repair and maintenance personnel, a stock of spare parts, and the purchase of maintenance manuals. However, the multitude of different devices from various countries makes systematic management impossible.

The third step is the actual procurement (3), meaning the ordering, freight, installation, and commissioning. Import, customs, and foreign exchange restrictions must be considered. Donated assets may also need to be taxed, and transport to remote regions can lead to significantly higher costs than, for example, in Europe.

During usage (4), maintenance is a larger problem, which we will address next. At this point, it should only be emphasized that maintenance is part of the life cycle

---

635 Weyrauch and Herstatt (2017).

and must be considered from the beginning. Maintenance personnel or teams, intervals, devices, spare parts, and costs must be included in the overall analysis.

Finally (5), disposal must also be part of the management cycle. Often, unusable devices (and buildings) in developing countries are simply deposited. However, this poses significant dangers, such as those caused by chemicals or sharp objects. If only the first four phases of the cycle are considered, for example, a solar system with appropriate battery buffering appears to be an applied technology. However, the fate of the exhausted batteries after a few years remains largely unresolved. Figure 4.2 shows the equipment life cycle.

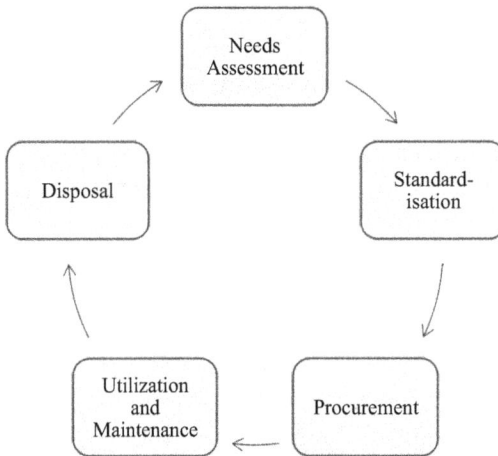

Figure 4.2: Equipment life cycle.[636]

The maintenance of buildings and equipment is a serious challenge. It is estimated that 1–2% of the construction costs of buildings and 2–5% of the acquisition costs of devices should be set as standard maintenance costs to guarantee optimal lifespan and functionality.[637] However, these figures are rarely achieved.

The lack of maintenance has various causes. On one hand, health budgets are often so low that only the medically necessary consumables and salaries can be paid. Funds for expenses that do not immediately endanger the basic functionality of the facility or programme are often lacking, so maintenance of buildings and facilities is postponed. In the future, this will necessitate higher expenditures, but in the short term, the healthcare facilities can maintain its performance, even without maintenance. On the other hand, the availability of maintenance materials and personnel is

---

636 Source: Own, based on Campbell and Jardine (2001).
637 Compare Halbwachs (2000) and Halbwachs and Issakov (1994).

not always guaranteed, so necessary maintenance is omitted. This usually indicates that the technology was not applied at the time of acquisition.

The omission or delay of maintenance often also has cultural reasons. In temperate climates like in Western Europe, the forward-looking storage of food and fuel and the functionality of the heating dwelling were vital for survival. During the long winter months, farmers also had time to maintain their equipment in order to produce enough food during the relatively short growing season. This developed a maintenance mentality.

In tropical regions, and especially in the traditionally populated fertile areas, food grows all year round and a solid dwelling with an adequate supply of fuel was unnecessary. Stockpiling was punished by rapid rotting, and maintenance of equipment or buildings was mostly pointless, as the climate overwhelmed even the best maintenance strategies. It was often easier to rebuild a hut after a relatively short time than to maintain it. Therefore, no maintenance culture developed.

The result of lacking financial resources, materials, and personnel for maintenance, and a lack of maintenance culture is visible in most healthcare facilities in developing countries: The potential factors of hospitals, health centres, and dispensaries are often in very poor condition, and there is a high need to catch up on replacement investments. Roofs need to be renewed, interiors renovated, beds and mattresses, as well as medical equipment and vehicles replaced. Particularly problematic in many hospitals is the power and water supply, as old cables have become unusable, generators have exceeded their lifespan, and wells have dried up.[638]

Figure 4.3 shows the life cycle of a typical hospital in a resource-poor country. During a build-up phase, sufficient financial resources are available to purchase equipment, construct buildings, or train personnel. These funds come either from the government budget or development aid. During this time, the institution's performance steadily increases. In the first few years, the institutions continue to be financially supported, so the performance level remains relatively high. However, after the expiration of the funding, the performance steadily declines until it reaches a level that can be financed with local resources. Typically, the quality of hospital services in this phase is so low that the population is unwilling to pay for it: The hospital buildings are beyond their technical lifespan, the equipment is unusable, and the vehicles are wheelless. Mattresses and medications are missing, and the staff is generally unmotivated.

In the past, the sustainability problem appeared to be solved by new financial aid (e.g. from abroad) at the end of the decline phase, allowing the health institution to be renovated. Typically, funds were also provided for personnel acquisition, vehicles, and medical equipment. Figure 4.4 illustrates this development. The cyclical financing of health services implies that patients receive poorer service during the build-up and

---

638 Compare Fleßa (2003b).

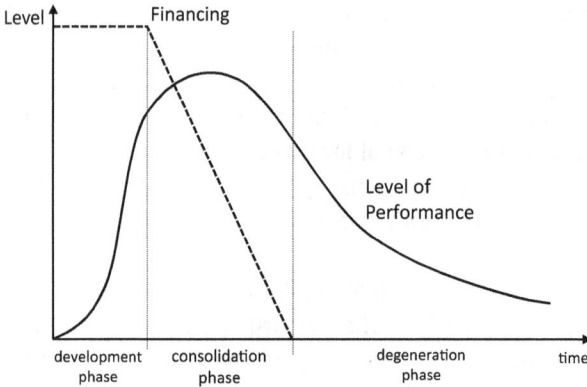

Figure 4.3: Single-period life cycle of a hospital.[639]

decline phases than those treated during the consolidation phase. This contradicts intertemporal justice and is inefficient. Uniform and long-term financing would secure a higher level of performance in the long run with the same budget, as postponed maintenance generally leads to higher costs than maintenance performed on time.

Thus, we can summarize that buildings and equipment are a significant factor in the poor structural quality of health services in low-income countries. Given the high investments (especially through development aid) in this area, one could expect better quality, i.e. international healthcare management must strengthen facility management.

4.1.1.2 Personnel

The basic personnel categories are similar in all countries with a science-based healthcare system, although the training programmes differ significantly, particularly the diagnostic-therapeutic service providers are trained differently. While in high-income countries, diagnosis and therapy are still predominantly reserved for licensed doctors with a 6-year academic study, many developing countries have introduced additional personnel categories to cover the high demand for experts. Figure 4.5 exemplarily shows the training of medical professions in Tanzania. In addition to the academic doctor, there are also the rural medical aid (RMA), who is primarily trained to provide care for dispensaries. In health centres and smaller hospitals, there is the clinical officer (CO; synonymously known as medical assistant, MA), who has better schooling and more intensive training than the RMA. Both work independently in diagnosis and therapy, where an RMA with work experience can be further trained as a CO.

---

639 Source: Own, based on Langenscheidt (1999).

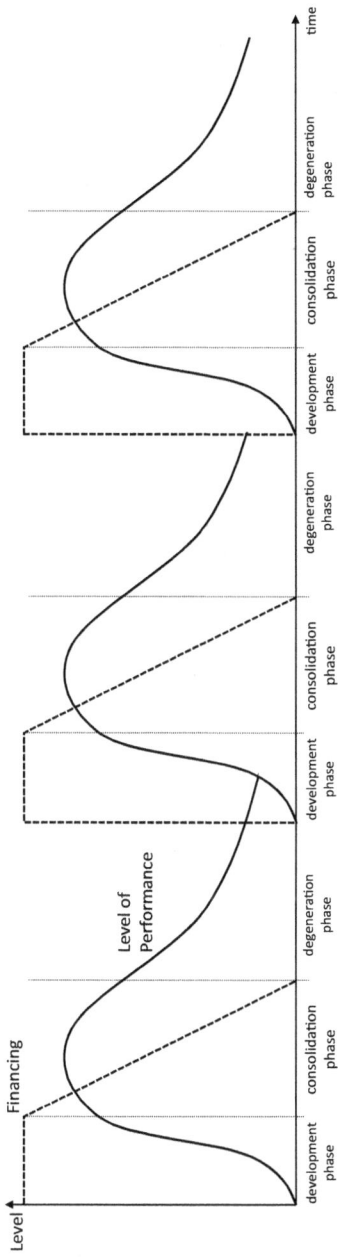

Figure 4.4: Multiperiod life cycle of a hospital.[640]

640 Source: Fleßa (2003b).

The CO may have the opportunity to further train as an assistant medical officer, who is considered a doctor and can independently run a smaller hospital. However, further specialization (e.g. as a gynaecologist) is excluded. Thus, the picture of medical professions is significantly more differentiated than typically the case in Europe. This is necessary because the extremely expensive and lengthy training of doctors in most low-income countries would prevent universal coverage of the population in all locations.

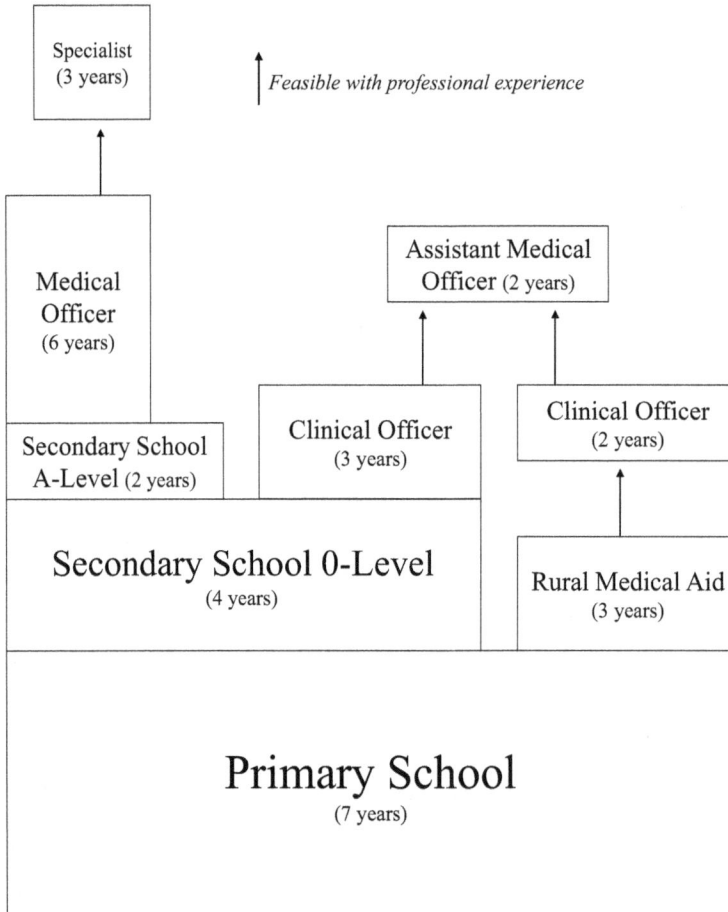

Figure 4.5: Training of medical professions in Tanzania.[641]

Nursing training is also often more differentiated in countries that follow other traditions and have a low density of qualified personnel. For example, in former English colonies, it is common for female nurses to add a fourth year of training to become

---

641 Source: Own.

midwives. A midwifery training as a separate professional branch usually does not exist there. Additionally, there are various categories of nursing assistants, with and without formal training. Figure 4.6 exemplifies nursing education in Tanzania. In Africa, untrained nursing attendants often take on tasks that would be performed by certified staff in high-income countries. Additionally, a large part of the tasks of nursing staff is taken over by family members, such as providing food.

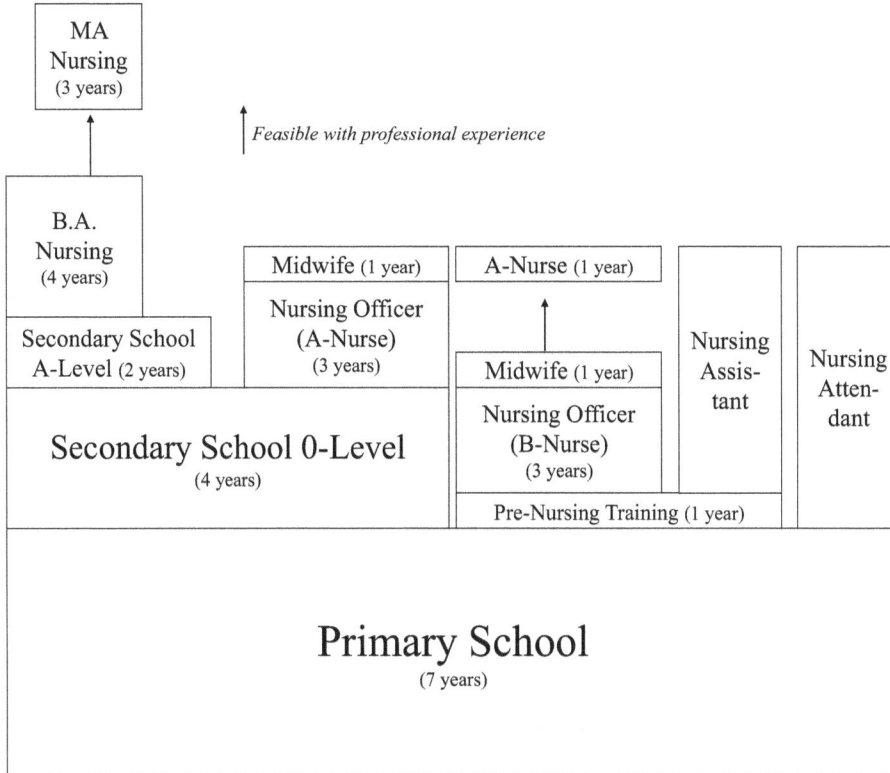

Figure 4.6: Training of nursing professions in Tanzania.[642]

In resource-poor countries, there is often the problem that positions cannot be filled with qualified personnel, so the proportion of untrained and semi-skilled workers is comparatively high. This problem has been exacerbated in recent years by the emergence of alternative employers for medical and nursing personnel. Especially, the so-called global health initiatives often pay significantly higher salaries than regular health services and deliberately recruit staff. Since many local facilities are not even able to comply with legal requirements (e.g. paying overtime), motivation often re-

---

642 Source: Own.

duces to remuneration. The qualified leave, and often those with lower performance remain. Leaders of these facilities face significant challenges in retaining and motivating their staff. Although money is not a motivator, it is a hygiene factor, i.e. irregularly paid salaries or a salary structure perceived as unfair prevent other factors from being motivating.[643]

4.1.1.3 Problems of International Cooperation

A significant portion of the resources in the healthcare sector in low- and lower-middle-income countries comes from development cooperation. The Overall Development Assistance for Health (ODA-health) was about US$10 billion in 1990 (public-private partnership (PPP) 2021, US$) and increased to about 40 billion in 2012. It was almost stable until 2019, but then it increased up to 70 billion due to COVID-19 and the global resources required to fight the pandemic.[644] A major, but declining share is allocated to HIV/AIDS programmes, other infectious diseases, reproductive and maternal health, as well as newborn and child health. Non-communicable diseases receive a negligible share of the ODA-health.[645] Low-income countries and in particular sub-Saharan Africa still receive a lion's share. In some countries, external aid contributes more than 50% to the total health spending, e.g. Somalia, Democratic Republic of Congo, Malawi, Mozambique, Tanzania, Laos, and Papua New Guinea.[646]

At the same time, voices are repeatedly raised complaining about the ineffectiveness of this aid. This includes the high costs of personnel cooperation, the overwhelming of local institutions by the multitude of partners, and the high dependency on their goals.

As an example of the problems of personnel cooperation, we will calculate the costs of a specialist doctor. The placement of doctors and nurses has always been a focus of development aid, but it represents only one variant of foreign personnel. Thus, people from developing countries are also working in other countries, partly for training and partly because these countries cannot cover their own needs and deliberately recruit skilled personnel from developing countries (brain drain).[647] Normally, this is relevant when there is also a difference in income levels between the countries, so that, for example, Indian doctors practice in the USA. In development aid, there is usually a charitable (or individually an adventure) motive, which, however, upon closer inspection, presents an efficiency problem. Table 4.1, for example, shows the (estimated) costs of a medical development worker.

---

643 Compare Mintzberg (1989).
644 Compare Apeagyei, Dieleman, and O'Rourke (2023).
645 Compare Apeagyei, Dieleman, and O'Rourke (2023).
646 Compare Apeagyei, Lidral-Porter, Patel, et al. (2024).
647 Compare Pang, Lansang, and Haines (2002).

Table 4.1: Costs of a development worker (doctor, 2-year assignment).

Cost category		Amount (€)
Preparation	Preparation course	15,000
	English course	15,000
	Local language course	10,000
	Transport	15,000
Ongoing expenses	Gross salary	180,000
	School fees children	48,000
	Insurances, etc.	5,000
Reintegration		18,000
Total costs		306,000

The preparation and reintegration time is almost a year, so the development worker must be paid for 36 months to be able to work on-site for 24 months. The salary is significantly lower than the corresponding compensation for a specialist doctor in Germany, but considerable additional costs arise, e.g. for international school (assumption here: two school-age children). Thus, the costs of a development worker amount to €12,750 per month of actual work on-site. The salary of a local doctor is often below €1,000 per month.

It is clear that personnel development aid can only be justified if no adequate force can be found either in the country or in South-South Cooperation (SSC), i.e. the exchange of resources, technology, and knowledge between low-income countries of the Global South.[648] It must also be analysed whether this sum could motivate a similarly qualified local who works abroad to return to his homeland.

The second criticism is the high number of institutions, programmes, requirements, conditions, etc., of development agencies. Table 4.2 provides a highly condensed overview of some important institutions and programmes relevant to the healthcare sector in low-income countries. Currently, an estimated over 500 partners are active on this 'market' – and even after the Paris Declaration (compare Section 2.4.2) with its call for alignment, most are poorly coordinated, each setting specific requirements for application and reporting as well as auditing. Thus, it can happen that a department in the Ministry of Health might have to create 25 different reports for the same programme because it cooperates with so many different donor organizations that cannot agree on a format.

The high dependence on foreign subsidies can also lead to the providers of a country's healthcare system aligning more with the requirements of international financial backers than with the needs of their own population. As the control loop (Figure 4.7) shows, in addition to the outcome relevant for the patients, there is a con-

---

648 Compare also Bandung Conference 1955, Appadorai (1955).

Table 4.2: Selected institutions and programmes of international development cooperation.[649]

Abbreviation	Institution
ADVENIAT	Bishop's Aid Action ADVENIAT
AGEH	Working Group for Development Aid
Bread	Bread for the World
CIM	Centre for International Migration and Development
DAAD	German Academic Exchange Service
DANIDA	Danish International Development Assistance
DIFÄM	German Institute for Medical Mission
DSW	German Foundation World Population
EPI	Extended Programme on Immunization
FCDO	Foreign, Commonwealth and Development Office[650]
GAVI	Global Alliance for Vaccines and Immunization
GFATM	Global Fund to Fight AIDS, Tuberculosis, and Malaria
GIZ	GIZ German Society for International Cooperation[651]
IMF	International Monetary Fund
JICA	Japanese International Cooperation Agency
KfW	Kreditanstalt für Wiederaufbau, German Development Bank
medmissio	Institut für Gesundheit weltweit (formerly Mission Medical Institute Würzburg)
MISEREOR	Bishop's Aid Action MISEREOR
PEPFAR	United States President's Emergency Plan for AIDS Relief
SIDA	Swedish International Development Cooperation Agency
TOWA	Total war against HIV and AIDS project
UNAIDS	Joint United Nations Programme on HIV/AIDS
UNFPR	United Nations Population Fund (formerly the United Nations Fund for Population Activities)
UNHCR	United National High Commissioner for Refugees
UNICEF	United Nations Children Fund
USAID	United States Agency for International Development
WB	World Bank, The International Bank of Development and Reconstruction
WHO	World Health Organization

trol variable analysed by the donors. If the dependence on foreign countries is very high, health politicians in resource poor countries will pay more attention to signals from abroad than to the statements of their own base. Since the goal systems of donors are not always identical with those of the patients, the flow of donations can lead to a complete neglect of the population in the catchment areas of the healthcare facilities.

A healthcare system in which the local population plays hardly any role as customers, and where the majority of financing occurs independently of service delivery,

---

649 Source: Own.

650 Formerly Department for International Development (DFID).

651 GIZ merged from German Technical Cooperation (GtZ), INWENT, and German Development Service as of 1 January 2011. It is responsible for technical cooperation, while KfW offers financial cooperation.

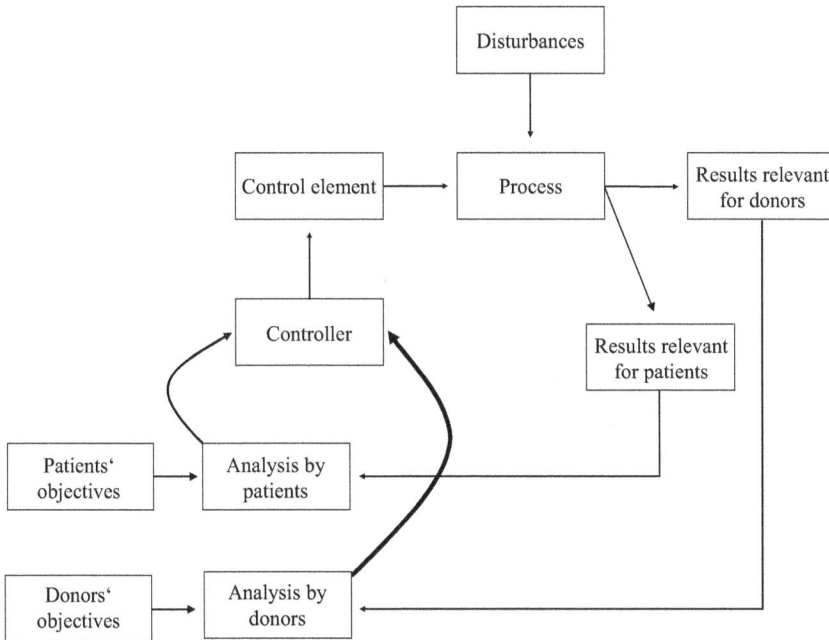

Figure 4.7: Feedback loop model for foreign dependence.[652]

is at risk of making decisions primarily based on the needs of donors rather than the desires of its own local population. Such a system is extremely fragile and may fail to notice increasing fluctuations because the healthcare system's crisis manifests primarily at the grassroots level, not in the flow of donations. International development cooperation is therefore always at risk of sustaining structures that should have been untenable long ago.

At this point, a distinction must again be made between development aid and humanitarian aid (compare Section 2.1.4.4). The latter does not aim to strengthen long-term capacities in developing countries but seeks to improve a humanitarian emergency in the short term. It can be justified, for example, during a drought disaster and in the face of the threat to the lives of millions of people to pay higher salaries and heavily burden government administrations. However, long-term development aid must analyse whether its activities weaken personnel capacities, regulatory systems, infrastructures, and institutional frameworks. The primary goal of sustainable development aid must be to strengthen the partner country's ability to manage its problems independently in the long run (compare Figure 4.8). This can be achieved through investments in infrastructure, by promoting the individual development of (future) decision-makers, by strengthening and developing efficient organizations, or

---

652 Source: Own.

by supporting the establishment of appropriate overall systems. Therefore, development aid in healthcare might finance hospital renovations, award scholarships, support the introduction of comprehensive quality management in the Ministry of Health, and promote a functional referral system.

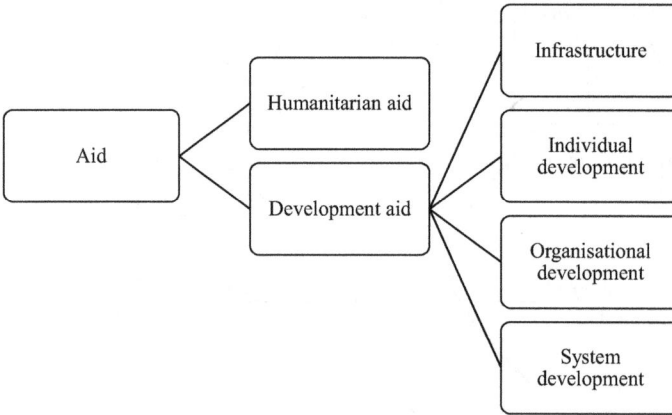

Figure 4.8: Humanitarian aid and development aid.[653]

In summary, it can be noted that the basic theory of production factors is fully applicable to international healthcare. However, each country has its peculiarities that must be considered.

4.1.2 Transformation Process

The transformation process of production factors into health services is fundamentally the same in all countries, i.e. diagnostics, care, and therapy follow the same 'laws of nature'. The availability of equipment, reagents, and specialists, however, determines the achievable standard. It is highly controversial what should be understood by a standard. Donabedian understands it as "professionally developed expressions of the range of acceptable variations from a norm or criterion" or "predetermined elements against which aspects of the quality of medical services may be compared".[654] Heidemann defines them as "a benchmark of achievement which is based on a desired level of excellence. As such, standards become models to be imitated and may serve, in turn, as the basis for comparisons".[655] For international healthcare manage-

---

653 Source: Own.
654 Donabedian (1982).
655 Heidemann (1993).

ment, it is crucial that the determination of standards can only occur with consideration of the specific situation and culture. In a low-income country, standards must be set lower than in the Western world – there is no global standard.

The definition of process chains, as well as the structured planning, implementation, and control of quality in healthcare facilities in resource-poor countries, is underdeveloped. There is mostly still an 'eminence-based medicine', i.e. a sole orientation on the expertise of the head physician. Initial individual approaches of guidelines, interface management, and structured quality management are likely to gain significant importance in the coming years and require attention from the international healthcare manager.

A fundamental problem is that many health service providers in areas with low population density are spatial monopolists. Consequently, they are unable to specialize and must offer the full range of services for their level of care. This leads to comparatively high case costs, as no specialization advantages can be utilized. Additionally, there is the risk that facilities either do not offer certain parts of the basic programme or provide services that are not part of their official portfolio. For instance, there is an example of a rural health centre where two German specialists worked, while only general practitioners were available at the district hospital. As a result, surgeries that could not be performed at the district hospital were conducted at the poorly accessible and inadequately equipped health centre. This created an unsatisfactory situation for the general population, while the sending organization and development workers were proud of their performance.

The transformation process thus implies both a clear definition of processes and quality management and the determination of a performance programme that corresponds to the level of care. Implementation requires leadership.

4.1.3 Leadership Process

Leadership is an interpersonal interaction process strongly influenced by values, interpretation patterns, and assumptions. Therefore, the culture of a country plays a significant role in the leadership process like no other area.

The term 'culture' is used in various ways. First, it is essential to distinguish between primary and secondary culture. The former describes the basic definitions of a cultural space, while the latter encompasses the institutions arising from it, such as forms of art. For the following discussion, only the primary culture is relevant, although it is generally accepted that only a very small part of culture is visible. The majority remains hidden but significantly shapes an individual's behaviour (iceberg model).[656]

---

656 Compare also Schein's culture model, Schein (1991).

Hofstede defines (primary) culture as the 'mental programming' of a population group, Kruse as the "deeper level of general basic assumptions and beliefs".[657] Cultural values are usually imparted in early childhood and affect adult behaviour for a lifetime. Therefore, healthcare workers in different cultural areas will always behave differently from their own cultural area. It is thus crucial for the international healthcare manager to know the dimensions of culture and the resulting problems.

Hofstede distinguishes six dimensions of national culture.[658] A high power distance exists when an unequal distribution of power is deemed appropriate, i.e. it is accepted and expected that the supervisor makes decisions alone, gives clear instructions, acts authoritatively, delegates little, demands obedience, and, if necessary, punishes. The supervisor must not be criticized, and his instructions can hardly be questioned. In the best case, he is paternalistically caring; in the worst case, he is a dictator, although this is not viewed negatively by his subordinates. According to Hofstede, the proportion of cultures with high power distance is comparatively high in developing countries.

The second dimension is individualism, understood as the right to self-determination, self-responsibility, proactivity, and self-realization. In contrast, collectivist cultures seek to integrate the individual into the network, a strong group orientation, and ultimately a merging into the community. Self-realization, the highest form of motivation according to Maslow,[659] is thus as insignificant as constant admonitions for individualistic proactivity according to Covey.[660] In extreme cases, the collectivist culture can lead to a victim mentality, as in times of collapsing social structures (e.g. in the slums of cities where original rural structures are missing, compare Section 3.5.7) the individual is overwhelmed to recognize the associated group and feels merely like a pawn. Indeed, according to Hofstede, the proportion of collectivism is comparatively high in many low-income countries.

As motivation towards achievement and success (third dimension, masculinity vs. femininity), Hofstede describes the emphasis on values traditionally attributed to men in European culture: competitiveness, assertiveness, heroism, aggression, self-confidence, and material reward. The counterpart is described with a preference for modesty, cooperation, caring, and work-life balance. In a more masculine culture, for example, a supervisor is expected to make decisions alone, assert himself against the competition with force if necessary, and occasionally be loud. A definitive statement on the presence of this dimension in developing countries cannot be made.

The fourth dimension according to Hofstede is uncertainty avoidance. Cultures that seek to avoid uncertainty require strict laws and tend to adhere to tradition as much as possible. Novelty and deviations from the previous path must be avoided

---

657 Kruse (1993).
658 Compare Hofstede (1983), Hofstede and Hofstede (2011), and Hofstede Insights (2024).
659 Compare Maslow, Frager, and Fadiman (1970).
660 Compare Covey (2004).

and, if necessary, combated. This results in a tendency to view innovations negatively and to prefer sticking to the existing standard. A typical tool of uncertainty avoidance, found in many traditional societies, is the orientation of society towards the older generation, who are expected to preserve traditions and customs and ensure survival in a constant environment – a control system that Blunt and Jones describe as typical for Africa.[661]

Long-term orientation also describes a culture. In cultures with a high present orientation, the future is systematically undervalued, so that the benefits and costs of the present are weighed much more heavily than those of the future. As a result, for example, prevention programmes that incur costs today (e.g. travel time) and only promise benefits in the future (e.g. protection from disease) are difficult to communicate in cultures with a high present orientation. Also, in leadership decisions, these cultures will always prefer the short-term advantage, even if this seems illogical to the future-oriented European.

The last dimension (indulgence vs. restraint) was added later. It describes the degree of freedom that a society offers to its members in fulfilling their human desires. If a society allows free gratification of basic and natural human desires, it has a high degree of indulgence. People are allowed to enjoying life, having fun, and even relax. A restrained society, on the contrary, has strict social norms that do not permit its members to be idle or have fun for the sake of fun. A high indulgence will lead to a high productivity, but likely also to a low creativity because the latter requires also free time of spinning new ideas. This might be seen as waste of time – but in reality, it is the foundation of innovation.

The goal of describing the cultural dimensions is by no means to evaluate the culture. Every culture is valid and has been – at least for longer periods – well adapted to its respective environment. However, the 'mental programming' also affects leadership behaviour, i.e. the selection and weighting of goals, assessment of risks and long-term consequences, decision-making, motivation, communication, and delegation are not just a matter of education but also of the deep-seated beliefs of the member of a culture, even if the respective employee is not at all aware of this. The culture shapes him, and under pressure, he will revert to his patterns, even if he has learned completely different theories during training.

The leadership process becomes particularly challenging because different cultures often meet within an institution and these cultures are subject to changes. For example, the workforce of a hospital in East Africa might consist of employees from different African tribes, descendants of Indian guest workers from the time of railway construction, descendants of Arab settlers, East Asian guest workers (e.g. doctors from the Philippines), and European development workers, all of whom must be led. Leadership thus becomes highly individual. Anyone who wants to take on leadership tasks

---

661 Compare Blunt and Jones (1992).

in such a situation must be aware of the multiculturalism of their employees and prepare accordingly.

The reader, who perhaps has never worked in a country with the mentioned challenge, will certainly wonder if a functional healthcare system can be established and maintained under these circumstances. Indeed, it is surprising at first glance that despite major structural weaknesses, a remarkable performance is achieved. This is largely due to planning often being substituted with creativity, structure with spontaneity, and professionalism with quantity. In many countries of the world, services are provided quite differently from the industrialized world – but they have worked remarkably well so far. The great challenges of rapid development (population growth, lifestyle demands, AIDS, etc.) require adaptation, i.e. cultures will change and new institutions and processes for managing healthcare systems will be created. A task of international healthcare management is to accompany this adaptation process.

4.2 Supply Structure

The provision of services in individual healthcare operations is not sufficient to effectively satisfy demand. Since the production and sale of services occur simultaneously in time and space, the spatial structure of the supply must also be considered. This includes the design of catchment areas, the determination of supply levels, and the provider portfolio.

4.2.1 Catchment Areas

The catchment area of a service provider is the space from which its customers come. Here, two concepts can be distinguished. The actual catchment area was described in Section 3.6.1. It is the space from which the patients of a healthcare provider actually come. The minimum distance catchment area is the space from which patients would theoretically come if they visited the provider closest to their location. Figure 4.9 illustrates the formation of this area using the example of two hospitals. The fundamental assumption here is that of distance friction (compare Section 2.1.3). A patient at location X will prefer hospital A and a patient at location Y will prefer hospital B. A patient on line EF is indifferent between the two locations. If one plots all health providers of the same level of care on a map and draws the respective circles, polygons are formed by connecting the intersection points, representing the respective minimum distance catchment areas.

Usually, the minimum distance and actual catchment areas will differ. Firstly, the minimum distance catchment area does not consider natural barriers, such as bodies of water, deserts, mountains, and national borders, which can limit the catchment areas. Secondly, there are cultural barriers, such as belonging to a specific tribe. A patient might be willing to travel longer distances to a more remote provider if treated by a doctor from the same tribe. Thirdly, health service providers on the same level of care with a higher reputation attract more, so the catchment areas of the better-quality provider are larger. Fourthly, maximum distances must be considered, meaning the actual catchment area is sometimes smaller than the minimum distance catchment area. Finally, transport routes and a different perception of distances must be taken into account.

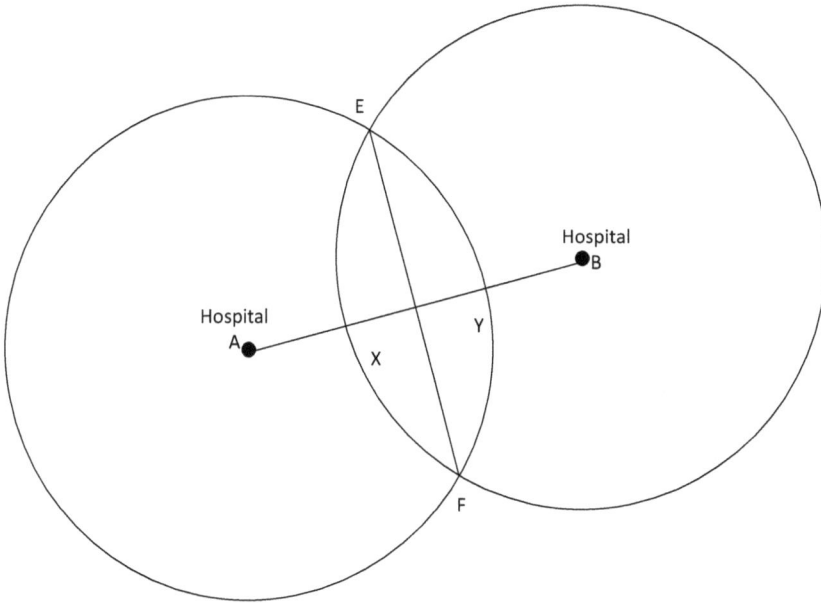

Figure 4.9: Minimum distance catchment area.[662]

Figure 4.10 sketches the actual catchment area of a hospital in southern Tanzania. It is noticeable that the catchment area to the west along the road and the lake is significantly larger, as here the population can more easily access the hospital using public transportation and boats. In contrast, a mountain range limits the catch area to the east. A river becomes a rushing torrent during rainy season and significantly hinders access to the hospital by motor vehicles, adding to the complexity of the region. The southwest area of the hospital is covered with rainforest and is uninhabited.

The perception of distance has changed significantly in recent decades, depending on infrastructure and cultural mobility. The living radius of the generation at the end of the colonial era was usually less than 50 km, meaning even a journey to a central town was a challenge. The next generation, however, regularly travelled to nearby

---

662 Source: Fleßa (2003b).

cities and sporadically to the main urban centres. For today's young generation, travel within the country and sometimes abroad is common, even in resource-poor areas. Therefore, distance friction depends not on the objective but on the perceived distance. This has far-reaching consequences for catchment areas: As people are increasingly willing to travel greater distances, the importance of smaller healthcare facilities tends to decrease. However, there will always be certain population groups (especially the elderly, disabled, etc.) who are less mobile. The thinning out of healthcare facility infrastructure thus systematically disadvantages these groups.

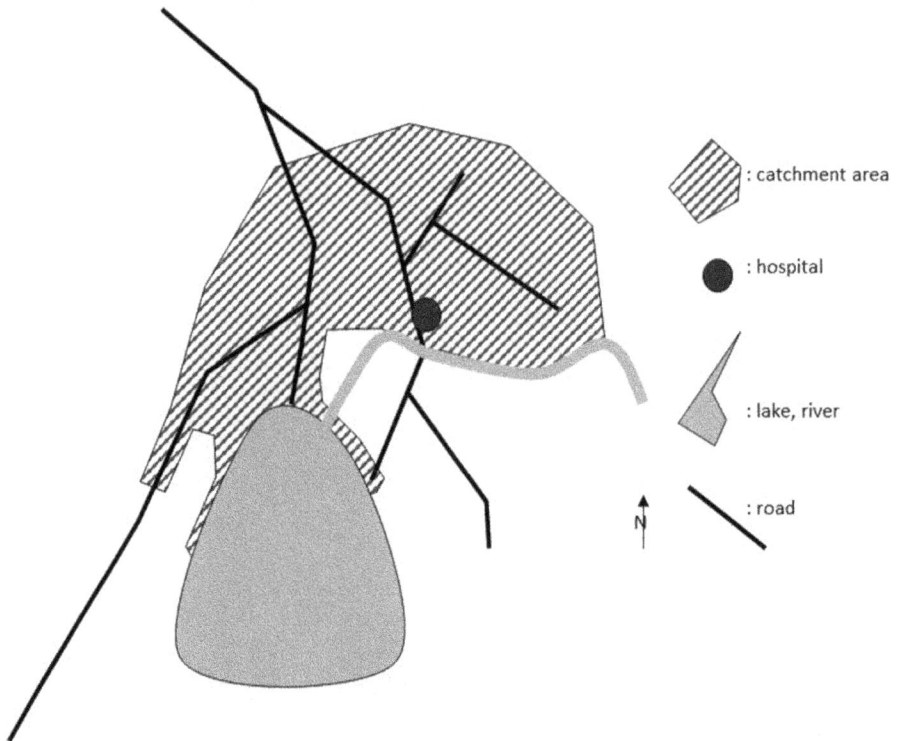

Figure 4.10: Actual catchment area of a hospital in southern Tanzania.[663]

Applying the principle of the minimum distance catchment area to multiple providers at the same level of care and assuming a uniform population density results in a pattern resembling honeycombs (compare Figure 4.11). These hexagons are actually the best compromise between equity and efficiency, meaning no other distribution of service providers in space leads to greater equality in travel distances, although not every resident has the same distance to their service centre.

---

663 Source: Own. See also Okundi and Varol (2024).

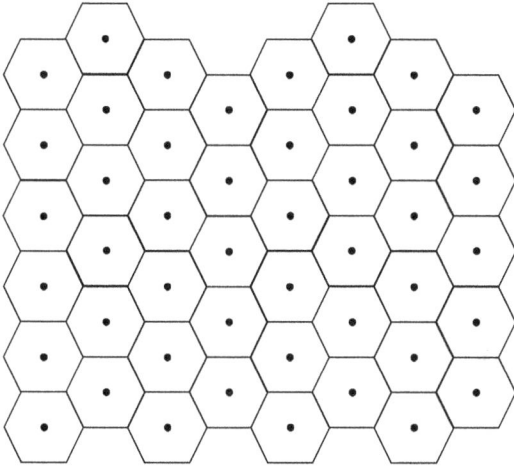

Figure 4.11: Hexagons.[664]

Higher population density should lead to greater capacity of each facility, but not to a different distribution in space. However, the actual catchment area often differs significantly from the theoretical conception. Figure 4.12 exemplarily shows the distribution of dispensaries in the Kajiado Health District in Kenya. It is evident that the facilities are predominantly concentrated at transportation hubs and settlement focal points. The southeast of the district is inhabited, but distances to the nearest health-care facility are (almost) insurmountable. Based on such analyses, suggestions can be developed for health planning, where healthcare facilities should be built to enable fair distribution. At the same time, it becomes possible to question why some areas have multiple facilities while others lack dispensaries. If the providers are private enterprises, this is understandable. For non-profit organizations (NPOs) or the state, opening a facility in an area already well-served is questionable.

4.2.2 Levels of Care

Section 2.1.3 demonstrated that the population's care is hierarchically structured. Diseases with high prevalence should be treated locally by village health workers and dispensaries. Rarer diseases with lower prevalence cannot be addressed at this level, so centres with larger catchment areas, better equipment, and specialization are formed, creating a multi-tiered care system. Typically, a higher-tier facility encompasses several catchment hexagons of the lower tier – a relationship proven by

---

664 Source: Own.

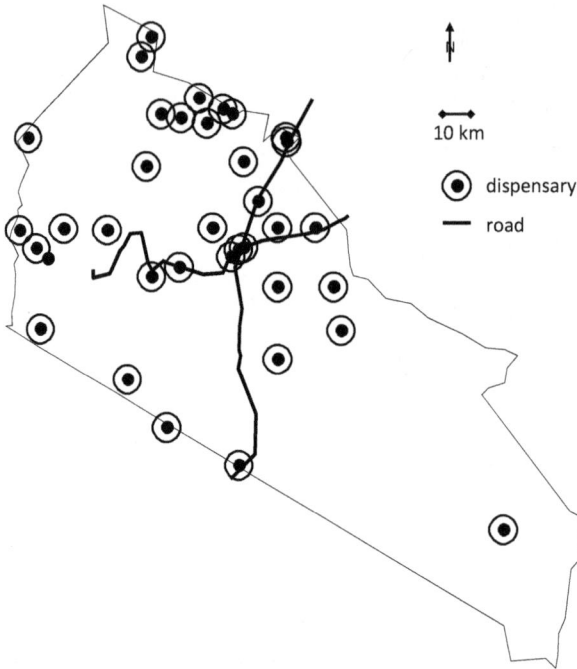

Figure 4.12: Dispensaries in Kajiado Health District, Kenya.[665]

Christaller in the 1930s for urban services.[666] Figure 4.13 illustrates this with two levels.

A fundamental problem is that the scope of services and quality are often less linked to the level of care than to the ownership and location. For example, 58% of primary care facilities in Nairobi had the minimum staffing level of three nurses per dispensary, while in all other 46 counties of the country more than 50% of facilities fell short of nurses. In the counties of Homa Bay, Kirinyaga and Samburu, all facilities did not reach the standard of three nurses per facility.[667] Private or faith-based health centres are often better equipped than state district hospitals. Thus, assigning a particular level of care is not always straightforward.

Another issue is the health centres, which often have the costs of small hospitals but deliver the quality of dispensaries. It has been repeatedly discussed to completely eliminate this level and instead equip dispensaries with beds. Here it has to be noted, that the terminology is not standardized. In some countries, the term health centre is used for the dispensary without beds, while health centres with beds would already be

665 Source: Ministry of Health (2009).
666 Compare Ritter (2001).
667 MoH Kenya (2023). Kenya Health Facility Census Report. Nairobi, Republic of Kenya.

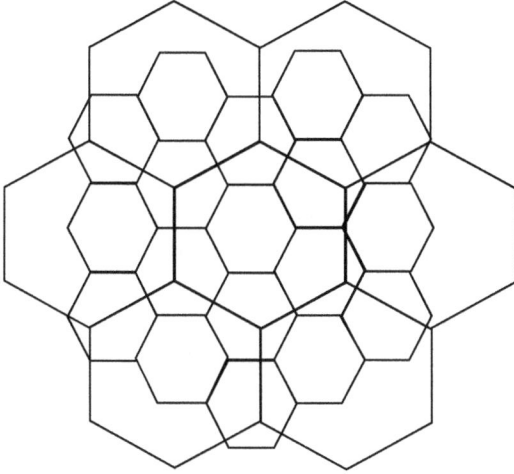

Figure 4.13: Hierarchical catchment areas.[668]

called level I hospitals usually without a surgical department. In this case, the same statement applies: small level I hospitals without surgical services frequently produce the same quality as health centres without beds but with the costs of level II hospitals.

A particular level of care is traditional medicine.[669] To this day, traditional midwives are a common form of childbirth assistance for a large part of the world's population. Herbalists also remain very popular. Neither traditional midwives nor herbalists have been displaced by scientific medicine, while traditional surgeons have almost completely disappeared. Apparently, healers offer benefits that Western medicine cannot provide. This may be because traditional medicine almost always has a spiritual dimension. In the minds of many people – including educated urban residents – disability, illness, and death result from violations of taboos, evil eyes, or the influence of ancestors. Consequently, a patient will first go to the hospital to treat acute malaria and then to a healer to 'remove the real cause', such as disrespecting an ancestor.

It is highly controversial how much traditional healers were truly capable of and what knowledge from them is still available today. In some Asian countries, traditional medicine is fully established and often integrated into healthcare facilities. In other countries, research institutes exist that analyse the ingredients of traditional medicine. There are particularly high hopes for diseases that are currently incurable by scientific medicine. As early as 1988, healers from Central Africa claimed they could cure AIDS and alleged that the rejection of their remedies by the World Health Organization was just another proof of how racist international organizations are.

---

668 Source: Reichart (1999).
669 Compare Feierman and Janzen (1992b).

This is an example of how international healthcare management must take into account the sensitivities involved.

4.2.3 Provider Portfolio

As providers of healthcare facilities, various levels of government (central, provincial, district, cities, etc.), NPOs, and commercial providers are possible. The provider portfolio corresponds to the composition of the individual owners at the various levels of the healthcare system. Normatively, it must be decided which provider should offer which services at which level and how cooperation should be designed.

Traditionally, the provider portfolio in developing countries was relatively simple. Church healthcare facilities and the government provided basic health services for the vulnerables, particularly poverty groups. Higher services (e.g. regional hospitals) were predominantly in the hands of the state. The ministries of health were primarily financing and controlling bodies for government dispensaries, health centres, and hospitals, and had few points of contact with faith-based or commercial providers. The latter focussed on the niche of the few wealthy who partially enjoyed insurance coverage, and offered high quality.

This simple division of labour has hardly been found in recent years. For one, the clientele of commercial providers has changed significantly. Increasingly, private individuals operate healthcare facilities that deliberately target poverty groups. Particularly in cities, waiting times also mean financial loss for day labourers, so private providers who treat quickly are preferred, even if they are more expensive than government or faith-based providers. The private sector of healthcare is booming, encompassing the entire spectrum of services from the simplest to complex treatment of chronic degenerative diseases.

Secondly, the subsidies from churches overseas have decreased significantly, causing church healthcare facilities to become distressed and, in some cases, to significantly increase their fees. As a result, they have excluded many poor and turned to the middle class. In addition, for about a decade now, other religious groups have been offering charitable health services, so today one often speaks of "Faith Based Healthcare Services".[670]

Thirdly, more and more collaborations between NPO, state, and commercial organizations are emerging, making the description of the provider portfolio increasingly difficult. This also necessitates that the Ministry of Health take on greater responsibility for regulating and controlling the entire sector than before.

Figure 4.14 provides an overview of the diversity of providers. An NPO here is an institution whose primary goal is to satisfy the needs of its clients. Profits may be gen-

---

670 Compare, e.g. DeHaven, Hunter, Wilder, et al. (2004).

erated, but they must be used for the original purpose of operation. Government institutions also belong to the NPOs.[671]

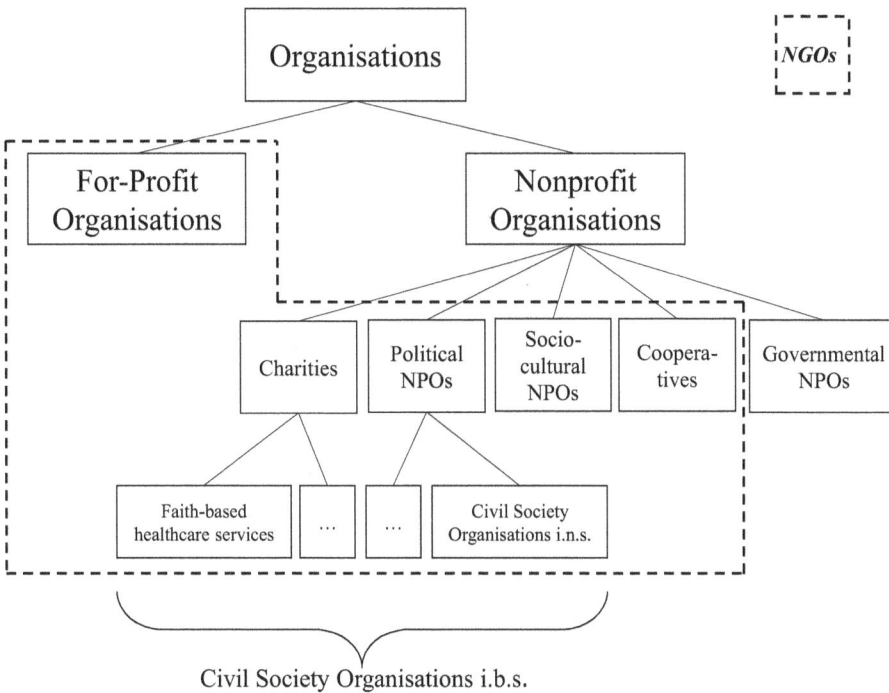

Figure 4.14: Diversity of providers.[672]

Non-governmental organizations (NGOs), on the other hand, refer to all non-governmental NPOs and all commercial private organizations. Often, however, only non-governmental NPOs are considered as NGOs. Within the NPOs, various groups can be distinguished, with charitable NPOs being the most significant group in healthcare. These include, among others, the faith-based health services. The political NPOs, which represent civil society and consciously influence politics, are becoming increasingly important. These include affected groups (e.g. lobbying work of HIV-positive individuals).

A major problem with the diversity of providers is cooperation. Figure 4.15 exemplifies the hospitals and dispensaries managed by Haydom Lutheran Hospital in Tanzania. If a doctor from Haydom wishes to fulfil his supervisory duties in all Lutheran dispensaries, he must undertake a journey of several hours, passing several govern-

---

671 Compare Schwarz (1992).
672 Source: Own. I.n.s: in a narrower sense and i.b.s.: in a broader sense.

ment healthcare facilities along the way. It would be significantly more efficient if the dispensaries were always managed by the hospital that is closest to them. However, this would require close cooperation, which is often not present. It is imperative to focus on the population's needs rather than the interests of the provider.

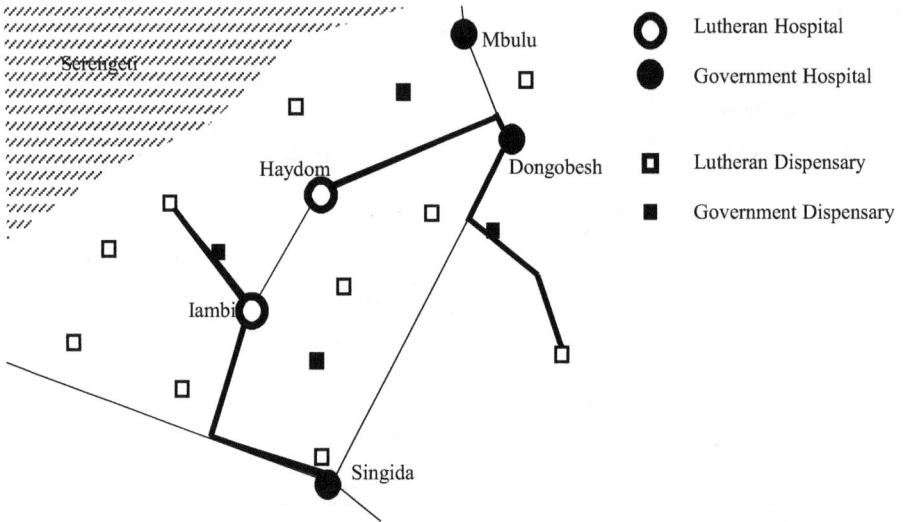

Figure 4.15: Catchment area of Haydom Hospital, Tanzania (sketched).[673]

Another innovation in the ownership structure is the PPP, which has been expanded in recent years especially in the healthcare sector in developing countries.[674] As shown in Section 2.1.3, health services are generally seen as public goods, the provision of which is the state's responsibility, as without its intervention, adequate care for certain (poverty-stricken) groups would not be possible. However, this does not imply that the government must act as the provider or financier. Instead, the government can collaborate intensively in the provision of public goods with the private sector, i.e. enter into a PPP.

The term PPP is used very differently. Some authors only speak of a PPP when there is a partnership between the government and exclusively commercial companies, while others also allow for partnerships between the government and NPOs. Sometimes, a PPP is demanded to involve purely market-based regulation through prices, at other times, a partnership based on long-term contracts and agreements is centre as a PPP. Many practitioners understand PPP as the undertaking of public tasks by non-governmental companies, while others see it more as the involvement of

673 Source: Own.
674 In regard to global PPP, compare Johnson (2011).

the private sector in state service provision (e.g. financing government hospitals through private leasing companies).

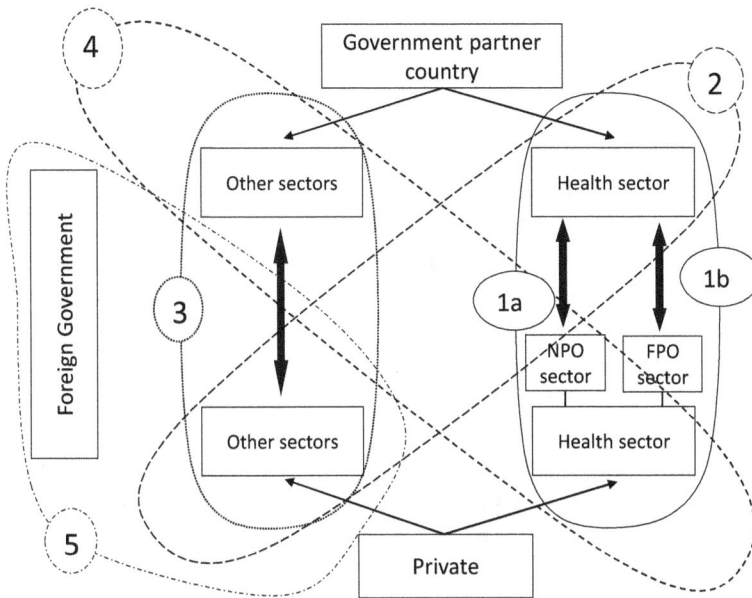

Figure 4.16: Public-private partnership.[675]

Figure 4.16 shows different concepts as they are applied in the practice of international healthcare management:
- 1.a. PPP is the collaboration of the Ministry of Health or government health services of a country with non-profit health organizations of the same country, e.g. a country designates the district responsibility to a church hospital.
- 1.b: PPP also includes the collaboration of the Ministry of Health or government health services of a country with commercial healthcare facilities in this country, e.g. a government delegates the responsibility for radiation therapy to a private hospital.
- 2. PPP occurs when the Ministry of Health or government health services of a country collaborate with facilities from other sectors, e.g. when a government hospital takes over the corporate healthcare management of an industrial company or a hotel provides rooms for patients who have been discharged but are not yet travel-ready, as long as this is done on a contractual basis.
- 3. PPP is also used for cooperations between the government and the private sector outside the healthcare sector.

---

675 Source: Own. NPO: non-profit organization; FPO: for-profit organization.

- – 4. Some authors use the term PPP even when non-governmental health organizations cooperate with government providers outside the healthcare sector, e.g. when a private hospital takes over the health counselling of employees of the Ministry of Finance.
- – 5. The term PPP is sometimes reserved in development cooperation for the collaboration of foreign government organizations with the private sector of partner countries.

It is evident that models 1.a, 1.b, and 2 are goal-oriented for international healthcare management. The responsible manager should clarify the terms to avoid confusion, but otherwise deal pragmatically with the definitions. More important than the definition is the use of the advantages of the PPP. Since NGOs are often more efficient, quicker, and closer to the people, they should always be involved to the extent possible under the principle of subsidiarity. However, when cooperating with commercial providers, one must not forget that their primary goal is profit maximization. Long-term commitments to corporate social responsibility do not change this. However, if they are so much more efficient than the government that they can provide better care for the population and their own profit with the same resources, there is nothing against this motive for their actions. This is not self-evident, however, and must be examined on a case-by-case basis.

With these brief remarks on service provision in international healthcare management, this section should be closed. The discussion on supply is shorter than that on demand, as the peculiarities of operations management are less than those of demand. Nevertheless, the international healthcare manager must be aware that the already high complexity of the health service provider and the healthcare system is further increased by cultural differences and extreme resource scarcity, demanding their full attention.

5 Healthcare Systems and Reforms

Supply, demand, and healthcare markets constitute the healthcare system. As discussed in Section 2.1.4.2, health policy goals require a high degree of regulation of this economic system, where especially the prices for health services are largely beyond the influence of individual providers or consumers. Instead, the government (or its appointed institutions) sets frameworks within which actors operate more or less independently, pursuing their own goals while aiming to achieve societal objectives. This necessitates continuous consideration of goal dimensions, weightings of goals, time preferences, risks, and interest groups, resulting in healthcare systems being subject to constant reforms.

The literature on healthcare systems and reforms is extensive, and this section will not attempt to comprehensively repeat general fundamentals. Instead, it will focus on some specifics that are either unique to international health or of particular relevance here. First, the fundamental concept of costs for economic evaluation will be explained. Subsequently, the reform alternatives will be briefly outlined, followed by a detailed discussion on certain key aspects.

5.1 Costs

In international healthcare management, it is crucial to emphasize that the direct treatment costs constitute only a fraction of the resource consumption caused by illness. The so-called National Health Accounts[676] (NHA) record expenditures for health services, typically core costs are captured. NHA are a top-down approach, i.e. the healthcare expenditure is recorded on the national level, but no consolidation with the real costs of healthcare services in the regions, the facilities and programmes is done. NHA are important for decision-making on the national or global level (e.g. total costs of drug imports), but they are almost useless to calculate a premium for an insurance, design a fee structure for healthcare services, or set a subsidy for the poorest. For this purpose, we need data that is calculated in the facilities, i.e. bottom-up data.

The degree of precision that is required determines the costing methodology. In rare events, this can be an activity-based costing calculating the resource consumption for every sub-process, e.g. of a Caesarean section.[677] For most decisions, a traditional cost accounting system (step-down costing) is sufficient, but the research question determines the methodology. For instance, full and marginal costs both have their right and relevance, but a full cost calculation might be misleading in the short run, while a marginal costing might be wrong in the long run. The respective methodology has been presented in the

---

676 Compare Berman (1997) and OECD (2000).
677 Compare Glaeser, Jacobs, Appelt, et al. (2020).

https://doi.org/10.1515/9783112217290-005

literature and is not significantly different to international standards of cost accounting.[678] The healthcare manager must, however, keep in mind the data situation in many healthcare facilities. It is frequently better to design a simpler system that can become a routine instead of applying highly complex costing methodology that will make only a unique snapshot but is far beyond the capability of the local healthcare facilities.[679]

The costs of research, education, training, and administration are rarely considered in costing studies, but a cost-of-illness analysis should include them. For example, the costs of staff training across all healthcare facilities must be accounted for if one wishes to determine the costs implied by an increase in stroke incidents in a country.

Even more important is the determination of household costs. Here, a distinction must be made between direct and indirect costs. The former represents outlays (e.g. for remodelling a house after a disability, for a special diet due to an illness, or for transportation to a healthcare facility), while the latter implies opportunity costs, i.e. reduction in income due to illness. The sick person and their family members cannot work and thus lose income, whether through a reduced harvest or salary. Frequently, indirect costs are at least as high as direct costs, yet they are rarely recorded. For some diseases, it has been proven that the loss of workforce due to illness represents a macroeconomic problem, i.e. the production factor of human labour in the production function is lower so that the production total is reduced.

Quantifying the costs is rather laborious, as national statistics often do not exist or are unreliable. Usually, a primary survey must be conducted.[680] This is particularly challenging for indirect costs. In countries with a fully employed, formal economy, net wages can be used as the cost of labour loss. In developing countries with a high proportion of subsistence agriculture or underemployed economies, the loss of labour does not automatically lead to a loss of production. For example, a work accident outside the planting and harvesting period in many African countries is not problematic, while during this period it can have serious consequences. An evaluation of these factors in an analysis is possible but requires a thorough investigation.[681] Common approaches in health economics (e.g. the human capital approach, friction cost method, and willingness-to-pay method) are of course applicable but must be adapted. Experiences show that collecting willingness to pay from illiterates who primarily make their living from subsistence farming is particularly difficult. Even more complex is the collection of intangible costs, i.e. the categorization of suffering and pain due to illness, disability, or premature death. Despite numerous research efforts, there is still no gold standard.[682]

---

678 Compare Flessa and Dung (2004), Flessa, Moeller, Ensor, et al. (2011), and Jacobs, Hui, Lo, et al. (2019).
679 Compare Jacobs, Hui, Lo, et al. (2019).
680 Compare Mushi, Krohn, and Flessa (2015).
681 Compare Fleßa (2016).
682 Compare Muennig (2002), Drummond, Sculpher, and Torrance (2005), and Edejer (2003).

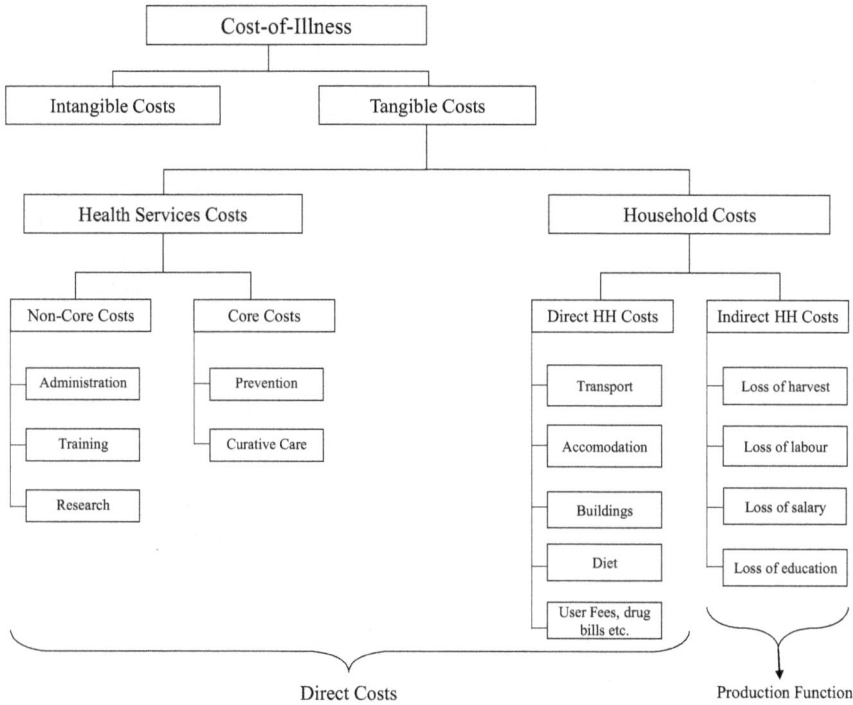

Figure 5.1: Costs of illness.[683]

Healthcare reforms must be based on facts, where tangible costs serve as input and the reduction of intangible costs as benefits play a crucial role. Especially in developing countries, these figures are often merely expert estimates. Healthcare reforms – as we will later argue – therefore always require a consensus process. The international healthcare manager must not present any database as an incontrovertible fact and thus as a condition if it is not really supported by comprehensive, current, and systematic studies.

5.2 Healthcare Reform Alternatives

5.2.1 Overview

Healthcare reforms, in a broader sense, encompass all systematic and targeted changes to the existing healthcare system,[684] i.e. they can fundamentally start at any

---

683 Source: Fleßa (2007).
684 Compare Garner (1995).

element of the economic framework model (compare *Figure 2.7*). On the supply side, this includes all measures to increase the efficiency of healthcare facilities, e.g. by increasing the autonomy of (state) healthcare providers, through targeted training and continuing education (e.g. of executives), by improving the supply chain (e.g. for medications), or through systematic asset management (e.g. through comprehensive maintenance services). Moreover, demand for health services can also be a target of healthcare reforms. For example, improving the accessibility of health service providers (e.g. through site selection, public transportation, or road construction) can be part of a healthcare reform as much as reducing the burden of disease through enhanced prevention.

Often, the term 'healthcare reform' is defined more narrowly. A healthcare reform in a stricter sense includes all legislative measures to change the organization of the financing of health services, the organization of the ownership of healthcare facilities, and interventions in health markets.

As described in Section 5.2.2, financing of health service providers can generally occur through the state, social insurance, private insurance, or direct user fees. Most healthcare reforms worldwide are actually financing reforms. For example, the 'major healthcare reform' in the USA(Patient Protection and Affordable Care Act, PPACA, 23 March 2010) was primarily a reform of health insurance. Also in Germany, the focus of healthcare reforms has often been on the financing side (e.g. the introduction of the Health Fund by the Act to Strengthen Competition in Statutory Health Insurance, GKV-WSG, 1 January 2009). In low- and lower-middle-income countries, there are currently numerous attempts to introduce social health protection (including social health insurance), and here too, healthcare and financing reforms are often equated.

Another variant of healthcare reforms in the narrower sense is the systematic and targeted change in the organization of the ownership of service providers. In some countries (e.g. in the USA), the majority of service providers are commercially operated, while in other countries the government still has a monopoly on health services. In other countries such as Germany, there is a plurality of owners. For example, hospitals are approximately one-third privately owned, non-profit, or state-owned, while medical practices are almost exclusively privately owned. Nursing homes are still largely non-profit, while rehabilitation clinics are predominantly commercial. The government has the obligation not to discriminate against any facility based on its ownership. For example, the funding of hospitals under dual financing is independent of ownership.

In many low- and lower-middle-income countries, the government's activities extend beyond merely indirectly controlling the supply and demand for health services. The government directly intervenes in the market as the operator of hospitals, health centres, and dispensaries. One goal of some healthcare reforms in these countries is to reduce the share of state-owned enterprises, particularly in curative healthcare. For example, until the 1990s, most African countries did not allow doctors to establish private practices, meaning they could only work as employees in government (or faith-based) facilities. However, most of these countries have undergone healthcare reforms, so that today private practices exist in nearly all countries, making an important contribution to healthcare not only for the upper classes. Another privatization reform was the (partial) return of previously expropriated hospitals.[685] Whether the privatization of the healthcare sector actually leads to improved care in rural, remote, and impoverished regions is highly questionable. However, in cities and for the emerging upper and middle classes, it is of central importance because, based on experience, the quality and especially the customer-friendliness in private facilities are significantly higher than in governmental institutions.

A third component of healthcare reforms in the narrower sense is the frequency and intensity of market interventions. There are countries, for example, where health service prices can be set completely freely, while in others the government fixes all prices. Often, social insurance organizations as semi-government entities are endowed with rights that allow them a monopolistic price dictate, so that providers of health services can only decide whether they want to treat patients at these prices at all. Table 5.1 shows examples of healthcare systems.

Another area in which the government intervenes is the setting and monitoring of minimum standards for health services. For this purpose, the government can act itself, establish semi-governmental organizations, or delegate self-administration. In all countries, specific licensing procedures exist, but not always is licensing carried out exclusively by the state. Partly, professional organizations are also of great importance, such as in the USA, where the associations of the respective disciplines have more weight than the government licensing authorities.

Another important field of reform is healthcare structure reforms. These refer to all structured and targeted measures to influence the share of health expenditures allocated to each level of the health pyramid (prevention, dispensaries, health centres, district hospitals, regional hospitals, tertiary hospitals, rehabilitation, palliative care, etc.) and to each region/province and district. Often, the share of the government health budget for certain levels and regions is intended to be changed because the current allocation of the national health budget is not suited to achieve the goals of government health policy. For example, if it is found that over 50% of the budget of the Ministry of Health is used to finance a single hospital in the capital city (compare Section 2.3.2), a healthcare structure reform might require less funding for this hospital and instead invest the funds in prevention programmes in rural areas.[686] Structure reforms lead to distribution struggles and thus to conflicts. Therefore, it is much more popular among politicians to develop alternative financing instruments than to make the fundamental structure of the healthcare system the object of a reform.

---

685 Compare Gilson and Mills (1995) and Giusti, Criel, and De Béthune (1997).
686 Compare Barnum, Kutzin, and Roemer (1993).

Table 5.1: Comparison of healthcare systems (examples).[687]

Country	Primary financing organization	Primary service organization
Austria	Social Insurance	Outpatient: private; inpatient: mostly public
Cambodia	Direct User Fees and Health Equity Fund	Mostly private; public services for the poor
Canada	National Health Service	Outpatient: private; inpatient: public
France	Social Insurance	Outpatient: private; inpatient: mostly public
Germany	Social Insurance	Outpatient: private; inpatient: public and private ownership
Greece	National Health Service with Contribution Financing	Mostly public
Italy	National Health Service with Contribution Financing	Mostly public
Kenya	Direct User Fees and Tax Funding	Mostly public and non-profit
Netherlands	Social Insurance with Basic Insurance and Additional Options	Mostly private
Philippines	Mixed	Mixed
Sweden	National Health Service	Mostly public
Switzerland	Private Health Insurances with Subsidization	Outpatient: private; inpatient: partially public; managed care organizations
United Kingdom	National Health Service	Mostly public
USA	Private Health Insurances	Private providers and managed care organizations
Uzbekistan	Government (through State Health Insurance Fund)	Mostly public
Vietnam	National Health Service	Mostly public

The following will delve deeper into financing and structure reforms, as they currently represent the focus of change efforts worldwide.

---

687 Source: Schulenburg and Greiner (2007). Direct user fees: out-of-pocket payments; HEF: health equity fund for the (officially) poor.

5.2.2 Healthcare Financing

5.2.2.1 Social Health Protection

As mentioned in Section 2.3.5, universal health coverage cannot be achieved by household out-of-pocket payments because the individual household has insufficient funds to bear the risk of catastrophic health expenditure in case of severe sickness. Thus, pooling of risks and the resulting health protection are essential to achieve UHC.[688] However, small risk pools are also at risk to be overburdened so that kinship-, clan-, or community-based health funds are likely to become insolvent particularly during an epidemic or a year of special weather events. Small-scale insurances need a re-insurance, or we need large-scale, social insurance schemes. It is generally accepted that UHC can only be achieved if the government takes responsibility for social health protection or a social insurance is established that covers the entire population and shares the individual health risks among millions.

Several countries have implemented different protection systems. For instance, Cambodia has started a national Health Equity Fund paying the user fees of government healthcare facilities for those living under the official poverty line.[689] Consequently, some 20% of the population are covered (on a low level). At the same time, Cambodia has launched a National Social Security Fund (NSSF) to cover all formal sector workers and civil servants. In the long run, the respective services are to be expanded to the entire population. The Vietnam Social Security (VSS) protects almost the entire population in case of illness.[690] Opposite to Cambodia, there is a degree of solidarity between social groups in Vietnam.

The biggest single social health insurance in the world is the Jaminan Kesehatan Nasional (National Health Insurance) of Indonesia.[691] With some 160 million members, it covers some 60% of the population. Services covered by the insurance reach from implants to MRIs. The social insurance from Indonesia has become a pattern to follow for many countries. These three examples show that solidarity-based social protection systems are developing all over the world.

5.2.2.2 Design of a Health Financing System

As shown in Figure 5.2, there are numerous variants for financing the healthcare system.[692] Fundamentally, it is stated that – with the exception of development aid – all health resources must first be generated by the population of a country. Involving ad-

---

688 Compare Nyamugira, Flessa, and Richter (2024).
689 Compare Wiseman, Asante, Ir, et al. (2017), Jacobs, Bajracharya, Saha, et al. (2018), and Fernandes Antunes, Jacobs, Jithitikulchai, et al. (2022).
690 Compare Reich, Harris, Ikegami, et al. (2016).
691 Compare Barrientos and Hulme (2016).
692 Compare, e.g. Laaser and Radermacher (2007) and Kutzin, Cashin, and Jakab (2010).

ditional institutions (e.g. the government and insurance companies) ultimately costs resources and is only justifiable if it offers significant advantages over direct user fees. The primary advantage of financing health services through the state or insurance is risk pooling.

If a system is chosen that is at least partially not based on direct user fees, the respective institutions have various functions to fulfil.[693] They need to raise funds (e.g. collect taxes or insurance premiums), operate a risk pool, purchase health services, and monitor the quality of services. The same or different institutions must, of course, also provide the health services. The bundling of these functions into one or more institutions enables the design of very different healthcare systems.

From the perspective of the healthcare services, three fundamental sources of funds can be distinguished: government, health insurance, and development aid. For a long time, development aid has primarily financed healthcare facilities or programmes. In recent years, however, there is an increasing move to directly support the population so they can afford health insurance and/or direct user fees (so-called cash transfers).[694] There are examples where the international donor community takes over the health insurance premium for poverty groups. Furthermore, it is possible to support social or private health insurances, for example, through consulting or reinsurance.

In countries without functional social insurance systems, the government traditionally plays a major role in financing healthcare facilities. As shown in Figure 5.3, there are several variants for government healthcare financing. In many countries, input-based financing is still primarily practiced today, meaning the government provides resources (e.g. personnel, medications, and financial funds) to healthcare facilities regardless of their performance. The resource transfer can, for example, consist of personnel being employed by the Ministry of Health and provided to the healthcare provider (partially independent of its ownership) free of charge. Health service providers often also receive standardized medication kits that they do not have to pay for. The extent of flat-rate input financing depends on certain parameters, such as the population number in the theoretical catchment area, the number of beds, or special needs (e.g. in areas with specific epidemic diseases). In exceptional cases, the input can also be adjusted ex-post based on performance. For example, antiretroviral medications are allocated based on how many patients have been enrolled in a corresponding programme. Fundamentally, however, neither the quantity nor the quality of the service plays a role in the allocation of funds. This can lead to patients being perceived and treated as a nuisance, since they do not generate additional revenue but do cause costs.

---

693 Compare Gottret and Schieber (2006).
694 Compare Rawlings and Rubio (2005).

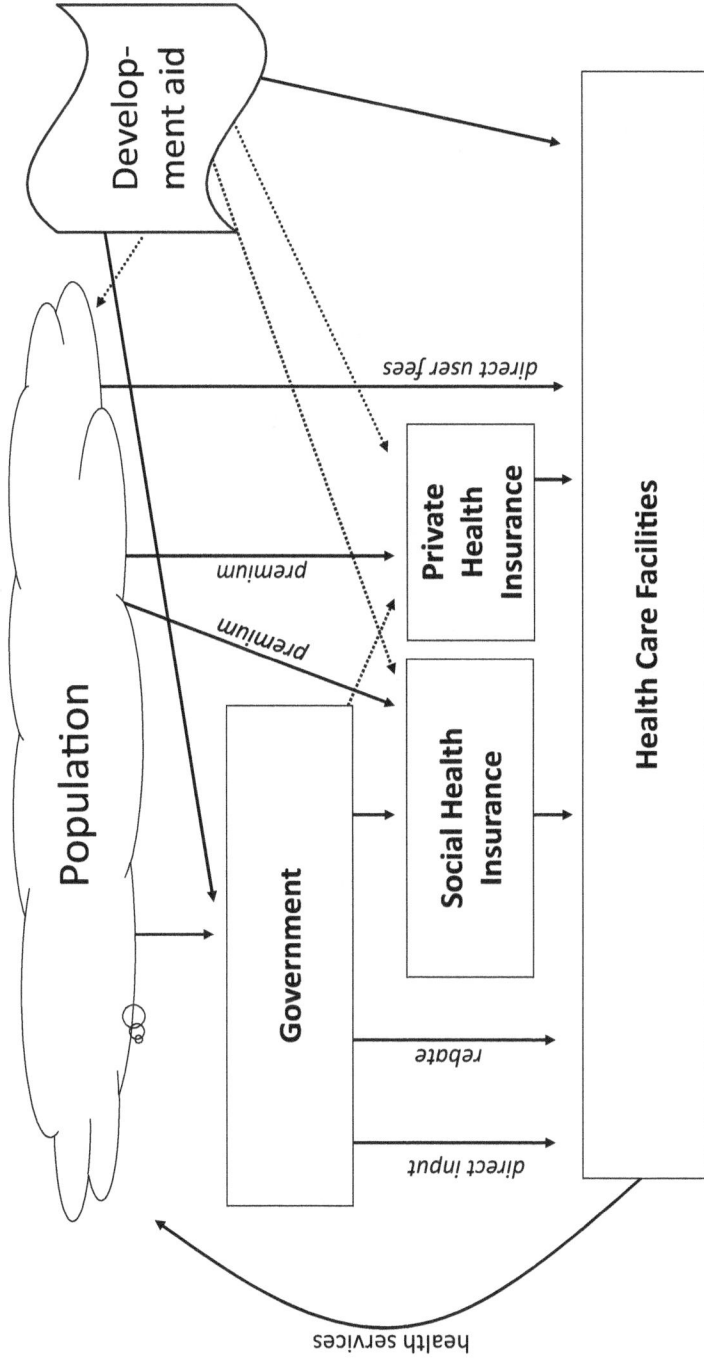

Figure 5.2: Financing options.[695]

695 Source: Own.

Alternatively, government transfers can be made dependent on the output of a health service provider, i.e. the state pays a predetermined price for each unit of service. The measure of output-based financing can be the number of patient contacts (e.g. in outpatient care), admissions, care days, or other service units. Particularly in hospitals with their broad spectrum of services, tying financing to admissions or care days leads to a preference for patients with simple illnesses or to extended lengths of stay. Therefore, the inclusion of diagnosis, case severity, and comorbidities is repeatedly demanded, as is the case with diagnosis-related groups (DRGs). The case mix would, therefore, be a measure for the government to allocate its budget to hospitals. Also, linking to quality indicators (p4p, pay-for-performance) is discussed and practiced in some countries (e.g. Rwanda).[696]

Furthermore, there is the possibility to combine input and output-based financing, e.g. by supporting infrastructure services (buildings and facilities) with flat rates and refinancing ongoing expenses (e.g. personnel and medications) based on performance. This would not yet correspond to a dual financing system as per the German model. Rather, the government would still be the only or primary financier but would have divided its transfers into a flat-rate and a performance-dependent component.

Government financial resources can reach the health service provider in various ways. On the one hand, the central government can transfer directly to service providers, or it can go through regions and districts. The latter has the advantage of greater autonomy for regional authorities but often leads to funds being 'lost' along the long way. Alternatively, the government could also involve associations (e.g. hospital association) or health insurance funds, which take over part of the accounting and quality assurance tasks.

The alternative is a (social) health insurance. As shown in Figure 5.4, the health insurance market is rather similar to a healthcare market. The starting point is again the needs of human beings. However, the need underlying the demand for an insurance is not physiological as such, but the main need addressed by insurances is the security need. People feel the need that they would like to have a safe future. They would not only like to be healthy today but also in the future. They would like to receive healthcare in the future if they are sick without fearing that they will not be able to pay for it. The underlying problem is uncertainty. Most future events are uncertain, i.e. they are subject to certain probabilities or even totally unknown. Most people are uncertainty-averse and try to avoid risks, in particular existential risks threatening their lives. The need to be 'on the safe side of life' is rather high and the driving force behind all insurances. As health is existential, the need for a protection against catastrophic payments to obtain healthcare services is also strong.

The need for certainty and protection becomes a want for health insurance if people are informed that such an institution exists and can protect them. Hopefully, the

---

696 Compare Kalk, Paul, and Grabosch (2010) and Ireland, Paul, and Dujardin (2011).

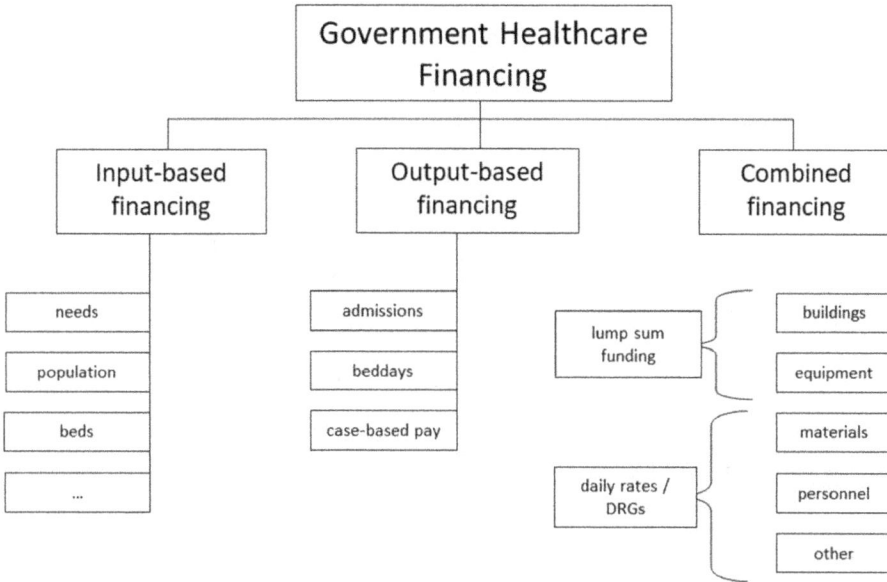

Figure 5.3: Variants of government subsidies for health services.[697]

need of certainty also leads to better prevention (resulting directly in lower risk of falling sick), but most people will not only fear sickness but also the financial consequences of it. Thus, they want a health insurance coverage. It is important to make a direct neuronal connection between 'certainty' and 'health insurance' by proper advocating, advertising, and learning.

The need for a health insurance becomes a demand if the filters (compare Section 3.6) are overcome, in particular if the insurance is affordable and has a high priority. Setting the right premium and the mode of payment (e.g. time and frequency of payment, payment in cash or in kind, payment per capita or per family, etc.) determines the ability and willingness to be insured. If the insurance coverage is free of charge (e.g. tax-financed health insurance), the price filter is turned off.

There is no natural need for a health insurance. There is a need for protection against future risks, but an insurance is an instrument to satisfy the needs, not the need itself. Consequently, the idea of risk-sharing in an insurance pool is brilliant, but it requires explanation and conviction.

Figure 5.4 also indicates that there are a number of decisions to be made. Table 5.2 expresses the decision field of a health insurance system. The first column holds the variables (e.g. legal form of ownership and number of insurances) while the other columns express certain alternatives. For instance, a country can decide to per-

---

697 Source: Own.

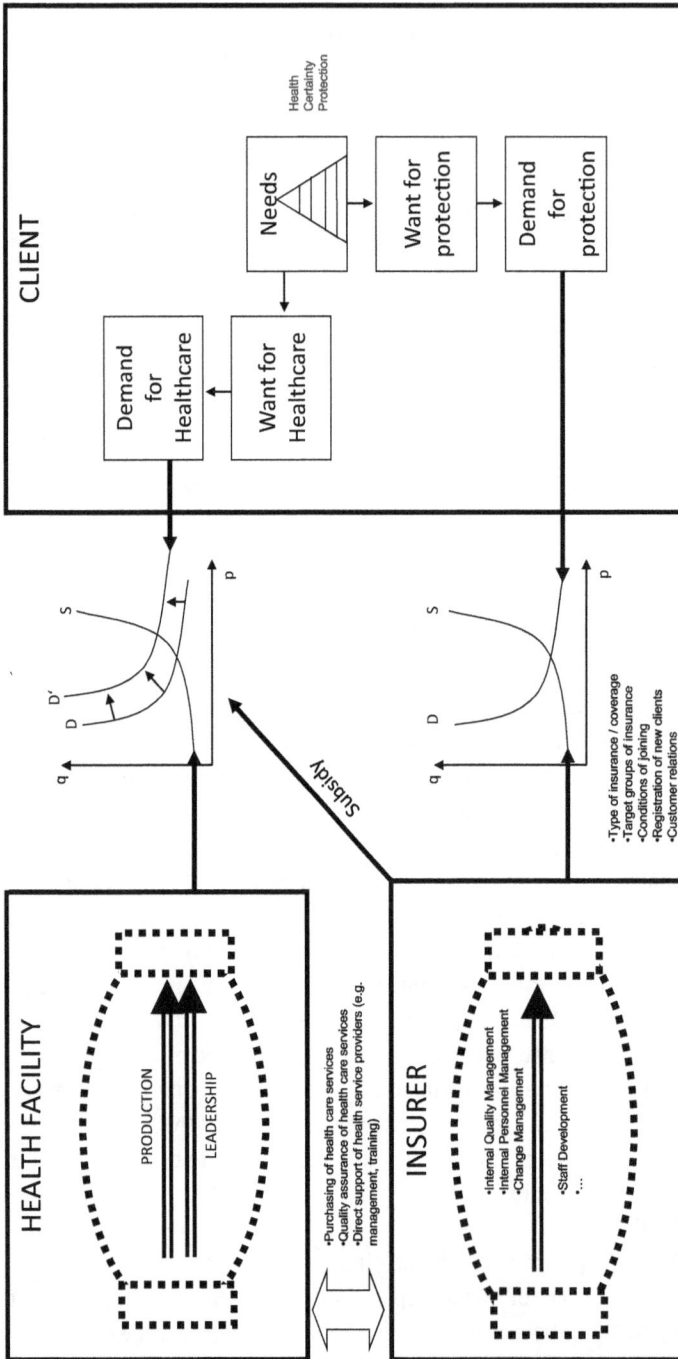

Figure 5.4: Healthcare and health insurance market model.[698]

mit only one single insurance fund for the entire country (monopoly), a few insurance funds (oligopoly), or several insurance funds competing for customers (polypoly or perfect competition). The table shows that a health insurance can be defined by many variables with many alternatives.

5.2.2.3 Payment Mechanism

Healthcare facilities must receive funds from the government, health insurance scheme(s), charities, or development aid. The respective amount and way of payment must be based on certain criteria. In principle, different alternatives are possible (and can also be combined):[699]

- Fixed budget: A fixed amount is paid to the facility irrespective of services. This system makes sense when the facility has no influence on the quantity and quality of services and in particular has to exist for emergencies irrespective of the performance. For instance, the police and the fire brigade are usually financed with a fixed budget and do not receive additional funds for arresting or putting fires out.
- Capitation: A fixed amount is paid to a healthcare facility for every member of the insurance selecting this facility as his primary point of service. For instance, the National Health Service of Great Britain traditionally (meanwhile the system changed) paid a capitation to general practitioners. Every citizen had to select his provider. The amount can depend on certain variables (age, gender, morbidity, and population density), but it does not depend on the number of visits or other performance indicators.

    A major problem of capitation is that it might be insufficient to finance smaller institutions in areas with a very low population density. If this healthcare facility is required to take care of the population in its nearest distance catchment area, but the population is too small, the total capitation might not cover the cost, in particular as fixed cost constitutes a rather high percentage of total cost. In this case, capitation will have to be supplemented by a fixed budget. In order to know the facilities that are required but likely to suffer a loss, a central healthcare facility planning is required (master plan).
- Daily rates: Inpatient services of hospitals are frequently paid by daily rates. In the simple form, the institution receives a fixed payment for each bed day a patient spends in the hospital irrespective of the department (e.g. same daily rate for surgical cases as for patients of internal medicine). In a more complex system, the daily rates differ between departments (e.g. daily rate of surgical cases > daily

---

699 A preliminary version of this section was first submitted to GIZ Uzbekistan.

Table 5.2: Decision field of a health insurance.[700]

Variable	Alternative 1	Alternative 2	Alternative 3	Alternative 4
Insurance system	Community-based	Social insurance	Beveridge system	Private for-profit
Administration	Part of national administration	Parastatal organization	Private	
Legal form of ownership	Public administration	Parastatal	Corporation	
Number of insurances	Monopoly	Oligopoly	Polypoly	
Services covered	Outpatient Prevention/promotion	Inpatient Curative medicine	Rehabilitation	Long-term care
Target group	Insured	Family	Social insurance	Entire population
Cost covered	Ceiling Co-payment	No ceiling No co-payment		
Conditions covered	Limited list of conditions	Exclusion of conditions	No exclusions	
Principle form of financing	General tax	Earmarked taxes (e.g. tobacco)	Payroll contribution	Other premium
Revenue collection	Tax collection	Own agents	Separate agency	Employers
Time of revenue collection	Monthly	Yearly	Event (e.g. show up in hospital)	
Revenues and means of payment	Cash	In kind		
Premium	Free-of-charge, not applicable	Subsidized premium	Full-cost premium	Subsidy for vulnerables
Basis for premium calculation	Income-based	Wealth-based	Risk-based	Capitation

700 Source: Schulenburg and Greiner (2007). Direct user fees: out-of-pocket payments; HEF: health equity fund for the (officially) poor.

Table 5.2 (continued)

Variable	Alternative 1	Alternative 2	Alternative 3	Alternative 4
Exemptions	Vulnerables	Not applicable		
Pooling of risks	National risk pool	Provincial risk pool	Smaller pools	Re-insurance
Actuarial accounting/ premium calculation	No actuarial accounting	Actuarial accounting		
Healthcare facility IT	Administration/accounting	Patient files	Tele-medicine	
Insurance IT	Member files	Claims settling	Administration	Other
IT integration	Transfer manually	Integrated platform	Full integration including MoH	
Target group	Entire population	Work force	Vulnerables	Civil servants and others
Registration of new clients	Own offices/agents	Third-party agents	Only online	At point of service
Time of registration	Every day	Certain times	Not in case of illness	Start of employment
Customer relations	Own customer office(r)s	Online only	No customer relations	Healthcare facility staff
Relation to healthcare facility	Insurance and healthcare facility are one (HMO)	Separate institutions		
Rebates based on	Actual full cost	Actual marginal cost	Estimates	Political prices
Rebates outpatient care	Fee for service	Capitation	Budgets	Mixed
Rebates inpatient care	Fee for service	Daily rates	Flat rates/DRGs	Budgets/ capitation
Budget	Part is fixed budget	Rebates only		
Insurance requires from healthcare facility	No quality management	Country-wide quality management	International quality management	
Insurance provides to healthcare facility	Training Other support	Management support	Management support	No support

Table 5.2 (continued)

Variable	Alternative 1	Alternative 2	Alternative 3	Alternative 4
Quality management insurance	No quality management	Own quality management system	National standard	International standard
Staffing	Personnel department	Part of public administration	No separate department	
Selection of staff based on	Professionalism	Kinship	Official rank	Other
Leading and directing	Leadership of professionals	No professional managers		
Staff development	Off-the-job training	On-the-job training	Academic training	
Strategy, control, and change management	Service portfolio management	Strategic cooperation	Strategic Resources	

rate of patients of internal medicine). A precise calculation of differentiated daily rates requires professional cost centre accounting.

– Case-based payment: A fixed price is paid for the treatment of a patient of a certain group. Usually, the payment is limited to one episode of a disease, i.e. two admissions of the same patient lead to two separate payments. The payment can be calculated by calculating the cost per bed day and multiplying them with the average length of stay of patients of the respective group. The difference between the daily rate and the case-based payment is, that in the latter case the payment for one individual patient is the same whether he stays more or less days.

Again, a case-based payment with a general cost weight and base rate does not safeguard that all necessary facilities can survive. There can be situations where the hospital is relevant for the catchment area, but its population is too small to produce a sufficient number of cases to recover the (fixed) cost. The case-based system is calculated so that the average hospital can recover the average cost. But small hospitals in lowly populated areas are not average – they might require additional budgets.

– Fee for service: It is also possible to record all services rendered and bill them one by one to the insurance. This system requires very precise documentation and bears the risk of supplier-induced demand resulting in over-consumption of healthcare services.

All of these systems have their advantages and disadvantages. Two aspects should be stressed here: Firstly, any case-based payment system requires the implementation of quality management systems. There is a risk that patients are discharged prematurely so that they will get sick again soon. If the payment depends only on the number of patients but not on the quality of services, doctors have an incentive to discharge as soon as possible. Consequently, healthcare facilities must install strict rules of quality control or even better systems of total quality management where the entire institution is geared towards quality of services.

Secondly, these systems constitute a different administrative burden. While fixed budgets are very simple to handle for the insurance and the healthcare provider, capitation is easy for the provider, but with some effort for the insurance which has to calculate the capitation. The other systems require very strong administrative capacity in both the facility and the insurance. A DRG system requires very complex algorithms and digital grouping. In all cases, cost accounting and costing of healthcare services are a prerequisite of a professional insurance system.

5.2.2.4 DRGs

The term 'diagnosis-related group' has become a buzzword in many countries attempting to implement it as the principal payment mechanism in particular for hospital services. Sometimes, one can have the impression that DRGs are not only a way of paying services, but they are perceived as the 'saviour' of the healthcare system. However, countries that have implemented a DRG system can confirm that DRGs are 'only' a payment mechanism, not more, and not less. Introducing this system has a number of prerequisites and obstacles.

The first DRG system was developed in 1965–1969 by Fetter at Yale University in the USA. He aimed to enhance the ability to describe the diversity of inpatient services. In his studies, he repeatedly encountered the problem that neither the number of cases nor the length of stay was a meaningful measure of a hospital's performance. Comparing hospitals on this basis was pointless. He therefore developed the DRGs to assign a corresponding, economically justified case severity to the cases.

It is important to note that the original DRG system was no tool of health financing, but of scientific analysis. The most important goal was comparing hospital services (between hospitals, departments, etc.). Later, the Health Care Financing Administration (HCFA) used the system for performance-based financing for Medicare and Medicaid. The 'Nordic DRGs' (Nord-DRGs) are a very early child of this original system for the Scandinavian countries (Denmark, Finland, Norway, Sweden, and Iceland) based on ICD-10 and the 'Nordic Classification of Surgical Procedures' (NCSP). Other countries (e.g. Estonia) followed and adapted the system. Compared to the Australian (AR-DRG) or German DRG system (G-DRG), the Nord-DRG are a simplified system with fewer complexities (see Figure 5.5), which makes them attractive for countries with limited administrative capacities.

In principle, a DRG system is a method to cluster cases with similar characteristics in one group. Internally, the groups shall be as homogeneous as possible (i.e. simi-

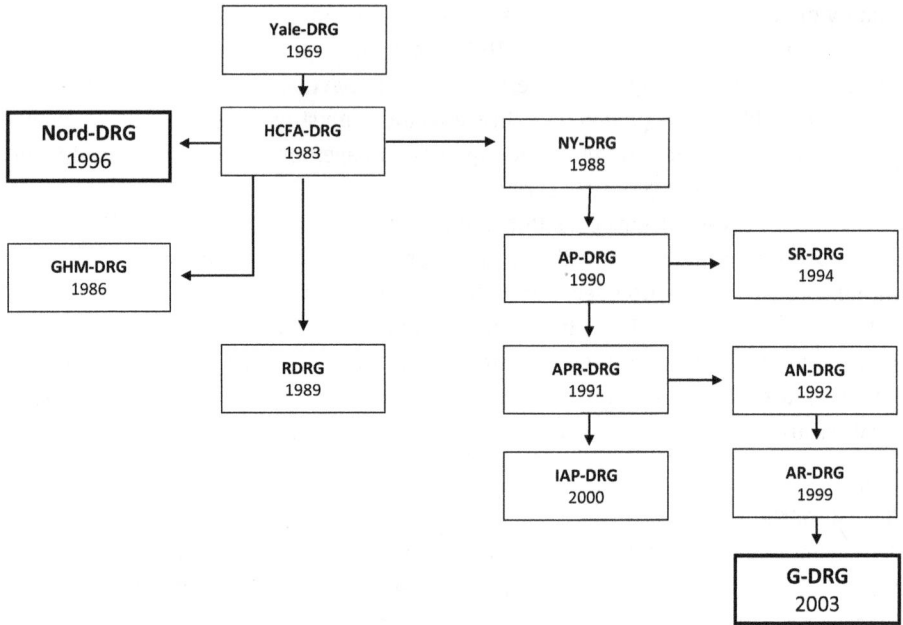

Figure 5.5: DRG systems.[701]

lar cases concerning the characteristic), and externally as inhomogeneous as possible (i.e. dissimilar cases concerning the characteristic). The main question is which characteristic is chosen to group the cases. All grouping systems use medical criteria. The most important criterion is the primary diagnosis, i.e. why this person was treated in the hospital. Other (secondary) diagnoses are also relevant from a medical perspective, but other medical characteristics, such as the procedures (surgery, conservative therapy, etc.), play a role as well.

DRG systems that should be used for health financing consider not only medical characteristics for grouping but also economic ones. The groups should be cost-homogeneous, i.e. cases within one group should have similar unit costs. Typical drivers of costs are the treatment intensity and the lengths of stay, but they are driven by complexity and comorbidity (compare Figure 5.6).

Comorbidity determines whether the treatment in a hospital is easy or intensive and whether the costs are low or high. If a patient has 'only' a broken leg, but otherwise he is completely healthy, the resources consumed for his treatment are lower than for a patient who has additionally many other diseases, such as diabetes, weak heart, obesity, and blindness. Thus, comorbidity is a major cost driver and must be reflected in a DRG system used for financing. However, comorbidity does not have

---

701 Source: Fleßa (2021).

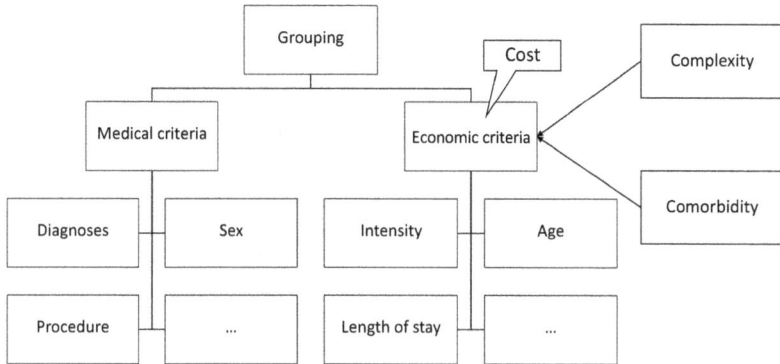

Figure 5.6: Grouping.[702]

the same influence on the costs of all major diagnoses. If a patient has a blood coagulation disorder as a secondary diagnosis, it makes a major difference in the costs of a surgical procedure, but not for a skin disease. Thus, the severity of a secondary diagnosis for the individual primary diagnosis must be analysed in detail and requires extensive codebooks.

Complexity is also a significant cost driver. Cases of the same disease can vary in severity, and the costs can be several times higher for a severely ill patient, even with the same secondary diagnoses. Thus, all DRG systems consider the complexity of each case and open different groups for different degrees of severity. Therefore, most DRG systems have more than 1,000 groups to do justice to this complexity. Only smaller countries (e.g. Estonia) limit the number of groups because otherwise the number of patients per group would be too small.

Figure 5.7 exhibits the coding process from a case to a DRG. The first steps are purely medical: Cases are allotted to major diagnostic categories based on their primary diagnoses. We could still call this case groups. What defines DRGs is the establishment of a patient clinical complexity level (PCCL). For this purpose, we individually analyse each comorbidity and assign a complication and comorbidity level (CCL). Afterwards all CCL are merged to a PCCL in a complex procedure. G-DRG uses a formula for that and Nord-DRG uses tables.[703] But in principle, both systems consider individual CCL and combine them into a PCCL. The economic grouping begins here, as similar medical cases with similar costs are grouped in specific DRGs. For this purpose, precise costing information must be provided for each patient, not just the 'average' patient.

---

702 Source: Fleßa (2021).

703 The Nord-DRGs do not consider the relevance of comorbidities for the main diagnosis, and the majority of DRGs appear in pairs (without CC: non-complicated; with CC: complicated). Based on this simplification one could challenge that Nord-DRGs are 'real' DRGs.

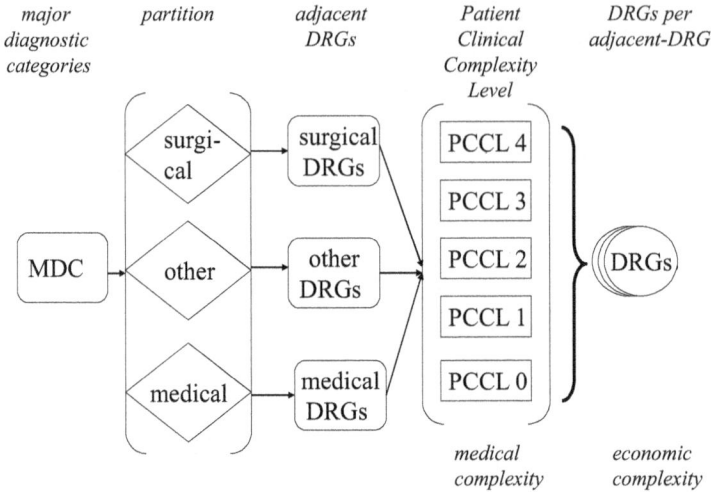

Figure 5.7: Coding.[704]

This highly simplified description of the DRG system demonstrates that its implementation has strict preconditions:

- Medical data: It requires detailed data on primary and secondary diagnoses, age, and sex.
- Health services data: It required detailed data on procedures, lengths of stay, form of admission, form of discharge, and special resources.
- Cost data: It requires calculating the financial value of resources consumed to treat patients of each DRG. It is insufficient to calculate the 'average' patient of a healthcare facility or a department, but the costs must relate to the DRG.

It is important to note that this data must be collected once to develop a county-specific system and annually to maintain it. This is completely infeasible without a digital information system in the three dimensions. However, even countries with strong administrative capacity struggle to provide meaningful data.

Consequently, introducing DRGs as a payment mechanism requires professional costing (e.g. cost per PCCL), standardization (e.g. precise definitions of diagnoses and procedures), quality management (e.g. reduce 'bloody discharge'), fraud control (e.g. detect upcoding) and staffing (e.g. professional coders and accountants) in the healthcare facilities. Furthermore, it requires the development of a 'DRG institute' in order to upkeep the system, including design of groups, calculation of cost weights, determination of base rate, and development of guidelines (e.g. coding and costing manuals). The respective health insurance funds also acquire profound knowledge of the system.

---

704 Source: Fleßa (2021).

5.2.2.5 Healthcare Financing Debts

The findings of the Commission on Macroeconomics and Health and of the Lancet Commission 'Global Health 2035: a world converging within a generation' (compare Section 2.4.2) prove that investments in health are profitable and pay back an interest rate that is far beyond normal interest on the financial markets. Thus, it might be worthwhile to take loans and finance better healthcare of the current generation. In future they will be able to redeem the loan because of their better health. If healthcare expenditure – so some argue – is not consumption but investment, it is very much appropriate to take loans for financing healthcare expenditure. For instance, lower-middle-income countries do not receive grants from development partners (e.g. World Bank, KfW) to buy medical equipment, but they are given loans which they have to pay back. Although the conditions are usually quite favourable for the partner country (low interest rate and long repayment period), these loans still mean that future generations have to pay for the better healthcare of the current generation.

As convincing as the argument of healthcare as investment seems, it must be challenged by arguments of intergenerational justice. Future generations have to pay for the healthcare expenditure of the current generation. If we take a loan today, they have no choice. Thus, this generation forces future generations and limits their freedom. On an individual basis, i.e. when an individual takes a loan for a certain medical treatment, it is very fair because the same person who takes the loan has to pay it back. But on a societal basis and for a longer time, taking loans for healthcare expenditure seems quite unfair. It is not the same whether we finance a harbour or a street with development loans, or whether we finance the purchase of drugs by loans. The harbour and street are (hopefully) still functional for the next generation. The drugs are consumed.

There are certainly cases where development loans for healthcare are appropriate, particularly for the establishment of buildings for healthcare facilities. But most expenditure will have to be financed by grants – or by increasing local sources. Thus, strengthening local institutions (e.g. insurance schemes), improving the efficiency of the government, and fostering the income basis of a nation seem more appropriate for the development of that nation than experimenting with loans to recover healthcare expenditure.

5.2.3 Healthcare Structure

The structure of the healthcare system can be evaluated based on the budget shares for the levels of the health pyramid. A central indicator is the share of prevention expenditures in the budget, but also the shares of dispensaries, health centres, and primary and secondary hospitals in the curative expenditures provide important clues about the chosen priorities in the healthcare system. Often, resource allocations consciously or unconsciously deviate from economic rationality, i.e. measures with low cost-effectiveness are seemingly preferred without justification.[705]

Determining the optimal structure is exceedingly complex but is the prerequisite for a healthcare structure reform. The complexity arises firstly from the fact that the optimal structure depends on the chosen goals of the healthcare system. Secondly, the optimal allocation depends on the disease panorama and thus on the phase of demographic or epidemiological transition. Thirdly, resource allocation is not only an absolute but also a relative function of health resources. Finally, in all structure reforms, it must be centred that the decision on the use of scarce health resources always implies rationing with life-relevant consequences. For example, resources allocated to prevention are no longer available for curative healthcare. Healthcare structure reforms consequently lead to some patients who were previously medically cared for suffering and dying without help. This is only justifiable if the structure reforms are democratically legitimized and transparently planned and executed.

The choice of the objective function of resource allocation has severe implications. Several objective functions can be considered:[706]

1. Minimizing the number of deaths: Health resources are allocated to the level of the healthcare system where they achieve the greatest reduction in the gross death rate. This means that diseases that cause suffering but do not lead to death will not receive resources. For example, rheumatism would be neglected under this objective function.

2. Minimizing the number of lost life years: Each death results in a loss of expected remaining years of life. Based on a given life expectancy, it is calculated for each death how many more years the deceased could have lived. Diseases that cause the maximum number of life years saved receive the greatest allocation of the health budget. Thus, the deaths of newborns are weighted much more heavily than the deaths of adults or seniors.

3. Minimizing incidence: Health resources are allocated to those levels of the healthcare system where the number of new cases is minimized. Therefore, the focus of the healthcare system is on prevention. Occasionally, curative services for infectious diseases are funded because curing an infectious individual can reduce incidence. However, the treatment of chronic degenerative diseases is neglected, as they have no impact on the rate of new cases.

4. Minimizing prevalence: This objective function implies greater attention to chronic diseases, as these patients are typically sick over the long term. For example, while a malaria patient suffers from malaria for only a few days on average, a diabetic suffers the consequences of his disease 365 days a year. Therefore, minimizing prevalence will, all else being equal, lead to combating chronic (and also

---

705 Compare Jamison et al. (2006).
706 Compare Fleßa, Laslo, and Marschall (2011).

chronic degenerative) diseases. Since the latter are often addressable at the higher levels of the healthcare system, this objective function also implies a stronger focus on hospital services.

5. Minimizing the loss of quality of life: Depending on the chosen concept for determining the quality of life, disease days and/or lost life days are evaluated with a quality of life weight. Severe diseases that cause significant suffering for the affected person are thus prioritized for resource allocation, while common but less painful or disabling diseases tend to be neglected. Agreement on which weights to use is difficult.

6. Minimizing the loss of workforce: This objective function values the disease time of an economically active person more than the corresponding value of a child or retiree. The DALY (disability-adjusted life year) concept implies a stronger weighting of middle years, i.e. resources are deliberately allocated to the health of productive age groups, while for example the fight against childhood diseases loses some weight.

7. Minimizing the loss of human capital: Since not all residents of a country contribute equally to the country's economic development, it makes sense to prefer those population groups that make special contributions. Thus, health services would be promoted in control centres and particularly for educational elites. For example, a portion of the budget could be reserved for the treatment of key figures in government and business abroad – services that are not offered to 'normal' citizens.

It is evident that these different objective functions lead to diverging resource allocations. Although the objective functions can be partially substituted (e.g. minimizing prevalence is included in minimizing the loss of quality of life), a complete consolidation into a single, universally accepted objective function is not possible. Therefore, a broad discourse involving the entire civil society on the goals and values of the healthcare system is required first and foremost.

Secondly, the available health budget also impacts the optimal allocation. Figure 5.8 illustrates the optimal allocation of a country's health resources based on a linear programming model. It shows that preventive spending not only increases absolutely with the health budget but also relatively. However, the relationship between the budget and the preventive share is neither linear nor monotonic. Consequently, one cannot rely on 'rules of thumb'.

The World Bank called in the World Development Report 1993 for an annual health budget in developing countries of $12 per capita.[707] This 'magic' number was long considered a standard for health policy in developing countries. According to the results of the model for optimal resource allocation, the $12 should be spent according

---

707 Compare World Bank (1993).

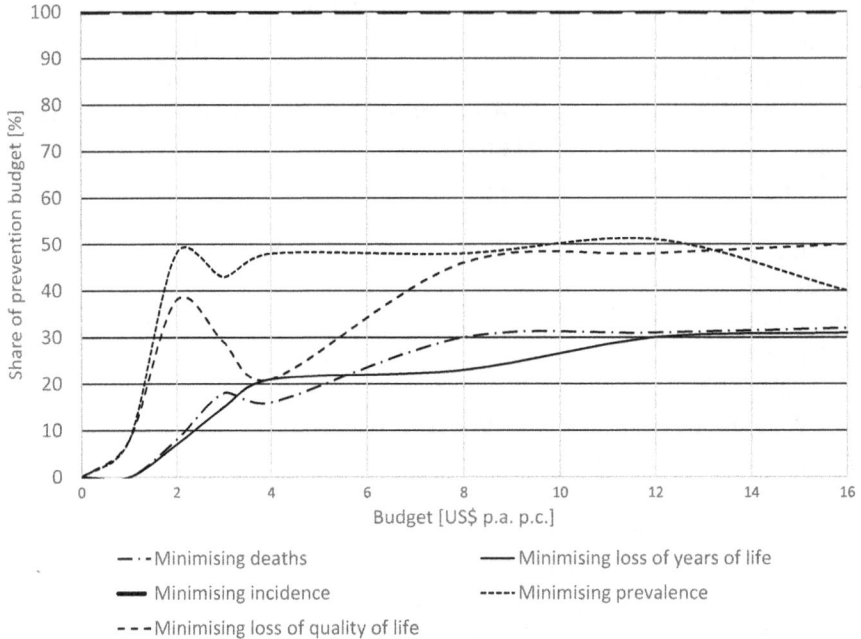

Figure 5.8: Prevention budget (relative to the health budget).[708]

to Table 5.3. It is clear that the World Bank implicitly gives the highest priority to minimizing mortality, as the allocation of about 33% of the $12 health budget to preventive measures is efficient only for the first two objective functions. The statement that the expenditures of most developing countries on hospital services are far too high remains valid, regardless of whether the relatively rough estimates of the World Bank or the results of this model are used as a health policy basis. A redistribution of health resources to basic health services is urgently required.

Finally, the disease panorama influences the optimal allocation. Countries in different phases of demographic and epidemiological transition must therefore have different structures of the healthcare system even if they have the same objective function. For example, a young population has a high proportion of infectious diseases, which are mostly preventable with relatively simple means (e.g. vaccination and hygiene). Older populations, on the other hand, have significantly more chronic degenerative diseases, the prevention of which often requires years of individual discipline

---

708 Source: Fleßa (2003b).

Table 5.3: Allocation of $12 per capita to the levels of the healthcare system.[709]

	Allocation of total budget [$ per capita (share of total budget)]		Allocation of curative budget [$ per capita (share of curative budget)]			
	Preventive medicine	Curative medicine	Dispensaries	Health centres	District hospitals	Secondary hospitals
Minimizing deaths	4.09 (34%)	7.91 (66%)	2.53 (32%)	1.90 (24%)	3.16 (40%)	0.62 (4%)
Minimizing lost life years	3.97 (33%)	8.03 (67%)	2.65 (33%)	1.69 (21%)	3.05 (38%)	0.64 (8%)
Minimizing incidences	12 (100%)	0	0	0	0	0
Minimizing disease days	6.57 (55%)	5.43 (45%)	1.79 (33%)	1.52 (28%)	2.11 (39%)	0
Minimizing lost quality of life	6.32 (53%)	5.68 (47%)	2.16 (38%)	1.42 (25%)	1.76 (31%)	0.34 (6%)

(behavioural prevention). Even with the best possible prevention, it cannot be guaranteed that the chronic degenerative disease will not develop. A young population will therefore invest particularly high budget shares in vaccination programmes, while this share steadily decreases during the third to fifth phases of the transition.

Based on the above model, it can be concluded that first, chronic degenerative diseases already exist during the first and second phases of the demographic transition, but they become increasingly important for resource allocation during the third to fifth phases. Second, the health costs for a population with numerous chronic degenerative diseases are higher than for a younger population with infectious diseases. This implies that the health status of an older population with the same budget will tend to be worse than that of a younger population. Consequently, satisfaction with the healthcare system tends to decrease as the population ages. Third, even within chronic degenerative diseases, there are significant differences in the cost-effectiveness of interventions. With scarce health resources, little or no funds will flow into interventions that are exclusively curative, benefit only a few, and are very resource-intensive. Chemotherapy or radiation therapy, for example, will hardly be funded, while establishing nationwide availability of insulin in the coming years is likely to be of great importance.

---

709 Source: Fleßa (2003b).

The optimal structure of the healthcare system is particularly important when the goal of fairness is defined such that equal opportunities and a minimum standard for every individual should be given. The resource allocation must then be 'pro-poor'.[710] If intergenerational fairness is also considered, the allocation of resources must also deliberate sustainability.[711] Corresponding models exist but often exceed the management capacity of decision-makers to handle complexity.[712]

In summary, it can be stated that healthcare reforms should not be reduced to financing options. The questions of which diseases should be treated in the public healthcare system, how different levels of the healthcare system should be equipped, and which regions or population groups should be prioritized are central to any healthcare reform. However, answering these requires a societal discourse that politicians in many countries have so far been unwilling to engage in. Indeed, the question 'Bismarck or Beveridge' is debated more vehemently in most governments than the decision "dialysis or ORT".[713] Ultimately, the analyses of international healthcare management lead back to the fundamental principles of primary healthcare as already formulated in the Alma-Ata Declaration in 1978. What follows will outline why this efficient conception of the healthcare system has hardly been implemented so far. This is an example of the health policy process.[714]

5.3 Health Policy Process

The history of healthcare in low-income countries can be described as a series of healthcare reforms, with the stable phases between reforms seemingly becoming ever shorter. The period from 1960 to 1980 was remarkably stable in many developing countries. National health budgets increased significantly, allowing new healthcare facilities to be built and the proportion of the population served by Western healthcare services to constantly grow. The young states had sufficient funds because they could sell their export products well on the world markets. In addition, there was a steadily increasing amount of development aid.

During this time, the prototype of a government healthcare system was created, i.e. not only in the former English colonies was the National Health Service of the United Kingdom elevated to an ideal. Financing was based almost exclusively on tax revenues and development aid. With few exceptions, all services of the healthcare facilities were without user fees, and the upper class also benefited from seemingly

---

710 Compare Gwatkin, D. R., A. Wagstaff and A. Yazbeck (2005).
711 Compare Soubbotina (2004).
712 Compare Fleßa (2009).
713 ORT: oral rehydration therapy, one of the most effective measures of reducing paediatric mortality in diarrhoea diseases.
714 A good summary is provided by Carrin, Buse, Heggenhougen, et al. (2009).

'free' services. The government financed the facilities almost always based on input, i.e. without reference to performance. Most healthcare facilities were state-owned, and in not a few countries, private and partially non-profit health service providers were nationalized after independence. A private economy in healthcare hardly existed at this time, which was also due to the fact that the freedom of establishment was severely restricted and prices were almost always fixed by the state. Hospitals were the focus of the healthcare system. Although there were already dispensaries and health centres, they were generally regarded as satellites of the hospitals, not as independent contributors to care.

The primary healthcare innovation fell into this period of stability in 1978. Its adoption was accordingly low, as the governmental, hospital-oriented system regime did not allow any distress to arise. Thus, this innovation was blocked before it could diffuse. In fact, the Alma-Ata Declaration should have acted as a macro-innovation that would have completely changed the healthcare system. But the macro-innovation was prevented, so that primary healthcare or community-based healthcare were only implemented as micro-innovations in some programmes additionally to a preserved hospital-based system.

During the 1980s, severe disturbances occurred in the previous growth path. On the one hand, export revenues, especially of agricultural raw materials, continued to decline, and on the other hand, the concept of hospital coverage for the entire population reached its limits. It became apparent that the previous model of healthcare, practiced in most countries, was no longer sustainable. Nevertheless, the adoption of the primary healthcare innovation was scarce and the previous system continued to evolve.[715] Instead of a structural reform, i.e. reallocating resources to prevention or basic healthcare services, there was a steady sequence of smaller reforms. These included the introduction of user fees, the licensing of private practices, the promotion of community-based health insurance, the strengthening of social insurance, or output-based aid.

As important as these reforms were in individual cases, they nevertheless failed to solve the fundamental problem that a state-dominated, input-based, and hospital-oriented healthcare system is not capable of adequately serving the population. Indeed, there is hardly any statement from the World Health Organization that does not emphasize this fact, yet the implementation in countries is minimal. Figure 5.9 gives a clue as to why a structural reform in the health policy process is so difficult to implement.

---

715 Flessa (2023c).

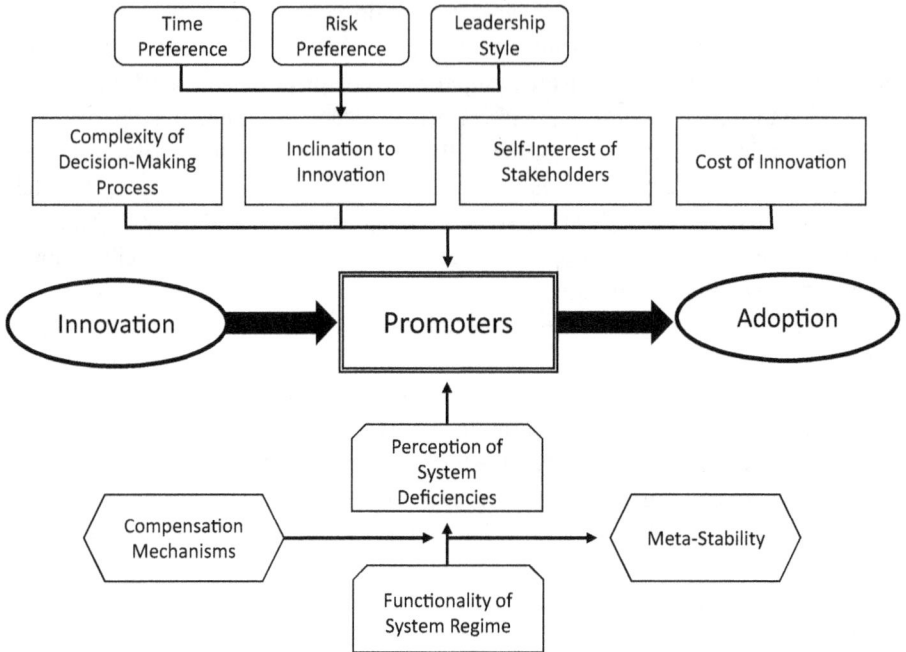

Figure 5.9: Model of innovation adoption.[716]

Next, the model will first be briefly described and then applied to the primary health-care innovation.[717] It is assumed that the innovation has already been matured in niches, so it is now available for diffusion as a standard.

According to Rogers,[718] the adoption of an innovation is a complex, multi-stage process that must overcome numerous barriers. In addition to uncertainty, there is particularly resistance from those affected and involved. Consequently, the adoption of an innovative seed primarily depends on the existence and functionality of key in-dividuals, who are recruited from the stakeholders of an organization. Their impor-tant role in the adoption of innovation necessitates first clarifying which stakeholders are involved in this process and what self-interest they pursue. Subsequently, it is nec-essary to analyse whether there is even a necessity for change. Every innovation means costs, risk, and inconvenience. Consequently, the functionality of the system regime must be examined. In a stable system, the likelihood of finding power pro-moters to implement a new idea is relatively low. Even in a crisis phase, the system control will first attempt to maintain the old regime. Initially, compensatory mecha-

---

716 Source: Fleßa (2008).
717 Huebner and Flessa (2022).
718 Compare Rogers (2003).

nisms within the existing structure are sought before particularly macro-innovations are adopted. This can lead to artificial stabilization (meta-stability) and thus fragility of the system. The pressure to adopt is particularly high during fundamental crises, while the pressure for innovation is not sufficient in times of minor crisis severity to effect profound changes.

Even if the system deficiencies are painfully perceived, this does not necessarily lead to the immediate adoption of the innovation. Complex innovations are less easily adopted than simple, manageable ones. Consequently, complex macro-innovations only have a chance to prevail if the crisis pressure is extremely high. The complexity of the decision-making situation must primarily be overcome by the technical promoter.

The costs of adopting an innovation are also of great importance. Besides the direct costs incurred by establishing new structures (e.g. purchasing operating resources), the indirect costs of the transition phase must be considered. During the transition phase, the performance of the organization may be lower than if the old system regime had been maintained. These costs are particularly high if the introduction is suboptimal. Here, the process promoter plays a crucial role, who can facilitate a quick return to a synchronous phase with his organizational knowledge. Without him, the implementation of an excellent innovation fails due to administrative problems.

Crucial to understanding the adoption of innovation in developing countries, however, is the individual inclination to innovate the promoters and decision-makers. The willingness to take the risk of an innovation depends on cultural values such as time preference or risk tolerance. In countries with high present orientation and high risk aversion, the suboptimal, current problem-solving approach is preferred to a better, but uncertain future option. From this, one can derive the thesis that innovations with a preventive function are very difficult to enforce.

The inclination to innovate the technical, process, and relationship promoters is also influenced by the leadership style. While there may be a power promoter in an authoritarian leadership style, agile and enthusiastic technical, process, and relationship promoters cannot develop because they lack any decision-making authority.

Using this model, it becomes understandable why healthcare reforms in most countries have not changed fundamental structures. Primary healthcare, in the sense of a complete reorientation of the healthcare system to meet the needs of the grassroots, has hardly emerged from niches and individual projects. This is primarily because there are hardly any decision-makers who see a personal advantage in implementing this reform.

The most important professional group in healthcare are medical doctors, who as chief physicians in hospitals, regional or district doctors, and senior administrative officials in ministries of health are so significant that there exists a "tendency to equate health with medicine".[719] Senior physicians would be ideal power promoters

---

719 Walt (1994).

for primary healthcare, as they are positioned very high hierarchically and their profession is attributed a 'natural' authority. Furthermore, many doctors could act as technical promoters.

In reality, however, there are few doctors interested in a profound structural reform. Rather, it has often been described that doctors advocate for maintaining the hospital-oriented healthcare system and against basic health services. For many physicians, the doctor and hospital are still inextricably linked, and health promotion and prevention are missing from the curricula of most medical faculties.

The possibility for patients to participate in the allocation of resources in healthcare is limited. Only urban minorities significantly influence governments, but these elites generally have no interest in basic health services, as they want to be treated with the best possible technology in case of illness. All health policy measures that reduce the performance of urban secondary and tertiary hospitals are politically opposed by them.

Attempts by the majority of the population to enforce basic health services at the expense of tertiary hospitals are often classified as politically 'left wing'. Indeed, pioneering experiences in community-based healthcare were gained in socialist countries, particularly in China, Mozambique, and Nicaragua, and liberatory pedagogy is considered one of their philosophical roots.[720] Accordingly, attempts by patients to influence the adoption of the primary healthcare innovation are suppressed by many governments.[721]

Further analysis of potential promoters is not much more promising: neither ministries of health, churches, development aid organizations, nor politicians can have a self-interest in reallocating health resources. The current system benefits the elites and allows the maintenance of existing procedures. Without civil society engagement, there will hardly be enough stakeholders to enforce structural reforms.

Another prerequisite for structural reform is the recognition of system deficiencies. Normally, system controls are only ready to take the risk of an innovation when the old system solution has clearly reached its limits and cannot be further developed.[722] In times of crisis, the risk of an innovation is more readily accepted because the current situation also has poor future prospects. Consequently, times without crises are relatively innovation-hostile. As mentioned above, the Alma-Ata Declaration fell into a synchronous phase of the healthcare system, so broad adoption of this innovation was not to be expected.

In a market economy, the crisis of a profit-oriented company can always be seen in its profits or losses. Competition ensures that innovations are quickly adopted, as otherwise, companies would become sub-marginal providers and would eventually

720 Compare, e.g. Klotzbücher (2006).
721 Compare Walt (1994).
722 Compare Perlitz and Löbler (1985).

exit the market. The healthcare sector in low- and lower-middle-income countries can only partly rely on this profit mechanism, as most providers of health services incur losses and are subsidized by the government or charities, such as churches. There is a risk that a crisis situation is not perceived or not centre in time, so that timely countermeasures cannot be taken.

Most health service providers in developing countries are financed based on input, meaning the local population hardly plays a role as customers. Thus, they are at risk of making decisions primarily based on the needs of the input providers, not the desires of their own catchment population. Since the crisis of the healthcare system primarily manifests at the grassroots level, but not at the input level, the increasing fluctuation is not noticed. The system regime has long reached an unstable phase, but the system control still feels the positive feedback from government subsidies or development aid. The system is artificially stabilized by foreign donations; it is metastable (compare Section 4.1.1.3).

Considering that some healthcare facilities depend on foreign donations for up to 80%, it becomes clear that the primary focus of the leaders of these institutions must be to satisfy the needs of the donors, not the catchment population. A crisis is not perceived because the transfers from overseas always come, regardless of the own performance.

From this analysis, it is clear that the relevant decision-makers see no need for a healthcare structure reform. Even if they do not attribute existing problems to technical inefficiency, i.e. minor flaws in the current approach that could be improved, they would hardly actively pursue a structural reform themselves, as it would bring them little benefits. Combining this with the tendency towards the present, risk aversion, and strict hierarchies described in Section 4.1.3, it becomes clear that profound reforms of the healthcare system will only have a chance when the supply situation has become catastrophic and civil society exerts pressure.

In fact, it has been regularly proclaimed over the last decades that this is now the case. However, new 'magic bullets' have always been found, with which attempts have been made to overcome the impending health crisis. These included the introduction of user fees, the promotion of social health insurance, privatization, and the World Bank's turn to direct support for poverty groups or the implementation of DRGs for hospital financing. While these activities are to be welcomed, there is still a danger that they prevent an orientation towards efficient structures. Ultimately, the constant sequence of reforms reflects frustration that healthcare for people in much of the world will only reach an acceptable minimum standard in many decades, even if their economy grows. Recently, therefore, there has been discussion of understanding health as a global human right and deriving a claim to international solidarity. Undoubtedly, these 'global health obligations' represent an important contribution to the discussion.[723] However, given the global financial problems, they should not lead

---

[723] Compare Gostin (2007) and Lowry and Schüklenk (2009).

to necessary healthcare reforms being postponed in individual countries. What is required is not just more money but above all an orientation of spending towards effectiveness and efficiency. In other words, what is needed is international healthcare management, which, with its tools, provides indications of where government, private, domestic, and international financial resources should be optimally deployed. For this insight to then become action-guiding, international healthcare management must enter into close cooperation with political science.

6 Outlook

Healthcare management uses the knowledge of business and economics as well as numerous other sciences to design, plan, organize, control, and evaluate healthcare systems and institutions of the healthcare sector so that they can best achieve health policy goals. It is always action-oriented and aims to enable leaders in ministries, associations, hospitals, medical practices, insurance companies, and other institutions to make practice-oriented and evidence-based decisions to put scarce resources at the service of life.

At the end of this book, one might ask whether it is necessary to conceive an international healthcare management. In principle, the above definition covers everything needed in an international context. In fact, the differences between countries are becoming smaller. For example, the upper class in the metropolises of low-income countries suffers from similar health problems and has comparable health resources as most people in richer countries. At the same time, structural problems of developing countries, such as spatial accessibility, are also found in peripheral areas of Europe and North America. The biggest differences today are not between North and South, but between rich and poor within a country.

Nevertheless, the analysis of the health problems of resource-poor countries can sharpen the focus on structures, as structural difficulties in these countries are more clearly apparent. The learning effect is thus comparatively low if international healthcare management only compares the United States, the United Kingdom, and Austria with Germany. The analysis of healthcare systems that are quite different is really exciting and promising because it allows a view of the essential relationships. Thus, international healthcare management should not only contribute to better care for the majority of the world's population but also consciously increase awareness of problems in Germany. There is much what we can learn from each other, such as the natural role of spirituality and religion for the majority of the world population in their health and healthcare.

This work aims to illuminate the basic interrelationships and invite more in-depth study. It is hoped that this book will help those working in international healthcare management. However, it is equally important that dealing with the foreign encourages one to perceive one's own problems differently and to initiate changes. It should now be up to the readers to decide which of their own problems as healthcare managers they can tackle creatively, having recognized from the international context that things can indeed be done quite differently!

https://doi.org/10.1515/9783112217290-006

References

Abel-Smith, B., and P. Rawal. 1992. "Can the Poor Afford 'Free' Health Services? A Case Study of Tanzania." *Health Policy and Planning* 7(4): 329.

Adams, F. 2022. *Airs, Waters, Places*. London: DigiCat.

Adams, J., et al. 2021. "The Conundrum of Low COVID-19 Mortality Burden in Sub-Saharan Africa: Myth or Reality?" *Global Health: Science and Practice* 9(3): 433–443.

Adegoroye, A. 1989. *Community Health Care*. London: Basingstoke, Macmillan.

Adhikari, A. 2018. *Strategic Marketing Issues in Emerging Markets*. Springer.

Adisasmito, W. B., et al. 2022. "One Health: A New Definition for a Sustainable and Healthy Future." *PLOS Global Public Health* 18(6): e1010537.

Affemann, N., et al. 1998. *Globale Herausforderung und Bevölkerungsentwicklung: Die Menschheit ist bedroht*. Böblingen: Deutsche Stiftung Weltbevölkerung.

Ahmed, S. A. S., et al. 2020. "Impact of the Societal Response to COVID-19 on Access to Healthcare for Non-COVID-19 Health Issues in Slum Communities of Bangladesh, Kenya, Nigeria and Pakistan." *BMJ Global Health* 5(8): e003042.

Akin, J. S., et al. 1987. *Financing Health Services in Developing Countries: An Agenda for Reform*. Washington, DC: World Bank Publications.

Alonso, S., et al. 2019. "The Economic Burden of Malaria on Households and the Health System in a High Transmission District of Mozambique." *Malaria Journal* 18: 1–10.

American Psychological Association. 2024. "Resilience." Accessed April 17, 2024. https://www.apa.org/topics/resilience.

Anand, S., and K. Hanson. 1997. "Disability-Adjusted Life Years: A Critical Review." *Journal of Health Economics* 16(6): 685–702.

Anchita, et al. 2021. "Health Impact of Drying Aral Sea: One Health and Socio-Economic Approach." *Water* 13(22): 3196.

Anderson, W. B. 1988. *The Church in East Africa 1840–1974*. Dodoma: Christian Council of Tanzania.

Andrade, M. V., et al. 2022. "The Economic Burden of Malaria: A Systematic Review." *Malaria Journal* 21(1): 283.

Apeagyei, A., et al. 2023. *Financing Global Health 2021: Global Health Priorities in a Time of Change*. Seattle, WA: Institute for Health Metrics and Evaluation (IHME).

Apeagyei, A. E., et al. 2024. "Financing Health in Sub-Saharan Africa 1990–2050: Donor Dependence and Expected Domestic Health Spending." *PLOS Global Public Health* 4(8): e0003433.

Appadorai, A. 1955. "The Bandung Conference." *India Quarterly* 11(3): 207–235.

Arhin, D. C. 1994. "The Health Card Insurance Scheme in Burundi: A Social Asset or a Non-Viable Venture?" *Social Science & Medicine* 39(6): 861–870.

Asante, K. 1998. *Sustainability of Church Hospitals in Developing Countries: A Search for Criteria for Success*. Geneva: Christian Medical Commission.

Aßländer, M. 2018. *Adam Smith zur Einführung*. Hamburg: Junius Verlag.

Audy, R. 1971. "Measurement and Diagnosis of Health." In *Environmental: Essays on the Planet as a Home*, edited by P. Shepard and D. McKinley, 140–162. Boston: Houghton Mifflin.

Baaseke, W. E. 2002. *Aufbruch zum Leben: Wirtschaft, Mensch und Sinn im 21. Jahrhundert*. Linz: Universitätsverlag Rudolf Trauner.

Bähr, J. 2004. *Bevölkerungsgeographie*. Stuttgart: UTB.

Baker, M. G., et al. 2020. "New Zealand's COVID-19 Elimination Strategy." *Medical Journal of Australia* 213(198): 10.5694.

Baltussen, R., et al. 2004. "Cost-Effectiveness Analysis of Cataract Surgery: A Global and Regional Analysis." *Bulletin of the World Health Organization* 82: 338–45.

https://doi.org/10.1515/9783112217290-007

Baly, A., et al. 2011. "The Cost of Routine *Aedes aegypti* Control and of Insecticide-Treated Curtain Implementation." *American Journal of Tropical Medicine and Hygiene* 84(5): 747–52.

Bandiera, O., et al. 2019. *The Economic Lives of Young Women in the Time of Ebola: Lessons from an Empowerment Program.* World Bank Policy Research Working Paper 8760.

Barasa, E. W., et al. 2020. "Assessing the Hospital Surge Capacity of the Kenyan Health System in the Face of the COVID-19 Pandemic." *PLoS One* 15(7): e0236308.

Barasa, E., J. Kazungu, S. Orangi, E. Kabia, M. Ogero and K. Kasera (2021). "Indirect health effects of the COVID-19 pandemic in Kenya: a mixed methods assessment." BMC Health Services Research 21(1): 1–16.

Barker, D. J., and C. Osmond. 1986. "Infant Mortality, Childhood Nutrition, and Ischaemic Heart Disease in England and Wales." *The Lancet* 327(8489): 1077–81.

Barnum, H., et al. 1993. *Public Hospitals in Developing Countries: Resource Use, Cost, Financing.* Baltimore: Johns Hopkins University Press.

Barrientos, A., and D. Hulme. 2016. *Social Protection for the Poor and Poorest: Concepts, Policies and Politics.* Springer.

Bauer, S. 2011. "Der Klimawandel als Entwicklungshemmnis und Sicherheitsrisiko: Neue Herausforderungen für die internationale Zusammenarbeit." In *Nachhaltigkeit in der Entwicklungszusammenarbeit,* edited by J. König and J. Thema, 120–37. Wiesbaden: VS Verlag.

Bedell, S. L., et al. 2020. "Cervical Cancer Screening: Past, Present, and Future." *Sexual Medicine Reviews* 8(1): 28–37.

Beiter, D., et al. 2023. "Improving the Technical Efficiency of Public Health Centers in Cambodia: A Two-Stage Data Envelopment Analysis." *BMC Health Services Research* 23(1): 912.

Berche, P. 2022. "History of Measles." *La Presse Médicale* 51(3): 104149.

Berche, P. 2022. "Life and Death of Smallpox." *La Presse Médicale* 51(3): 104117.

Berger, J., et al. 2022. "Sozioökonomische Benachteiligung als Risikofaktor für Krebserkrankungen: 'Closing the Care Gap'." *Forum.* Springer.

Berger, P. L. 1994. "The Gross National Product and the Gods." *The McKinsey Quarterly* 1: 97–110.

Berman, P. A. 1997. "National Health Accounts in Developing Countries: Appropriate Methods and Recent Applications." *Health Economics* 6(1): 11–30.

Bertz, J. 2010. *Verbreitung von Krebserkrankungen in Deutschland: Entwicklung der Prävalenzen zwischen 1990 und 2010.* Berlin: Robert-Koch-Institut.

Bhutta, Z. A. 2006. "What Does Absorption Capacity Not Measure?" *The Lancet* 368(9534): 428–30.

Bichmann, W. 2010. "Potenziale des Privatsektors für 'Primary-Health-Care'-Strategien." *Prävention und Gesundheitsförderung* 5(1): 23–28.

Blacker, C. P. 1947. "Stages in Population Growth." *The Eugenics Review* 39(3): 88–.

Blakely, T., et al. 2020. "The Probability of the 6-Week Lockdown in Victoria (Commencing 9 July 2020) Achieving Elimination of Community Transmission of SARS-CoV-2." *Medical Journal of Australia* 213(8): 349–51.

Blunt, P., and M. L. Jones. 1992. *Managing Organisations in Africa.* Berlin and New York: Walter de Gruyter.

Bobek, H. 1959. "Die Hauptstufen der Gesellschafts- und Wirtschaftsentwicklung in geographischer Sicht." *Die Erde* 90: 258–97.

Boerma, J., and S. K. Stansfield. 2007. "Health Statistics Now: Are We Making the Right Investments?" *The Lancet* 369(9563): 779–86.

Bommer, C., et al. 2018. "Global Economic Burden of Diabetes in Adults: Projections from 2015 to 2030." *Diabetes Care* 41(5): 963–70.

Bonita, R., et al. 2008. *Einführung in die Epidemiologie.* Bern: Huber.

Bonnet, F., et al. 2024. "Spatial Disparities in the Mortality Burden of the COVID-19 Pandemic across 569 European Regions (2020–2021)." *Nature Communications* 15(1): 4246.

Borgetto, B., and K. Kälble. 2007. *Medizinsoziologie: Sozialer Wandel, Krankheit, Gesundheit und das Gesundheitssystem*. Weinheim: Juventa.

Bosanquet, N., and K. Sikora. 2006. *The Economics of Cancer Care*. Cambridge: Cambridge University Press.

Bouma, M., et al. 1994. "Climate Change and Periodic Epidemic Malaria." *Lancet* 343(8910): 1440.

Bradfield, L., et al. n.d. "Raised Temperatures over the Kericho Tea Estates: Revisiting the Climate in the East African Highlands Malaria Debate." *Malaria Journal* 10.

Brady, K. T. 2020. "Social Determinants of Health and Smoking Cessation: A Challenge." *American Psychiatric Association* 177: 1029–1030.

Brandt, A., et al. 1979. *Cost-Sharing in Health Care*. Berlin and Heidelberg: Springer.

Breman, J. G., et al. 2004. "Conquering the Intolerable Burden of Malaria: What's New, What's Needed: A Summary." *American Journal of Tropical Medicine and Hygiene* 71(2 Suppl): 1–15.

Bremer, S. 1996. *Der Wirtschaftsethische Ansatz in der Theologischen Ethik von Helmut Thielicke*. Münster: Lit.

Brienen, N. C., et al. 2010. "The Effect of Mask Use on the Spread of Influenza during a Pandemic." *Risk Analysis: An International Journal* 30(8): 1210–1218.

Briggs, A. H., et al. 2012a. "Model Parameter Estimation and Uncertainty Analysis: A Report of the ISPOR-SMDM Modeling Good Research Practices Task Force Working Group–6." *Medical Decision Making* 32(5): 722–732.

Briggs, A. H., et al. 2012b. "Model Parameter Estimation and Uncertainty: A Report of the ISPOR-SMDM Modeling Good Research Practices Task Force–6." *Value in Health* 15(6): 835–842.

Brizuela, V., and Ö. Tunçalp. 2017. "Global Initiatives in Maternal and Newborn Health." *Obstetric Medicine* 10(1): 21–25.

Brößkamp-Stone, U. 2003. *Systeme und Strukturen der Gesundheitsförderung*. In *Das Public Health Buch*, edited by F. W. Schwartz, 243–254. München and Jena: Urban & Fischer.

Bruce-Chwatt, L. J. 1988. "History of Malaria from Prehistory to Eradication." In *Malaria: Principles and Practice of Malariology*, vol. 1, 1–59.

Bruchhausen, W. 2020. *Global Health in the Colonial Era: The Expansion of European Medicine*. Mainz: Leibniz Institute of European History (IEG).

Bruni, L., et al. 2023. *Human Papillomavirus and Related Diseases Report*. Barcelona: HPV Information Centre.

Bruni, L., et al. 2022. "Cervical Cancer Screening Programmes and Age-Specific Coverage Estimates for 202 Countries and Territories Worldwide: A Review and Synthetic Analysis." *The Lancet Global Health* 10(8): e1115–e1127.

Burton, M. J., et al. 2021. "The Lancet Global Health Commission on Global Eye Health: Vision Beyond 2020." *The Lancet Global Health* 9(4): e489–e551.

Busbee, B. G., et al. 2002. "Incremental Cost-Effectiveness of Initial Cataract Surgery." *Ophthalmology* 109(3): 606–612.

Butter, I. 1967. "Health. Manpower Research: A Survey." *Inquiry* 4(4): 5–41.

Caballero, B., and B. M. Popkin. 2002. *The Nutrition Transition: Diet and Disease in the Developing World*. Academic Press.

Calwell, H. G. 1993. "Tropical Medicine and Hygiene in Tanganyika Territory." *The Ulster Medical Journal* 62: 1–42.

Cambodia Ministry of Health. 2013. *Clinical Practice Guidelines Type 2 Diabetes*. Phnom Penh: Ministry of Health.

Campbell, J. D., and A. K. S. Jardine. 2001. *Maintenance Excellence: Optimizing Equipment Life-Cycle Decisions*. Basel: Eastern Hemisphere Distribution.

Caradonna, J. L. 2022. *Sustainability: A History*. Oxford: Oxford University Press.

Carrin, G., et al. 2009. *Health Systems Policy, Finance, and Organization*. Amsterdam et al.: Academic Press.

Cattaneo, A., et al. 2015. "The Seven Sins and Seven Virtues of Universal Health Coverage." *Third World Resurgence* 296/297: 13–15.

CDC. 2024. "History of Smallpox." Accessed August 28, 2024. https://www.cdc.gov/smallpox/history/his tory.html.

CEBM. 2024. "Basic Reproductive Number." Accessed August 13, 2024. https://www.cebm.net/wp-content /uploads/2020/04/KM-4.png.

Cervellati, M., and U. Sunde. 2007. *Human Capital, Mortality and Fertility: A Unified Theory of the Economic and Demographic Transition*. Centre for Economic Policy Research.

Chianca, T. 2008. "The OECD/DAC Criteria for International Development Evaluations: An Assessment and Ideas for Improvement." *Journal of Multidisciplinary Evaluation* 5(9): 41–51.

Claeson, M., et al. 2002. *Health, Nutrition and Population: A Source Book for Poverty Reduction Strategies*, edited by J. Klugman, 201–230. Washington, DC: The World Bank.

Cleveland Clinic. 2025. "Cryosurgery of the Cervix." Accessed March 24, 2025. https://my.clevelandclinic. org/health/treatments/9120-cryosurgery-of-the-cervix.

Cliff, A., and P. Haggett. 1988. *An Atlas of Disease Distribution*. Oxford: Blackwell.

Cobb, C. W., and P. H. Douglas. 1928. "A Theory of Production." *American Economic Review* 18(1): 139–165.

Conteh, L., et al. 2021. "Costs and Cost-Effectiveness of Malaria Control Interventions: A Systematic Literature Review." *Value in Health* 24(8): 1213–1222.

Cook, G. C., and A. Zumla. 2009. *Manson's Tropical Diseases*. London: Elsevier.

Corsten, H. 1998. *Grundlagen der Wettbewerbsstrategie*. Stuttgart: Teubner.

Corsten, H., and R. Gössinger. 2007. *Dienstleistungsmanagement*. München and Wien: Oldenbourg Verlag.

Covey, S. R. 2004. *Seven Habits of Highly Effective People*. London and New York: Free Press.

Crabtree, J. 2005. "Patterns of Protest: Politics and Social Movements in Bolivia." *Capital & Class* 88: 164.

Creagh, N. S., et al. 2023. "Self-Collection Cervical Screening in the Asia-Pacific Region: A Scoping Review of Implementation Evidence." *JCO Global Oncology* 9: e2200297.

Creese, A., and J. Kutzin. 1997. *Lessons from Cost-Recovery in Health*. Geneva: World Health Organization.

Crossin, R., et al. 2023. "The New Zealand Drug Harms Ranking Study: A Multi-Criteria Decision Analysis." *Journal of Psychopharmacology* 37(9): 891–903.

D'Aquino, L., et al. 2019. "Introducing a Sector-Wide Pooled Fund in a Fragile Context: Mixed-Methods Evaluation of the Health Transition Fund in Zimbabwe." *BMJ Open* 9(6): e024516.

Dars, L. 1971. *The Demand for Health and the Demand for Medical Care: An Econometric Model*. New York: New School for Social Research.

Davies, R., et al. 1975. "Planning Patient Care with a Markov Model." *Operational Research Quarterly* 26: 347–362.

De Allegri, M., et al. 2009. "Community Health Insurance in Sub-Saharan Africa: What Operational Difficulties Hamper Its Successful Development?" *Tropical Medicine & International Health* 14(5): 586–596.

DeCanio, S. J. 2003. *Economic Models of Climate Change: A Critique*. New York: Palgrave Macmillan.

DeHaven, M. J., et al. 2004. "Health Programs in Faith-Based Organizations: Are They Effective?" *American Journal of Public Health* 94(6): 1030.

Delvos, A. 2008. *Warum ist Demografie, Alterung und Gesundheit ein wichtiges Thema für das Gesundheitsmanagement?* München: Grin.

Desai, M. A., et al. 2004. *Indoor Smoke from Solid Fuels: Assessing the Environmental Burden of Disease at National and Local Levels*. Geneva: World Health Organization.

Destatis. 2024. "The Largest Cities Worldwide." Accessed July 25, 2024. https://www.destatis.de/EN/ Themes/Countries-Regions/International-Statistics/Data-Topic/Population-Labour-Social-Issues/Demo graphyMigration/UrbanPopulation.html.

Deutsche Gesellschaft für Hygiene und Mikrobiologie. 2010. "Selbstverständnis." Accessed May 15, 2010. http://www.dghm.org/red/ueberuns/.

Diamond, J. 1999. *The Wealth and Poverty of Nations: Why Some Are So Rich and Some So Poor*. New York: Norton.

Diesfeld, H. J., and W. Bichmann. 1989. "Primary Health Care: Primäre Gesundheitspflege oder Utopie."
    In *Medizin in Entwicklungsländern: Handbuch zur Praxisorientierten Vorbereitung für Medizinische
    Entwicklungshelfer*, edited by H. J. Diesfeld and S. Wolter, 120–134. Frankfurt a.M.: Lang.

Diesfeld, H. J., et al. 2001. *Gesundheitsversorgung in Entwicklungsländern: Medizinisches Handeln aus
    Bevölkerungsbezogener Perspektive*. Berlin et al.: Springer.

Dinkel, R. H. 2002. *Demographie: Fertilität und Mortalität*. Vahlen.

Donabedian, A. 1982. *Explorations in Quality Assessment and Monitoring: The Definition of Quality and
    Approaches to Its Assessment. Vol. II, The Criteria and Standards of Quality*. Ann Arbor: Health
    Administration Press.

Donabedian, A., and R. Bashshur. 2002. *An Introduction to Quality Assurance in Health Care*. Oxford: Oxford
    University Press.

Dossa, R., et al. 2001. "Impact of Iron Supplementation and Deworming on Growth Performance in
    Preschool Beninese Children." *European Journal of Clinical Nutrition* 55(4): 223–228.

Drehsen, V., and M. Baumotte. 1995. *Wörterbuch des Christentums*. München: Orbis.

Drummond, M. F., et al. 2005. *Methods for the Economic Evaluation of Health Care Programmes*. New York:
    Oxford University Press.

Dümbgen, L. 2009. *Biometrie*. Wiesbaden: Vieweg & Teubner.

Edejer, T. T. T. 2003. *Making Choices in Health: WHO Guide to Cost-Effectiveness Analysis*. Geneva: World
    Health Organization.

Editorial, L. 2006. "The Business of HIV/AIDS." *Lancet* 368(9534): 423.

Egbendewe-Mondzozo, A., et al. 2011. "Climate Change and Vector-Borne Diseases: An Economic Impact
    Analysis of Malaria in Africa." *International Journal of Environmental Research and Public Health* 8(3):
    913–930.

Egger, M., et al. 2017. *Public Health Kompakt*. Berlin: de Gruyter.

Elkeles, T., and A. Mielck. 1997. "Entwicklung eines Modells zur Erklärung gesundheitlicher Ungleichheit."
    Gesundheitswesen 59: 137–143.

En'Ko, P. 1989. "On the Course of Epidemics of Some Infectious Diseases." *International Journal of
    Epidemiology* 18(4): 749–755.

Enayati, A., and J. Hemingway. 2010. "Malaria Management: Past, Present, and Future." *Annual Review of
    Entomology* 55: 569–591.

Erazo, D., et al. 2024. "Contribution of Climate Change to the Spatial Expansion of West Nile Virus in
    Europe." *Nature Communications* 15(1): 1196.

Esenwein-Rothe, I. 1982. *Einführung in die Demographie: Bevölkerungsstruktur und Bevölkerungsprozeß aus
    der Sicht der Statistik*. Stuttgart: Steiner.

Evans, D. B., et al. 2013. "Universal Health Coverage and Universal Access." *Bull World Health Organ* 91:
    546–546A.

Ewert, D. M. 1990. *A New Agenda for Medical Missions*. Brunswick: MAP.

Farrar, J., et al. 2023. *Manson's Tropical Diseases E-Book*. London et al.: Elsevier Health Sciences.

Feachem, R. G. 2002. "Commission on Macroeconomics and Health." *Bull World Health Organ* 80(2): 87.

Feierman, S., and J. Janzen. 1992. *Therapeutic Traditions in Africa: A Historical Perspective. The Social Basis of
    Health and Healing in Africa*, edited by S. Feierman and J. M. Janzen, 163–174. San Francisco: University
    of California Press.

Feierman, S., and J. M. Janzen. 1992. *The Social Basis of Health and Healing in Africa*. San Francisco:
    University of California Press.

Feldstein, M. S. 1967. "An Aggregate Planning Model of the Health Care Sector." *Medical Care* 5(6):
    369–381.

Fenner, F. 1982. "Global Eradication of Smallpox." *Reviews of Infectious Diseases* 4(5): 916–930.

Ferlay, J., et al. 2010a. "GLOBOCAN 2008 v1.2, Cancer Incidence and Mortality Worldwide." Accessed
    February 1, 2012. http://globocan.iarc.fr.

Ferlay, J., et al. 2010b. "GLOBOCAN 2008 v1.2, Cancer Incidence and Mortality Worldwide: IARC CancerBase No. 10." Accessed December 17, 2011. http://globocan.iarc.fr.

Fernandes Antunes, A., et al. 2022. "Sensitivity Analysis and Methodological Choices on Health-Related Impoverishment Estimates in Cambodia, 2009–17." *Health Policy and Planning* 37(6): 791–807.

Fernandes Antunes, A., et al. 2024. "Revisiting a Decade of Inequality in Healthcare Financial Burden in Cambodia, 2009–19: Trends, Determinants and Decomposition." *International Journal for Equity in Health* 23(1): 196.

Ferranti, D. d., et al. 1999. Preface. In *Health Expenditures, Services, and Outcomes in Africa: Basic Data and Cross-National Comparisons, 1990–1996*, edited by D. H. Peters, v–vi. Washington, DC: Human Development Network, Health, Nutrition, and Population Series.

Ferrari, A. J., et al. 2024. "Global Incidence, Prevalence, Years Lived with Disability (YLDs), Disability-Adjusted Life-Years (DALYs), and Healthy Life Expectancy (HALE) for 371 Diseases and Injuries in 204 Countries and Territories and 811 Subnational Locations, 1990–2021: A Systematic Analysis for the Global Burden of Disease Study 2021." *The Lancet* 403(10440): 2133–2161.

Ferreira, L. 1994. *Poverty and Inequality during Structural Adjustment in Rural Tanzania*. Washington, DC: World Bank.

Flanigan, D. A. 2007. *Malaria Research Trends*. New York: Nova.

Fleßa, S. 1998. "Many Worlds of Health: A Simulation of the Determinants of the Epidemiological Transition." *Z Bevoelkerungswiss* 23: 459–494.

Fleßa, S. 1999. "Decision Support for Malaria-Control Programmes: A System Dynamics Model." *Health Care Management Science* 2: 181–191.

Fleßa, S. 2003a. *Arme Habt Ihr Allezeit! Ein Plädoyer für eine Armutsorientierte Diakonie*. Göttingen: Vandenhoeck & Ruprecht.

Fleßa, S. 2003b. *Gesundheitsreformen in Entwicklungsländern*. Frankfurt a.M.: Lembeck.

Fleßa, S. 2005. "Disease Dynamics. Simulation Epidemiologischer Prozesse mit Methoden des Operations Research." *OR-News* 23: 18–20.

Fleßa, S. 2006. *Das Computer-Gestützte Managementplanspiel Moshi (= Management of Small Hospitals) als Strategische Waffe im Kampf für eine Effiziente Gesundheitsversorgung in Entwicklungsländern*. Nürnberg: Forschungsgruppe Medizinökonomie, Universität Erlangen-Nürnberg.

Fleßa, S. 2007. *Gesundheitsökonomik: Eine Einführung in das Wirtschaftliche Denken für Mediziner*. Berlin and Heidelberg: Springer.

Fleßa, S. 2008. *Grundzüge der Krankenhaussteuerung*. München: Oldenbourg.

Fleßa, S. 2009. *Costing of Health Care Services*. Frankfurt a.M.: Lang.

Fleßa, S. 2010a. *Grundzüge der Krankenhausbetriebslehre*. München: Oldenbourg.

Fleßa, S. 2010b. *Planen und Entscheiden in Beruf und Alltag*. Berlin: Walter de Gruyter.

Fleßa, S. 2016. "Gesundheitsökonomische Evaluation in der Entwicklungszusammenarbeit." *Gesundheitsökonomie & Qualitätsmanagement* 21: 11–12.

Fleßa, S. 2021. *Systemisches Krankenhausmanagement*. Berlin: De Gruyter.

Fleßa, S. 2022. *Systemisches Krankenhausmanagement*. Berlin: De Gruyter.

Fleßa, S. 2023. "Zur Ökonomie von COVID-19: Allgemeine Überlegungen mit Schwerpunkt Afrika." In *Covid-19 pandisziplinär und international: Gesundheitswissenschaftliche, gesellschaftspolitische und philosophische Hintergründe*, 151–86. Berlin and Heidelberg: Springer.

Flessa, S. 2002. *Malaria und Aids: Gesundheitsökonomische Analysen auf Grundlage von Disease Dynamics Modellen*. Lage: H. Jacobs.

Flessa, S. 2016a. "Christian Milestones in Global Health: The Declarations of Tübingen." *Christian Journal for Global Health* 3(1): 11–24.

Flessa, S. 2016b. "Future of Christian Health Services—An Economic Perspective." *Christian Journal for Global Health* 3(1): 25–35.

Flessa, S. 2022. *Cataract Surgery in Low-Income Countries: A Good Deal! Healthcare* (MDPI).

Flessa, S. 2023a. "Place Matters: The Spatial Diffusion of Contagious Diseases." *International Journal of Business and Systems Research* 17(6): 677–702.

Flessa, S. 2023b. "Primary Health Care: Historical Failure or Innovation Seedling for Future Healthcare Systems?" *Z'GuG Zeitschrift für Gemeinwirtschaft und Gemeinwohl* 46(4): 487–509.

Flessa, S. 2024. "Sector-Wide Approach (SWAp) in Healthcare: A Mixed-Methods Assessment of Health SWAps in Nepal and Bangladesh." *International Journal of Environmental Research and Public Health* 21(12): 1682.

Flessa, S., and N. T. Dung. 2004. "Costing of Services of Vietnamese Hospitals: Identifying Costs in One Central, Two Provincial and Two District Hospitals Using a Standard Methodology." *The International Journal of Health Planning and Management* 19(1): 63–77.

Fleßa, S., and W. Greiner. 2020. *Grundlagen der Gesundheitsökonomie: Eine Einführung in das wirtschaftliche Denken im Gesundheitswesen*. Berlin and Heidelberg: Springer Gabler.

Fleßa, S., et al. 2011a. "Zielfunktionen und Allokationsentscheidungen im Krankenhaus." *Ethik in der Medizin* 23(4): 291–302.

Flessa, S., et al. 2011b. "Basing Care Reforms on Evidence: The Kenya Health Sector Costing Model." *BMC Health Services Research* 11(1): 128.

Flessa, S., and A. Zembok. 2014. "Costing of Diabetes Mellitus Type II in Cambodia." *Health Economics Review* 4(1): 1–15.

FluTracker. 2012. "Tracking the Progress of H1N1 Swine Flu." http://flutracker.rhizalabs.com/.

Ford, N., et al. 2011. "The First Decade of Antiretroviral Therapy in Africa." *Global Health* 7: 33.

Forrester, J. W. 1964. *Industrial Dynamics*. Cambridge, MA: Wright Allen Press.

Forrester, J. W. 1971. *World Dynamics*. Cambridge: Wright-Allen Press.

Forsythe, S. S., et al. 2019. "Twenty Years of Antiretroviral Therapy for People Living with HIV: Global Costs, Health Achievements, Economic Benefits." *Health Affairs* 38(7): 1163–1172.

Frenk, J., et al. 1991. "Elements for a Theory of the Health Transition." *Health Transition Review*: 21–38.

Fricke, W. 1987. "Geographische Erklärungsansätze für die Geomedizinische Forschung: Räumliche Persistenz und Diffusion von Krankheiten." In *Heidelberg*, edited by W. Fricke and E. Hinz, 3–13. Heidelberg: Selbstverlag des Geographischen Institutes der Universität Heidelberg.

Fu, S., et al. 2011. "Influence of Central Obesity on Clustering of Metabolic Syndrome Risk Variables among Normal-Weight Adults in a Low-Income Rural Chinese Population." *Journal of Public Health*: 1–7.

Fuchs, V. R. 1974. *Who Shall Live? Health, Economics, and Social Change*. New York: Basic Books.

Gaag, J. v. d. and T. Barham. 1998. "Health and Health Expenditures in Adjusting and Non-Adjusting Countries." *Social Science & Medicine* 46: 995–1009.

Galey, P. 2019. "Climate Impacts 'to Cost World $7.9 Trillion' by 2050." Accessed November 11, 2024. https://phys.org/news/2019-11-climate-impacts-world-trillion.html.

Garber, G. 2001. "An Overview of Fungal Infections." *Drugs* 61(Suppl 1): 1–12.

Garner, P. 1995. *Health Sector Reform in Developing Countries*. Boston: Harvard University Press.

Geyer, S. 2001. "Krankheit und Soziale Ungleichheit: Untersuchungen mit Krankenkassendaten." *Forum Public Health* 9(33): 6–7.

Ghaderi, A., et al. 2018. "Explanatory Definition of the Concept of Spiritual Health: A Qualitative Study in Iran." *Journal of Medical Ethics and History of Medicine* 11.

Gilliam, B. L., et al. 2011. "HIV in Africa: Challenges and Directions for the Next Decade." *Current Infectious Disease Reports*.

Gilmurray, J., et al. 1979. *The Struggle for Health*. London: Catholic Institute for International Relations.

Gilson, L., and A. Mills. 1995. "Health Sector Reforms in Sub-Saharan Africa: Lessons of the Last 10 Years." *Health Policy* 32(1): 215–243.

Giusti, D., et al. 1997. "Viewpoint: Public versus Private Health Care Delivery: Beyond the Slogans." *Health Policy and Planning* 12(3): 193.

Gizaw, M., et al. 2019. "Uptake of Cervical Cancer Screening in Ethiopia by Self-Sampling HPV DNA Compared to Visual Inspection with Acetic Acid: A Cluster Randomized Trial." *Cancer Prevention Research* 12(9): 609–616.

Glaeser, E., et al. 2020. "Costing of Cesarean Sections in a Government and a Non-Governmental Hospital in Cambodia: A Prerequisite for Efficient and Fair Comprehensive Obstetric Care." *International Journal of Environmental Research and Public Health* 17(21): 8085.

Globocan. 2024. "Population Factsheets." Accessed October 8, 2024. https://gco.iarc.who.int/today/en.

Goldie, S. J., et al. 2001. "Policy Analysis of Cervical Cancer Screening Strategies in Low-Resource Settings." *JAMA: The Journal of the American Medical Association* 285(24): 3107–3115.

Goleman, D. 2006. *Social Intelligence*. New York: Bantam Dell.

Goleman, D. 2008. *Emotionale Intelligenz*. München: Deutscher Taschenbuchverlag.

Goodchild, M., et al. 2018. "Global Economic Cost of Smoking-Attributable Diseases." *Tobacco Control* 27(1): 58–64.

Goodman, C., et al. 2000. *Economic Analysis of Malaria Control in Sub-Saharan Africa*. Geneva: Global Forum for Health Research.

Gordis, L. 2008. *Epidemiology*. Philadelphia: Saunders.

Gordis, L., and R. Rau. 2001. *Epidemiologie*. Marburg: Kilian.

Gostin, L. O. 2007. "Meeting Basic Survival Needs of the World's Least Healthy People: Toward a Framework Convention on Global Health." *Georgetown Law Journal* 96: 331.

Gottret, P. E., and G. Schieber. 2006. *Health Financing Revisited: A Practitioner's Guide*. Washington, DC: World Bank Publications.

Greenwood, B., et al. 2005. "Seminar Series: Malaria." *The Lancet* 365: 1487–1498.

Grimes, C. E., et al. 2011. "Systematic Review of Barriers to Surgical Care in Low-Income and Middle-Income Countries." *World Journal of Surgery* 35(5): 941–950.

Grimes, D. A., et al. 2006. "Unsafe Abortion: The Preventable Pandemic." *The Lancet* 368(9550): 1908–1919.

Grundmann, C. H. 1992. *Gesandt zu Heilen*. Gütersloh: Gütersloher Verlagshaus.

GtZ. 2007. *Extending Social Protection in Health*. Eschborn: Gesellschaft für Technische Zusammenarbeit.

Günal, M. M., and M. Pidd. 2010. "Discrete Event Simulation for Performance Modelling in Health Care: A Review of the Literature." *Journal of Simulation* 4(1): 42–51.

Gurbaxani, B. M., et al. 2022. "Evaluation of Different Types of Face Masks to Limit the Spread of SARS-CoV-2: A Modeling Study." *Scientific Reports* 12(1): 8630.

Habitat, U. 2010. *State of the World's Cities 2010/2011: The Millennium Development Goals and Urban Sustainability*. New York: United Nations.

Halbwachs, H. 2000. "Maintenance and the Life Expectancy of Healthcare Equipment in Developing Economies." *Health Estate* 54(2): 26.

Halbwachs, H., and A. Issakov. 1994. *Essential Equipment for District Health Facilities in Developing Countries*. Eschborn: Deutsche Gesellschaft für Technische Zusammenarbeit.

Hale, T., et al. 2023. "Variation in Government Responses to COVID-19. BSG-WP-2020/032, Version 15." Accessed August 26, 2024. https://www.bsg.ox.ac.uk/sites/default/files/2023-06/BSG-WP-2020-032-v15.pdf.

Hamisi, N. M., et al. 2023. "Global Health Security amid COVID-19: Tanzanian Government's Response to the COVID-19 Pandemic." *BMC Public Health* 23(1): 205.

Hang, S., et al. 2023. "Feasibility, Accuracy and Acceptability of Self-Sampled Human Papillomavirus Testing Using careHPV in Cambodia: A Cross-Sectional Study." *Journal of Gynecologic Oncology* 35(1): e6.

Hauff, V. 1987. *Unsere gemeinsame Zukunft: Der Brundtland-Bericht der Weltkommission für Umwelt und Entwicklung*. Ascheberg: Eggenkamp.

Hay, S. I., et al. 2002. "Climate Change and the Resurgence of Malaria in the East African Highlands." *Nature* 415(6874): 905–909.

Heidemann, E. 1993. *The Contemporary Use of Standards in Health Care*. WHO.

Heineberg, H. 2000. *Grundriss Allgemeine Geographie: Stadtgeographie Paderborn*. München, Wien, Zürich: Ferdinand Schöningh.

Helmert, U., and W. Voges. 2001. "Herz-Kreislauf-Krankheiten: Von der Managerkrankheit zur Krankheit der sozial Benachteiligten." *Forum Public Health* 9(33): 5–6.

Heudtlass, P., et al. 2016. "Excess Mortality in Refugees, Internally Displaced Persons and Resident Populations in Complex Humanitarian Emergencies (1998–2012): Insights from Operational Data." *Conflict and Health* 10: 1–11.

Hey, J. D., et al. 2010. "The Descriptive and Predictive Adequacy of Theories of Decision Making under Uncertainty/Ambiguity." *Journal of Risk and Uncertainty* 41(2): 81–111.

Hinz, E. 1987. "Persistenz, Expansion und Regression durch tierische Nahrungsmittel übertragener Parasitoren." In *Räumliche Persistenz und Diffusion von Krankheiten*, edited by W. Fricke and E. Hinz, 43–72. Heidelberg: Selbstverlag des Geographischen Institutes der Universität Heidelberg.

Hoebel, J., et al. 2025. "Die Lebenserwartungslücke: Sozioökonomische Unterschiede in der Lebenserwartung zwischen Deutschlands Regionen."

Hoerauf, A., et al. 2003. "Onchocerciasis." *BMJ* 326: 207–210.

Hofstede, G. 1983. "The Cultural Relativity of Organizational Practices and Theories." *Journal of International Business Studies* 14(2): 75–90.

Hofstede, G., and Hofstede, G. J. . 2011. *Lokales Denken, Globales Handeln: Interkulturelle Zusammenarbeit und Globales Management*. München: DTV.

Hofstede, G., et al. 2005. *Cultures and Organizations: Software of the Mind*. New York: McGraw-Hill.

Hofstede Insights. 2024. "Compare Countries." Accessed May 29, 2024. https://hi.hofstede-insights.com.

Homann, K., and F. Blome-Drees. 1992. *Wirtschafts- und Unternehmensethik*. Göttingen: UTB.

Horton, R., and S. Lo. 2015. "Planetary Health: A New Science for Exceptional Action." *The Lancet* 386(10007): 1921–1922.

Horton, S., et al. 2017. "Ranking 93 Health Interventions for Low- and Middle-Income Countries by Cost-Effectiveness." *PLoS One* 12(8): e0182951.

Hosseini, K., et al. 2022. "Role of Fungal Infections in Carcinogenesis and Cancer Development: A Literature Review." *Advanced Pharmaceutical Bulletin* 12(4): 747.

Hotez, P. J. 2021. *Forgotten People, Forgotten Diseases: The Neglected Tropical Diseases and Their Impact on Global Health and Development*. Hoboken, NJ: John Wiley & Sons.

Howdon, D., and N. Rice. 2018. "Health Care Expenditures, Age, Proximity to Death and Morbidity: Implications for an Ageing Population." *Journal of Health Economics* 57: 60–74.

Hsiao, W. C., et al. 2007. *Social Health Insurance for Developing Nations*. Washington, DC: World Bank Publications.

Huber, M., et al. 2011. "Health: How Should We Define It?" *BMJ* 343(7817): 235–237.

Huchko, M. J., et al. 2014. "A Comparison of Two Visual Inspection Methods for Cervical Cancer Screening among HIV-Infected Women in Kenya." *Bulletin of the World Health Organization* 92: 195–203.

Hudson, P. J., et al. 2002. *The Ecology of Wildlife Diseases*. Oxford: Oxford University Press.

Huebner, C., and S. Flessa. 2022. "Strategic Management in Healthcare: A Call for Long-Term and Systems-Thinking in an Uncertain System." *International Journal of Environmental Research and Public Health* 19(14): 8617.

Hunt, J. M. 2005. "The Potential Impact of Reducing Global Malnutrition on Poverty Reduction and Economic Development." *Asia Pacific Journal of Clinical Nutrition* 14: 10–38.

Hurrelmann, K., and O. Razum. 2012. *Handbuch Gesundheitswissenschaften*. Weinheim, Basel: Juventa.

Iacobucci, G. 2019. "Life Expectancy Gap between Rich and Poor in England Widens." *British Medical Journal Publishing Group*.

Iannaccone, L. R. 1998. "Introduction to the Economics of Religion." *Journal of Economic Literature* 26(3): 1465–1496.

IAPD. 2022. "Vision Atlas." Accessed February 3, 2022. https://www.iapb.org/learn/vision-atlas/.

IDF. 2021. *IDF Diabetes Atlas 2021*. International Diabetes Federation.

IFC. 2008. *The Business of Health in Africa*. Washington, DC: International Finance Corporation.

IFPRI. 2021. "COVID-19 School Closures and Adolescent Mental Health: Evidence from Mozambique." Accessed January 11, 2022. https://www.ifpri.org/blog/covid-19-school-closures-and-adolescent-mental-health-evidence-mozambique.

Ignatius, R. 2006. "Parasitosen." In *Springer Lexikon Diagnose & Therapie*, 1217–1228. Berlin, Heidelberg: Springer.

IHME. 2024. "Disease, Injury, and Risk Factsheets." Accessed August 5, 2024. https://www.healthdata.org/research-analysis/diseases-injuries-risks/factsheets.

IHME. 2025. "Global Burden of Disease Results." Accessed August 31, 2024. https://vizhub.healthdata.org/gbd-results/.

Ijaz, S., et al. 2023. "Relationship between the ABO Blood Group and Rhesus Factors with COVID-19 Susceptibility." *Expert Review of Hematology* 16(4): 297–303.

Ireland, M., et al. 2011. "Can Performance-Based Financing Be Used to Reform Health Systems in Developing Countries?" *Bulletin of the World Health Organization* 89(9): 695–698.

Ivinson, A. 2002. "Macroeconomics and Health: Investing in Health for Economic Development." *Nature Medicine* 6: 551–552.

Jaberi, A., et al. 2019. "Spiritual Health: A Concept Analysis." *Journal of Religion and Health* 58: 1537–1560.

Jackson, J., et al. 2021. *Global Economic Effects of COVID-19*. Updated November 10, 2021. R46270. Washington, DC: Congressional Research Service.

Jacobs, B., et al. 2018. "Making Free Public Healthcare Attractive: Optimizing Health Equity Funds in Cambodia." *International Journal for Equity in Health* 17: 1–11.

Jacobs, B., et al. 2019a. "Costing for Universal Health Coverage: Insight into Essential Economic Data from Three Provinces in Cambodia." *Health Economics Review* 9(1): 29.

Jacobs, B., et al. 2019b. "Costing for Universal Health Coverage: Insight into Essential Economic Data from Three Provinces in Cambodia." *Health Economics Review* 9: 1–14.

Jain, K. K. 2015. *Textbook of Personalized Medicine*. Berlin, Heidelberg, New York: Springer.

James, W. 2008. "WHO Recognition of the Global Obesity Epidemic." *International Journal of Obesity* 32: 120–126.

Jamison, D. 2006. *Disease and Mortality in Sub-Saharan Africa*. Washington, DC: World Bank Publications.

Jamison, D., et al. 1999. *The World Health Report 1999: Making a Difference*. Genf: Weltgesundheitsorganisation.

Jamison, D. T., et al. 2006. *Disease Control Priorities in Developing Countries*. New York: Oxford University Press, USA.

Jamison, D. T., et al. 2013. "Global Health 2035: A World Converging within a Generation." *The Lancet* 382(9908): 1898–1955.

Janson, M. 2022. "89% der Corona-Toten waren im Alter 70+." Accessed January 3, 2022. https://de.statista.com/infografik/23756/gesamtzahl-der-todesfaelle-im-zusammenhang-mit-dem-coronavirus-in-deutschland-nach-alter/.

Jay, P. 2000. *Das Streben nach Wohlstand*. Berlin, München: Propyläen.

Joarder, T., et al. 2020. "A Record Review on the Health Status of Rohingya Refugees in Bangladesh." *Cureus* 12(8).

John, T. J., and R. Samuel. 2000. "Herd Immunity and Herd Effect: New Insights and Definitions." *European Journal of Epidemiology* 16: 601–606.

John, U. 2003. *Bewegung und Gesundheit. Gesund und bewegt ins Alter*. In K. Eisfeld, U. Wiesmann, H.-J. Hannich et al., 25–27. Butzbach-Griedel: Afra.

Johnson, S. A. 2011. *Challenges in Health and Development*. Heidelberg, London, New York: Springer.

Jones, A., and J. Kirigia. 1999. "Health Knowledge and Smoking among South African Women." *Health Economics* 8(2): 165–169.

Jones, K. E., et al. 2008. "Global Trends in Emerging Infectious Diseases." *Nature* 451(7181): 990–993.

Kaiser, A. H., et al. 2023. "Extending Universal Health Coverage to Informal Workers: A Systematic Review of Health Financing Schemes in Low- and Middle-Income Countries in Southeast Asia." *PLoS One* 18(7): e0288269.

Kalk, A., et al. 2010. "'Paying for Performance' in Rwanda: Does It Pay Off?" *Tropical Medicine & International Health* 15(2): 182–190.

Karimizadeh, Z., et al. 2023. "The Reproduction Rate of Severe Acute Respiratory Syndrome Coronavirus 2 Different Variants Recently Circulated in Humans: A Narrative Review." *European Journal of Medical Research* 28(1): 94.

Karnon, J., et al. 2012. "Modeling Using Discrete Event Simulation: A Report of the ISPOR-SMDM Modeling Good Research Practices Task Force-4." *Medical Decision Making* 32(5): 701–711.

Kasiloo, O. M. J. 2000. *African Forum on the Role of Traditional Medicine in Health Systems*. Harere: WHO Regional Office for Africa.

Kazibwe, J., et al. 2022. "The Use of Cost-Effectiveness Thresholds for Evaluating Health Interventions in Low- and Middle-Income Countries from 2015 to 2020: A Review." *Value in Health* 25(3): 385–389.

Keeling, M. J., and P. Rohani. 2011. *Modeling Infectious Diseases in Humans and Animals*. Princeton and Oxford: Princeton University Press.

Kermack, W. O., and A. G. McKendrick. 1927. "A Contribution to the Mathematical Theory of Epidemics." *Proceedings of the Royal Society of London. Series A, Containing Papers of a Mathematical and Physical Character* 115(772): 700–721.

Khafaiea, M., and R. Rahim. 2020. "Cross-Country Comparison of Case Fatality Rates of COVID-19/SARS-CoV-2." *Osong Public Health and Research Perspectives* 11(2): 74–80.

Khaibullina, Z., et al. 2022. "Socio-Economic and Public Health Impacts of Climate Change and Water Availability in Aral District, Kyzylorda Region, Kazakhstan." *Asian Journal of Water Research* 8: 177–204.

Kickbusch, I. 2003. "Gesundheitsförderung." In *Das Public Health Buch*, edited by F. W. Schwartz, 181–189. München, Jena: Urban & Fischer.

KieraCampbell. 2024. "Basic Reproductive Rate." Accessed August 13, 2024. https://commons.wikimedia.org/w/index.php?curid=79523883.

Kim, J. J., et al. 2008. "Modeling Cervical Cancer Prevention in Developed Countries." *Vaccine* 26, Suppl 10: K76–K86.

Kiple, K. F., et al. 1993. "Bubonic Plague." In *The Cambridge World History of Human Disease*, edited by K. F. Kiple, R. R. Graham, D. Frey et al. Cambridge: Cambridge University Press.

Klein, R., and A. Scholl. 2012. *Planung und Entscheidung: Konzepte, Modelle und Methoden einer modernen betriebswirtschaftlichen Entscheidungsanalyse*. München: Vahlen.

Klotzbücher, S. 2006. *Das ländliche Gesundheitswesen der VR China: Strukturen, Akteure, Dynamik.* Frankfurt a.M.: Peter Lang.

König, A., et al. 2024. "The Impact of the Health Microinsurance M-FUND on the Utilization of Health Services among Migrant Workers and Their Dependents in Thailand: A Case-Control Study." *Journal of Migration and Health* 9: 100236.

Kotz, M., et al. 2024. "The Economic Commitment of Climate Change." *Nature* 628(8008): 551–557.

Koum, K. 2019. "Project Progress Report." Accessed May 25, 2025. http://scgo-kh.com/wp-content/uploads/2019/11/1-Project-progress-Prof.-Koum-Kanal.pdf.

Kourti, A., et al. 2021. "Domestic Violence during the COVID-19 Pandemic: A Systematic Review." *Trauma, Violence, & Abuse*. https://doi.org/10.1177/15248380211038690.

Krauss, H., et al. 1997. *Zoonosen: Von Tier zu Menschen übertragbare Infektionskrankheiten*. Köln: Deutscher Ärzte-Verlag.

Kruse, P. 1993. "Der Mitarbeiter als Mensch." In *Der Mensch im Mittelpunkt*, edited by R. Schatz, 8. Bonn, Fribourg, Ostrava: InnoVation.

Kuper, H., et al. 2010. "Does Cataract Surgery Alleviate Poverty? Evidence from a Multi-Centre Intervention Study Conducted in Kenya, the Philippines and Bangladesh." *PLoS One* 5(11): e15431.

Kuruvilla, S., et al. 2016. "The Global Strategy for Women's, Children's and Adolescents' Health (2016–2030): A Roadmap Based on Evidence and Country Experience." *Bulletin of the World Health Organization* 94(5): 398.

Kutzin, J. 2013. "Health Financing for Universal Coverage and Health System Performance: Concepts and Implications for Policy." *Bulletin of the World Health Organization* 91: 602–611.

Kutzin, J., et al. 2010. *Implementing Health Financing Reform: Lessons from Countries in Transition*. Genf: Weltgesundheitsorganisation.

Laaser, U., and R. Radermacher. 2007. *Financing Health Care: A Dialogue between South Eastern Europe and Germany*. Lage: Jacobs.

Lachmann, W. 2003. *Entwicklungspolitik. 1. Grundlagen*. München: Oldenbourg Wissenschaftsverlag.

Ladkin, D. 2020. *Rethinking Leadership: A New Look at Old Leadership Questions*. Cheltenham: Edward Elgar Publishing.

Laenderdaten. 2024. "Megacities." Accessed November 11, 2024. https://www.laenderdaten.info/megac ities.php.

Lampert, T., et al. 2018. "Health Inequalities in Germany and in International Comparison: Trends and Developments over Time." *Journal of Health Monitoring* 3(Suppl 1): 1.

Landes, D., et al. 1999. *Wohlstand und Armut der Nationen*. München: Siedler.

Langenscheidt, P. 1999. "Ausbildung zum Distriktchirurgen." In *8. Symposium der Deutschen Gesellschaft für Tropenchirurgie, 'Eine Welt – eine Chirurgie'*. Jena: Deutsche Gesellschaft für Tropenchirurgie.

Lansingh, V. C., et al. 2007. "Global Cost-Effectiveness of Cataract Surgery." *Ophthalmology* 114(9): 1670–1678.

Lauterbach, K., et al. 2005. "Auswirkungen der ersten und zweiten Stufe der Tabaksteuererhöhung." Accessed January 2, 2012. http://www.uk-koeln.de/kai/igmg/sgmg/2006-03_kostenreduktion_tabakste uer.pdf.

Lawson, J., et al. 2021. "Speculation and Food-Grain Prices." *Applied Economics* 53(20): 2305–2321.

Lederman, Z., et al. 2021. "Stamping Out Animal Culling: From Anthropocentrism to One Health Ethics." *Journal of Agricultural and Environmental Ethics* 34(5): 27.

Lee, R., and A. Mason. 2010. "Fertility, Human Capital, and Economic Growth over the Demographic Transition." *European Journal of Population/Revue européenne de Démographie* 26(2): 159–182.

Legood, R., et al. 2005. "Screening for Cervical Cancer in India: How Much Will It Cost? A Trial Based Analysis of the Cost per Case Detected." *International Journal of Cancer* 117(6): 981–987.

Leiniger, M. 1970. *Nursing and Anthropology: Two Worlds to Blend*. New York: John Wiley & Sons.

Leiniger, M. 2005. *Culture Care Diversity & Universality: A Worldwide Nursing Theory*. New York: Jones & Bartlett Pub.

Leon, D. 2008. "Cities, Urbanization and Health." *International Journal of Epidemiology* 37(1): 4.

Lerner, R. M. 2018. *Concepts and Theories of Human Development*. Milton Park: Routledge.

Lewis, M. 2006. *Governance and Corruption in Public Health Care Systems*. Washington DC: Center for Global Development.

Li, Q., et al. 2020. "Early Transmission Dynamics in Wuhan, China, of Novel Coronavirus–Infected Pneumonia." *New England Journal of Medicine*.

Lim, K., et al. 2011. "Comparing Visual Inspection with Acetic Acid to Cytology in Detection of Precancerous Lesions of the Cervix in HIV-Infected Cambodian Women." *Journal of the International Association of Physicians in AIDS Care* 10(5): 283–286.

Lindfield, R., et al. 2012. "The Challenges in Improving Outcome of Cataract Surgery in Low and Middle Income Countries." *Indian Journal of Ophthalmology* 60(5): 464.

Lindsay, S. W., et al. 2000. "Effect of 1997–98 El Niño on Highland Malaria in Tanzania." *The Lancet* 355(9208): 989–990.

Liu, Y., and J. Rocklöv. 2022. "The Effective Reproductive Number of the Omicron Variant of SARS-CoV-2 Is Several Times Relative to Delta." *Journal of Travel Medicine* 29(3): taac037.

Liu, Y., and F. Wu. 2010. "Global Burden of Aflatoxin-Induced Hepatocellular Carcinoma: A Risk Assessment." *Environmental Health Perspectives* 118(6): 818–824.

Lopez, A. D., et al. 1994. "A Descriptive Model of the Cigarette Epidemic in Developed Countries." *Tobacco Control* 3: 242–247.

Lorenz, R. J. 1996. *Grundbegriffe der Biometrie*. Stuttgart, Jena, Lübeck, Ulm: Gustav Fischer.

Lotka, A. J., and James, A. 1956. *Elements of Mathematical Biology*. New York: Dover Publications.

Lowry, C., and U. Schüklenk. 2009. "Two Models in Global Health Ethics." *Public Health Ethics* 2(3): 276.

Lu, R., et al. 2020. "Genomic Characterisation and Epidemiology of 2019 Novel Coronavirus: Implications for Virus Origins and Receptor Binding." *The Lancet* 395(10224): 565–574.

Lyman, P. N., and S. B. Wittels. 2010. "No Good Deed Goes Unpunished: The Unintended Consequences of Washington's HIV/AIDS Programs." *Foreign Affairs* 89(4): 74–84.

Macdonald, G. 1957. *The Epidemiology and Control of Malaria*. Oxford: Oxford University Press.

MacKellar, L. 2005. "Priorities in Global Assistance for Health, AIDS, and Population." *Population and Development Review* 31(2): 293–312.

Mahler, H. 2016. "The Meaning of 'Health for All by the Year 2000'." *American Journal of Public Health* 106(1): 36–38.

Mailu, E. W., et al. 2020. "Factors Associated with the Uptake of Cataract Surgery and Interventions to Improve Uptake in Low- and Middle-Income Countries: A Systematic Review." *PLoS One* 15(7): e0235699.

Malthus, T. R. 1888. *An Essay on the Principle of Population: Or, A View of Its Past and Present Effects on Human Happiness*. London: Reeves and Turner.

Marques, A. P., et al. 2021. "Global Economic Productivity Losses from Vision Impairment and Blindness." *eClinicalMedicine* 35: 100852.

Marseille, E., et al. 2002. "HIV Prevention before HAART in Sub-Saharan Africa." *The Lancet* 359(9320): 1851–1856.

Marshall, S. J. 2004. "Developing Countries Face Double Burden of Disease." *Bulletin of the World Health Organization* 82(7): 556.

Maslow, A. H., et al. 1970. *Motivation and Personality*. New York: Harper & Row.

Mbiti, J. S. 1992. *Introduction to African Religion*. Nairobi: Heinemann.

Mbiti, J. S. 1994. *African Religions and Philosophy*. London: Heinemann.

McCormick, I., et al. 2022. "Effective Cataract Surgical Coverage in Adults Aged 50 Years and Older: Estimates from Population-Based Surveys in 55 Countries." *The Lancet Global Health*.

McGilvray, J. C. 1979. *The Quest for Health. An Interim Report of a Study Process*. Tübingen: German Institute for Medical Missions.

McGilvray, J. C. 1982. *Die Verlorene Gesundheit: Das Verheißene Heil*. Tübingen: Deutsches Institut für Ärztliche Mission.

McKenzie, F. E., et al. 1998. "Discrete-Event Simulation Models of *Plasmodium falciparum* Malaria." *Simulation* 71(4): 250–261.

McKeown, T. 1979a. "The Direction of Medical Research." *Lancet* 2(8155): 1281–1284.

McKeown, T. 1979b. *The Role of Medicine: Dream, Mirage or Nemesis*. Oxford: Blackwell.

Meade, M., and M. Emch. 2005. *Medical Geography*. New York, London: The Guilford Press.

Meade, M., and M. Emch. 2010. *Medical Geography*. New York, London: The Guilford Press.

Meessen, B., and W. Van Damme. *Reaching the Poor*. Washington, DC: World Bank Publications.

Mentis, A. 2019. "Social Determinants of Tobacco Use: Towards an Equity Lens Approach." *Tobacco Prevention & Cessation* 3: 5–7.

Metelmann, I. B., et al. 2020. "Does Health Securitization Affect the Role of Global Surgery?" *Journal of Public Health*: 1–6.

Meyer, M. 1996. *Operations Research – Systemforschung: Eine Einführung in die Praktische Bedeutung.* Stuttgart et al.: Gustav Fischer.

Meymen, M. 1985. *International Geographical Glossary.* Wiesbaden, Stuttgart: Steiner.

Midgley, J. 2020. *Inequality, Social Protection and Social Justice.* Cheltenham: Edward Elgar Publishing.

Mielck, A. 2000. *Soziale Ungleichheit und Gesundheit: Empirische Ergebnisse, Erklärungsansätze, Interventionsmöglichkeiten.* Bern, Göttingen, Toronto, Seattle: H. Huber.

Minde, A. 2007. *Demographischer Wandel in Deutschland bis 2020.* GRIN Verlag.

Ministry of Health. 2009. *Mapping Study.* Nairobi: United Republic of Kenya.

Mintzberg, H. 1989. *Mintzberg on Management: Inside Our Strange World of Organizations.* New York: Free Press.

Moller, A. B., et al. 2019. "Monitoring Maternal and Newborn Health Outcomes Globally: A Brief History of Key Events and Initiatives." *Tropical Medicine & International Health* 24(12): 1342–1368.

Möller, J., et al. 2004. "Gesundheit der Ökonomie und Ökonomie der Gesundheit." *Journal of Public Health* 12: 3–9.

MoH Kenya (2023). Kenya Health Facility Census Report. Nairobi, Republic of Kenya.

MoPoTsyo. 2012. *MoPoTsyo Patient Information Centre: Annual Report 2011.* Phnom Penh: MoPoTsyo Patient Information Centre.

Moran, M., et al. 2009. "Neglected Disease Research and Development: How Much Are We Really Spending." *PLoS Medicine* 6(2): e1000030.

Morgan, J. A. T., et al. 2005. "Origin and Diversification of the Human Parasite *Schistosoma mansoni.*" *Molecular Ecology* 14(12): 3889–3902.

Morley, D., and H. Lovel. 1986. *My Name Is Today.* London: Macmillan Education.

Morrow, R. H. 2002. "Macroeconomics and Health. Despite Shortcomings the Plans in This Report Deserve Strong Support." *BMJ* 325: 53–54.

Msemburi, W., et al. 2023. "The WHO Estimates of Excess Mortality Associated with the COVID-19 Pandemic." *Nature* 613(7942): 130–137.

Mtani, F. A., and J. Ngohengo. 2023. "Africa at the Crossroads: An Overview of the COVID-19 Pandemic and Its Drama in Tanzania." *African Journal of History and Geography* 2(1): 1–16.

Muennig, P. 2002. *Designing and Conducting Cost-Effectiveness Analysis in Health and Medicine.* San Francisco: Jossey-Bass.

Müller, O. 2011. *Malaria in Africa.* Frankfurt a.M.: Peter Lang.

Murray, C. 1994. "Quantifying the Burden of Disease: Technical Basis for Disability Adjusted Life Years." *Bulletin of the World Health Organization* 762: 429–445.

Murray, C. 1994. *Quantifying the Burden of Disease: The Technical Basis for Disability-Adjusted Life Years.* In *Global Comparative Assessments in the Health Sector*, edited by C. Murray and A. D. Lopez, 3–20. Geneva: WHO.

Murray, C. 1994. "Quantifying the Burden of Disease: The Technical Basis for Disability-Adjusted Life Years." *Bulletin of the World Health Organization* 72(3): 429–445.

Murray, C. 1998. *Income Inequality and IQ.* Washington, DC: AEI Press.

Murray, C. J. 2024. "Findings from the Global Burden of Disease Study 2021." *The Lancet* 403(10440): 2259–2262.

Murray, C. J. L., et al. 2002. *Summary Measures of Population Health: Concepts, Ethics, Measurement and Applications.* Geneva: World Health Organization.

Mushi, L., et al. 2015. "Cost of Dialysis in Tanzania: Evidence from the Provider's Perspective." *Health Economics Review* 5: 1–10.

Nabyonga, J., et al. 2005. "Abolition of Cost-Sharing Is Pro-Poor: Evidence from Uganda." *Health Policy and Planning* 20(2): 100.

National Cancer Institute. 2024. "Dictionary of Cancer Terms." Accessed September 20, 2024. https://www.cancer.gov/publications/dictionaries/cancer-terms/def/neoplasm.

National Health Commission of China. 2020a. "COVID-19 Prevention and Control Plan (Seventh Edition)." Accessed December 16, 2020. http://www.nhc.gov.cn/jkj/s3577/202009/318683cbfaee4191aee29cd774b19d8d/files/f9ea38ce2c2d4352bf61ab0feada439f.pdf.

National Health Commission of China. 2020b. "Press Conference of National Health Commission of China." Accessed December 16, 2020. http://www.gov.cn/xinwen/gwylflkjz122/index.htm.

Nazarnia, H., et al. 2020. "A Systematic Review of Civil and Environmental Infrastructures for Coastal Adaptation to Sea Level Rise." *Civil Engineering Journal* 6(7): 1375–1399.

Nefiodow, L. A. 2001. *Der Sechste Kondratieff: Wege zur Produktivität und Vollbeschäftigung im Zeitalter der Information. Die Langen Wellen der Konjunktur und Ihre Basisinnovation.* St. Augustin: Rhein-Sieg Verlag.

Nelson, R. R. 1956. "A Theory of the Low-Level Equilibrium Trap in Underdeveloped Economies." *The American Economic Review* 46: 894–908.

Neumann, M. 1990. *Zukunftsperspektiven im Wandel. Lange Wellen in Wirtschaft und Politik.* Tübingen: Mohr.

Nimmannitya, S. 2004. "Dengue and Dengue Haemorrhagic Fever." In *Manson's Tropical Diseases*, edited by G. C. Cook and A. Zumla, 765–772. Philadelphia: Elsevier Health.

Normand, C., and A. Weber. 2009. *Social Health Insurance: A Guidebook for Planning.* Bad Homburg: VAS.

Notestein, F. W. 1945. "Population: The Long View." In *Food for the World*, edited by T. W. Schultz, 36–57. Chicago: University of Chicago Press.

Nutt, D., et al. 2007. "Development of a Rational Scale to Assess the Harm of Drugs of Potential Misuse." *The Lancet* 369(9566): 1047–1053.

Nyamugira, A. B., et al. 2024. "Health Insurance Uptake, Poverty and Financial Inclusion in the Democratic Republic of Congo." *Sustainable Development* 32(4): 3293–3312.

Oaks, S. C. 1991. *Malaria: Obstacles and Opportunities: A Report of the Committee for the Study on Malaria Prevention and Control: Status Review and Alternative Strategies, Division of International Health, Institute of Medicine.* Washington, DC: National Academies.

Obiako, O. R., and H. M. Muktar. 2010. "Challenges of HIV Treatment in Resource-Poor Countries: A Review." *Nigerian Journal of Medicine* 19(4): 361–368.

OECD. 2000. *A System of Health Accounts.* Paris: OECD Publishing.

OECD. 2005. *Paris Declaration on Aid Effectiveness, Ownership, Harmonisation, Alignment, Results and Mutual Accountability.* Paris: Organisation for Economic Cooperation and Development.

OECD. 2011. *Benefits of Investing in Water and Sanitation: An OECD Perspective.* Paris: OECD Publishing.

Okosun, I., et al. 1999. "Abdominal Adiposity in Six Populations of West African Descent: Prevalence and Population Attributable Fraction of Hypertension." *Obesity Research* 7(5): 453.

Okundi, A. O., and C. Varol. 2024. "Spatial Analysis of Primary Healthcare Accessibility Patterns in Migori County, Kenya." *SSM–Health Systems* 2: 100005.

Oladipo, E. K., et al. 2020. "Laboratory Diagnosis of COVID-19 in Africa: Availability, Challenges and Implications." *Drug Discoveries & Therapeutics* 14(4): 153–160.

Oleribe, O. O., et al. 2021. "Possible Reasons Why Sub-Saharan Africa Experienced a Less Severe COVID-19 Pandemic in 2020." *Journal of Multidisciplinary Healthcare* 14: 3267.

Omran, A. R. 1971. "The Epidemiologic Transition: A Theory of the Epidemiology of Population Change." *The Milbank Memorial Fund Quarterly* 49(4): 509–538.

Omran, A. R. 1977a. "A Century of Epidemiologic Transition in the United States." *Preventive Medicine* 6(1): 30–51.

Omran, A. R. 1977b. "Epidemiologic Transition in the United States: The Health Factor in Population Change." *Population Bulletin* 32(2): 1.

Omran, A. R. 2005. "The Epidemiologic Transition: A Theory of the Epidemiology of Population Change." *Milbank Quarterly* 83(4): 731–757.

Orem, J. N., et al. 2012. "Impact of Malaria Morbidity on Gross Domestic Product in Uganda." *International Archives of Medicine* 5(1): 1–8.

Ostfeld, R. S. 2009. "Climate Change and the Distribution and Intensity of Infectious Diseases." *Ecology* 90(4): 903–905.

Oswald, M. 2009. *Innovation und Diffusion: Geographische Basiskonzepte und ihre Anwendung in der Kulturgeographie.* München: GRIN Verlag.

Ouedraogo, L.-M., and S. Flessa. 2016. "The Potential Contribution of Community-Based Health Financing Schemes towards Achieving Universal Health Coverage in Sub-Saharan Africa." *African Journal of Health Economics* 5: 01–24.

Palomo, S., et al. 2023. "Flattening the Curve: Insights from Queueing Theory." *PLoS ONE* 18(6): e0286501.

Pang, T., et al. 2002. "Brain Drain and Health Professionals." *BMJ* 324(7336): 499–500.

Peace, J., and J. Weyant. 2008. "Insights Not Numbers: The Appropriate Use of Economic Models." Pew Center on Global Climate Change, Arlington.

Perlitz, M., and H. Löbler. 1985. "Brauchen Unternehmen zum Innovieren Krisen?" *Zeitschrift für Betriebswirtschaft* 55: 424–450.

Pesut, B., et al. 2008. "Conceptualising Spirituality and Religion for Healthcare." *Journal of Clinical Nursing* 17(21): 2803–2810.

Philippe, C., and N. Marques. 2021. *The Zero Covid Strategy Protects People and Economies More Effectively.* Paris, Bruxelles: Institut Économique Molinari.

Phillips, D. R. 1990. *Health and Health Care in the Third World.* New York: John Wiley & Sons.

Pitman, R., et al. 2012. "Dynamic Transmission Modeling: A Report of the ISPOR-SMDM Modeling Good Research Practices Task Force-5." *Value in Health* 15(6): 828–834.

Podolski, P., and H. S. Nguyen. 2021. "Cellular Automata in COVID-19 Prediction." *Procedia Computer Science* 192: 3370–3379.

Polack, S., et al. 2010. "The Impact of Cataract Surgery on Activities and Time-Use: Results from a Longitudinal Study in Kenya, Bangladesh and the Philippines." *PLoS ONE* 5(6): e10913.

Preker, A. S. 2005. *Spending Wisely: Buying Health Services for the Poor.* Washington, DC: World Bank Publications.

Pschyrembel, W. 1993. *Pschyrembel. Klinisches Wörterbuch.* Berlin-New York: Walter de Gruyter.

Pschyrembel. 2022. "Katarakt." Accessed February 4, 2022. https://www.pschyrembel.de/Katarakt/K0BGL.

Queen, P. M. 1911. "Sleeping Sickness in Uganda." *Bulletin of the American Geographical Society* 43(3): 181–184.

Ramke, J., et al. 2022. "Grand Challenges in Global Eye Health: A Global Prioritisation Process Using Delphi Method." *The Lancet Healthy Longevity* 3(1): e31–e41.

Rao, G. N., et al. 2011. "The Global Burden of Cataract." *Current Opinion in Ophthalmology* 22(1): 4–9.

Rauner, M. S., et al. 2005. "The Use of Discrete-Event Simulation to Evaluate Strategies for the Prevention of Mother-to-Child Transmission of HIV in Developing Countries." *Journal of the Operational Research Society* 56: 222–233.

Rawlings, L. B., and G. M. Rubio. 2005. "Evaluating the Impact of Conditional Cash Transfer Programs." *The World Bank Research Observer* 20(1): 29–55.

Razum, O., and S. Voigtländer. 2010. "'Primary Health Care' und Urbanisierung." *Prävention und Gesundheitsförderung* 5(1): 29–36.

Razum, O., et al. 2006. *Globalisierung – Gerechtigkeit – Gesundheit: Einführung in International Public Health.* Bern: Huber.

Reich, M. R., et al. 2016. "Moving Towards Universal Health Coverage: Lessons from 11 Country Studies." *The Lancet* 387(10020): 811–816.

Reichart, T. 1999. *Bausteine der Wirtschaftsgeographie.* Bern, Stuttgart, Wien: Haupt.

Reliefweb. 2022. "Six in Seven COVID-19 Infections Go Undetected in Africa." Accessed January 3, 2022. https://reliefweb.int/report/world/six-seven-covid-19-infections-go-undetected-africa.

Rheumatology, The L. 2023. "Alcohol and Health: All, None, or Somewhere in-Between?" *The Lancet Rheumatology* 5: e167.

Rice, D. P. 1967. "Estimating the Cost of Illness." *American Journal of Public Health and the Nation's Health* 57(3): 424–440.

Rich, A. 1991. *Wirtschaftsethik, Band 1: Grundlagen in Theologischer Perspektive*. Gütersloh: Gütersloher Verlagsgesellschaft.

Rieckmann, H. 2005. *Managen und Führen am Rande des 3. Jahrtausends*: *Praktisches, Theoretisches, Bedenkliches.* Frankfurt a.M.: Peter Lang.

Ritter, W. 2001. *Allgemeine Wirtschaftsgeographie. Eine systemtheoretisch orientierte Einführung*. München: Oldenbourg.

Rogers, E. M. 2003. *Diffusion of Innovations*. New York and London: Free Press.

Rojas-Rueda, D., et al. 2021. "Environmental Risk Factors and Health: An Umbrella Review of Meta-Analyses." *International Journal of Environmental Research and Public Health* 18(2): 704.

Romanello, M., et al. 2024. "The 2024 Report of the Lancet Countdown on Health and Climate Change: Facing Record-Breaking Threats from Delayed Action." *The Lancet*.

Rösch, P. 1995. "Der Prozess der Strukturanpassung in Tanzania."

Rösner, H. J., et al. 2011. *Handbook of Micro Health Insurance in Africa*. Münster: LIT Verlag.

Ross, R. 1908. *Report on the Prevention of Malaria in Mauritius*. London: Churchill.

Roth, G. 2005. *Das Gehirn und seine Wirklichkeit: Kognitive Neurobiologie und ihre philosophischen Konsequenzen*. Frankfurt a.M.: Suhrkamp.

Roth, M., and K. Heidenberger. 1998. "Strategic Investment in HIV/AIDS Control Programmes: A System-Dynamics-Based Economic Evaluation." In *Operations Research Proceedings* 1997, 575–580. Springer.

Royal Government of Cambodia. 2014. *National Strategic Plan for the Prevention and Control of Noncommunicable Diseases*. Phnom Penh: Ministry of Health.

Rubinstein, R. Y., and D. P. Kroese. 2011. *Simulation and the Monte Carlo Method*. Hoboken, NJ: Wiley.com.

Russell, P. 1955. *Man's Mastery over Malaria*. London: Oxford University Press.

Sachs, J. 2002. "An Economist's View of Health." *Bulletin of the World Health Organization* 80: 67–169.

Sachs, J. D. 2001. *Macroeconomics and Health*. Genf: World Health Organization.

Sankaranarayanan, R., et al. 2009. "HPV Screening for Cervical Cancer in Rural India." *New England Journal of Medicine* 360(14): 1385–1394.

Say, L., et al. 2014. "Global Causes of Maternal Death: A WHO Systematic Analysis." *The Lancet Global Health* 2(6): e323–e333.

Scarborough, W. 1873. "Medical Missions." *Chinese Recorder* 6: 137–152.

Schaeffer, D., et al. 1994. *Public Health und Pflege*. Berlin: Edition Sigma.

Scheel, M. 1987. *Partnerschaftliches Heilen*. Stuttgart: Verlagswerk der Diakonie.

Schein, E. H. 1991. *Organisationskultur: Ein Neues Unternehmenstheoretisches Konzept*. Stuttgart: C.E. Poeschel.

Schiller, J. T., and D. R. Lowy. 2014. "Virus Infection and Human Cancer: An Overview." In *Viruses and Human Cancer: From Basic Science to Clinical Prevention*, 1–10.

Schleidgen, S., et al. 2013. "What Is Personalized Medicine: Sharpening a Vague Term Based on a Systematic Literature Review." *BMC Medical Ethics* 14(1): 55.

Schöpf, A. 1984. "Grundzüge der Verteilungsgerechtigkeit." In *Energie und Gerechtigkeit*, edited by R. Kümmel and M. Suhrcke, 102–109. München, Reinbek.

Schott, H. 2000. *Die Chronik der Medizin*. Gütersloh: Chronik Verlag.

Schulenburg, J. M. G. v. d., and W. Greiner. 2007. *Gesundheitsökonomik*. Tübingen: Mohr Siebeck.

Schuster, R. 2009. *Biomathematik*. Wiesbaden: Vieweg und Teubner.

Schwartz, F. W., et al. 2003. *Gesundheit und Krankheit in der Bevölkerung. Das Public Health Buch*. München, Jena: Urban & Fischer, 23–47.

Schwarz, F. W. 2022. *Public Health. Das Public Health Buch*. 4th edition. München, Jena: Urban & Fischer, 3–6.

Schwarz, P. 1992. *Management in Nonprofit Organisationen: Eine Führungs-, Organisations- und Planungslehre für Verbände, Sozialwerke, Vereine, Kirchen, Parteien usw*. Bern: Paul Haupt.

Schweikart, J. 1992. *Räumliche und soziale Faktoren bei der Annahme von Impfungen in der Nord-West Provinz Kameruns. Ein Beitrag zur Medizinischen Geographie in Entwicklungsländern*. Heidelberg: Selbstverlag des Geographischen Instituts.

Sedgh, G., et al. 2007. "Induced Abortion: Estimated Rates and Trends Worldwide." *The Lancet* 370(9595): 1338–1345.

Seidell, J. 1999. "Obesity: A Growing Problem." *Acta Paediatrica* 88(s428): 46–50.

Seinfeld, J. 2013. "Cost-Benefit Analysis of Cancer Care and Control: The Case of Cervical, Colorectal and Breast Cancer in Low and Middle Income Countries." Accessed from http://isites.harvard.edu/fs/docs/icb.topic1011506.files/CCC%20-%20Breast_Cervical%20and%20Colorectal%20cancer%20cases_AB.pdf.

Sellors, J. W., and R. Sankaranarayanan. 2025. "Colposcopy and Treatment of Cervical Intraepithelial Neoplasia: A Beginners' Manual. Chapter 12: Treatment of Cervical Intraepithelial Neoplasia by Cryotherapy." Accessed March 24, 2025. https://screening.iarc.fr/colpochap.php?chap=12.php&lang=1.

Semba, R. D., and M. W. Bloem. 2008. *Nutrition and Health in Developing Countries*. New York: Humana Press.

Sen, A. 1983. *Poverty and Famines: An Essay on Entitlement and Deprivation*. New York, Oxford: Oxford University Press.

Shaffer, R. 1987. *Beyond the Dispensary*. Nairobi: African Medical and Research Foundation.

Shattock, A. J., et al. 2024. "Contribution of Vaccination to Improved Survival and Health: Modelling 50 Years of the Expanded Programme on Immunization." *The Lancet* 403(10441): 2307–2316.

Shengelia, B., et al. 2003. *Health Systems Performance Assessment*. Genf: Weltgesundheitsorganisation.

Shiffman, J. 2006. "Donor Funding Priorities for Communicable Disease Control in the Developing World." *Health Policy and Planning* 21(6): 411.

Siadat, B., and M. Stolpe. 2005. *Reforming Health Care Finance: What Can Germany Learn from Other Countries?* Kiel Economic Policy Papers 5. Kiel: Institut für Weltwirtschaft.

Sibley, L., and T. Ann Sipe. 2004. "What Can a Meta-Analysis Tell Us About Traditional Birth Attendant Training and Pregnancy Outcomes?" *Midwifery* 20(1): 51–60.

Sickles, R. C., and V. Zelenyuk. 2019. *Measurement of Productivity and Efficiency*. Cambridge: Cambridge University Press.

Siebert, U., et al. 2012. "State-Transition Modeling: A Report of the ISPOR-SMDM Modeling Good Research Practices Task Force-3." *Medical Decision Making* 32(5): 690–700.

Siegrist, J. 2005. *Medizinische Soziologie*. München: Elsevier.

Singh, M. P., et al. 2019. "The Economic Cost of Malaria at the Household Level in High and Low Transmission Areas of Central India." *Acta Tropica* 190: 344–349.

Skinsnes, C. C. 1952. *Scalpel and Cross in Honan*. Minneapolis: Augsburg Publishing House.

Sloan, F. A., and C.-R. Hsieh. 2017. *Health Economics*. Cambridge, Mass., et al.: MIT Press.

Smith, N. R., et al. 2018. "Agent-Based Models of Malaria Transmission: A Systematic Review." *Malaria Journal* 17: 1–16.

Snow, J. 1854. "Cholerafälle in London." Accessed from http://de.wikipedia.org/w/index.php?title=Datei:Snow-cholera-map.jpg&filetimestamp=20051106111039.

Socialist Republic of VietNam. 2002. *Health Statistics Year Book 2001*. Hanoi: Ministry of Health.

Soubbotina, T. P. 2004. *Beyond Economic Growth: An Introduction to Sustainable Development*. Washington, DC: World Bank Publications.

Soy, A. 2020. "Coronavirus in Africa: Five Reasons Why Covid-19 Has Been Less Deadly than Elsewhere." Accessed December 30, 2021. https://www.bbc.com/news/world-africa-54418613.

State Council. 2020. "China's Actions to Fight Against the COVID-19 Epidemic (White Paper)." Accessed December 13, 2020. http://www.scio.gov.cn/ztk/dtzt/42313/43142/index.htm.

Staude, L. 2022. "Schulbeginn: Nach 83 Wochen." Accessed January 11, 2022. https://www.tagesschau.de/ausland/afrika/uganda-schulen-corona-101.html.

Stavenhagen, G. 1969. *Geschichte der Wirtschaftstheorie*. Göttingen: Vandenhoeck & Ruprecht.

Sterman, J. 2016. *Business Dynamics*. Boston, et al.: McGraw-Hill.

Stern, N. H. 2007. *The Economics of Climate Change*. Cambridge: Cambridge University Press.

Stokes, C. J. 1962. "A Theory of Slums." *Land Economics* 38(3): 187–197.

Suhrcke, M., et al. 2006. "The Contribution of Health to the Economy in the European Union." *Public Health* 120(11): 994–1001.

Szmigiera, M. 2021. "Impact of the Coronavirus Pandemic on the Global Economy: Statistics & Facts." Accessed January 5, 2022. https://www.statista.com/topics/6139/covid-19-impact-on-the-global-economy/?utm_source=browser&utm_medium=push-notification&utm_campaign=EN-cleverpush-2022-01-03T16%3A35%3A34#dossierKeyfigures.

tabacconomics. 2019. *Economic Costs of Tobacco Use. Policy Brief 2019*. Baltimore: Johns Hopkins University, School of Public Health.

Tarimo, E. 1991. *Towards a Healthy District*. Geneva: Weltgesundheitsorganisation.

Tarimo, E., and E. G. Webster. 1996. *Primary Health Care Concepts and Challenges in a Changing World: Alma-Ata Revisited*. Geneva: World Health Organization.

Tartalja, H. 1981. *Die Erste Quarantäne in der Stadt Dubrovnik*. Basel: Internationale Gesellschaft für Geschichte der Pharmazie.

Tefera, D. R., et al. 2020. "Economic Burden of Malaria and Associated Factors among Rural Households in Chewaka District, Western Ethiopia." *ClinicoEconomics and Outcomes Research*: 141–152.

Teller, C., and A. Hailemariam. 2011. *The Demographic Transition and Development in Africa*. Springer.

Thay, S., et al. 2019. "Prevalence of Cervical Dysplasia in HIV-Positive and HIV-Negative Women at the Sihanouk Hospital Center of HOPE, Phnom Penh, Cambodia." *Asian Pacific Journal of Cancer Prevention: APJCP* 20(2): 653.

The World Bank. 1994. *Better Health for Africa*. Washington, DC: The World Bank.

Thompson, W. S. 1929. "Population." *Journal of the American Statistical Association* 34: 959–975.

U.S. Census Bureau. 2025. "International Data base (IDB)." Retrieved 18.12.2025, from http://www.census.gov/population/international/data/idb/informationGateway.php.

UN. 2003. *Indicators for Monitoring the Millennium Development Goals: Definitions, Rationale, Concepts and Sources*. New York: United Nations Publications.

UN. 2015. *The Millennium Development Goals Report*. New York: United Nations Publishing.

UN. 2020. "Global Indicator Framework for the Sustainable Development Goals." Accessed July 24, 2024. https://unstats.un.org/sdgs/indicators/indicators-list/.

UN. 2024a. "Least Developed Countries Category." Accessed July 12, 2024. https://www.un.org/ohrlls/content/ldc-category.

UN. 2024b. "Sustainable Development Goals." Accessed July 24, 2024. https://sdgs.un.org/goals.

UN. 2024c. *The Sustainable Development Goals Report 2024*. New York: UN.

UN. 2024d. "Sustainable Development Goals. Goal 6: Clean Water and Sanitation." Accessed November 2, 2024. https://www.un.org/sustainabledevelopment/water-and-sanitation/.

UNAIDS. 2010. *Report on the Global AIDS Epidemic 2010*. Washington, DC: Joint United Nations Programme on HIV/AIDS (UNAIDS).

UNAIDS. 2024. "Global HIV & AIDS Statistics: Fact Sheet." Accessed August 15, 2024. https://www.unaids.org/en/resources/fact-sheet.

UNCTAD. 2024. "UN List of Least Developed Countries." Accessed July 16, 2024. https://unctad.org/topic/least-developed-countries/list.

UNFPA. 2005. *Sector Wide Approaches: A Resource Document for UNFPA Staff*. New York: United Nations Population Fund.

UNFPA. 2007. *State of World Population 2007: Unleashing the Potential of Urban Growth*. New York: UNFPA.

UNHABITAT. 2010. *The State of African Cities 2010*. Nairobi: UNHABITAT.

UNHCR. 2024. "Refugee Data Finder." Accessed November 11, 2024. https://www.unhcr.org/refugee-statistics.

UNICEF. 2021a. "40 per Cent of Children in Eastern and Southern Africa Are Not in School." Accessed January 11, 2022. https://www.unicef.org/where-we-work.

UNICEF. 2021b. "Learners in South Africa up to One School Year Behind Where They Should Be." Accessed January 11, 2022. https://www.unicef.org/press-releases/learners-south-africa-one-school-year-behind-where-they-should-be.

United Nations. 2010. *Millennium Development Goals Reports 2005–2015*. New York: United Nations.

Vaillancourt, D. 2009. *Do Health Sector-Wide Approaches Achieve Results?* Washington, DC: World Bank.

van Pelt, M., et al. 2012. *Yes, They Can: Transforming Health Markets in Asia and Africa – Improving Quality and Access for the Poor*. G. Bloom, B. Kanjilal, H. Lucas et al. London: Routledge.

VanderWeele, T. 2024. *A Theology of Health: Wholeness and Human Flourishing*. Paris: University of Notre Dame Press.

Vázquez-Serrano, J. I., et al. 2021. "Discrete-Event Simulation Modeling in Healthcare: A Comprehensive Review." *International Journal of Environmental Research and Public Health* 18(22): 12262.

Venkatesan, P. 2024. "The 2023 WHO World Malaria Report." *The Lancet Microbe* 5(3): e214.

von Both, C., et al. 2008. "Costing Maternal Health Services in South Tanzania." *The European Journal of Health Economics* 9(2): 103–115.

Vuong, D. A., et al. 2014. "Determining the Impacts of Hospital Cost-Sharing on the Uninsured Near-Poor Households in Vietnam." *International Journal for Equity in Health* 13: 1–8.

Vutuc, C., and H. Flamm. 2010. "Dreißig Jahre Weltweite Ausrottung der Pocken durch die Weltgesundheits-Organisation." *Wiener Klinische Wochenschrift* 122(9): 276–279.

Walker, R., et al. 2010. "Stroke Incidence in Rural and Urban Tanzania: A Prospective, Community-Based Study." *The Lancet Neurology* 9(8): 786–792.

Walt, G. 1994. *Health Policy: An Introduction to Process and Power*. Johannesburg: Witwatersrand University Press.

Walter, U., and F. W. Schwartz. 2003. *Prävention. Das Public Health Buch*. F. W. Schwartz. München, Jena: Urban & Fischer, 189–214.

Wang, M. M., and S. Fleßa. 2021. "Overcoming COVID-19 in China Despite Shortcomings of the Public Health System: What Can We Learn?" *Health Economics Review* 11(1): 1–18.

Wang, W., et al. 2024. "Computational Approaches of Modelling Human Papillomavirus Transmission and Prevention Strategies: A Systematic Review." *arXiv preprint* arXiv:2404.19235.

Weber, M. 1958. *Politik als Beruf*. Max Weber: Gesammelte politische Schriften. J. Winckelmann, Tübingen: Mohr Siebeck, 493–548.

Weinstein, J., and V. K. Pillai. 2015. *Demography: The Science of Population*. Lanham, MD: Rowman & Littlefield.

Weishaupt, M. 1936. *Krankendienst in Afrika*. Leipzig: Leipziger Mission.

Weiss, G. H., and M. Zelen. 1965. "A Semi-Markov Model for Clinical Trials." *Journal of Applied Probability* 2(2): 269–285.

Weltbank. 1994. *Better Health in Africa*. Washington, DC: The World Bank Press.

Weltbank. 1999. *Tanzania: Social Sector Review*. Washington, DC: The World Bank Press.

Weltbank. 2010. *Entwicklung und Klimawandel. Weltentwicklungsbericht 2010*. Washington, DC: The World Bank Press.

Werner, D., et al. 1997. *Questioning the Solution: The Politics of Primary Health Care and Child Survival with an In-Depth Critique of Oral Rehydration Therapy*. Palo Alto, CA: Healthwrights.

Weyrauch, T., and C. Herstatt. 2017. "What Is Frugal Innovation? Three Defining Criteria." *Journal of Frugal Innovation* 2: 1–17.

WHO. 1948. *Constitution*. Geneva: World Health Organization.

WHO. 1978. *Alma-Ata 1978: Primary Health Care. Report on the International Conference on Primary Health Care, 6–12 September 1978*. Geneva: World Health Organization.

WHO. 1986. *Ottawa Charter for Health Promotion*. Geneva: World Health Organization.

WHO. 1992. *The Hospital in Rural and Urban Districts. Report of a WHO Study Group*. Geneva: Weltgesundheitsorganisation.

WHO. 1994. *AIDS: Images of the Epidemic*. Geneva: Weltgesundheitsorganisation.

WHO. 1996. *District Hospitals: Guidelines for Development*. Geneva: Weltgesundheitsorganisation.

WHO. 1998. *The World Health Report 1998. Life in the 21st Century. A Vision for All*. Geneva: Weltgesundheitsorganisation.

WHO. 2003. *WHO Framework Convention on Tobacco Control*. Geneva: World Health Organization.

WHO. 2005. *Make Every Mother and Child Count: The World Health Report*. Geneva: Weltgesundheitsorganisation.

WHO. 2006. *Comprehensive Cervical Cancer Control: A Guide to Essential Practice*. Geneva: World Health Organization.

WHO. 2008a. *2008–2013 Action Plan for the Global Strategy for the Prevention and Control of Noncommunicable Diseases*. Geneva: Weltgesundheitsorganisation.

WHO. 2008b. *The World Health Report 2008: Primary Health Care: Now More Than Ever*. Geneva: World Health Organization.

WHO. 2008c. *World Malaria Report 2008*. Geneva: Weltgesundheitsorganisation.

WHO. 2011a. *Prevention and Control of Dengue and Dengue Haemorrhagic Fever*. Geneva: Weltgesundheitsorganisation.

WHO. 2011b. *Scaling Up Action Against Noncommunicable Diseases: How Much Will It Cost?* Geneva: World Health Organization.

WHO. 2011c. *WHO Report on the Global Tobacco Epidemic, 2011: Warning About the Dangers of Tobacco*. Geneva: Weltgesundheitsorganisation.

WHO. 2012. "World Map Gallery." Accessed June 12, 2012. http://www.who.int/gho/map_gallery/en/.

WHO. 2013. *Comprehensive Cervical Cancer Prevention and Control: A Healthier Future for Girls and Women*. Geneva: World Health Organization.

WHO. 2017. *WHO Methods and Data Sources for Global Burden of Disease Estimates*. Geneva: World Health Organization.

WHO. 2019a. "Emergencies: International Health Regulations and Emergency Committees." Accessed August 15, 2024. https://web.archive.org/web/20210815072835/https://www.who.int/news-room/q-a-detail/emergencies-international-health-regulations-and-emergency-committees.

WHO. 2019b. "Universal Health Coverage." Accessed June 26, 2019. http://www.who.int/health_financing/en/.

WHO. 2021. *WHO Guidelines for Screening and Treatment of Precancerous Lesions for Cervical Cancer Prevention*. Geneva: World Health Organization.

WHO. 2022. "Blindness and Vision Impairment." Accessed February 3, 2022. https://www.who.int/news-room/fact-sheets/detail/blindness-and-visual-impairment.

WHO. 2023. *World Malaria Report 2023*. Geneva: World Health Organization.

WHO. 2024. "Abortion." Accessed November 2, 2024. https://www.who.int/news-room/fact-sheets/detail/abortion.

WHO. 2024a. "Deaths by Sex and Age Group for a Selected Country or Area and Year." Accessed June 18, 2024. https://platform.who.int/mortality/themes/theme-details/topics/indicator-groups/indicator-group-details/MDB/cervix-uteri-cancer.

WHO. 2024b. "Global Cancer Burden Growing, Amidst Mounting Need for Services." Accessed September 18, 2024. https://www.who.int/news/item/01-02-2024-global-cancer-burden-growing–amidst-mounting-need-for-services.

WHO. 2024c. "Global Health Estimates." Accessed August 5, 2024. https://www.who.int/data/global-health-estimates.

WHO. 2024d. "Global Health Estimates 2021 Summary Tables." Accessed August 16, 2024. https://cdn.who.int/media/docs/default-source/gho-documents/global-health-estimates/ghe2021_deaths_global_new2.xlsx?sfvrsn=e1f725b1_2.

WHO. 2024e. "Global Health Estimates: Leading Causes of DALYs." Accessed August 21, 2024. https://www.who.int/data/gho/data/themes/mortality-and-global-health-estimates/global-health-estimates-leading-causes-of-dalys.

WHO. 2024f. "Hygiene." Accessed November 2, 2024. https://www.afro.who.int/health-topics/hygiene.

WHO. 2024g. "Malaria Vaccines." Accessed August 21, 2024. https://www.who.int/news-room/questions-and-answers/item/q-a-on-rts-s-malaria-vaccine.

WHO. 2024h. "Malnutrition in Children." Accessed November 1, 2024. https://www.who.int/data/nutrition/nlis/info/malnutrition-in-children.

WHO. 2024i. "Maternal Mortality." Accessed November 2, 2024. https://www.who.int/news-room/fact-sheets/detail/maternal-mortality.

WHO. 2024j. "Sanitation." Accessed November 2, 2024. https://www.afro.who.int/health-topics/sanitation.

WHO. 2024k. "SDG Target 3.8 | Achieve Universal Health Coverage (UHC)." Accessed July 25, 2024. https://www.who.int/data/gho/data/major-themes/universal-health-coverage-major.

WHO. 2024l. "Social Determinants of Health: Key Concepts." Accessed July 12, 2024. https://www.who.int/news-room/questions-and-answers/item/social-determinants-of-health-key-concepts.

WHO. 2024m. "Tobacco." Accessed November 2, 2024. https://www.who.int/news-room/fact-sheets/detail/tobacco.

WHO. 2024n. "WHO COVID-19 Dashboard." Accessed August 26, 2024. https://data.who.int/dashboards/covid19/cases.

WHO. 2025a. "Medical Doctors per Population." Accessed February 14, 2025. https://www.who.int/data/gho/data/indicators/indicator-details/GHO/medical-doctors-(per-10-000-population).

WHO. 2025b. "One Health High-Level Expert Panel (OHHLEP)." Accessed April 17, 2025. https://www.who.int/groups/one-health-high-level-expert-panel.

WHO. 2025c. "Water, Sanitation and Hygiene (WASH)." Accessed February 26, 2025. https://www.who.int/health-topics/water-sanitation-and-hygiene-wash#tab=tab_1.

WHO African Region. 2024. "Coronavirus (COVID-19)." Accessed August 28, 2024. https://www.afro.who.int/health-topics/coronavirus-covid-19.

Williams, R., et al. 2020. "Global and Regional Estimates and Projections of Diabetes-Related Health Expenditure: Results from the International Diabetes Federation Diabetes Atlas." *Diabetes Research and Clinical Practice* 162: 108072.

Wiseman, V., et al. 2017. "System-Wide Analysis of Health Financing Equity in Cambodia: A Study Protocol." *BMJ Global Health* 2(1): e000153.

Woodruff, B. A. 2006. "Interpreting Mortality Data in Humanitarian Emergencies." *The Lancet* 367(9504): 9–10.

Wootton, R., et al. 2009. *Telehealth in the Developing World*. Ottawa: Royal Society of Medicine Press.

World Bank. 1993. *World Development Report: Investing in Health*. Washington, D.C.: The World Bank Group.

World Bank. 2019. *World Development Indicators*. Washington, DC: The World Bank.

World Bank. 2024a. "World Bank Country and Lending Groups." Accessed July 16, 2024. https://datahelpdesk.worldbank.org/knowledgebase/articles/906519-world-bank-country-and-lending-groups.

World Bank. 2024b. "World Development Indicators." Accessed May 30, 2024. https://databank.world bank.org/source/world-development-indicators#.

World Bank. 2025. "World Development Indicators." Accessed December 13, 2025. https://databank.world bank.org/source/world-development-indicators#.

World Health Organization. 2019. *World Report on Vision*. Geneva: World Health Organization.

World Population Review. 2024. "World Population by Country 2021 (verschiedene Länder)." Accessed August 28, 2024. https://worldpopulationreview.com/countries.

Wu, F., and P. Khlangwiset. 2010. "Health Economic Impacts and Cost-Effectiveness of Aflatoxin-Reduction Strategies in Africa: Case Studies in Biocontrol and Post-Harvest Interventions." *Food Additives & Contaminants: Part A* 27(4): 496–509.

Wu, F., et al. 2020. "A New Coronavirus Associated with Human Respiratory Disease in China." *Nature* 579(7798): 265–269.

Wu, H. C., and R. Santella. 2012. "The Role of Aflatoxins in Hepatocellular Carcinoma." *Hepatitis Monthly* 12 (10 HCC).

Wu, S., et al. 2021. "Aggressive Containment, Suppression, and Mitigation of COVID-19: Lessons Learnt from Eight Countries." *BMJ* 375.

Xia, Q., et al. 2024. "Case Fatality Rates of COVID-19 During Epidemic Periods of Variants of Concern: A Meta-Analysis by Continents." *International Journal of Infectious Diseases* 141: 106950.

Yang, S., et al. 2020. "Early Estimation of the Case Fatality Rate of COVID-19 in Mainland China: A Data-Driven Analysis." *Annals of Translational Medicine* 8(4).

Yingi, E. 2024. "War in Foreign Lands, Hunger at Home: The Implications of the Russia-Ukraine War on Hunger and Food Security in Africa." *International Journal of Research in Business & Social Science* 13(6).

Young, N., et al. 2019. "Integrating HIV, Syphilis, Malaria and Anaemia Point-of-Care Testing (POCT) for Antenatal Care at Dispensaries in Western Kenya: Discrete-Event Simulation Modelling of Operational Impact." *BMC Public Health* 19: 1–12.

Young, T. K.-H. 1973. "A Conflict of Professions: The Medical Missionary in China, 1835–1890." *Bulletin of the History of Medicine* 47: 250–272.

Yudkin, J. 1999. "Tanzania: Still Optimistic after All These Years?" *Lancet* 353(9163): 1519–1521.

Zahr, C. A. 2007. *Verbal Autopsy Standards: Ascertaining and Attributing Cause of Death*. Geneva: World Health Organization.

Zhang, X. 2018. "Application of Discrete Event Simulation in Health Care: A Systematic Review." *BMC Health Services Research* 18: 1–11.

Zhou, P., et al. 2020. "A Pneumonia Outbreak Associated with a New Coronavirus of Probable Bat Origin." *Nature* 579(7798): 270–273.

Zhu, N., et al. 2020. "A Novel Coronavirus from Patients with Pneumonia in China, 2019." *New England Journal of Medicine*.

Zsichla, L., and V. Müller. 2023. "Risk Factors of Severe COVID-19: A Review of Host, Viral and Environmental Factors." *Viruses* 15(1): 175.

Zuckerman, A. J., et al. 2009. *Principles and Practice of Clinical Virology*. Chichester: Wiley & Blackwell.

Zweifel, P., et al. 2014. *Health Economics*. Berlin, Heidelberg, New York: Springer Science & Business Media.

Index

access 8, 19, 29, 41, 84–85, 123, 161, 205, 247, 253, 293, 297, 310
age 8
agents of production 279
AIDS 157
alcohol 249
ANC 247

basic reproductive number 148–149, 186
Beveridge 271, 320, 332
birth 246
Bismarck 2, 271, 332
blindness 62, 150, 222, 244, 324
burden of disease 104, 116, 131, 134, 207, 251
business administration 16–17, 279

cancer 214
cardiovascular diseases 212
cataract 222
catchment area 267–268, 270, 273, 290, 296, 299, 304, 314, 319, 337
CBHC 77
cervix uteri carcinoma 211, 228
climate change 256
Commission on Macroeconomics and Health 46, 64, 104–105, 327
community medicine 14
community-based healthcare 77
comprehensive primary healthcare 78
cost 8, 18, 25, 52, 67, 76, 85, 91, 133, 237, 244, 250, 255, 266, 269, 273, 280, 293, 295, 300, 307, 314, 319, 324, 331, 334–335
cost of illness 309
COVID-19 12, 118, 144, 156, 182
CPHC 78

DALY 95, 104, 116, 126, 207, 246, 253
Declaration of Alma-Ata 77–78, 85, 92–93, 95, 243, 246, 333, 336
demography 12
development 45
development concept
– dynamic 59
– static 53
development trap 48, 105
diabetes 52, 83, 102, 130, 194, 208–209, 217, 240, 262, 265

distance 19, 25, 30–31, 83, 91, 116, 151, 153, 244, 247, 259, 266, 296, 319
DRG 323, 337
dynamic concept of health 8

economic framework model 16, 43, 87, 115, 310
efficiency 11, 16, 38, 59, 61, 84, 92, 106, 118, 143, 288, 298, 310, 327, 337
environment 255
epidemic 70, 94, 142, 146, 152–153, 162, 178, 184, 252, 275, 313
epidemiology 13, 143
equality 25, 40–42, 79, 100, 262, 270, 298
equipment life cycle 282
ethics 22

financing 313
friction of distance 267
frugal innovation 281

geography 12, 19, 44, 82
global health 112, 157

health 5
health economics 16, 23, 87, 95, 113, 115, 134, 308
health insurance 19, 22, 26, 85, 124, 261, 269, 271, 302, 307, 310, 313–314, 319, 326–327, 333, 337
health policy 22, 45, 77, 81, 87–88, 119, 130, 242, 246, 307, 311, 330, 332
health promotion 78
health risks 236
health science 9
healthcare financing system 313
healthcare management 16
healthcare pyramid 81
healthcare reform 36, 262, 309, 332
healthcare structure 327
healthcare system 11, 16, 22, 47, 57, 73, 76, 82, 88, 109, 113, 131, 162, 184, 216, 250, 271, 284, 289, 296, 302, 307, 312–313, 323, 327, 332
Hofstede 44, 68
host 144
HPV 211, 214, 228
hunger 96, 100, 189, 239–240, 251, 264
hygiene 11, 74, 77, 80, 102, 123, 153, 162, 243, 261, 330

https://doi.org/10.1515/9783112217290-008

international cooperation 288

justice 25, 27, 75, 79, 284

Kilbourne model 156, 193

leadership 293
levels of care 299

maintenance 38, 175, 281, 296
malaria 170
Malthusian trap 47
Markov model 136, 212, 219
maternal and child healthcare 78
MCH 78
MDG 95, 100, 105, 243, 246
megacity 259
metabolic syndrome 242
modelling 133, 143, 216
multiple-cause-multiple-effect model 132, 211, 232,
    237, 255

National Health Accounts 307
nutrition 239

One Health 112
output-outcome-impact model 30

pandemic 146, 153, 157, 171, 182, 288
Paris Declaration 106, 289
pathogenesis 78
peer educator network 219
PHC 77
PHEIC 157
planetary health 112
portfolio 273
poverty 19, 31, 37, 50–51, 54, 62, 95, 100, 109, 239,
    251, 255, 262, 269, 302, 313–314, 337
pregnancy 101, 116, 122, 161, 246
prevention 9–10, 18, 73, 80, 82, 85, 90, 102, 107,
    131, 152, 216, 264, 266, 274, 295, 310, 317, 327,
    333

primary healthcare 75
provider portfolio 302
public health 7, 10–11, 27, 74, 112
pyramid of healthcare services 18

Rawls 40
regional health planning 81
resilience 7, 34–35

salutogenesis 78
SARS 152
SARS-CoV-1 147, 182
SARS-CoV-2 182, 189
SDG 86, 100, 243, 246
SDGs 100
selective primary healthcare 78
slum 96, 205, 244, 263, 294
smoking 249
Snow, John 14
stunting 242
substance abuse 249
system dynamics model 137

transformation process 292
transition 59, 94, 120, 210, 212, 240, 259, 328, 331,
    335
Tübingen 76

UHC 84, 102, 313
underweight 242
unstable population 263
urbanization 124, 137
Urbanization 259

value 24

wasting 242
water 243
WHO 5, 17, 46, 72, 75, 82, 92, 95, 104, 214, 301, 333

zero COVID 183, 186
zoonosis 144–145, 156

www.ingramcontent.com/pod-product-compliance
Lightning Source LLC
Chambersburg PA
CBHW081045220326
41598CB00038B/6990